Revisiting
Wertheimer's Seminars

Revisiting Wertheimer's Seminars

Abraham S. Luchins and Edith H. Luchins

VOLUME I:
Value, Social Influences, and Power

Lewisburg: BUCKNELL UNIVERSITY PRESS
London: ASSOCIATED UNIVERSITY PRESSES

Associated University Presses, Inc.
Cranbury, New Jersey 08512

Associated University Presses
Magdalen House
136-148 Tooley Street
London SE1 2TT, England

Library of Congress Cataloging in Publication Data

Luchins, Abraham S
  Revisiting Wertheimer's seminars.

  CONTENTS: v. 1. Value, social influences, and power.—v. 2. Problems in social psychology.—
  1. Social sciences—Methodology—Collected works. 2. Wertheimer, Max, 1880-1943. 3. Social psychology—Collected works. I. Luchins, Edith Hirsch, joint author. II. Title. [DNLM: 1. Psychology, Social. HM251 L936r]
  H62.5.U5L82   300′.1′8   72-3525
  ISBN 0-8387-1227-4 (v. 1-2)

PRINTED IN THE UNITED STATES OF AMERICA

To
Muzafer Sherif,
for his scholarship, friendship, and sincere interest in man as
Homo sapiens

Contents of Volume I

Preface

The task of reconstructing Wertheimer's social psychology seminars at the New School for Social Research was more difficult than that of reconstructing his seminars on problem solving and thinking for the following reasons. Sometimes the seminar was attended by several professors of the New School's Graduate Faculty (University in Exile). One or more of them would present for discussion a preliminary formulation of an idea or a rather formal thesis. In addition, other refugee scholars, as well as American scholars, addressed the seminars. The students varied in their background and training, ranging from professional people with advanced degrees to adult education students with little formal education. The topics, which varied from seminar to seminar, were discussed from the points of view of a variety of disciplines and in terms of the personal beliefs of the professors and students. They frequently expressed their concern with the social, political, and economic problems of the 1930s and freely brought up matters that interested them, for example, a current event, a recent Gallup poll, a research idea, an experiment in progress, a preliminary draft of a paper, a recently published paper. At times the discussions seemed to lack organization because there was a tendency to go off in many directions. Social, political, and philosophical ideologies were expressed, sometimes with considerable intensity. In some sessions Wertheimer presented a thesis and then attacked or defended it. In other sessions he systematically discussed what was said after the speaker had finished or he repeatedly interrupted to express his reactions to what was being said. In still other sessions he said little, but provoked arguments by a look or a remark or a question. He did not appear so neutral as in the seminars on problem solving and thinking. He passionately believed in certain ideas and expressed his convictions by voice or by expressive movements. As one of his students wrote, "His involvement in the issues was often reflected in his voice and manner. . . . Easily aroused to indignation by approaches which he regarded as *blind* or as not making sufficient allowance for the human capacity for intelligence, curiosity, altruism . . . he directed his anger at ideas rather than people." Another student wrote that Wertheimer once gave "a seminar with Karen Horney, the psychoanalyst, Bernard Glueck, Sr. (and others) of which I remember . . . that there were occasional typical Wertheimerian explosions." (The reference was to a seminar on power in which Hans Speier, Kurt Riezler, and Abraham Maslow were among the other par-

9

ticipants who presented papers.) Wertheimer's spontaneous reactions sometimes encouraged others to speak freely to him during and after class.

Although Wertheimer is the central figure in the reconstruction, other
people also contributed to the stimulating intellectual atmosphere of the
seminars. We are particularly indebted to the seminal ideas learned from the
original faculty members of the University in Exile. Despite their language
difficulties and the problems of establishing a new university in a foreign
country, during the depth of the economic depression, they transported the
best of German university life to America and kindled ideas and generated
research that contributed to the revolutionizing of the social sciences in
America. In *Verlorenes Paradise (Paradise Lost)*, Wolfgang Metzger (1970) described the Psychological Institute of Berlin during 1917-1931. When we read
his description of the facilities and of the teaching and research by Köhler,
Lewin, and Wertheimer, as well as the work of their students and research
assistants, some of us who were privileged to study with Wertheimer in
America might wonder what made us feel that the New School was *Paradise
Regained.* Since there was no laboratory, no laboratory equipment, no office
space, and no research rooms (and a library that lacked most of the books
and journals of psychology), we suspect that what was important was not the
physical facilities in Berlin or the lack of them at the New School, but the
teachers and the teaching methods. Wertheimer and the other eminent refugee scholars created an intellectual and social atmosphere in the University
in Exile that made us oblivious to the physical surroundings; they were able to
transfer to the United States features of the intellectual paradise that Metzger
described.

Wertheimer came to America at a time when cultural relativism was the
stylish doctrine and psychology was very self-conscious about its status as a
science. Many students and visiting professors had been nurtured on cultural
relativism and were convinced that in order to be scientific psychologists must
use certain methods and must renounce interest in certain topics. Yet some of
them returned week after week to learn from Wertheimer another approach
to psychology and to hear him talk about the so-called forbidden topics. Even
with customary, conventional topics he did not deal with them in the customary academic manner but often provoked discussions that stirred the heart as
well as the brain. Many found his ideas disturbing, perhaps because they went
against their cherished beliefs about what topics and methods were scientific
or about how psychology should be taught. Some left; but others came back
to listen and to argue. Wertheimer did not ask that the students become his
disciples; he wanted them to face the issues that were at stake, issues that he
believed had consequences for the treatment of man and the world.

His teaching came as a breath of fresh air to those of us who were seeking
answers to the questions of what is the nature of man, the nature of society,
the nature of the physical world, and the required relationships among them.
Wertheimer made us realize that these were not just theoretical questions but
that the answers to the questions implied certain doctrines of man and that
the acceptance of one or another answer could affect what is done to man.
He taught during the Great Depression, in which people were spiritually as
well as financially impoverished. Some of the students had become alienated
·from their parents' traditional beliefs and sought a new outlook, hoping to
find it in science. Some students were content with the answers that the scien-

tific study of man gave them, but others felt that something was lacking. For example, cultural relativism freed them from certain beliefs and of many traditions, but it also made Hitler's doctrines possible. They were ambivalent to the notion that value had no ontic existence, that values and norms were a result of arbitrary social influence in which those who had the power could mold people to believe in their doctrines. Science's answer to their search for the Truth was like Pontius Pilate's answer when he was asked what truth is; he remarked, "What is Truth?" and walked away. He did not have to answer because he had the Roman Legions to enforce whatever he willed to be true.

Wertheimer was to many of us the first psychologist who not only stopped to answer but told those who were unconcerned about Truth to face the question. He made us feel, believe and think that questions of value and ethics were of paramount importance, that they were not only of theoretical significance but also had consequences for the fate of individual men.

In attending and in reconstructing the seminars, it was helpful to Abraham S. Luchins to have had the privilege of having been introduced to the field of personality and social psychology in Hadley Cantril's courses. It was in one of these courses, *The Social Psychology of Everyday Life*, that Muzafer Sherif, one of Cantril's former students, described his now classical experiment on social norms. Sherif's experiments were often the focus of controversial discussions in Wertheimer's seminar. The severe criticism of Sherif's work by Wertheimer provoked many of the experimental outgrowths that were conducted with Wertheimer, and later, alone, in order to reach experimental decisions. During all this time, regardless of the fact that ASL was associated with his main antagonist, Sherif maintained warm friendly relations with us. As a token of our appreciation of what his friendship meant to us for nearly forty years, we dedicate this volume to him.

The reconstruction is based on ASL's lecture notes taken during the seminar as well as on the discussions of the seminar material with his adult education and college students. The material was organized by ASL so that it revolved around doctrines that had been proposed throughout the ages to questions about the nature of man, of society, of the physical world, and of the relations among them. This orientation had been shaped by ASL's undergraduate teachers: Sol Blum in history, Edwin Spengler in economics, and Isidore Kayfetz in education. The erudition of these men prepared ASL for the concepts and names that were alluded to in the seminars. In reconstructing the seminars, ASL filled in the details because his students asked questions or seemed to be baffled by what had been said. It is at present difficult to separate the seminars and after-class discussions at the New School from the lectures and discussions in ASL's classes, which served as sounding boards for the seminar material. We are grateful to our students in the WPA Adult Education classes as well as to our students in Yeshiva University, McGill University, the University of Oregon, the University of Miami, and the State University of New York at Albany for keeping alive the discussion of the topics, for the many hours of stimulating class and after-class discussions, and for companionship in research along the lines suggested by Wertheimer. For heuristic purposes, we present some of the experimental outgrowths. Perhaps they will stimulate the research that still needs to be done in order to test Wertheimer's conjectures.

We are also indebted to the Natural Science Project Science Courses for

Baccalaureate Education, Rensselaer Polytechnic Institute; V. Lawence Parse-gian, its chairman and Rensselaer professor; Alan S. Meltzer, professor of physics and astronomy at Rensselaer; and others on the project who created a stimulating social atmosphere that reestablished many features of the intellec-tual climate of the New School for Social Research and made us realize that the topics dealt with by Wertheimer are still with us, and that events in the past 30 years have made them more timely than ever.

The research reported in this monograph was terminated in 1970 by factors beyond our control. We express our appreciation to the National Institute of Mental Health for assistance in the preparation of the first draft of this monograph which appeared as a series of technical reports between 1970-1973 and was supported by Mental Health Grant Numbers MH-1269204-05.

We are grateful to Mr. Dell H. Warnick, ASL's graduate student at S.U.N.Y.-Albany, for compiling the name and subject index of this volume.

Abraham S. Luchins
State University of New York at Albany

Edith H. Luchins
Rensselaer Polytechnic Institute

Introduction: Recollections of a Master Teacher,* by Austin B. Wood

Max Wertheimer was one of "Hitler's gifts to America," a bit of silver lining to the dark cloud of Nazism.

I attended the first set of lectures he gave at Columbia (date ?) shortly after his flight to this country. We young American graduate students were just beginning to hear about the new trend of thought in psychology, stemming from the German Phenomenologists, Gestalt psychology. It was an enlightening experience for us. But, in my own life, the really unique experience came a term or two later when he moved down to the New School and became one of the first of those scholars and scientists who were to become the "University in Exile" under the aegis of Alvin Johnson. You know what the typical student composition of New School classes was: 1) under graduates endowed with a bit of vision, or restive under the more or less ossified curriculum of the colleges in the city, 2) Ph.D. candidates from universities in the area (I was one of these), 3) Post-doctoral students wishing to keep abreast of new developments in their field, and 4) a few of that group which we at the University of California in the twenties had called the "Pelicans"—older people, usually college graduates who wished to maintain their self-image as educated and cultured intellectual individuals mostly *without too much effort,* so they attended a course or two from time to time. A few of them were quite serious and did all the homework quite conscientiously, but the majority were far less dedicated, did little work but nevertheless convinced themselves that they were serious intellectuals.

Well, the first class Wertheimer gave at the New School had all these types in it. He spent considerable time at the beginning ascertaining the interests, wishes, background preparation (or lack of it) of his group, and then he proceeded to give a course that gave something meaningful to every single person in that heterogeneous conglomeration of "scholars." I have never, before or after, experienced anything like it. His presentation was at many levels simultaneously. It was at once simple and complicated, obvious and profound, professional and lay, technical and nontechnical. He used lecture, discussion, quiz, demonstration, and various techniques that he seemed to have de-

* Reprinted by permission of Austin B. Wood, Professor Emeritus, CUNY: Brooklyn, N.Y.

13

veloped on the spot. I remember once when he was introducing us to the elementary, essential Gestalt concepts when he went over to the piano and played a series of passages which he asked us to identify. No one could. He replayed them, maintaining the same tones but very gradually altering the temporal values of the tones until we all had an "aha" experience and recognized "Yankee Doodle" or a fragment from Mozart or Verdi. Then he made sketches on the blackboard. He projected the signatures of famous people on the screen and discussed the common qualities of their signatures and their personalities, suggesting that a signature is, among other things, a product of a person(ality) in action. Then he made up synthetic signatures on the blackboard and asked us to try to describe their writers.

In my six decades as a student, I have had three teachers who truly inspired me and whom, I may say, I revered. The first was Exum Percival Lewis who taught a "physics for non-engineering students" at Berkeley in the twenties. At the end of each lecture, he was mobbed by students clamoring for answers to questions his lecture had elicited. He made introductory physics so exciting, we were often quite late for our next class. The second of my trio was William Kirk, economist. His subject was, U.S. Immigration Policy. At that time, I couldn't care less about U.S. Immigration Policy but all who had taken Econ 34 reported that he related our Immigration Policy to contemporary political and economic conflicts, and that it became, in effect, one man's view of contemporary institutions. He was also said to be taking some lusty swings at the powers that were in the course of his account and analysis of U.S. Immigration laws and their effects. His iconoclastic attitude naturally appealed to us young ones. This attitude stiffened and, while I was in his class, it came to his being ordered, under penalty of dismissal, by the university administration, acting under pressure from the Regents, to cease criticising official U.S. policy. He refused and was fired. He concluded his last lecture by quoting Kipling's "if" ("if you can keep your head when all about you. . .") Corny, yes. But deeply moving to young idealists distressed to learn of the exploitation of man by man.

Third in my trio was Wertheimer, and he was head and shoulders above all others. He did not publish very much. Neither did he perish! He TAUGHT. When some student 200 years from now writes the history of American psychology, from the point of view of the *sources* of the most significant ideas, ideas later refined, developed, tested, researched, etc., by others, but first excogitated, intuited, evolved (in a process of "emergent evolution") by the "sources," I am sure Wertheimer will be among the foremost of them. My own favorites on such a list would include also Edward Tolman and Abraham Maslow. It was Tolman, by the way, who became the leader of the "Oath Non-Signers" at Berkeley, putting his pension on the line, when he was within a few years of retirement, because of his opposition to a fascistic action by the administration that was ultimately outlawed by the California State Supreme Court. Wertheimer approved Tolman's stand, I am sure.

Did you know that, but for an accident of fate, the author of *Mentality of Apes* would have been Wertheimer rather than Köhler? Wertheimer was originally scheduled to go to Teneriffe but something, illness, or whatever prevented his going and Köhler took his place. Don't you wonder how the volume would have differed from the one we know had Wertheimer authored it?

An illustration Wertheimer used in one of his lectures that sticks in my mind was the account of a German anthropologist who lived for some time in an Indian Village deep in the Amazonian jungle. He was studying, among other things, their songs and considered himself fortunate in obtaining as informant, a talented and personable young man who promised faithfully to sing to the anthropologist all the songs of the entire tribe. In session after session, the two collaborated until the young man declared that he had sung absolutely all the songs. "Are you sure?" pushed the anthropologist. "Absolutely," said the young man. From the fact that the young man had sung nothing like a love song and from other lines of evidence, the anthropologist was just about to conclude that these people knew the sexual act and its relation to the production of babies, that they enjoyed erotic experiences, but that they were strangers to the tender emotion of LOVE. It was on the eve of departure for the return home when, strolling on the village outskirts at twilight, he heard a male voice singing a song he had not heard before. It was his informant serenading a young woman. When taxed with his apparent repudiation of his promise to "sing all," the young informant said, "But, Sir, I could not possibly sing a love song to you. You see, I do not love you."

An hour with Wertheimer was an excitement, "a thing of beauty and a joy forever." His examples and illustrations were so varied, so imaginative, so apt, so illuminating—you were constantly acquiring new perspectives, new insights. Aha experience followed an aha experience. There was a teacher! Socrates may have been a better teacher than Wertheimer but I doubt it.

He was a gentleman, too, and a gentle man. An hour at his dinner table or an evening in his home convinced you that his heart was as big as his mind. I remember one debate we had on the basic nature of human nature and the relation of that to better methods of child rearing. "Was the untutored child selfish, egotistical, anarchic, annoying? Or was he (she) generous, outgoing, warm, loving?" I was a freshly minted coin of the American behaviorism —materialism—Calvinism—pessimism and I supported the first point of view. The Master supported the latter. Certainly, his own family seemed to have been living proof that he had been much closer to the truth than had I.

Life has been good to me. And one of the most precious gifts it has given me was my association with Max Wertheimer.

Revisiting
Wertheimer's Seminars

1
The Place of Value in Science

The Joint Seminar on Methodology in the Social Sciences, held at the New School in the Fall of 1936, was conducted by the entire faculty of the University in Exile. *The professors often outnumbered the students, who were undergraduates, graduate students, post-doctoral students, and intelligent laymen with no college education. In these as well as later on in Wertheimer's seminars in Social Psychology, there were often passionate discussions of value. What was said in these discussions was presented by Abraham S. Luchins to his students and their reactions were often discussed with Wertheimer. In reconstructing the discussions on value we have tried to preserve Wertheimer's comments but have taken the liberty to revise the contributions of others and to add the results of the discussions in ASL's Adult Education and Yeshiva College Classes. The discussions reflect our collating five years of commentary on each topic.*

In the first session one of the professors gave a brief but vivid description of current events. He concluded that people were bewildered by what was happening as one calamity after another befell them, their country, and their community. They did not know what to do as their cherished beliefs, institutions, and their very lives seemed to be threatened. They sought salvation but no longer believed in the efficacy of prayer. The world had lost its enchantment. They no longer believed in magic. Some of these people believed that any salvation would have to come from science and not from God. Therefore, they turned to the scientists as their ancestors had turned to the priest and the magician for help. They believed that science was power and that only the scientist had the means to straighten out their lives and the social scene. "What is, and what can be, the answer of the social scientists?" He directed this question to everybody.

Nearly everybody including Wertheimer expressed an opinion in the informal discussion that followed. Some made it clear that they were not expressing their own beliefs but were attempting to bring before the seminar the diversity of opinions and the possible answers social scientists would give to the question which had been presented. The professors spoke informally, interrupting each other to add, to modify, or to illustrate what was being said. The following reactions of social scientists emerged:

19

1. There were scientists who admitted that we lived in troubled times but they pointed to recorded history and said that the present was not unique. Man had always had such crises and would continue having them "until the last syllable of recorded time." It was just like bad weather, we talked about it, we complained about it but we could do nothing about it. It was, however, comforting to know that similar problems had existed in ancient times, in the Middle Ages, and even in modern times. One could just look at the history of the Jews in the Biblical times or in the Middle Ages as well as in the present; they had survived and so would we. We just had to sit tight in our storm cellars until the cyclone passed. Some of these social scientists, therefore, told us not to get unduly alarmed, to have patience and fortitude, and to resign ourselves to what had been and would be the lot of man in human history. Others were more optimistic; they said that things would soon normalize themselves. There would not only be good weather again, but there would even be some benefits derived from the present tempests. Every cloud had a silver lining.

2. There were other social scientists, however, who said that science had no business meddling in mundane things. Science should instead continue in its tradition of seeking the Truth. This had been the tradition of Ancient Greece in which science had been born. This had been the tradition that had led to science's greatest discoveries and theories. These scientists asked to be left alone in their cloistered campii or in the quiet studies of their ivy-covered towers so that they could devote themselves to studying what really mattered, the Eternal Truth. They were not overly concerned with the ephemeral phenomena that comprised but flickering shadows without substance. Some of these people were proud of being pure scientists and looked down on the applied scientists, the technicians. They did not want to become corrupted by dealing with practical problems.

3. There were still other scientists who wanted to do something about the ills of the world. They felt that science not only could, but should, do something about current social, political, and economic problems. They believed that science could lead mankind to progress in its pursuit of life, liberty, happiness and prosperity. Some of them said that society should use the scientific method to collect useful information on which to base public policy. Just as the physical scientists had helped society so could the social scientists. In the writings of the technocrats, of the New Deal's Brain Trusters and of the Marxists, they saw examples of scientists who were proposing that certain ideas and institutions should be preserved, that certain ideas and institutions should be abolished, and that certain new ideas and new institutions were needed to further mankind's quest for progress.

Although many social scientists were willing to participate in this, there were social scientists who were more cautious or timid about becoming involved. They claimed that science was value free. Social scientists, therefore, could only present the facts as they found them. They could not make statements about what ought to be or what should be. This was reflected in the work of the physician. He, the physician, was concerned with curing patients; but science did not tell him to cure patients. He turned to science only for the means to cure patients. The methods of science told him which means were the most efficient ones to help him meet his goal. They could not tell him whether his goal was good or bad because such matters were basically foreign to science. Science did not evaluate ends but only evaluated and constructed means. In the social sciences there were men like Max Weber, who maintained that all that a scientist could do was to say that these were the means which would produce such and such consequences, but he could not determine which goal one should choose, because there were no criteria for such an endeavor. A society could adhere to any goal it pleased to pursue. These social scientists went on to point out that there was a difference between dealing with what was and what ought to be. The former involved matters of fact and could be dealt with scientifically; the latter, however, involved matters of personal taste and therefore could not be dealt with through science. Thus there were limits to what science could do. For example, it could not deal with ultimate facts, values, purposes, etc.; such questions belonged to metaphysics and not to science.

Wertheimer seemed to be disturbed by what was being said. Two or three times he walked to the window. Finally, he interrupted to challenge the idea that science was divorced from life. The Greek scientists and philosophers might have placed a higher value on *Theoria* than on *Praxis* but they were not recluses who removed themselves from society to seek personal enlightenment; for example, some of the Cosmologists preached doctrines that they believed would lead to a way of life in which man would live in harmony with nature and with other men. They not only sought to enlighten people about the true or real nature and causes of things but were active in the political and social life of the community to the extent that they often got into trouble with the community. (Socrates was not the only philosopher who got into trouble.) Plato's *Republic* did not propose a vague, mystical retreat but dealt with the question of how to create a good Society on this earth.

A student said that he agreed, that Plato had sought the True and the Beautiful and the Good in order to lead men to virtue, to proper conduct. The purpose of Plato's metaphysics was to establish a foundation for ethical conduct and not to direct men to a mystical and other-worldly way of life. Plato, it could be said, had been a social reformer, not a mystic. The other-worldliness of Greek philosophers might have been due to the fact that they had been cast into the role of the Christian saints who walked off into the desert to commune with God. But the early Christians had not regarded them (the Greek philosophers) in this light. Greek philosophy had been associated with the materialism and sensuality of paganism and therefore had been rejected by the Church. Only after a thousand years had passed and the Church's ideas had come to dominate the minds of men, had the Greek philosophers been rediscovered and used to rationalize church doctrines. (This was not the first time that Greek philosophy had been related to religious ideas. The Jews of Alexandria, especially Philo, had rationalized the Jewish religion with Plato's philosophy.) Many of the problems of Greek philosophy had been seen to be of value in dealing with theological problems. The Greek philosophers were now seen to be concerned with the search for the Truth, and this search was equated by some Scholastic philosophers with the seeking of Him. Socrates, Plato, Aristotle and even some of the Pre-Socratic Philosophers were then assumed to have lived like ideal Christians, perhaps because Christianity and Christian were synonymous with virtue. This rehabilitation of the Greek philosophers overlooked the fact that they had been men of affairs who had sought to convert people to their philosophy in order to lead them to a better life. They were pagans to whom the mystical ideas that were attributed to them would have been foreign (cf. Collingswood, 1965).[1]

A student questioned the idea that the Christians were, in contrast to the Greek philosophers, other-worldly and mystical. The Christians also were preaching a doctrine that was offered as a solution to man's ills. One could find sentences in the Gospels that showed that they were offering advice about how people should behave on earth even though earth was but a vestibule to an eternal world to those who were true believers. In one sense they were different from the Greeks. The laws had already been revealed to them. Their duty was but to carry them out. The early Christians were aggressive in putting these laws into practice. They were social reformers who busied themselves with conquering in His name. They were not content just to commune with Him. Perhaps we needed to reevaluate the role of other worldliness and mysticism among the masses of the early Christians. While they yearned for salvation, many of them went about the business of this world's concerns and this world's problems. The other world constituted the idealized way of life. It was put on a pedestal and worshipped as an Ideal, but it played little or no role in the actual lives of most people, laymen, scholars, and even some of the clergy. Perhaps the notion of a dispassionate, objective search for the Truth, with no concern for practical matters, was actually quite a modern idea. It was the ideal of science that had replaced the mystic's communion with Him.[2]

One of the professors said that facts and scientific ideas became more objectively viewed as they were separated from values, as they were studied apart from moral questions regarding man's place in the universe. In view of this, social scientists should not become involved in ideological issues about what ought to be done. Furthermore, it was not possible to deal with the question of value in a scientific manner because it did not deal with what was, with facts, but with ends. Max Weber had pointed out that there could not be any genuine knowledge of the ought. Values could not be studied in an empirical or rational manner. There were varieties of values and they often conflicted with each other. The social scientist could indicate the conflicts but he could not offer a solution. The solution was up to each person. (Some of ASL's students said that Weber's thesis was a safe course to take in a troubled world,

1. James K. Morrison, ASL's student who had been a Catholic priest commented: It should be pointed out that Paul did not simply regard the pagan Greeks as materialistic and imbued with sensuality. He often preached to them (for example, at Athens) in their own language. He seemed to respect their integrity and fought against Peter and others (during what is called the first ecumenical council at Jerusalem) so that the non-Jews could have the gospel preached to them and could become followers of Christ. Timothy and others also took a more liberal outlook on the non-Jews and this outlook eventually prevailed. It should also be pointed out that too often authors have interpreted Plato and his Socratian dialogues (for example, Phaedo, Symposium, etc.) as indicative of Plato's convictions regarding life after-death, immortality, virtue, etc., whereas in actuality there is some evidence that Plato wrote most of these as a farce, hoping that the reader would see how the arguments put in the mouth of Socrates in favor of, for example, immortality were actually poor and fallacious arguments. (JKM).

2. The early Christians were not as other-world oriented as some think. There seemed to be much doubt, even in the gospels, regarding when Christ would come again. At first the Christians thought he would come again soon after Christ's death. When this did not happen early Christians began speaking of living in the world and meeting Christ in the next life. But even still, Paul, for example, speaks often of many practical matters (for example, respect for the laws and traditions of non-Christians) which were important to the this-world life of the Christians. (JKM) See Max Brod, *Paganism, Christianity and Judaism,* 1970, for a detailed discussion of this and related questions (ASL).

especially when one's salary depended on the state. It reflected the Scholastics' doctrine of the two-fold truth as well as Kant's solution to the problem of value.)

Wertheimer remarked that those who did not wish to become involved would not be allowed to stay in their storm cellars or cloisters. They would at some time be asked to take a stand. They would be told that science serves the state. What was true and good was what was of value to the state. He who was not involved in the pursuit of the state's goals was its enemy. Because of modern methods of communication and coercion, the state would compel everyone to obey. This was the policy of the Nazis. If they succeeded in conquering the world, there would be no science devoted to the pursuit of Truth but only a technology to serve the state. Social science would become merely a technology to control the minds of men. Perhaps it might be wiser for the scientists to become involved if they wished to preserve the goal of science, the pursuit of Truth.

Someone doubted Wertheimer's dire predictions by pointing out that in the year 400 pagan philosophers would never have believed that in the years 1600-1700, the Church would be persecuting as heretics philosophers who rejected or criticized Aristotle's philosophy. Nor would the pagan men of letters have believed that the Church would be a patron of the pagan classical writers. They would never have believed that there would someday be a Renaissance of paganism, led by churchmen, in which the cultures of ancient Greece and Rome would be considered to be the Golden Ages of Mankind, and that there would be a war between the ancients and the moderns in which the ideas of the pagans would be defended by the very Church that was saying in the year 400 that philosophy was a tool of the devil. Similarly we could not refuse to believe that the Nazis, Fascists, and Communists would in the distant future rediscover and idealize the ideas that were at present being rejected, that they would reprint the books that they had burned and teach the ideas that they had banned.

Wertheimer challenged this by saying that before the Nazis got into power people said that Hitler's program was just propaganda. They said that once he got into office he would be like the rest of them, that what he was proposing was just campaign talk. What evidence is there that he will not carry out the program he has described in *Mein Kampf?* A student interrupted to say that it was wrong to assume that Greek knowledge had been common knowledge in Europe and that the Church had burned the books of the Greeks or banned them from the European universities. There had been no Greek universities in Western Europe and the Greek philosophical doctrines had not been the dominant ideas in Western Europe. Moreover, Greek philosophy and science had persisted in certain places. During the Middle Ages, Arab and Jewish scholars had kept it alive by studying and translating their texts. Certain Christian scholars, including churchmen, had studied with them and obtained from them translations of the Greek texts. It was, therefore, too superficial a view to say that what was happening now was similar to what had been the fate of Greek science and philosophy in the year 400.

Someone said that we had to face the possibility that if the Nazis were successful they would really do a thorough job of burning the books. They would, for example, be more systematic and efficient than those who had burned the Talmud, suppressed Hebrew scholarship and exiled and plundered the Jews in the Middle Ages. The Nazis were opposed to the most basic values of our civilization. They frankly said that they planned to change them and that they wanted to create a new kind of man. In view of this, could social scientists say that they must do nothing? When social scientists said that they were sorry about the ways in which their ideas were used but had to remain neutral in the battle over men's minds, they did not realize that their scholarly pursuits might create conditions favorable for a Nazi take-over. They said that social science must remain value free; yet some of them said that science could not deal with values or goals because such things did not relate to matters of facts but were based on the arbitrary whim or will of individuals, and that all values were arbitrary and meaningless expressions, mere emotive noises. Such comments destroyed the belief in values, and life became as Hobbes once said, nasty, brutish, and short, as man warred against man in pursuit of personal pleasure. But as Hobbes had also said, such was not a livable state of affairs, and, in order to preserve themselves, people would agree to let a sovereign preserve and/or make peace. The Third Reich was the Leviathan, the sovereign state of the twentieth century. The Führer would determine what was True, Beautiful and Good. He would give meaning and purpose to life and to the world which science said had no meaning and purpose.

Wertheimer pointed out that science required certain social conditions, for example, the very freedom to seek the truth it claimed was its goal. The seeking of truth involved decisions about value, about ethics.

Someone interrupted to say that no scientist, qua scientist, might say that he would work for X and not for Y because X's goals were better. It was just a matter of his taste. He went on to say that contemporary social scientists were drawing back from the grand programs to explain, to predict and control societies and mankind in order to lead them to Utopias. They now had a more modest view of what science could do. They were more critical of their pronouncements and more aware of the limitations of their methods. This did not mean that they had renounced the world. Just as Plato had gone to help the tyrant of Syracuse, the social scientist could serve as a consultant to governmental agencies, to educational and other institutions of the community, and to industry in order to help them function more efficiently. All this could be done in the tradition of science. But once a scientist started to determine the goals of the institution, he was no longer a scientist but a propagandist.

Wertheimer asked the speaker whether he really believed that the social scientist had no responsibility other than that of finding more efficient methods for the institution or the state. Was it scientific for German professors and physicians to develop better methods for the Nazi race program? To find better methods to kill and to torture people? Was it scientific for German professors and scientists to find better methods to arm the German army so that it could conquer the world?

The speaker answered that he saw no scientific reason why it was better for American scientists, physicians, or professors to do such things for the U.S.A. than for Germans to do them for the Third Reich.

Wertheimer asked the speaker if this meant that a scientist must give up his sensitivity to the relation of means to ends. The speaker answered, What proof do you have that he has, to begin with, such a sensitivity? Such a sensitivity is developed by one's society, and different societies develop different tastes and different sensitivities. Wertheimer said that perhaps it was but a dogma that man had no sensitivity about the adequacy of means-end relations in the course of his selecting and judging a course of action or a method to solve a particular problem. Had it been proven to be a universally valid thesis? Maybe we needed to reconsider the whole question of what was value, and to take another look at the doctrine of cultural relativism. It might not only be invalid but dangerous for human survival to say that one might pursue any goal he wished, and that there was no objective way to decide whether certain goals were better or worse for man to pursue.

The speaker said that one old view considered that man had many natural goals, in another view there had been only one goal, but now we knew that both views had been wrong. Man had as many goals as he wished, and science could not determine which were better or worse goals. Wertheimer said that such a view was blind to this question. "Is there a proper or improper relation of means to goals?" That is, was there or was there not in a concrete particular situation an inner relationship between goals and means?

After-Class Discussion

After class a few students engaged Wertheimer in a discussion. A student pointed out that in particular mathematical problems certain methods were required because of the admissibility conditions for a solution, and that there were problems with more than one solution. Wertheimer said that this did not mean that just any solution or any method solved the problem. It was a confounding of issues to say that because there were several ways to solve a problem that the solution chosen was arbitrary. It was a superficial view of matters to say that because a variety of means could achieve a certain goal that the relation of means to ends was arbitrary.

ASL said that the idea that it was not possible to decide between goals was not new. It was an ancient doctrine; for example, Protagoras had argued that everything was equally good, Gorgas had argued that everything was equally bad. Although Plato had thought that he had demolished their arguments, the arguments kept haunting all discussion of ethics. Maybe this testified to the validity of the doctrine. A student said that the doctrine had been used whenever someone wished to change the values of a group. It was used to unstructure the situation, to make things fluid so that the person could then propose his value system as a way out of the confusion. Since all value was merely custom, one might just as well accept his proposed value system. Usually the people who did this had the power to assert their will over others. Thus the ultimate determiner of value was power; what was true was what the boss said was true.

Wertheimer said that he was not denying that certain goals were arbitrarily imposed, but the question was whether there were goals that were required by the particular social system. He asked, What are the consequences for mankind as well as science when the scientist says that there are no inner relations between means and ends, that all goals are arbitrary, that man is free to do whatever he pleases and that science can only help one impose his goals on others but has nothing to say about the goals? A student pointed out that science did not know what should be the long- or even the short-range goals of mankind. It was not even sure about the goals for science. How could one, therefore, expect the social scientist, qua scientist, to determine the goals of society? A scientist was not like a Biblical prophet or a priest. Wertheimer pointed out that he was not saying that science should decide the ultimate or long term goals of society or mankind, but that in particular situations the scientist was able to, or should at least have tried, to make a decision about the consequence of his action or inaction. Moreover, there was nothing unscientific about a scientist's asking himself, What kind of world is needed for the pursuit of science in terms of its ideal, to seek the truth? This did not mean that the scientist should believe that he had the ultimate truths and proceed to create the kind of world that would reflect them. Someone said that the scientists had been doing this, and pointed out that the dogmatism of the Age of Reason's and the Enlightenment's epigones of science still existed. It represented a world view that had clashed openly with other views. It wanted to become the new universal religion of mankind. He challenged the idea that the pursuit of knowledge for its own sake was good. Maybe it had to be restrained, because it also created evil. This view was shocking to everybody. Wertheimer remarked that the student had challenged a prevalent idea and asked us to write to him our reactions to the statement.

Comments

The seminar's main points were used as a basis for a lecture to ASL's Adult Education class. The students' discussion and questions led to several concluding remarks (by ASL) that are presented in order to highlight some of the issues discussed in the seminar which are pertinent to present-day discussions. What is presented below reflects statements or answers ASL obtained in his reading of the history of science in order to answer these questions.

1. The notion of detached scientists seeking the truth may be a myth. The men who were involved in the scientific revolution were interested in the world around them. Men like Bruno, Galileo, Gassendi, Mersenne, Descartes, and Leibnitz did not separate themselves from life but aggressively attacked scholastic philosophy and sought to convince people of the truth of their doctrines. The early discussion of scientific ideas took place in what we would today call literary clubs. The discussion in these clubs dealt with political, social, and economic problems of the day. The scientific societies that were founded in the seventeenth century discussed metaphysical and theological problems as well as reports of experiments, novels, trade, industry, agriculture, education, mathematical problems, and even music and dancing. The so-called history of the war between science and religion is replete with examples of the interaction of science with the ordinary world. The scientists were concerned not only with religious problems, but also with the political problems of the day, such as the development and control of industry, trade, taxes, and legal matters. Scientists did not object when the philosophes and the literati popularized their ideas. The pioneers as well as the popularizers of science wanted to extend the scientific method to every aspect of human thought, social life and technology. It may be said with some justification that the passion to convert people to Christianity had been transferred to convert people to Science.

There were social reformers who believed that just as there were natural laws that determined the motion of the heavenly bodies and objects on earth, so there were natural laws that determined social behavior. They proposed a social physics (for example, the Physiocrats) to explain man's behavior. Laws derived from such a social physics were to replace the prescientific laws and customs which were man-made, unnatural, and therefore the cause of mankind's ills. They sought to establish political, economic and juridicial policies in terms of the natural laws that they claimed to have discovered. In fact, the idea of extending the mechanistic model of physics to social life was considered to be more feasible to men like Diderot and other Encyclopaedists than were the proposals to apply it to biology and chemistry. Thus the social science emerged as a movement to transform society in the image of science. In view of all this, when social scientists are now being asked to help solve social problems they are being asked to do what they had done in the past. Why therefore do some social scientists claim that it is not their traditional role? Perhaps the pioneers of the social sciences bit off more than they could chew. Contemporary scientists have learned from history that they have been wrong. A host of problems and social ills followed in the wake of the acceptance by the state of the policies that they had proposed, for example, the doctrines of the Philosophical Radicals. Some social scientists now say that the so-called natural laws of social, political, and economic behavior were actually rationalizations for the emerging capitalistic society. At present, social scientists frankly admit that they do not know what are *the* laws. Some say that the errors of the pioneers of social science were due to their lack of objectivity and their involvement in the social scene. In order to gain a proper perspective it would be necessary for social scientists to withdraw from the social scene, to avoid participating so that they might observe it as objectively and dispassionately as possible. Thus they have renounced the role of social reformers and are focusing on collecting facts; and only in this way, it is believed, will it be possible to obtain valid laws for the building of a sound theory. At present, therefore, they prefer to seek the truth and not techniques for social use. They have no concern with the use of their ideas by society because the true scientist is happy to be left alone in the pursuit of the Truth. He does not propagandize his ideas.

2. Wertheimer agreed that the early social philosophers had made mistakes. The messianic hopes of religion were replaced by the belief in Progress. Science was going to turn the earth into Paradise. Bacon believed that there was a definite number of fundamental facts that could be discovered in a few generations by the use of his methods, and that man would soon live in the Utopian world described in the *New Atlantis*. Descartes was also certain that his methods had general applicability and that if they were used they would lead men to the indubitable truths. Similarly, Leibnitz believed that he had developed a universally applicable method of calculation that could replace disputation and error in decision-making in society as well as science. But, by the end of the nineteenth century, it had become clear that things were not as simple as they were believed to be in the early days of the scientific revolution. Physics and mathematics were shaken at their foundations. Some of the literati who were the epigones of the scientific world view were disillusioned because things had not gotten better; national war still followed national war; class war and poverty were on the increase as more and more people left or were driven off the land into the crowded industrial cities where culture and

morality were not higher, but lower than ever. Nor did the Golden Age preached by the Age of Reason and the Enlightenment arrive. Just as the Philosophes of the mid-seventeenth century had espoused science and proclaimed her virtues and fecundity, the intelligentsia in the mid-nineteenth century began to urge divorce, denouncing her as barren or as the mother of all of mankind's ills. Some students argued that science was not at fault but that it was being corrupted by its ties to technology and to the capitalistic states. They pointed with approval to the use and development of science in Russia. Others argued that only in a truly democratic society could science be truly fruitful and bring no evils.

Only one student expressed the belief that science was potentially dangerous because it had destroyed the values, ethics, and traditions of the past and had not replaced them with anything. He pointed out that the Manpower Commission of the U.S. Government was harnessing science to fight Hitler. In the last war, however, the government had not made much use of scientists. Thomas Edison had to suggest that a physicist be placed on the Defense Board which he chaired, just in case some calculations would have to be done. Science has much greater status now than in 1917. We must not forget that science, a product of the human mind, would destroy man unless we checked it now. It was destroying the cultural values that man had evolved throughout the long course of human history. Man was to science but another machine, as Huxley had described in his *Brave New World.* (ASL as well as the entire class thought that his remarks were outlandishly exaggerated and were in fact ridiculous. Now, thirty years later, his assertion is the common one and the other opinions are the uncommon ones. The atom bomb and automation of industry and of education seem to have created comments like those of this lonely prophet of doom in 1938.)

3. Just as Descartes and others had called for and had initiated a reexamination of philosophers' fundamental ideas, the philosophers who are concerned with science have proceeded to reexamine the foundations of science. Some social scientists have listened to these philosophers and have agreed that more attention must be paid by social scientists to their fundamental assumptions. Science must purge itself of all unscientific ideas. They have argued that when a sound foundation of science exists, then they would be able to be of real help. Other social scientists, however, have wondered whether the solutions of particular problems of society depended on the solutions of the fundamental problems of science. The scholars in the physical sciences and mathematicians have not stopped their work to wait for the end of the crisis in the foundations of their disciplines. Does the study of and concern with foundational problems require that social scientists withdraw from life and avoid dealing with particular social problems? Someone attempted to draw an analogy between what these social scientists were doing and what Saint Augustine did to solve a crisis in Christian theology. He separated the secular realm from the sacred realm. God and His Church were not concerned with the political and economic affairs of man but with man's salvation. Science, the God of modern man, was not concerned with mundane things, but with the Truth. Those who have the intellectual ability are predestined to find it; the others are doomed to confusion and ignorance. Just as the descendants of the children of Abel, the elect, were predestined to be saved, so were the pure scientists, the elect of science, predestined to reach the Truth, the Heaven of Science. Unfortunately modern man did not believe that there was an eternal

City of Science similar to the City of God. Science was a perpetually moving stream of ideas that men created. Science had destroyed the belief in the City of God in order to replace it with the City of Science with the hope of bringing the City of God down to earth, but it had not succeeded because science called for perpetual doubting.[3]

Science seems to have given up the doctrine that it can get at the ultimate truth. Scientific theories are now viewed as ephemeral opinions, not the eternal truth. It now seems that man is doomed to ignorance. He just changes its forms. In the past two thousand years he has sought the Truth in Christianity and in Science, now he seeks it in the varieties of Communism, Socialism, Fascism, Nazism. Just as he was disappointed with Christianity's and Science's schemes for stabilizing his world and giving it meaning, man will find that whatever "ism" he chooses will lead to disappointment. So why should we get excited over what we should or could do? It all boils down to the same thing. Ecclesiastics had the answer; all is vanity. Maybe Epicurus had the right idea. Man should seek happiness in small communities, in fellowships, and lead a life that will not stir up the desires and passions. He should seek happiness in simple things and gentle sensations and thoughts.

Informal Discussions on Value

Wertheimer asked ASL what he thought about the discussion in the seminar. He said that he was surprised to hear Wertheimer say that the social scientists should involve themselves in arguments about value. When Wertheimer asked why, ASL said that when physics rejected the teleological world view of Aristotle it became a successful science. Similarly the social scientists would become successful. The various theories of optics and sound did not destroy art and music. Why therefore should a value-free science of man imperil man? Another student who had joined the discussion at this point said that it was a myth to say that science was value free. It stressed reason, rationality. What was not reasonable, for example, an intuitive revelation, was not acceptable as evidence or data even though many people might have experienced it. A million people might see a miracle, but unless a rational basis for it was established it would not be accepted. Thus rationality had a high value in science. It valued only the attitudes of this world and rejected the supernatural, for example, if someone tried to convince a scientist of the truth of his creed by showing that all of Jeremiah's prophecies came to be as foretold, the scientist would not accept it because he rejected the supernatural. In addition to these values there was the high value placed on liberalism and rejection of authority, for example, the scientist had to see or understand for himself what was what, and not accept an authority. He was free to decide, to accept or to reject authority. It was essential for academic freedom. It guaranteed productive, genuine thinking. Tradition blinded and hindered. Another value was the stress on actively striving to progress, to advance knowledge, the prediction of and control over natural events instead of the passive contemplative attitude of the mystic.

Wertheimer asked whether each of these values really represented science

3. I think it is quite questionable whether Augustine actually intended to separate the secular and sacred realm, except for the purpose of analogy and comparison. Plato is often accused of being idealistic for separating the material world from the world of ideas. But neither Augustine nor Plato were quite so naive.(JKM)

as it existed in the flesh and blood of human beings. He then went on to say that the thesis of a value-free science was a doctrine that might lead to nihilism. The cynical scientist would sell his services to the highest bidder. ASL said that a scientist had no scientific justification to refrain from selling his services other than to say that he did not like to do such and such a thing. The government could rightfully ask him, By what authority do you do this? A Hebrew prophet could say that God had instructed him. A Shaman could say that the spirits had instructed him. But what could the scientist answer? It became a question of who had more will power or might. A student said that the doctrine of a value-free science left the way open for idealistic and religious philosophies. Thus there was the realm of nature that science could deal with and there was a realm of ideas that was inaccessible to science. The scientist could refuse to act because of a greater commitment to the latter realm. Thus science took second place to religion, supernaturalism, etc. In order to avoid this dilemma, science must deal with value.

Wertheimer did not comment because he had to leave. Perhaps he would have agreed with Goldner (1960), who in discussing Weber's thesis concerning sociology pointed out that it represented a solution to "two tensions in Western Tradition: reason and faith; between knowledge and feeling, Classicism and Romanticism; between head and heart." Weber, Goldner says, proposed a truce by "the segregation of the contenders, by allowing each to dominate in different spheres of life." It did not lead, however, to a respect for both realms but to the destruction of human values and the turning of science into a technology.

2
Economics and Value

[During some of the sessions of the Joint Seminar and occasionally during Wertheimer's seminars, discussions of value in the context of economic doctrine were held. These discussions were used by ASL in his lectures. What follows reflects the organization of the discussions in ASL's classes.]

One of the professors said that despite what had been said last time about the aim of social sciences to be value free, economics had always been concerned with the problem of value. In ancient times and in primitive society reflection on and discussions of economic activity had been intimately related to ethics, morality, and politics. The Bible and Oral Law of the Jews contained numerous examples of economic doctrines related to commandments from the Deity. To the Greeks of ancient times economics had dealt with household management. The household was often involved in the production and/or exchange of goods and services as well as in their consumption. These economic activities of the household had often been regulated by the mores and ethics of the society. Therefore, economic activities had to some extent been regulated by laws and customs that were moral in nature.

The members of the seminars gave examples from history to illustrate the role of value in economic thought. [What follows is a more detailed statement of what was actually said on each point.] According to Plato, cooperation and interdependence of man were the basis of the economy and the state, and the division of labor led to more efficient production of the goods and services needed by the state and its members. That society was best in which each person did what he was by nature best suited to do. Some of Plato's notions of the good society are similar to the ideas of contemporary (1936-37) economic planners as well as to the ideas of Classical Economists. Although it has been said that Plato's *Republic* was a communistic state because the warriors were not allowed to have private property, he had many ideas which were similar to those of the classical (capitalistic) economists. He presented these ideas in the course of discussing various doctrines concerning what was the way to reach the Good, because Plato was not seeking knowledge about economics but of the eternal verities, the True, the Beautiful, and the Good. He did not,

31

however, neglect economic activities. In Plato's discussion of the exchange of commodities one can see certain features of modern utility concepts of value. Plato's conception of token currency for trading purposes reflects some of the modern Utopian economic doctrines that regard money as an evil.

Aristotle also stressed the role of the division of labor because of its productive efficiency in a way that reminds one of Adam Smith's *Wealth of Nations.* He justified private property on the grounds that people will take better care of property when it is theirs than when it is held in common, an argument that was used by Adam Smith and is still used today against communism and socialism. One can also find many other modern economic doctrines in Aristotle's work, for example, the labor theory of value, the concept of marginal utility, the concept of value in use and value in exchange, and even some arguments against monopoly. He believed that banking and trade produced social evils, that they corrupted man, and that agriculture led man to virtue. Like Plato, Aristotle's interest was not in economics per se. These economic doctrines and concepts were presented in the course of discussions about ethics and government and are found in Aristotle's books on ethics and politics. Like Plato, he was not describing economic activities so much as he was prescribing certain ways of acting. As did his contemporaries among the Hebrews, though to a lesser extent, he stressed that economic activities and economic relations should be ruled by justice. In an exchange between parties, neither party should make a profit or suffer a loss. These views of Aristotle's did not reflect what was actually taking place. Aristotle's ideas were the impractical or ideal ways of life; they were concepts of philosophy and not of life. It has been said that trade, not philosophy, was the ordinary Greek's way of life and the Roman's forte, and therefore Aristotle did not influence the economic activities of the ancient world. But, even the Romans produced moralists who tried to justify their rapacious economic activities in terms of their society's mores and folkways. Aristotle's philosophical ideas, however, fitted in with the Church Fathers' ideas; then churchman began to say that Christianity's ideas were compatible with Plato's and Aristotle's. They claimed that merchants could not please the Deity. On religious grounds they approved of certain economic activities and objected to others. They based their economic doctrines on theological or church doctrines. In their view, economic activity was subservient to the goals of salvation. The Church was opposed to usury (money lending) and trade because they were occupations that led men to sin against the Diety's laws. Poverty, not wealth, humility, not self-aggrandizement, and spirituality, not materialism were idealized. When Aristotle's philosophy became acceptable once more in the Middle Ages, the Churchmen used their authority to support their negative appraisals of money lending and of trade, and to support their doctrine that one should seek to maximize justice in the exchange and distribution of goods and services. Since the emphasis was on organizing the economic activities in line with the Church doctrines, economics was moral theology. They did not describe what was actually occurring in the social world, but what should be. Although the church tried to enforce these ideals, men did indulge in trade, usury, etc., for example, Venice and other Italian cities and Christian countries had good Christians who were bankers.

The Scholastic philosophers, however, were aware of the actual world. Some of them formulated what we would today call the utility and marginal utility theories of value. They recognized that the value of a commodity and/or a service was not in the commodity or service but in the mind of the evaluator, the mind of man. Scarcity, utility, and desirability contributed to the value of a commodity. Even though their discussions of value might have had elements similar to those of modern economics, the Scholastics were oriented toward the maintenance and furthering of church law. They were moralistic, not scientific. Even with the rise of science in the seventeenth century, economics (political economy) was still moralistic. It was now called Moral Philosophy, but the moral philosophers, for example, Adam Smith, taught economics in terms of natural law. It was, however, in terms of a different world view from that of the Greek or of the Scholastic philosophers. To the Greek philosophers the world was an organism not a mechanism; the idea of inert matter was foreign to them. Everything, mineral, vegetable, and animal, was part of an organism and had a definite part to play in it. Moreover, every part existed in the organism for a purpose. The failure of a part to fulfill its purpose set into action compensatory or retributive activity to restore the situation to what it was before it was upset.

Aristotle's work was the culmination of the teleological view of the universe, in which there was a chain of being from unformed matter to pure form and each being had a purpose to fulfill. It will be recalled that the Scholastic philosophers recast Aristotle into the Christian view of nature. Because of the concern with the *City of God* rather than the secular world, the stylish intellectual values and goals of man became otherworldly. But this was not an abrupt departure from the Greek philosophical tradition because they too were not concerned with *Praxis* but with *Theoria*, which led them to abstract otherworldly concepts; for example, the Good, the True, the Beautiful, Justice, Welfare, had been used by men like Plato and Aristotle as they sought to rationalize human behavior and to reconstruct or construct it. The actual behavior of man, however, lost some of its concreteness when it was dealt with in terms of abstractions and became even more divorced from the mundane world when it was discussed in terms of eternal laws. The theological discussion of these Ideals focused on the mystical feature of the Ideals. They lost their social significance in some of the theological formulations into which they were cast.

When the scientific revolution in physics rejected Aristotle and the Scholastic philosophy, some moral philosophers and scholars who were interested in government, politics, and economics also rejected the Aristotelian ideas of nature. They regarded the state and the economy as operating in terms of natural laws and not in terms of the supernatural laws of Aristotle or of the Scholastics. They claimed that just as there were laws regulating the movement of the stars in the heavens and the movement of bodies on earth, there were natural laws governing the lives of men and of societies. The social and political evils of the day were said to be due to the violation of these natural laws. (Note that they still viewed natural laws and the violation of them just as had the Greeks and the Scholastics; certain behavior was required and violation of the requirements led to punishment.) The early scientists, however, claimed that man and nature were ruled by natural laws (made by the Deity) which man's reason knew or could discover. In such an intellectual milieu economics came into being as an independent science. It still was moralistic and ethical in its approach as it propounded laws concerning the ways in which government should regulate (or not regulate) the economy of the nation, but it was believed by their proponents that the proposals were based on scientific discoveries of certain natural laws. The laws and proposals were soon criticized by their opponents as being neither natural nor beneficial, but the governmental policies were nevertheless established as if they had been derived from natural laws, and it was claimed that adherence to them would further the welfare of the nation and mankind. There appeared a plethora of contradictory doctrines—socialism, anarchism, capitalism—all appealing to the concept of natural law. It became evident to some social scientists that these doctrines of the nature of society and of man were human conjectures. Some even began to doubt that there were any intrinsic or necessary connections in what are called cause-and-effect relations in scientific theorizing. Thus the mechanistic view, which stressed determinism and rejected teleology, led to a conception of the world with no authority or requiredness. But this need not be so, claimed certain social scientists. To regard nature, man, and society from the mechanistic point of view elevated man to the place he had once reserved for the gods. It was a humanistic view. It did not mean that there were no longer any goals or values, but that they were human artifacts. It pointed to a concern with the actual lives of people and it took men away from concern with eternal, timeless, placeless values. It told man to create Paradise on earth. These scientists, as well as many other people, believed that science has led man to progress to the present state of knowledge and technology and could lead man to greater heights. Present-day social ills (1936-37) were due to the lack of absorption of ideas from psychology, sociology, anthropology, and economics. For example, if everybody had known that there were no pure or inferior races, facts discovered in anthropology, Hitler's doctrine would have had less of a chance of being accepted. If the government had utilized the plans and programs of the economists, there would have been no unemployment and no poverty in society; there would have been a surplus of goods, staples, and building material. One-third of the nation was ill-housed, ill-fed, and ill-clothed because we had not utilized the discoveries and talents of the social scientists.

When someone said that there is the possibility of life becoming meaningless as the Good became represented in goods, an economics major argued that even if it did become represented in goods, the problem of value would still exist because people would still be buying and selling goods. How would they make the exchange? Moreover, in civil suits, how would they be able to determine the value of the goods or services? Any system of civil and even criminal law would have to deal with and make decisions about value. He went on to say that we should not get lost in the problem of the Good, but should stick to the problem of economic value. [A discussion followed that continued throughout the next session. Although it was informal, many of the economist's statements were at times elliptical and highly technical so that many of the noneconomics majors did not fully understand them. However, the students did not interrupt; they were amazed at the display of erudition and debating skills. Because of personal reasons ASL did not take notes during this seminar but reconstructed the discussion at night in order to present it to his class. What follows may therefore have been affected by the purpose for which he wrote the notes as well as by his undergraduate courses in intellectual and economic thought.]

The history of economic thought may be said to be a record of the struggle with the problem of what determines a service's or a good's value. To some ancient Greeks the value of a thing lay in the thing itself as well as in its evaluation by the user. Thus objective and subjective features were involved. Because of the difficulty of properly evaluating the subjective features, the stress was on what there was about the thing that gave it its value. Aristotle said that a thing got its value from the amount of work crystallized in it. This doctrine has persisted until today. The socialists and communists claim that the value of a commodity is derived from labor. The laborer creates all the value an object possesses, and the worker is at present exploited because he does not receive the full value of his production. One could point to things that are very valuable but which require little or no work in order to dismiss this assertion as invalid. This concept, however, was used by Karl Marx in his interpretation of history and in proposing programs of social reform. One can disprove it, but it is a force in the minds of men that has transformed the world.

The labor theory of value per se is not a communistic doctrine. It is also a doctrine of the Classical Economists and has played a great role in shaping capitalism. Perhaps it is a common idea of our culture. In the beginning there was a Golden Age, according to a Greek myth (as well as in a more ancient Sumerian myth). Man was happy and had free access to sustenance. The Bible (Genesis III, 17-19) also describes a time when man did not have to work in order to produce what he needed to satisfy his needs. But, because of his sin, Adam was expelled from the Garden and was cursed to earn his livelihood by the sweat of his brow. Thus one paid a person for the suffering he endured in making goods or in performing a service. Work was a calamity.

One of the professors pointed out that not only did different economists use the labor concept of value in a variety of ways, but that even the same economist might use it differently. In one place, Adam Smith claimed that "labor is the fund that originally supplies the nation with all the necessities and conveniences of life—it is the original purchase money of all things." Profits and rents were deductions from the products produced by labor. In another place, he rejected this labor theory of value as he went on to point out that the value of a commodity was not related to the amount of labor needed to acquire or produce it, but to a variety of personal and social factors. Perhaps Adam Smith was not contradicting himself. He used this idea as a cudgel with which to beat the Mercantilists' notion that money was the source of a nation's wealth. He also rejected the Scholastics' idea of *use value* because there were commodities like water that have the greatest use but have a lesser price or value than diamonds, which have less use. (The Scholastics called this the *Paradox of Value*.) Smith used the cost of labor in two ways; the absolute cost of labor in the process of producing the commodity and the relative cost of labor, which reflects the competition of different users for the productive capacity of the labor. The absolute cost of labor was stressed by David Ricardo, who held that the essence of value was the pain of labor. But he too changed his mind about this.

Some economists have rejected the labor theory of value because it was not a scientific notion but an ethical one. They claimed that it assumed that labor or sacrifice ought to be the basis of value. It has also been described as a theological concept because it reflected the Christian concept of the sin of

Adam. Wertheimer remarked that perhaps it reflected a general cultural concept of our society, that work was a calamity. The aim of life was to be free of care and toil. He went on to suggest that the concept of work, of doing, needed to be more carefully examined to see whether labor was really a curse.

The discussion went back to economics when somebody pointed out that Ricardo had a relative and absolute labor value theory. The absolute value of a good was the quantity of labor it contained, but its exchange value was relative. Karl Marx, however, conceived of the exchange value of a commodity as absolute and equal to its labor content.

Someone pointed out that Aristotle too did not have just one value theory. Aristotle talked about value in use and value in exchange. Aristotle said that in order for goods to be exchanged every commodity must possess some amount of a measurable quality, a common quality, value. There also had to be a means of measuring this value of the commodity. Social need made all commodities commensurable, and the exchange value of a commodity was proportional to the work necessary to produce it. In the process of exchanging it, however, the commodity's value was not increased. After a just exchange everybody must come out without gain or loss.

The idea of a *just exchange* (and a *just remuneration*) reflected Aristotle's teleological view of nature and fitted in with the Hebraic Oral Law, but not with Roman Law. It also fitted in with aspects of early Christian doctrines, even though Greek philosophical ideas were considered pagan artifacts. But when the churchmen began to use Aristotle's philosophy to justify the faith, they found Aristotle's ideas compatible with church doctrines. But as the church became more organized and became a part of the Roman world, and perhaps because of the recession of Judaic ideas in the Christian outlook, some scholastic philosophers turned away from this aspect of Aristotelian Economics. They asked what value was, and not what it should have been. Thus they reflected a modern approach to value. Saint Antoninus posited the thesis that a thing's value rested on a variety of factors, for example, its comparative equality with other articles of similar nature, its scarcity and its *complacibilitas*. The last criterion was similar to the thesis that value was an idea in the mind of an individual. It was the balance in one's mind between possession of one thing and another. Thus it was not something in the commodity but something in man's mind that comprised the only constant standard of value. He also pointed out that the desire for prestige and status was greater than the desire for luxuries and that the desire for luxuries was greater than a hungry person's desire for food.

As the market price became the dominant determinant of value, Aristotle's idea of the cost of production, of labor costs, began to be ignored. The Scholastic philosophers developed ideas similar to the modern idea of a free market in which supply and demand determine price. Therefore, they were against guilds (unions). One could find many features of the classical capitalistic doctrines in the Scholastics if one looked at them with an open mind instead of the frame of reference of the Ideals of the Church Fathers and of the Bible, and perhaps it would help one realize that the present day defense of capitalism in the name of Christian Ideals has some justification in the teaching of the Church, at least in the later Middle Ages.

Someone commented that it was strange that the Greek philosophers who thought that work coarsened the mind as it did the hands saw labor as the determinant of value, but that the Christian theologians whose Church sanctified labor rejected it. What was the status of the worker in the late Middle Ages in comparison to ancient times? Perhaps the theory of labor in no way affected the way the laborer was treated. Why wasn't the laborer respected and paid for being the source of all value?

Instead of answering, someone pointed out that one could trace the utility theory of value in the work of the Scholastic philosophers. This is not surprising if we keep in mind the influence of Greek thought on them. One finds reference in Plato to pleasure and to fun as the determinants of human decision-making and to the thesis that the calculation of future pleasure and pain make life humanly livable even though he objected to the thesis that this was all that there was to life and value (*Protagoras, Philebus*). Aristotle also formulated notions that are similar to aspects of modern utility theory. The Scholastic philosophers of the late Middle Ages, who proposed utility theories of value, represent the resurgence of the hedonistic view of human nature. It was not the ethical hedonism of Epicurus, who was an ascetic individual compared to some of these Scholastic philosophers. It was psychological hedonism, the doctrine that it was the nature of man to seek pleasure and to avoid pain. It prefigured Bentham's assertion in the eighteenth century that "nature had placed man under the governance of two sovereign masters; pleasure and pain," and that "all men sane or insane calculate with pleasure and pain and thereby do that which will give them the least pain and the most pleasure." Bentham said that that which gave one a quantitatively greater amount of pleasure over pain was better than something that gave one less. Bentham as well as others devised mathematical calculi for the determination of *felicity,* the property of an object that can produce benefits, pleasure, happiness. Psychological hedonism was considered to be for man what the laws of motion were for kinematics in physics. Each person found his place in society because of felicity, just as each planet found its place due to gravity and the laws of motion. Since each person always acted to maximize pleasure, it resulted in the greatest good for the greatest number of people; it produced the good society.

Objections were raised against psychological hedonism from the very beginning, for example, what was pleasure to one person was pain to another, and what was pleasure at one time or place for a person might be pain for the same person at another time or place. Pleasure was usually incidental to an act and not its cause, and it was not always possible to foresee the pleasurable or painful consequences of an act. Moreover, man acted irrationally at times. Variations of the utility theory were made to meet such objections. For example, it was added that a man's choice was not made by pleasure but was guided by expected pleasure, which was based on the recollection of the pleasure he had experienced in an activity or with an object in the past, that is, one sought to reestablish a past pleasurable experience. Some economists pointed out that with each additional unit of the commodity one did not increase felicity; one became satiated. This objection was answered with the theory of marginal utility, and it was argued that expected pleasure could be measured just as could weight and length if it were properly conceptualized. However, so many personal and individual factors were found to influence motivational behavior that some economists rejected the idea that the measurement of utility involved the measurement of motivational factors. There developed a movement in economics to do away with the explanation of economic phenomena in terms of motivation. It was said that just as physics sought empirical laws and did away with explanations, economics must develop empirical laws. This eventually led to a variety of mathematical and statistical economic theories.

Wertheimer remarked that it was necessary to know what one was measuring in order to use proper methods. If one did not, there was the danger that one would get numbers that were not only meaningless but that blinded one to the actual structure of the phenomena. A student said that mathematics might be the queen of the sciences, but not the father of scientific progress. He went on to object to the quantification of human behavior, particularly values. What was human, real and vital, got lost in the numbers. For example, the focus on getting curves of business trends, and on the analysis of these curves, made one forget that business was only one part of a society's culture. Moreover, such mathematical trends were only phenotypical descriptions of behavior, and they ignored the genotypical dynamic features that gave rise to them. The economy was embedded in a society which contained cultural patterns in which certain values were central and others were peripheral. The patterning of these values and goals gave direction to the economy.

Some students objected to this formulation. They presented the Marxian thesis that values were in the society's superstructure that had evolved from the effects on people of the methods of production. One of the professors said that this was not necessarily a Marxian thesis. Aspects of it could be found in some of the universal histories that were written around the eighteenth century. Human history was then seen as the unfolding and development of culture and reason; for example, people living in the hunting and fishing stages were on a lower level of mental and social development than people living in the industrial stage. The fine arts, philosophy, and science emerged when man left the hunting and fishing (economic) stages.

The doctrine of economic determinism was questioned. Someone asked whether the methods of production of our society created the waste and the misuse of human and natural resources, the placing of property rights over human rights, the higher value placed on property than on life, the high regard of aggressiveness and competitiveness. Someone pointed out that the Etruscans, Romans, Greeks, Phonecians, and Carthagenians, and others in ancient times, had many of these traits and values, but they were not capitalistic societies. Perhaps these and other values were not due to the state of a society's economy and technology, but these values created our technology and industry. The idea that Science, the modern Prometheus, was power, reflected these values. They were held in check by old customs and ancient gods, but modern science and technology gave a new world view to those who wished to exercise fully these values in industry and trade. It helped to free the forces of reform that also expressed these values. Furthermore, the idea that Christianity was the highest spiritual level reached by man and that it was man's duty to conquer in His name might reflect these values. Thus a certain combination of cultural values of our society constituted good soil for the growth of our economy. Someone said that it had been argued that capitalism grew out of Judaism, the Protestant ethic and St. Augustine's doctrines. But the truth was that we had allowed it to grow because it was bringing us an abundance of goods and services even though it was also bringing in its own wake various kinds of problems that have seemingly destroyed the sacredness of life and nature. Since this world was not important to the Deity but was merely a place for us to stay until we went to heaven or to hell, we acted in it in a way that would lead us to our predestined place in heaven or hell. The traits were the traits of sinful followers of the murderer, Cain.[1]

A student said that if we accept the thesis that the economy was part of a culture, then the question arose whether man was able to plan and order the society intelligently so that it maximized the development of certain cultural values set by scientific analysis. Therefore, there was a need for social planning, to set up priorities as to what man should strive for in life. When someone alluded to some of the current proposals for social planning, one of the professors said that men did not live by bread alone. He argued that the present unplanned economy gave one a wider horizon and a greater chance to develop. It created needs for the society and for its members to fulfill in order that the economy could grow. The economy was thus the engine of the society. It was the source of energy for growth just as Freud's libido was for the personality's growth. Someone added that as was the libido, it was blind! It just wanted what it wanted without concern for the consequences of its action.

Wertheimer objected to the idea that material and technological values were the main goals of mankind. How did we know that it was the best or primary goal of man? In support of the idea that it was, someone pointed out that more and more countries sought to become industrialized. Wertheimer asked why it was that people in technological societies had felt that they were being alienated from themselves and nature by the industrial society. Someone asked whether people readily or willingly gave up their old value orientations or whether it was done by force of the state, by its educational system, and by advertising and propaganda.

Wertheimer asked what the real wants of the man in the street were, and not those of an owner of a plant who was of necessity oriented to the economic values of his factory. Moreover, what were the real or other values of the average businessman who seemed to be so occupied and lost in his business? How does this affect him as a person? Someone answered that history would show that man had not readily or even happily accepted technology or any other innovations. It was man's nature to resist change. Man was a creature of habit. Once he got used to the changes he had once resisted he felt that they were just as natural as the conditions they had replaced. As long as we had progress and industrial growth there would be discontent. It was the price we paid for progress. Modern science had institutionalized change. In the past, innovation and change had been left to chance, but now, by means of research, we plan development and growth; therefore, the rate of change had become faster. When people would become oriented to the technological world view of our society and view things in terms of scientific tenets rather than in terms of custom and old beliefs, fewer people would feel alienated. Someone said that institutionalized change meant that we would have change for the sake of change and that people who could not change so readily

1. I would not say that it is a Christian tradition that the world is not important to God. The gospel of John says that "God so loved the world that He sent His only Begotten Son. . . ." Many texts like this show man is God's greatest creation and is important to God. The letters of John are further examples of this tone. (JKM)

would be called abnormal. The agents of change would control man's behavior.

Someone said that maybe it would lead to a world in which life would be meaningless. He pointed out that men like Condorcet and Godwin had preached such a doctrine of progress in the eighteenth century. Science had taken over and we all worshipped progress, but there was alienation and despair. Socialism, Communism, Nazism, Fascism were attractive to people because they gave them a meaningful world apart from the search for material goods and wealth. Liberalism had not liberated man's spirit but the individual's willfulness, and science had not filled man with a greater spirit but had emptied man of his soul. Man was just another object with no purpose or reason for existence. Someone said that the society had utilized only the ideas and methods of the physical sciences and not of those social scientists who realized the need for a more humanistic approach. This was the cause of much of our trouble. The government and even industry, however, were beginning to use more and more social scientists as consultants, and, therefore, the damage would be rectified. Someone said that the social scientists would become social engineers and would do what their bosses told them to do because, like the physical scientists, they did not worry about value. They believed that whatever was scientific was inherently good.

A professor remarked that the discussions so far had expressed problems and ideas that were not unique to the social sciences. They were also found in discussions in theology and in philosophy. He then outlined the problem in the following way:

Some said that value was in the object that was being evaluated; it was something objective. Others said that it was not objective but that it was in the mind of the person who did the evaluating; he projected it into the object. Values were thus actually subjective. Some said that value was related to some constant feature or quality of the object. Others said that it was not an absolute quality or feature but a relative feature of the object. Something was not all good or bad, but was more or less good or bad than something else. Some said that value dealt with the eternal features of things. Others said that there was nothing permanent about values; they were temporary feelings or sensations of the person. Some said that values involved objects, people, events. Others said that values do not deal with anything concrete. You could not point to a value because values were abstractions, ideals. Some said that values were the habits of people, a series of responses. Others said that values were not habits but referred to the goals and aspirations of people. Some said that values were features of man as a rational being, Homo sapiens. Others said values had no reasonable basis but only an emotive basis. They were feelings, not thoughts. Some said that values were related to natural or divine laws. Others said values were man-made and that man was free to make them as he wished.

Comments

1. Some students in ASL's adult education course pointed out that the professors seemed to make a sharp separation between the Good and goods. The two ideas are on different levels of abstraction; the Good represents an idea in philosophical discussions of value and goods represent concrete things that

we use in daily life. Perhaps no decision can be reached as to what is the Good, but one can decide in concrete cases whether a certain object fits, is needed, or is required for certain situations of daily living. A few students argued that many goods and services are seen by people to fit, to be needed, or required because they have learned to regard them that way. Modern advertising and education cultivate needs, and even create needs and values, so that people buy goods and services that may be required for a certain sector of the economy to make a dollar, but these goods and services may not in themselves be naturally required by people. Men are being trained to be manipulated by the various sectors of the economy so that they will be consumers of their goods and services. Thou shalt consume is the first commandment in the modern code that scientific technology has set up. Perhaps it is not a new value. Economic reality has always been important, but, in the past, traditions and customs had directed it. At present it apparently directs itself. In a sense it represents the spirit of the times. Modern man's morality and ethics are based on his own reason and not on an outside authority. Autonomous forces, not heteronomous external forces, control him.

A few students raised the question of whether the social scientists' collaboration with industry would help it become even more efficient in manipulating men in order to sell them its goods and services. They feared that it would destroy the soul of man and turn him into a being that lived to consume. Most students brushed aside this fear by pointing out that the scientific enterprise had controls built into it and that science created no evil. Evil was a product of man's ignorance alone.

This was the view of students between 1936-39. The minority opinions of these students have become the majority opinions in 1966-69. Do the present-day students really reject the values of economy?

2. The discussion concerning the determinants of a thing's value was seen by some people as a scholastic exercise, an excursion into sophistry. Why was it not possible for the government to set up price control and arrange for everybody to get what he needed? They pointed to the gross inequality that existed in our society despite the ideal that all men were created free and equal and had an inalienable right to life, liberty, and the pursuit of happiness. They argued that just as the New Deal had set up price supports for the farmer, it should set up income supports for the laborer. They went on to illustrate how commercial interests and the seeking of pecuniary gain were not only destroying our human resources and traditions but also wasting our natural resources. If we really believed in the ideals we preached, why could the government not guarantee them for all people? Some openly sided with various revolutionary doctrines, including Communism and Nazism, because they believed they were creating a meaningful life for youth and the masses of people.

A professor who was visiting ASL's class commented that much of the talk of value was an attempt to rationalize morality. Morality, however, was essentially irrational. Men lived their way into living; after they had acted, they sought to justify their actions. The class ended on this note.

After-Class Discussion

Some students from the seminar sat in the lounge above the library and discussed the question of whether it was possible to have a society which did not allow economic values to be the most dominant feature of its culture. Someone contrasted the culture of Sparta with that of Rome. Sparta had remained primitive and had been overpowered because it had not allowed economic growth, even though it had valued warriors. Ancient Judea, which had valued certain so-called spiritual values more highly than economic values, had also disappeared as a state. Perhaps China and India had lost to the Europeans because they had not greatly esteemed the values that allowed for economic development and growth. Japan was in the process of conquering China because it had become a modern industrial state. Its values had allowed for economic growth.

The discussion turned to Ruth Benedict's *Patterns of Culture* when Wertheimer joined the students. A student told him that the book represented a Gestalt approach to anthropology. Societies were not just a sum of people and of cultural artifacts. A culture was not an and-sum of elements. A society's culture had a pattern, and the ways in which the people behaved and the values they possessed were what they were because of the culture's pattern. Different societies were organized differently because of their cultural patterns; therefore, they created different kinds of persons who were differently oriented to the social and physical world. Wertheimer remarked that the book did not represent the Gestalt thesis. A student said that another book, Sherif's *Psychology of Social Norms*, did use Gestalt concepts. Wertheimer suggested that the student present Sherif's experiment to the seminar.

3
Social Norms and Laws

The student began his report on Sherif's experiment by saying that Sherif had brought the study of social values and norms into the laboratory so that their formation could be studied experimentally. His basic experiment involved the use of a perceptual phenomenon, the Autokinetic Effect (AK). If one sat in a dark room and fixated on a stationary point of light, the light would appear to move. The dark room could be compared to an unstructured situation, one in which there were no main structural features. The subject therefore had no standard against which to judge the movement. At first he made erratic judgments, but after a while he saw it move consistently for a certain distance because he developed a subjective frame of reference or norm from which he could view the AK light.

One of the professors said that once while he was mountain climbing he had been overtaken by fog. He had decided to stay where he was because it had been too dark to return. As he had sat looking around him, he had noticed below him a light. At first he had thought that it was a street light, but when it had begun to move he thought that a lamplighter was walking in the valley below, putting on the street lights. When the fog had lifted he had noticed a cabin a few feet away from where he had been sitting and it had had a light burning in its window. This must have been what had served as an AK light for him. Someone gave as an example of AK the apparent movement of street lamps on a foggy day, and added that when one was in a fog the world became unclear or unstructured; therefore, things moved.

The student continued with his report by saying that Sherif had first had subjects view the AK light alone until they had developed a frame of reference which they used to judge the movement in a consistent manner, that is, the subject developed a personal frame of reference. Then he had put two of these subjects at one time in the dark room and had asked them to judge the AK movements. At first each one had judged the movement from his own personal frame of reference and therefore they had disagreed. After awhile both subjects' judgments had again become erratic. Eventually, however, both had begun to make the same judgment. For example, in the beginning one subject had said that it had moved one foot and the other had said that it had moved eight feet; at the end they both had said that it had moved three feet.

43

Wertheimer interrupted and said that after this Sherif had each of the subjects again judge the AK light individually. Each person was now in the room alone; how did he now judge the light? After a pause, Wertheimer asked whether or not the subjects would use their previous personal frames of reference for judging the movement. Some students said that they would have; Wertheimer then told them that the subjects had not; they judged the light as they had done in the group situation even though they were now alone. Wertheimer asked, "What does this mean?" ASL said that it showed that when one became a member of a group, it might change his perception of an objective situation. [ASL really believed this; he was not playing the devil's advocate.]

When Wertheimer asked why Sherif had used AK movement to study the development of social norms, the student said that social norms developed in unstructured or unclear situations. Several professors gave examples of how politicians and advertisers first unstructured and made situations unclear before they proposed a structure. Someone gave some examples from the tactics of the Nazis and concluded that Sherif was correct in his assumptions. He went on to give examples from anthropology and sociology to illustrate how people from different societies or cultures clashed because they saw the same thing differently. ASL interjected several remarks to the effect that Sherif's study followed from Gestalt psychology's work on perception. There was no difference between illusionary and real perceptual experiences; what one saw depended on his frame of reference.

Wertheimer pointed out that the students were assuming that values were never based on evidence, that the material being judged or evaluated was as neutral and indifferent as the AK movements. One could say that it moved one inch, one foot, one mile. The assumption was that a value was arbitrarily connected to the object being evaluated. Because of personal preferences or social pressures any value could be attached to the object being evaluated. When someone interrupted and referred to the previous discussions on utility, Wertheimer asked whether food which was evaluated positively by a hungry person was neutral to his evaluation. Could he be given a brick and told that it was bread, could he be made to evaluate it as a loaf of bread? The fact that there were cases in which values were unrelated to the qualities of the object of evaluation did not mean that there were no cases in which values were intrinsically related to the object. When the object that was evaluated was neutral, it could be called good or bad, just or unjust, but what of the objects that were not neutral to the way in which they were evaluated?

Someone pointed out that Wertheimer was taking a moralistic position and went on to say that all discussions of law which discussed concepts such as justice as intrinsic qualities of things were not scientific. The scientific study of law was a study of the objective behavior of judges and the behavior of people with regard to rules. This comment sidetracked the discussion. Wertheimer asked whether it could be just for a court to condemn the prisoner and then send out its agent to execute the sentence on the first person they met whose name began with a letter selected out of the judge's hat. Someone pointed out that Wertheimer was forgetting that court trials were not conducted for discovery of the facts or for enlightenment, but for deception and concealment. We admired clever lawyers and did not condemn them because of our culture's values. Yet, because of the same values, we would think that it was unjust if the following occurred. In some Indian tribe, when a person died it was considered to be due to magic. If the dead man's body deteriorated quickly, then it was a woman who was the magician and the first woman that was seen on the road would be seized and killed. If a man stole something in ancient Judea, he had to return it or compensate the owner for it; in nineteenth-century England even little children would be hanged for stealing a handkerchief, but the person whose handkerchief was stolen never got it back. To the ancient Judeans this would have been unjust; to the Englishmen it was just. Could we say that one law was just and the other unjust? In some states adultery was a felony; in other places it was not at all improper. The Jews called it adultery; the people of Canaan considered it to be a religious ritual.

Wertheimer said that if all this were true, then what was called the law represented some sort of capricious behavior of people. If one just looked at the responses, their behavior, it was possible to get such a view. It was necessary, however, to study the place, role, and function of the person's behavior in terms of the situation in which the action took place in order to see how it fitted the situation. Sometimes when this was done the law or behavior did not seem to be so arbitrary.

Someone said that according to sociologists the criminal could tell the judge that from his (the prisoner's) point of view and from the standards of his group, the judge was the criminal. Unfortunately, he had been caught and was being tried by the standards of the judge's group. This remark led Wertheimer to present examples from German courts before Hitler came to power in which the Nazi party members had displayed just this attitude. They had not accepted the jurisdiction of the court, yet now that they had taken over they were punishing these judges. He went on to ask whether a just judge or a just court was one that merely did what the party that controlled it said was correct. Was that which was correct and just merely what one's group said was correct and just? Were values merely one's group's norms? Did one use them mechanically, blind to the facts of the evaluation? Was justice another name for the arbitrary exercise of power?

Someone pointed out that justice was defined by a certain code. In one code the same act might be judged differently than in another. Insofar as we realized the need for order, we would accept the ruling of each code when we were in places in which law and order functioned on the basis of one of these codes. It was possible that one might not wish to live under any particular code and might be able to do what he wished because of his power, prestige or influence. He would, however, try to legitimatize his behavior by getting people to change or abolish the code. What determined a people's agreeing to change of their code? One factor seemed to be what Sherif's experiment illustrated: a disagreement over the judgment of the same situation could arise which would lead to an unstructuring of the peoples' frame of reference, and out of this fluid situation would emerge new norms.

Wertheimer said that this was a superficial description of the process of the development of norms. Just what were the processes that were involved? Was it as simple as the manner in which it had been described? Was it just a matter of force, of blind thoughtless behavior? Such questions had to be faced, not merely for theoretical reasons, but because the answers might affect the concrete situations in which we were living. It was at present stylish to say that what was right was what the group called right, and that what was called right in one place might very properly be called wrong in another. An elderly student said that she had heard this argument used by students in a sociology class to justify immorality and delinquency. She gave as an example the statement of a lady in her adult education class who in a discussion of morality and ethics, said that years ago when someone stole a piece of bread he was hanged, but we have become enlightened and we no longer hang people for such things; at present adultery is a sin but when we will become enlightened we will see nothing wrong in it. The lady seemed to be using sociology to justify adulterous behavior. Someone interrupted to say that everybody rationalized his behavior. Morality is essentially irrational and any attempt to make it rational is futile. The elderly lady went on to say that there was a danger that people would begin to believe that everything was all right as long as you could get away with it. The session ended with this comment. It seemed to most students to be a rather naive view but Wertheimer seemed to take it seriously because he remained to talk with her. Some students listened to her criticize the social sciences for destroying respect for law, morality, and authority, and for encouraging children and young adults to believe that there was nothing more sacred than expressing themselves and having a good time. She wondered what they would do when they grew up. Someone told her that they would settle down because when they assumed adult responsibilities they would realize facts that they now ignored. Someone pointed out that this might be the case because they still lived in a world that had been shaped by the ideas which they rejected at present. They would, however, not really believe in what they did. What would happen if they just used the old words but did not mean them? What would happen when they tried to raise their children in a laissez-faire atmosphere? Would their children feel a need for and seek intrinsic values or would they just fall in the rut as had their parents? If Wertheimer were correct, we should expect trouble even though the New Deal created a world in which all men's needs were cared for.

ASL left the room and did not hear Wertheimer's answers. When Wertheimer came out of the room ASL told him that he was puzzled by what he had said about Sherif's work. He had met Sherif in Cantril's class and from talking with him, he could see no basis for Wertheimer's objections. When ASL told him about Sherif and Cantril's experiments in which prose and paintings had been judged, Wertheimer said that these studies also had not given subjects evidence on which to make their judgments. ASL, who at that time believed in cultural relativism, said that the same results would be obtained with evidence as well as without evidence. ASL proposed an experiment involving the judgment of a series of pictures, line segments, music, odors, liquids, weights, colors, curves, temperatures, and strengths of electric shock to test whether people really were oriented to evidence when evidence was given to them. Wertheimer objected to the use of the noxious stimuli because they might hurt people. Therefore, ASL designed a series of pictures which began with a profile of a face that deteriorated in successive pictures, until there was a very unclear drawing. Then, in subsequent pictures, there gradually emerged the drawing of a bottle. The series ended with a clear, unambiguous drawing of a bottle. From the results, it was clear that the subjects became set in the first half of the series to see a face. Because of this set they saw a face in the ambiguous pictures and did not see the bottle in the second half of the series until it became very clear. Moreover, when the same subjects were immediately afterwards given the series of pictures in reverse order, starting with the bottle, they now saw the bottle in pictures in which they had previously not seen it, and they did not see the face in pictures in which they had previously seen it. This experiment led to ASL's PhD thesis (see Luchins & Luchins 1970c) and the techniques were also used for experiments on social influences on perception of complex drawings which Wertheimer supervised.

In a discussion at the next meeting, Wertheimer remarked that the AK effect should be studied more systematically instead of accepting the assumptions implied in Sherif's use of it. This led to a long-term study on the factors that minimized and maximized the AK effect. [The results of the project have recently been published (Luchins and Luchins, 1969)] Wertheimer raised several other problems that ought to be studied. They are presented below to stimulate research.

He proposed that we look at what was actually happening in concrete social situations and then try to formulate the processes that result in the development of particular norms in group situations.

How did a particular child actually discover that there are standards? What was his understanding of them, after he learned that certain objects were judged in terms of inches, feet, ounces, pounds, monetary values? Were there certain ways of learning or experiencing them that led to an understanding of the concepts so that he used them in a genuine way, not in a blind way? Did he realize that one standard might be better than another to measure certain things, for example, an inch instead of an ounce of a certain piece of candy? What could be done to make him realize the superiority of one standard over the other? One could learn social norms either by rote or by understanding. What were the consequences of each type of learning? How did rules or standards emerge in the daily lives of children? What was the nature of the situation and the nature of the relation of the child to the group and the task? Was there a difference when the rule or standard was imposed and when it was discovered by the children as a solution to a problem?

ASL once asked Wertheimer: Why is the question of value so important now? Why do we not find it discussed in primitive groups, by people in isolated communities? Is it because in primitive groups there is more agreement? Is it that discussion arises only as a result of discrepancies? Is it that thinking emerges only when blind habits are not capable of handling a situation? Unfortunately he has forgotten Wertheimer's reactions. What are yours?

After-Class Discussion

In an after-class discussion, ASL argued that Sherif's experiment opened the way to study the formation of social norms in an exact manner and what had been found in the laboratory fitted what happened in daily life. Wertheimer pointed out that it holds only for certain but not all cases; not all values and norms came into being in the way that the autokinetic effect is judged. When a student argued that it is better to be exact and to deal with quantifiable aspects of norms than to talk loosely about them, Wertheimer told him that to get a number is not the end of science, one can get lots of numbers that are meaningless. The same student then said that norms and values become matters of fact when they are reduced to quantitative formulations.

Another student changed the discussion, saying that social norms and values are conventions; what is ugly or beautiful, good or bad, kind or unkind, honest or dishonest depends on the society's stereotyped ways of reacting to things. Things do not have these qualities; we impute them to things. In Africa fat girls are beautiful and so are kinky hair and black skin but in the USA they are not beautiful. In the USA girls like to be whistled at but in some European countries they do not. In Germany and in the USA, Communism is bad but in the USSR it is good. What is fashionable dress one year is not fashionable the next year because the dressmaking industry lowers or raises the hemline and the suit manufacturers pad or unpad the shoulders or change the size and shape of the lapel or the number of buttons. In church people are concerned about having been honest, kind, chaste, dutiful sons or daughters, or faithful wives or husbands but in the social and business world they are not concerned about these values and may even violate the church's values when doing business. One may get into trouble when he uses church values in non-church groups. A normal person's mind is compartmentalized; he acts differently and uses a different set of values at home, school, church, and business. He gave as an example of compartmentalization, a strike of the maintenance staff at Columbia. The Dean sent out on a rainy day coffee and umbrellas to the men on the picket line, although the reason why they were out in the rain was because he would not grant them the raise that the trustees had already approved. ASL said that in a study of adolescence which he did for his master's degree, he found only a few youths who were concerned about the contradictory roles they had to play at home, church, street, school, and work; most of the youths were not even aware of their contradictory behavior. The process of growing up in our society calls for the ability to adapt and to shift to the norms and values of the various institutions and groups in which one lives; when in Rome act like the Romans, is the motto of our society. In response to Wertheimer's questions, ASL said that one does not have to understand or know the historical or situational reasons for norms or values but must learn to use them. Many members of a group neither know nor question the reasons for its social norms and values. Moreover, they are not concerned or even aware that their behavior in terms of the values of one group is contradicted by their behavior in other groups. When it is called to their attention they say that they see no contradiction or rationalize their behavior by saying that one must adjust, be polite, be friendly or cooperative. He went on to say that Sherif's experiment and thesis about the effects of learning a social norm adequately account for the value orientation of the subjects of his adolescence study. When certain children joined the gang that he was studying, they began to see the world in terms of the gang's norms. Joining a group and learning its norms affects one's cognitive grasp of the world to the extent that one's virtues are turned about. Wertheimer objected to the sweeping generalizations about compartmentalization, asking for a systematic study to validate it. After a pause he remarked, It is true that social norms and values are sometimes used arbitrarily and that men have certain social values and norms which they use in a stereotyped, unthinking, blind manner; parents and the schools teach the stereotypes of these values. Children and even adults learn to repeat the stereotypes of the values and are blind to the place, role, and function of their behavior in a social situation. The type of education that does this exists. But there are also cases where one does not learn the stereotype of the value and where one does not use it blindly and arbitrarily. Sherif's experiment is based on the thesis that such cases are special cases of the former kind. How valid is this assumption; maybe it is the other way around?

A student said that Wertheimer is applying the Gestalt psychologists' criticism of the use of nonsense syllables in learning to the learning of social norms. He is assuming that the laws derived by studying the learning of meaningless material cannot account for the learning of meaningful material and that if we developed laws based on meaningful material we would find that the laws which have been based on nonsense syllables were special cases of these laws. There is no proof for this; the work of Hull and his students show that the laws that hold for meaningless material also hold for the meaningful. Wertheimer remarked that this was a superficial view of what was actually being studied by Hull and his students. He suggested that the student go into a classroom or into a home where there is a baby and see how learning actually takes place. Are the laws adequate to account for the child's learning? Some teachers and parents who have learned child psychology might use these laws. What happens when they do; what is the effect on the child, on the social atmosphere; what consequences does it have for learning and thinking in subsequent similar situations in which what was learned is possible and is not possible? Wertheimer then returned the discussion to the learning of social norms by asking what is the consequence for the person and society when he learns the stereotypes of norms and values. When someone said that most children learn social norms with no understanding and do not care to know why, Wertheimer retorted that it is a dogma not a fact. The same student then described an experiment by Tresselt in which watchmakers judged the same weights as heavy which blacksmiths had judged as light. Such experiments show that good, bad, long, short, light, dark are determined by the frame of reference of one's experiential background. In response to Wertheimer's question he said that in one society a thing could be called good which in another society would be called bad. Wertheimer asked, Suppose a person who calls a certain thing bad is in a situation with a person who comes from the society where it is called good. What would happen if the thing was required in the situation; would the person from the society in which it is called bad say that it is bad and not use it? When ASL said the person would not use it, Wertheimer referred to the Einstellung experiments and said that people may become so set by a method that they are blinded to what is needed in a situation. This is due to the kind of education they have received, it is not due to a fundamental tendency to repeat blindly what one did before. He added that there is a drive in men to know, a desire not to do things blindly, not to be a robot. This tendency is destroyed by certain educational and social situations. In response to ASL's argument he said that calling a thing black will not make it black. It is possible for you to use the word black instead of the word white if you are in a situation where such things are called white. It is like learning to say *pomme* instead of *apple* to a French storekeeper.

Someone said that Wertheimer is substituting the dogma that people are thinking beings for the dogma that men learn to think. He went on to say that all theories start with axioms that are accepted on faith; it is a matter of taste which axiom one uses. It is proper to say that the basic substance of nature is cream cheese as long as it generates hypotheses that are experimentally validated. Wertheimer objected to the thesis that one is free arbitrarily to pick any axiom and went on to say that observation of little children and even animals shows that they are curious. Little children ask questions, they are interested in what is happening around them to the extent that they annoy adults. They are given tasks to do that keep them from thinking and bothering adults. Eventually they learn not to ask questions. When someone said that child psychologists have proven that little children do not naturally think, Wertheimer told the student to observe the behavior of infants and children in order to see for himself what is the case. An elementary school teacher offered some observations in support of Wertheimer's conjectures. Some children in her first-grade class overwhelm her in the first few days with questions and comments but by the end of the term many of them become rather taciturn so that they do not even ask questions when she asks for them. A child guidance worker said that children ask questions for many reasons: to get attention, to validate what they see or know, to show off, as well as because they are curious and want information. In response to ASL's question she said that classroom routine, the social atmosphere, and the method of teaching as well as the textbooks destroy the child's curiosity. In order to adjust in school, to get a good report card, one must not ask questions that disturb the routine. She said that perhaps the home also becomes less tolerant of questions and less patient to answer the child because he is now in school and it is the school's responsibility to deal with such things. In response to questions by Wertheimer she said that it would be of interest to ask mothers to keep a journal of all questions and remarks that a child makes starting from the day he first learns to talk or starting at least a year before he goes to school. Would there be an increase or decrease of questions? In what places and about what subjects would there be an increase or a decrease, and what could be the possible reason for this? What happens the first year the child goes to school; how do the questions compare with those he has asked before going to school? Wertheimer suggested that the teachers' and parents' reactions to the questioning should also be studied, that not just the number of questions but the questions' place, role, and function in the situation should be studied. When he suggested that we also study older children and adults, a visitor said that maybe there are situations in which nearly everybody asks questions and that there are situations in which no one does. What is the nature of these situations? Similarly, perhaps there are some children and adults who always ask questions and others who do so rarely; why? This led to the suggestion that one of the requirements in teacher's education should be assignments to homes, playgrounds, and classrooms to study systematically the questions that children ask. Also a particular individual should be studied in this way from birth to adulthood. Each year a different student should be assigned to observe and record the same individual's questions and the consequences of his questions in a situation. The visitor concluded that one cannot learn if he is afraid or cannot ask questions. If we found out why some children ask questions and others do not, we would know how to appeal to children's curiosity. Wertheimer brought the discussion back to social norms by asking, Suppose you knew nothing about the psychology of social norms, how would you go about studying the development of social norms? Some proposed to have a group of children meet in the same place day after day. In order that they do not interfere with each other and do not work at cross purposes, they will have to develop social norms. He agreed with someone who interrupted to say that the effects on the group and on the person may be different when one enters an already existing group and has to learn the existing norms; therefore, we also must study what happens when a person joins an already existing group. What conditions of learning, what social and personal factors cause a child or an adult to learn a stereotyped way of reacting instead of realizing the place, role, and function of the norm in the situation? [This suggestion was tested during World War II in group psychotherapy when ASL compared the growth of social structure in *closed* and *open* therapy groups (Luchins, 1964) and when patients were told the rules of the ward, or of the group, or discovered them for themselves. Wertheimer's conjectures seemed to be validated to the extent that certain procedures and social atmospheres more often created thinking beings and other procedures created robots (Luchins, 1959).]

Wertheimer proposed that we study the effects when a person learns a social norm by being told that this is the way to behave, with the stress being on the importance of the procedure or when he is given an interesting problem to solve or is put in a social situation in which he discovers the rules for himself. One could teach the norm in terms of a formula and have the person memorize it until he knows it by heart or give him a variety of examples or put him in a variety of situations whose structures are so clear that he can discover the rule and understand how it fits and is required by the situation. After a pause he said, Suppose a child learned how to measure length with a ruler and then was given the task of measuring the volume of something. What kind of instruction, what kind of learning would lead to the use of the ruler in a manner that was adequate for length but not for volume? He suggested that we think of other social standards, norms, and values that are taught so that they are blindly and not blindly used. Wertheimer said that it was not merely a question of learning by rote or by understanding; what is involved is a doctrine of man: whether he is a vessel into which the leader pours rules and he blindly does what the leader wants or whether he is a thinking being.

On the way to the subway station ASL told Wertheimer that he found Sherif's work to be of great value in teaching psychology to students in the WPA Adult Education Project. After he had critically evaluated various concepts of human nature, he developed the thesis that man was a product of his society's culture. After raising the problem of how the culture entered the person he presented Sherif's (1936) concepts and related ideas. In order to illustrate how the biological man became transformed into a person who reflected the culture into which he was born, the growth of an individual was studied in terms of the institutions and groups of which he had been and was a member. A specially prepared life history was read to and discussed by the class in order to illustrate how a particular person had been molded by the groups and institutions of his society. Although the life history illustrated the role of social factors which were stressed by sociologists and anthropologists, its major theme was the acquisition and modifications of frames of reference as a consequence of one's coming into contact with various groups and institutions. All students were encouraged to write their own life histories so that they could get some understanding of the social forces that had molded their own personalities. The students seemed to enjoy doing this and claimed that it helped to concretize and make meaningful to them the concepts that had been used in the earlier lectures (cf. Luchins, 1946).

When Wertheimer wanted to know the students' reactions to the first part of the course, ASL told him that many students had been upset when the various popular concepts of human nature, particularly the instinct concept, had been criticized. Most objections had come from students who had gone to high school and to college. Some of these students had appealed to the fact that they had learned these concepts in their formal education, which they considered to be more authoritative than the WPA Adult Education courses which were not taught by professors. They resisted the thesis that every person was a reflection of his culture and that there were no universal invariant features in human behavior. Their objections changed when they had begun to work on their own life histories. They then began to appreciate the validity of the cultural approach to human behavior and personality.

Wertheimer remarked that the course may be teaching them to realize the importance of social field conditions but it is also teaching them a particular doctrine of man, that man was nothing but a creature of his culture, that men were creatures of habit that had been imposed on them by their society. He pointed out that there was a danger that the students would use the idea of frame of reference and social norms in a superficial way, that they might use it as a neat formula to account for behavior.

The next day ASL asked the students to write the ideas that they had learned from the lectures and the study of their life histories. Their answers were collected and the following report was sent to Wertheimer. Unstructured situations were most often the places in which they had become aware of the need to learn about or had become aware of the inadequacies of their habits, values, and norms. Among the situations in which this occurred were: moving into a new neighborhood or apartment house, transferring to a new school or to a new class in the old school, the birth or death of a member of their family, their marriage or divorce, and loss of employment by themselves or their parents. The new situations were at first strange and confusing, they were apprehensive and anxious but after a while, things again became normal as they learned new outlooks and habits. They gave examples of how becoming a member of a group or wanting to become a member of a group had resulted in their developing a new outlook about things, for example, a group's way of doing things was contradictory to the values of the home, church, or school but in order to be accepted by the boys or girls, they did what the group did with the result that they saw their old values in a different light. Sometimes this resulted in a conflict with parents and teachers. However, many of the students reported instances in which they changed their ways of doing things and their values in each group that they had joined, and they were not aware or concerned by the fact that the different groups required adherence to contradictory values. They had learned in each case to act, feel, and think in terms of the group's requirements. A few students reported that they felt guilty or uneasy about being a different person in different situations. Some of these students sought a unifying set of values by joining a political party's youth group. Generally speaking, the students' reports indicated that from their earliest childhood there had been a tendency to structure their worlds in terms of the groups of which they were or wished to be members. They also gave examples of how their standards or norms had changed with age. When they had been little children, a walk or ride around the block had been a big walk or ride, their fathers and mothers had been tall, two or three pennies had been a lot of money; but now these were very short distances, small sizes and amounts. They attributed these changes to the acquisition of different frames of reference which were outcomes of specific experiences, growing up, changing needs, and formal learning of the standards of measurement and meaning of the concepts which they had previously used blindly and rather grossly. The reports indicated that the students had acted their way into believing or thinking rather than thinking their way into acting.

When ASL met Wertheimer a few days later to talk about the students' reports, he remarked that the students might have written as they did because of what they had been taught, the students might have written different life histories had their instructor used a different theory. ASL agreed that this might have been the case because in his course on personality the students had been told after the presentation of each theory to add to their life histories any new information that was suggested by what had been taught in class. Therefore, they often added new things after learning Freud's, Jung's, and Adler's theories. Looking at themselves from a different frame of reference had revealed different features of their personalities.

An outgrowth of the discussion was the following project. Students were asked to reread their life histories in order to see whether there was a theme or themes in their lives. We asked them to experiment with their histories in the following manner. Read the early childhood days to someone and ask him to tell you what is the general impression of the individual. What sort of a child is he? Then ask the person to predict how he will behave in the next five years at home, in the neighborhood and in school. After this is done, read to him the next part of the life history and again ask him to give his impression and to predict how the child will behave in the next part of the life history, and so on for each part of the history. When ASL reported to Wertheimer that some life histories seemed to have a central theme and others seemed to have a variety of themes, Wertheimer suggested that after each impression was read, the subject should be asked to give his reasons for each prediction and that more than one person should be asked to judge each life history. It was also planned to make a systematic study of the goals, traits, expectations and habits of the person in each part of the life history in order to see what had remained invariant and what had changed. Wertheimer suggested also that a description of the structure of the person should be made at each stage of development, in order to identify the central and peripheral traits at each stage. The different descriptions could then be studied to see what had remained and what had not remained central and peripheral, and to try to determine the factors that might have been responsible for the change or lack of change. [These suggestions led to a long-term project on the forming of impressions of personality. A brief description of some of these studies is available upon request.]

The discussion led to ways of introducing the students to other ways of studying their personalities. The students were told to keep a diary of all social contacts during the day, every other day, for four weeks. They were to record who had initiated the contact, where it had taken place and what had occurred, including what they had done and how they felt about it. The students then analyzed their diaries to find out how many groups they had participated in and the kind of roles they had played in each group. Were there groups in which they always did the same thing and felt the same way; were there groups in which they did not, and what was the difference between these groups' structures, memberships, and goals that might have produced the constant or variable behavior? In discussing his students' diaries with Wertheimer, ASL pointed out that some people readily changed as they went from group to group but only a few did not. This raised the question of why they behaved differently as well as the question whether the social influences on the behavior, mood, and thoughts of the person were functions of his personality, the structure of the situation, or of the kind of togetherness they formed. Wertheimer did not like the dichotomy. He also expressed concern over the passivity of most of the students in the face of social pressure. ASL pointed out that this passivity might have been due to the fact that schools train children to be cooperative, to become good American boys and girls, and to the fact that the subjects were second generation or first generation Americans who were oriented toward becoming assimilated to the mainstream of American life. They or their parents had rejected their Old World cultures' values and were eager to do what was right, to be real Americans. Thus they were oriented toward following and accepting suggestions from their membership groups. When ASL said that they were being realistic and that perhaps these attitudes were necessary for success, Wertheimer said that critical-mindedness in following and becoming an American was also possible. As an illustration, he mentioned that Carl Shurz had once been asked whether he believed in the motto *My country, right or wrong*. Shurz had answered that if his country was right, it was right; but if his country was wrong, it was his duty to make it right. ASL said that the students' life histories indicated that because of economic reasons it was difficult for them to act as Carl Shurz had done. Some of the students had thought in their early childhoods that their parents were right but when they met boys and girls in school who were doing things that were not right in terms of what they had learned at home, they had to choose between being social outcasts or doing what the others were doing or what the teachers demanded. They soon realized that what they were being told to do was perfectly all right and even thought that they had been stupid or foolish for believing that such behavior was wrong. Moreover, with age, they realized that everybody was entitled to his beliefs and that in order to get along in this world one must compromise. To insist that one was right was to assume that he knew more than others; such an attitude made one appear willful, disrespectful, insolent, and/or intolerant of the beliefs and customs of others.

Experimental Outgrowths

ASL presented to his Adult Education classes Wertheimer's criticism of Sherif's work and asked them to think of ways of testing Wertheimer's conjectures. They raised the question whether the adolescents' diaries of ASL's project contain evidence that norms were learned and changed on a reasonable basis, that social norms were not stereotypes, and that people were not compartmentalized. ASL told them that only one youth seemed to fit Wertheimer's reflective person. He was always wondering why people behaved the way they did and was worried about his standards and the pressures on him to change them. Most of the youths were not at all concerned as they rushed headlong into new experiences, they showed no concern about the effect of their behavior on other social situations or people; they lived it up now. (cf Luchins, 1954) The psychology majors in ASL's class said that it proved Sherif's thesis and disproved Wertheimer's, but a woman who had little formal education asked what conditions produced these two different kinds of people. She also challenged the conclusion that most youths are not reflective, pointing out that most adolescents are moody, reflective, and have conflicts over norms and values because of becoming aware of them; adolescence is a period of value reorientation. She suggested that the results might have been different if the youths had been studied differently. She proposed a study which would find out the various places a youth lives in and would find out the public views of the standards, values, and norms of these situations, as well as what the youth regards to be the standards, values and norms of these situations. No one did this, but other projects grew out of this discussion to which we turn.

Several students in the class kept a record of what happened each time they had to learn a rule or norm of a group, focusing on such questions as these; did they just do as they were told, did they wonder what their behavior meant in terms of their other values, were they curious why things were done this way, did they have an opportunity to decide what the value or norm should be? They also wrote of situations in the past year where they had to learn a norm or rule of conduct. The outstanding feature of their results was that there were few situations in which they had participated in the formation of the norm and in which they had questioned the norm or had tried to find out its purpose or rationale. If they did not like the way things were done they tended not to go back to the group. If it was not possible to leave the group or if they could not vary, they did what they were told to do. Some said that at first they found it irksome but after awhile they got used to it. There were a few individuals who did try to find out the reasons and some of them got in trouble at home, at school and with the gang because they questioned the values. The only place where they could be reflective about things was in the WPA Adult Education classes, where they felt free. The results led the class to conclude that people were compartmentalized and were content to follow or do mechanically what most groups demanded of them, that people do not think their way into norms or values but live their way into them, chaste girls or boys gradually find themselves doing things that are against their former values. When their parents call it to their attention they often openly announce their rejection of or feel alienated from the old values. The students' reports showed that most youths gradually or abruptly accepted the norms of the street and school gang even though they were counter to their religion and home values. Many still acted at home in terms of the old values and were not concerned with their contradictory behavior.

When ASL told Wertheimer about these results he asked whether there were cases in which the youths rejected the values of the street and school for the values of the home. Were there cases where a youth revolted against the values of the street even though the home encouraged him to be one of the boys? ASL said that he rarely came across a youth who became devout, rejecting the values of the street and his irreligious parents. ASL went on to say that one must go along with what is being done in the groups of which he is a member and may not deviate unless he has the power to do what he wishes. Wertheimer objected to the idea that following or not following a norm is a matter of power or might. When ASL hypothesized that maybe the results reflect the lower social class's subservient attitude to the world, Wertheimer objected to the idea that the lower classes have a servile attitude. He went on to say that it is often said that one learns and/or follows a norm because of force, that it is forced behavior. How true is it? He suggested that we study the actual values and beliefs of particular people and groups; how do certain norms come into existence, what do they mean to the person, and to the social field?

Someone suggested that it would be of interest to study the recent refugees who were moving into his neighborhood to test the hypothesis that people had to accept the standards of the dominant people in the community. These refugees are pious East European Jews whose customs and beliefs are outlandish and an embarrassment to the Jews who live in this neighborhood. The refugees are dependent on the Jewish community because they are destitute, they cannot go on Home Relief because paupers are deported. Will these people, who find themselves in a world where even their so called coreligionists mock and reject their behavior, change and conform to the standards of the majority, of the people who have power? A visiting instructor said that it is an unfair test of Sherif's thesis because these people believe in the power of God, they would rather go to heaven than live in an irreligious manner. A student pointed out that most pious Jews who came to the USA after 1919 conformed. Wertheimer stopped the argument by suggesting that they study these people and said, Suppose these people change the community's, the majority's, values instead of adjusting to them; what would it mean? When ASL said this would never happen, Wertheimer predicted that these people would maintain their values. He asked, What factors in the social field and in their personalities could be the reason for this? [Wertheimer's prediction seemed absurd but the past 30 years have proven that he was correct. Not only these pious people but also the religious German refugees from Frankfort have preserved their ways of life and are at present converting nonobservant Jewish intellectuals and youths whose parents had rejected religion. Why did they succeed? An answer may be found in the missionary work of Lubavitch-Chabad among nonobservant Jewish college youths.]

In an attempt to disprove Wertheimer's conjecture, ASL made a content analysis of the diaries of the adolescents whom he had studied. The results indicated that they behaved in terms of different social values in the gang than when at home, the values of the home and church were not used in athletic and social activities, on dates and at work. Some youths sometimes protested against the aggression, coldness, shrewdness, and taking advantage of others but occasionally acted in these ways in their athletic and social activities. The diaries of seven of the ten boys of one group suggested that the youth were compartmentalized into a home self, school self, street self in their value orientation. Only two of the seven youths were worried about their contradictory behavior, the contradictions between their ideals and their practices. When each youth was shown the results of the analysis of his diary, only one of them spontaneously remarked about his different behavior in different places and the contradiction in values and norms. When the youths were asked why they believed in the traditional virtues and defended them at home and in discussions but acted in a contrary manner in the gang and on dates, they said that what they did was appropriate, that they never think of such things when on a date; in a party one seeks sexual gratification, in a game one wants to win. It is natural to act differently in such situations, it is not a contradiction.

Wertheimer said that maybe the results were due to the piecemeal analysis of behavior. It was necessary to know more about the structure of the social situation in which the actions took place and how the youths saw the situations, and what were the reasons for the youths' narrowed view of things. He went on to say that the thesis of compartmentalization was based on a superficial view of people's behavior. It ignored the place, role, and function of the act in the situation. If one acts the same way in all situations one may violate the requirements of a situation and act arbitrarily. A student who had joined the discussion gave examples of mothers who always show love to their children to the extent of condoning and encouraging socially destructive acts. He also gave examples of boys and girls who are good to people to the extent that they are exploited. ASL defended the thesis of compartmentalization by giving examples from his psychiatric case work with truants and his observations of high school and college students. There were members of the Socialist and Communist youth groups who did not mind doing business and making a profit, who did not mind exploiting their fellow students. Although they were against competition and aggression they were very competitive, uncooperative, and aggressive in achieving their personal ends. The conservative students who were against the New Deal went on Home Relief in order to get WPA jobs and sided with the radical students when they needed favors from them. Some even went to meetings of radical groups because of the opportunity for sexual gratification, entertainment, and free-loading. Some religious Christian students who argued for love and forgiveness uttered anti-Semitic and anti-Negro statements and were just as materialistic, aggressive, and self-centered as the students whose behavior they criticized as materialistic.

Someone who had sat down while ASL was talking added examples of contradictions that are taught in the schools, in political parties, and in churches, for example, the Jews are cursed in church services for having killed God and at the same time He is asked to forgive them (the worshipers) as they forgive others; the New Deal has destroyed crops and animals because there is an abundance while people are starving; he went on to give other examples. ASL said that one of his pupils had been arrested for stealing. When he asked the child why he stole, the boy said that he was not stealing but helping his mother. Another pupil had been running around with sailors and she was arrested on the charge of delinquency. She told him that she was doing nothing wrong, that it was patriotic to do this. He went on to say that life is full of contradictions; the movies, radio, newspapers, magazines, and the entertainment industry idealize and present as normal what the school, church, and home regard to be deviate and immoral behavior. In view of all this people have to compartmentalize or else go mad.

When ASL presented to his students the results of the content analysis, some said that the results were like their own experiences. They gave examples from their own or friend's experiences in which they acted in terms of the norms of the group in which they were, and thus contradicted the norms they had learned at home and at school. Some said that they did not want to be told about the contradictions; they expressed resentment that their parents were trying to make them behave on the outside in terms of the home's values. A few of them said that the parents' demands were paradoxical, that they were damned if they did or did not do what the home wanted. The home wanted them to be a success in school, to be popular, go on dates; to do all this they had at times to violate the family's code of conduct. One comment summarized it as follows. They want you to walk through the fire and not get burned; they yell at you if you get burned and yell at you if you do not walk through the fire. Some students concluded that to grow old means to become a hypocrite, to be all things to everybody. Others said that the conduct of their parents and their own contradictory behavior is a reflection of social disorganization. When one student complained that things were not like this, an argument arose which ASL used to motivate the following assignment. Keep a record for a month, at least every other day, of all experiences you have in which a norm, standard, or value is involved, in which you or others use norms or are aware that it is a value-making or using situation.

Of the thirty-seven students every student kept a record for at least two days and twelve kept it for a full month. The diaries were collected and analyzed by ASL and the results were presented in class. About half of the diaries reported contradictions between their own or other people's ideals and actions. These observations were often made by students who were members of liberal, radical, or conservative organizations. Most of the contradictions were between the values of the home and church and the values of the business and social world. Also there were times at home, school, church, and work when people acted contrary to the institution's values and it was considered to be proper conduct or when they were not aware that they were not living up to the norms. In the discussion most students rejected the thesis that there were two kinds of social norms, the ideal and the real. They said that the discrepancies were due to social disorganization. A few students were surprised to hear that people did not live up to the norms of their church, but others pointed out contradictions between the theory and practices of Christians toward coreligionists and people of other faiths. Some students said that all this illustrated the tendency of people not to notice contradictions. When they were asked why some are aware of contradictions, someone said that they are noticed by people who are set by their ideologies to find them. The following method was suggested for testing this hypothesis. Give liberals, radicals, and conservatives a copy of a daily newspaper, ask them to read it for 15 minutes and then to summarize the important news. Because of different ideologies they will make different reports. When given the same editorial or news story they'll notice different contradictions and different misrepresentations of the facts because they pick out what fits their ideology and leave out or do not even see what is against their ideology. Moreover, they tend to believe the newspaper which fits their party's ideology; a Communist believes the *Daily Worker* and not the *New York Times*.

ASL pointed out that there were contradictions which liberals, radicals and conservatives of the class had noticed, for example, starving people amidst a surplus of food; the religious values of poverty, charity, chastity, and the acceptance of the values of the business and social world which contradicted them. The radicals and conservatives were quick to point out that the contradictions meant different things to them, that they were due to different causes. A student who had frequently visited Wertheimer's seminars pointed out that the results indicate that people do what they do for a variety of reasons. Therefore we must understand the reasons why people who are church goers and who believe that charity is a virtue put on their doors signs that say *Beggars Not Allowed*. Offhand, it looks like a contradiction but the sign does not mean that they do not believe in charity; they do not want strangers in their buildings. Someone argued that according to the Bible one should be good to strangers but the Bible does not say that one should not protect oneself against people who might harm them. Someone insisted that such signs actually rule out the possibility to give charity; it makes no difference why they put the sign on their door, it's unchristian. The student then said that according to Wertheimer it does make a difference. She went on to give an example from his lecture. You might say that one man is charitable because he always gives to the poor and that another man is uncharitable because he never does. The first man's behavior may be due to the fact that he is good-hearted or wants to help or that he really does not want to give but was drilled by his father to do it and he gives charity to please his father. The latter person's behavior may be due to the fact that he is stingy, selfish, or that he has no money or has the conviction that one should not give money but should help the man get a job. Wertheimer has said that we should not study a response per se but should try to find out the process that produced it. Wertheimer claimed that it is not merely a theoretical argument; one will judge people differently when one knows the reasons for their behavior. There are different consequences for the person and the social field if he is charitable in one or in the other way. The student proposed that the class study people who are charitable because they are sensitive to situational requirements and who are charitable because of a blind mechanical habit.

When Wertheimer was told about what had happened in ASL's class he raised the question whether the awareness of contradictions was due to previous class discussions. Therefore, ASL made another study in another class. After telling the students that it often happened in life that we evaluated or judged things in terms of certain ideas, values, standards, or norms, he told them to write down the various standards that were used. After the papers were collected, they were given the assignment to bring in next time as many words denoting standards as they could recall. All the words were then tallied and the list was consolidated into about 80 items. Ten items of the list of value terms were given to them at a time and each time they were told to indicate their awareness of the use of these value terms in a life situation during the past month. After their papers were collected the following task was given for homework: they should indicate where, when, why, and how they used the term at home, in places of recreation, occupation, in religious institutions, in their neighborhood, in the community at large, or in any other place that was not included in these categories. In this way, for the next two months, they were given ten of the values from the list each time. After this the list was readministered. This time they were asked to answer the questions in terms of where, when, why, and how most people use these values in the same places. The data became the basis of a discussion of value. It was used to answer such questions as: are certain values used in all situations, are certain values used by nearly all people, which values are used more often or least often in certain places and by certain people? The results showed that there were a few students who acted in terms of the traditional home and church values wherever they went, no matter what the others were doing and regardless of the pressure put on them by their peers, employers, or teachers to act differently. Most students tended to act in terms of a cluster of values that were arranged in a different order of importance at different times in the same situation or in different situations. Some of these students were ego-oriented and ambitious to succeed but others were oriented to the requirements of the social situation; they were not concerned or worried about their acceptance or success in the place where they used the values. Some students were not unaware of being compartmentalized; they were aware at one time or another of trying to be consistent. Some knew that they were acting differently in different places but they did not consider it to be contradictory behavior; they thought that they were doing what was proper in each place. A few students expressed feelings of guilt, of disloyalty, of shame or a general uneasiness when they reflected on what they had done, said, or thought. Some did not regard their own behavior as being compartmentalized but when they discussed the behavior of other people they said that people act without awareness of their contradictory behavior, that most people are different kinds of selves in different places and operate in terms of the values and norms of the place in which they find themselves and that to grow up means to learn to become a segmented person who plays the prescribed role in each place with no concern about the fact that the roles demand contradictory norms, values, loyalties, and beliefs.

When ASL told Wertheimer about this study he raised questions about the method. He objected to the questionnaire, suggesting that the actual behavior of people be studied and that factors be introduced in the situation to test whether there is awareness, and to help them become aware of the contradictions. When ASL said that the results would be the same because most people use norms and values unthinkingly and are compartmentalized role players, Wertheimer remarked, Suppose only a few subjects act in a genuine manner? Does this mean that all people act unthinkingly and blindly? Maybe most people act in terms of the stereotype of the social norm or value because of the structure of the social field or because of attitudes, assumptions, and needs which narrow or blind them. Maybe it is due to their education or to propaganda. Your students' finding that in different situations the values were arranged in a different order of importance might be a function of the social structure of the situation. We need to understand the structure of the situation in order to understand why the person is using or is concerned with these rather than those values. An act of behavior cannot be understood without taking into account its place, role and function in the situation. He asked why is it that many subjects did not list charity and honesty as norms in business. Someone asked why is it that the Jewish students did not list charity as a norm in the synagogue. If they went to the synagogue daily they would have dropped each time a few pennies into the collection box for food for the poor. Moreover, when walking into and out of the synagogue they would have met at least one beggar. How is it possible that the subjects did not mention charity? Was it because they went to synagogue on Saturdays or holidays when money is not collected? Another student rejected this because appeals for pledges for charity are made on these days too. He conjectured that they did not mention charity because they never thought of it as *charity*. He said that he has recently found out that he was a polyglot when he was a child because he spoke four languages. The same can be said for charity. People who give charity may not see themselves as charitable but as fulfilling a duty or doing what is natural. The student went on to say that people in business also contribute to charity, nearly all storekeepers give to various funds and to beggars but the students did not mention acts of charity in the business world; even many department stores give charity. Maybe the results reflect the students' negative attitude toward business or maybe when one thinks of business one does not think of charity because it is not a central activity of business.

The discussion of the study led to other class projects. In one project the students asked their subjects to list the values or norms they use in each of the following situations and why they use it there: home, school, playground, library, place of work, on the street, on dates, with boy friends, girl friends, in the family, business world, educational world, recreational world. After this they asked their subjects to list the values that are socially accepted in each of these places and to give the reason why it is so. In still another study they asked the subjects to give the reasons why people have to cooperate, to be good, honest, diligent, trustworthy, faithful, chaste, responsible, and other value terms from the original list. Could they imagine situations in which it would violate the values to apply them literally? What would happen if a person always told the truth in each situation? Could it cause trouble, hurt people, destroy the faith of people? What would happen if somebody always wanted to be good to people? Are there situations where it might lead to personal and social trouble? Similarly, they were asked about diligence, efficiency, love, forgiveness, charity, etc. Some years later a variation was conducted by ASL's class at Yeshiva College. Instead of the value terms they used the lists of duties, obligations, and aspirations expressed by Jews in their daily prayers. These activities were substituted for the value terms in the above described procedures. (The study was not repeated because of the unpopularity of religion in those days and the results are not available.)

After the list of value terms were collected, two lists were made, a list of negative terms and of positive terms. The list was printed in a column on a sheet of paper followed by empty columns in which the subject was to put a number that represented his awareness of the use or of the existence of the value in home, school, neighborhood, place of work, dates, parties, beach, park: (1) always (2) very frequent (3) frequent (4) infrequent (5) never. After this he was given a similar sheet but this time he indicated how he applied the value: (1) rigorously (2) with some exceptions (3) as many exceptions as no exceptions (4) with little rigor (5) no rigor at all. Another blank was given to him in which he was told to check off the values that he found in each of the situations and then to rank them in terms of the importance of the use of the value in each situation. After this he ranked them in terms of the importance of the value to him in each situation. A few weeks later the same forms were presented but this time he answered them in terms of how he thought other people would answer them. When ASL told Wertheimer about the study, he suggested that the subjects be given a chance to explain why they answered the way they did and that they be allowed to add other values which the list lacked and be allowed to add other institutions and places for the values that were listed. This suggestion was passed on to the class. The data is not available to us but recently a graduate student at SUNY-Albany undertook to replicate it in modified form.

Some aspects of the study have been used as projects in ASL's courses on Adolescence at the University of Oregon and in studies that were conducted for the Yale University Attitude Changes and Communication Project. In order to find out what people of different ages and backgrounds meant by contradictions, dilemma, and paradoxes, junior high school, high school, college students, and non-college adults were asked to record on alternate days of a two-week period all contradictions, dilemmas, and paradoxes that they noticed in their own and other people's conduct (cf. Luchins and Luchins, 1964a, 1964b). In a variation of this study the students were given a list of contradictions, dilemmas, and paradoxes involving ordinary life situations with which they were and were not ego-involved. The results of these studies led to an investigation on the application of principles in In-Groups and Out-Groups, which will be presented later in this monograph.

Also of interest here are some studies on problem solving and thinking in which situations were contrived so that a child had to learn or had to devise a standard of measurement (Luchins and Luchins, 1970a). In discussing these studies Wertheimer again suggested studying values and norms in ordinary life situations, to find out when standards arise or change in a group. What are the structures of the situations, the attitudes, assumptions, and needs of the group or of the persons that give rise to the development of social values or norms? This led to studies in which ASL asked children of a Brooklyn slum area, some of them delinquents, why certain rules were necessary in their school, home, community, classroom, and in games. He started out by asking them: Suppose there was no rule that you may not speak or walk around the classroom whenever you wanted; that there was no rule that the umpire's decision must be accepted in a punch ball game; that automobile drivers could ride wherever they wished on the streets and on the sidewalks. After they accepted each supposition he encouraged them to give cases or examples of what would happen if it was in effect. The subjects, the delinquents as well as the nondelinquents understood the need for most of the rules. They said that the rules kept order, made it possible for the group to function, kept people from interfering with each other. When ASL presented the same questions to high school and college youths there was more negative reaction to the rules of the school and especially of the home. Their first reaction was to say that they were restraints on a person's freedom of expression and kept one from doing what was best for him, that they were arbitrary. When ASL gave examples of what may be negative consequences to them for violation of the rules they then realized the functional value of the rules, but they still felt that something was wrong with the home, school, and community because they did not allow opportunities for free self-expression.

Wertheimer doubted that many of the youths really considered the social norms and values as arbitrary. Perhaps their reaction was due to the nature of the social field and their education. ASL said that maybe it was in part due to being told that when they grew up they would be free to do what they want. They were grown up in terms of the social norms for physical growth but they found that they were still treated like children. They were physically mature adults but were not allowed the adult responsibilities which would give them opportunities to gratify their biological and personality needs. Moreover, the home, school, and community stimulated their desires but blocked gratification. Perhaps they were fed up with the entire society because of this. When ASL referred to Durkheim's concept of anomie Wertheimer remarked that one must beware of substituting words for research.

Investigating the Autokinetic Effect

Wertheimer's criticism of Sherif's work included the statement that it is a fairytale that the light does not move; a quiet object on the retina will be unstable; because of the condition in the eye it will be seen as moving. The frame of reference is important. If there is none, the object is labile to the least motion. This led to an investigation to find out the factors that extremize the Autokinetic (AK) Effect. Because there was no laboratory at the New School the investigation began with the study of conditions that could be studied at home, where all that was required was a box, a bulb, and a darkened room. When ASL joined Yeshiva College in January 1940 there were no laboratory facilities but the variation he had already conducted could readily be duplicated by the students. Therefore it became the principal phenomenon that was studied in experimental psychology. The students compared AK to real and Phi movement, central and peripheral, monocular and binocular viewing of the AK light. They studied the effect of size, color, and meaning of the stimulus, the effect of sex, social suggestion, psychopathology, frame of reference on AK movement, etc. (Luchins and Luchins, 1969, surveys the project). Early in this work ASL told Wertheimer that it would be of interest to study the effect of increasing the illumination of the background in which the AK light was set. If it is found that subjects have a threshold in terms of the amount of light needed to stop AK movement then we will have a new way to study social influences that will overcome some of his objections about what the change of the subject's judgment means. Suppose a subject who needed, when judging it alone, five-foot candles for the cessation of AK movement then overhears someone consistently report that the light moves even though the illumination of its background is increased so that it is no longer a light but a black dot. Would the subject's threshold change in the direction of seeing movement with more light when he is later tested alone? Moreover, as the light increases on the background it will cast light into the room in which the experiment is being conducted, will the subject report seeing more things in the room when the background is illuminated? Wertheimer laughed when ASL said that he had criticized Sherif for not being a good behaviorist when he wanted to know whether the subject really saw things differently and asked, How do we know what he sees, maybe it's all verbal agreement? In this new procedure we do not need to depend on the subject to tell us whether he agrees with the other person in order to find out if his perception had been influenced; the change in the threshold can be measured by a dial reading on a Variac. This study had to wait until 1947 when the Physics Department lent him a Variac and Dean Isaacs built the apparatus for ASL in his home (cf. Luchins, 1954).

Conflict between Social Norms

Wertheimer objected to the assumption that social norms and values are arbitrary artifacts and in turn implied that values or norms have a certain function in the situation that can be grasped or understood. It was therefore decided to test this by using children who did not know about the metric system. These elementary school children of a Brooklyn slum had learned measurement by the usual drill methods of instruction. A ruler based on the metric system was *doctored* so that only half centimeters were marked on it. One child was given such a *doctored* metric ruler and another was given a *doctored* linear ruler in which only the quarter of inches were marked. First one child and then the other child was asked to measure the line on the card that was handed to him and to report how many units long it was in terms of his ruler. In this way ten lines were measured. For some cards the children gave the same report but for others they differed by more than one unit. All the cards were repeated five times to see whether the children would agree; ASL urged, Let's see if you both can get 100%. Of a class of 32 children not one agreed all the time, although they both changed their judgments of a line which was slightly above or below a full unit of the ruler; 6¼ became 6, 4¾ became 4 or 5. In some variations ASL told the child with the linear ruler that he had 100% but to measure them again in order that the other child would also get 100%, or the child with the metric ruler was told that he had 100% and the cards were readministered so that the other child would get 100%. Except where the difference was less than one half a unit of the respective rulers there was no agreement. It is of interest to note that they tried to agree and were concerned, but after measuring and remeasuring a line the child would give the results of his measurement. A few children in all variations spontaneously protested that they were measuring correctly and wanted to know what was wrong. One child, usually the one that had 100%, sometimes volunteered to watch how the other child measured in order to help him or show him how he did it. In spite of this, not one child realized that their rulers were different. When ASL asked them to change rulers a few immediately noticed that their units were skinnier or fatter. In many cases ASL had to place the rulers side by side before the children became aware of the difference in the rulers. When this happened, some said that both rulers were fakes and asked permission to go to their classrooms for their own ruler. A few became so upset that they would not trust the ruler that ASL gave them even though it was the standard classroom ruler. When the children realized that they had gotten different results because the units were different, he introduced them to the metric system and used this experience to give them a lesson on measurement.

When ASL told Cantril about these results, he said that such situations were too clear-cut and therefore it was possible for people to be guided by the evidence and argued that the ambiguous situations were fruitful for the study of the formation of social norms. When told of this, Wertheimer disagreed saying, Social norms and standards also develop in situations in which there is evidence; the history of the use of weights and measures is replete with such cases. He went on to suggest that variations be made where the subjects realize themselves that the trouble is due to the differences in standards. Therefore, two children were told that their task was to complete a house. One child was the lumberman and on his side of the table were pairs of doors and windows; the other child, the builder, measured with his ruler, gave to the lumberman the dimensions of a door or a window. The lumberman measured a door or window and delivered it. Because one had the doctored English linear and the other had the metric ruler, the builder always received a door or window that did not fit. The first few times they measured and remeasured when they found that the door or window did not fit; but after a while they agreed that the rulers were no good; they discarded the rulers and tried to fit the parts by inspection. This led to success. In short, when the standard interfered with the completion of the task they did not use it. ASL varied the instructions so that the children had to develop new standards in order to complete the house.

When these results were presented to Wertheimer he suggested that variations be conducted to discover factors that hinder or help the children realize that the standards are the source of trouble. He also asked that experiments be devised where the standards were more natural, where they were not like our arbitrary unit of measurement. He pointed out that these experiments may hold for cases where values and standards are conventions but there are values and standards which are more intrinsically related to the event or object being studied. When ASL said that all frames of reference are arbitrary, Wertheimer said that we must not overlook the question of the referent of a frame of reference, one does not use an acid when a base is needed (Luchins and Luchins, 1963). [This is a neglected problem.]

When we were writing the report of the Einstellung experiments, Wertheimer pointed out the possibility of setting in different ways two or three people by different experiences with similar problems and then bringing them together in similar situations to solve a problem or to make a judgment. This led to a series of experiments that were later replicated and reported elsewhere (Luchins and Luchins, 1959, p. 536-571). Before ASL left for the Army he discussed with Wertheimer these as well as other studies on imitation. ASL said that many of his experiments support Sherif and Cantril's position. The thesis that people act the way they had been habituated, and do it with little or no understanding, is supported by experimental evidence as well as daily life. He agreed with Wertheimer who said that there are two extreme possibilities in handling a problem, in making a judgment in a social situation, or in assessing a situation in terms of social norms and values: (A) trying to face structurally the actual situation, dealing intelligently with it according to its structural requiredness (B) acting on the basis of the unity of the group, more or less blindly carrying over, repeating what one had done before instead of thinking. ASL pointed to one of the variations in the studies on social influences on judgment (Luchins, 1945) and social influence on perception (Luchins, 1945), which Wertheimer had helped edit for publication, as proof and concluded that man more often acts blindly and unthinkingly than the way Wertheimer implies. Wertheimer said that when one looks at the social scene this is in fact very prevalent. What does this mean? When ASL said that it means that one may expect injustice rather than justice in life, Wertheimer said that even if only a few people most of the time act as in A, it means that such behavior exists and should be studied for the understanding of ethical behavior. He added that many people sometimes act in terms of A. What is the nature of such situations, how do they differ from situations in which the same person acts as in B? [ASL's personal experiences in the New School during the previous three years tempted him to give many examples of type B behavior. Instead he bid Wertheimer good-bye and left in a pessimistic mood. If men like Wertheimer can be blind to what was going on among his own students and the people whom he trusted, the tendency to act in terms of B is much greater than A.]

4
Philosophical Speculations about Value

In the beginning of the session a visitor remarked that value had once been an economic term but was now applied to all aspects of human life. In 1885 Lotze had introduced the word value into philosophy and proposed a new branch of philosophy, axiology, which was usually associated with the philosophies of Personalism and Idealism. To these philosophers, value was *in, of,* and *for* a person; it was neither a Platonic Ideal, an eternal norm, nor a condition or quality of intrinsic nature. Value was a clue to the nature of reality. Lotze said that the true beginning of metaphysics lies in ethics. Axiology did not study value per se, it was an attempt to apply science to life. It was claimed that not nature but man was the cause of all value, of all felicity as well as of man's ills, and that value theories were attempts to change values themselves because modern man believed that his destiny was in his own hands, that he did not need the concept of God to direct it. As the scientific study of value proceeded, some philosophers and social scientists realized that the methods that had proven to be successful in the natural sciences were not applicable in the social sciences. Neither the inductive approach nor the deductive approach seemed applicable. The men of the Age of Reason and the Enlightenment were certain that their methods would deliver signed and sealed the answer to the question of what is nature. But their methods and the immutable laws of nature that were proposed in the name of science tore apart the fabric of human life and did not reveal what is nature. Therefore some philosophers became anti-scientific, anti-rationalistic, as they pointed to the failure of the empirical and mathematical methods of science to yield an understanding of human values. Some blamed the failure on the mechanistic, analytic, and atomistic methods that were already giving the natural scientists trouble in understanding certain aspects of the physical world. Just as in these regions of the physical sciences there was a search for new methods, the social scientists began to look for more appropriate methods. Men like Dilthey proposed new methods to deal with the special features of the social sciences. Dilthey drew a distinction between the social and natural sciences. The latter merely described and made generalizations from the descriptions of phenomenal and external events, but the social sciences dealt with the realm of goals, values, and meaning which could not be understood by such an extrinsic point of view. The aim of the social sciences was not merely to predict or to control, but to understand, *verstehen*. In order to achieve understanding, we needed to comprehend the nature of the consciousness, the inner unity, the *Strukturzusammenhang* of the individual and of social life, as well as the historical development of this inner unity in art, religion, and science. This view was opposed to the emphasis on prediction and control of social and individual behavior as exemplified in the work of Comte and the Utilitarians. Dilthey raised the problem of the conservation and objective reevaluation of cultural forms. He stressed that men understood each other and were interested in each other because of their individuality, their uniqueness. Human behavior and experience involved value judgments, preferences, and choices that could be understood only by first comprehending the structure of the experience. Such comprehension led to seeing human behavior from within. The methods of the physical sciences, however, gave us a view from without, not from within. The focus on isolated parts had been useful in the physical sciences, but it had not been useful in the social sciences because it destroyed the inner unity, the essential nature of social and human behavior.

Wertheimer pointed out that not analysis per se was at fault but piecemeal analysis, that reason and logic were not at fault but a certain kind of logical thinking. Someone interjected that Hitler also rejected logic and science and stressed intuition, empathy, inner unity, and structure. The proposed approach did not necessarily yield any better results for mankind than the use of and faith in the traditional scientific methods and in reason. Wertheimer added that new logical and mathematical tools were being devised to deal with structure in physics and mathematics. The natural scientists were aware of the need to develop more adequate approaches but the social scientists stuck to certain traditional methods of science. Someone remarked that it might be due to the fact that the earliest application of science was for human welfare. Voltaire, not Newton, who was a religious man and wrote books on theology, used the Newtonian world machine as a social doctrine. Hobbes, not Galileo, used the laws of motion to develop a political doctrine. The social scientists have been concerned with the issues and problems that these early social reformers and philosophers developed and have not kept up with the development of physics. They have seemed to assume that the methods of the natural philosophy of the seventeenth and eighteenth century were the methods of twentieth-century science. Because of the technological success which was attributed to these methods, the social scientists believed that they were *the* methods of science.

The discussion changed when Wertheimer said that Dilthey's doctrine of Historicism (a society's values, mores, institutions, customs, and the thought of its people are determined by its history) was similar to the doctrine of Cultural Relativism. To say that what a person believed was true depended solely on the place and time in which he found himself meant that no objective knowledge was possible, that everything was subjective.

The visitor pointed out that Dilthey, the Personalists, and the Phenomenologists placed a high value on the individual. Man was seen as an end in himself while this was not the case according to some of the modern adherents to the doctrine of Cultural Relativism. A student pointed out that according to Dilthey and others, one saw and evaluated things and people in terms of his *Weltanschauung*, which was the result of the structure of his beliefs and judgments about the nature of man and of reality, these in turn being determined by the time and place in which he was living. Because of one's *Weltanschauung*, one person might value something in a way different from that of another person. No objective decision was possible, because each evaluation was equally valid from its respective point of view. Naturalism, Subjective Idealism, and Objective Idealism were different *Weltanschauungen* that led to regarding man as an impersonal mechanism, as a unique free agent or as part of an organic whole in nature, respectively. This doctrine could be used to deal cynically with people and events, even to justify Hitler as merely the expression of behavior that reflected his *Weltanschauung*. One could condone the Nazis' behavior as being the result of a certain world view. When the visitor protested, the speaker said that the rationalistic doctrine based on traditional science might also be used cynically. The liberal doctrines which were based on the mechanistic view of nature and society, resulted in a world similar to what happened in the barnyard when the elephant yelled *Everybody for himself!* as he trampled among the chickens. At present, the Nazis and Fascists were using anti-rationalistic concepts to wreak havoc with man and society. Perhaps all the talk about the superiority of one approach to the social sciences over another was just an attempt to rationalize one's faith or ideology.

The visitor went on to describe how Dilthey's concepts had been used by Spranger to develop a theory of ideal types, of men who strove to actualize certain values. The theoretical man's aim in life was the discovery of the truth by observation and reason. He was empirical, critical, and rational as he sought to order and systematize his knowledge. The economic man was interested in what was useful. He was interested in the production, marketing, and consumption of goods, in the development of methods of exchange and credit, and in the accumulation of wealth. He valued utility and the kinds of education, art, science, and religion that yielded tangible results. He was a pragmatist: truth was what worked; what was true was what was useful. The aesthetic man valued form and harmony most highly. Life to him was composed of events or episodes that yielded enjoyment. To him truth was beauty. The religious man sought unity with the cosmos. He was directed to the creation of the highest and the most absolutely satisfying value experience. Truth was the communion with this value experience. The political man was interested in power. He sought personal power; he wanted renown and to influence people. His attitude to truth was like that of Pontius Pilate, who had the Roman legions behind him. The social man loved mankind; he valued each person as an end in himself and therefore saw the values of the previously described types of people as inhumane insofar as they did not deal with a person as an end in himself. The truth, to him, was what furthered mankind's welfare.

A student objected to these types. He claimed that when he gave Allport's test, which was based on these types, to pious Jewish students, they tended to rank high on the theoretical and social but very low on the religious values. Why was this so? Wertheimer said that Spranger's types were idealized types based on certain theoretical conceptions and ideas of science, religion, art, and politics; they did not necessarily reflect the actual behavior and beliefs of scientists, artists, businessmen, and religious people. He asked, Just what kind of understanding does one get about a particular individual by comparing him to these types: Does it deepen our understanding of him?

A student pointed out that tests like Allport's were of value in placing students. By giving a student such a test we could place him in the type of school in which he could actualize his ideal self instead of arbitrarily forcing him into schools that would not further his self-development. Since self actualization was important for mental health, such tests were valuable diagnostic instruments. Another student asked whether it would be wise to send the above-mentioned Jewish students to social work or science schools because of their test scores and not allow them to go to religious schools. The former student protested that the latter was raising an unfair question. The latter went on to ask if it would not be better to find out the actual values of particular people. What were the actual goals for which particular people strived? Just what did they hope to achieve? What did they call valuable? What were their concerns and interests? Instead of categorizing people's answers to such questions in terms of a theory, should we not ask each person to rank or to make a hierarchy of what he said were his goals or values in order to see how they were structured in him? Similarly we could ask people to make a ranking or a hierarchy of what they thought were the goals, values or interests of their society, community, or institution. The student proposed still another way to study value. What were the various situations in life in which we used value terms and in which we experienced a value, a goal? What were the situations in which they did not arise? What was the difference in the structure of the two kinds of situations and what were people's relations to them and to each other? This might help to clarify what was meant by the words. It might suggest the social and personal factors that were involved in the phenomenon of human values.

The visitor and some students said that the proposal would yield a plethora of bits of information but that it would lead nowhere because it was an atomistic approach. The student who had made the proposal argued that at least his method involved a concern with actual people, with their hopes and aspirations, instead of spinning tales about what they were. The modern approaches to value were not any less abstract and divorced from life than the laws and values of mankind posited by the Age of Reason and the Enlightenment. Dilthey and others had rejected Positivism, but had fallen into the same trap of skepticism, subjectivism, or absolutism of values. Wertheimer ended the session with the suggestion that the students write to him about the ways in which they would go about studying value.

The Source of Values

In the next session the visitor said that some people viewed the various ideas of the nature of value as arranged in a scale from the absolute good or God to Humanism. Even religions were at present arranged on such a continuum, from myths and gods to reason and humanism. The more advanced ideas of value were based on humanism. Those who stressed the absolute Good or God felt that we could not have any morality or values without an authority, a force behind the order. A student interrupted to ask why God was on one end and man was on the other end of the continuum, as if they were antithetical. And why was the order from God to Man assumed to be from the lower to the higher end of the continuum and not in the opposite direction? The visitor said that it would lead to a different hierarchy of values if the order were reversed or if different concepts were used at the extremes of the continuum. This led to several remarks by students in support of the visitor's remarks that the concept of god was a restriction on man's behavior, one that might have been needed in man's infancy, but that modern man had reached a stage of intellectual maturity such that he no longer required a god to enforce morality.

The same student objected again to the idea that God and Man, Absolute Good and Humanism were at opposite ends of a continuum.[1] Man had been made in God's image; the laws of God were the laws of life. He argued that there would be no need for a League of Nations, for armies, or for police forces; there would be social justice and cooperation if everybody kept the last five of the ten commandments, which were based on a very primitive code of law. Why did modern man believe that his generation was the wisest of all that had preceded him? In the eighteenth century, they had said that science would create a paradise on earth. It had created a hell ruled by Hitlers, Mussolinis, and Tojos; this Hell is on the earth not beneath it.

The visitor explained that the concept of God and the values based on a belief in gods had arisen when man had had only primitive and rudimentary knowledge of nature. Man had been a naive realist due to lack of abstract-mindedness; his ethics and morality had been based on the restrictive force of an outside authority. But with the development of science man had found that natural laws and not the wills of capricious gods regulated the physical world. He found that man was a part of nature, not some special being with the spark of the Divine in him. As a part of nature his conduct was also regulated by natural laws. Modern man no longer believed that one's existence depended on the caprice or favor of a god. Moreover, various religions had assumed that mankind's values had been determined once and for all. But from knowledge currently available we know that that is not true. We know now about the unity of mankind, and that every society has a unique system of values that regulates it and keeps it together. The unity of mankind is based on man's biological make-up and his values are cultural artifacts of societies. We now understand why people steal, rape, covet, murder, and reject authority. These actions are symptoms of personality or social malfunctioning. Because of this new knowledge, we are developing a therapeutic approach to such behavior in place of the primitive, and often inhumane, methods that have been based on the laws of gods.

Someone interrupted the discussion by asking the class what punishment God had commanded in the Bible for stealing a cow. No one answered. He said that restitution and not punishment had been required. If you killed a thief while he was robbing you, you were guilty of murder unless you could prove that the act had been one of self-defense. Moreover, torture and other methods to wrest a confession or testimony were forbidden. The student said

1. It is absurd to argue that humanism and God-believing philosophies are at opposite ends of the continuum. Although in some people the concept of God restricts their humanistic breadth, still for so many (for example, Francis of Assisi, Jesus, Pope John, Billy Graham, etc.) the concept of God seems to give them an extra added incentive to help their fellowmen. (JKM)

that he wondered whether *Genesis* had been written after or before the Nazi Doctrine, in view of the visitor's comments which linked the concept of the unity of mankind and the humane treatment of prisoners with scientific knowledge. The Nazis were using, as a basis for their beliefs and programs, modern biological concepts, not the Biblical myths. The Nazi elementary school primer taught the so-called laws of genetics. It taught the theory of evolution by natural selection and survival of the fittest, not the myths of *Genesis*. He concluded by saying that the Code of Hammurabi, which was over 3,000 years old, compared favorably to the laws of modern European countries. The intellectual development of Western man had not made him more moral than the late Neolithic man, the naive realist, who was considered so concrete-minded.

The discussion returned to the question of why God-based values were to be thought of as inferior to those built on a humanistic foundation. It was said that God demanded blind obedience.[2] He was arbitrary and prevented man from being a free agent. Someone said that the same features could be found in certain humanistic doctrines, and he went on to say that all value was based on some kind of authority: that of God, of natural necessity, a monarch, a legislative body, or some other group. The authority could demand blind obedience and be arbitrary, or it could demand study and decision-making and be reasonable in making its will known to men in the sense that they would see that the demands fit the exigencies of the situation. A humanistic-centered value orientation need not be more humane than a deistic or authoritarian one. During this exchange Wertheimer made two remarks. He told the story of Y in ancient times who had refused to accept the conclusion of a discussion group that had supported X's interpretation of a point of law. X said that he could prove that he was right; for, if he were correct the tree in the court yard would jump to another place. It jumped, but Y refused to accept it as proof. X said that if he were correct, it would rain. It rained, but Y still refused to accept X's interpretation as correct; Y argued that its raining had nothing to do with the case. Each time, X proposed that a miracle would prove that he was correct, and, each time, it occurred; but Y refused to accept it as proof. Finally, X said that if he were correct, a voice from heaven would announce it. When a voice proclaimed that X was correct, Y pointed an accusing finger heavenward and said that God had given men the law to study it with their reason, and, therefore, His saying now that X was correct was irrelevant. A few weeks later Y met an angel in the marketplace and asked him what had happened in heaven when he had argued with X and had rejected both X's and His decision. The angel said that God had laughed and said that His children were smart. Wertheimer asked the class to tell him where the story came from. When no one spoke, he told them that there were several versions of it in the Talmud. What did such a story indicate? [ASL's students would not believe it. He asked them whether there were examples in the Bible of a man talking back and arguing with God. They mentioned Job, but no one recalled the times Abraham and Moses

2. Only the more primitive religions would seem today to think of God in such a narrow fashion that he would be demanding blind obedience. Most religions admit that the real problem is to know when God commands or what His Will really is. This remaining ambiguous, it would seem rare that one could think of God demanding blind obedience. (JKM)

argued with Him. Nor did they recall having ever read in the Bible instances in which God had used evidence to justify his actions and was dissuaded from a course of action because of possible effects on public opinion.[3]]

The other remark Wertheimer had made was that in the Bible's story of creation God started with creating light and not darkness, with order and not chaos. The student who had objected to the God-Humanism continuum said that before God had created the world He had created the Law and that He could not thereafter change or violate it without destroying the world. This conjecture was found in the Talmud. Someone remarked that the continuum presupposed a certain definition and concept of God and of man. He went on to say that to Epicurus the gods were tangible and were made of the finest atoms; to Anaxamenes god was an eternal unknowable. Neither of their gods had concerned themselves with man. To other people the gods had been capricious lords, demanding masters, or like loving parents. Generally speaking, the gods had been self-activated. Plato's soul or the humanist's self was a self-activating entity and thus godlike. Depending on the definition one used, one could make God out of man or man out of God. The continuum, therefore, got one involved in the arguments of what was God and what was man. Someone else pointed out that humanists have objected to the conception of a person as a collection of roles and have stressed that a person was a self. But what is a self? Thus we are just going from one mystery to another. We are finding new labels for the unknown and kidding ourselves that we are somehow closer to reality. Someone said that he had been doing some reading on the topic and found that the term value was a loose and vague concept. He then proceeded to give examples of what he had learned about value in his reading. He gave definitions from Whitehead, Dewey, Brightman, Marx, Perry, Russell, Sellars, Santayana, Durkheim, Patterson, Leighton, and Moore. He concluded that despite all the time and effort these scholars had spent, they had not been able to arrive at a universally acceptable idea of what was value. How could we study something that we could not define? Wertheimer interrupted to say that in mathematics and science many things were studied which were not defined. Mathematicians do not agree on what is a number, biologists do not agree on what is life. The student ignored Wertheimer's statements and said that value was used in a variety of ways and that if we were to have a fruitful discussion, one that actually got somewhere, we had to know what we were talking about. Were we talking about preferences, goals, expectations, decisions, feelings, or thoughts; about subjective or objective phenomena; about social, personal, or natural phenomena? One of the professors agreed that we must not deal with value in a vague way and that we must define the criteria. When Wertheimer said that the various theses that had been stated in class were bound by a traditional set of ideas and assumptions, one of the professors remarked: Why not describe a concrete case, instead of just talking about abstractions? The session ended at this point.

After-Class Discussions

1. The student who had objected to the God-Humanism continuum continued his arguments after class. Someone told him that it was a well-known

3. The New Testament part of the Bible has no instances I can think of where saintly figures argue with God. Some Christians say this points out that the evolution of the concept of God had changed. (JKM)

fact that morality that sprang from inner controls was more effective than enforced morality. A person who was honest because of external forces would steal when the forces were removed but if the forces were within him he would not do it. Freud and other psychoanalysts had shown that morality depended on the development of a superego which could be viewed as an inner mechanism that brought about moral behavior. Studies on moral development by Hartshorne and May as well as by Piaget had shown that real or normal moral behavior came into being with maturity. These results seemed to fit in with theories of social evolution. The last remark led to some critical remarks about cultural evolution. The student who objected to the continuum pointed out to the discussants that although they were against the idea that certain cultures could be placed on a continuum, that some cultures were more advanced than others, they were not against placing on a graded continuum of cultural artifacts, God and man. Perhaps they were covertly ethnocentric insofar as they were using the standards of the Enlightenment, in which it was assumed that modern man had reached a stage of mental maturity in which he was the master of all he surveyed. The same student asked whether the Humanism of modern man had in the past three hundred years really helped the common man, the widow, the orphan, the pauper, the stranger. It was one thing to strike a blow for the doctrine of Humanism and another thing to help one's fellowmen in particular situations. When someone said that Humanism was a naturalistic doctrine, whereas the God idea was a supernatural one, the student asked: Why is it essentially bad or good to be one or the other? The ideas of man and of God are both artifacts of a culture. Why is one idea better than the other?

2. Some students sat with Wertheimer in the lounge above the library discussing the question of whether there were absolute values. The students gave examples from anthropology to prove that what was moral, beautiful and true in one society was considered immoral, ugly, and untrue in another. They also gave examples from history and sociology illustrating that in the same society at different times and places that which had been called lawful or moral was considered unlawful or immoral; for example, the Volstead Act had made possession and sale of liquor unlawful and the repeal of the law again made it lawful; twenty years ago kissing was immoral, today it was moral. Wertheimer said that anthropological and sociological evidence is often presented to show that values or the systems of values of one society contradict those of another society. From such evidence it is concluded that there is no way to decide which values or systems are better. All that we can do is to state and to compare them. We may develop axioms for each group and we may compare them but we may not decide which are better. This thesis is very popular. It is found in the philosophy of Dewey and in many social psychology texts. The thesis is accepted unquestioningly by many students. Why?

A student said that some people accepted it because it was a point of view that rationalized the breaking away from the traditions of the past, from one's parents, from the church. It might also be that it was assumed to be a philosophy that encouraged and supported social reform. It was a doctrine that liberated one from social ties because it served as a basis for changing customs. If the laws and customs were man-made, and if we had a truly democratic society, we could not demand that a person abide by laws concerning the formulation of which he had had no say. Man was a value-creating animal, and a society that was based on absolute eternal laws was arbitrarily restricting the person's performing in a natural way by preventing him from participating in the formation of the values.

Wertheimer said that the fact that man makes customs and laws and that they may be arbitrary has been known throughout the ages. But the fact that they are customs does not mean that one may arbitrarily decide to disobey them. Someone said that in the past each group thought that its laws were natural and that the other group's were unnatural, and each group tried to force the other to believe that their laws were natural. ASL pointed out that some groups in ancient times seemed to have a greater respect for the customs of different people and to have recognized the power of customs more than was the case with modern man, if we were to believe the Biblical stories and the legends and myths of the synagogue. Even the Romans, who were efficient administrators, had usually respected the customs of the people they had conquered.

Before he left, Wertheimer made a number of remarks which questioned the validity of Cultural Relativism. Was it logical to infer from differences in facts that the underlying axioms were different? Were we allowed to deal with the facts superficially, without studying their sources and dynamics? Perhaps the facts demonstrated a transition from one system to another; because of differences in conditions there was different behavior, but the differences might not be arbitrary. After a pause he remarked: Suppose in one culture thunder is a god and in another culture thunder is a devil. Can these attitudes to thunder be explained as conditioned responses? Can we say that it is like a CR to food in one man and a CR to shock in another man? A student said that the thunder was like the buzzer and the god was like food, a positive reinforcement; and the devil was like electric shock, a negative reinforcement. Wertheimer asked him whether equating the god to food and the devil to shock explained the behavior of the people toward thunder. He suggested that the students think over the examples he had given instead of being so sure that they were just instances of conditioned responses. He also suggested that we reread the evidence for and against Cultural Relativism and keep in mind that a truth (T) might be composed of little truths (Tt), as well as of little falsities (Tf), and that a falsehood (F) might be composed of little truths (Ft) as well as of little falsities (Ff). A student thereupon said that Wertheimer was suggesting that we must take the whole culture or situation into account if we wanted to understand an act of behavior. Another student objected that it was impossible to know the whole; Truth or Falsity spelled with capital letters meant nothing because Ideals were by definition, unknowable.

Wertheimer said that we could at least make an effort to study what is Truth, humbled by the realization that we did not know the answer. We should seek an answer in an honest and sincere manner. Thereupon someone said that this meant that everybody was entitled to his understanding of what was true and false and should be allowed to act in terms of it. By what authority or on what objective basis might X be stopped from polluting the stream which he was using as a latrine while Y was drinking from it? Freedom for everybody to do what he thought was right might sometimes lead to chaos. Wertheimer noted that there was a relation between genuine productive thinking and ethics. In response to a student's objections to discussions of ethics, Wertheimer said that perhaps we had to examine carefully the system of ethics we now choose because it might influence the world in which we later lived.

5
Absolute versus Relative Ethics

The session started with a student saying that in the Middle Ages the Christians had regarded usury as a sin, but that at present bankers were honored church members and were even churchmen. Was this not an example of Cultural Relativism? Wertheimer said that Karl Duncker had pointed out that such examples ignored the possibility that the same behavior might have different meanings at different times and in different places. In the household economy of the Middle Ages people borrowed for necessities, for consumption, but in the modern commercial economy people borrowed in order to engage in business enterprises, to make a profit. Somebody said that usury had been forbidden in the Bible. If the Church were consistent, it would still evaluate it negatively. The Bible had presented an absolutistic code of ethics; therefore, whoever accepted the Bible must not lend money for interest.

Wertheimer asked for specific examples of usury from the Bible. None were given. He went on to say that the instances in the Bible were usually situations in which one had profited from his neighbor's plight. Even at present such actions were not considered proper.

A student pointed out that if an unwed woman gave birth to a child in our society, it was evaluated as bad but in Borneo, it was evaluated as good. Even in the USA there were places where it was evaluated as good. This illustrated Duncker's thesis that the situational context determined the evaluation. It was a well-known fact of perception that a piece of gray thread on a white shirt looked black but on a black suit it looked white. It was possible in the laboratory to make a lighter and a darker gray thread look the same by changing the amount of light of their respective backgrounds. Thus the same object might not look the same when displayed against different backgrounds, whereas different objects might appear to be alike. Similarly, different behavior might look the same within the contexts of their respective cultures, and the same behavior might look different due to their respective cultures. People of different cultural backgrounds acted or evaluated things and behavior differently because of the various cultural patterns from which they were perceived. If we wished to understand the behavior of a person, we had to understand his culture's value system. Social norms and values could only be understood in terms of a society's cultural pattern. We might say that the people of society X were uncouth and barbaric but they might say that we were uncouth and barbaric; furthermore, both could be correct.

Another student said that morals or values had different functions in different societies just as the same concept or axiom played a different role in different mathematical systems. One would not say that the parallel line postulate was correct in Euclid's geometry but not in non-Euclidean geometry. To understand the postulate, one had to understand the system of which it was a part. Since morals and values had different functions in different situations, there were no universal ethics, there were no universal laws of conduct. Everybody acted in terms of the way in which he was conditioned to act by his society.

One of the professors said that the thesis of relativism was an absolutistic one because it judged behavior in terms of the absolute nature of the responses or of the behavior, and assumed that the cultural difference in interpretation was due to the attaching of meaning to the behavior. The meaning came from one's background. It was like the traditional conception of perception: a percept was the sum of sensations plus meaning from one's past experience. It could also be said that this thesis gave a logical basis or reason for cultural absolutism; each culture's value system was absolutely correct because its cultural pattern was absolute. Thus, although it denied the existence of universal norms, the validity of values was nevertheless justified by an absolute value system or absolute fact.

Wertheimer questioned whether the thesis of absolute values had ever been as well established as the Cultural Relativists claimed when they attacked it. They assumed that there existed a widely accepted doctrine of absolutism and proceeded to invalidate it. When Wertheimer said that it was like saying that no cat had three tails, therefore, no cat had one tail, a student interrupted to say that Wertheimer was forgetting that in science we never proved a hypothesis but only disproved it. The opposite of the thesis of Cultural Relativism had to be Absolutism. The Cultural Relativists had set up Absolutism as the hypothesis to be disproven; if they disproved it, they could maintain their hypothesis. A student asked whether this meant that one could keep on believing that a cat had no tail, without even looking at a particular cat, after the initial study supported his thesis. The student added that it was one thing to prove deductively whether this or that act was good and another thing to experience whether or not it was good. The carpenter did not have to prove deductively that he could trisect an angle, but actually trisected certain angles. That he did so did not disprove the geometric proposition that all angles cannot be trisected with a straight edge and a compass.

Wertheimer challenged the idea that people in particular value experiences evaluated in terms of a logically complete and consistent system of values. He differentiated between the axiomatic approach and the nonaxiomatic, practical approach to value. He pointed out that sometimes a concrete demonstration was primary and basic and that it might even help the development of an axiomatic approach. One was at a loss if one confounded the concrete case with general axioms. A student supported Wertheimer's remarks by saying that the deductive approach sought the fewest principles or axioms from which to generate the world of facts, just as Euclid had done with geometry. Spinoza had tried to do this in his ethics; the result was a good book to read. It showed the power of the deductive human mind but it did not necessarily tell the man in the street how to conduct himself. Neither did Euclidean geometry tell a carpenter how to cut a piece of wood.

A visitor took the discussion away from the question whether there was proof in our experience that there were absolute values. He said that in certain situations we experience a demand to evaluate and to judge. We feel that the demand comes from the outside and recognize that it is different from the experience in which the demand comes from us. We sometimes experience such a demand to evaluate in spite of our personal likes or feelings. If evaluation were an arbitrary act, would we have such feelings of requiredness? Would we ever experience a feeling that a standard or scale of judgment was not arbitrary? It sometimes happens that we have difficulty in meeting a situation's demands until we realize that our standards are interfering with our dealing with it.

Someone said that the experience that evaluation was necessary constituted proof for Absolutism. In such a case, the person had a direct experience of value; he felt that a certain thing had to be done, and that nothing else would do. According to the theory of Relativism, such feelings were illusionary, mere projections of the way in which the person, because of his cultural background, had learned to structure events.

Wertheimer asked, What do we mean when we say that we evaluate something? A student said that it meant that we compared it with a certain criterion to see whether or not it contained certain features, or we tried to determine how much of a certain feature it contained.

Two students discussed Wertheimer's question in terms of examinations. One argued that the only way to grade a student was on a relative basis and not in terms of an absolute amount of knowledge. The other student said that grading students in terms of the normal distribution curve was a method that was blind to what the students did on the examination. The highest grade could be 40%, yet students would get As. Students were often graded in terms of the average ignorance of the class rather than in terms of what they knew. The other student argued that no teacher had a right to set 65% as passing. Wertheimer remarked that during this discussion neither of them had raised the question of what was required by the course, by the curriculum, and by life situations. Moreover, neither of them had talked about the knowledge the students had to obtain in order to be able to do the work in another course. He then asked whether comparing a thing with a standard was the same thing as trying to understand the thing. He went on to ask, What does it mean for the thesis of Cultural Relativism that the state of one's knowledge about something brings about a different evaluation? For instance, what does it mean that the white stuff that looks like poison is really sugar or vice versa? When students said that these questions had nothing to do with value, Wertheimer said that ethics required that we should not be blind to the situation; ethical behavior required knowledge and understanding. Suppose X and Y judge the same thing differently because they have different frames of reference. Could we by the Socratic or other methods open their eyes to the structural features of the thing so that they would arrive at the same judgment? A student said that when somebody calls a certain stuff *rocks* and another person calls it *coal,* it is possible to decide, but we cannot decide whether this or that act is moral.

Someone said that Wertheimer was assuming that people would listen or look at the object of judgment. Many people, however, would judge in terms of their own purposes and needs even to the extent of working at cross purposes with each other. The student doubted that people could be deflected from their personal goals and become interested and concerned with the phenomenon per se.

Wertheimer said that this might be rare but that it did happen. He suggested that the students find cases in daily life where it did and did not happen. After remarking that one could set up experiments to study the conditions under which it occurred, he asked us to consider the following example. Suppose there were two cultures, A and B. In A the act of killing was called bad but in B the act of killing was called good. A member of Culture A deems his culture's evaluations of the act as good and that of Culture B's as bad, but a member of Culture B deems his culture's evaluation as good, and Culture A's as bad. Is this kind of evaluation Absolutism? He added that some Cultural Relativists point to the same behavior without regard to the context of the evaluations and say that killing is killing: calling it good or bad does not change the act, it is still killing. A visitor pointed out that this is actually a kind of absolutism, the act of killing is the same to these Cultural Relativists. In order to get away from such an absolutistic point of view some Cultural Relativists say that we must not focus on the material contents of the evaluation, the killing, but must focus on the relation of the act to the culture. But if this is done each culture becomes the absolute determiner of the evaluation. It seems that one may say that the thesis of Absolutism is in a certain sense a relativistic thesis. The very terms *absolutism* and *relativism* are good or bad words in terms of an ideological fight for the minds of men. The real question is whether there are constant features in human value experiences and behavior. Should one envision these constants in terms of the identity of the contents of the behavior, or in terms of the identity of the relations among the contents?

Somebody suggested that the answer lay in the research on relational learning and went on to present Spence's and Köhler's thesis. Wertheimer brought the students back to ethics by asking them to consider the following example. *A* asserts that a shoemaker has to make good shoes and *B* asserts that a tailor has to make good clothes. What do they mean? If B says that the shoemaker is not a good shoemaker but that the tailor is a good tailor, would you agree that *B* evaluates shoes negatively and clothes positively and that it is not possible to refer to the identity of the shoemaker's making·shoes and the tailor's making clothes? The visitor elaborated the example. He said, Suppose that in order to be called a good man one must be a good shoemaker in Society A but in Society B one must be a good tailor. According to the Cultural Relativists the members of Society B would see no goodness in shoemakers but only in tailors. Was it possible for the members of Society B to see an identity, goodness, in making a good pair of shoes and in making a good suit of clothes? A student pointed out that the history of mankind proved that people did not see such identities. When people of different cultures met they thought that all virtue lay in their ways of doing things and that no virtue lay in the other culture's ways. This is seen in the history of the spread of the universal religions and in the destruction of the artifacts of the civilized Indians in Central and South America by the white man.

Wertheimer agreed that people could be blind to identity of relations, that they might have a narrow view of an act or of a situation because of the kind of education they had received or because of propaganda, group pressures of various kinds, or personality factors. But the history of mankind also showed that there were people who did see identity of relations, who did see righteousness in the behavior of people or other cultures who acted differently from them. Someone said that Wertheimer's argument was substantiated by certain traditional ancient religious views. He asked why is it that 2,500 years ago people saw identity of relations and not now? Wertheimer pointed out the need to find out the conditions under which people do and do not see identity of relations. Thereupon, the visitor asked, Suppose a member of Society A who called only shoemakers good men found himself in Society B and needed clothing. After several tailors had failed to fit him properly, he found a tailor who did. Would he consider him to be a good tailor in the sense that other people in that society did and would he realize that the tailor is in some way *good* as shoemakers are *good* in his society? A student argued that the person might have such a feeling but that it would not change his conception of the Good, because he believed that all virtue resided in shoemaking and not in tailoring. Somebody said that the student was confounding what happened in a concrete particular situation with general axioms. Some people might think that in general all Swiss cheese eaters were bad but they might nevertheless see some goodness in concrete actions of particular Swiss cheese eaters. Similarly, other people might think that Swiss cheese eaters were good but see nothing good in the behavior of a particular Swiss cheese eater. Wertheimer's example points to a neglected aspect of value in the controversy between Absolutism and Relativism, the relation of what a particular man does to the requiredness of a particular situation. He argued that when a shoemaker made a good pair of shoes and a tailor made a good suit of clothing they were both doing something good. He went on to say that Wertheimer's example illustrated Moore's thesis that something was good if it fulfilled the definition of its concept. It also reminded him of Socrates' thesis that a good man did what was required of him. Someone objected to the metaphysical notions in the example. The example was of no help to those who were concerned with the problem of what was good. It was a simplistic solution to the problem. The visitor remarked that it was not a simple thing to try to understand the structural features of an act and its place, role, and function in the situation in which it occurred. The example did not intend to serve as an answer, it merely pointed to one way of looking at value. The former student answered that examples proved nothing. How could one study a concrete situation per se? Moreover, were there not always some assumptions? Was it not better to make them explicit? [One assumption of Wertheimer's example, it seems to us, was that the general case might have nuances not found in the particular case, and vice versa.]

Wertheimer said that the term evaluation was used in a variety of ways. To some psychologists an act of evaluation consisted of some thing or some act to which was attached a positive or a negative evaluation. It was an and-summative structure. A positive or negative evaluation was attached to a thing or an act in the same way that two sentences were connected with the word *and*. It was a perfectly logical sentence to say, Hitler is the Führer and two plus two equals four. In this thesis the act and the value that was attached to it belonged to two heterogeneous classes of phenomena, there was no intrinsic connection between them. Someone objected that Wertheimer was assuming that an action required a plus or minus evaluation but it was well known that the same act may be evaluated one way or the other. It had been demonstrated in conditioning experiments; by rewards and punishments people attached positive and negative evaluations to actions and to things. This demonstrated that values were learned and that they were not innate. We get sick when we drink blood, but certain African herdsmen bleed their cows and drink their blood. A religious Hindu would retch if he were told that his food had meat in it; we would not. There was nothing essentially sickening about the blood or the meat. The behavior was due to conditioning.

Wertheimer said, We may learn to like and dislike things because of our own personal experience or the customs and traditions of our society but the question of liking is different from that of ethical evaluation. Liking or not liking must be separated from the idea of just, unjust, good, not good, fit, not fit. Whether we like it or not, we may feel that a thing is just or unjust. We need to study the inner connection between an act and the ethical judgments of it and not focus only on the question of liking it. Whether or not a shoe is a good shoe has nothing to do with liking or not liking shoes. When a child is sick there are many things the parents may do; play the piano, spank the child, or call the doctor. The parents may act arbitrarily or do what fits the situation, what fits is not merely that which they like to do, but doing what is called for in the situation.

Someone objected that Wertheimer was assuming that the problem for the parent was to cure the child's sickness and that doctors had the cure. The parents might not see it this way. They might regard the child as being cantankerous and soothe or spank him depending on how they felt or had been conditioned to act in such situations. A student said that the parents might be stupid or irrational but the question was whether playing the piano or spanking the child cured the illness. He pointed out that Wertheimer was raising the question of which action fitted the requirements of the situation. The previous student then turned to Wertheimer and said, If a gunman needs a gun to kill someone, would you give it to him? Wertheimer said that he would not. The gunman was not in a closed system but was part of a social system in which his act did not fit. Somebody from the seminar on Productive Thinking said that Wertheimer was using the same idea that he had used in the parallelogram problem. There was a gap and it required a certain solution. What was good was filling the gap in a genuine manner. The gunman in his relation to the social world had a problem that he felt is best solved with a gun. In the parallelogram problem it was rather obvious that the problem had certain definite limits. It was a system with rather well-defined boundaries but the gunman's situation was not so well-defined. He might be a Robin Hood who was protecting the poor from the wicked sheriff and tyrannical noblemen.

Wertheimer remarked that it was important to study each concrete situation in order to understand its structure and its relation to the field of which it was a part in order to find out what was actually required. In the social field as well as in problem solving, there might be blind, mechanized and stupid behavior. People might learn and believe that a certain series of responses was of value. [A student in ASL's class said that values were formulas that helped us decide, select, and judge. It seemed to the student that Wertheimer rejected this idea and instead proposed that value was an attribute of the world and of people. Values had a directional or selecting quality and were related to cognitive as well as emotive behavior. It reminded him of MacDougal's concept of instinct, a predisposition to become aware of certain things in the environment and to experience a tendency toward or away from them. To MacDougal, the core of the instinct was feeling; to Wertheimer the core of value was cognition. But both notions weie similar in that each had affective, conative, and cognitive elements. Did we really need such a complex concept to explain people's interests, judgments, choices, preferences, and other actions which were related to the concept of value? We might feel in life that values served as the criteria for much behavior, but this did not mean that we had to study values to predict and to control behavior. Psychology as a science might be better off not to deal with the problem of value. The natural sciences had developed only when man turned away from the notion that nature operates in terms of such qualitative or phenomenal features.]

A visitor said that in psychology we knew that it was not the situation but the libido that had demands; he asked Wertheimer whether he denied this. Wertheimer said that the thesis that the organism or the ego was the center of the world was not true for all cases of human behavior. There were experiments with children that showed that there were vectors in the system of which the person was a part, and that these caused his behavior. [This point is related to Wertheimer's views about egocentrism, which are presented in Volume II: *Problems in Social Psychology.*]

When someone wanted to know whether it was true that ethics dealt with conflict situations, Wertheimer said that there were such situations but that the study of conflict situations was not the same thing as the study of value. He rejected the proposal that it was better to start the study of value and ethics with conflict situations. In conflict situations there were two requirements that were opposed to each other. Therefore, why not first deal with less complicated situations? Later on we could study the more complex situations in which there were opposing requirements. He said that there were situations in which all factors worked in one way on judgments, a habit, or an attitude. Why not start with a clear-cut case of value and see how one deals with it, whether one deals with it in a mechanized manner or in a genuine way? What could be done to the situation and the person to extremize either kind of behavior and what were the effects on the person and the situation when one went from judging blindly to genuinely or from judging genuinely to blindly? He ended the session by saying that we needed concrete experiments and not only philosophical discussions of ethics and value.

After-Class Discussion

After class some students sat in the lounge discussing problems raised by Wertheimer's remarks. If there were intrinsic as well as extrinsic connections between the object and the value, how did one determine them? Someone said that there were facts and values. People misinterpreted the facts because of value judgments or because the facts had values hidden in them. Facts were things or events as they were; values were characteristics not of things or events but of a certain culture. One could regard them as historical facts. One might even regard them as final and absolute within the culture's history.

Someone argued that it made no difference scientifically speaking whether one focused on facts or values because the concept of what was a fact was an artifact of science, and science was a social institution. If we said that there were facts as opposed to values, we were implying that science had its own autonomous culture, but science was a social institution and the society's culture controlled it. One of the students said that the issue was not whether we had a world of facts or of values but whether the world had intrinsic or arbitrary meaning and whether the connections of things and meanings in it were arbitrary and meaningless.

Someone said that Wertheimer's concept of intrinsic connections reminded him of Spinoza's idea of necessity. What proof had we that what one saw was really ruled by necessity? Wertheimer sat down among the students when the question was asked. He asked the students for examples in specific situations in which events or things were intrinsically and not extrinsically related. He went on to ask the students to study such situations in order to determine what were the differences between them. This led to a discussion of the concept of cause. When we used the word in these situations, did we mean that something was the factor that produced an effect or that something merely followed something else? Wertheimer said that there were both types of situations. It would be of value to study them and to see what was the structure of each instead of assuming that cases of intrinsic, or rho connections, between events were similar to the cases of extrinsic non-rho connections (Luchins & Luchins, 1970b).

Someone remarked that values seemed to radiate meaning; a thing took on a different meaning when one or another value was attached to it. Did this mean that the value gave it its quality or that the value directed us to different qualities in it? For example, the same boy or girl may be seen differently when it becomes known that he or she is *bad*. Even though you may never see them do anything immoral yet your view of them changes. Wertheimer suggested that we study such cases in order to see what brings about the changes instead of speculating. A student said that the value might be used to rationalize our behavior toward a person or a thing. The thing really does not possess the quality but because we wanted to treat it in a certain way we said that it had such and such a quality. Wertheimer said that the issue was not just whether or not one rationalized; rather, it was the direction of the rationalization which was important. How does rationalization affect the person or the situation and the object being evaluated? Sometimes rationalizations make it possible for a person to go on living and hoping; they may not do violence to the object being evaluated or they may. Someone added that the word rationalization was often used as a bad word, but it might be a method of obtaining a meaningful word. Wertheimer said that the psychologist who says that a person is rationalizing might himself be rationalizing the other person's behavior in terms of his theory and be blind to what the person is really saying or doing.

A student argued that we like an individual because he has the virtues which we have learned to like; we seek out in the world people and events that are in line with our values and ignore people and events that are not in line with them. Values make us see what we like and ignore what we do not like. After a pause Wertheimer said that this might be the case, but instead of getting involved with the question of whether or not one learned to like certain values, we should find out in a specific case whether we like a particular person because he actually has the value. He added that one might like something because of certain values and one might really like the thing, too; they might reinforce each other. There might also be situations in which we liked only the thing or only the value and the factors could actually oppose each other. What are needed are empirical studies instead of mere speculations and dogmatic assertions.

Wertheimer Elaborates on Value

In the next session, one of the students said that he was confused by what Wertheimer had been saying. Wertheimer remarked that various issues had been thrown together in the discussion and that it might be of help if we focused on some of them separately. What was a productive way to view value or evaluation? From one view the content of value was a feeling or an evaluation. He drew $A\vert\;\vert^{\pm}$ and said that on the one hand there were objective facts, A, and that on the other hand there were values or evaluations, + or −; they were in two different realms; A belonged to the world of facts and the plus or minus belonged to the world of subjective meaning or feeling. When he paused for questions, one of the students said that the schematic representation looked structurally similar to the Associationists' assumption that the stimuli and the sensations were heterogeneous. There was no blue in the light waves that were the stimuli for the sensation of blue; similarly, there was no goodness in the object that gave rise to the value of good. This doctrine seemingly had some support in experiments with primitive people. When South Sea Islanders were given a color-sorting test, they classified the colors differently from the way we did because they viewed the stimuli differently. Thus the objects of the color test, A of the schema on the blackboard, were evaluated differently because of the people's different social norms. They saw the world differently from the way we saw it because of the culture in which they had grown up. Values were cultural products and therefore people from different cultures evaluated A differently. The student went on to say that values and norms were man-made and since man had made the values and norms man could change them—that a person was not committed to values and norms which he did not create. Values and norms were impositions on a person's freedom to act. A student objected to these remarks. He argued that because customs and traditions were man-made did not necessarily mean that they were arbitrary or that everybody was free to select and to obey only those customs which he liked or had helped to create. The idea that they were man-made was not new but the idea that one could therefore do as he pleased was perhaps new.

Wertheimer said that some of the students' remarks represented the stylish point of view that the family, religious, and other institutions arbitrarily attach positive or negative evaluations to things. The same thing could just as well be evaluated negatively or positively. It was not possible for us to say that one evaluation was correct and the other one was incorrect. To say that one evaluation was better was pointless because it was just a personal preference due to the values one had learned to connect to it. When a visitor pointed out that it was an external connection, it was blind to the nature of A, Wertheimer inquired, What are the consequences of this thesis? One of the professors said that it meant that science could study value and the process of evaluation without getting mixed up with metaphysical questions about the True, Beautiful, and Good. It indicates the kind of problems that are solvable by science. Science can study just how A is evaluated in different places and at different times. It has already yielded valuable information about the diversity of ways in which A is evaluated so that the thesis of Absolutism is no longer tenable.

Someone remarked that it had led to the assumption that the purposes for which one strives and the meaning one sees in his existence are culturally determined. This means that there is nothing outside of oneself and one's culture that may offer valid guidance for decisions about how to act and what to strive or hope for. Life has become meaningless because there are no intrinsic and objective goals to strive for. One is alone with his feelings of anxiety over the senselessness of existence.

Someone interrupted to say that the goals and meanings still existed but that they were external to the person. Science had found out that they were cultural products of the society into which one was born and that they had meaning in the context of the culture. Insofar as one understood his place and role in his society, his life was meaningful; the traditions of his society bound him in a meaningful way to his fellowmen and to the world. Just as the wisdom of his mother's body has led to his development before his birth, the wisdom of his society's culture leads to his development after birth. The culture does not impose a biologically alien way of life on the infant: What is done reflects the past experience of the society in creating conditions for the survival of neonates as well as adults. He added, Why should the fact that different societies have developed different cultural patterns mean that there are no values? A student remarked that the trouble lay in modern man's loss of historical perspective. It is ironical that we know more facts of the history of ancient times than did the people living in those times. It seems that knowledge does not lead to understanding.

A professor pointed out that science constituted an ahistorical approach to phenomena. If we knew the place at which a planet was at present and the speed with which it was moving, we could predict where it would be in the future and could say where it had been in the past. This idea from astrophysics had been used by some social philosophers and social scientists to lessen the importance of history. Another professor suggested that they had used the mechanistic model of Newtonian Physics to rationalize their rejection of the Ancient Regime and the Christian concept of history. However, the men who made the scientific discoveries in the field of astrophysics had not preached the mechanistic social doctrines attributed to them. He went on to say that in ancient times it had been known that people had different customs or gods and that because one was raised by a certain society, one learned its customs and believed in its gods. Ancient man, generally speaking, had not believed that his gods or customs were universal laws of mankind or of nature. If he was an Athenian, it was his duty to believe and to act like an Athenian and not as a Spartan and vice versa because that was the way he had been nurtured. One cut himself off from the community when he rejected its value system; he was excommunicated, ostracized. He became an outlaw, no longer did he have the protection and privileges of his group, when he refused to live by its norms and values. This great respect for customs was reflected in Socrates' choosing death instead of banishment. It was also seen in the codes of the early civilizations of Asia Minor and in primitive tribes. The modern rediscovery of the diversity of human values and customs might present a problem to those modern men who believed that there was a certain way of living that was in accord with Natural Law and that all enlightened men, men liberated from the cake of custom that encrusted them, would do what was natural. With the same zeal with which their ancestors had preached that Christianity was the only true and universal religion and that the Church's laws were the only valid laws of conduct, the philosophers and intelligentsia of the past three centuries had preached a new universal doctrine. Just as their ancestors had destroyed idols, opposed false beliefs and heathen customs because they were evil and the work of the devil, the epigones of science opposed the customs, beliefs, and institutions of their times and preached a new age of faith. An example of this was Comte's proposal for a new scientific religious hierarchy to replace the Roman Catholic church. His church would also have a Pope, Cardinals, and priests but would teach scientific doctrines. Although such a church had not developed, science and the ideas of Positivism and Utilitarianism had become a way of life in our society. Just as there developed heresies in the Church, there developed different points of view among the adherents to the scientific faith. Some scientists no longer believe that their laws are the eternal and absolute laws of human conduct and argue for Cultural Relativism, one of the doctrines of the ancients. Just as it might have confused and bewildered some of the ancients to see their cherished beliefs about their customs destroyed by the growth of the Universal Church and just as some true believers had been confused by the doctrines of the Age of Reason and the Enlightenment, the children of the Enlightenment's parents were now confused by the doctrines that there did not exist absolute natural laws of human conduct and that man was a creature of his culture. Those individuals who have grown up to believe that their goals, values, and customs are dictated by nature may feel that their lives are meaningless because nature has dictated different ways of living to people in other societies but nature moved in mysterious ways its wonders to perform.

Someone objected to the statement because it reflected a negative attitude toward science. There was a danger in what was said; it implied that science was not the way to the truth. The professor remarked that there was a difference between pointing out that science was not the only way to the truth and saying that it was not a way to the truth. He went on to say that the doctrine of Cultural Relativism could lead to a genuine belief in Cultural Pluralism. Such a belief was necessary at present when technological culture is spreading throughout the world and wiping out one culture after another. Cultural diversity is disappearing as more and more societies become industrialized; technology is succeeding where the Church has failed. Soon all mankind will believe and act in the same way; they will be united with each other in the name of Technology.

A student pointed out that if Technology would lead to the unity of mankind, there might be no more wars and poverty. The professor said that the idea of the unity of mankind had been preached for thousands of years. It had not arisen out of the scientific view of man and life. The question was not if mankind would be united or not, but how it would be united. He expressed doubts that the ideas of Technology would succeed where the idea of God had failed. Someone said that it would succeed because the idea of God was a personal and vague feeling and did not involve a detailed blueprint for society. Industry has developed more efficient ways to control and to predict human behavior. It can create a world in which everybody does the same thing just as Ford has made identical Model-T cars.

Wertheimer resumed speaking, saying that the fact that the same thing was evaluated differently in different societies did not necessarily substantiate the thesis of Cultural Relativism. It could be that A was evaluated differently in Culture B than in Culture C because it did not mean the same thing in the two cultures. He drew $\underset{A\;|AB\;\diagdown\;A\;|AC}{\big|\diagdown\big|\big|}$ and said that in Culture AB, A meant B and in Culture AC, A meant C; therefore, in one society A as B was positively evaluated and in the other society A as C was negatively evaluated. A student interrupted to say that Wertheimer's schema was supported by experiments on brightness contrast (he was referring to Wertheimer's experiment on Stumpf's paradox which will presented in the Perception Seminars). Another student said that this might be true for perceptual phenomena but that it did not hold for values, meanings, or goals. Wertheimer said that piecemeal analysis of value might lead to errors. We must not be blind to the context in which the action takes place. Suppose one walked into the theater and heard laughter at the hero's predicament. It would seem heartless, but had he come in two minutes earlier, he too would have been laughing. The same scene seen in a different context means a different thing and therefore is evaluated differently. A student gave this example from law: a man in some states was allowed to get married immediately after his divorce but a woman had to wait three months. He asked the class why this was so. Most of the answers referred to the discrimination against women. The student then told the class that the reason for the law was to protect her and her baby. If she was pregnant at the time of her divorce, her former husband had to support them and the child was entitled to share his father's estate. The student concluded that there were many examples in law in which a rule seemed to be cruel and inhumane but when the situational context was learned it became humane and just. This seems to indicate that there might be some objective basis for evaluation. Some students objected that it did not prove that values were objective.

Wertheimer said that so far the focus had been on the reasons one ascribed a negative or positive evaluation to an action. There was another way to look at it. He drew SITUATION └───ir───┘ DOING and said that ir stood for inner relations. He compared this new schema with the one that he had drawn before and pointed out that the former thesis (I) dealt with external and blind connections; the new thesis (II) dealt with connections that were ruled by inner structural qualities. In response to students' objections, he said that he was not discussing whether the connections in Thesis I and II were learned or not learned, subjective or objective but whether the connections were logically or structurally similar. The student then said that most situations fitted Thesis I and not II. Wertheimer answered that even if there were only one case of II it would serve as an objection against Thesis I and would demonstrate Thesis II. A professor remarked that what had been said did not invalidate the idea that on the one hand there were factual things and on the other hand there were such nonfactual things as oughtness, goals, and desires. During the argument, Wertheimer objected to the professor's razor-cut distinction that dissected an act into responses and goals and motives. Not only was the structure of the concrete act ignored by such a procedure but the place, role, and function of the act in the social context was also ignored. A visiting professor objected that Thesis II came dangerously near to being a metaphysical doctrine. It involved questions of what ought to be and such questions were not in the domain of science. He went on to say that even if there were cases that were in accordance with the second thesis, he would prefer to deal with them in terms of Thesis I because Thesis II was not in line with scientific traditions. Mankind had advanced when it rejected the world outlook from which Thesis II stemmed. In Thesis I man was a free agent who could shape his own destiny. Just as he had learned from the physical sciences to transform the earth and harness the forces of nature for his welfare, he was now learning from the social sciences and psychology how to create societies in which each human being would actualize his individuality.

Somebody said that he had recently read Huxley's *Brave New World,* which depicted a world run by scientific principles; it was a frightful picture. The scientific view of nature and man as value-free had destroyed the mystique of man and nature. Its success had led to the misuse of natural and human resources. A student said that these destructive tendencies had existed before, that man had always been the earth's most destructive creature. It made no difference to the earth's flora, fauna, mineral deposits, or human beings whether they were destroyed by beliefs in supernatural or in natural forces. The person who had alluded to Huxley said that perhaps there were limits beyond which the earth would not tolerate man's destructiveness, and that man's present behavior was reaching the point of no return. The student said that this had been said in ancient times as well as throughout man's history, but that man progressed despite the prophets of doom. The unfettered spirit of man had produced a world never dreamed of by the pioneers of science. [It is of interest to note that most seminar members and most of ASL's students believed that science had the key to most of man's problems. Science has produced even greater miracles in the past 35 years but a feeling of disquietude exists at present. Students may not believe in God but in supernatural experiences, in astrology, in mind-expanding drugs, oriental religions, and magical practices. Is it all due to just the A-bomb?]

A psychiatrist raised the question of whether values were determined by the personality of the individual. The person was a self-actualizing creature; in the process of actualizing himself certain values were created or were discovered to be important for one's development. If we focused on the individual's personality and not on God or the group or on the society, we would discover what was required for self-actualization. Wertheimer said that this view did not necessarily do away with Thesis II. He added that it was not a question of desiring or needing something but doing it blindly, arbitrarily achieving one's goal in a way that did not fit, that did violence to the situation. The psychiatrist argued that the needs, values, and goals of man are expressions of unconscious forces that are cut off from the environment; they reflect the demands of deep inner forces. These forces, deep within the person, determine all of his behavior, including values.

Wertheimer rejected the assumption that on the one hand there were the person's needs and on the other hand there was the situation and that the person's ego had to battle to satisfy or to repress these inner demands. This view of man might be true for certain situations, but we must not overlook the possibility of cases existing in which the *radix* of the individual met the *radix* of the situation. (*Radix* refers to the principle governing a structure.) In these cases there might be sincere attempts to meet each other on the basis of mutual requirements, with no trickery from either the situation or the person.

Someone interrupted to say that Wertheimer was assuming that there was a mutuality between the basic needs of a person and all situations which he was in, as well as a desire in the individual to act in terms of this mutuality. It reminded him of the attitude of certain mystics who sought communion of their inner spirit with the spirit of the world. It was the ideal Homo sapiens man trying to come to grips with what was real, genuine, not an imitation and who was seeking to actualize in his behavior the Eternal Ideals. Such a conception of man belonged to Speculative Philosophy but not to science. A student remarked that the concept of self-actualization did not necessarily imply that there was a conflict between man and society. Every society had as its goals the actualization of certain kinds of persons. A society could be compared to a system of positions, just as in Ford's factory. In order for the factory or the society to operate, each person had to do what was required of him at his station. Just as Ford's factory's personnel office sought to fit people into positions whose requirements they would meet because of their aptitudes and abilities, so did society select and place different kinds of individuals in different positions. When each person actualized himself and developed to the maximum of his ability, society's needs also would be best met and its positions adequately filled.

Before dismissing the class, Wertheimer asked the students to think over this formulation. In a certain situation a gunman needed a gun. The gunman made a positive evaluation of Mr. X's giving him a gun but the victim evaluated it negatively. Was it enough just to note that the gunman called it plus and the victim called it minus? Were the gunman and victim parts of a system in terms of which the act of giving the gun could be understood regardless of how one evaluated the sub-systems of the gunman and victim? Was it possible that in terms of this system both gunman and victim would evaluate negatively the giving of the gun? How would you proceed to study such systematic relations?

6
Experimental Outgrowths on Value

Wertheimer repeatedly referred to the research of Hadley Cantril and Muzafer Sherif as examples of studies that were not dealing with value but with evaluation. Moreover, Wertheimer often pointed out that the thesis underlying their work denied the reality of value. His criticism led to a negative feeling toward their work among many members of the seminars, particularly among those who assumed the roles of acolytes, converts, and disciples. The negative evaluation of Sherif's and Cantril's work overlooked the fact that both of them were interested in value and were seeking to develop conceptual and methodological tools which would deal with the problem of value. Because ASL had been introduced to *Social Psychology* and to *Personality* in Cantril's courses in the summer of 1936, Wertheimer's criticisms were a challenge to him to reexamine the research which he had begun under Cantril's supervision.

Values of Youth

In the summer of 1936 ASL was a student in Cantril's courses *Social Psychology of Everyday Life,* and *Personality,* in which the problem of value was presented as an important and perhaps central issue for the understanding of the social and individual behavior of man. Two research projects were undertaken under Cantril's supervision: a research project which centered on the study of a group of adolescents and a study of the values of youth which was supported by the National Youth Commission. In a discussion of the methods to be used in these studies, Cantril suggested that Kurt Lewin's method of studying the level of aspiration might be a fruitful approach to study certain aspects of values and ideals. The following procedure was finally used. A series of interviews was arranged with a subject. In the first interview he was asked what he valued most at present. If he gave more than one answer, which was usually the case, he was asked to rank the items, and each of the values was then discussed in the following manner. He was asked to give reasons that the particular value was one of his most important values. He was asked whether it always had been one of his most important values. If he said that something else had previously been his most important value, he was asked what it was and what had been the reasons for the change. He was questioned to find out whether something on the outside or a personal factor had brought about the change. He was also asked how he had felt when he had made the change, and what he felt and thought now about the old value. In the same way he was asked what had been the value before this previous one, until he came to a value that had not been preceded by another one. Some subjects were questioned in the reverse order, from the earliest values they could remember to their present values. Before or after these interviews on what he valued most, the subject was asked to list all his values and ideals. He was questioned about each value and ideal in the same manner as that used for ascertaining his most important value. In another study the subjects were asked about their ideals of an occupation, a recreational activity, school subjects, teacher, mother, father, brother, sister, boy friend, girl friend, man, woman, religion, political system, community, group, and family, as well as for their ideal conceptions of God, truth, justice, goodness, honesty, friendship, love, and happiness. They were questioned in the same way as in the previous studies.

Some subjects agreed to keep a diary in which they would record everything that happened. They wrote five times a day; after first describing their dreams, they wrote at about 10 AM, 2 PM, 6 PM, and just before they went to sleep.

The reports of all these studies were used to base a discussion of value, including Wertheimer's thesis of fit, in ASL's Adult Education Courses and college courses on adolescence. Some of the results and conclusions are presented to stimulate research with present-day populations. One could raise the objection that the results below represent the values, ideals, and aspirations of a certain type of student, many of them were first-generation Americans, who were attending the WPA Adult Education classes in 1936-1937. Most of the subjects' values and ideals reflected the philosophy of the New Deal. The fervor with which they expressed their values reflected their personal commitment to one of the current ideological views: Liberalism, Communism, Republicanism, Fascism, or Nazism. But their examples of value and ideal usually involved particular people, events, behavior, and things. Although some subjects stated different general or abstract values and ideals, they usually gave many similar concrete and particular examples. Although they differed ideologically, they valued similar things. Those subjects who were not committed to an ideology tended to give more particular and concrete examples. Those who had gone on to high school and college were found to have changed their values and goals more often than those who had not. Regardless of their education, the subjects of the lowest economic level tended to change their values more often because of external factors than did the middle-class subjects. The middle-class subjects changed their values more often because of personal factors—they outgrew them, obtained more information, and developed new desires or interests. The middle-class subjects seemed to be moved more often by ego desires, while the lower-class subjects seemed to be moved more often by factors in the external situation. The former tended to have a more Faustian attitude, whereas the latter seemed to be more resigned and contented to come to terms with the facts of life and settle for something within reach. A few of the latter looked back on their childhood values and goals as foolish, naive, unrealistic, childish ideals. The middle-class subjects tended to know more ways of getting and doing things to advance themselves, for example, they knew more about the resources and opportunities for student aid and scholarships. They were more knowledgeable about job opportunities, public works programs, civil service programs and jobs. They even knew how to get on the WPA and relief roles. Some of the youths of the lower socioeconomic levels who were intellectually oriented and successful in school seemed to be more passive about pursuing careers than the middle-class youths. More of them were willing to settle for a small job that would give them economic security on an economic level that was not much more advanced than that of their parents; they did not seem to be so success-oriented. Was this because their parents had accepted a certain status in life and had taught their children not to move out of their class or status?

Generally speaking, the subjects, regardless of their socioeconomic level or education, started out with the virtues taught by the home and church. School experiences were sometimes the instigators of the changing of these values. Although the curriculum contributed to some changes, most changes were related to recreational or extracurricular activities in which the subjects had met children with other values. Friendship and falling in love were major sources of value changes. Going to work and observing the workday world of people, becoming curious about sex, thinking of death, of one's status, of one's future and occupation, as well as joining a gang, club, or political party were also sources of value change.

The social atmosphere of the school and the teacher's values were felt by some youths to be counter to those of their parents, for example, to be accepted or successful in the school meant to do things that were against the values of their parents' religion. Some adjusted to the demands by developing one set of values for the home and another set of values for the school. Some did this after first feeling disloyal, sinful, or concerned about what their parents would think of them, but others did not. They readily learned to live in each place or with each person in terms of the value orientation of that place or person. They learned to play different roles in each place in terms of its requirements. A few students were disturbed by their different value orientations and sought a unified orientation but most of the subjects were content to behave in each place in terms of its standards. It was even regarded as a sign of maturity to be able to behave in these ways without qualms. Many changed their old values with a feeling of liberation; they felt that they were now really living. A few felt that their worlds had been shattered, even though they accommodated themselves to the different value orientations. A few felt a need for, or a sense of responsibility toward, the traditional values. They expressed a desire for continuity of traditions. More subjects, however, totally rejected their old values as parochial superstitions and old ways of viewing the world. A few of these subjects saw no intrinsic worth or meaning in the old values. Progress, even the future of mankind, depended on abolishing them. A few were estranged to the extent of being hostile to their parents and religion. Among these subjects were ideologues and children of parents who were strenuously trying to become Americanized. A few youths were pragmatic and realistic to the extent of being cynical; they said that they used political and social ties to advance themselves. Among them were a few who said that money, sex, friendship, and other interpersonal relations should be used to advance oneself. Nearly all the youths reported the greater importance of clothing, money, good looks, and the greater need for mastery in interpersonal relations, sexual gratification, and self-aggrandizement in their later years than in the earlier years of their lives.

Some youths had several values, even contradictory values, which were equally important to them, but a few had one guiding value to which everything was subservient, for example, sexual gratification or the ideals of a revolutionary party. A few subjects reported that a change in one value brought about a change of meaning in other values, even though the initial change did not require a change in the other values. Some youths who had lost their old values sought new ones, going from one new value to another. Others said that they still believed in their old values but saw them as ideals, as abstract ideas; thus they separated their ideals from the world of everyday life.

There were a number of youths who were attracted to different organizations on the campus such as the Popular Front Against War and Fascism because of the opportunities for social and sexual experiences and not because of any ideological convictions. Similarly, a few had joined the Bund and other groups.

Some of these studies were replicated in 1956 by ASL's students in a graduate course on adolescence at the University of Oregon. The students concluded that the 1956 youths were more interested in self-development and self-actualization, and that there was less concern with political and socioeconomic conditions than in the 1936-1937 (New York) study. There was also a greater emphasis on competition and on the idea that the social group was the source of value. There was somewhat more stress on religion, morality, sociality, and cooperation even though their diaries indicated more intense striving for self-expression, sensual gratification, status, and material goods.

Some Oregon high school teachers made a content analysis of the 1936-1937 diaries and presented the tabulation of values, needs, hopes, and goals to their colleagues who were asked to indicate whether the particular items were alike or different from those of their high school students. They also made a content analysis of the 1947-1949 protocols of ASL's group psychotherapy sessions held in the New York City Veterans Administration's Mental Hygiene Clinic. The tabulated goals, values, and needs of the veterans were also given to their colleagues. In both cases, the teachers saw little difference or no difference between the youths of 1936-1937, the veterans of 1947-1949, and the high school students of 1956 in the state of Oregon. But when the same items were given to the students, they saw themselves as better adjusted, less pessimistic, more social, and more knowledgeable, sophisticated, and sexually experienced.

We discussed the teacher's findings with the students who had replicated the study with college students. Several reasons were advanced for some of the discrepancies. One possibility was that face-to-face interviews might lead to different impressions. Another was that the teachers were ideologues of the social living philosophy, while the students were not. For example, the students saw injustice in the arrest of the Bishops of the Brethren Church's Communities for not giving their children the approved social living curriculum in their schools. The teachers said that the churchmen were robbing the children of their rights as Americans. The students also could not understand the teachers' condemning parents who would not allow their children to participate in the social dancing program of their physical education department in their high school. The teachers tended to believe that all values stemmed from one's peer group.

In discussing some of the 1937 results with Wertheimer, ASL pointed out that the social field could foster a philosophy of life in which values were seen as a subjective quality of existence with few or no bases in the objective world. He pointed out that some of the protocols indicated that some subjects had not started as egocentric individuals; they had first been oriented to the requirements of situations outside of themselves. First they had been sensitive to the demands of situations. Then they had become egocentric, and finally they had become sensitive again. Who were these subjects? Were these trends due to personality changes, to field conditions? What kind of personality factors and what kind of social field conditions led to egocentricity? He raised such questions as: Why were some youths sensitive to discrepancies between their values and their actions while others were not? Why were some youths more aware of such discrepancies in other people than in themselves? Why were so many youths rejecting their parents' value orientations? Why did some youths feel that they had to do something to change the values and goals of people while others did not?

ASL pointed out that most youths were interested primarily in their own needs, in creating a personally satisfying world, and that even the ideologically oriented youths were interested in their own status and sought material goods and services. They seemed to be playing the game according to its rules even though they were against the social system and its economic doctrine. They seemed to know how to further their own interests.

Wertheimer rejected the implied thesis that it was human nature to look out for oneself. Perhaps it was an artifact. Social interest, sympathy, and cooperation were also natural. He added, after a pause, that if a person in our society were not for himself, no one would look out for him, but if a person centered primarily on what was a profit to him, there was a danger that he would develop a narrowed view of the physical and social world. This too could get him into trouble because it gave him a distorted view of things. A world in which everybody optimized his own profit was an impossible world. When ASL said that because there were sheep to be shorn there were sheep shearers, Wertheimer rejected that idea—that society was possible because some people were dominant and others were submissive.

ASL pointed out that some of the youths' value orientations were primarily sensual, while others were primarily conative, and still others were intellectual. This was seen in the fact that the situations that these youths entered were acted upon in terms of the possibilities for sensual gratification, status achievement, or intellectual stimulation. A few even transformed the situations to fit their value orientation. Their personalities, needs, or goals determined their values, which, in turn, created a social field for realizing them. Wertheimer rejected the conclusion that the personality per se was the source of value. He pointed out that the types of behavior were examples of *crippled doing* brought about by situational factors or the social development of the person; they did not represent prototypes of natural ways of behaving. The discussion ended when ASL said that Wertheimer was postulating the Homo sapiens ideal as the prototype of behavior but modern anthropology had shown that it was a myth. Wertheimer did not deny that he was assuming the Home sapiens doctrine of man. He added that there was a need to find out the common values of man and not to keep on pointing to the differences and losing sight of the fact that all men had characteristics in common because they were members of the same species. [Some thirty years later, Hadley Cantril (1966) published the *Concerns of Men,* which studied the values and aspirations of millions of people throughout the world, and found that there were some common concerns.]

The Meaning of Value Terms

Wertheimer once remarked that although the experts did not agree about what value was, the man in the street—and even the expert when he was acting like an ordinary man—knew what value was. This remark led to questioning the students in ASL's Adult Education Classes in order to test Wertheimer's remark. The following questions were asked one at a time, on different days.

1. What do you mean when you use the word *value?* Give some examples.
2. How do you distinguish between what has and what does not have value? Give some examples.
3. What do you mean when you use the word *good?* Give some examples.
4. What do you mean when you use the word *bad?* Give some examples.
5. How do you distinguish between good and bad? Give some examples.
6. What do you mean by *truth?* Give some examples.
7. What do you mean by *untruth?* Give some examples.
8. How do you distinguish between truth and untruth? Give some examples.
9. What do you mean when you say that something is *not beautiful?* Give some examples.
11. How do you distinguish between something that is beautiful and something that is not beautiful? Give some examples.
12. Are there any situations that create values? If so, what types of situations are these?

First the general question was asked and then the request for examples was made. After the students answered all the questions, they were told to give the questionnaire to children of various ages and to youths and adults of different educational backgrounds. The same questionnaire was given again in 1957 to students in ASL's courses on adolescence and problems of youth at the University of Oregon, and in 1967 to his students at SUNY at Albany. Each time all students answered all the questions. In their replications of the study, the students also found that all adults and youths were able to answer all the questions. They found, however, that some children below the fifth grade had trouble understanding the first question, but they too were able to answer all the other questions. In a recent replication (1969), there were a few college students who refused to answer. They argued that the words were empty of meaning. Although in 1937, 1957, and 1967 there were subjects who also said this, they had, however, given examples to illustrate the use of the word. The 1969 subjects, however, refused to give examples. They seemed to be bored by or contemptuous of or indifferent to the experimenter's request.

The results of all these studies were similar in the following ways. The student experimenters who timed the subjects found that responses wer quicker to the terms *bad, untruth,* and *ugliness* than to the terms *value, good, truth,* and *beauty.* The subjects gave more and even different responses in the second half of each question. They were more varied when they were asked for examples than when they were asked the general question. Children tended to give fewer and less varied examples and to be even more concrete than the noncollege youths and adults who in turn gave less-varied and less-abstract answers than the college students. But in all age groups and in all educational levels, the most frequent responses referred to concrete or particular objects, people, and events. Value was most often something that was important or useful to themselves or to others. It also meant worth in terms of monetary value. Value was a social or personal matter to many subjects. The mention of nature, God, or philosophical principles was infrequent but was found more often among the responses of the college students. In 1937 more students regarded value as natural, inherent in nature, in the physical world, and in society. In 1957 more students regarded values as social norms or standards of conduct. In 1967 more individuals viewed value as personal preferences. In 1937, 1957, and 1967 material goods and personal services were most often given as examples of what value was. Generally speaking, the subjects were materialistic and sensual in their orientation.

More subjects in 1967 said that there were no situations that created value because values were based on personal likes and dislikes or on common sense or on living naturally. In 1957, however, many subjects had pointed to social situations as value-creating situations. The answers reflect a moving away from the idea that value is objective to the idea that it is purely subjective.

In 1937 many subjects gave examples of behavior of people in the socioeconomic and political scene that did not fit or indicated situations that required some kind of behavior. The 1957 and 1969 subjects also mentioned *fit* or *requiredness,* but it was mostly in terms of what fulfilled their needs and desires. In 1969 particularly, the college students saw value in terms of what fulfilled them and were not so concerned as the 1957 group with the effect of their value orientation on others. The 1969 students gave more abstract answers than non-college students. The subjects made less mention of the broad humanistic, religious, and traditional moral precepts than had the 1937 and 1957 subjects. They gave more psychological concepts to illustrate the nature of value.

In all three studies, truth and untruth were related to matters of fact, beauty and ugliness were about something on the outside, but good and bad were subjective matters. However, in 1969, more students regarded good and bad as merely subjective than in 1937, and more in 1969 judged goodness or badness in terms of their likes and dislikes or in terms of what fulfilled them.

The meanings of value terms were studied in another way. Subjects were asked the following questions in an interview and asked to give reasons for each answer. What do you value most? What is good? What is true? What is beautiful? What is right? A week later they were asked: What is bad? What is untrue? What is ugly? What is wrong? A week later they were asked for experiences in which something had first been good but changed to bad, and were asked about the circumstances of the change. In the same way they were asked about changes from true to untrue, beautiful to ugly, and right to wrong. Finally, a week later they were asked for examples of changes from bad to good, untrue to true, ugly to beautiful, and wrong to right.

The results corroborated the previous study. About one-third of the subjects valued material things or possessions most. Fifteen percent said that they valued most highly that which was important to them; ten percent valued knowledge or education; five percent valued love, friendship, and self-respect; about two percent valued, respectively, sports, games, religious virtues, and God most highly. Young children and noncollege adults gave more examples of good and moral than of ugly and beautiful. College students more readily gave examples of beautiful and ugly. Good was more often illustrated by abstractions like God, nature, and morals; truth was more often illustrated by matters of fact; and beauty by nature, the fine arts, and human physical features. They gave more examples of going from negative to positive values. A replication in 1969 indicated that people still valued most highly goods and personal services, but there was a greater emphasis on individual preferences and likes, and less reference was made to social and situational factors. More subjects gave examples of beauty and much fewer gave examples of good. Some explained this by saying that good was a personal thing but beauty was found in the relationship of someone to some external object. Truth still was seen to be related to matters of fact.

In discussing the results of the 1937 interviews, Wertheimer raised the question of whether the results were due, in part, to the interviews. He suggested that we make naturalistic observations of pupils and students in school, on the playground, and in the street, and of adults at their place of work. He believed that doing what was fit or required was more prevelant than one would be led to believe from the results of the interviews. [There was little evidence in ASL's observations of his students and colleagues to support Wertheimer's conjecture, but several years later ASL found several examples of people responding to the demands of the situation in the closed wards of the U.S. Army Hospital's Neuropsychiatric Wards.]

ASL raised the question of whether the situations that were related to Wertheimer's thesis of fit were situations that people often thought of when they think of value. Value to many people was the worth of something or the measure of something in terms of a standard of conduct. There were cases of fit with no evaluation of good or bad, but they were actually matters of fact, not value. What was fit in terms of good or bad was often in terms of ideals, hopes, desires, and the expectations of the person. It was the filling of a need or a gap in the person. Wertheimer challenged the implied thesis that evidence or factual matters did not play a role in such cases of fit. He asked whether the object or deed really met the situation's requirements or filled adequately the felt need or gap. He did not deny that one might be deceived into believing that something fitted which did not fit. The discussion ended with his suggesting that experiments be devised to study the sensitizing and the desensitizing of people to the requirements of a situation. (Cf. Luchins 1951, on methods used to change patients' social perception.)

At another time Wertheimer said that fit was related to understanding the place, role, and function of an act in the system of which it was a part. In recent years, due to ASL's participating in the development of a science course of study (Parsegian et al., 1968, 1970), Wertheimer's notions of fit have seemed to make sense in terms of contemporary systems-analysis concepts. The systems engineer has to be careful not to optimize a part of a system at the expense of the total system. Did Wertheimer view each human being as a potential systems engineer? In what kinds of situations are people aware of the total systems of which their behavior is a part? What are the effects on the person and the situation when he acts in a manner that is blind to the system as a whole? Some direct answers to this question may be obtained by asking workers in a plant to describe the place, role, and function of their job in the job structure of the plant, or by asking students the place, role and function of their various activities in the total college setting. Is there a certain amount of awareness needed for successful functioning at work, school, and in the community? Perhaps modern division of labor in industry and specialization in school make it possible for a person to function efficiently in his position without knowing just how his behavior fits in the total situation. [Luchins (1959) describes a systematic approach to the study of a mental hospital that is, in part, an outgrowth of these suggestions.]

A student activist who was told about the 1969 study at SUNY at Albany, was asked why the students, in contrast to the 1937 students, leaned toward individualism. He said that the individualism that they expressed was not the individualism that the 1937 subjects had rejected. In the 1930s the rational man of Liberalism was rejected for the social man of the various social and political doctrines. The present-day students felt that everybody was on his own trip. College students in 1969 could work for a few days or months and earn enough to live separated from the normal social world. Moreover, most of the 1969 students came from affluent homes and did not need to worry about how to get along in the world. They did not need to reconcile themselves to the established ways of doing things; when they did not, they got away with it. They were by-products of an educational system that stressed self-expression and made them verbally articulate, a system that was based on a solipsistic phenomenalism which denied that there was evidence for value and value judgment. Values and evaluation were bad words to some educators and psychologists. Their schools stressed a naive egalitarianism, for example, some teachers believed that no matter what the child drew in the art class, it was as good as what was drawn by the other children because everybody had a right to express himself. This had already existed in the 1930s, but the children's parents had then still felt the effects of the old traditional way of doing things and demanded it in their children's behavior. But the students of 1930 had raised their children without stressing the old virtues, and when the children came to school, they continued in a more intensified way the self-expression which had been encouraged at home. In 1937 it was called expressing oneself; now it is called doing one's thing. When the professors criticize certain literature, drama, and art, the students protest that they like them; they protest that the analysis kills the feeling. Everything is a matter of personal taste and one has to learn to tolerate different people's taste and must let everybody "do his thing." The students are concerned with the fact that many people, especially among the lower classes and minority groups, are not allowed to do their thing. They see a discrepancy between the egalitarianism and permissiveness as the ideal that was preached to them and the establishment's real ways of doing things. They want to change it so that everybody will be free to do his own thing. This is required if we are to live up to the values that we have preached for so long a time.

The value words are meaningless because words have lost their meanings due to advertising and propaganda; the same amount of X is called king size, giant size, family size, and extra large. The word democracy is used by all isms. Words like imperialism and peace-loving are used for different kinds of behavior. Perhaps some of the results of the study are due to the loss of the classical education that stressed the understanding of culture, civilization, history, and philosophy and that may have made people think more critically about the meaning of words.

More students go to college and the colleges meet the problem of mass education by textbooks and workbooks that dish out facts to be memorized and tests that are graded by IBM machines. The student is allowed to express himself in class and to voice his opinions, but this does not count. What counts for the student's grade in the score on these tests. People are becoming more similar and bland. As a professor once said, they are becoming like the various blends of Kraft cheese; they all taste alike.

Modern technology requires certain things. One can't change the fact that the machine has certain requirements in order to produce and to go on producing. These requirements are producing the values, but the old value words are used to rationalize them. If we look at the USSR and the USA, we will see that both are doing the same thing, pursuing the same material and technological goals because both are modern, industrial societies. We see here an example of Wertheimer's concept of value as the requirement of the system as a whole. As more and more men get used to and desire the goods and services that the industrial society produces, they will have to accommodate themselves to the values of the machine-based society. Since we still use the old value words, each person has to struggle to attach meaning to the words. Since the old value words have been used in relation to the values that are determined by the machine, people struggle to make a private world. As people do this, they may in effect accentuate the meaninglessness of the value words and make more possible the idea that machines may be the ultimate values.

Studies on Value

When Wertheimer's seminars on value were used as a basis for a discussion in ASL's Advanced Social Psychology class in 1969-1970, several class and individual projects developed. The following reports illustrate the nature of the projects.

1. At the beginning of the term each student was told to keep a diary for two weeks in which he recorded every time he came across the word *value* or related words such as *valued, valuable, value-free.* The diaries were collated for class discussion by Margaret Brown, ASL's assistant. The number of entries in the 12 diaries ranged from 4 to 45 and totaled 163, averaging about 14 entries per diary or one entry a day per student. Over two-thirds of the entries occurred in conversation or lectures and about one-quarter of them in reading material. Most of the entries (78%) involved evaluation and normative behavior. About a third of the items occurred in business transactions, another third involved social or moral standards as well as expressions of *requiredness* or *oughtness,* and the other entries referred to abstract principles or ideas (18%), or to desires, goals, and expectations (11%).

2. Another class project was a modification of one of the prewar studies that had been described before. Sixty subjects were interviewed individually

by the students. In order to obtain a varied sample, there were ten subjects in each of the following categories: 5-7 years, 8-12 years, 13-15 years, 16-18 years, college students and young adults with college education (College), and adults with only some high school education (Adults-High School) who ranged in age from 35 to 45 years. The subject was asked, What is value? Give examples of value? In the same way he was questioned concerning the words *good, bad, true, false, beautiful,* and *ugly.* The verbatim answers to each question were first tallied by Paul S. Cowan, ASL's assistant, and then classified according to whether they referred to the subject (Personal) or to something outside of him (External). The latter responses were further classified as Concrete or Abstract. Another category was made up of words relating to action. Thus there were four categories: A. External-Concrete, B. External-Abstract, C. Action, D. Personal. The numbers of responses to the words and the number of responses in the various categories were as follows:

	5-7	8-12	13-15	16-18	College	Adults-H.S.	All Ss
Value	12	16	22	22	28	36	136
Good	27	29	24	23	32	32	167
Bad	27	25	21	17	32	48	170
True	10	31	20	25	35	31	152
False	14	27	21	27	27	29	145
Beautiful	21	31	22	29	26	42	171
Ugly	22	32	26	27	29	43	179
A Ext.-Concrete	81	99	57	42	86	108	473
B Ext.-Abstract	18	53	54	76	83	97	381
C Action	26	33	29	16	11	16	131
D Personal	8	6	16	36	29	40	135
Total	133	191	156	170	209	261	1120

Most subjects in all age groups were able to give examples of each of the terms. The total number of responses for all the questions was 1120, about 20 per subject. There was a tendency for the number of responses to increase with age, with the smallest number (133) contributed by the youngest subjects and the largest number (261) by the oldest ones. For each term the largest number of responses was made by the college and adult subjects. For all subjects combined the number of responses increased in the following order: *value* 136, *false* 145, *true* 152, *good* 167, *bad* 170, *beautiful* 171, and *ugly* 179. With the exception of the two older groups, the terms *value* or *true* received the smallest number of responses in each group. In contrast, the College group gave the word *true* its largest number of responses. It is of interest that the 5-7 year olds and the Adults-High School subjects gave their largest number of responses to the word *bad* and that the 8-12 year olds and College subjects gave their second largest number of responses to this word whereas the remaining groups gave it their smallest or next-to-the-smallest number of responses.

The percentages of the various categories of responses are given in the subsequent table. The External-Concrete responses predominated for the group as a whole and for every age group with the exception of the 16-18 year old for whom External-Abstract responses predominated. As in the previous studies, the younger subjects gave relatively fewer abstract responses and more concrete responses than the older subjects; they also gave relatively more action responses. In view of the alleged egocentricity of young children, it is of interest that they had about the same or smaller frequency of personal responses than the older groups; the largest frequency of such responses was

TABLE 6. 1

Percentages of the Various Response
Categories within Each Group

Concept	Category	Groups				Adults		
		5-7	8-12	13-15	16-18	College	H.S.	All
Value	A	75	63	73	32	43	61	56
	B	8	12	14	23	43	22	23
	C	17	25	4	4	0	0	6
	D	0	0	9	41	14	7	15
Good	A	63	38	9	10	28	32	31
	B	4	24	29	38	44	28	28.
	C	26	38	45	30	3	12	24
	D	7	0	17	22	25	28	17
Bad	A	37	32	33	29	31	37	34
	B	19	44	33	47	50	42	39
	C	37	24	29	18	6	4	17
	D	7	0	5	6	13	17	10
True	A	40	39	25	28	37	22	31
	B	10	36	30	44	57	65	45
	C	40	19	35	8	0	3	13
	D	10	6	10	20	6	10	10
False	A	50	48	33	22	24	38	35
	B	36	33	48	74	40	48	28
	C	14	19	19	4	32	14	16
	D	0	0	0	0	4	0	1
Beautiful	A	76	74	36	31	54	40	51
	B	19	26	50	34	27	38	33
	C	0	0	0	3	0	5	1
	D	5	0	14	31	19	17	15
Ugly	A	82	69	46	22	73	53	57
	B	4	16	38	48	10	26	24
	C	4	3	0	4	10	7	3
	D	9	12	15	26	17	14	16
Grand	A	61	53	36	25	41	41	42
Means	B	13	28	35	45	40	37	34
	C	20	17	19	9	5	6	12
	D	16	3	10	21	14	15	12
TOTALS		100	100	100	100	100	99	100

given by the 16-18 year old subjects. Concrete responses were given to the words value, beautiful and ugly by three-quarters or more of the youngest age group and by over half of the subjects as a whole. The word true yielded the largest percentage of abstract responses (45%).

3. Values were studied in another way with the assistance of Robert Meshanic, a student who was a counselor at one of the state colleges. He interviewed individually five adults who had completed high school but had no college education (Adult-High School) and five who had a college degree (Adult-College). They were questioned concerning value and non-value, good and bad, true and not true, beautiful and not beautiful. They were asked about each of these concepts in the following way: What is beautiful? Give examples of beautiful. What is not beautiful? Give examples of not beautiful. In the same way they were questioned about each of the terms. There were 466 responses which were categorized as Concrete (61%), Abstract (37%), and Unclassified (2%). It is of interest that the first question about each of the terms yielded more abstract responses and fewer concrete responses than the second question that asked for examples of the term. As expected, the subjects with more formal education gave more abstract responses; of the 247 responses made by the Adult-High School subjects, 72% were classified as Concrete and 26% as Abstract whereas the 219 responses made by the Adult-College subjects were about evenly divided between the Concrete and Abstract categories. Of the abstract responses, a total of 64 (an average of about 13 per subject) were contributed by the Adult-High School group and a total of 105 (an average of about 21 per subject) by the Adult-College group. Of the concrete responses, a total of 179 (an average of about 36 per subject) were made by the Adult-High School group and a total of 108 (an average of about 22 per subject) by the Adult-College group. Whereas 38% of the abstract responses were from subjects with no more than a high school education and 62% from subjects with a college degree, precisely the reverse was the case for the concrete responses. Moreover, the Adult-College group gave as many or more abstract responses than the Adult-High School group and as few or fewer concrete responses on about 90 percent of the questions. Thus educational level was apparently reflected in the nature of the responses.

4. Another study was conducted with the assistance of George Burstein, ASL's student who taught a management class to 19 graduate engineering and science students at Rensselaer Polytechnic Institute. They were questioned in six consecutive sessions of the class about the terms value and not value, good and bad, truth and untruth, beautiful and not beautiful. At the beginning of the session a questionnaire was given to each subject which asked, What do you mean when you use the word beautiful? Give some examples. During the class break another questionnaire was distributed which asked, What do you mean when you say that something is not beautiful? Give some examples. At the beginning of the next session another questionnaire was given to them which asked, How do you distinguish between something that is beautiful and something that is not beautiful? Give some examples. In the same way they were questioned about the other terms.

The 19 subjects were males ranging in age from 22 to 46 with a median age of 29; nine were either only children or first born. When asked to give their opinion on the generation gap and to rate their agreement or divergence from their parents on basic value perceptions and on social and political issues, they indicated only moderate divergence; 10 of the 19 or 53% had rather complete value identification in line with both parents and political identification with their fathers. Thus, the so-called generation gap was not found in this group. Most subjects gave more than one response to each question, contributing a total of 371 responses to the twelve questions, an average of about 20 responses per subject. Of the total responses, 21% were abstract (general or philosophical) and the remaining 79% were concrete or specific. The latter responses were further categorized as social (oriented around social values, beliefs, norms, or interpersonal relations); personal (internal or individualized); materialistic (pertaining to money, possessions, or hedonistic values). The numbers and percentages of responses in these categories were as follows:

Type	Number	% of Total
Abstract	78	21
Social	119	32
Personal	98	27
Materialistic	76	20

In comparison with results obtained in ASL's WPA Adult Education classes during the Depression, the present group showed fewer abstract responses, more social, interpersonal and personal responses and fewer materialistic responses. The WPA classes' responses (although not analyzed in quite the same way) were about evenly divided among the following three categories: abstract responses, social and interpersonal responses, and personal and materialistic responses. The WPA classes were composed of working people or people seeking employment for whom jobs, food, clothing, rent were important; one WPA subject spoke for many when he said that his aim was to be a well-fed man. The relatively smaller frequency at present of materialistic responses may reflect the difference between an economically depressed and an affluent society. Also, the greater overt concern in the present group with social, interpersonal and personal values may reflect the greater emphasis at present on sociality as well as doing one's own thing, ideas stressed by the mass media, the educational institutions and youth movements. Although the emphasis during the Depression was on sustenance, on getting or holding a job and supporting oneself, one's parents, or one's family, the materialistic or economic concerns did not exclude or overpower all others. This is seen in the fact that the WPA students were enrolled in a variety of cultural courses and that they contributed more abstract and philosophical responses than did the present group. But, economic and materialistic values seemed to underlie even some of the abstract responses because of the general social atmosphere. It is possible to speculate that their concern with the abstract and philosophical was an escape from pressing economic worries.

In the present study, the largest number of responses occurred in the social classification for all questions except the three questions pertaining to beautiful, not beautiful, and the distinctions between them. For these three questions, materialistic responses predominated and accounted for over half of such responses. These three questions also accounted for about one-third of each of the abstract responses and the personal responses. About one-third of the social responses were made to the three questions concerning good, bad, and the distinctions between them.

5. Another study was undertaken with the assistance of an undergraduate student, Miss Sifrim, who interviewed individually ten radical (Left) and ten conservative (Right) students on the campus in the Spring of 1970. Each subject was asked to name five goals or objects that were most desired and then was asked to name five goals or objects that were least desired. In the same manner, each time being asked for five responses, he was questioned concerning the personal values that he evaluated positively, the personal values that he evaluated negatively, the values commonly held by Americans that he evaluated positively, the values commonly held by Americans that he evaluated negatively, the goals that America should achieve and the goals that America should not achieve.

The responses were analyzed in detail because of their relevance to current campus unrest. On the whole, the conservatives (Right) gave a greater variety of responses. There seemed to be more agreement and less variability within the radical (Left) group than within the conservative group (Right). About one-third of the responses were similar in the two groups, although the frequencies differed; 22% of the Left and 8% of the Right mentioned hatred, wars, and fighting when asked what they least desired. When asked what they most desired, the two groups gave three responses in common: love (14% and 6% for the Left and Right respectively), peace (10% and 6% respectively) and realistic happiness (2% and 4% respectively). The conservatives emphasized family, personal achievement and material possessions while the radicals emphasized interpersonal relationships, self-knowledge, and social justice. For the latter, the most frequent responses were as follows: love, honest relationships (14% each); peace, freedom for all (10% each); to be respected (8%); self-knowledge, freedom from hangups, happiness of others (6%); and an end to human starvation (4%). For the Right, the most frequent responses were as follows: family, graduation (8% each); acceptance, experience, interesting job, money, health, love, peace (6% each); and friends, security, success (4% each). While some conservatives said that they most desired specific material possessions, for example, lovely home and saxophone, with these constituting 10% of their responses, these were not mentioned by the Left. Christian ideals of salvation, grace, and heaven were mentioned by some members of the Right group, constituting 8% of their responses, but were not mentioned by the Left. Goals America should achieve yielded eight common responses which constituted 38% of the Left's replies and 30% of the Right's replies. Included were these goals: end poverty (10 and 8% for the Left and Right respectively), social equality (8 and 4%), freedom and democracy and preserve the environment (6 and 4% each). For the Left the most frequent replies for goals America should achieve were socialism (16%), end poverty (10%), redistribution of wealth, social equality (8% each), love for mankind, freedom and democracy, preserve the environment (6% each), legalize drugs, tolerance, do good with technology, end imperialism, and end military intervention (4% each). The most frequent responses for the Right were respect abroad (12%), good government, economic growth, end poverty (8% each), peace within America, solution to race problem, slash budget (6% each), abolish warfare, patriotism, freedom and democracy, social equality, decent standard of living, preserve environment, scientific gains, and strengthen moral fibers (4% each).

Surprisingly, the Right referred to ending the war and to world peace more often than did the Left.

Goals America should not achieve yielded six common items which constituted 48% of the Left's responses but only 14% of the Right's responses. These included laws to restrict freedom (18% for the Left and 2% for the Right); takeover of the world (12% and 4%); building more weapons (8% and 2%); forcing American values on the world; and more discrimination (4% and 2% each). For the radicals, the most frequent responses were laws to restrict freedom (18%); takeover of the world (12%); building more weapons, extending capitalism (8% each); indifference (6%); forcing American values on the world, maintaining ruling elites around the world, more discrimination, more ignorance, and more poverty (4% each). Goals America should not achieve which were most frequently mentioned by the Right included more social programs (10%); end to free enterprise (8%); black power, high inflation, decline in prestige (6% each); anarchy, disrespect for parents, too wealthy a populace, overly powerful military, economic control of foreign countries and takeover of the world (4% each). Surprisingly, conservatives mentioned big business, concern only with economic growth, protection of other countries, absolute success in foreign policy, and end of communism. Some conservatives referred to leniency in law enforcement, disrespect for law, disrespect for God, bowing to minorities, and sexual license, none of which was mentioned by the radicals.

In summary, the replies to the questions largely reflected the two groups' political and social convictions. However, there were some crossings of the lines not only in the common responses but also in other responses. The largest differences in the common responses occurred with reference to goals America should not achieve (48% and 14% for the Left and Right groups respectively, a difference of 34%) and with reference to personal values, positively evaluated (58% and 30% respectively, a difference of 28%). The most agreement on common items occurred for personal values, negatively evaluated (26% for each group), and for goals America should achieve (38% and 30% for the Left and Right groups respectively, a difference of 8%).

After the results were tabulated, ASL suggested that the radicals should be asked to predict how the conservatives would answer each question and the conservatives should be asked to predict how the radicals would answer. The student investigator was not able to do this because of the tensions that the questions produced. Was it because the subjects suspected that they had common specific goals or because they were afraid to reveal their personal likes and dislikes? Another possibility is that the student investigator was ego-involved about the results.

Do the radicals and conservatives have different conceptions of man? In an attempt to answer this question, Miss Sifrim conducted a second part of the experiment which was similar to previous studies on personality impressions (Luchins and Luchins, 1970). The subject was told that the purpose was to study the formation of impressions of others based on what was read about them. He was then given the questionnaire of the usual study and asked to answer it before he received a description of Jim, a college student; in life we usually have expectations about a person before we meet him, please write your impression of him before I give you the reading material. After this, the subject received a paragraph that described extrovert or introvert behavior by

Jim, followed by a detailed questionnaire concerning Jim (Hovland et al., 1957). Half of the subjects in each of the radical and conservative groups received a paragraph that described extrovert behavior (E paragraph) and the others received a paragraph that described introvert behavior (I paragraph). The descriptions of Jim written before the paragraphs were read were analyzed with regard to content and level of complexity. The questionnaires answered after the communication were analyzed for the frequency of responses suggestive of extrovert (E) or introvert (I) behavior.

The descriptions written before the communications, when the only information given was that Jim was a college student, showed some similarities as well as some striking differences between the two groups. In each group, 60% referred to Jim as a fraternity man. However, while the conservatives usually described Jim mostly in terms of physical characteristics and manner of dress, the radicals usually described him mainly in terms of his values. Members of the Right who referred to Jim as a fraternity man mentioned that he dressed in a clean, conservative manner, wore his hair short, had a good body build, tall stature, and was athletic, popular, and of medium intelligence. Members of the Left who described Jim as a fraternity man usually wrote about his desire for a high-paying job, his concern about his social image, his respect for authority, and his unquestioning mind. The remaining descriptions of the Right referred to Jim as a confused young man, as a liberal and as achievement-oriented, but the remaining descriptions in the Left referred to Jim as an unsure person, as a conformist and as friendly and open-minded. The results suggest that radicals and conservatives may have different conceptions of the average college student. This raises the question of whether the reactions of the students to each other on the campus may be related to these conceptions (cf. Secord and Backman, 1964).

As in the other experiments, the subjects who received the extrovert paragraph tended to give predominantly extrovert responses and those who received the introvert paragraph tended to give predominantly introvert responses. For the Left and Right subjects respectively, extrovert responses averaged 76% and 74% for those who received the E paragraph (compared to 79% for 44 high school and college subjects in previous experiments) and introvert responses averaged 62% and 64% for those who received the I paragraph (compared to 73% in the previous experiments). In short, prior to the communications the subjects tended to form their impressions more on their preconceptions of a college student which were colored by their political orientations whereas their subsequent impressions were based more on the information contained in the communications. The results support Wertheimer's contention that when evidence is provided, it tends to be taken into account in shaping one's impression.

[Margaret Brown's students in her course on adolescence at the SUNY-Oneonta are at present replicating several studies that have not been mentioned here.]

6. Margaret Brown, who has been replicating many of the studies that had been reported in Wertheimer's seminars, conducted an interesting modification of one of them. She told the students in her classes on adolescence that a value in a situation was the resultant of feelings, thoughts, and opinions which help a person to make judgments or choices. They were asked to think of the standards or bases which they use in making a choice between two or more

actions, how they evaluate what someone is doing and how others evaluate what they are doing. Then they were asked to write their answers to the following question. What values will you meet or use in classrooms, in the dorms, in church, with your friends or other places in the next week?

The number of values listed by the 61 students ranged from two to sixteen. Most students listed five to eight values, the mean number being six and the total number 383. The values were tabulated and then categorized by Mrs. Brown as follows: personal and social values, 74%; abstract principles, 13%; community and citizenship values, 8%; economic values, 5%. A more detailed categorization of personal and social values is given in the tabulation. Some of these items were also grouped together as follows: honesty (34), friendliness (15), understanding (21), appearance (20), monetary values (19), ambition (18), morals (17), and religion (15). It is noteworthy that no artistic, musical, or other aesthetic values were mentioned.

In order to get another picture of the results the values were reclassified in terms of the Vernon-Allport-Lindzey categories (economic, aesthetic, political, religious, social, and theoretical) but the categories were used in terms of the ordinary language meaning of the words. The reclassification raised such questions as this: should the 20 items which pertained to appearance and which previously had been classified as social now be placed in the social or aesthetic category? It was decided to place them in the latter. Similarly, there were questions about how to classify items that pertained to morality, physical abilities, use of alcohol and of drugs, and abortion; with some misgivings, each was placed in a category. The resulting classification of all the 383 responses showed that most of them were categorized as social, 68%, the theoretical category accounted for 9%, the political for 8%, and the economic, the aesthetic, and the religious for 5% each.

The subjects were asked to rank, in the order of the importance of the values in their lives, the four main categories into which the answers had originally been placed as well as the Vernon-Allport-Lindzey categories. Only 47 of the original 61 students were available for this inquiry. Although responses remained anonymous, they were asked to indicate their sex; one failed to do so. The tabulations showed the rankings for the 47 subjects (T) as well as for the 14 males (M) and 32 females (F). The category of personal and social values which had accounted for about three-fourths of the items was ranked first by about four-fifths of the subjects (79% of the males and 84% of the females); no one ranked it last. In contrast no one ranked the economic category first, about one-third of the subjects ranked it last. The ranking of the Vernon-Allport-Lindzey categories showed that social values were most important; about half of the students (57% of the males and 50% of the females) ranked it first and no one ranked it last. Political values were ranked last by 36% of the total subjects but by only 14% of the males and by 47% of the females. Sex differences were also found in some of the other rankings, for example, the religious category was ranked first by only one male, 7%, but by seven females, 22%.

Because problems had arisen in placing some responses into the Vernon-Allport-Lindzey categories, the subjects were asked how they would place moral values, appearances, physical abilities, use of drugs and alcohol, and abortion in these categories. There were varied classifications, with some subjects placing a response in more than one category, for example, 45% said that moral values belonged to the social category and to another category, usually the religious, while 26% and 21% placed them solely in the social and religious categories respectively. Appearances were placed solely in the social category by 68% and jointly in the social and another category, usually the aesthetic, by 17%, while 6% put them only in the aesthetic category. The use of drugs and alcohol was put solely in the social category by 72% and jointly in the social and another category by 17%, while no one put it solely in the religious category and only 4% placed it jointly in the religious and another category. In contrast, the response of abortion was put in the religious category solely by 43% and jointly by 19% who also placed it in the social category, while only 15% placed it solely in the latter category.

Because the students had been discussing the development of sex-role identity, they were also asked to place the terms masculine and feminine in the Vernon-Allport-Lindzey categories. There were some striking differences in results compared to the classification of the other words as well as sex differences. Whereas no one had failed to categorize moral values and there were only 2, 3, 4, and 6 failures to respond to appearances, physical abilities, use of drugs and alcohol, and abortion respectively, there were 17 and 18 failures to categorize masculine and feminine respectively. Only two of the 14 males did not classify the latter two words whereas 15 of the 32 females did not classify them; the difference was statistically significant (p = .05) using the Chi square with 1 df = 4.40. Moreover, the female students who responded never put either of these words in more than one category whereas each of six males classified feminine in several categories and each of three males did so for masculine (see tabulation). Previous words had been placed in more than one category by 12 of the 17 females and by six of the 12 males who classified masculine and feminine.

There was a possibility that the results were influenced by previous class discussions of the male and female roles in our society. (There had been discussions of Lynn's hypothesis that males are instrumental and versatile problem solvers and females passive and expressive lesson learners. Protests by women's liberation groups against traditional classifications of femininity had also been discussed.) To test this possibility, the tasks of putting masculine and feminine in the Vernon-Allport-Lindzey categories were given by Mrs. Brown to two other classes (taught by a male instructor) which had not had a discussion of the male and female roles. The 31 students did not put either word in more than one category; there were few failures to respond and they were not significantly higher for the 20 females than for the 11 males (two or three failures compared to one failure per word; see tabulation). These findings suggest that the results in the experimenter's classes may have been influenced by previous class activities, including the discussions about sex roles and the classification of the previous words. The only notable sex difference found in the male instructor's classes was that females put the words in the theoretical classification more frequently than males (five and seven times compared to one per word). In all classes the social category accounted for the largest number of classifications (60% for the experimenter's classes and 38% for the other instructor's classes) with the aesthetic category next and the theoretical category third. It is of interest that there were no classifications in the economic category in the other instructor's classes and few or no entries in the political and religious categories in any of the classes. [This study has been presented in order to highlight some of the problems in the study of values.]

TABLE 6. 2.

Ranking of the Vernon-Allport-Lindzey Categories (T=47, M=14, F=32)

Rank

	First			Second			Third			Fourth			Fifth			Sixth		
	T.	M.	F.	T.	M.	F.	T.	M.	F.	T.	M.	F.	T.	M.	F.	T.	M.	F.
Economic	3	1	2	13	4	9	6	0	6	5	1	4	15	6	9	5	2	3
Aesthetic	4	1	3	11	2	9	9	2	7	9	1	8	8	3	5	6	5	1
Political	1	0	1	3	1	2	9	5	4	9	5	4	10	1	9	17	2	15
Religious	8	1	7	8	4	4	10	3	7	6	2	4	4	1	3	11	3	8
Social	24	8	16	7	1	6	9	3	6	3	1	2	3	1	2	0	0	0
Theoretical	7	3	4	5	2	3	4	1	3	15	4	11	7	2	5	8	2	6

Ranking of the Values Categories Developed from the Listings (T=47, M=14, F=32)

Rank

	First			Second			Third			Fourth		
	T.	M.	F.	T.	M.	F.	T.	M.	F.	T.	M.	F.
Personal and social values	39	11	27	5	2	3	3	1	2	0	0	0
Abstract principles	5	3	2	13	4	9	10	3	7	19	4	14
Community and citizenship	3	0	3	21	5	15	12	5	7	11	4	8
Economic values	0	0	0	8	3	5	22	5	16	17	6	10

Placement of Masculine-Feminine Categories+

Instructor Ss: Word	Economic ½	1	Aesthetic ½	1	Political ½	1	Religious ½	1	Social ½	1	Theoretical ½	1	No Response
Mrs. B 47													
Masculine	1*	3	3	1	3	0	0	0	3*	17	3*	3	17
Feminine	1	1	2	5	0	0	0	1	2	16	1	3	18
Mr. W 11M													
Masculine	0	0	0	3	0	0	0	0	0	6	0	1	1
Feminine	0	0	0	5	0	0	0	0	0	4	0	1	1
Mr. W. 20F													
Masculine	0	0	0	4	0	1	0	0	0	6	0	7	2
Feminine	0	0	0	7	0	0	0	0	0	5	0	5	3

+ ½ refers to a word placed in two categories; five and three male students placed masculine and feminine respectively in two categories.

* one male student placed masculine in three categories: economic, social, and theoretical.

7. In a study of the concept of *Imitatio Dei* (Imitation of God), which is presented in another section of Wertheimer's seminars, a list of characteristics or traits were compiled which are regarded in the Judaic-Christian tradition as stemming from this concept. The list was read to students in ASL's WPA classes and they were asked: Which are religious ideas? Which are social ideas? Which are political ideas? In the same manner they were asked to indicate if a

characteristic belonged to a particular religion, for example, Buddhism, Catholicism, Paganism, etc. A modification of this study was recently conducted in a graduate class on guidance and counseling at SUNY-Albany with the assistance of David Houston. All the traits were presented on one sheet of paper and the class was asked to check which characteristic belonged to the various religions and which were religious, social, and political ideas.

The survey table presents the percentages of the 15 students who checked the various characteristics as being religious, social, or political concepts. For example, Love your neighbor was regarded by 100% as a religious concept, by 40% as a social concept, and by only 7% (one S) as a political concept. Equal justice was regarded by 40% as a religious concept, by 60% as a social concept, and by 73% as a political concept. Fight injustice was regarded by 33, 93 and 53%, respectively as religious, social, and political concepts. Just measurement was considered by 53% each to be a religious and social concept but by 60% to be a political concept. Similarly, 60% thought of correct balances in measuring as a political concept but only about one-third to one-half classified it as a religious or social concept. Were they thinking of government weights and measurements inspectors? On the average, 63, 56, and 25% of the subjects classified the characteristics as religious, social, and political concepts re-

TABLE 6.3
Percentages Who Classified Characteristics as
Religious, Social, or Political

	Religious Concepts	Social Concepts	Political Concepts
A. Loving kindness	67	53	7
B Mercy	87	47	7
C Follow His ways	80	20	20
D Pity	53	60	7
E Graciousness	33	73	7
F Be merciful as I am merciful, gracious as I am gracious	80	20	7
G Be holy because I am holy	87	20	7
H Compassion	87	47	7
I Just	60	47	27
J Fight injustice	33	93	53
K Reverence for parents	80	53	7
L Consideration for the needy	53	93	27
M Care of widow, orphan, stranger	47	93	27
N Consideration for beast of burden and other animals	53	60	20
O Honorable dealings	53	73	47
P No tale-bearing	73	87	27
Q Do not be malicious	73	53	20
R Love your neighbor	100	40	7
S Equal treatment of alien and stranger	53	67	40
T Equal justice to rich, poor, laymen, king, clergymen	40	60	73
U Just measurement	53	53	60
V Correct balances in measuring	33	53	60
W Do justly, love mercy, and walk humbly with your God	80	27	7
Mean	63	56	25

spectively. The table also shows the percentages of subjects who checked the characteristics as belonging to various religions. For example, Love your neighbor was regarded by only 13% as belonging to Buddhism and Mohammedanism, by 20% as belonging to Hindusim, Shintoism, and Paganism but by 47, 60, and 80% as belonging to Judaism, Protestantism, and Catholicism, respectively. On the average, 48, 39, and 36% classified the characteristics under Catholicism, Protestantism, and Judaism, respectively but only about 20% under each of the other headings.

TABLE o. 4
Percentages Who Listed Characteristics as
Belonging to Various Religions

	Buddhism	Mohammedanism	Catholicism	Protestantism	Judaism	Hinduism	Shintoism	Paganism
A*	20	13	53	46	40	20	20	20
B	13	20	73	53	47	20	20	13
C	47	33	67	47	33	27	27	13
D	13	13	40	47	33	20	20	20
E	13	13	27	33	27	20	20	20
F	13	13	60	40	33	20	20	7
G	27	27	53	33	40	20	20	7
H	13	13	60	53	47	27	20	20
I	20	20	40	33	40	20	20	27
J	13	20	40	33	33	20	20	33
K	33	20	67	47	47	27	27	20
L	13	20	40	33	33	20	20	27
M	27	20	53	40	33	27	27	27
N	13	20	40	33	27	20	20	27
O	27	13	33	27	33	27	27	20
P	13	20	40	33	33	20	20	27
Q	20	13	40	33	33	27	27	27
R	13	13	80	60	47	20	20	20
S	20	20	33	27	33	20	20	20
T	13	13	33	27	33	20	20	27
U	20	20	33	27	33	27	27	33
V	13	13	33	27	27	20	20	33
W	13	13	67	67	40	20	20	7
	19	18	48	39	36	22	22	21

* Table 6.3 lists the characteristics.

The results of the present study are in some respects different from the prewar study. Although then as now most traits were seen as religious and social, in the WPA classes more traits were classified as religious ideas and fewer as political ideas. For example, *Graciousness* and *Fight injustice* were then listed by most students as religious ideas whereas only one-third of the present Ss did so. On the other hand, relatively few students then classified as political such characteristics as *Fight injustice, Equal justice, Just measurement,* and *Correct balances,* which were now classified by over half of the Ss. The answers to the religious orientations also differed. Except for Paganism, most of the religions were seen to be more alike than at present in involving *Loving kindness, Mercy, Pity,* etc. Thus there were fewer differences between each of Buddhism, Mohammedanism, Hinduism, and the three major religions than at present. Why these differences in results? Are they due to the religious, educational, and social backgrounds of the Ss or to differences in the social atmospheres between the 1930s and the 1970s? Are they due to increases in secularization and politization? Are there at present more misconceptions about the various religions? It would be of interest to conduct the study with Sunday school students, theological students, and people who are members of or who have knowledge about various religions. (It would be advisable to ask the person to rate or rank the characteristics according to their importance or value to him and to his religion). It is also of interest to compare the results with the recent work by Milton Rokeach and his colleagues on the value orientations of different religious groups.

7
Other Discussions on Value and Evaluation

In the beginning of one of the sessions in the seminars in social psychology a visitor remarked that one starts out in life as a malleable biological organism with needs which are common to all organisms, that the society transforms one into a person who reflects his society's culture. Therefore one sees the world, society, and himself from the frame of reference of his culture because it has been inculcated in him by the social institutions in which he has been raised. Many psychologists accept the view that a person and his values are cultural products. Why does Wertheimer not accept these modern ideas about man and his values? Wertheimer replied that his objection to Cultural Relativism did not mean that he rejected the notion that the culture played an important role in the development of a person and his values. To say that values are learned is not enough; we need to know just how they are learned. He is objecting to the stylish thesis that value is something arbitrarily, blindly attached to what is evaluated. One learns what is right because one's teachers and parents say that it is right, one learns what is wrong because they say that it is wrong. Because the adults give him pleasure or pain the child learns to be submissive, to have blind confidence and trust in others, learns to conform to the culture's ways of evaluating things. Is this what really happens?

Some students said that it is a valid description. Children first act because of biological needs, and out of the social and personal consequences of their actions they learn what is required of them. Most of the time the consequences are rewards and punishments. In order to get and/or to avoid disapproval the child often acts with no understanding. Therefore, values are seen by the child in terms of the adults' rewards and punishments. Although he may understand or see a reason for a value, most of the time he reacts in terms of learned habits. The source of all value are one's repertoire of habits. Most people are content to act in terms of mechanical habits; there must be a tendency in man to act in terms of habit. Even if God Himself were to command them to study critically their values in order to understand and apply them understandingly, they would not do it. Somebody said that it was not a natural tendency to be tradition bound but that it is due to the social control exerted by the church and state.

An undergraduate visitor pointed out that there were religious groups that considered it the duty of all their members from the earliest days of their lives to study their culture's customs and laws, and not merely to carry them out in a blind manner. Would a study of these groups show that the people preferred to do things blindly by habit? Some students dismissed the statement, doubting that any religion would long endure if this were the practice of its people; when custom is confronted with reason custom is annihilated. A rational man is free of traditional customs because he follows the dictates of his own reason and not those of an authority.

The discussion changed when a student said that the ideal of truth or honesty was merely a culturally defined series of responses. What was called honesty or truthfulness in one society might be called dishonesty or untruthfulness in another society. Wertheimer presented a thought experiment. Suppose that there were two groups, A and B, that lived next to each other, and that it was a virtue in each group to tell the truth only to members of their group and that it was a virtue for members of Group A to tell only untruths to Group B, and vice versa. He drew on the blackboard [Truth A — Lies — Truth B] to represent the state of affairs. He then said suppose there were two other groups, C and D, that lived next to each other. In both C and D it was a virtue for its members to tell untruths to each other and it was a virtue for members of Group C to tell the truth to members of Group D, and vice versa.

He drew on the blackboard [Lies C — Truth — Lies D]. He then asked the class whether all four situations were possible. Student X said that according to Thesis I that had been discussed previously, all four possibilities could occur, Wertheimer asked him to describe the conditions that would make them possible. Student X said that it was merely a matter of conditioning, of organizing rewards and punishments to bring about and to maintain the desired behavior. Wertheimer said that he doubted that any society could exist in which the rule was that one must deceive his fellowmen. If there were such a law, people would not follow it. He conjectured that Groups A and B were more probable than Groups C and D. He added that there are businessmen who have the rule that the better you deceive your competitors the better off you are. But, it often happens among them that a businessman will keep his promise to his competitors. Why? A student said that there was a tendency to be sympathetic; little children of different religions and races play with each other in a very friendly way even though their parents and the community teach them racial and religious hatred. Student X remarked that Wertheimer was assuming that people had an innate proclivity to be social, but sociality was learned. He described cases of children who were reared in isolation and who did not have the traits that we associated with human beings. Another student remarked that there was an empathic relation between adults and infants that served as the basis of the development of later interpersonal relations. He went on to say that even the Nazis show sympathetic behavior when confronted with babies and children. The Nazis have put adults but not children into concentration camps; they shoot adults but do not hurt little children. The worst fate for a young girl was that she might be forced to be a prostitute, and for a boy, that he become a slave laborer. A visitor said that he saw no reason to believe that they would not slaughter babies, children, and women; it had been done throughout the ages. Hitler was leading a new crusade in the name of his race doctrine; he wants to purify the white race. When one killed bed bugs, one did not think of them as God's creatures; similarly, when one is purifying the human race, one does what is required even if one has to shoot defenseless women and children. Most students were shocked at these wild, irrational statements. The visitor was accused of being an interventionist, of spreading pro-war propaganda.

Someone said that if one wanted to understand someone's behavior, one must understand his motives. People spoke the truth or told lies because it paid. Whatever one said was a self-serving statement; the deception might be carried out consciously or unconsciously. It is well known that emotions and motives played a role in what one said or did. This was recognized in ancient and modern codes of law; for example, in one code of law a person whose occupation involved aggressive or cruel behavior such as the slaughtering of animals or the lending of money was not considered an acceptable witness. A person who had served as a judge in a case in which the defendant had been condemned to death was not allowed to try another case involving a capital crime. An argument over psychoanalysis was stopped when Wertheimer asked the class what they thought of this occurrence: Mr. A argued that the company should buy a certain machine from X and not from Y. After A had told them that X's machine not only cost less but was a better machine, someone said that Mr. A had an ulterior motive in proposing that they buy from X; he was a stockholder of the firm. Some students said that it was a reasonable argument. Wertheimer asked them whether Mr. A's motive was all that mattered; why were they overlooking the possibility that X's machine might actually have been better and cost less than Y's machine. He went on to say that it was such a popular doctrine to say that one should focus on people's motives to understand their behavior that it had led to the neglect of the question of what the action accomplished in the situation, that we focus on the question of unconscious motives served by a person's behavior and are blind to what is actually being done. He added, This is even considered to be a scientific doctrine in some circles. What consequences does it have for enforcing the law in terms of justice and for the role of evidence in making a decision in a particular situation?

A visitor said that the thesis made it impossible to arrive at a decision in terms of the evidence in the situation. He went on to say that when A claims that B's proposal is due to his motives, B may in turn question A's motives. This means that no one can be trusted to tell the truth in terms of the evidence. This has made *argumentum ad hominem* respectable. Perhaps an examination of motives is of help as a therapeutic device but it may be valueless in juridical and decision-making situations. Someone defended the thesis by enumerating various ways in which it helps determine who is a proper witness and a judge. He concluded that some of these procedures had existed prior to the advent of psychoanalysis. The visitor argued that the thesis would not pervert justice; it would lead to another way of dealing with law breakers. The courts at present were based on ways of doing things that had existed before there was psychoanalysis. One problem faced by a court was to find out what had been the accused's intentions. The motives of the defendant are important in determining the court's decision. The idea that there were unconscious motives did not destroy but rather furthered the rule of Justice. The use of psychoanalysis would lead to a scientific determination of the person's motives by people who had studied motivation. It would be an objective determination of motives in terms of scientific knowledge. Someone remarked that the same action might be interpreted differently by people who had different theories of motivation. Whose theory should the court accept as the valid one? One of ASL's students said that intent was an important factor in judging a person's crime and that such judgment could not be left to conjectures or inferences. In one ancient code of law, two reliable witnesses had had to tell the criminal not to commit the crime and to warn him that if he did, he would be given a certain kind of punishment. If the criminal then said that he did not care about the penalty and immediately proceeded to commit the crime before the witnesses, it was considered proof that he had committed the crime intentionally. No circumstantial evidence or unconscious motives were acceptable as proof of the person's intentions. Someone dismissed the student's statement as a myth because people would very rarely be punished under such circumstances and there would be no deterrent against crime.

A student said that in every society there were times and places where the same behavior was evaluated differently, for example, it was proper in our society to tell lies in certain situations and to certain people. If one consistently told the truth, he would get into trouble. In order to get along we learn to tell lies, it is both polite and sociable to lie. In wartime killing is a virtue and in peacetime it is a crime. During a war, extramarital sexual behavior is allowed and even adultery is condoned. Business ethics often contradict religious ethics; the values and morals of the recreational industries are not the same as those of religious institutions. Every value has its antivalue just as there are positive and negative particles in an atom. Someone thereupon commented that perhaps the contradictions illustrated people's ambivalence toward the values. He suggested that we had to distinguish between values as timeless, placeless ideals and values in terms of what happened in concrete situations. There seemed to be an uncanny ability in people to do what was required or fit in particular situations despite the abstract ideals which they professed. People learn that they have to be realists and not idealists; to be obsessed by an ideal gets one into trouble. In view of this, would it not be more honest to say that there were no ideals? Man lived by facts, not by Ideals or by Values. Someone observed that this reflected Thesis II that Wertheimer had once presented. Its emphasis on the fit of the action or on the means in the situation was a realistic view of value. One of the previous speakers said that a Nazi could say that what he was doing fitted the particular situation and that the means which the party used was required to get Germany out of its economic difficulties. A visitor protested that the Gestapo was used to enforce certain ideas and conduct, and that the Party decided what fitted and what did not fit in terms of its ideology and not the situation's requirements. If the Gestapo did not enforce the party's decision, people might have different ideas and do things differently in certain situations. In Thesis II one acted because he understood or saw a certain meaning in the value. It was a cognitive, not a conative or mechanical act. A student remarked that it made no difference to the victim if he was killed by a cognitive, conative, or mechanical conception of value.

Wertheimer proposed an experiment. Let a group of individuals develop a group structure of some kind during the course of meeting daily to do certain things (children in a class, patients in a mental hospital's ward). Then introduce problems for the group that have to be solved in order for the group to maintain its structure as well as to meet the requirements of the larger social structure of which it is a part. What could happen to the group when a member tried to impose his ideas or his methods of doing things? Would the group respond the same way to his ideas whether or not they fit the needs of their problem situation or the larger social structure? Someone said that such experiments were not necessary because we saw such things occurring in daily life. There were political parties that preached that their policy was the true solution to the problems of poverty and of war. Whoever did not believe in the policy was branded as an enemy of the people and was imprisoned or shot. The schools of these countries claimed that they were teaching the truth but they actually taught what was good for the maintenance of the party's power. Another student added that religious and even scientific groups were dominated by cliques that controlled the beliefs of its members. All this reflected the tendency in man to select and to edit his experience in terms of his groups' needs and not to face freely the situation's evidence. It had produced good things as well as bad things. If people stuck close to the facts, there would be no scientific theories, no generalizations, no social values, and no social progress. Man lived in a world of ideas as well as of facts; the ideas and not the facts moved him.

Wertheimer proposed another thought experiment. He asked what would happen in these situations. In Group A only the leader or the leading clique is aware of and feels responsible for meeting the goals of the group. In Group B every person is aware and feels responsible. Would the groups' structures and processes be different? Would the individuals in each of the groups behave and feel different? Someone remarked that in our society we valued more highly the type of leadership of Group B, but we often acted as if we really believed in the leadership of Group A. In the long run, all groups develop cliques which control everybody and decide that they know what is best for everybody.

Toward the end of the session, Wertheimer reminded the seminar of his first thought experiment and suggested that they think it over, to make predictions as to what would happen within and between the groups and to devise experiments to test their predictions. [A preliminary study was planned with the cooperation of teachers in the evening play center in the local elementary school. Four clubs of five children each were organized to play a certain game. The groups were given tasks that sometimes called for cooperation in communicating information to each other in the group and/or between groups. The experiment had to be stopped because the children revolted when the counselors began to strictly enforce the rules. However, the greatest revolt and disorganization occurred in the groups whose members had to tell lies to fellow group members. It seemed easier to enforce telling lies to members of another group than to one's own group members. Telling the truth within a group was more easily enforced, telling lies to outsiders was less easily enforced.]

Wertheimer also suggested that the class think over and plan experiments to test the following: (1) There is a tendency for two opposing fields under certain conditions to form one unified field. It has been argued that Fascism and Nazism are the last stand to resist this tendency. (2) The bigger the distance between the laws and justice, the greater were the oppressive forces. Oppression was a function of the deviation from the necessary field conditions. The more injustice there was in a country, the more courts it had and the larger was its police force.

8
Motives, Needs, and Values

Before class, some students met with Wertheimer and discussed the presentations of papers in another seminar. Reference had been made in it to a report on the effects of insulin on mental patients' sensitivity to sweetness. Immediately and for some hours after recovery from insulin shock, the patients would be given sugar-saturated solutions of tea or drink. When they were asked how it tasted, they reported that it tasted pleasant, but when their blood sugar returned to normal, they said that it tasted unpleasant. It was also reported that men who worked in the boiler rooms of ships ate salt herring which was unpalatable to ordinary people. Thus, the sensation of sweetness or saltiness was not a result of happenings on the end organs, the taste buds on the tongue, but of the sugar or salt level of one's blood. These observations were related to experiments with animals which demonstrated that when given free choice of a diet, they selected the kind of food needed for healthy body growth. Thus what was valued by an animal or by a man might be a function of the systemic requirements of the body; the needs of the organism were sources of value. Everybody agreed that these were mechanisms that functioned to maintain a healthy body. When conditions within the organism produced a deficiency within it or conditions outside produced a dangerous situation for it, the organism acted to preserve itself.

Someone proposed that the personality also had needs and that there were mechanisms in its structure to maintain a healthy personality. These mechanisms were the sources of social values. He added that Kurt Goldstein and Alfred Adler had been theorizing along these lines and he went on to report on Maslow's ideas about motivation which had been discussed with him informally. Because the organism was an integrated and organized whole, the whole organism, and not a part of it, was motivated. The person, not his stomach, wanted food; the person, not his stomach, was satisfied after a good meal. Moreover, when one was hungry his perception, thinking, and memory were affected because his needs made him see and evaluate things differently. Different things or actions fitted the requirements of the total organism when it had this or that need. In describing the needs of men, Maslow rejected the idea that the physiological needs were the primary needs and that such needs as having to read a book or going to the movies were secondary; perhaps the reverse was true. He proposed that it might be better to take the desire for money instead of hunger as the basic drive. Maslow has also said that the pattern of all needs was not analogous to the physiological drives, nor were they localized in some somatic drive; we would never understand love by focusing on physiological drives. The student proceeded to read from his notes of Maslow's lectures. In daily life we find that drives are means for certain ends and not ends in themselves. To understand motivation we have to understand what the person is trying to do. The behavior of a person is symptomatic of the functioning of the needs and goals of the whole organism. Therefore we need to study the dynamics of these symptoms. In studying behavior we soon find that there are goals that are ends in themselves and that could not be seen directly. Therefore, we have to look for them in the unconscious. In different cultures these unconscious goals are expressed differently; the deep needs of men are satisfied by different means.

In response to Wertheimer's questioning the student said that Maslow's theory did not focus on specific desires as the basic motive. It was unusual that a certain behavior be motivated by only one desire; for example, sexual desire might assume a desire for masculinity, closeness, dominance, love, and safety. Thus one motive could serve as a channel for other desires. The usual theories of motivation implied equipotentiality of drives when they were listed. Maslow, however, was arranging the drives in a hierarchy. Human beings were rarely satisfied; when one want was satisfied others arose. Maslow had said that when one wanted something of a cultural nature, it was indicative of the more basic wants in the hierarchy being satisfied. An unusual aspect of Maslow's theorizing is that he was seeking the fundamental goals and needs of man qua man instead of building a theory on the usual organismic drives that are common to all organisms. The student concluded that if Maslow was successful in developing his theory it might solve the problem of what was value because it would spell out the ultimate goals of men. Maslow's theory would lead to a conception of value that was more like Thesis II than Thesis I because it would deal with requirements of the human personality as a system. Values might be considered to be the psychological analogue of Cannon's *wisdom of the body* or of Claude Bernard's *homeostasis*.

Wertheimer made the following remarks about Maslow's theory of motivation. Several problems were neglected; the theory was based on studies of abnormal and maladjusted college students. One has to separate the common sense use of the word unconscious from the psychoanalytic idea of the unconscious; there is a difference between a naive man's saying that he does not know the motives, reasons, or causes of someone's behavior and a psychoanalyst's saying that it is due to unconscious factors. The question of whether it is unconscious or conscious actually has nothing to do with the idea of the place and function of the item of behavior in the structure of the personality or of the social field. For example, in the Hartshorne and May study a child's response might mean a different thing depending on the processes that bring it about, also a response has a different meaning if it occurs in a different situational context. To seek a motive behind an act is a different thing from trying to understand the structure of the act in terms of its situational context; such meaning may not be related to the unconscious. After a pause he asked, What about the strong desire for freedom, for justice, and the desire not to do things blindly? Maslow's theory does not say anything about this because of the methodology and point of view of the investigation It is assumed that all behavior is egocentric. Moreover, Maslow did not observe the actual behavior of people; he interviewed them. Perhaps some results on which the theory is based are a consequence of the method of inter viewing. After a pause for reactions to what he had said, Wertheimer added, Of course a person's view of the social field is colored by his point of view and personality factors. People may be blind to various things and happenings in the social and physical world. What is in the world for people depends on their possibility of acting and living in relation to it; people have different kinds of relationships to the world. We need to know the various types of relationships that exist between people and their social (and physical) fields. On one extreme, there are cases in which a person's behavior is shaped and determined by the field. On the other extreme, people command and create their fields. The same individual may at certain times or in certain places behave in terms of one or the other of these extremes. We need to study the factors that bring about these extreme types of relationships instead of assuming that all behavior is egocentric. A person is a part, a sub-whole, of a field. Certain relationships between the person and his environment bring about a stress in the person, in the sub-part, and/or in the whole of which he is a part. What are the factors that make a person the center of the world so that he sees the whole field in terms of his ego and acts as if only he existed? What makes him blind to the requirements of the system of which he is a part and what are the effects of his behavior on the system? What are the factors that destroy the uniqueness and individuality of a person? After this Wertheimer asked, What is lacking most in Maslow's list of human needs? Maslow lists what is required by the person from the field, but how about the requirements of the field? With Maslow there is only a one-way traffic, from the person to the field. Is this a proper picture of the person and his field (cf. Maslow, 1970)?

The last remark led to a discussion in which Wertheimer proposed that we study situations in which a person behaves as if he were the center of the world, as a closed or isolated system, and situations in which the person's behavior is determined by the social or physical world. We should find out what happens to the person and the social field when the requirements of the person are counter to that of the social field and vice versa. And we should see what happens when the requirements of the person and the social field are in the same direction. [Wertheimer had hoped that some of the work on perception would clarify these issues; Witkin (1954) and Sherif (1957) are steps in this direction. The monograph on Wertheimer's perception seminar as well as other sessions in this series indicate specific problems that still need to be studied.]

Comments

To some students Wertheimer's criticism seemed to overlook the fact that Maslow's work was being done in the context of his search for a proper theory of human nature on which to base a valid theory of value. The theory was in line with the humanistic tradition that goes back at least to the Renaissance and probably beyond. To the Humanist, value stems from man's essential nature and not from an external authority. The Enlightenment preached that modern man had reached intellectual maturity and could now use his own reason to decide what is moral. Therefore, he no longer needed an authority to impose a code of ethics on him. He had outgrown this. It was assumed that there was reason in nature and because man was a part of nature his reason could guide him to the laws of nature from which he could realize the rules of his own behavior. Man's reason is now the sole authority for human conduct and not a God or a sovereign. The demand quality of things, the feeling of oughtness, the sense of duty, requiredness, or necessity stems from man's own rationality and not from physical nature or a heteronomous authority such as God. Man's fate is in his own hands; progress is possible by the use of reason and man can transform the earth into paradise by making use of his reason. The Enlightenment shattered man's belief in God as an authority and shattered his respect for traditional ways of doing things. Modern man saw himself as the apex of an evergrowing tree that was on the verge of reaching the perfection which was once relegated to his immortal soul. Twentieth-century man no longer has such complete faith in reason and progress; some even doubt that man and nature are regulated by reason. Man's scientific orientation, however, does not allow him to return to the supernatural authorities or to extrapersonal factors for guidance. Men are in desperate need of a valid theory of value and of man. Instead of despairing because we have not reached an understanding of human nature, Maslow has been trying to develop one that will do justice to the uniqueness of man and his experience of value.

Although Wertheimer seemed to endorse aspects of the Humanistic doctrine, he objected to the assumption that value stems only from man's nature. Because Wertheimer was vehemently opposed to the idea that people act only because of their dear egos, he was concerned with the possibility that Maslow's theory could be interpreted to mean that man is egocentric by nature, a view not held by Maslow.

Wertheimer's use of the words *field, system* and *sub-part* seemed vague to many students. The idea of motivation in terms of a person or organism seemed to be rooted in biological science whereas Wertheimer's concepts merely had vague resemblance to field theory of physics. But modern systems engineering students would not find his ideas to be so strange. It makes sense to them to talk about the sub-parts of a system and the effects of the functioning of a sub-part on the total system. A theory of value which is based primarily on the study of the sub-part, the individual, is not only a one-sided view of things but may optimize a sub-part of the system, the individual man, and thus destroy the system. The needs of man, therefore, could not serve as the basis of a theory of value, according to Wertheimer's thesis.

Wertheimer implied that it was possible for people to understand the systemic requirements of the social or physical systems of which they were parts. But when one looks at the social scene, one may wonder at the validity of this assumption. In view of what he had said in his course on logic, one may conclude that he would not claim that people always understand their relationship to the field or that such understanding would always be absolutely or entirely correct. He stressed that one should seek enlightenment rather than to assume that one was enlightened. Wertheimer agreed that people act blindly, stupidly, willfully and selfishly. But, he asked, What can be done to open people's eyes and make them face the structural requirements of the situation and not to be blinded by their passions, habits, and personal goals?

Wertheimer's stress on the social field seemed to some students to challenge the liberal's view that morality is possible without an authority. It fitted in with the ideas of Hobbes, who had pointed out that man's pursuit of self-interest leads to an intolerable state of affairs, that for the sake of self preservation men realize that they need peace and therefore make a contract with the sovereign to enforce peace. Wertheimer's ideas also seemed to fit Durkheim's thesis that human desire is an abysmal chasm that can never be filled and that only in the collective conscience does man find a feeling of self-fulfillment. Wertheimer's ideas also reflected the growing rejection of the philosophy of individualism and the growing focus on man as a social being with the stress on society and not the person, with its insistence that values are just group norms of conduct. Yet Wertheimer rejected the idea that insofar as one is a good member of a group one does what his group requires him to do. Is it because it implied that value needs an external authority, that the group's sanctions, not God's, is the force behind morality?

A few students saw in Wertheimer's thesis the deification of the group, the endorsement of the idea that the individual has to obey because he realizes the constraints of the system. The system, an external authority, decides what value and moral behavior are. This thesis runs counter to the principle of increasing the number and the range of choices rather than decreasing them. Wertheimer did not believe that it is generally true that the system of which one is a part constituted a constraint on the person. Some systems and even some kinds of authorities, maximize instead of minimize human freedom. In discussing this thesis with Wertheimer, a student once gave the concept of God as an example of an authority that limits man. Wertheimer asked the student why he did not give Hitler or Mussolini instead. He went on to say that in human history the concept of God has often been used by people to protect themselves against the state and the group to which they belonged. He added that instead of getting involved with ideological issues, we should find out what authorities and groups at present offer people opportunities and are concerned with people's freedom to think and act understandably and which do not. When the student persisted in objecting to God, Wertheimer said that certain concepts of God have sometimes given certain people the freedom to oppose acts of injustice even when it seemed or was said that God had proposed them. Someone said that instead of arguing it would be better to make a content analysis of myths of different people to see how their gods act. This led another student to say that since the Deity in the Bible is often referred to as cruel, vengeful, deceitful and merciless, visiting the iniquities of the fathers upon the children and dealing arbitrarily in giving punishment, it might be a good idea to catalog His behavior in it as well as in the legal traditions that grew up based on it. [What would a content analysis of the *Pentateuch* and the *New Testaments* reveal?]

The last discussion led to a preliminary study in ASL's class in which students were asked to record the every day usage of the word authority, to record the sentence and to describe the context in which it was used. A month's record by the students revealed examples that fitted Wertheimer's thesis that certain authorities narrow, restrain, and blind while others expand and develop one's mental horizons, that the same authority at different times or places could lead to either kind of effect.

The same adult education class kept a record of their value conflicts and choices. The analysis of the protocols indicated that there were situations in which they acted in terms of inner desires and others in which they acted in terms of situational requirements, but either type was capable of being arbitrary or of fitting the situation. Discussion of these results raised several problems for research. One may assume that a theory of value must be based on a theory of human nature and that all value stems from man's essential nature. One may, however, assume that a theory of value must rest on an authority outside of man. The former approach to value leads us to the problem of the nature of man and the latter approach leads us to the problem of the nature of authority, but do either of these conjectures reflect what happens in concrete situations? Should a conjecture be accepted because it fits in with a broader conception even though it neglects what is vital in many concrete situations? Are we to dismiss the particular case as mere opinion and seek for the truly universal truths? Is one of these approaches more scientific and fruitful than the other? Must we assume that only one approach leads to the truth? Wertheimer once remarked that it is important to try to understand why a conjecture was made and how it was used in concrete situations and not to dismiss it because it did not fit in with one's assumptions. He seemed to call for a need to separate the problem of what are the universally valid principles from whether or not a judgment is correct in particular judgment situations. He dismissed as beside the point questions as to whether this means that one is accepting the philosophy of pragmatism or is a realist or a nominalist. The question is whether the person is acting blindly rather than in terms of the given evidence.

9
Justice

In the beginning of the session a visitor said that in recent years there has been increasing criticism of the courts: the court's sentences did not stop crime; the crime rate and delinquency were increasing. Some psychiatrists and sociologists claim that a criminal is a sick person, he needs treatment not punishment and that we have to remove the social and developmental conditions that produced criminals. Why were lawyers against these new ideas? When someone said that the courts existed to mete out justice and not necessarily to punish, the visitor asked whether it was a sacrifice to the ideal of justice to put a man in jail for stealing. Of what value was the sentence? It deprived the family of a breadwinner and gave the criminal a postgraduate course in crime, but did not restore the stolen goods to the proper owner. Moreover, the sentence depended on the state in which the crime has been committed and the cleverness of the criminal's lawyer. This led to an exchange between the visitor and a student who argued that the courts were oriented toward the ideal of justice. The visitor insisted that courts merely administered the laws laid down by a legislature or a monarch. Wertheimer stopped the argument by saying that one view of the law equated it with what was legal, with the rules of the court. According to this view, the law was not an attempt to approximate justice; the reverse was true, justice was what the law was. Someone interrupted to say that this seems to be what happens in courts; the courts do not make the laws, they carry them out. When an illegal group gets political power it changes the law and legitimizes itself; for example, the Nazis have changed the laws and have appointed or retained only those judges who carry out the laws that they have promulgated. Everything in Germany is being done according to law; people who do not like the Nazis' laws say that they are unjust but they are just because they are lawful.

Wertheimer remarked that justice is not the same thing as legality. One can say that a law is a law and not look to see whether it fits the situation nor bother to examine its quality of justice or injustice. A law could be 100 percent legal and yet be unjust. Someone interrupted saying that Wertheimer is using a vague word, justice, whereas those who equate legality with justice are dealing with objective facts. The word justice is merely an emotion-laden word. Wertheimer remarked that this is the Positivist's point of view; after a pause he said that legality could be viewed in terms of evaluation (Thesis I) or in terms of fit (Thesis II). There are instances in which judges have spoken out in court that their decisions, though forced upon them by the laws, were miscarriages of justice. What does a judge mean when he says that a miscar-

riage of justice has occurred? Does he mean that the law has not been carried
out?

ASL remarked that Justice is an ancient idea and is even found among
primitive people. It is sometimes related to the survival of the soul and its
destiny. The gods are often the guardians of human justice and people appeal to them for justice on earth as well as in the hereafter. Justice is also
inherent in the life of the group, in the sense that it is related to the discipli-
nary actions necessary for a group's functioning. It preserves the proper interpersonal relations of the group members as well as their relations to their
God. Someone interjected that a popular notion among the Greeks was that
the gods demanded that men observe justice in their relation to each other
but that the gods were not required to observe justice in their conduct toward
men. The gods were capricious; they had free will. In some Scholastic
theological disputes, God was also considered to have such free will. Some
modern theorists say that the law is the power of the state and that the state
is free to make any law it wants. Others say that the ruling class is also free
from the rule of justice; it has the power to do what it wants. He concluded
that the state, like the gods, does not have to observe justice in its relation to
ordinary people because the state has power—the machine gun knows no justice. Justice is a glittering generality used by the machine gun holders to make
them appear respectable.

The last sentence led to a discussion in which the following points were
made. The concept of justice is not merely a word used by the powerful to
fool the weak or vice versa. It is a concept which has played a great role in
human history and is also a common-sense notion. Some of our culture's ideas
of justice can be traced to Greek philosophy, to the *Pentateuch,* to Roman law
and to Christianity. In Plato's *Republic* and the *Pentateuch* justice is the ideal
element in all laws. Justice is the supreme or most general virtue from which
everything flows. In the former, the harmony of the state and in the latter,
the harmony of the universe, rests on justice. To Plato, justice is the regulator
of all other virtues; it maintains an equilibrium that results in their harmonious functioning. In the *Republic,* Plato demonstrated the nature of justice by
describing what produces a harmonious state. It exists when every member of
a society does well that task which the society assigns him. Society to Plato is
like a huge animal. In order for the animal to live, its parts must function
properly in their naturally assigned places and must perform properly those
roles necessary for the maintenance of the animal. When parts do not function properly or do not play the role assigned to them, there is chaos, disharmony. Justice is the *sine qua non* for the harmonious functioning of the
state. Similarly, if each part of a person's psyche does its job, there results a
harmonious functioning of the individual; he then does what is required of
him as he actualizes himself. Plato's *Republic* describes an educational system
that is aimed at creating order in the public lives of men by creating discipline
in their private lives, by establishing the supremacy of reason in the state and
in the individual. Generally speaking, injustice occurs when a part of an organism does something that disrupts the harmony of the whole of which it is
a part. Justice calls for self-discipline in the interest of the whole of which one
is a part. In the long run, this self-discipline, which is in the interest of the
whole, promotes the interests of the part; what is good for the whole organism, be it the individual or the state, reflects back on the welfare of its

parts. Because Plato's aim was to develop a logically consistent and complete theory, he was led to postulate an ideal world of Forms (Idios) which was the real world, a world in which things were genuine and not imitations of something else. What exists in the mundane world is an imitation of this Ideal, real world. Thus Justice became a transcendental object to which man is related through his soul, because man's soul comes from the real world, the realm of Ideals. Man must seek the knowledge of the Ideal even though it is not possible to realize it fully in the mundane world. Plato assumed that knowledge leads to virtue. Therefore, proper education, formal discipline, will lead to liberation of the soul, to the actualization of harmony, justice, in the individual and in the state.

The visitor said that what has been said fitted in with what Hitler was doing, that Plato's philosophy could be used to rationalize the maintainance, reformation, or nullification of existing laws. Plato's thesis does not prevent one from saying, What I call just, is just; what the other fellow calls just, is unjust.

Wertheimer asked the students whether it is just for a court to render a verdict in a case without a search to determine what happened, to condemn a person without a trial and to conduct a trial in which only the state or the defendant is allowed to speak. He then added, Why is it that a court may use laws that are just and the verdict could be just but people would still feel that something is wrong, unjust? After a pause for comments he remarked that, even in ancient times, it was considered in certain countries unjust if the defendant had not been able to find out or to understand the meaning of the law; if he was not told the charges against him; if torture was used to obtain evidence; if evildoers served as witnesses; if members of the court were either directly or indirectly related to one of the litigants or if they could even in some remote and indirect way benefit from the verdict. Wertheimer added that in some codes very detailed procedures were prescribed to ascertain whether the testimony was valid and whether the witnesses and the judges were impartial. Violations of these procedures were considered to be acts of injustice. The visitor pointed out that there are examples in social anthropology that speak against what Wertheimer said. Among certain Eskimo tribes, a hunter who concealed the fact from the group that he had made a kill would be killed if it was discovered that he had hidden food from the group; there would be no trial. Wertheimer replied that the situation of these people has to be examined to understand the gravity of the hunter's crime. This is not usually done; it is done during periods of starvation. Because they do it under certain conditions does not mean that they always condemn a man without a trial, without confronting him with the charges. Wertheimer proceeded to give examples from European legal codes. He said that offhand it seems arbitrary that in certain legal codes theft from an isolated farm is treated more severely than the same theft in a populous area. However, when one considers the greater danger and susceptibility to theft on the farm, one can see the reason for the law. Moreover, what may appear at present as an unjust law may be due to the fact that the situation has changed and we no longer know the reason why the law was enacted. Wertheimer did not deny the fact that laws remain on the books long after the need for them has disappeared and are used at certain times and in certain places in an unjust manner. He concluded, To carry out the laws with justice is not the same thing as blindly enforcing the rules of the legislature or monarch.

One of ASL's students compared Plato's view with the Hebrew conception of justice. In the Hebrew conception justice is the supreme virtue, the foundation of the universe; God cannot violate it without undoing what He has created; to act justly is an attribute of God. It is, however, not His only attribute; loving kindness and even sensitivity to public opinion temper His execution of justice. Because this conception of justice is not defined in terms of certain rigid rules, some people have the impression from superficial reading of the rules and commandments in the *Pentateuch* that it involves mechanical application and blind obedience to fixed laws. Examples can be cited from the *Pentateuch* where the opposite is true, where God reasons with man and bases His commandments in contractual terms. One traditional view holds that the commands and laws are examples and exhortations that guide one in particular concrete and practical matters to what is required of man, justice. The stress is not on seeking a grand soul-filling revelation but on seeking understanding which is commensurate with one's knowledge and experience in the process of fulfilling and studying His laws and commandments. Therefore, there must be constant study of past decisions and judgments which were made in the name of the *Pentateuch*. Thus justice is not something in a transcendental realm; it is not an abstract ideal divorced from mundane matters as in Plato's philosophy. It is a way of life on this earth in which the group and its members try to fulfill their obligations to Him. In return He fulfills His part of the contract. The chain of command is not only from above down but also upward from man to God. Some see in the Hebraic concept of law a limit on God's free will but others say that the idea of arbitrary, unlawful free will is a remnant of the idea of the capricious Greek gods. God is reasonable and acts according to the law which He created before He created the world. Since man's knowledge is limited to the information available to him there must be a constant reexamination and reinterpretation of the laws and rules of procedure for each case in order to actualize His law. There is no final answer as to what is His will. Different opinions and judgments have been rendered by courts, tribunals, and scholars about the proper way to fulfill the contract with Him. Thus varied and even contradictory opinions are not dismissed as in Plato's philosophy. [The Principles of Contradiction and the Excluded Middle of Greek logic are not used in Hebraic logic.]

A visitor said that this viewpoint had led to a legalistic approach to justice which was based on authority and was concerned with the letter and not the spirit of the law. The student asked the visitor for specific examples of this in the actual interpretation and application of Judaic laws. The visitor answered that what he had said was the reasoned opinion of authorities. The student asked him, Who were the authorities; what evidence did they give to back up their claims? When the visitor did not answer, the student went on to suggest that we investigate the written records of past and current activities of Rabbinical Courts in communities that have used these laws. In order to guard against ethnocentric bias it was recommended that the researchers use the same open-minded and empathic approach utilized by anthropologists among primitive people. Just as some anthropologists are worried about the contamination of primitive cultures and are trying to study them before they disappear, we ought to study the existing religious communities that are regulated by the Biblical-Talmudic laws before Hitler destroys them.

Someone said that the popular or commonly held idea of Hebrew law has been promoted by certain Christian dogmas and the dogma of social evolution. To both, the Hebrew codes are seen to be on a lower level than Christian law. This sparked some comments about the concept of justice in Christianity. In Christianity, justice was subordinated to charity and love. Justice no longer was the supreme regulator of all virtues as in Plato; nor was it the foundation of creation as in the Hebraic idea. The focus of concern was with the last or final things and not the mundane matters of man as the theologians discussed problems related to salvation and the nature of divinity. Justice became an eschatological idea. Some theologians said that one does not earn or demand justice from Him; it was a gift based on grace. Thus justice was separated from morality. According to St. Augustine, justice was not realizable on earth but only in the *City of God*. Justice was the harmony of the mystical body composed of heaven and earth. The functioning of the state was not based on justice but on the social norms and methods of brigands. The state was similar to an association of brigands while the church was the stronghold of Justice on earth; it reflected the *City of God*. Justice had to do with matters of the ideal, supernatural realm and not with the everyday affairs of politics, with the laws and customs of human institutions (cf. Kahler, 1968). This doctrine has played an important role in the advancement of mankind. From the evolutionary point of view, it was considered the highest stage of human thinking about value. It led to the rejection of the Naive Realism of primitive people who considered laws to be real, to be natural (cf. Strauss, 1953). It reflected the abstract attitude of modern scientific man who realizes that laws are created by man. It led to a separation of morality from justice and thus reflected the nominalistic and relativistic views of human laws. The doctrine made possible the modern secular state in which man's will and not God's will determined the law (cf. Hirsch, 1962). God is not concerned with the temporal matters of man but with eternal matters. He is concerned with the salvation of men's souls and not the social rehabilitation of men on earth; that is man's business. This view helped psychology and sociology come into existence as disciplines separate from theology. When someone said that the doctrine made religion lose its relevance, another student warned that we must look at St. Augustine's doctrine in terms of present-day ideas. The message of Christianity, its central theme, was salvation; and it had come when people thirsted for it.

A sociologist said that this doctrine constituted an advance from the older ideas of justice because the law was located in society and not in the heavens and the vague ideas of values were relegated to the heavens. It gave those who were oriented to the *City of God* an escape from the misery of this earth but it also allowed others to say that the law was merely a man-made means of social control and of preserving the social order. The sociologists have not found it necessary to agree with St. Augustine that there is a *City of God*, nor do they despair that the state is a kind of brigandage; there is honor among thieves, even bands of brigands have rules or laws of conduct for their members. Someone said that this doctrine was a dangerous one; it implied that the Church could shut its eyes to what Hitler was doing. He went on to argue that the Church must reject such doctrines in order to become socially relevant. Another student said that the doctrine was not at all shocking to the people of St. Augustine's time because the world had then been considered to be a vestibule to heaven in which people waited for "the end of days." Further-more, it was a realistic picture of the state and of many social institutions in those days. There was no justice on earth and many people could not accept the doctrine that God had created the world and had gone off leaving man and other creatures to stew in their own juices, as Epicurus said of the Greek gods. St. Augustine had at least given people hope that they were among the elect and would be saved through His grace.

A professor said that the Augustinian doctrine was only one stream that fed Scholastic philosophy; Aristotle's, the Stoics', and the Roman legalist's doctrines had been used by the Church and were all finally incorporated by St. Thomas into a different orientation toward justice. He took from Aristotle the idea that justice implied a certain degree of equality, that commutative justice is expressed arithmetically and distributive justice is expressed geometrically, that the ideal is to achieve a just mean or equilibrium, and that justice is immanent in man's conduct and is not transcendental. St. Thomas's ideas also reflected the Stoics' idea that Justice was the general law of the universe to which all members of the human race must submit. This idea of the Stoics had been assimilated by the Roman legalists into their conception of justice as the fulfillment and realization of existing Roman law, the letter of the law. St. Thomas, however, distinguished between human justice which stems from natural law and divine justice which stems from God. Some Scholastics of the Thomistic tradition said that natural law would exist even if God did not exist. Besides St. Thomas, there were Scholastic philosophers as well as religious leaders who stressed the older Hebraic ideas of justice and thus reunited value with the world of everyday life. But with the advent of modern science in the seventeenth century the idea of justice was completely separated from such theological ideas. Justice was to be based on what is apprehended by man in nature and not on doctrines that related it to the supernatural and to revelation. Machiavelli and Hobbes tried to develop a rational account of what led to social harmony. According to Hobbes, man's awareness of the miserable existence that would follow from the pursuit of his own interests, coupled with his desire for self preservation, led to a search for peace which resulted in men contracting a sovereign to maintain order. Thus, the state was the force behind the order; without it, there would be chaos, death, and destruction. However, others like Locke and Rousseau started out with the premise that man's goodness, not his beastliness, led to the covenant that resulted in the state. To Hobbes, justice was the command of the state but to Locke and Rousseau it was the synthesis of liberty and equality. Later on, justice was regarded by some advocates of Romanticism to be a subjective feeling and not an objective order. Some of them declared that if the laws of public authorities ran counter to a person's feelings of justice, he was not obliged to obey them. Since all people were supposed to have an identical consciousness of justice, an egalitarian state was the best guarantor of law and justice.

The visitor pointed out that Hitler claims that all justice-loving people would agree with him. Perhaps the Utilitarians, the Socialists, and the Communists were correct when they said that justice was but a smoke screen to mask the exploitation of the people by the state. Someone said that he had in the past thought that Mill had been correct when he had said that what was just was what was useful. But what bothered him now was that an act that brought goods, services, and happiness to one person sometimes resulted depriving another person of them. And so, he was now wondering whether he had returned to the problem of Plato's *Republic*, that of determining what was the Good. Is it that which gave one profit, got results or was it that which produced a harmony among the parts of the society?

Wertheimer pointed out that through the ages there had been wise men and philosophers who had believed that there was a common-sense notion of justice, that people sensed what was just and unjust in concrete situations. He proposed, therefore, that the seminar members find out how the words just and unjust were used when a person said, "This is unjust"; "This is not fair"; "This is just"; "This is fair." If we took the criteria used by philosophers and theologians, one by one, would we find that they explained all cases of the use of the words? He conjectured that such a study might yield some examples of justice that indicated that justice was related to the operation of a law or rule in terms of meeting the requirement of the situation; that injustice meant that the operation was blind to the structure of the situation.

Someone remarked that Wertheimer was assuming that men could differentiate between what was just and unjust; but he was overlooking the fact that it was possible to get people to call something which they would ordinarily call unjust, just, and vice versa. Wertheimer said that this statement implied that we could get 100 percent agreement if we changed the value around. He challenged the student to devise an experiment to see whether this was possible. He went on to say that the student's thesis implied that by manipulating the situation it was possible to change the evaluation. Just what kind of situation would produce such a radical change? What effect would the change have on the situation and on related situations as well as on the people in them? The student answered that Wertheimer was also assuming that when you gave a person evidence he would invariably look at it, but the person might be more interested in his own status than in that of the object of judgment. Wertheimer agreed that this might be the case and suggested that an experiment be conducted to show the factors that brought about such behavior. Just as he was about to dismiss the class, the following examples were presented to the class to think over. Suppose someone wished to hang a picture on the wall and needed to drive a nail in it; could one just as easily teach him to use the head of a live chicken as a hammer? Suppose a certain medicine had proved itself to be good for someone; could you teach him to call it bad? Suppose that somebody made something that a person needed and said that it was well done; could one teach him to say that it was badly made? What do the following cases have in common? I mix up the words of a book and say that the resulting sentences are good literature. I take two melodies, a_1, a_2, a_3, a_4 and b_1, b_2, b_3, b_4 and make a third melody out of them by randomizing the letters of the two sets of letters that stand for their notes. Is something being ignored? What?

Students' Reactions to the Seminar

What follow are ASL's students' reactions to the seminar and Wertheimer's comment on some of their reactions. One student said that in the classical biblical view one gave charity because it was dictated by justice. Righteousness and charity were the same word in Hebrew but in the Christian tradition charity as well as love was a value in its own right. These human values were autonomous expressions of the human spirit as it sought communication with Him. Charity therefore did not necessarily mean alms-giving or supporting the widow, orphan, and stranger. Nor did love mean physical union with others but the expression of a spiritual tie with one's fellowmen, *Agape*. Someone said that his ancestors had been burnt in autos-da-fé in the name of love for Him. Armies in Christendom had fought each other as an expression of love for Him. He wondered therefore whether this abuse was a consequence of separating love and charity from justice.

A student said that in contrast to the beliefs of Plato and the Hebrews, Erich Fromm claimed that love was the supreme value. It made life meaningful. Modern man feels that he is alone in a cold, indifferent world because his reason no longer allows him to seek refuge in the shelter of the church. He knows that he is a part of nature, yet he feels separated from it and powerless before its forces. Man foresees that his ultimate end is death. His reason has freed him but he finds freedom intolerable. Therefore, he escapes to authoritarian social movements. As he unites himself with them, he is able to gain a new sense of meaning and power. "One subordinates his little light to be part of the brilliant sun of an illustrious figure." The student continued saying that Fromm had proposed a concept of love that was close to the Christian idea of *Agape*. Love united one with someone else, yet in the union each person preserved his individuality and integrity. Since the union in love led to creation, one felt that he was a creator. Another student said that Fromm's idea was not the same as that of Christian love. Individual man, not a supernatural being, was the key figure in the drama of human history. Fromm was not talking about a relation to God but of interpersonal relations. His concept was something like Adler's idea of social interest and Durkheim's idea of *conscience collective*. Another student argued that although Fromm was a Humanist, his position with regard to man's salvation through love was identical to Christianity's. It did not make much difference; just substitute for the words *soul-seeking communion with God,* the words *Nature, Mankind,* or *Community* and you get the same thing.

Someone said that Fromm's thesis about modern man's reason leading him to loneliness did not mean that reason must inevitably make one feel alone. Ancient people in Greece and Asia minor, including Judea and Egypt, had been rationalists, yet their reason had not made them feel lonely. Perhaps the trouble was that the faith in reason of the Age of Reason had led to a new religion, but its God had turned out to have clay feet. Moreover, man was God's partner in creation according to the Judaic roots of Christianity; man was given knowledge, wisdom, and intelligence in order to understand His law. Reason, incidentally, had not made Socrates feel alone, even on the day on which he had to drink the hemlock. Greeks like Anaxamenes and some Jews had not felt estranged when they reasoned that God and ultimate values were eternal unknowables. Nor had these scholars, when reason had led them to believe that they did not know the ultimate answers, turned to the various social movements and mystery cults that promised salvation. Someone pointed out that a case could be made for the thesis that man's escape from reason was due to the failure of the Age of Reason and of the Enlightenment to lead man to an earthly paradise. It could be argued that the faith of the believers in the Enlightenment and the Age of Reason was a mass movement similar to the one in which Jews and others converted to Christianity had waited for

Jesus to return and take them to heaven. When Jesus did not return they were confused, but men like Paul and Augustine and other church fathers and even the leaders of the so-called heresies sought ways out of their perplexities. Modern man needs such leaders to save his faith in reason and science. The student who has presented Fromm's doctrine argued that man had to learn to love again. His salvation lies in love, not in reason because real wisdom is in the heart and not in the brain.

Wertheimer remarked that love might open one's eyes or blind one. It might liberate or enslave, strengthen or weaken the individual. The notion that love could not lead to harm was not valid. He added that some believers in the supremacy of Justice warned that man would be wiped out in a moment if His justice were permitted to rule, untempered by loving kindness. Perhaps the converse of the statement was also true.

A student who had heard Wertheimer's lecture on love some weeks before this discussion said that it seemed to him that the question raised by Thesis II might be asked about love and charity; it was a question of how the act fitted the requirements of the particular situation. What did it do to the situation, to the giver and the recipient of love? He went on to say that to hold Thesis II one did not have to assume the supremacy of Justice in the Platonic sense, as maintaining a universal harmony. Someone said that the concept of requiredness did not mean that we had to know the absolute, eternal requiredness of the whole. There are some wholes we could never know surely and completely. Everything was not necessarily related to everything else; we did not need to conceptualize the whole universe's harmony to know what was required in a particular place. It meant that we had to act insightfully, with understanding and awareness of the effects of what we were doing in particular situations. This could be treated as a scientific quesion. When someone objected saying that this meant that Thesis II was a pragmatic approach to ethics, the student said that it was common sense, and went on to say that Thesis II did not mean that we should not try to understand the whole or not try to get as complete and consistent a view of everything as was possible; rather it meant that we must separate the problem of the search for universals from the task of trying to do justice in particular cases and places. It called for a realistic appreciation of our ignorance and knowledge. Someone added that there must be a continuous search because we do not live in a static world, events and knowledge of them change continuously. Since no two men have the same experiences and each man continues to learn as long as he lives, men are bound to feel tensions that lead to questioning and to wondering about the nature of things. Even if one believes that the Truth has been revealed in the Bible, on rereading it every week one may find questions and puzzling contradictions that have not been noticed before. Even here the whole truth is not known. A visitor said that in all human endeavors, including science and religion, the belief that it is more important to seek the truth than to believe that one has found it has brought about originality, creativity and growth in understanding. The aim of life is to learn, to gain knowledge, wisdom, and understanding.

The last point raised was that Thesis II implied a demand quality in things. In the past, a heteronomous agent, an authority outside of man, had done the commanding and man's commitment to it had ensured obedience. Modern science had destroyed this commitment but had not given man a new one. It was assumed that man was a part of nature and just as man's reason had discovered the laws of physical nature, reason would discover the laws of human nature. This would inevitably lead to ethical and moral behavior. Although some people rejected reason and science as the sources of the Good, other men were willing to accept them. Because of the goods and services provided through science, it was possible to transfer to science the authority that prescientific man had given to such external powers as God. It was assumed that control of behavior was inevitable as long as man lived in groups. Science had the means of basing the control on intelligent planning for the satisfaction of the individual as well as for mankind at large. It would not use threat and punishment as was now the case but rather rewards and an appeal to reason. A few students wondered whether it will be possible for science to remain science when this happens. What guarantee did we have that scientists playing the role of God would never abuse their position? In the old ideas each man had a spark of God in him and therefore was able to know what was good but in the new idea the scientist had superior knowledge. He was the expert.

Someone said that at present we could claim that such and such was correct because science had proved it. Modern man has faith in science to the extent of not questioning its assertions. Thus the will of science and not the will of God often keeps us from looking to see just what is actually the case. He went on to say that the use of the fruits of science in this manner might be more dangerous than the ancient idea of the will of the gods, because the gods really had not existed. The scientists not only exist but are transforming us and the world. Science as an institution might eventually become more successful and efficient than the God of the Bible in getting people to conform to its will. Any self-respecting scientific technologist would be ashamed of his record as an agent of social control if the *Pentateuch* were a report of his attempts to control the behavior of a people.

A student said that Wertheimer had once remarked that we must differentiate between science and technology. Science was based on a search for the Truth and not merely prediction and control of behavior. Science did not assume that it has the eternal absolute truth. In view of this, how could science give us guidance in particular situations? The scientist could only inform us of the probability of occurrence of certain events or things. A world based on scientific fact would still be a world based on uncertainty, on the fear of being wrong or making a mistake. In concrete situations people would still have to make up their own minds because neither the results nor the methods of science were infallible formulas to get into an earthly heaven. This attitude of doubting and wondering was not peculiar to science. Even in certain religious sects it was encouraged. Just as certain religious, political, and social institutions have taught blind, unquestioning obedience and the mechanical carrying out of certain acts and rites, so has science been taught to get obedience. Science education sometimes does not reflect the spirit of scientific search for the Truth but rather the memorization of what has been discovered in its search. Such education ignores the fact that there is Truth, and that man's search for values is related to this drive. The student concluded that in view of Wertheimer's remarks it was important to encourage people to seek the Truth in all walks of life and to teach people that scientists were not sacred cows.

10
From the Seminar on Value

[For over a period of five years various aspects of value and value judgment were discussed in most of Wertheimer's classes. These discussions culminated in a seminar on value which was attended by psychologists, psychiatrists, sociologists, philosophers, and other professions. It was conducted in an informal manner. Different people presented their ideas in a rather informal way and Wertheimer as well as everybody else commented and argued about what had been said. Some of the speakers later published their papers but what Wertheimer said was never published. What follows is a summary of his remarks in the context of comments and arguments that were made by the seminar members and by ASL's students to whom Wertheimer's remarks were presented for discussion.]

Wertheimer began the seminar saying, People have notions of right and wrong, honesty and deceit. What are they? After a pause for comments he said, Some people are convinced that such notions refer to or mean something objective. They believe that it is possible to make a decision as to whether something is right or wrong just as they are sure that they can show that $6 + 7 = 13$ and not 15. There has developed in recent years the belief, the thesis, that all such things are illusions and that people who believe such things are deceiving themselves; they are blind to the facts. What is good or bad is determined by the social norms of the society into which one has been born; what is good in one society may be bad in another. There are no objective standards concerning what is good or what is right; an objective decision as to what is good or right is not possible. There is only what your society says is true or good. This thesis is at present being taught as the truth about values.

He then read to the class from Cantril's chapter on social behavior in Boring, Langfeld and Weld (1940) and asked, Is such a picture correct? Is something lacking? When someone said that it was a scholarly and objective account of human behavior, Wertheimer said that such a picture lacks elements which are important and which we cannot afford to omit. It was not just another theoretical point of view that was being taught by Cantril. It could produce practical consequences. Such a psychological description of values and social influences might help to bring people to believe in men like Hitler. It produced a climate in which their propaganda could be effective because it claimed that existing values had been arbitrarily determined by a group in the first place and always would be. What justification did a person who believed

133

in this theory have for rejecting Hitler's values?

A visitor proposed that one could try to get people to accept his value orientation by convincing them of his point of view. If he was adept in leading people, he might get a following and thus be able to fight Hitler if his values ran counter to Hitler's. A professor pointed out that this proposal assumed that there was freedom in a state like Hitler's to organize groups to oppose the official policy of the state or of the party in power. It also assumed that all groups had equal access to the means of communication and education, to military and police power. But even if such opposition were possible, what reason would we have for expecting a person to ever challenge the norms that nurtured him? Could it not be said that he did it because of perverse and selfish desires, that he believed that the expression of his will was more important than the values of the group or the will of its leader? Since there was no objective decision possible as to who was right, it would all boil down to a battle in which people tried to impose their wills on each other. But even Hitler has not dared to say this openly. He has claimed to be the leader of the wave of the future and has insisted that Providence is behind him, that his is a just and righteous cause. A student said that the doctrine that values were merely the social norms of the group did not have to lead to a situation in which one would have to believe in a Hitler. The doctrine of Cultural Relativism does not tell a person that his church's values or his family's values are not to be followed. In fact it tells him that if he wants to be a good member of the group to which he belongs, he must act in terms of their norms. If the churches and business institutions told their loyal members that Hitler's doctrine was incompatible with theirs, then the people would have to make a choice to be loyal to their church or loyal to Hitler. Another student pointed out that Wertheimer was not objecting to the ideas that values are social norms but to the commonly resulting inference that they were arbitrary, blind responses to things. The issue was the thesis of the essential arbitrariness of the value response and not its origin.

Wertheimer resumed his remarks on Cantril's chapter saying that it reflected a number of theses that were the basis of contemporary social psychology, and went on to comment on them. Value had something to do with evaluation. In evaluation, a positive or a negative value was added to a neutral content which might be evaluated negatively or positively. How one evaluated it made no difference to the thing or the situation itself. The same mechanism held for all things that were evaluated, be they beefsteaks or justice. The person *per se* was a cultural product, the very idea of what was an individual was a cultural product; the culture made possible the idea of individuality. All evaluation was ethnocentric; individuals and social groups were connected by the social values of their cultures and all evaluating was done in terms of the group's culture and its norms. After a pause for comments Wertheimer remarked that Cantril wrote that social influences were due to emotional and nonintellectual factors. He paused again and asked, Is it permissible to make such a razor-cut distinction between the emotions and the intellect? No one answered; he asked, May we treat all evaluation in the same way; beefsteak, democracy? Is it allowed? A student answered that it was a proper procedure; it was done in other sciences. Burning, rusting, and rotting are all considered to be cases involving oxidation. The psychologists are also seeking the dynamics that underlie diverse behavior. He concluded that what the social psychologists were saying was that values were learned. They were not innate ideas.

Wertheimer replied that the issue is not the innateness of value. He added, Cantril was applying a certain theory of learning to describe the connection between the value and the object being evaluated. Cantril believes that these connections are formed on the basis of habit. One calls this thing good and that thing bad because of habituation. Value is something that is externally attached to a certain event, object, person, or behavior; the evaluation itself is brought about in a way that is basically blind to the structure of the object of evaluation. According to Cantril, one could be readily conditioned to believe that the same thing was bad or good. People are conditioned to judge one way rather than another because of customs, tradition, and social conformity which are also arbitrary in nature.

When he paused for comments, a student pointed out that just as the associationistic thesis had led to the experimental study of learning instead of speculations about what was learned, the application of associationism in its modern form had led to the experimental study of social behavior and was resulting in better prediction and control of the phenomena of human values, interests and needs. Moreover, much of what took place in evaluation was due to rote learning and constituted mechanical, blind responses. Another student pointed out that current work in social psychology was bearing out the generality of the thesis of the learning theorists. They seem to have universal principles that hold for all behavior. Someone remarked that no learning theory has been universally accepted, that there are controversies about the nature of associations and conditioned responses as well as about the processes that bring them about. Nor are the learning theorists themselves in agreement when they are asked to explain a concrete case of habituation in problem solving. The student asked, Could we assume that we know just how learning occurs; Are we allowed to use what we learned about learning of rats in human social situations? Was there not the danger that we could create social conditions that were in line with our theories? Instead of learning about the processes that were involved in social learning and evaluation, we would be producing people who acted and evaluated in a blind and mechanical manner. This was happening in the schools in which the rat-learning model had been used to create mechanized individuals in problem-solving situations.

Wertheimer said that there are cases that fit the associationistic thesis but that it does not hold universally. There are other kinds of situations in which a person has reasons for his evaluation, where it is not a mechanical or blind response, where thinking is involved, where the evaluation is based on evidence and intelligent assumptions about the object of evaluation and the situation in which the evaluation is being made. The evaluation in such an instance is not always an arbitrary connection between the value and the thing. In response to a student's objections he said that thinking and evaluation were not arbitrary processes; perhaps psychologists and sociologists have underestimated the role of reason in evaluation.

A visitor pointed out that Wertheimer's thesis was founded on the discredited *Rational Man Model* of the Enlightenment and of the Classical Economists. He alluded to the social problems that arose when this model had been used by the Philosophical Radicals and other social reformers. He argued that Wertheimer had said that certain theories were dangerous because they would make a Hitler possible, but his own thesis had led to the exploitation of millions of men as well as to the destruction of their lives and property. He concluded that either Wertheimer's or Cantril's thesis could be used to justify the same social dogma. What was at issue was not which ideology was good for mankind. The scientific question was the real issue. We need to know which theory could serve as the prototype for all judgment situations. Was it possible to explain all or at least a greater number of cases of evaluation by one or the other thesis? Wertheimer answered that those who posited the first thesis (the thesis of habit) assumed that it was the prototype containing the one true psychological mechanism and they bent and twisted it in every which way in order to make it account for those situations that were usually said to be cases of the second thesis (the thesis of rational assumptions). This was usually accomplished by focusing on the responses rather than on the processes that led to the responses.

A professor pointed out that the second thesis had shifted the issue. He went on to say that Wertheimer was talking about means-ends relations. Whether one evaluated a course of action as good or bad, depended on whether he evaluated the ends as good or bad. Evaluation begins when one says that he wants a certain end, and then the end is labeled good, not bad. The professor went on to say that evaluation is mixed up with the problem of ultimate ends. As long as one has not solved the problem of what the ultimate ends are we cannot solve the problems of evaluation. The problem of ultimate ends or the purpose of existence, however, is not a scientific problem because we cannot deal with values in science. A scientist can only state what is; can tell us the factual consequences of certain acts but cannot tell us that it is good to do this or that. The professor reiterated that Wertheimer was dealing with the question of the connection between means and ends and not with evaluation; thus his proposals did not constitute a scientific thesis.

A student wanted to know why Thesis II or the problem of evaluation of necessity led one to the question of ultimate ends. Just because Plato had been led to a transcendental world when he had found it logically impossible to assume that form was immanent in matter did not mean that we too have to postulate a world of pure forms in order to understand what to do in a particular time and place on this earth. Why did we have to get involved in the issue of ultimate ends or eternal values in order to deal with a particular concrete situation? Someone pointed out that the problem of morality was always discussed in terms of such philosophical and religious doctrines. ASL's student pointed out that in Talmudic civil and criminal law the discussion of particular cases did not lead to the question of ultimate ends. Someone said that this was because the discussants (the rabbis) were laymen and not philosophers. In order to have a consistent philosophy, Christian theologians had been led to the problem of whether value was immanent in or transcendent of the thing being evaluated. It was interesting to note that both theses led to difficulties but that the Scholastic philosophers had persisted in seeking a solution just as the Greek philosophers had done before them. Moreover, modern and contemporary philosophers also believe that a solution to the problem of ultimate ends is basic to an understanding of morality. A student asked why it is not possible to assume that one does know the ultimate end for man and to assume that there is an Eternal Unknowable that demands that we do justice, be righteous, show loving kindness and mercy when we make evaluations. Since they are eternally unknowable we can never be sure how adequately we apply them. Therefore, we have to examine and reexamine the concrete cases of our evaluations to see whether we have actualized them. When a beggar holds out his hand he is not appealing to ultimate ends but for righteousness, justice.

When a student said that it was impossible for a rational man to act this way, ASL's student replied that a large literature exists that describes the results of such an attitude in religious life as well as in science. Perhaps it is not in line with certain notions of what is good philosophy and theology but millions of people have lived and are living this way. Someone said that a contradiction was involved in ASL's student's proposal. How could one claim to have an understanding of what are the ultimate values for man and at the same time believe that they were unknowable? ASL's student said that people who cannot accept the possibility that they err in their evaluations have sought the one or more principles that are absolutely correct. Some of them have become so obsessed with seeking absolute knowledge of the ultimate ends that they refuse to do anything in the concrete situations of daily life or they do anything they please, not bothering to study because they know that they will remain ignorant of the ultimate ends. Thus the idea of ultimate ends becomes a snare and/or a delusion. He went on to say that some Greek philosophers speculated about ultimate ends to the extent that they had neglected examining the decision-making processes in particular, concrete situations. They could afford to do it because they belonged to the leisure class; their slaves and servants worked while they speculated. The results of their speculations seem to indicate that the more a value is related to the search of the ultimate the less it is available in man's experience as a reality. A visiting professor said that the student's remarks reflect the American worship of action rather than reflection, the American stress on science as technology rather than the search for Truth.

A student raised the question of whether we always need to know the whole system before we can deal with it and understand any of its parts. Perhaps every part can, to some extent, be understood without knowledge of the whole. Some parts of a system or a machine may be understood for prediction and control without really knowing what place, role, and function it has in the structure of the system as a whole. Someone interjected that some parts may be well understood but with the increase of knowledge of the whole, we may see new, overlooked, features of the part. Increasing knowledge of the whole might lead also to awareness of anomalies or irregularities in a part's functioning which were not seen before and these in turn might lead to the discovery of aspects of the entire system that were not noticed before or to the discovery of its relationship with parts to which it was not previously thought to be related. One of ASL's students said that perhaps we ought to stop confusing the word *whole* with *holy*. It confused matters to say that the problem of the means-end relations in a certain situation brings one inevitably to an issue of ultimate ends which must then be resolved before anything else can be done. This is mixing up a particular problem in a concrete situation of everyday life with the philosophical search for a logically consistent and complete theory of ethics.

Wertheimer went to the blackboard and wrote, <u>Operation Situation</u>, and said that it stands for a certain operation (behavior) in a certain situation, a rho connection (cf. Luchins and Luchins, 1970b). The relation between the operation and the situation is called good or bad depending on whether it fits the situation. There are concrete situations in which the main question is whether the action fits the situation. One must separate evaluations that are based on preferences, whether or not one likes the fit, from the question of whether the operation fits in the situation. We must differentiate between judgments of the fitness of an act and the preference for an act.

A visitor said that this thesis was different from the others that had been discussed. In the other theses there was a separation of the ordinary world from the world of values. In the other theses, values and being had nothing in common; being had no value and value had no being. Values were related to something the person did in the course of his evaluating an object or discovering its value. It was therefore subjective and relative to the person. The source of the oughtness or demand quality was in the person's feelings for value or in some ideational hierarchy of values in his phenomenal world or personality. Thus value had no objective existence in the world of facts; it was an ideational element and could be thought of as an intuition into a world of pure thoughts or ideas. To Plato it was the thirst of the soul for the Good, the True, and the Beautiful; to the Christians it was the yearning of the Divine spark in man for communion with God. To the philosophers of the Enlightenment it was the faculty of reason. Since modern man does not believe that he has a faculty of reason or a soul, he uses words like ego, personality, and self, which are nevertheless similar to Plato's conception of the soul as a self-actualizing agent. In contrast to these views, Wertheimer is proposing that we seek the source of value in the situation in which the evaluation is being made. Value exists in the situation's structure; it is an essential feature of the structure. Value thus had ontic existence. Someone pointed out that the previous theses led to problems about the nature of the evaluation but Wertheimer's new thesis leads us to the problem of the nature of reality.

Wertheimer said that he agreed that the new conjecture was different from the previous theses. He went on to say that he saw no need to get involved with the broad theoretical and philosophical problems of ontology and epistemology in order to deal with concrete cases of the fitness of an operation in a particular situation. His conjecture involves empirical questions which we must face. Someone interrupted to say that just as the previous theses had led to the development of certain scientific methods and concepts to deal with evaluation, the new conjecture could lead to the development of new methods and concepts to study value. It was not a formula describing what value was or ought to be, but was a heuristic to study what was required in a situation. He concluded by saying that Wertheimer's conjecture was similar to his formulation concerning the relation of a problem's solution to the problem. If we assume that the problem of the nature of value is related to what occurs in genuine problem solving, then we can look for such processes as centering, recentering, and concentric narrowing of the visual field. This calls for experiments with social and personal problems that occur in the daily lives of people, in the school, in the courts, and in business in order to find out what factors influence these processes that Gestalt psychologists claim occur in genuine problem solving.

A professor said that the student was confusing issues of ethics with mathematical problem solving and that according to Max Weber we could not deal with value on a rational scientific basis. Wertheimer remarked that even in Max Weber's thesis of the nonevaluative nature of science there was implicit evaluation. Scientists believe that one must face a problem with an open mind and be objective if he wishes to solve a scientific problem, and that it is proper for a scientist to do this and this but not to do that and that, if he wants to be objective. Objectivity is one of the values of science. In Nazi Germany, however, science is a tool of the state. The Nazis say that scientists may be objective only in certain situations but not in others, that scientists may decide objectively whether this or that method makes a better machine gun but they may not objectively evaluate whether it is better for the people to be blindly obedient to the leaders or to investigate whether what the leader says is a fact or a big lie.

Someone pointed out that science is grounded on a belief in the rationality of man whereas Nazi philosophy is based on the doctrine that all human actions were based on irrational factors. Some social scientists, Pareto and the Freudians, seem to lend support to this doctrine when they say that both rational and irrational factors are involved in man's behavior but that behavior rested ultimately on the irrational factors.

Someone pointed out that the Positivists in philosophy, in psychology, and in the social sciences asserted that value had an irrational basis and that only facts were subject to rational consideration. Those who opposed the Positivists were labeled irrationalists insofar as they claimed that human behavior, human beings, and the world could not be understood by reason but only through intuition, empathy, and unconscious feelings. It seems that modern man has finally realized that reason has its limitations, that all systems of thought are based on assumptions that one accepts on faith. Wertheimer remarked that some psychologists have made a blind and arbitrary separation between thinking and emotions; it has never been universally accepted that thinking is *cool hearted*. Throughout the ages people have regarded thinking as connected with a strong passion to get at the truth, connected with a strong emotion against lies and deceit. He went on to say that one may be blinded by reasonable, intelligent assumptions as well as by emotions and feelings and that emotions and feelings are not necessarily always blind. He wrote on the blackboard: *Thinking: Thinking-Emotions: Emotions* and said that because of philosophical and historical reasons we talk about thinking and emotions as two distinctly different kinds of behavior. There are cases in which there is thinking without emotions, it is found in a machine, in a calculator but not in a human being. There may even be cases of behavior that seem to be pure emotional responses, emotions without thinking. Both are, however, artificial, extreme forms of behavior. The middle case, *Thinking-Emotion*, is real, natural, and exists in genuine thinking.

In response to questions, he said that some people who stress the irrational claim that it is not good to be rational and that it is best to rely on your instincts, drives, feelings. They say that you weaken your position in a decision-making situation when you say that on the one hand this may be done and on the other hand that may be done. To be effective, do by an act of will what is needed. To cross a brook you must jump over it; if you stop to figure out how deep it is, how fast is its current, and how wide it is, you will never cross it.

Someone said that the irrationalists sometimes seem to advocate impulse gratification in the present instead of in the future. Yet for social reasons it is better to do something in terms of the long-run considerations or consequences of the action. Someone protested that every man lives in the short run and not in the long run. The irrationalists' advice, therefore, is more in line with the actual needs of particular people. Of what benefit is it to the starving worker to be told that the public policy or the industrial changes that have deprived him of his livelihood benefit mankind? It does not benefit him. The men of the age of Reason and the Enlightenment talked about the progress of mankind, not the welfare of particular people. Wertheimer remarked that pointing out to a person the long-run consequences may result in making the person act in a genuine manner and not being blinded or narrowed down by petty things. He agreed with a professor that it may also lead to conforming to the authority or majority and even blind one to the real consequences of what is being done. He went on to suggest that there is a need to find out what factors make a person refuse to adapt to the demands of the authority or majority when an appeal is made to long-run consequences. When does one agree or not agree to such social factors when they are against the structural requirements of the situation?

A student said that Wertheimer's conjecture implies that a scientist can say that this goal is better than that goal in terms of the system as a whole. Thus, notwithstanding Max Weber's thesis, scientists can make decisions about goals. But a scientist cannot say that he is absolutely sure that this is the best goal to pursue. Therefore, of what use is his advice? Someone said that neither can the scientist say that such and such a means is absolutely the best method to obtain a certain goal. The same tentativeness exists for both kinds of decisions. He went on to say that the scientist must set up a continuous process of analysis and study of the situation in order to see what are the effects of the means and goals that are being used. A student interrupted to say that there is a difference between a scientific law or decision and a law or decision made by a legislator. The scientist does not deal with *thou shalts* and *thou shalt nots*. The former student retorted that one can formulate the laws of physics in legal terminology without too much loss of change in meaning. Just as in science, the legislature's laws are subject to change with change in knowledge of what is happening in the social structures and in the condition of daily life. Neither the laws of physicists or politicians are Eternal Laws. When someone said that there is a certain inflexibility in legal rules, the student retorted the same holds for gravity and thermodynamics. When someone argued that legal rules are authoritarian, that they call for obedience to the will of the legislature or the sovereign, the student said that if you want to move something you will obey the laws of physics as formulated by physicists. In such a case the physicists are the final authorities. [ASL's students wanted to know whether it is possible that several goals may fit equally well in one situation; whether several methods may be equally fit to obtain the same goal. ASL responded that Wertheimer's thesis does not mean that there is a unique solution to the problem of what is fit in a certain situation.]

11
Relativism and Values

After a few sessions on other topics in which his remarks about value were repeatedly challenged, Wertheimer presented his position in one of the last sessions of the value seminar. He first said that he agrees that many people do not act as he has described. He then went on to say, We must differentiate between value and evaluation. In evaluation the majority plays a role but it is not the value that is determined by the group. After a pause for comments he read a letter that had been sent to the editor of the *New York Times* in order to illustrate the confusion that results when people present as arguments for cultural relativism cases of different evaluations in different situations and in different social groups. After a few remarks about the ambiguity of the relativistic thesis, he reformulated it into two theses. *Thesis I:* There are differences in evaluation. People evaluate things in terms of the customs and standards of their respective societies or groups. Society A evaluates X positively but Society B evaluates X negatively, therefore, we say that they contradict each other. It seems to be a contradiction, but can we be sure that the situation is so simple? We can say that it is a contradiction as long as we look only at the naked facts. It may really not be so easy to decide from the naked facts that they are really contradictory evaluations. If we try to grasp what is meant by these evaluations, we may realize that they touch on very complex situations.

What do evaluations mean? He drew on the blackboard $\left|\begin{smallmatrix}a\\ac_1\end{smallmatrix}\right. \neq \left|\begin{smallmatrix}a\\ac_2\end{smallmatrix}\right.$ and said, Maybe a in context ac_1 is not the same thing as a in ac_2. If we agree that this may be the case, then our conclusion (from the differences in evaluation) for relativism is not valid. We must realize the situational meaning of a in Society A and in Society B; we must seek the bases of evaluation in societies A and B. Suppose that in Society A both parents are slain by the children but in Society B both parents are cared for by the children. Why the difference in the treatment of the parents in A and B? On can offhand say that it is due to a different evaluation of old age or to a difference in esteeming your parents. But, when the actual situation is examined it may be that it is best for them in the particular situation and also is based on their religion. A student illustrated this remark with a custom among certain Eskimos. When the community is starving, the old people strip themselves of all their clothing and walk out into the snow. It is the duty of their children to club them into unconsciousness. This is considered an act of kindness, not patricide. Wertheimer continued, saying that by studying the situational meaning and seeking the basis of the evaluation we might discover

141

that similar evaluations of the same thing are really different and that different evaluations of the same thing are the same, in terms of the processes underlying the evaluation.

There followed a discussion in which someone said that Wertheimer is proposing that we try to understand the processes and the frames of reference from which the evaluations are made instead of just taking the responses at face value. This proposal reflects a common-sense view of customs. If one wishes to be polite, one does not insist that picking up one's hat and letting a cold draft of air pass over his head is the proper thing to do in a society where one puts his right thumb to his nose and extends the other fingers of his hand toward the person whom he is greeting. Someone else said that Wertheimer's formulation calls for a reexamination of the examples of folkways and mores in text books in order to understand them instead of listing them to prove cultural relativism.

Thesis II: Wertheimer said that his proposal to study the situational meanings of the actions actually leads to another kind of thesis of cultural relativism. Various societies have different contexts. Each society has a certain structure, and things in it have meaning in terms of its structure. This formulation led to the following remarks by students. Thesis II shifts the emphasis from responses to processes. It raises new questions: Who sees these processes, the members of the society or the anthropologists who study them? One could say that an evaluation is not just a positive or negative response but is based on a reason which is a verbal statement that the person or actor repeats by rote or applies as a rationalization for his evaluation. The second thesis is like those in Ruth Benedict's *Patterns of Culture* and Sherif's *Psychology of Social Norms*. Different cultures are patterned in different ways and its members see the world from the point of view or frame of reference of their culture's pattern. It is a Gestalt theoretical view of evaluation and social values; there is evidence for it in the Gestalt Laws of Perception.

In response to the questions and arguments directed to him, Wertheimer made several remarks which are presented in the order in which they were given, although it was not possible to record the questions themselves: It is not important that everybody in the group conform to or be aware of the structure. It is possible that some parts of the cultural pattern as well as some members' relations to the pattern may be an external attachment. But there may also be evaluations in which there is some kind of justification for the evaluations. It may have a reasonable basis; it is not merely attaching a + or − value to a thing but having some relation to the thing; the value may have some structural relation to the thing. After a pause, Wertheimer said that according to Thesis II, people from different societies evaluate things differently because they have different philosophies of life. We can find out a society's philosophy of life and its axioms but we cannot go any further. Justice is created by the rules of the state. Each society has its own axiom system and therefore what is seen as justice in one society may not be the same thing as in another society because of the differences in axioms. We cannot say that a rule in one society is just or unjust; we can only say whether it is consistent or inconsistent with its society's axioms or philosophies of life. After a pause Wertheimer asked whether Thesis II can serve as a basis for value. A student said that it helps one appreciate what value is, for example, being rich may be viewed differently because of the philosophy of life of the society. It may be positively evaluated because it gives one leisure or shows that one is efficient. It may be negatively evaluated because it means that one cannot go to heaven or because it is a bothersome way of life. The student went on to say that according to the theory of relativity in physics everything is judged in terms of a frame of reference.

Wertheimer remarked: Both Thesis I and II deal with evaluation but have no basis for value. He then said, Suppose you are on a boat; the mast breaks off and the captain and officers are killed. Will you proceed to elect a leader to save the boat and reject the services of someone who steps forward and commands you to help him erect a mast? No one spoke. Wertheimer then gave another example. A fire breaks out. Everybody is confused. A man steps forward and calmly commands that everybody stand still and then proceeds to organize a bucket brigade from a well outside of the building. Would you evaluate his behavior negatively or positively in terms of your society's conception of how a leader is determined? [Wertheimer's stories were told to kindergarten, fifth grade, high school, and college students. All of the children and most youths said that the man who spontaneously became the leader did the correct thing. His behavior fit, it was appropriate, good, and helpful. Some college students, however, made comments about the possible motives of or reasons for the man's behavior. A few thought that such persons were domineering or authoritarian people and that they could have or should have first asked the people if they wanted to follow him. One student said that even in the Bible, the prophets say: Who is for the Lord follow me. It would be of interest to assess the reactions of present-day student populations to similar stories.]

When one of the professors said that the examples that had been presented were extreme cases, Wertheimer remarked that we have to begin with clear cut cases. Someone interrupted to say that sometimes in emergency situations a person who likes to be in the limelight steps forward and may be inept. Wertheimer remarked that in such cases the people realize that he is a fake; the fire rages, the ship wallows in the water and someone else steps forward. He went on to say, in such examples we see that there is a situation with a gap and the question is how the action fits its requirements. This is an example of value. This is an issue that may have nothing to do with one's liking or not liking the man, but with the value of the man in the situation. The difference between a bad or good general depends upon the worth of the man in terms of the situation's requirements. The question is not whether one likes the man who is the general; the requirements of the concrete situation may determine the man's value. After a pause for questions he said, Let us separate these two evaluations of the general: 1, the general is apt and is therefore positively evaluated; 2, he is engaged in a war, which is negatively evaluated by us and therefore we hate the general. The last remark touched off an objection by a professor that the separation makes possible the justification of Hitler's generals' behavior; moreover, a gangster's behavior becomes a thing of value.

Wertheimer remarked that in Greece they esteemed the arts but not the artist. They believed that manual labor coarsened men's souls as well as their hands, therefore, they did not evaluate the artist highly but his work had value. They spoke highly of the ability of the slave but not of the slave *per se*. In such cases we have a miscentering of the situation. When someone inter-

rupted to ask how it is possible to say that a gangster's behavior fits a situation, he said, One may focus on a subwhole of the social system; in such a
narrowed view, the situation seems to require certain behavior. A safecracker
therefore may not be seen as a burglar but as an efficient person who is doing
his job well as he is opening a safe. But this situation is not a closed system; it
is part of a larger system in which the safecrackers' behavior does not fit
properly; his behavior is a disturbance, a disruptive factor, in the larger system of which it is a part. After some arguments by students he added that the
question is whether it is possible to act because of the demands of a situation
regardless of one's likes and dislikes. Someone pointed out that if one considers the philosophy of life of certain devout Christians, a general is bad because all army men, all war, all violence, and killing are bad. These people say
that if someone strikes you on one cheek, you should turn to him the other
cheek. Are these people blind to situational requirements? Someone said that
such a philosophy is unrealistic; it allows aggressive individuals to kill and
maim at will whomever and whenever they please. One of ASL's students said
that a truly religious person, regardless of his faith, will thank God that he is
the victim rather than the murderer because the religious person is oriented
toward Eternity and not this world. This view of life is reflected by Socrates'
behavior. Before he died he gave one of his friends money to buy a sacrifice
to the gods, a gift for being freed of his *mortal coil*. Wertheimer remarked
that the students' statements raise the question of how one's philosophy of life
fits the reality of man, the reality of society, and the reality of nature.

In response to someone's question about Gandhi's doctrine of nonviolence,
Wertheimer raised the question of whether the doctrine can be successful in
the face of Hitler's stormtroopers. Perhaps Gandhi's methods worked because
he dealt with the English and not the Nazis. After a pause for comments he
said that doing nothing may sometimes be more effective than doing something, in bringing about a certain result. It is not just a matter of whether it is
better to act or not to act but whether we want the results of our doing nothing, whether the results will be what we think they should be. After waiting
for students' reactions, he raised the question of whether certain, and not
other, philosophies of life are required by the nature of man, of society, and
of physical reality. No one responded to this question. [In ASL's class that
night his students complicated the issue by wanting to know from whose point
of view we were to regard the requirements of the physical world, of society
or of man. They pointed out that Wertheimer had once said that paganism
leads to an empty existence but a pagan of ancient times or of the present
would not agree. One could say that it was empty in ancient times because it
was replaced by Christianity. But if we look at the world at present, we see
that paganism is becoming a dominant way of life, replacing the Christian way
of life. Some students argued that Christianity is not being replaced; it has
just recently taken roots but has not yet penetrated the hearts of men. If it
really had become the way of life there would be no Hitlers, no social evils. A
student objected to bringing religion into the discussion and argued that what
is crucial in evaluating a philosophy of life is whether the view of nature and
men leads to survival. ASL then told them that according to this thesis the
neolithic cultures that have persisted until the present day are best adapted. A
student pointed out that they exist because they never had any competitors.
ASL challenged his class to name a culture that had survived for over 1,00C

years in face of competition. Someone mentioned the Chinese, the Indians of India, and the Jews, and asked, Did these cultures survive because they were based on intrinsic, on real values or because of the power of their agencies of social control? What is the nature of their agencies of social control? What is the nature of their values? In what way are they similar, in what ways are they different from the Roman Empire's, Sparta's, and Athen's agencies of social control and values? No one was satisfied with the idea that survival is the criterion, but it was agreed that there must be some system of relationships that allows people to live in security and freedom as individuals. This raised the question of whether these are universal values of man.]

Wertheimer summarized the main points of his presentation, while being repeatedly interrupted. He drew the following table on the blackboard.

I	A+ (assumed to be a good medicine)	C− (assumed to be a poison)	C+ (assumed to be a medicine)	A− (assumed to be a poison)
II	B+ (medicine +)	D− (poison −)	B+ (medicine +)	D− (poison −)

In the first meaning of relativism (I) it is claimed that the same thing is evaluated differently in different places. In the second meaning of relativism (II) it is pointed out that there is agreement in the evaluation when we understand the axioms on which they are based. The question of whether or not a certain herb or other agent is actually a medicine is outside of the culture's evaluation and outside of historical changes in it. It depends on the facts. Does it cure the person of the disease for which it is used? He ended the session after suggesting that we mail him arguments and examples for and against the points in the outline.

After-Class Discussion

Some students talked to Wertheimer after class. They said that his thesis of fit seems to hold for trivial situations. They told him that it does not help one understand the reactions of members of the seminar to the .Moscow Trials, to the Hitler-Stalin Non-Agression Pact, and to Hitler's bombing of London. Because of their ideological convictions some individuals see no difference between the Nazis and the English; they regard the war in Europe as a struggle between capitalists. They do not believe that Hitler will attack the USSR as soon as England is defeated and that after that he will attack the USA. Someone was bold enough to say that Wertheimer had been able to convert some of the seminar members to Gestalt psychology because they had no strong commitments to another theory or were seeking some ideas to launch them into successful careers or give them fame. Although they seemed to accept some of his ideas about social psychology, they have not been moved from their ideological positions. Wertheimer ignored the arguments and suggested that the students take a simple situation and find out what has to be done to the people in it and to the situation to blind the people to the demands of the situation. One should also take a simple situation in which people act blindly and arbitrarily and try to discover what can be done to open their eyes to the demand of the situation. [ASL's students presented case histories that indicated that it is much easier to make people act blindly than to open their eyes. The examples were simple ones involving pupils, students and teachers in school situations, friendships, love affairs, community activities. The students agreed that the study made them appreciate the saying: The devil runs the universe.]

After Wertheimer left, some of the students remained to comment on the social-political scene, on the politics of university appointments, and the power politics of members of the seminar. They could find little evidence in them for Wertheimer's idea that people act in terms of situational requirements.

When Wertheimer's remarks were presented that night by ASL to his students, the class's discussion centered on these points:

1. Man's reactions to particular situations sometimes redefine the requirements of the situation. The means whereby a requirement of the situation or a basic need of man is met may become institutionalized and after a while become an end in itself. Moreover, the methods produce certain demands of their own, which may eventually hinder the functioning of the original means or demand or value.

2. The culture and its philosophy of life may be compared to a complex pattern of means-end relations that a society has developed in history. It has a certain structure that tends to perpetuate itself in spite of changes in the physical world. Because of the culture's demands, all of its members may perish as they try to live in accordance with its dictates. There are cases in history in which this has occurred. But there are also cases where the members of a society have refused to accept their culture's values and its maladaptive philosophy of life. They seem to have had their own ideas and values and thereby destroyed their society's ancient culture or joined another society. They did not act in terms of the requirements of their social situation. What makes a person act in terms of his inner convictions or in terms of another group's values and against the group that nurtured him, against all societies, or against the world? Whose demands is such an individual meeting? Does he see the requirements of a historical or physical process that others do not see? Are there individual differences in the susceptibility to becoming a creature of one's culture?

3. People of different cultures often do clash because they view the world differently. The European settlers transformed North America in terms of their cultural pattern and thereby destroyed the physical bases for the cultures of the Indians. They justified their actions in terms of their own philosophy of life. At present we see that this philosophy of life has created dust bowls, floods, etc. The short-ranged pragmatic policy of the settlers and of present day Americans is now on the verge of destroying the world; yet we go on plundering the planet. Why do we not see that the very existence of our culture is imperiled by the methods we use? Does this not prove the irrationality of man and social action? Rarely is it that different cultures can exist together in the same society and not destroy each other even though there are from time to time clashes between them as seen with the Jews in Eastern Europe, the Swiss Cantons, etc.

4. We do not know what is required of mankind but only the officially stated needs or demands of each man or each society. The entire discussion

of what is required of man is an echo of the idea that the gods require this or that action. It also reflects the Enlightenment's belief in reason in nature. Wertheimer believes that there is reason in nature, that nothing is done arbitrarily. It is a faith and not a fact. What would happen if people no longer agreed to be reasonable, to reason together, but confronted each other instead with *faits accomplis,* with force and violence? Would we have the world that Hobbes described as man's state of nature?

5. Wertheimer assumes that when an inept person takes over in a group or is put in charge of a situation, he removes himself or is easily removed when the need for him no longer exists. He overlooks the possibility that the person may maximize his tenure in a variety of ways. We see this in business, in government, and even in scientific organizations. There is leeway in the means that a group may use to meet its goals; therefore, the inept person may remain in control or create new structures to ensure his control. He may even change the character and goals of the group. If he is replaced, it may be long after he has gotten what he wanted. The students gave examples from their gangs, school clubs, and community organizations to illustrate these points. Wertheimer seems to ignore that there are people who have the ability and/or means to maximize their own private needs, to optimize the subpart of the system which they occupy and to focus on reaping benefits from it before the total system reacts against or protects itself from them. They are modern Louis XIV's who say, "Après moi le déluge." Perhaps a social system is possible because in addition to such kinds of people, it contains many others who are passive or content with their lots or who do not want or like to rock the boat. Wertheimer seemed to object to Maslow's concept of dominant personalities. But they exist; of course, a group composed only of these kinds of people might not be possible, but what will happen if we develop a society by means of our educational methods in which most people are dominant, self-centered, self-actualizing people? Wertheimer seems to think that it is not possible. But maybe it is.

6. Wertheimer is assuming that men hate deceit and do not desire to do evil; whenever they do evil, it is due to field conditions. He is assuming that man is by nature good; only bad conditions create bad men. This argument is used to excuse all kinds of evil behavior. Maybe man is a microcosm that reflects the tensions of the world. Just as the atom is made up of negative and positive particles, man too has positive and negative features in his psyche. The psychoanalysts, especially Jung, have stressed this. The liberal-minded psychologists might benefit from studying the folklore of mankind to see how they have dealt with the problem of evil instead of insisting that it is a phenomenon peculiar to bad social conditions or to societies based on pre-scientific principles. Even Wertheimer is aware of evil when he tells us to resist Hitler. But what is evil? Some of the more religious students agreed that to do evil was to miss the mark toward becoming the kind of human being demanded by man's essential nature; all men are directed toward certain divine attributes. Man knows when he has missed the mark because these attributes maximize living conditions that lead to Justice. However, most students were disillusioned; they could see no purpose in the life of man; their belief in Marxism had been shattered by Stalin's pact with Hitler and/or the Moscow trials. Maybe the best way to characterize man is as a creature who *rolls with the punches* hoping that he would eventually make some sense out of what is happening to him even though it appears to be hopeless and absurd.

12
Telling the Truth

An elementary school teacher said that in a previous session Wertheimer had implied that telling the truth was a natural way of behaving, that people had a moral sense or faculty. This was not supported by recent studies on honesty and other traits of character. In one study the same child had been given four tests of honesty. Pennies had been placed in certain places in his home to see if he would take them. An examination which had been marked in invisible ink was returned to him and the child was asked to grade it himself, thus giving him a chance to cheat. In another situation, he had been called *safe* in a ball game when he had obviously been *out*. In another, he had been asked how many chin-ups he had done after the teacher had walked out of the gymnasium. This study by Hartshorne and May found some children would cheat in one situation and not in another. The children had showed no consistent trait of honesty. These findings illustrate what happens in daily life; we learn to be honest in certain situations and our honesty is restricted to these situations.

Wertheimer challenged the results of this study because the responses alone had been considered; no attempt had been made to find out the processes that had led to the responses. How could we be sure that a child's *not* changing the answers on the test was due to his being honest? A child could have been too naive to realize that here was a chance to cheat, he could have seen the opportunity but did not change the answer because he had suspected a trick, or he could not have changed the answer because he had really been honest. Was it permissible to lump all these cases of not changing answers together as cases of honesty? A child might have naively felt the need to change the answer and did it with no thought of cheating, whereas another child had realized that he was cheating. Were both of these children equally dishonest? It would have been of interest for the experimenter to have questioned the children, or to have tried by other methods to find out the reasons that a child had changed or not changed his answer, stolen or not stolen pennies, and cheated or not cheated on the playground or in the gymnasium. The children's attitudes towards schoolwork, toward teachers, parents, and fellow students might also have been the reasons for their having cheated in one but not in another situation, or for having remained honest or cheated in all of them.

A student said that according to Wertheimer's thesis of meeting the demands of the situation, it could be said that those children who had changed their answers had acted in a way that ran counter to the requirements of the situation and that the children who had not changed their answers had acted in accordance with the requirements. He therefore saw no reason for getting involved in finding out the child's motives or intentions. The way to hell is paved with good intentions. Wertheimer replied that we would treat a child in a different way depending on the process that had brought about the honest or dishonest behavior. Just saying that a child was honest or dishonest was not enough if one wished to recify the child's behavior. A teacher protested that cheating was cheating and that what mattered in life most of the time was the response itself. People most often react to our behavior and do not stop to think about our intentions. She went on to say that certain responses were required in certain places; adults as well as children were expected to make them if they were to be considered honest.

Wertheimer asked, Does honesty mean to do what an arbitrary power tells you to do or does it mean such things as to be friendly, not to deceive others, and not to be treacherous? He urged the class to find out the ordinary everyday usage of the words *honest* and *dishonest* and went on to comment that Hartshorne and May's study of honesty had correlated the children's responses in different situations and concluded from this that the child had or had not been consistently honest. What was needed, however, was to study the place, role, and function of each response in the context in which it occurred. In doing this, it might be discovered that some children who had acted differently on the tests, at home, at school, in the gymnasium, and on the playground had actually been doing the same thing; that some children who had acted the same way in all the test situations had been doing different things. When a student protested that Wertheimer wanted the investigator to be a Gestalt psychologist instead of a Behaviorist, he said that there was a Latin aphorism found in old logic books that went like this: When two people are doing the same thing, they may not be doing the same thing; and when two people are doing different things, they may not be doing different things. It was not a matter of being a Behaviorist or a Gestalt psychologist but of finding out what brought about the responses. He then gave this example, Suppose a child is stubborn and you are asked to propose methods to change him. If you want to do something about the stubborness, you have to consider the conditions under which it occurs. The child's stubborness might be due to the ignorance or stupidity of the child or of the people. The method one uses in dealing with the child depends on such factors as well as the social situation.

Someone said that what Wertheimer was saying fitted in with the modern psychiatric approach that stressed that one should not treat the symptoms but the causes of abnormal behavior. This led to an argument between two students; one claimed that symptom removal had cured or relieved more people of their troubles than had psychoanalysis, which had purportedly treated the causes of the symptoms. This controversy led to a discussion of the questions of what was a symptom, of what was a cause, and whether it was always possible to treat the causes even if they were known (Luchins, 1959, pp. 157-207).

The seminar returned to the question of honesty when a student said that in order to be honest one had to be true to one's self. Thereupon, Wertheimer asked, Does this mean that if one is a liar he must lie in order to be true to himself? The student said that by definition the self does what is fit.

Someone said that if we assumed that the self was the core of the person in the sense of Plato's concept of the soul, then the self knew and yearned for the True, the Beautiful, and the Good which it had known in the world of Forms before it had come down to earth into a body. If we assumed that the self is like Anaxagoras's *Nous,* which was the organizing rational principle that brought order out of the primordial chaos, we would get into trouble because the *Nous*, as Socrates so dramatically said in the *Phaedo* was nonteleological in nature. But the term, *Nous,* has been spiritualized so that we often think of it in a teleological manner. A visitor pointed out that if the self was just a system of habits that the organism had developed in its interaction with its social world, then it was possible to be true to one's self by being a liar in those situations that required one to lie. To be true to one's self was to be a true reflection of one's society's culture. When a student protested that the formulation was the basis of the Nazi doctrine, the visitor remarked that it was a doctrine of cultural anthropology and not a political doctrine.

Wertheimer stopped the argument over what concept of the self inevitably led to truthful responses by proposing the thesis that honesty was a quality of the person's interactions with the social and physical world. It was an attitude toward conduct in the social realm. He then asked what it meant in a particular situation to tell a lie. A student suggested that the class read Bojer's *The Power of a Lie* for an example of what a lie can do to people. Wertheimer said, Suppose a man asks you how to get to a certain street because he has a gap in his knowledge and sees you as the source of the means to fill this gap. If you fill this gap with the wrong information and the man does not reach his goal his relation to you is changed. You are no longer to him what you had been before, a source of information about how to get to a place. What you told him had consequences for him and in turn has consequences for your future relation to him. An elementary school teacher gave as an example of Wertheimer's thesis the story of the shepherd boy who cried "Wolf!" because he wanted company. People at first came running to his aid but found no wolf. After several such false alarms, one day a wolf did attack the flock and the shepherd boy called in vain, no one came to his aid.

Wertheimer returned to his example, saying, What is the difference between giving a man wrong directions because you want to trick him and giving wrong directions because of faulty knowledge? From a certain point of view, in both cases a falsehood was told. But despite the fact that both situations involved a falsehood, the processes that led to them were different and your relation to the man and his problem was different. In the first case you deliberately set out to keep him from filling the gap in his knowledge; you tricked him, you were treacherous and you failed to live up to his trust in you as a source of information. In the second case you felt the other person's needs and tried to fill it. A kindergarten teacher interrupted to say that Piaget asked children of different ages to tell him who was the bad boy in stories like the following. A man asked Johnny what trolley car would get him to a certain place. If he did not get there on time he would lose his head. Johnny wanted to help the man but gave him the wrong directions. Therefore, the man took the wrong streetcar, did not arrive where he had to go, and eventually lost his head. Another man in a similar predicament asked Henry how to get to the same place. Henry purposefully gave him the wrong directions but while the man was riding on the wrong trolley car, he became worried and therefore asked the conductor who redirected him so that he arrived at his destination on time. The man did not lose his head. Piaget found that little children would say that Johnny was a bad boy and Henry was a good boy because of the consequences of their actions and not because of their intentions. Someone said that Wertheimer was not asking us which boy would be labeled as bad by subjects of different ages. Wertheimer's concern was not at what age most children judged in terms of intentions or consequences. He wanted us to examine the structure of the two cases; a social situation where someone deliberately sets out to fool someone and fails in his attempt and a situation in which one sets out to help someone but unwittingly causes trouble for the person. Several students said that it made no difference for the man who did not reach his goal whether he was intentionally or unintentionally misled. If one was killed by malice or by stupidity, one was equally dead. The teacher said that Piaget found that adults took the children's intentions into account but young children judged solely in terms of consequences. A visitor remarked that the question of judging people in terms of the consequences of their behavior or their intention was an old problem in ethics and law. In the most ancient codes of law, intentions had been taken into account but the philosophical problem of which was more important, intentions or consequences, was a relative newcomer in Western thought. It was a pseudoproblem that reflected certain aspects of Greek and Scholastic philosophy. Some psychologists who are concerned with this problem consider judgments in terms of intentions to be a sign of mental maturity reflecting the ability to assume the abstract attitude. Wertheimer cut short the visitor's description of abstract-mindedness by asking, What is the difference in concrete situations between telling the truth and telling a lie? Some students said that the different behavior represented different attitudes toward the world which in turn reflected certain personality needs. Others pointed out that it involved different kinds of relationships to the world. Still others said that one's relationship to a person changed when he told him lies, that he was no longer a helpful person or a source of information but a trickster or an ignoramus. Someone interrupted to say that all this presumed that one had a relationship with the person that he wished to maintain or that he wished to develop such a relationship with him. We often meet people once and for certain restricted purposes. Such situations need not necessarily be affected by our telling a person a lie rather than the truth; one might only affect the recipient of the lie. The visitor said that sometimes one's relations to the social situation also changed when he told a lie; he was considered to be an unreliable witness or an inefficient consultant, a perjurer, a troublemaker, or a public nuisance. He might be ostracized or ignored because of it. [Some of ASL's students said that there were people who were unmindful about the consequences of their statements for other persons or for the social situation. All they focused on was their own interests, either their desires of the moment or the future advantages which such behavior might afford. Some people saw such behavior as a form of sport; it was fun to fool people. It would be of interest to study such people, those who were successful in life despite the telling of lies, and see how they compare with those liars who are unsuccessful.]

Wertheimer suggested that the students study actual cases in which lies were deliberately told, cases in which the truth was deliberately told, cases in which lies were unwittingly told and cases in which the truth was unwittingly told. He asked, What are the differences in these four kinds of cases? A student said that neither one's attitudes nor one's relationships were the significant factors in such cases. The group and the group's norms determined what was honest and what was dishonest, what was a lie and what was the truth. To be called correct one must act in terms of his group's norms. Violations of the norms are treated differently, depending on the status and power of the violator in the group or in other groups. Wertheimer asked what would happen if we, as a group, established the law that we had always to tell lies or had always to tell the truth to each other. What would be the difference in their effects on our functioning? A student said that if we consistently told lies instead of the truth, there would be no trouble because we would eventually learn to believe the opposite of what we were told. We would learn to operate on two levels. Another student said that it would complicate matters, that it would be impossible in some situations to keep up the pretense. It might bring about personality disorders or grievous trouble in certain social situations. Most students seemed content with the notion that as long as we would be consistent there would be no trouble. Wertheimer therefore suggested that each student try to live, first one way and then the other way, for a day or a week in order to see what difference it made.

A visitor said that young children often live in a fantasy world. They get so absorbed in their fantasies that they really believe them. Because of this they tell stories or make statements that are considered by adults to be lies. Is there a difference between telling a lie and acting out such a lie or fantasy? Someone said that fantasy became a lie the moment one took it for reality. This was challenged by other students who argued that some people acted out their fantasies so compellingly and coherently that other people changed their behavior toward them, thus supporting their fantasies. Another student said that there were examples in history in which untruths had been told about people, nations, and religions in order to glorify the king, the god or an ideology, and people still believe in these fabrications. He added, if Jesus appeared and told us that certain statements He was purported to have made were not true, people would not change their beliefs; cf. Dostoyevsky's *The Brothers Karamazov*. A lie becomes a truth when everybody believes it. Other students gave examples from the psychology of testimony to prove that people often told untruths in the name of the truth. [The difference between pretense and reality and the question of the difference between fantasy and a lie were the subjects of several sessions in Wertheimer's seminar on perception, which will be presented in another monograph.]

Someone returned the class to Wertheimer's illustration when he asked whether it would constitute a lie if the man in Wertheimer's example who had been given the wrong information had nevertheless managed to find the way. This led him to ask whether a statement's truth or falsity should be judged in terms of its logical structure, the motives of the person making it, its consequences, or in terms of whether or not it fitted the situation. After a pause Wertheimer noted that in logistics we were told that one could only know the truth of a statement in a system but not its truth *per se*. This led to a brief discussion of whether there were relative truths or absolute ones. A visitor gave Fascism as an example of a relatively closed system in which the welfare of the state was equated with honesty. If one told a lie for the good of the state, he was doing a virtuous thing. Thus we see that a statement is true depending on the system in which it has been made. Someone objected that this was not true. He claimed that Nazism was a social system in which it was not honesty but brutality that was highly evaluated. Wertheimer remarked that perhaps a person who was brutal and was evaluated highly was not evaluated because of his brutality per se but because the evaluator's mental field was narrowed to see only the purported results. All he focused on was the purported good it did for the state. He added that the act or item of behavior should be studied in relation to its structure in order to find out its meaning in the situation and to see its role in it before we called it an example of honesty or brutality. Labeling it Nazism or Fascism or Communism was not enough; we need to understand it. The session came to an end with a student's saying that according to what he had heard in class, if we knew that a statement was made for the Glory of God, or the state or one's political, social, or scientific ideology, it was irrelevant to judge it in terms of its truth. The system which it supported would determine how we should judge it. [A student in ASL's class commented on Wertheimer's statement that a lie disturbed the relationship between people; he said that this statement had not been thoroughly explored by the members in the original seminar. They overlooked the fact that the structure of our society is based upon the expectation of truthfulness. Even though two people have not had any previous contact, when one asks the other for information, an honest answer is expected; otherwise he would not have bothered to ask in the first place. If he does not receive a truthful answer, the structure is violated. If violations were very frequent in a society, they would destroy the structure of the society and would prevent the exchange of information for common purposes; personal relationships and working toward common goals would be impossible. Were the structure of our society based upon the expectation of untruth, it would be necessary to reverse one's answer to every question. This would not destroy relationships but would seriously hamper the formation and development of relationships. (An example of this is the situation in George Orwell's *1984,* in which the authority in power attempted to control the minds and the relationships of the masses by using double-think.) The student also asked, What do people mean when they say they are telling the truth? Illusions of perspective lead us to a conclusion which reflects how we *see* a phenomenon but not how it actually *is.* The possibility is immediately apparent that many people can be placed into situations where they would tend to acquire a certain perspective and believe it to be the truth. Others with other experience may consider these people blind or even liars, but they would be mistaken. There is a difference between giving an answer from a singular point of view and giving an answer without looking at all. It is advisable to be tolerant when one realizes that another person is giving answers from a restricted point of view. This permits the individual to retain his basic faith in the structure of society. It is also advisable not to ask those with a singular point of view, or lack of certain experience, to give you any answers. Piaget's study illustrates that an older person should not abrogate his responsibility for his own welfare by asking a younger, less-experienced person the road to travel.]

After-Class Discussion

A few students sat in the lounge discussing the question whether ethics can be studied by science. Someone said that Wertheimer's theses about values are common-sense notions. In ordinary life when we hear people say that this is good or that is bad or that this person is honest or dishonest we often are able to tell whether or not they are true statements. We often assume that there is objective evidence on which the statement is based. If we do not see the evidence we may reject the person's statement or refuse to act in accordance with it unless he can give us a reason. Furthermore, people want to know why they are right or wrong and why certain actions are required. Wertheimer's ideas of fit and acting in terms of understanding of the situation reflect this in concrete situations. Another student said that people often also say that they feel that something is right or wrong, good or bad but they cannot tell exactly why they feel this way. This is daily life evidence for the subjective nature of value, the egocentric thesis that Wertheimer has been attacking. The first student said that sometimes people say that they think when they mean that they have a feeling about what is required or fit. We need to know the context in which such assertions are made; this is also needed for the assertions in which one says that he sees, feels, and believes. Someone who had overheard the discussion recommended that we read Korzybski's *Science and Sanity*. It would save us from confusion. When Wertheimer sat down ASL assumed the role of the devil's advocate and defended the thesis of subjectivity of value and ethics saying that statements about value are devoid of what is called logical thinking; they are neither false nor true because they cannot be justified in terms of logic or facts. When Wertheimer suggested that the students collect cases which were clearly of a subjective nature and cases which were clearly of an objective nature, someone interrupted to say that it would be very difficult to find cases of the latter kind. Wertheimer remarked that an empirical study has never been made to find out whether there are more or fewer of the latter cases in life situations. When he challenged the dogma of Logical Positivism a student pointed out that the Logical Positivists have brought clarity into philosophical thinking by the analysis of language. Carnap and other Logical Positivists have shown why we have to reject the questions that are usually asked in discussions of ethics. The statements in these discussions are meaningless; they are expressions of emotions and can be neither true nor false. Such statements are simply nonsense, like singing in the bathtub to give vent to one's emotions. Such vocalizations of feelings do not even state anything about feelings. Bertram Russell in *Religion and Science* argues convincingly that value judgments are merely expressions by which we try to persuade other people to adopt our desires and that ethics is either an attempt to bring the collective desires of a group to bear on an individual or an attempt by the individual to cause his desires to become acceptable to his group. Recently Ayer in *Language, Truth and Logic* has demonstrated that ethical terms are unanalyzable because they are pseudo-concepts of an emotive language which express the feelings of the speaker or try to get others to feel as he does.

Wertheimer said that Wittgenstein once remarked regarding the search for an intellectual basis for ethics: This is a terrible business, just terrible. You can at best stammer when you talk of it. Wertheimer asked, What do you think of this remark? A visitor said that Wittgenstein is correct. If we look at the history of philosophy we can find no intellectual decision about what is the Good. Value and ethics seem to have eluded the intellect of man. One of

ASL's students said that it is really scandalous when one considers the situation. The intellectuals and moral philosophers have not been able to found ethics on a sound logical or philosophical basis, yet many schools of philosophical or social thought make claim to an answer. The visitor said that it is even more of a shocking thing if one realizes that the philosophers and intellectuals who claim that there is no valid basis for ethics and values make ethical demands on others in daily life and expect people to act in terms of certain conceptions of values. Why should the Logical Positivists expect others and even themselves to act ethically? The student who had referred to Russell's book said that Russell has said that even though it is true that science cannot decide questions of value, because they cannot be decided intellectually, they do rest on a kind of moral emotion which protects us from anarchy.

The last statement led some students to point out that values and ethics have adaptive values. For example, Thomas Hobbes had pointed out that due to self-preservation people were driven to make a social contract with a sovereign who was given the authority to decide what was right or wrong, good or bad, just or unjust. In recent years the theory of evolution has been used to show how under the pressure of the struggle for existence a person and a people develop a moral code. Even though intellectual or logical analysis has not given us an answer, biology has in the meantime come up with the answer, a naturalistic theory of ethics devoid of metaphysical assumption. Someone remarked that this biological doctrine of the nature of ethics has been used by Marxists, Fascists, Anarchists, Democrats, and Republicans; it can be used by anyone to justify as natural his doing whatever he wishes.

Wertheimer interrupted to recommend that the students read Schlick's *Problems of Ethics*. This book, which was written by the founder of the Vienna Circle, presents a modification of the Logical Positivists' position. Schlick writes that ethics must be applicable to problems of life, that negative reactions concerning ethics are not enough. Wertheimer went on to say that the Logical Positivists reject data of human experience on logical and not on empirical grounds. Moreover, they are using traditional logic, which has been found to be inadequate to deal with many problems in the foundations of mathematics and science. Their view of science and the logic they use may have contributed to their results. Perhaps their methods destroy the possibility to come to positive results. He left after he again suggested that we study actual situations in which people say that this is good, bad, right, wrong, just, unjust, required, not required. What are the reasons they give for such statements? Moreover what difference does it make for them and the social field when they make one or another assertion? Someone said that such a study will show that the basis for people's assertions about value is some divine or human authority or their feelings or some other seemingly arbitrary or subjective factor. After Wertheimer had left, one of the students said that Wertheimer had been mixing up issues. Moral philosophy in the tradition of the Greeks seeks the one or the few principles from which to deduce ethical behavior. What he has proposed is that we reject this approach; like Dewey he is telling us to focus on concrete ethical situations. Such an approach will never give us a theory but a lot of unrelated facts. Another student added to the criticism by pointing out that Wertheimer seems to believe that ethical situations are like problem-solving situations and productive thinking in that there are genuine solutions to problems of ethics that fit the structure of the situation. This leaves us with the problem of what is a genuine solution and what is the structure of the situation. Are they not emotional appeals? One of the students tried to answer these objections by referring to the arguments in the seminars on productive thinking. He pointed out that to many psychologists the solutions of problems in creative problem solving are due to nonlogical or irrational factors. Just as Wertheimer has been arguing for the need to develop a logic or logics of discovery for arithmetic, geometrical, and algebraic problems, he is making a plea for including problems of daily life where people have to make moral, ethical, or value judgments and decisions. Perhaps out of the study of such situations some theorists will get clues for a theory of value. The discussion ended with a student remarking that Wertheimer's view is like that of a poet or an artist but not of a scientist. The discussion reminds him of Robert Blake's poem in which he says that if one wants to do good one must do it in minute particulars and that the general good is the refuge of the scoundrel.

ASL left with his student. On the way to the subway the student said that Wertheimer's approach to ethics is similar to certain trends in traditional Jewish discussions of the oral tradition. He was curious about the relation of Gestalt psychology to those traditions, which seem to him to reflect the teaching of Rabbi Judah Loew of Prague (deceased 1609). When ASL told him that Wertheimer grew up in Prague, the student said that he would try to see him next time and talk with him. [When the student asked Wertheimer about the relation of Gestalt psychology to religion in general and Judaism in particular, he referred him to Professor A., saying something to the effect that Dr. A. might be more knowledgeable about such matters. The student did not pursue the question any further. The student has asked a question that has been asked by other people in recent years. ASL had not been able to answer it because of lack of information which is in part due to his reluctance to enter into discussion with Wertheimer about religious beliefs even when Wertheimer made inquiries. Thus several opportunities were lost to find out something about Wertheimer's religious background and beliefs. We are, however, at present trying to obtain more information about his early education and the relation of his paternal and maternal grandparents to the Jewish community of Prague.]

13
Hartshorne and May Studies

One day several students were discussing Wertheimer's criticism of the research of Hartshorne and May. It was pointed out that the former was head of research in Yale's Divinity School and the latter was director of the Institute of Human Relations of Yale University. The study was conducted under the general supervision of Thorndike and it had been planned to answer such questions as the following. If a child or youth is dishonest in one situation can we predict that he will be honest in another situation? What is the relation of honesty and socioeconomic background? What is the relation between knowledge of what is right conduct and conducting oneself accordingly? They studied about 800 children and used about 36 different tests. In order to complete their study in a definite time they had to use tests and situations that took a short time. They were also aware of the need to devise reliable and objective methods to study the results of character education, for example, the outcomes of Sunday School education. Among the tests used were tests of moral knowledge. After a description of an action, the subjects were asked to list everything that could happen, good as well as bad. After the description of a situation, the subjects were given a multiple-choice question and were asked to select the sentence that describes what was best to do. Another kind of test, a provocations test, was designed to find out just where the child would draw the line when tempted to commit an immoral act. They were given a one or two sentence story of what children had done under certain circumstances and were asked to vote on whether or not the behavior in these circumstances was right, wrong, or excusable. On the way to Sunday School Johnny matched pennies with other boys in order to obtain money for the Sunday School collection. Helen knew that if she ate the salad it would make her sick but she ate it in order not to offend her hostess. In still another test the child was tested to see what he regarded the most sensible, useful, and helpful thing to do in a wide variety of social situations. A boy is being teased by some children. What is the most sensible thing to do: (a) tell them that they ought to be ashamed to pick on him; (b) tell the child who is being teased to go home and not to play with the children; (c) propose that they do something else so that they won't think about teasing; (d) pick out the ringleader of the teasing and fight him. In addition to these tests of moral knowledge or judgment there were tests of conduct such as those described in the seminar. There were twenty-three such simple situations involving deception or dishonesty, five situations involving giving service, four involving inhibition of impulses, five involving persistence. Generally speaking there were 500 samples of imaginary situations in which the child had to make some kind of intellectual decision and 350 situations where he had to express a preference or desire, in addition to the 37 conduct tests. Wertheimer's comment in the seminar had ignored most of these tests. He had focused on four of the twenty-three conduct tests of deception. Moreover, his criticism ignored the fact that the tests were validated. The results were checked against the child's reputation among his teachers, classmates, and others who knew him, and against pen portraits of one hundred children based on all available data. The pen portraits were arranged by six to three judges according to the desirability of the character described. The reputations of the children were obtained by objective tests instead of collecting gossip about the child's reputation.

The results of the study showed that there was little evidence of unified character traits, that there is no such thing as a trait of honesty residing within the individual; what seemed to be a trait was actually habitual responses to various situations. Very few children cheated but very few children were honest in all of the twenty-three chances given to them. Most of them were honest in some but dishonest in other situations. There was no difference between the cheaters and noncheaters in the conduct tests in the way they answered the question designed to elicit their attitudes to cheating. There was very low correlation between moral knowledge and conduct in specific situations. Hence, there was no significant relation between moral knowledge and judgment and conduct.

Generally speaking there was a negative correlation between age and conduct except in the persistence scores. Older children tended to be more persistent than younger ones. The older children were much more inclined to be deceptive than younger children. When it came to moral knowledge or judgment, the picture was quite different: there was a positive correlation with age. As children grew older they became more appreciative of the ideal standards of society and their opinions and attitudes therefore conformed more closely to those of educated adults.

There were some sex differences, too. On the tests of helpfulness, cooperation, charity, moral knowledge, attitudes, and opinions the girls were slightly better than the boys, and on tests on inhibition the girls were consistently much better than the boys. They also found a high positive correlation between honesty and IQ. Inhibition, persistence, and service were also correlated with IQ. The correlation between intelligence and moral knowledge was as high as the correlation of one intelligence test with another; thus, intelligence plays a great part in the development of a child's social concepts and the ability to make ethical discriminations. Just as intelligence showed a very significant relation to honesty and moral judgment, so did the socioeconomic background of the child. The fifty highest and fifty lowest honesty scores were studied and it was found that the least-honest children came from home where there were family discord, bad discipline, and an unsocial attitude to children. These homes were in an impoverished community and subject to changing socioeconomic situations. The most honest children came from homes of an opposite nature. Siblings correlated around .50 on the honest test and children who went to Sunday School showed a general tendency to exhibit more desirable conduct than those who did not. But there was no correlation between these traits, including honesty, with frequency of attendance in Sunday school. Children who attended private schools, especially the progressive kind, were markedly more honest in their school work than children in the conventional public school.

Wertheimer had sat down during the recital of the results. After the student had finished, he asked: What do the results mean? A discussion followed in which Wertheimer raised questions from time to time. The main points of the discussion were as follows. One student said that it was assumed that the knowledge of moral behavior and the understanding of what was right or wrong or required in the situations used in these studies meant the same thing to all the children. Maybe in order to get children of lower IQ's or of the lower socioeconomic levels to understand moral behavior it is necessary to put the principle in a different act or situation. Due to a different frame of reference the actions may have meant different things to them; examples of moral behavior of one social group or person may not mean the same thing to people of a different social group. Hartshorne and May set up the study to disprove the thesis that there are no general moral principles but they may have shown that the meaning of a moral principle may be influenced by the situational context or by the actions in which it is expressed. Moreover, why should the children of one social class recognize the meaning of behavior that is common in another class? It is possible to clarify matters and to make children of the lower class realize that a certain principle is involved in a certain action which at first is seen to mean something else. Why did they not do this? Moreover, their tests may have been invalid. The judges who were used to validate the tests were of the same socioeconomic group as the makers of the tests and the subjects were upper- or middle-middle-class children. It would have been of value to ask the children the reasons for their answers in the knowledge test and to interview them to find out their reactions when the conduct tests were discussed with them. Different answers might have reflected the same moral principles and similar answers might have reflected different moral principles.

When we ordinarily think of an honest man we do not think of a person who will show 345 reactions to the 345 situations which are called honesty-provoking situations in our society. Honesty involves a certain conception of a person and his relation to his fellowmen. Just what is an honest man may therefore have eluded the investigators because of their thinking of certain responses that are called honest in certain segments of our society. Why should consistency of acting in terms of their conception of situational requirements be a sign of the trait of honesty? Does the everyday idea, the ordinary language use of the trait of honesty mean that one must show it in $\frac{2}{3}$, $\frac{1}{4}$, or in all situations? Is it just a question of the number of times one shows it in different situations?

It is well known that people's answers on attitude and personality tests may not reflect their behavior. Situational factors during the test, interpretations of, attitudes toward, and assumptions about the test, the test situation, the test items, and the examiner may influence one's answers. Thus the lack of correlation in their study between knowledge and conduct is no miracle. That they expected a correlation reflects the assumption that knowledge of moral principles makes one virtuous. An honest person may not know many of the ethical principles but still be honest. Just as the devil could quote the Scripture, people can prattle phrases about morals and act immorally. Moreover, an immoral and delinquent act may be committed by a child or a youth in the name of an ideal or principle. The question can therefore be raised as to what one learns when he learns a moral principle or an ideal. Does he really understand the principle or does he just memorize and repeat what he hears? To understand a principle one must be able to recognize it when it is transposed into another situation like Wertheimer's A-B experiments which test genuine understanding in problem solving and learning. Maybe there is a relation between knowledge of ethics or value and conduct when one really understands what the principle or value means in the living concrete situations of everyday life. The correlation with age fits the idea that moral behavior and knowledge are a repertoire of habits. As we grow older we learn to relate verbal rules because of the school courses and the principles of ethics that are preached to us. We learn the categories of verbal utterances just as we learn abstract terms like fruit. This is not a sign of real abstraction, but is just mechanically learning by rote.

Some students were interested in the fact that some children became more dishonest with age. What kind of social atmosphere does this reflect? On the one hand we are taught to have a consistent verbal ideal about value and conduct and on the other we are taught dishonesty in certain phases of social life. It seems that the subjects' upbringing on the one hand fostered an increasing commitment to ideal values and on the other hand demanded a realistic pragmatic attitude. Wertheimer said that he once had discussed a similar question with a lady who claimed that her boy was a very noble individual. When he asked her whether the boy would act in a noble manner in a number of concrete situations she exclaimed, After all, you do not expect him to be an Idealist. ASL described how he nearly lost his job because he refused to steal. The boss-baker told him to steal the baked products left at a certain grocery store by a competing baker because that baker had stolen from one of his customers and he had been blamed for being negligent in making deliveries. Some students said that there are numerous examples in business, in school, in love, and in play where cheating, lying, or stealing is considered the thing to do. Only naive individuals do not compromise and because of that they often lose out in the competition for love, fame, and material goods. Someone pointed out that the study reflects what exists in our society. People learn moral principles but they also learn that when confronted with a concrete situation they must react to its requirements, to the pressure of the situation, and the needs of the moment. We see this every day. People do not tell the truth; they withhold information and help; they indulge themselves sexually and violate the moral code concerning sexual conduct. Yet these same people will know what is good and proper to do. Moreover they have learned that it is not only not fashionable to tell the truth but that it often gets one into trouble. One must learn not to give people everything they ask for or to go out of one's way to help others. One knows what he should or shouldn't but that does not mean that he would or wouldn't. With age we not only learn to say in public what is considered proper but we also accommodate ourselves to the various pressures of the social and business world and learn to live to the norms of what is proper.

The sex differences reflect our society's attitude to women. Women a either on pedestals or in the gutter. A slight flaw in a woman's character makes her a candidate for the gutter but the same flaw in a man is considered to be a sign of manliness. Because of our society's double standards the woman learns from an early age to be inhibited and cautious. Boys are allowed, in fact encouraged, to sow their wild oats.

The discussion turned to the relation of intelligence with immorality. The results fit in with the thesis that criminals are born, that people are immoral because they are moral idots. Wertheimer pointed out that some studies in Europe and in the USA indicate that some people in jail may be lower but others may even be higher in intelligence than people outside of jail. Referring to the Hartshorne and May results, someone said that the results seem to support the idea that the poor and the immoral are what they are because of their lack of intelligence. Wertheimer asked whether it is true that only the well-to-do are honest, helpful, and kind to others. Perhaps the so-called criminal acts or immoral behavior of poor people is different from the acts of the well-to-do and this could be explained by examination of their social conditions. He then asked who were the children of the study? When someone told him, he said that maybe the results hold just for the two schools of New Haven and for the three schools fifty miles from New York City. Perhaps it reflects the social atmosphere of the communities and the kind of education the subjects have received at home, at school and in Sunday School. He repeated the criticism given in the class that the study focused on the responses and not on processes that led to them and went on to say that other groups of children should be checked before we accept the conclusion as generally valid. One of ASL's students wagered that the results would not be the same among the Chasidic parochial school children of Brooklyn and added that the results would not be the same if the students were from the Amish of Pennsylvania and communities where people do not separate ideals from practice.

Wertheimer asked the students to think of other possible explanations of the results of the Hartshorne and May studies. It is too sweeping a generalization to say that what we call traits of character are just an and-summation of specific habits. Of course there are people who are deceitful and put on an act of honesty; the same goes for being helpful and kind to others. But there are people who are genuinely honest, helpful, and kind. Even little children are sometimes able to detect who is genuine and who is putting on an act. They know the difference between the aunt who gives them money and candy but does not like them and the aunt who may not give them money and candy but loves them. Before he left, he told the students about a group of children he had observed in a certain institution in Germany. They were considered to be moral idiots and were restrained and treated in a very strict manner since it was believed that they were unable due to lack of intelligence to control their impulses, to see the consequences of what they were doing, and to understand what was right. But when a new director who did not believe this theory took over the institution and gave the children freedom and opportunities to learn to control their lives in the institution, the children changed for the better. Their delinquent behavior was not due to their lack of ability to realize and to understand what was moral; rather, they had been narrowed down in their view of themselves and the social situation by the social atmosphere of the institution. The way they had previously been treated in the institution helped to perpetuate their animal behavior. The change in the social atmosphere of the institution helped broaden their mental horizon and elicited moral behavior. He went on to say that he too once had some experience with such children. He found that instead of their lacking a moral sense they were very sensitive to injustice, to wrong done to them and to others.

After he left, some students said that Wertheimer had expressed a romantic attitude but others said that there was evidence from the treatment of delinquent children in school and at home that bear out his thesis. ASL, who had been a social worker for the WPA Truant Case Work Project of the New York City Board of Education gave examples to support Wertheimer. He also gave examples from his own personal experience. (He had grown up in a slum and a tough neighborhood and some of his best friends and protectors were the gangsters.) Few children and youths really enjoyed being cruel and bad. The ones that broke rules did so for a variety of reasons: to be noticed, to be a Somebody, to be popular, not to lose status, because it was a form of play, or even because it was a way of obtaining money for their own needs or their parents' needs. Sometimes they just started out to have some innocent fun but it ended up in a delinquent act. Some of the things for which these children were arrested were sometimes dealt with in an informal manner in middle-class schools and neighborhoods. What may be a naughty prank in the middle-class school or neighborhood may be a delinquent act in the slum. Also sometimes a child may get a reputation of being a delinquent or being bad. Then people may regard him as a delinquent and treat him as such even when he is good. Other people in the community may support or encourage his delinquent behavior because of profit or gratification to themselves. Sometimes the only friends the delinquent may have are these very people who exploit him sexually and financially. A few students argued that although there are factors on the stimulus side, there may also be factors on the reactive side, such as the personality characteristics that are expressed by the immoral behavior. Furthermore, because of other personality characteristics perhaps some get caught and others do not get caught. The discussion ended with someone saying that just giving such individuals freedom and being kind and considerate to them does not lead to their becoming moral; sometimes they take advantage of such treatment to do what they darn please.

A few days later the same students were again discussing morality. Someone pointed out that Wertheimer is of the opinion that people are nice and kind, good, honest, and helpful but it is true that most people are looking out for themselves and will do what pleases them. Some will be more careful not to hurt others while they are doing it because of their past learning. Someone said that it is all a matter of conditioning when Wertheimer sat down. He asked those present to suppose that it were true that morality is a conditioned response or a series of conditioned responses. Would a person become conditioned not to make responses which we call dishonest and to make responses we call honest just as a rat learns to avoid certain stimuli and approach others? A visitor remarked that Wertheimer seemed to be implying that there was an innate moral sense in man. Wertheimer said that questioning the validity of a certain theory of how one learns morality does not impl innateness. A student pointed out that the conditioning theory was attractive to him because it rejects the idea that man is constrained to behave morally. It is a theory that increases the possibility of human freedom. ASL's student objected to this by saying that the student was assuming a certain conception of genetics that had been challenged in recent years. Moreover, one may think of the social field as a set of constraints that molds behavior in a certain way and builds certain constraints into the brain. Wertheimer stopped the argument by saying that he could understand why the visitor objected to the idea of innate reflexes or patterns of behavior but why should he assume that if learning is involved in the development of moral behavior that it is similar to what occurs when a rat or a dog is conditioned? The visitor said that Wertheimer seemed to be implying the discredited rational man model. Such a model is not as scientific as the model that implies that man is a creature of habit, of cultural conditioning. Someone pointed out that people experience guilt feelings, remorse, anxiety and even grief because of not acting in terms of the moral standards or rules of conduct but rats or dogs do not. The visitor went on to say that according to Hartshorne and May there appears to be a greater consistency of honesty at adolescence. By then the child had integrated the specific habits around certain verbal statements or rules of conduct. Moral principles do not stem from one's conscience but are learned rules or principles that reflect the values of the society. In fact values can be conceived of as formulas for handling conflicts.

The student said that the issue was not whether morality is innate or is a system of rules or values developed by a society's culture and that a member of society learns these ready-made formulas. The issue was how one learns or what one learns. He asked whether the culture is stamped into the person by rewards and punishments and whether or not moral behavior was a mechanical playback of what was put into the person. He asked whether the cultural pattern is a structure that stamps out behavior like a die stamps out coins. This is implied when one says that morals and values are imposed by an outside authority on a passive child.

The visitor pointed that it is not as bad as some make it sound. The adult is not imposing his will on the passive child. Adults have a greater understanding of the consequences of an action and are in a better position to judge that certain behavior is harmful and therefore bad and that other acts are beneficial or good. There seems to be in man a natural tendency for empathy, a need for social agreement, an ability to realize what is good for others and an ability to generalize rules. But all this is learned behavior.

Wertheimer was called away as an argument developed over whether or not morality is basically a matter of respect that grows out of fear for an authority. Without the fear of an authority's disapproval of violation there would be no adherence to the morals or values of a culture. Morality is associated, therefore, with punitive sentiments and not with the idea that it leads to welfare. In prescientific times the authorities were gods; now the authorities are natural laws. Since the appeal to the gods and to natural laws has proved inadequate, we now relate morality to human welfare and enlightened self-interest, but it is the same appeal to punitive sentiments.

14
Discipline

In his class on teaching and learning Wertheimer asked the class how they would deal with a pupil who disrupts the class by talking, fighting, and who is willfully disobedient. A graduate student said that a recent study by Wickham has shown that such behavior is not bad. He went on to say that the study showed that teachers are overly concerned with such behavior and do not realize that from a psychological point of view such behavior may be good and natural in terms of normal personality functioning. In the Wickham study teachers and mental hygienists were asked to rank various kinds of behavior from the worst downward. The teachers ranked as worst behavior fighting and talking but ranked lowest such behavior as shyness. Mental hygienists, however, ranked the behavior in the reverse order. In view of this study it is advisable that teachers be taught mental hygiene and be sensitized to real personality problems instead of having a rigid moralistic attitude that restrains the children from acting naturally. An elementary school teacher protested that the student is overlooking the fact that such behavior disrupts the classroom. It interferes with teaching and thus the teachers were being honest in their answers. She predicted that in view of the fact that mental hygiene is now a required course for a teaching license, teachers in the future might rank the conduct the same way as the mental hygienists. This would mean that they had learned the values of the mental hygienist or that they were expressing the stylish philosophy about education, but it would not mean that shyness would be more of a problem to them in the classroom than talking and fighting. This led to an argument about whether it is possible to assume that what is considered natural behavior in terms of a theory of personality is proper behavior in all life situations. Maybe what is permissible in psychotherapy is not permissible in teaching because different situational requirements exist in the classroom than in the therapist's office.

Someone brought the class back to Wertheimer's question by saying that before one can answer it one must ask to whom the child is a problem: to himself; to the teacher; to his classmates? From the teacher's point of view the child may be disruptive but he and his classmates may enjoy it. The elementary school teacher protested that the reality of the classroom is being ignored. In order for teaching to go on such behavior is not allowable. It is all right for a child to act out his hostility in the therapist's office or in therapeutic situations but in order for teaching to go on such behavior is not permissible. ASL illustrated the teacher's argument with what happened when he was doing practice teaching in an elementary school in the slums of Brooklyn.

There were several bad boys in the class that he was teaching. Since he believed that it was important to make the lesson more interesting in order to gain the attention of the bad boys he ignored the noise they often made. One day the children in the front of the room told ASL to tell the boys in the back of the room to stop making so much noise. Thereupon the troublemakers began to make more noise. Luckily it was toward the end of the lesson; the regular teacher took over and bawled out the boys for misbehaving and sent one boy to the principal's office for being bad. ASL's supervisor (college professor) thought that he had done the right thing and said that it is best to ignore the noisy children and to concentrate on the lesson. He also suggested that ASL tell the regular teacher to permit him to rearrange the seating of the children so that the troublemakers were in front of the room and were separated from each other. When he told the teacher what his supervisor had said, she said that she had tried this plan but it did not work. She had isolated them in the back of the room so that they would not disturb those who wanted to learn. She added that these children were of low IQ and did not belong in the class with the other children. She also described her efforts to be nice to these children and said that it all seemed so hopeless. Maybe they belonged in a special class or were in need of individual attention. ASL told her that he grew up in a tough neighborhood and went to a school in which some of the pupils were gangsters. Once they helped elect him captain of the school's police force. He made them members of a special task force and found that not only did they not cause any trouble but they helped the police force and the teachers to maintain order on the playground, in the hallways, and even in the classroom. He wondered whether something like this could be done to the troublemakers in this school. She said that the principal would object to rewarding the children for being troublemakers. Wertheimer thereupon asked the class whether such a plan really rewards the troublemakers. Why look at the matter of disobedience and discipline problems in terms of rewards and punishments of the individual? What attitude or doctrine of man and society does such a statement reflect?

Another elementary classroom teacher said that ASL had been successful because he was the gangsters' friend. They had elected him and in order to keep him in office they had to behave. Moreover, as members of a gang they obeyed their leader and had rules to help them function. They applied the same techniques to keep their gang in line and to keep the other school children in line in order that ASL be a successful police captain. She went on to say that she would not be surprised to hear that these gangsters were stricter in enforcing the school's rules and handing out punishment in the pupil's court. ASL said that she was correct. There were times when he had had to beg the gang's leader, who was his friend, not to be so severe because the parents, teachers, and the children themselves would protest. Incidentally, the leader several times reported himself and asked ASL to give him a demerit because he had violated the school's rules but had not been caught or noticed. The elementary school teacher said that although it may be true that children will do what is required when given the responsibility in social situations, it does not always work. In her school the gangsters would never agree to such a plan and if they did they would terrorize the children in order to get what they wanted. They were basically hostile and aggressive. It was therefore necessary to use external controls with them. However, if someone would develop the kind of relation that ASL had had with his gangster friends it might be different. In her school a boy such as ASL would be called teacher's pet and other names. He would lose the respect of the others because he had joined the teachers. ASL said that he appreciated her remarks because when he had been in the fourth grade he had found out that his cousin was studying to be a school teacher. He had said to her, Please do not be a teacher, children will hate you.

Someone said that ASL's story was a special case and showed that bad children know how to manipulate the good ones. He went on to say that the best procedure in a case of willful disobedience is to expel or to isolate the child, or to send him to the child guidance clinic for treatment. After psychotherapy the child would be able to behave in school. We have to treat the causes of the child's behavior and not the symptoms. When Wertheimer asked the student what may be the causes of disobedience in school, the student said that psychoanalysis would be needed to find out what they are. The elementary school teacher challenged this student's faith in psychoanalysis by pointing out that studies of the effectiveness of psychoanalytic therapy had been carried out. And, these studies did not show that it was any better than symptom removal therapy by conditioning or other common-sense methods of habit formation and habit breaking. Another student said that psychoanalysis does not remove the causes because it cannot remake the personality. What is necessary is the proper education of parents and teachers so that they will behave properly toward the growing organism and not create traumatic situations. A visiting college professor rejected psychoanalysis as mysticism. He referred the students to Knight Dunlap's *Freudianism, Mysticism, and the Scientific Method.*

A child psychologist pointed out that when it comes to child development, Thorndike's and the Behaviorists' ideas, as reflected in the Hartshorne and May studies, are in agreement with psychoanalysis. A child, even an infant, is not a passive piece of putty but is a dynamic organism with basic drives which makes him react to things as they affect his sensorium. The child is capable of indulging in rather complex forms of behavior or mental activity. Freud has spelled them out in his theory of psychosexual development and Susan Isaac's books have shown that they actually occur in nursery school children. Moreover, if one reads Piaget's books one can see that he too has spelled out mechanisms of mental functioning that are similar to Freud's. Someone supported the speaker by saying that recent work at Yale shows that Freud's ideas can be reduced to drive reduction concepts of the Behaviorists; but another student objected by saying that Piaget's theory is a cognitive theory not an instinct theory. During this discussion Wertheimer said that perhaps the doctrine of man that Piaget's work reflects is closer to psychoanalysis and to drive reduction theories than it looks at firsthand.

The child psychologist said that she agreed that Piaget, Freud, and the Yale researchers have a common theoretical core; they are against the theologically oriented view of man which posits innate ideas of morality. The Hartshorne and May studies showed that one learns morality and that moral principles are a product of mental maturity. Freud's and Piaget's work also point to the fact that the understanding of moral principles and behavior depends on mental maturity. Children are not born moral but rather gradually learn the moral code and moral behavior. The fact that the adolescents and older children in the Hartshorne and May study showed consistency in moral judgments but the very young did not, is in line with Piaget's finding that with age one develops the mental mechanisms needed for acquiring and appreciating the abstract principles on which moral judgments are based. Susan Isaacs has shown that Piaget's findings about mental mechanism fit in with Freud's, for example, Piaget's egocentric stage of development (egocentrism) is similar to the psychodynamics of the personality prior to the development of the child's super ego. The super ego develops out of the child's experience with adults; he introjects their behavior as he sucks in nourishment. He first sees no difference between what is outside or inside of him but gradually he learns to differentiate between himself and others. This is precisely what Piaget describes when he describes the mind of the infant and the role of what he calls imitation in learning about the world. Psychoanalysts talk about the child incorporating and identifying with others, particularly adults in the process of the development of a super ego, which is the source of moral judgment. Piaget seems to be saying the same thing when he talks about how the child assimilates and imitates the world outside of himself. Both say that the child goes from an organism-centered being to a social being due to his experience and both stress developmental stages that all humans pass through as they go from animality to sociality. This led to some examples of behavior of infants to illustrate that the infant is not the innocent creature that it is commonly supposed to be. Someone interjected that instead of having less of what we ordinarily call animal or beastly behavior man has more. The young infant is a seething sea of sensuality and destructiveness.

Wertheimer interrupted to remark that maybe it is unfair to animals to say that men behave like animals. Why are psychologists so certain that willful, destructive, and blind behavior is characteristic of animals? Maybe the behavior just described is not beastly behavior but behavior manifested by men under certain conditions and is not at all typical of animals. He challenged the students to look at actual behavior of animals and of little children instead of accepting it as a dogma that animals behave like a man does when we say that he is acting like a beast. Wertheimer also rejected the notion that a child is just an immoral egocentric creature. Maybe the child is not born as a rugged individualist who is blind to the requirements of the situation which he is in; maybe from the beginning he is a social creature showing sympathy, kindness, love. Someone remarked that what Wertheimer was saying fits Alfred Adler's ideas of social interest and Harry Stack Sullivan's idea of the empathic relation between the infant and the mothering adults in its environment. But these theorists have been shown to be dealing with superficial aspects of behavior. The real dynamics are what Freud and Piaget describe. The session ended with Wertheimer pointing out that in discussing what to do with the disobedient child they seemed to assume that the behavior stemmed from the child's personality, his lack of intelligence, and that little mention was made of the social field. When mention was made of the social situation it was viewed as restraints on the expression of the child's natural behavior. He ended the discussion by asking whether they believed the idea that bad children are moral idiots.

While ASL was walking with Wertheimer to the subway station he told Wertheimer that he seems to differ from Freud and Piaget in assuming that man is naturally good and that man is born with a moral sense. This belief went against anthropological knowledge that shows that in different societies people have different moral principles. Wertheimer pointed out that the issue is not whether or not people learn moral principles or whether all societies have the same verbal generalizations or principles about morality but what the people do in concrete situations. One may do violence to a particular situation and not meet the requirements because of a general moral principle just as one may not do violence and meet its requirements without knowledge of moral principles. He rejected the idea that knowledge of principles leads to moral behavior. ASL asked whether this means that knowledge does not lead to virtue. It has been the belief of scholars from Plato to present-day scientists that the pursuit of knowledge leads to goodness. Wertheimer said that there are examples in which scientific and philosophical pursuit of knowledge led to nonsense as well as to evil.

15
Piaget's Thesis

A few weeks later the same students were sitting in the school's lounge discussing Piaget's work on moral development. One of the students was acquainted with Piaget's work. In response to questions, he said that Piaget was not interested in child psychology but in how man gains knowledge from the world and that his aim was to develop an experimental approach to the problems that have plagued philosophers. It is a kind of genetic experimental epistemology. When ASL said that experimental psychology can also be called experimental epistemology, the student said that Piaget is approaching the problem via the social and biological evolution of man. Just as a human being develops from a one-celled into a multicellular animal and reflects aspects of human evolution in his development so does each person reflect the mental development of the human race.

Someone interrupted to argue against this approach by saying that it reflects Haeckel's biogenetic principle, that ontogeny not only of man but also of every living creature is a recapitulation of its phylogeny, that the development of the embryo is an abstract of the history of the genus (this doctrine had previously been proposed by Meckel; Darwin also referred to it in the *Origin of Species;* it was developed in detail by Fritz Müller). Contemporary biologists, however, have rejected it; it is biologically invalid. Moreover, why should we assume that a completed human organism who has recapitulated the biological evolution of the species reflects in its development the evolution of man's mind or the history of his society's cultural evolution? Hitler believes this because of his race doctrine but what justifies Piaget's assumption? Suppose we exchange at birth a child who represents 200 generations of pure Andaman stock with a child who represents 200 generations of pure North German stock. The former would grow up to be a German and the latter to be a primitive person. Why should we assume that early in human history man was a sensual creature, that he was stimulus-bound and that due to mankind's historical experience man slowly evolved into an ethical creature? The first altruistic man would have been killed by the savage ones. Someone said that he was taught that before the advent of Christianity there were no universal ethical principles and that there was no concern with humanity. The former student said that the ethical codes of ancient Sumeria reflected more humanism than the codes of laws promulgated by some Christian governments of modern as well as ancient times. He went on to describe accounts of anthropologists, among them churchmen. Father Schmidt indicated the existence of a high moral sense in a so-called neolithic culture. Another student said that he was taught by his Christian school teachers that man was once perfect and that the so-called primitive people's beliefs and conduct were deviations from what was once an ideal way of living. Man has deteriorated. Modern science has rejected the idea that men were first perfect and became corrupted in time; social scientists instead developed the thesis that men are now reaching perfection, that modern man is a superior being, that there is an increase of humanism and ethics as man develops along the road revealed by reason and science. He went on to say that the philosophes of France rejected Christianity but replaced it with themselves as the élite of mankind. Another student said that Lowie's *Are We Civilized* demonstrates that it is untenable to talk of higher and lower stages of cultural development. Piaget seems to be reflecting the bias of European man. Just as some religious people regard Christianity as the apex of the evolution of ethical principles so do agnostic intelligentsia see European man as the apex of human mental development. The writers of universal histories have claimed that mankind has reached mental maturity in European man and even social anthropologists until recently have believed that European man is on a higher stage of social evolution than men of other continents. Contemporary anthropologists have rejected such ideas of the evolution of moral and mental development of mankind but Piaget has not. Another student also attacked Piaget's doctrine of development by referring in a negative way to Lévy-Bruhl's thesis of primitive mentality. He said that such doctrines have been used to justify imperialism and race doctrines.

Wertheimer sat down when ASL was arguing that it was unfair to criticize Piaget because of his use of an outdated model of evolution. It is a fact that children develop from one kind of being to another. The previous speaker said that this was known before Piaget's time. Shakespeare's King Lear and the Sphinx in *Oedipus Rex* talk of the ages of man; men have always been tracing the growth of man from a baby to a corpse. Moreover, in ancient times and at present in primitive as well as in modern society one is held responsible for one's actions only after a certain age, the age of understanding. Little children, the feebleminded, and some others are considered not to have the ability to make moral judgments, and are not held accountable for their delinquent actions. A student said that it has been generally assumed that a child is a miniature man. Just as he is physically smaller so is he mentally smaller. Except for size there is no essential difference between an adult and a child. Wertheimer asked whether it is true that ordinary people believe that a child is a miniature man mentally and physically. He asked, Who in our society say this and when and why do they say this? Someone pointed out that the clothing manufacturers who are making long pants for children are making miniature men out of little preschool boys but mothers and fathers who raise them know that they are not miniature men. Someone raised the question of whether the idea is connected with the concept of equality before the law. A child like an adult is equal before God and the law. He has equal rights as a human being. Adults have to protect and care for him as for any other human being. Wertheimer asked whether wearing long pants makes a child think like a man. He went on to say that maybe the miniature man thesis is a dogma that students of psychology are inculcating in the minds of men. He suggested that we study ancient and modern literature and history as well as their laws and their conception of moral responsibility to see whether a bad child was considered to be a little bad man, a small-sized edition of the same contents. Someone remarked that they might find the reverse to be true, that the children are considered to be innocent, good beings, and that when adults are good they are compared to the perfect sinless infant. He went on to say that Freud's doctrines of infant sexuality and the death instinct reject this idea. Infants and children are amoral creatures who become moral because of the rewards and punishments of the adults. Psychoanalysts see the child as a being bursting with behavior that we call bad. When adults are bad they are often said to behave like children. It seems that in our culture the common man thinks that the child is an angel but the psychologists think that he is a devil.

Someone pointed out that Thorndike has argued that the minds of men, children, and rats are essentially the same; there are no qualitative differences between them but only quantitative differences. This reflects modern science's view of nature and is counter to Aristotle's, which focused on the qualitative instead of the quantitative features of a phenomenon. According to modern science quantitative changes lie at the basis of qualitative changes. Because of difference in the amount of experience the infant is qualitatively different from a two year old, the two year old is different from a three year old, etc.

Someone defended Piaget by saying that Piaget could say that at each stage of development there is a change in mental structure, not merely a container with more matter in it. There is always a certain kind of structure that results out of the organism's adjusting (assimilating and accommodating) to its environment. The structure changes when it cannot deal with new experience. This change produces the qualitative features of the organization of the human mind at each stage of development. Piaget has rejected the idea that the child's mind is a piece of blank paper on which experience is enscribed. The mind is an organization, a system of some kind that tries to maintain itself under changing conditions. It is an active organism not a passive receptacle. The student went on to compare Piaget's conception of the levels of development with Köhler's idea of *Physical Gestalten*. He concluded that the only difference is that Piaget prefers to use words from biology and Köhler uses concepts from electrodynamics and quantum mechanics.

Wertheimer said that it is possible to water down the differences but he prefers instead to sharpen the differences because it might lead to clearer understanding of what is involved. He went on to object to Piaget's idea that there are higher and lower levels of mental functioning. They reflect a certain philosophical orientation rather than the actual state of affairs. ASL interrupted to say that Köhler (*Mentality of Apes*) wrote that the apes could not master the problem of dynamics that was involved in one of the tasks that required building a stable structure out of several boxes in order to reach the banana. Studies with nursery school children show that little children also fail to solve such a problem. Furthermore, some of his own examples of productive thinking show children need a certain mental maturity to solve certain kinds of problems. Wertheimer answered that it is possible sometimes for parents and teachers to use methods which will reveal to little children the structural requirements of some of these problems. A method of teaching that works for an adult or an older child may not work for a little child. He rejected the implication in Piaget's thesis that it is not possible to arrange situa-

tions to produce higher functioning in children or in others who are functioning on the so-called lower level of mental ability. He gave Gelb and
Goldstein's work with brain-damaged patients as an example of what he
meant.

During another discussion a few days later a student said that he had been
reading Kurt Lewin's *Dynamic Theory of Personality* and could now see why Gestalt psychologists reject Hartshorne and May and Piaget's studies. They reflect
the Aristotelian approach to science. Their concepts are dominated by the
idea of regularity in the sense of frequency. They seek what is the common or
the average kind of behavior at a certain age instead of seeking the dynamics,
what brings about the particular concrete case of behavior. Because of this
they are interested in how the average and not the individual child behaves
on their tests. The individual child behavior is fortuitous and unimportant;
lawfulness is a matter of the frequency of the occurrence of an event of behavior at a given age or state. Piaget in particular considers his abstractly defined classes of behavior as the essential nature of the particular children in
the class. The idea that a human passes through certain stages into an adult
also reflects Aristotle's chain of being. At first the child shows a vegetative
soul and finally he actualizes his rational soul. Someone protested the parody
on Aristotle and the misinterpretation of Piaget's stages of development but
the proponent of Lewin dismissed the remarks as minor details. He went on
to say that Piaget's approach is not like the Galileian approach of modern science in which the focus is on the full concreteness of the particular situation.

Someone interrupted to say that Gesell's and Hartshorne and May's approach may be Aristotelian but Piaget's is not. Piaget openly rejects Aristotelian logic and Aristotle's philosophy. The previous speaker said that the
rejection of Aristotle's ideas does not mean that he does not use them. In fact,
most biologists and psychologists reflect the Aristotelian approach to science;
but they reject his metaphysics. Wertheimer pointed out that Piaget's work
uses traditional logic's approach to thinking. Abstraction and classification are
used the same way as in Aristotle's logic. He went on to say that Piaget's description of the structure of the mind is in terms of mechanisms in the person
that grow due to experience. There is a relative neglect of the social field in
which the child is growing up, for example, that the child judges in terms of
consequences may be a result of the social field of his home. The concept of
egocentrism is an organism-centered view of the child's behavior which neglects the factors in the social field of the child or the test situation that
brought it about. He suggested that we read the second and third chapters of
Lewin's book and compare his approaches with Piaget's methods.

A student said that one cannot put Piaget into the same pot with
Hartshorne and May. The former used a clinical approach and the latter used
a psychometric approach to study the moral judgment of children.
Hartshorne and May gave children several items on a multiple choice test
after presenting them with a moral judgment situation. Piaget also gave children a moral judgment situation but let them answer at will. Someone
pointed out that Piaget analyzed the children's responses in terms of his
theory; he looked in the children's responses for clues to support his theory.
Hartshorne and May were also theory-centered; they made test items that reflected their theory and the child had to select the answer from them. Thus
in both studies the experimenter had certain conceptions of what was moral.

But Piaget tested the children by use of methods similar to the old-fashioned subjective tests whereas Hartshorne and May used modern objective tests. A visitor interjected that it is significant how masterfully Piaget is able to organize the children's answers to fit his theory. He went on to say that Piaget rarely cites negative instances; for example, it is well known that some children show at a very early age mathematical ability and some master two or three languages by the age of five. Such behavior contradicts Piaget's ideas of mental development. Someone pointed out that only a few children are able to learn two languages and that Forlano's and Pintner's studies have shown that children from bilingual homes have lower IQ's. It seems that learning two languages confuses children and may even thwart their growth. One of ASL's students pointed out that it is not uncommon for Jewish four year olds to speak Yiddish as well as English and that traditional schools among Jews have taught children two languages by the age of five with no adverse effects. Since Piaget lives in Switzerland, it is surprising that he did not study the language development in children in homes that use both French and German. Thereupon the child psychologist asked why replications of Piaget's work with American children have generally supported Piaget's findings. It is a fact that children are animistic, everything is alive to them, physical objects just like people are good, bad, hurtful, and helpful to them. Goodness and other perceived qualities are in the object. The child does not differentiate between himself and others and is egocentric in his demands and desires. His early conception of space is in terms of his ego; he acts as if he is the center of the system of coordinates for localization of things in space and things exist only when he sees them. He believes that his behavior produces many natural events in his environment. Space, time, causality, and even objects are often seen in terms of his actions and his immediate sensory-motor experience. Below the age of six children do not adequately use speech as a means of conveying information to each other. They repeat what the other person says or just engage in collective monologues. They cannot pass on information to others when asked to do it, they distort and make idiosyncratic transformations of the statements they are asked to convey. They demonstrate magical thinking, for example, they believe that some human or divine agent created natural events and that human actions and natural processes are related. To children inanimate objects and animals are alive in the same sense that a human being is alive. They group apparently unrelated things or events together into a mixed-up classification and they fail to see the connection between events or things. They cannot consider several aspects of a situation simultaneously. In social behavior the child often fails to follow the rules of a game and yet at the same time he believes that the rules are sacred and inviolable. They make moral judgments in terms of the consequences of an act and not the intentions of the actor. On the one hand the child is egocentric and on the other he manifests a unilateral respect for adults. The child's behavior generally speaking does not reflect the fundamental laws of logic; only with age does his thinking become regulated by the principles of identity, contradiction, excluded middle, and of sufficient reason. This is due to having developed the mental structure needed for understanding them. One can say that at first the child does things with little or no adult understanding and that with experience there develops mature mental structure analogous to the structuralization of function in biological development. In response to an objection she said that perhaps we should accept Piaget's theory of the evolution of the mind as we accept Darwinian evolution even though it is as full of unanswered questions. We have no other theory and it gives us a consistent and complete picture of human development; Koffka's *Growth of the Mind* and Werner's *Comparative Psychology of Mental Development* do not offer psychologists a better alternative.

Wertheimer said that Aristotle's theories dominated men's minds for nearly two thousand years perhaps because it seemed to be a complete and consistent view. Although in the early Middle Ages facts were known that contradicted Aristotle's theories the facts were overlooked because of the desire for a consistent view and also because Aristotle's theory became a kind of faith. Should we ignore the facts that are against Piaget's theories because of faith? Before Wertheimer left he said that it is of importance to remember that child psychologists who are believers in Freud's theory find evidence for it in their observation of children and that those who believe in Adler's and in other theories find evidence for their theories in the behavior of nursery school children. He then suggested that we take a naive look at children and forget theories for a while.

On the way to the subway ASL told Wertheimer that he is teaching a course, Psychology of Children and Youth, to parents in a middle-class neighborhood. He was planning to present to them Piaget's studies and to ask them to predict what they would expect to find among their own children. They would also be asked to replicate with their children Piaget's study of moral development.

Experimental Outgrowth and Suggestions

A few weeks later ASL reported to Wertheimer what had happened in his class. The results and Wertheimer's comments were incorporated in ASL's lectures in educational psychology in the spring semester at Yeshiva College and were used to stimulate research projects. What follows is based on the lecture notes.

The parents tried out on their own and their friend's children the story of the two boys X and Y who gave the wrong directions to a man; X did it unintentionally and Y did it purposely. Most children (aged four to six) said that Y was a bad or not a nice boy and some spontaneously expressed shock at his conduct. When the children were asked to give their impression of the two children, some said that X should have told the man to ask someone else or should have asked his mother or big brother or sister to tell the man the directions. Some children said that both X and Y had done wrong; X for assuming that he knew the directions or because he did not think before talking and Y for trying to fool the man. Further questioning revealed that a few children who said that Y was bad added that since nothing bad happened to the man, Y would or should not be punished and that the man himself would think that Y did not really know the directions. Some of the same children said that the man would scold X or Y when he saw him or would tell X's or Y's mother that he had misled or tried to mislead him. The few children who had said that X was bad said that the man might think that the boy wanted to fool him and that the man might become angry and not think that the boy did not mean it; he might even hit him when he saw him next time. Nearly all the children differentiated between the behavior of X and Y in terms of their intentions.

The parents varied the story by asking a child to imagine that he was asking the directions of X and Y. Some children said that they would never again ask either of them for help because it was no good. A few said that they would never play with them again. A few would regard Y's behavior as a joke. Some blamed themselves for not asking the conductor of the trolley car. Many of the children said that they would not ask X or Y for directions but would ask an adult or a policeman. When they were asked what they think about the man who asked X and Y, they said that the man should not have asked children because they do not know enough, he should have asked a policeman or an adult. In discussing these results with Wertheimer it was planned to change the instructions so that a child would be free to give his impressions of what the children had done before being asked who is the bad boy. Wertheimer also suggested that more meaningful situations be created that involve ordinary life experiences.

In order to obtain some meaningful situations we asked children of different ages as well as adults to relate incidents in which they had tried to be helpful but were not of any help, incidents in which they unintentionally hurt someone or broke something as well as situations in which they intentionally tried to hurt, to fool, and to do damage. The instances are not now available to us. We gave them to students to base their studies of moral judgment after we had tabulated them in order to make some generalizations about the number and variety of acts of intentionally or unintentionally doing damage or hurting someone. The children between four and seven years of age gave very few examples of intentionally doing such things but beginning with the age of eight there was an increase of such conduct. There was a sharp increase of intentionally deceiving, trying to get even and doing harm to others. Unintentionally doing such things seemed to be somewhat more frequent among the younger children. What do these results mean? Is it merely due to the older subjects' better memory and more opportunities to do such things or could it be that little children are more sympathetic, kind, and helpful and that they get into trouble because of their good intentions? Our students hypothesized that the results prove the proverb that the way to hell is paved with good intentions. Wertheimer, however, pointed out that perhaps there is a fundamental error in viewing moral behavior in terms of intentions and consequences. Instead of trying to understand the place, role, and function of the act in the social situation of which the actor is a part, it focuses on issues that are related to theological and philosophical disputes. An adult who sincerely believes that only intentions should be considered, would in certain circumstances react violently because of the consequences for him of another person's unintentional behavior. He might get angry at the person, call him a bungling stupid fool, and even strike him. On the other hand, a person who is committed to the doctrine of consequences would under certain circumstances excuse a person whose behavior resulted in negative consequences to him. The meaning of consequences and intentions may be a different thing to a five year old from that which it is to an adult. We need to reconsider the question by finding out what children really do. Perhaps adults too should be studied in situations which involve them and others in acts of so-called immoral behavior in order to find out how they view such situations and their behavior in them. We have to find out what people understand by the idea of intentions and consequences in their every day use of the words instead of the philosophical discussions and definitions of the terms.

Our students as well as Wertheimer objected to Piaget's assumption that the marble game is a valid test of a child's understanding of rules. The marble game is an existing cultural artifact like baseball and football and not something the child himself has created. It is a complex game for a child to understand; the rules are not his but are imposed on him by an authority. Moreover to win a game might under certain conditions seem to him to be an aggressive and mean act; therefore, he changes the rules. He might not like to lose his marbles nor like to take the other child's marbles. He might give the other child his marbles as a sign of friendship, sympathy, etc., and he might expect and desire that the other child not take his marbles or give him marbles. He might not like to be a loser and might not feel competitive. The marble game is an and-summation of behavior; there is no structural requirement that demands that this or that rule be adhered to. Since one rule does not necessarily lead to changes of the other rules, the child could change one without regard to the others. Instead of focusing on the change the child makes in the rules we should ask what is the direction of the change. Just what does it do to the interpersonal situation? Some children might be more concerned with the interpersonal situation of the game than with the mechanical application of rules, especially when a rule interferes with the interpersonal situation. In short, the game is a ritualized role with no inner connection between its parts except as they affect the child in the giving or taking away of marbles. Some adolescents playing football, chess, or checkers sometimes show the same reactions to rules as Piaget's children did to the marble game. Some see the rules as absolute, natural principles and would never dream of modifying them to make a more interesting game or to avoid taking advantage of the other person's errors. Some American adults argue about baseball as if the rules were laws of nature. In view of this Wertheimer suggested that we study how children learn to play together and study the rules that they spontaneously make when left to their own devices. He conjectured that they may invent rules or change the rules to make a better game in which one does not take advantage of someone's errors nor tries to trick the other person in order to win. He also said that the rules they make and change may reflect their social relations, their attitudes toward each other and to people in their social world. Someone pointed out that Wertheimer's proposals imply that it is natural to be social and cooperative and that competition is due to certain kinds of social conditions. His view reflects the doctrine of the Utopian Socialists, the Marxists, the Anarchists, and the Social Democrats, but the history of mankind shows that victory and success go to those who are good at seizing the opportunity to advance themselves. Wertheimer reminded him of some studies among primitive people that belie this thesis. The student remarked that these people have lost out to aggressive, individualistic European man.

Wertheimer objected to the idea that man is from the beginning an egocentric person and gradually becomes socialized. ASL said that according to Piaget the child is first an individual and later a social being. Because of this difference in the doctrine of man's original nature, they differ in their ideas of moral development. Wertheimer answered that it is not just a matter of an abstract doctrine of man; it has consequences for treatment of people. Children, even little ones, seem sometimes to know when they made an accident, when something happened that they did not mean to produce. They expect to be treated differently at such times than when they purposely do something bad. Moreover, even when they make an unintentional accident they may feel sorry and want to help to fix up the mess, to rectify the consequences of their behavior. Of such things Piaget's work tells us nothing.

When ASL pointed out that Piaget's stages of development could be reinterpreted in terms of processes like physical Gestalten, Wertheimer said that to do this is to ignore the essential differences in their approaches toward human behavior. ASL then asked him why he objects to the developmental levels. Maybe they represent certain equilibria states under certain social conditions. It is therefore necessary to find out what maximizes and minimizes them instead of to reject them. Wertheimer pointed out that perhaps the different stages are not higher or lower stages of mental development but represent various ways in which an equilibrium results under different field conditions; they may be aspects of one genotypical process, one underlying phenomenon. Furthermore, adults may show egocentrism under certain conditions. Animistic thinking, juxtaposition, syncretism, and other so called lower-level behavior can be found among adults. Why stick to what happens in Piaget's tests? Why not observe people and children in daily life in order to find out how frequently or infrequently as well as when and where they show such kind of behavior instead of saying that certain kinds of behavior are characteristic of children or adults? When ASL argued that Piaget's work may be of value to get norms for teachers and parents so that they would know what to expect from children, Wertheimer said that maybe the results could lead to rationalization of certain curricula and methods of teaching.

Informal Session on Evolution of Morality

Wertheimer was discussing with ASL the results of a study in which children of pious parents were asked who was the bad boy, the one who intentionally or the one who unintentionally gave the man the wrong instructions. Most children of the first through the fifth grades of their religious school said that the boy who intended to fool the man was a bad boy. No one said that the boy whose good intentions led the man astray was naughtier than the boy who intended to do it. A few, however, felt that he was somewhat responsible because one should not give directions if he is not sure, but the children would not say that it was the same thing as fooling people. The little children, aged 5 to 8, spontaneously expressed shock that somebody would intentionally deceive someone under such circumstances. Some of the older boys, aged 11 to 13, tended to be more jurisdictional in their judgments. They quoted the Talmud to base their decisions. Some said that the two children are too young to be held legally responsible for their actions, that they represent different ways of responding to the needs of people. They wanted to know more about the children's backgrounds and what could have led to their conduct. Wertheimer was making suggestions for variations of the study when the student who had been defending Piaget's thesis in class walked by. He called her over and told ASL to read some of the protocols to her. She said that the children seemed to be very sympathetic, they sounded like the ideal children one hears about in Sunday School. ASL told her that they were Chassidic children who from early childhood live according to certain laws and rituals. She was surprised at the reasoning of some of the young children and wondered whether they really understood the laws that they were applying. ASL said that their education encourages questioning and thinking of hypothetical cases when they study the *Oral Law*. It is not unusual for a ten year old to challenge and even stump his rabbi (teacher) with a tough question. When she raised questions about the consequences for their future personality development, Wertheimer said that it would be of interest to study the kind of person this kind of education produces. How would they get along in the world in future years? He added that they showed the kind of sympathetic behavior that he has often seen in children. The student said that she is puzzled by the data and by Wertheimer's assumption of a natural moral sense. Children are not born moral. In early childhood their world does not contain moral principles because they are in the sensory motor stage. When they learn moral principles, these principles are sacred rules like the laws of a Divinity or nature. The laws are fixed eternal restraints. The child does not know that they are man-made values. They are absolutes because of his inability to differentiate between the objective and subjective features of his experience. The child is a naive realist. The child is unable to differentiate between the view of things from his own perspective and from other people's points of view; he cannot take the view of others and cannot shift perspectives because he is egocentric.

Wertheimer interrupted to read a protocol of a six-year-old child who discussed the two boys' conduct in a rather judicious manner. The child gave arguments pro and con his decision. The student wondered whether the child really understood what he had learned in school or was just repeating it. ASL said that the principles were not taught to him in terms of behavior of little children or of the modern world. They were learned during the study of the *Oral Law,* which dealt with civil law cases of adult life about 2,500 years ago. She then wondered whether the parents and teachers ever used contemporary examples in disciplining or exhorting the children. ASL told her that the models they used were East European people from small peasant villages in which there were no buses or policemen. She was troubled by the results but went on to say that there may be evidence in the protocol that the rules are regarded as sacred, absolute, unchangeable and that the parents and adults are all knowing people; children see rules as commands, external principles. ASL said that these children are encouraged in their studies to question the adults and to challenge them for reasons for the statements or rules. They believe God's laws are absolutely true and eternal but they study them with a questioning attitude. The adults, those who are ignorant as well as those who are philosophically minded learned scholars, also have this belief. The adults as well as the children discuss, interpret, and reinterpret these laws and apply them to various concrete and hypothetical cases. A child may contradict an adult in these discussions. She wondered whether this attitude of questioning was actually the same process in the child's mind as in the adult's mind; due to experience with children his own age, the child transforms the adult's authoritarian principles and the external restraints, to internal principles. As the child matures to the level of abstract reasoning he begins to transform them into rules of justice. Only then the rules become immanent conditions of social relations. They are the laws governing the social equilibrium, to use Kurt Lewin's field theory, and in order to obey, the child no longer needs external restraints. The initial respect and feeling of solidarity that exists in their interpersonal relations are seen to require the laws. Thus justice becomes a concern because of the reciprocity and equality between individuals.

Wertheimer pointed out that apparently the children ASL had studied were functioning on the adult level at the age of 5 or 6. She said that Piaget has shown that the child's conception of justice is related to his idea of how violation of the laws governing the reciprocity between people should be dealt with. First there is expiatory punishment in which one has to be severely punished for doing wrong. This occurs during the stage when rules are seen as restraints by adult authority. She brushed aside Wertheimer's counter-examples from the protocols and went on to say that later on punishment is not merely for the sake of expiating the offense but there is sensed requirement in the situation for compensatory action or behavior in order to reestablish the bond of solidarity or reciprocity that has been broken by the violation. This occurs when the rules have become inner principles of action. The child finally goes from an attitude of concrete reciprocity to ideal reciprocity. Now the child does not think of punishment or revenge for the violation. He now realizes that there is no end to vengeance, therefore he forgives the wrong-doer. Thus the child first goes from blindly reacting to what is bad to a realization that the punishment should be related to the action and the actor's intention, and then finally he develops the idea of forgiveness instead of punishment. There evolves a morality of forgiveness and understanding because the individual has the mental structure that enables him to put himself in the shoes of the transgressor. Since he can realize what the other person's intentions may have been, he is able to show a deep concern for justice. He is no longer concerned with punishment but rather with making the transgressor realize how he has broken the bond of reciprocity. ASL pointed out that it is significant that Piaget's evolution of moral judgment in the child follows the beliefs of some Christian theologians. Piaget's first stage fits their description of the behavior of mankind before the Mosaic laws were revealed to man, the next stage, that of reciprocity, reflects the idea of the Old Testaments and the last stage is the law as given in the New Testaments which stressed forgiveness for sin instead of punishment. Wertheimer objected to the classification of the levels of moral behavior as higher and lower. Perhaps this description of moral development reflects a certain cultural point of view. He challenged the idea that little children usually seek vengeance for wrongs done to them and that only those who have interiorized our culture's ideal principle of justice will forgive wrongs done to them. He pointed out that perhaps this may be true for the illustrations Piaget used in his studies but in daily life there are many examples of forgiveness and of genuinely trying to help others to do what is required among children as well as among adults. Such behavior may even be more common in children than adults. We need to study actual behavior in the daily lives of children and adults to validate Piaget's conclusion before we assume that this is the way people learn to be moral. Instead of worrying whether his age levels are correct or whether there are three, five, or seven stages, let's find out why individuals behave the various ways they do and what can be done to change their behavior.

After Wertheimer left, the student said to ASL that she cannot understand Wertheimer's objections to Piaget, who is demonstrating that there is a progressive concern in development with the needs and feelings of others; a sense of justice develops with this progressive concern. One develops a respect for authority out of realizing that it produces reciprocity and equality of treatment of human beings. ASL said that Wertheimer does not deny that experience molds the person but experience may blind one or open one's eyes to the requirements of situations. He rejects the idea that one is first a greedy grabby creature who gradually grows into an altruistic creature. The self is an outgrowth of field conditions and therefore we need to know more about the field conditions that produce different types of egos or selves. Instead of assuming that a certain type of self is the ideal self and then looking for the age at which most children or people show behavior that reflects this kind of ideal self, why not study the actual behavior of people of different ages and find out what is similar, what is different, and how such behaviors are brought about?

ASL said that Wertheimer is reflecting the attitude of contemporary biologists and anthropologists when he rejects the idea that certain levels are higher than others. Perhaps from a certain theological point of view one can justify the arrangement of the levels as higher or lower but those who have another theological view might arrange the levels differently and/or object to the descriptions of the levels. She pointed out that Wertheimer seems to be placing the concrete-minded behavior of children and naive and primitive people at a higher level. ASL said that at times it seems that he is doing this. But he has never said that it is a higher level. He merely says that it is not a lower level. To understand what he means we have to understand his concept of genuine productive thinking. He is arguing that even little children can act in a productive and genuine manner.

After class the group resumed the discussion of Piaget's work. The same student defended Piaget's use of the recapitulation theory by insisting that just as biologists have not rejected Darwinian evolution because of the many questions it raised we should not reject Piaget's theory of moral evolution because of certain complicating facts. The idea that the mind of man evolved may prove fruitful for and will give focus to research. The development stages may be aspects of an equilibria state and perhaps can be explained in terms of physical Gestalten but this does not preclude Piaget's thesis. Furthermore his thesis is not contradictory to Gestalt psychology because Piaget is not proposing that the basic elementary bits of the mind are the sensa of traditional psychology or that experience is accumulated in the brain in the way that the associationists have proposed. At each stage there is a unified system and there exist certain characteristic ways of behaving that are due to the nature of the particular system's structure. Kurt Lewin, Koffka, Werner, and even Wertheimer have said similar things but Piaget has been painstakenly describing the characteristics of the system. His concept of developmental stage is similar to Kurt Goldstein's idea of capacity level.

ASL pointed out that Wertheimer had in the 1936 class on logic criticized in a very sharp manner Kurt Goldstein's thesis of abstract and concrete mindedness. One objection was that he is neglecting the field conditions that bring them about. Wertheimer objects to the idea of a capacity level when it is described as if it were independent of the field conditions of the organism.

He is not denying that children and adults may at times function at different capacity levels. Wertheimer would want to see those who talk of levels to describe under what conditions children of one level can act at different levels. That children normally all act in a certain way is not enough; we have to discover what are the variables that bring it about. To put it in terms of physics, we need to minimize and maximize the so-called characteristic behavior of a level and to find out what transformations in the present field are needed to produce in children the behavior of the various levels of behavior instead of describing them as fixed maturation levels through which one must pass because of some inner organismic growth tendency. She said that such an approach is impossible at present; we have to settle for what Piaget is doing. Before she left she said that Wertheimer's attitudes would keep psychologists tied down to their data and keep them from theorizing. It is easy to criticize a theory. It is difficult to make a theory if one has such a critical attitude to his data. [In retrospect, it seems that Wertheimer was objecting to a possible use of Piaget's data and the support it would give to adherents of certain ideological points of view with which he disagreed. One can read into Piaget's theory the ideas of the social evolutionists of the nineteenth century, certain ideas of Christian theology, as well as ideas of the Enlightenment, of Associationism, of Psychoanalysis, and even of Pragmatism and John Dewey's ideas of ethics. Wertheimer often liked to ask what the world would be like if a certain theory were true. In view of this, what would the world be like if Piaget's theory were true? How would it affect the treatment of children if this theory were true?]

16
Experimental Outgrowths

Justice

1. In an after-class discussion of Piaget's theory of moral development, Wertheimer objected to the thesis of higher and lower stages, saying that it reflects a dogma about morality and justice. He added that it is important to understand the field conditions and the reason why one reacts in one of the three ways when wronged: retribution, reciprocity (restitution), and forgiveness. Some students pointed out that many people would agree with Piaget if they were asked to rank retribution, restitution, and forgiveness; they would rank forgiveness highest. ASL said that this may be true because of certain ideological and religious principles but the judgments of concrete situations may show different results. Wertheimer remarked that this calls for investigation, not dogmatic assertions. ASL therefore told his WPA Adult Education class that there are various ways in which people react to injury that is done to them by others and that in the history of mankind there are various ways in which societies have, by custom or by law, reacted to crime. Generally speaking, there are three ways: retribution, restitution, forgiveness. As an example of what each meant he read sentences from Piaget's description of the three levels of morality. No reference was made to Piaget's theory. He then asked them to rank a court's verdict by indicating which one they thought was the best, the most moral way of acting, which was next, and which was least ethical and moral, in a case in which a man's cow was stolen. All thirty-five students placed retribution in the last rank; 20 students (57%) ranked forgiveness first and 15 (43%) ranked restitution first. Many students who put forgiveness first said that it is the ideal taught by their church. It is the thing Jesus would do, it is in line with the Sermon on the Mount, and it is the most humane thing to do. A few said that maybe the man needed the cow for food or milk or that he had no cow whereas the other fellow had many cows and therefore would not mind the loss too much. Some students ranked forgiveness first because it was what they would do if someone had wronged them; they were not concerned with violation of social laws or property taken from them. Some of the students who ranked restitution first did so because they thought that it avoided the issue of morality. Some saw the matter as a choice only between retribution and forgiveness. The same day ASL had conducted the study with 15 adults and youths who were well versed in Talmudical and

biblical law. At first they balked and asked, What cows or situations do you have in mind? When ASL refused to elaborate, most said that forgiveness is of very high value but that if one's cow was stolen it would be unjust to tell the robber to keep the cow and to go and sin no more. They said that the victim should forgive the wrong done him but that justice requires that restitution be made for damage done or for the stolen property. They refused to rank the verdicts.

When the answers were discussed in ASL's class, some of the students objected to the view that restitution avoided the moral issue. They claimed that it was the thing to do in terms of the Pentateuch. Other students rejected what they said and pointed out that the Old Testaments' Ten Commandments state that thou shalt not steal and an eye for an eye and a tooth for a tooth. Since it is a sin to steal, one must be punished; restitution does not suffice. ASL stopped the discussion and read from *Exodus* the laws concerning theft. One of the students noted that in Hebrew law theft was treated more like a civil than a criminal case and the thief did not have to bring a sin offering to the temple for theft. ASL asked the class again to rank the three modes of reacting to the crime. There was now an increase in ranking restitution as first. Six students changed from forgiveness to restitution and one changed from restitution to forgiveness. The seven students who shifted were interviewed the next day. The student who changed from restitution to forgiveness said that he does not believe in religion and private property. The class discussion made him realize that he had really meant forgiveness and not restitution. The six who had shifted from forgiveness to restitution said that they now realized that forgiveness would not return the stolen property or repair the damage; restitution seemed more just. Forgiveness meant that the offender was let off scot-free and that the victim was penalized. He would like to have what was stolen from him returned to him or the damage repaired even though he forgave the person and would not like to have him jailed or beaten for the crime. When asked why they had judged differently before, they said that they did not think of concrete wrongs but of an ideal; that it is ideal to forgive. One student said that he had thought that the Bible would demand retribution and had believed that our penal codes are due to our society's not living up to the Sermon on the Mount but enforcing the Mosaic Code.

In view of the above findings it was decided to concretize the three modes of reacting to crime and injury. The subjects were told that a man stole a cow and sold it to a butcher who slaughtered it. The thief was eventually caught and brought to court where he confessed to the crime. Three people saw him lead the cow to the slaughter house and the sheriff had found the cow's hide in his house. Such thefts have occurred through the ages and in different countries different verdicts have been handed down by their courts. Here are four court verdicts for such a crime: (a) the thief is sentenced to a two-year jail term; (b) the thief is sentenced to have his hands cut off; (c) the thief is commanded by the court to pay the owner an amount equal to the current price of his cow so that the victim could buy another cow; (d) the court tells the thief not to steal and tells the victim to forgive the thief the wrong that was done to him because vengence breeds more crime and injury. The subjects were asked the following questions and were encouraged to give reasons

for each answer. Which sentence of the court was just? Which was unjust?
Which sentence do you think the victim of the crime would prefer? What sentence do you think the defendant would prefer? If your cow had been stolen
which sentence would you have preferred? Which verdict was the verdict of a
civilized court? Which verdict was the verdict of a biblical court? Which verdict is from our country's court? Are we a Christian country?

The subjects were 20 students of another of ASL's WPA Adult Education
class. All were high school graduates and about half of the class had 1 to 4
years of college. All were Christians and members of the liberal church in
which the class was being conducted. The percentages of responses to the first
two questions were as follows.

Verdict	Just	Unjust
pay money	45	0
forgiveness	25	0
jail	30	5
cut off hands	0	95

Several subjects who selected forgiveness as a just sentence commented that
Jesus said that it was the thing to do; Christians should forgive. They gave as
an example the woman caught in adultery. Those who selected payment (restitution) were concerned with the loss suffered by the victim of the theft and
those who chose jail were concerned with rehabilitating and/or punishing the
thief so that he would not do such things again.

The percentages of responses to the questions which dealt with who would
prefer each of the verdicts, were as follows:

Verdict	Victim	Defendant	Subject
pay money	25	0	80
forgiveness	0	100	20
jail	75	0	40
cut off hands	0	0	0

Their reasons now reflected the feelings of the persons involved. Some of
them reasoned that the victim would expect that the thief would want to clear
his conscience and therefore would accept the light two-year sentence as pen-
ance, since he expected to be punished. Some said that the victim would not
expect restitution; a man steals and keeps his loot and pays by going to jail.
However, most subjects said that if their cow had been stolen they would want
their cow back or at least an equivalent amount of money. And all said that
the defendant would like to go scot-free; therefore he would prefer forgiveness.

The answers to questions which required identifying the courts were as follows:

Verdict	Civil	Biblical	USA
pay money	35	5	0
forgiveness	35	80	0
jail	35	0	100
cut off hands	0	15	0

Most of the subjects interpreted the term biblical to mean New Testament; the others answered in terms of stereotypes of the Pentateuch in Christian ideology. Twelve said that the USA was a Christian country and eight said that it was not.

This study has been replicated recently by an Albany High School student, Karen Smith. Her subjects were 80% Protestant, 10% Catholic, and 10% Jewish respectively. The results were similar to those obtained in 1938.

2. We have often used the following demonstration on which to base a discussion of justice. Each student is told to interview a few people and to give them the following questions and tasks. What is justice? Give examples of it. What is injustice? Give examples of it. In discussions of ethics with regard to juridical matters, the concepts of restitution, retaliation, repentance and forgiveness are often used. (The concepts are defined.) How would you rank these concepts from the most ethical to the least ethical? Which would be most preferable for the victim of a crime?

Last year the students of the course the Doctrines of Man in the Behavioral Sciences interviewed individually 45 Ss, mostly college students. (The last question was not asked of 12 Ss.) Robert Giblin tabulated the protocols submitted by the class and we present the summary to stimulate research. It is interesting to compare the results with current discussions concerning morality and justice in developmental psychology. It is also interesting that in many years of teaching we find for the first time that restitutuion is ranked so high: 40% ranked it first (most ethical), 21% ranked it second, and 54% thought it would be most preferable for the victim of a crime, thus giving it higher rankings than the other concepts. Perhaps this is indicative of a trend of thought in our country which has led recently to the introduction of bills in the Congress of the United States and in some state legislatures to provide restitution for victims of crime.

Percentages of answers which implied presence for justice and absence for injustice of various characteristics were as follows:

	Justice	Injustice
equality, fairness, forgiveness	37	22
law and order, social responsibility	27	35
protection of moral and civil rights	25	19
just punishment or just desserts	11	24

Percentages of various rankings from most ethical to least ethical:

Rank	Restitution	Forgiveness	Retaliation	Repentance
first	49	28	7	9
second	21	30	7	42
third	25	26	14	30
fourth	5	16	72	19
Preferable for victim of crime	53	26	15	

Kindness

In 1938 ASL tested some of Wertheimer's conjectures concerning the judgments of kindness and goodness by telling children stories that described people's activities and asking them various questions. After hearing a discussion of the results Mrs. Margaret Brown became interested in knowing how contemporary slum children would react to such stories and questions. She therefore asked Alice Kanouse to present the stories ASL was using in a class project to children in a New York City slum. (She questioned older children in the same neighborhood about morality.) The stories, which were told to each of 12 third-grade children and 10 kindergarten children, most of whom were black, were as follows:

A. In a neighborhood where poor children lived there was a sale in a store that was selling candy. A child was looking through the window at the candy. He wanted some very much but he had no money to buy it. A man walked out, saw the boy and gave him some candy.

B. In the same neighborhood another poor child was looking at the candy in the window when a man walked out. Some candy fell out of his shopping bag. The man picked up as much as he could. He did not notice and therefore did not pick up a few pieces. The little boy picked up the candy and ate it.

When the stories were told to girls, they were sometimes worded so that they were about a girl. We present the questions together with a summary of the answers given to them by the seven girls and five boys in the third grade. Immediately after the first (A) story, the subjects were asked, What do you think of the man? What kind of man was this person? What do you think of the child? All five girls said that the man was nice, kind, generous. Five of the seven boys also said this, some of them adding explanations and elaborations, for example, I think the man was generous to give him candy; He was nice, he was the candy man of the store; He's a nice man and I'm going to pay him back; He's a nice man and a gentleman. But two of the boys were suspicious of the man, questioning his motives. One said, I think the man stole the candy, he could be a robber or a thief or something; the other said, I think the boy shouldn't have eaten it because the man could have put poison or something in it, he maybe was a nice man but maybe he was an old junky that gives candy to kids to have poison. The five girls' comments about the child were that he was a good boy, OK, poor, wanted candy, got candy. Two of the boys said that he was poor, another said that he was nice and still another said that he was very sad. Other reactions were that the child appreciated what the man did and that he should thank the man for giving him candy.

After the second (B) story, the subjects were also questioned about the man and child in it. The reactions were mixed, including positive and negative evaluations as well as neutral statements. Two girls said that the man was nice to leave some candy and another thought that he would have given the child some of the candy that fell, a few pieces not all of it. Still another girl said that the man didn't know that the candy fell out. Only one girl said that the man was mean. The boys were more critical; one said that the man was nice to drop the candy, another said that the man didn't know he dropped it, and a third merely noted that the man was a candy eater. Four of the boys criticized the man for not noticing that he dropped candy or for not picking i up; for example, I think the man should have looked at the bottom of his bag to see if there was a hole and should have got two shopping bags; I think the man should have looked back to see if he dropped any candy on the ground; the man should have picked up all the candy—he could have known that someone would take the candy. Reactions to the child were mixed. Three girls said that the child was poor, hungry, and ate the candy; another girl said that the child was not too kind because he should have told the man that he dropped the candy; still another girl didn't think one should eat candy from the ground. Five of the boys criticized the child; for example, for eating the candy because it dropped on the ground, because it was not his, for not giving it back, for stealing it, and (quite irrelevantly) because the boy could have "fell off the roof and had no business on the roof." Another said that the boy was so hungry that he couldn't stand it and had to eat the candy; another simply commented that the boy wanted the candy.

After both stories the children were asked, How is one man the same or different from the other man? One girl said that the men were the same; three girls said that one man gave candy and the other didn't; one of them added that the first man was nice enough to give candy and the second man could have done better than he did. Another girl said that the men were not the same because their names were not the same. Physical appearances were the bases of differentiation for three of the boys; they don't look the same and they're not alike; one man has one face and the other man has a different face; because of the way the face looks, if it got a scar or something. Another boy said that they differed because everyone is not the same or alike. The other boys described something that happened in the stories or evaluated the men. When the subjects were also asked to compare the boys in the first and second stories, they gave a variety of answers. Some answers stressed poverty or hunger; for example, I think he was poorer than the boy in the first story; he was hungry and couldn't help himself so he ate the candy. Some just mentioned the boys' behavior or evaluated the behavior. A subject's answer was not always consistent with what he said in the previous questions about the boys.

The final questions asked were the following: Who is kind? Who is not kind? Who is good? Who is not good? Who did the right thing? Who did not? Which man would you be like? All five girls said that the man who gave the candy (story A) was kind and that they would be like him. Four of the girls referred to this man when asked who was good and who did right, and one girl referred to the boy in the first story. All the girls answered that the man in the second story (B) was not kind; four of them also said that he was not good and did not do right, and one girl referred to the boy in the B story. The tendency to give positive evaluations to the characters of the A story and negative evaluations to those in the B story was also found in the boys' responses, but it was not so pronounced. For example, in response to the questions of who was not kind and who was not good, three boys referred to the man and three referred to the boy in the B story and one referred to the boy in the A story. To the question of who did right, five referred to the man in the A story and one each to the boy and man in the B story. Five said that the man and two said that the boy in the B story did not do right. Six said that the man and one said that the boy in the A story was kind; four said that the man and the others said that the boy in the A story was good. Thus about nine-tenths of the boys' responses to these questions differentiated between the acts in the two stories. Their responses to the last question were more ambiguous. Three said that they would be like the first man and another apparently meant this when he said that he would be like the nice man who tried to help people and tried to cooperate with people. But two boys said that they would be like the man in the second story; one of them gave an irrelevant but revealing answer, that he would be like a nice man who works all the time.

It is of interest that the answers to the last series of questions showed more of a dichotomy in evaluation of the two stories than the preceding answers; for example, immediately after the B story only one girl gave a negative evaluation of the man, saying that he was mean, but in the later questions four or five girls referred to this man when asked who was not kind, not good, and did not do the right thing. Moreover, the responses to the later questions did not yield as much concern with the character's motives, or as many neutral responses, or as varied a basis for differentiation, as did the answers to the earlier questions. These results suggest that the nature of the questions may make a difference. To ask who is good or not good, who did the right thing, who did not, etc. invites certain types of answers and may direct the child's thinking to external actions or consequences instead of to intentions or motives. When you ask someone how much a sack of potatoes weighs, he often tells you the weight without mentioning the quality of the potatoes or how they were grown or how they are going to be used; this does not mean that he may not be concerned with or aware of such matters or that he does not know the answers to questions regarding them. Analogously, if the questions had been limited to the last series, we might have concluded that the children tended to evaluate the first story positively and the second story negatively because we did not have the information which was given by the earlier questions.

The subjects' reactions to the two stories were even more varied among the ten kindergarten children. Two of the children referred to white and black people; for example, when asked how one man was the same or different from the other man, they said because one man is white and the other man is black; their answers to the last series of questions repeatedly referred to the black and white man or black and white boy; and one of these children had said after the A story, when asked what kind of person the man was, that he was a black man. Some children gave very brief answers but others elaborated their answers into stories. In some stories a child asked his mother for money with which to buy candy. One child said that the boy went home to ask his mother and father and both bought him candy; when asked who was kind, this child said that the mother and father of his story were kind and later referred ambiguously to a man in a third store. Another child referred to the two boys in the stories but added that one cried and wanted candy because his brother had gotten some. The children were critical of the boy in the B story for eating the candy because it did not belong to him, because he would get sick, or because he should tell the man who dropped it. Some negatively evaluated the man in the B story because he dropped the candy, for example, immediately after the B story, one child said spontaneously that he thinks that the man would go back and pick up the candy; when he was later asked who was not kind, this child said that the man who dropped the candy wasn't kind because he should go back and pick it up. Negative evaluations of the man in the B story were given for varied reasons, for example, because the man wasted the candy by dropping it, because he could get the boy sick by letting him eat the dirty candy, because he did not give the boy candy.

Generally speaking, these results again contain counter-examples to Piaget's thesis. These children as well as the slum children of the prewar studies showed that some children were aware of intentions and motives and judged behavior accordingly. Even the other children's responses, although not strictly counter-examples, contained features that were counter to Piaget's thesis that little children judge in terms of consequence. Although the results support the hypothesis that someone's acts, which by accident benefits another person, may not be judged as an act of kindness, the results also support Wertheimer's conjectures about kindness. At minimum, the children were not as egocentric and blind to the social situation as would be expected from Piaget's concept of egocentrism.

Moral Judgment

In the same school as in the previous study, three girls and three boys in the third grade and five girls and two boys in kindergarten were interviewed individually by Alice Kanouse in order to get their reactions to being asked to lend a toy to a friend who had refused to lend them one, to having their toys taken away, and to being hit (by a little or big child) intentionally or unintentionally. The following stories and questions were given (the words *John, ball,* and *boy* being used for boys, the words *Ann, doll,* and *girl* used for girls) with three sessions held for some children.

> Suppose you asked John (Ann) to lend you a ball (doll) but John (Ann) would not lend you the ball (doll). [Pause for comments.] The next day, John (Ann) asked you to lend him (her) a ball (doll). What would you do? Why? Do you think it is fair to do this? Why? Do you think it is right to do this? Why? Would friends do such things? What would you do if you lost someon e's ball (doll)?
> What would you do if a little boy (girl) hit you? Why? What would you do if a big boy (girl) hit you? Why? What would you do if a boy (girl) ran up to you and said, I do not like you, and hit you? What would you say to him (her)? What would you do if a boy (girl) walked over to you, hit you, and said, Oh, I'm sorry my hand shot out while I passed you—I did not mean to hit you. What would you say to him (her)?
> You are playing in your backyard. A big boy (girl) comes in and says, You are rich, I am poor; therefore, I'm going to take away your toys. He (she) then did it. What would you think of the boy (girl)? What would you do?
> You left your toys in the playground. A boy (girl) thought that you did not want them and took them after you left. What do you think of the boy (girl)? What would you do?

Responses to some of the questions may be summarized as follows:

Question	Kindergarten	Third grade
Lend ball (doll)	2 yes, 4 no, 1 ask mother	1 yes, 5 no
Is it fair?	3 yes, 4 no	3 yes, 3 no
Is it right?	4 yes, 3 no	2 yes, 4 no
Would friends do it?	1 yes, 4 no, 2 sometimes	3 yes, 2 no, 1 no answer
You lost someone's ball (doll)	4 find it, 2 buy another or pay, 1 go in house	1 find it, 3 pay or buy if can't find, 2 buy another
A little child hit you	7 hit back	4 hit back, 1 tell her mother, 1 I'm bigger and wouldn't hit back
A bigger child hit you	3 hit back, 1 hit back when bigger, 3 tell mother	5 call for protection, 1 tell child's mother
Said do not like you and hit you	6 hit back, 1 say stop	2 hit back, 3 verbal retort, 1 walk away
Hit you and said I'm sorry	3 say its OK, 3 say don't do that, 1 hit back and say I'm sorry	4 say it's all right, 2 say watch it next time

The three children who would lend the toy were girls. One kindergarten girl would lend the doll because she liked the other girl, another did no know why she would lend it and the third-grade girl would lend it because i is better to be nice than bad. Those who would not lend the doll or ball usu ally justified this on the ground that the other child had refused to lend it to them. One boy said that he could not lend the ball because he needed some toys. The questions about its being fair, right, and whether friends would do it were referred by some subjects to the other child's actions and by other sub jects to their own reactions. When asked what they would do if they lost th toy, the most frequent response by kindergarten children was that they would find it because they lost it, but most of the third-grade children realized tha they might not find it and would have to pay for it or buy another toy, fo example, I'd go find it and if I couldn't find it I'd buy another; I'd give ther the money 'cause I lost it.

In response to the questions about being hit, more kindergarten childre replied that they would hit back. When asked what they would do if a littl child hit them, all 7 kindergarten children said that they would hit back, b cause he hit me first, whereas 4 of the third-graders would hit back, or would not hit back because he was bigger than the child and one would te his mother. When asked what they would do if a bigger child hit them, thre kindergarten subjects would hit back, for example, because my mommy said someone hit me I should hit them back; I'd get a rope and hit her back cau she hit me. One said that he would wait until he was bigger before he hit ba and three would tell their mothers. One third-grader would tell the child's mother but all the others would call for help from their mothers, sisters, or brothers, for example, I'd go get my big sister cause I can't beat a big girl. When asked what they would do if someone said, I do not like you, and hit them, six of the kindergarten children would hit back and some of them would add a verbal retort, for example, I would say the same thing back to her and hit her back; I'd hit him back and I'd say, you'd better stop hitting me or I'll tell my mother. The one kindergarten child who would not hit back said, I don't like to hit him first because he hit me, not all the time; I'd say, Stop. In response to the same question, one third-grader would just walk away and three would resort only to verbal threats or remarks, for example, I'd say, I don't like you either—don't hit me; I'd say, You'd better stop hitting me cause I don't want to hurt you. Two mentioned hitting the child back: This time I think I would hit her back and say, What do you hit me for?; I do not like you and I'm going to hit you back. When hit by someone who apologized, only one kindergarten boy would hit back; I'd hit him back and say, Sorry. Three kindergarteners and four third-graders would say it was all right or OK and some of them elaborated, for example, I'd say that's all right—some people's hands do slip and they don't mean to hurt you; I would say that's all right as long as you didn't mean to hit me. The remaining subjects would tell the child not to do it again or to watch out next time; some of them would say that it was all right this time, for example, I'd say OK, the next time watch it; I'd say I'll let you go this time. Thus the children in both classes seemed to distinguish between intentional and unintentional hitting.

The distinction was less clear in the situations in which their toys were taken away deliberately or mistakenly. Reactions to having the toys taken away varied as the following responses show (T denotes a third grade and K a kindergarten child, 1 refers to the backyard situation and 2 to the playground situation):

K1. 1. The girl is bad. I'd call my mommy and say that girl took my toys. 2. Her took my toys. I want it. I'd call my mother and say someone took my toys.

K2. 1. I think he was bad. I would tell my mother or my father. 2. I think he was bad. I would tell my mother to buy me some more toys.

K3. 1. She stole something of mine. I would tell my mommy and she would get her. 2. I think she was very *stoldes*. I would forget I lost them.

K4. 1. I tell my mother. She's too bad. 2. Bad girl. I don't want the toys. I don't like toys. I punch her in the mouth.

K5. 1. I think she'll give me my toys back. I'd take them back. I'd hit her. 2. I think she'll give them back to me. I'd ask her to give them back to me.

K6. 1. I'd cry. I'd tell my mother he took all my toys. 2. I think it's gone. I'd cry and I'd tell my mother.

K7. 1. I'd tell her mother. I would go get some more toys from Santa Claus. 2. I think I'd go get my toys from her. I'd slap her and beat her up and kick on her.

T1. 1. She was poor. I'd give her some of my toys and my money. 2. She was a cheater. She stole. I would say give me my toys.

T2. 1. I think she's evil. I make her buy me new ones. I'd go tell

her mother and she'd spank her. 2.   I think she's a thief. I'd go look for
her and get my toys.
    T3.   1.   I think she's not nice. I take them back. 2.   I think that she
ain't nice. I go to her home and tell her they're mine.
    T4.   1.   He's a thief. I'd take my toys back. I'd take my toys back.
2.   He's a criminal and he don't have no toys. I'd clip him in the jaw.
    T5.   1.   I think he was very poor and don't have toys. I could buy
toys cause I'm rich and he's poor. I'd say give my toys back. I'll tell my
mother. 2.   I think he's a thief. I'd say, Hey boy, hey boy and run after
him and say why do you want these toys? I'd give him a little, not all of
them.
    T6.   1.   I would think that he wouldn't have money and no one
would give him. Maybe he would take them. I would call my mother and
tell her that a big boy stole my toys. 2.   I would think that the boy must
want some toys. I would tell the boy, Hey boy, may I have my toys back?
If not, I would call my mother. It's not good to take my toys.

Some children reacted similarly to both situations, for example, K1, K2, K6,
T3. Some children would show mercy in the first situation to the poor child
but not in the second, for example, K7, T1. Some would hit or have someone
spank the child only in the first situation, K5, T2, and others only in the second situation, K4, K7, T4. While the desire for the return of the toys was the
usual motive for violence, K4 maintained that she did not like or want the
toys but still would punch the girl in the mouth in the second situation. The
children did not refer to the second child's notion that they did not want the
toys, which was a mistaken notion (except possibly in the case of K4). Children who referred to motives, that the child was poor or wanted toys,
nonetheless wanted all or some of their toys back, for example, T5, T6. Some
children described the taking of their toys in one or both situations as theft,
for example, K3, T2, T4.
    In short, the reactions did not show a consistent distinction between the two
situations. Most of the children, whether they were in the kindergarten or
third-grade class, acted on the basis of the consequences when their toys were
taken but most of them acted on the basis of intentions when they were hit
intentionally or unintentionally.

Concluding Remarks

    The discussion here arose because in Piaget's study of moral judgments the
subjects were asked to evaluate someone's behavior and Piaget's assumption
reflect the Cultural Relativist's thesis that different individuals in differen
stages of development use different standards. What one calls good the othe
one may call bad because their standards are different; moreover, an ind
vidual at one stage may not be able to understand an individual at anothe
stage because they are like members of two different cultures. Therefore th
arguments that Wertheimer leveled against Cultural Relativism hold fc
Piaget's work. Wertheimer would say that subjects may disagree because
different experiential backgrounds but that the situation could be clarified
that they could understand each other's point of view, so that they cou
grasp the structure of the act in the context of the particular interperson
and social field and judge whether the act fits or does not fit its requiremen
Wertheimer believed that children in different stages of development, li

people of different cultures, can come to an agreement as to whether something is good or bad, fits or does not fit, if the situation is clarified so that they can see its structure. One may have to clarify the situation differently for a child who is functioning in one stage of development than for a child who is in another stage. Wertheimer was not content with saying that this is what the child can or cannot do in terms of the standards set up by an experimenter but wanted to know what can be done to bring about a judgment that fitted the situation. He wanted to know what kinds of transformations were needed at different stages to bring about a certain judgment; he would not object to the thesis that different transformations were needed at different stages to get the same response. One of the German refugee professors once said (apropos of Wertheimer's criticisms of Piaget, Freud and others) that Wertheimer was looking for the good man and wanted to know how to make man good. Some seminar members said that this was a moral problem and not a question of science. [How valid is this argument?]

Wertheimer was concerned with what actually takes place in the judgment situation and not with testing a theory of mental evolution by studying the frequency with which a certain type of response is made at a certain age level. Piaget was interested in whether the judgment was being made in terms of intentions or consequences as defined by his theory. Wertheimer once said that centering on cues that indicate intentions or consequences has the danger of focusing the investigator on those features of the situation that are relevant for his theory and may blind him to what is actually happening. Our results seem to indicate that with different types of questioning it is possible to show that what apparently looks like judgments in terms of intentions may involve consequences and what looks like judgments based on consequences may involve intentions. Just as an adult will offhand judge in terms of consequences when something goes wrong the child also does it. And just as an adult, when questioned in order to find out if he is able to make a judicious judgment in terms of the meaning of the act to the person, the actor, or the meaning of the act in the social situation, may show that he is capable of doing it, so it is possible for the child also to do likewise if the questions are framed in a certain way. Just as the adult may not be aware of features of the situation which he did not take into account when he judged or was narrowed down in his judgments by what seemed to be intentions or consequences, so the child may be narrowed down. For example, when one of ASL's truant casework students was accused of stealing oil, the little boy said that he wasn't stealing but was helping his mother. He was innocent of intentionally trying to steal; nor was he aware that arrest for theft would be the consequences for climbing into the oil man's yard and draining off the few remaining drops in each of the hundreds of cans that were stacked in it. The owner of the oil withdrew the charges when ASL explained to him what the boy had done. Obviously at first the owner reacted in terms of the consequences, what the child was doing, and not in terms of the child's intentions. He was angered that someone had broken into his yard and he saw the possibility of thievery. He was not aware of the child's intentions, of what the child's act really involved, and what the act meant. After all, the cans were practically empty and the child was merely drawing off oil from what had remained in the cans when they were returned from the customers.

According to Wertheimer, a judicious judgment would try to do justice to the situation. Justice involves such things as understanding the place, role, and function of the individual's behavior. Wertheimer once pointed out that the problem of consequences versus intentions as a basis of judgment had been involved in theological or philosophical disputes in the Middle Ages and that according to certain theologians and certain Christian sects, intentions were important but according to other theologians and other sects consequences were important. Consequences and intentions in both these cases are not the consequences and intentions that Piaget is talking about; we have to make a distinction between theories of intentions or consequences and actual acts involving intentions or consequences. We have to make a distinction between judging a particular act in order to do justice to it and trying to formulate a theory of ethics which is based upon the axiom that intentions or consequences are the important thing from which decisions should follow. As far as Wertheimer was concerned, the theological and philosophical arguments for basing an ethics on one or another axiom may be irrelevant to or may miss the point of what may take place in an actual situation. He was interested in doing justice, in understanding an act of another's behavior, in not acting arbitrarily and not being blind to what the situation demanded. Moral judgments to Wertheimer involved a certain view of a person's act in a social context. Because one is blinded by emotions, needs, or general abstract principles of intentions or consequences, one might structure the situation in such a way that he judges it in a manner that does not fit the situation. In the case of a child given the stories used in some of our projects, to ask who is the bad boy is to center the child on an evaluation rather than to find out what the child thinks about the situation. Because of this, even the studies reported here do not meet Wertheimer's requirements. The stories should be dramatic so that the structure would be clear, so that the direction of the act would be understood in terms of its place, role, and function in the situation. Some of the slum children understood the act quite differently than middle-class children or Piaget's children would understand it because of the social context in which they placed the stories.

All this is not to say that Piaget's theory of moral development is without value. He has pointed out very ingeniously, in terms of the responses made in their judgments that children develop according to a certain theory. Incidentally, it is similar to a theory that was made popular during the Enlightenment. It is ironic that Piaget, who has criticized the Gestalt psychologists for being Kantian, was most Kantian in embracing the Enlightenment conception of morality.

Studies on Fit

1. In the seminars and lectures on thinking and learning, Wertheimer repeatedly made use of the concept of filling a gap in terms of its structural requirements. For example, in Figure A subjects would put a' into a and b' into b, in B they would put a and not b into the gap. He conjectured that it would take more repetitions to learn to put together these forms in the counter-structural manner. We therefore made a form board in which rectangular doors and square and circular windows of a house were missing. The subjects' task was to finish the house with the parts given to them. Kindergarten as well as fifth-grade children readily completed it correctly, but

were told then that they were wrong, that they had put the wrong pieces into the gaps. All the children protested that the parts did fit the holes. When they were told to try again, many of the kindergarten children did not know what to do, but there were a few fifth-grade subjects who began shuffling the parts in order to guess what the experimenter would call correct. They realized that what went into the gaps depended on what the teacher called right. When the experimenter put the pieces together in a counter-structural manner, the subjects said that it was a hard test because they had not learned to do it this way. A few protested that the pieces did not fit well.

The experiment was varied. The subjects were asked to select the parts that fitted the windows and the doors, and each time they were given a pair of doors or windows, one of which fitted into a gap in the house, while the other was larger or smaller than the gap. Nearly all of the subjects selected the member of the pair that fitted snugly. Afterwards, when they were told that they were wrong, they changed the piece for the other one. When the piece was larger, they usually were content with the answer but when the smaller piece was called correct, they complained that it would not stay in place, that a new frame was needed, that air and rain would come into the house. The results indicated that it was possible to make some subjects focus on the social requirements instead of the task's structural requirements. The results also supported a conjecture that Wertheimer had made, that is, that the social atmosphere generated by methods of teaching that focus the child on what the teacher calls right, might blind the child or make him insensitive to the requirements of problem situations. (See Luchins, 1942, pp. 90-92, and the first two monographs on Wertheimer's seminars; also Luchins and Luchins, 1956, 1959).

The same results were obtained when we used arithmetic problems (Luchins and Luchins, 1959, pp. 56 ff.). However, when the problem could not be solved because of the social requirements, some subjects solved the problem and ignored the authority and/or the majority's ruling on what was the correct way to proceed. Preliminary experiments with social problems showed the same trend of results. Our results indicated that it may be easier to get people to focus on the social requirements than on the structural requirements of the task. Even when they realized that the problem is not solved they do not wish to violate the group's rules; to solve the problem requires changing the admissibility conditions. The results also indicate that some people seem reluctant or do not like to be called wrong on psychological tests.

2. The concept of fit is related to Wertheimer's conjecture that there is a tendency in man not to do things blindly and arbitrarily. He criticized existing tests and studies of concept formation for ignoring the question of fit and for assuming that one might arbitrarily put together into one class things that were structurally different because they had certain elements or features in common. Several experiments were conducted to test this conjecture.

a. A collection of objects was presented to children to sort into groups that went together. For example, they were given two of each of the following objects, most of them toys: cat, dog, horse, lion, boat, locomotive, knife, plate, cup, pot, scissors, hat, coat, book, pencil, and pen. The members of each group were written in columns on a large sheet of paper as the subject grouped them. After a subject grouped the objects, he was asked for the reasons for each grouping. The subjects were then asked to group them in another way. This was done five times. Fifth-grade children tended more often to make a class in terms of pairs than college students. Few subjects put horse, ship, and locomotive into a class (means of transportation) or put locomotive, scissors, knife, and pot into a class (made of metal) or put the toys into two classes (replicas of living things and of man-made objects) or put pencil, book, coat, hat, cat, dog, horse, and lion into one class (organic substances). When these possibilities were presented to them, some children and some college students objected that it was senseless. Other college students, however, thought that these were clever ways to group the objects.

b. In another study the same procedure was used but the collection of objects, most of them toys, consisted of the following: a metal disc and a wedge-shaped piece of metal that fitted the sector that had been cut out of the disc, an open bottle with its cork, an open jar with its metal cover, a headless doll and its head, a cup, a saucer, a knife, a spoon and a fork, a paper clip and loose sheets of paper, a car with a wheel missing and the wheel, and an open wooden pill box and its cover. Most subjects put together pieces that belonged together; for example, they put the head on the doll, the wedge into the disc, the wheel on the car, and also clipped the papers, covered the wooden box, corked the bottle, and covered the jar. Nobody put the head, the cork, the cap, and the box covers into one class. When they were told that these objects all top something, most subjects, especially the children, thought that it was a senseless grouping.

Although in both studies the subjects put together what ordinarily went together into a common structure, they also made some classifications on the basis of common elements and ignored the structure. It was possible to increase the number of artificial classifications and to reduce the more natural classifications by giving the subjects prior experience in making logical classifications and telling them that concrete and functional answers get one credit while abstract classes get two credits on intelligence tests, and that it is a sign of superior intelligence to subsume things that appear to be different under some general principle. When the subjects were urged to find general principles, they gave more abstract classifications; some even made up stories in which all the parts were related. Pressure to give abstract answers sometimes resulted in bizzare and funny answers. It was our impression that it was relatively easy to make generalizations once the subjects got into the mood to invent classes without regard to the functional use of the object or its structure as a whole.

Instead of using a collection of objects we used names of historical figures and celebrities; for example, Mohammed, Jesus, Hitler, Moses, Washington, St. Paul, Pershing, Napoleon, Luther, Stalin, Lenin, Father Divine, Hoover, F.D. Roosevelt, Einstein, Ford, Clara Bow, and Florence Nightingale. Now the results were not as clear-cut as before. The subjects' knowledge of history and the role of the person in history affected their groupings. Moreover, the interpretation of history they had learned determined whether certain people were seen to belong together. Furthermore, there were subjects who made one or two groupings and could not go on. The subjects did not show as much ease in shifting the people into different groupings as they had shown in the object sorting test. They protested that the groupings were absurd or preposterous when ASL put Jesus, Moses, Hitler, Stalin, Luther, Father Divine, F.D.R., and Hoover into one group and told them that they are or were leaders of men. Some refused to play the grouping game because it violated their feelings about these people.

c. In another study the subjects were given ten paragraphs that had gaps in them. They were given fifteen phrases and were told to use them to complete the paragraphs. The paragraph completions were more varied because of the different interpretations the subjects gave to the sentences and/or to the paragraphs. Those subjects who focused on the meaning of the paragraph as a whole and who recognized that the paragraph was from a biblical or historical or newspaper story more often correctly fitted the correct sentence into the gap. In those paragraphs that described a mood or a type of person, the subjects who focused on the mood or the type fitted the sentence correctly. The type of person or the mood was sometimes misinterpreted with rationalizations such as "He's a mixed up kid" or "He's a mental patient." This sometimes led to fitting in the wrong phrase or sentence. These studies demonstrated to ASL's students the importance of the meaning one sees in the object in determining what does and does not fit. If Stalin and Hitler were seen as evil men or dictators, one grouped them together; if they were regarded primarily as leaders of men, they might be grouped with F.D.R., Moses, Luther, and Jesus; if Jesus was seen primarily as the son of God, he would not be grouped with the others.

d. In another study the subjects were given descriptions of historical or current events; an Indian massacre, the lynching of a Negro, a pogrom, a riot, a sit-in strike, a religious celebration of a primitive people, a church service, etc. Many subjects found it difficult to group the descriptions. They reacted to the contents of each event. Their attitudes toward and knowledge of the events played a role in making the groupings. As in the grouping of the names, the subjects refused to put together into an abstract grouping, events that had different social significance to them. When ASL put riot, massacre, pogrom, and lynching into a group called aggression, some thought that it made no sense to say this. Similarly, some rejected the grouping of a church service, a ritual of a primitive society, and a sit-down strike as gatherings of people.

In another study, children were given pictures in which something was required. For example, the subject was shown a picture in which a baby was reaching out of the crib to get a milk bottle which was out of reach. The subject was asked to describe what was happening in the picture and then was asked what he would do. Several scenes were used: a child in the river yelling, Help, while two boys are playing ball on the river bank; a child standing near a telephone booth while a hold-up man is demanding money from a man; children throwing stones at an old bearded man; two boys fighting on a sidewalk strewn with their school books; and an old lady standing in the middle of the street while cars are riding by, her groceries spilled all over the street behind her. Kindergarten children as well as college students recognized the plight of the persons in the pictures and usually spontaneously remarked on what ought to be done.

Wertheimer raised the question of whether it would be possible to train subjects to be so abstract-minded that they would not notice the nature of the objects or events which were used in the studies. We were reminded of the sophomores who became so enamored with their science courses that they ate chemical compounds instead of food, of doctors who focused only on that part of the body that was related to their specialty and overlooked other aspects of their patients, of the psychology students and psychoanalysts who saw everything in life in terms of their concepts, and of the engineers who focused on the production of a product to the extent that they minimized human factors and other aspects of the physical world. These were examples of being blind to the requirements of the total system. Wertheimer proposed that the actual social and political situations in which such blindness had occurred be studied to find out what had brought about and maintained the blindness. This led to several conjectures concerning the determinants of seeing what was fit. The place in time or space from which a thing or event was viewed might determine what was fit. Moreover, the requirements of the particular system might be met adequately in a variety of ways, perhaps in an infinite number of ways. Mathematically speaking, the question of what fitted might be a problem with just one solution, a problem with a nonunique solution, a problem for which no solution had yet been found, or a problem that could not be solved under the given restrictions or admissibility conditions for a solution. The definition of the situation might lead to one conception of what is fit rather than another, and the definition might be due to habit or custom, the needs of the person or the needs of the social group. Not responding to the requirements might be due to the personality of the individual. He might be inhibited, timid, or unsure of himself. He might fear the consequences of acting, lack knowledge, feel powerless, or feel it was not his business. Social factors might also not allow the person the freedom to act or to survey the situation in order to find out what was required, thus imposing a certain solution which might otherwise have been counter to his judgment.

Wertheimer seemed to assume that if a man was not inhibited by social and personal factors, he would do what was fit in the situation. He would realize the consequences of his actions and modify them to fit the situation and system of which he was a part. He did not deny that it was an ideal case and that it was counter to the popular idea of human nature which regarded man's behavior as due to arbitrary and blind forces. He said that there was some evidence from the behavior of little children and naive people that went counter to the popular conception of man and lent support to his conjecture.

Conflicts over What Fits

Wertheimer was aware that people disagreed over what fitted in a particular situation but he believed that these differences could be resolved. ASL conducted some preliminary experiments with Wertheimer's help in which people who had been set to view or to judge differently were brought together to see or to judge the same thing. What follows were outgrowths of this preliminary work.

1. Two children were seated next to each other and measured, independently, the same object. They gave two different answers because, unknown to them, one child's ruler was based on the metric system and the other child's ruler was based on the English linear system. Children were able to reconcile their differences by discovering that their rulers were different (Luchins, 1947). In another study, two children who were seated at different ends of the table had the task of putting together a house. One child meas-

ured the dimensions of a window or a door that was needed and asked the
other child to give him the required door or window. Due to the fact that his
ruler was different, the child gave him the wrong sized door or window. The
children soon realized that they could fit the doors and windows properly if
they discarded their rulers (Luchins, 1947; Luchins and Luchins, 1956, 1957).
Experimental variations of this study to make each child stick to his ruler's
results have not been as successful as experiments in which children were set
by previous experience to solve problems in a certain way. In the problem-
solving situation, the children could be made to generalize that their method
was the rule or the correct way to solve the problem (Luchins and Luchins,
1959, pp. 536-566).

2. When alone, each of two children was given a series of pictures in different order so that one developed a set to see a bottle and the other developed a set to see a face in the same ambiguous picture. After they developed the set, they were seated together and told to react to the same task.
They were then given one at a time the same series of pictures. (In addition
to the pictures, anagrams, word blocks, and the water-measuring problems of
the Einstellung rigidity tests, as well as a series of descriptions of a person
named Jim, have been used.) Usually the subjects agreed that both their answers were correct. Some of these subjects overlooked the gradual changes in
the subsequent drawings so that they did not see things that a naive person
would see; for example, they did not see a goblet in a series of pictures, or
did not see a word that was written in the usual way in the anagrams or word
blocks. (However, when one subject developed a set to use the E method,
which involved three jars, and the other to use the D method, which involved
two jars or one jar, for the solution of a water-measuring problem, the subjects usually agreed to use the direct method and not both methods. This may
have been because problems are supposed to have one solution, and one of
the solutions was better than the other.) It seems that they agreed to view the
stimulus from both frames of reference instead of examining each in terms of
its own structure. Wertheimer, who helped ASL design the word block study,
suggested that factors be introduced to make the subjects look for new words
instead of just agreeing to use both frames of reference. We have also conducted experiments aimed at getting each child to stick to his answers; e.g., by
telling him to generalize a rule or that he would get extra credit on the test if
he persisted in his original view. Some of these studies have been recently replicated at SUNY at Albany and will be presented in the section on social influences.

3. Two children were seated at the same table, facing each other. In front
of them was a pile of pieces of two jigsaw puzzles that had been mixed up.
(Each jigsaw puzzle was made up of 24 pieces and had different colors as well
as pictures.) Each child was given a piece of the puzzle and was told that he
should put together the picture to which the piece belonged. The children
usually interferred with each other but eventually they each completed a puzzle. They were then asked to do it again, but this time to try to decrease the
time it had taken them before. Some children now separated out the pieces
before getting to work so that they would not get in each other's way. Others
were so intent on what they were doing that they did not even put a wrong
piece back into the pile, with the result that one or both of the children were
not able to complete the task. Wertheimer suggested that variations should be

conducted which would make the children devise methods of not getting into each other's way. It was usually found that stress on competition hindered while stress on cooperation facilitated the solution. (These experiments will be presented later.)

4. Two subjects independently read a descriptive paragraph about a person named Jim and then wrote their impressions of him. Afterwards, they were asked to tell each other their impressions of Jim. They disagreed because they had read a different description. The experimenter asked them why they disagreed. Some subjects got so involved over what they had written that they failed to find out that they had read different information. Most subjects realized, some spontaneously and others after a few hints, that the paragraphs were different. They were then told to imagine that they had independently observed Jim, that each had seen what their initial paragraph contained, and that each had therefore reported a different impression. Their task was to reconcile their differences and make a description that would include both observations. Usually the subjects could be made to agree on six trait names. But when they were later asked to write independently their new impressions of Jim, they tended to revert back to their first impressions. Thus, their first view did not readily change. It seems that people tend to resist restructuring their impressions in the face of new and contradictory information or, at least, tend to revert back to their first impressions (cf. Luchins and Luchins, 1970b).

Early in his work with Wertheimer, ASL was struck by the persistence of beliefs in the face of contradictory evidence. In one study we asked subjects to describe or tell the meaning of the *mark of Cain, Noah's curse,* and God's action in various places in *Exodus* when the Jews violated his commandments. They were asked where in the Bible were located the phrases "Love thy neighbor," "Proclaim liberty throughout the land," etc. Religious as well as irreligious subjects sometimes gave factually wrong answers. Even though the portions of the Bible were subsequently read to them, they would afterwards revert back to their original erroneous answer, perhaps because of their ideological view of God and the Old Testament.

Doing What Is Required

Wertheimer once discussed a study by Kounin and Adler in which children were given a choice to complete a house that someone had not finished or to build their own. This led to several studies by members of the seminar, including Helen Block Lewis. We shall briefly describe a few studies conducted to test Wertheimer's comments about these studies. Wertheimer conjectured that if the dynamic quality of the test was increased, the subjects would respond to it and would attempt to complete the task left undone by the other person.

1. In one study, a subject was waiting for the experimenter in the chemistry laboratory. Another student entered and remarked that he was going to make coffee. He then put a pot of coffee on a burning Bunsen burner and walked out. The coffee pot boiled over, but the student who was waiting usually did not turn off the Bunsen burner. In ten replications, only two subjects turned off the gas. In another study, a student was waiting for the experimenter in a room where another student, who was unknown to him, was

hanging streamers on the walls. He was having trouble with the streamers because the window was open and they blew the streamers around the room. In two of the five replications, the student who was waiting did not volunteer to help. In still another study, a student waited alone in ASL's office while the telephone repeatedly rang. Six of the fifteen subjects answered. Those who did not answer said, when later asked, that it had not been their business, that it would not have been proper to answer. Those who had answered thought that it might be the experimenter calling them.

When the experimenter asked the students what had happened while they were waiting for him, many of the students at first did not mention the coffee or the streamers. When they were asked why they did not turn off the coffee or close the window, they said that they had never thought of it, it had not been their affair, or that they had wondered when the fellow would return to put out the coffee or when he would have the sense to close the window.

2. When the experiments were conducted with sixth-grade children and high school students, we found even fewer subjects responding to the task's requiredness. We therefore changed the procedure to one of presenting hypothetical cases and asking the subjects what they would do in them: If you saw a lady carrying a large bag of groceries and something fell out of her bag, what would you do? If you saw a package fall off a truck, what would you do? In both cases, the subjects said that they would call to the lady or the truck driver and/or bring the object to them. When asked what they would do if they saw a fire or if they saw a group of men breaking into a house, they said that they would call the fire department or tell a policeman. When asked what they would do if they saw a big boy hurt a little boy, most said that they would mind their own business or run away. When they were asked what they would do if a boy was messing up the books in the library or fighting with a girl, many said that they would do nothing because they did not want to get into trouble. Children were also asked three questions: A man stops you and tells you that people want to kill him. What would you do? A baby is crying in its carriage; its rattle is on the ground. What would you do? In both cases most subjects would not do anything. When they were asked what they would do if a child in their class cheated or stole a piece of chalk or paper, a few said that they would tell the teacher, but most of them said that they would not be snitchers.

Their answers were used as the basis of an interview to find out when, where, and how they would help someone. A common theme in their answers was that there were certain things they would not do because they feared that the consequences might be bad for them, their behavior might be misunderstood, or they might get hurt or ridiculed.

The Arbitrariness of Laws and Rules

It will be recalled that Wertheimer conjectured that rules and laws might be fit or required in the situation. One method of demonstrating this was to describe a law or rule, to ask the subject what he thought about it, and then to give the reason for the law or rule. We told the subjects about the rule that allowed men to get married immediately after a divorce but required women to wait three months. After the subject gave his view of the rule, he was told that the reason for this was that the divorcee might be pregnant and therefore her former husband would be responsible for the care of the child. Another example of an apparently arbitrary rule was that Pythagoras forbade his disciples to eat beans. Yet this rule was not really arbitrary since the people of the Mediterranean Region were allergic to the fava bean.

The work of Muzafer Sherif has many suggestions for the study of laws and group norms. It is of interest to note that in the Wertheimer seminars his work was criticized for not coming to grips with the problem of value. Yet in the past thirty years his approach to the study of group behavior has yielded many examples of what Wertheimer meant by fit.

Wertheimer's examples of fit were simple ones. To some of the students who attended his adult education courses, his idea of fit was a common-sense notion, but the psychologists who attended the courses usually read into them theoretical problems and issues. Wertheimer often tried to disentangle them from these theoretical and ideological arguments. He wanted the students to face the example and ask themselves whether the traditional answers did justice to the particular example. This approach was used not only in the discussion of ethics but in the study of music, art, perception, and learning. It was our impression that on the one hand he had faith that beneath the phenomenal diversity there was a structure in which the diversity made sense and had meaning; but, on the other hand, he was critically reexamining his own and other people's assertions about the nature of this unity. A student who had come to learn theories from Wertheimer and was getting annoyed at the repeated examples he used to illustrate his point of fit said that all he was telling us was to deal righteously with particular things, people, and events, to show loving kindness, and to walk humbly with our conception of the Truth. All these were nice slogans, but they reflected a moralistic and not a scientific view.

Other Studies on Fit

One day while some students were discussing Wertheimer's conjecture about doing what was fit in a social situation, someone related a childhood experience. While climbing a backyard fence, his body slipped through two boards and his head got stuck; some neighbors saw him but did nothing. A recent immigrant to the USA rushed to his aid. The man later told the child's mother what had happened and said that had this happened in his town in the old country, everybody would have rushed to the child's aid instead of looking out of the windows and talking. The student went on to describe peoples' behavior in the subways and on the streets and then concluded that these cases do not support Wertheimer's conjecture about doing what was fit. Wertheimer, who had sat down while the student was talking, remarked that it had been said that if you want to get lost or to be alone, go to a big city. Why is this so? What is there about the structure of the social field of a city that is different from a small town's social field? Why do people not help in a big city? A visitor said that maybe they have a narrow view of the social situation because they are interested in their own business and are not aware of things that are happening around them. In small towns everybody minds everybody's business. Wertheimer remarked that we have to study cases in the city where people do help and to find out the reasons why they help in then but not in the other situations.

When ASL walked with Wertheimer to the subway, he told him that h would ask his Adult Education class to keep a record for the next month of instances or accidents in which someone needed help, to record what and where it happened, who saw it, whether bystanders came to the person's help. They would also be told to observe the reactions of all bystanders and to speak to them to find out why they did or did not help. Wertheimer said that maybe the students themselves would sometimes rush to help the person. In what situations would they do it and in what situation would they not? ASL went on to say that years ago all druggists would take a cinder out of someone's eye when asked, but now they do not; years ago a doctor would rush to help in a street accident, but now he would be reluctant to do so. In the former case they are not allowed by law, in the latter case they fear that they may be sued for malpractice. It would be a good idea to interview old-fashioned druggists and physicians as well as modern ones to find out why they help and do not help.

When the students of ASL's class were told about this discussion, some of them volunteered to keep records of cases in which bystanders helped and did not help and to speak to their druggist and physician to find out when, where, and why they would and would not help someone. Some students made up a list of critical situations and asked people what they would do in them and why. For example, you are walking in the street and see a fire; you are walking in the street and see a hooded man run out of a jewelry store and rush into a car which drives off; you see a young man and girl struggling in front of a house, on the beach, in a lover's lane, in the park; you see two boys or two girls fighting; a baby is crying in a carriage; a dog is jumping and biting a little boy; boys are stealing the bread or milk that had been put in front of a grocery store by the delivery man; a man is annoying a girl in the subway train; a lady dropped a bundle; a package fell off a delivery truck; two cars collided; an old lady is walking and struggling with a big bundle of groceries that she can hardly hold; a child, an old man, an old lady, a blind man is waiting for someone to help him or her across the street. The students found many cases in which people were kind, helpful, and even went out of their way to be of help. In many of the situations it was a matter of good manners, of being thoughtful and considerate of others, for example, picking up a book or a package that a woman drops, helping a blind person or an old lady across the street. Some involved civic responsiblity, for example, turning in a fire alarm, calling an ambulance, the police. The students who had recorded accidents or incidents of violence or quarrels had fewer cases of helping than of not helping. Some bystanders who had not helped said that they did not see it as a situation requiring their help, that they did not want to embarrass the people, did not want to get involved or mixed up in what was not their business, felt intimidated, scared, or lacked the boldness to act. Some frankly said that they did not want to get involved in others' business; a few of these people seemed to imply that they were embarrassed, felt inhibited, did not want to be conspicuous, feared the possible consequences for themselves. Some said that it was not their responsibility, that people should mind their own business if they want to get along or to live long. Some said that they were not competent and did not have the power or authority to act; some said that it was the job of a professional or an official person whose duty was to help in such cases, for example, the police, an ambulance attendant, a doctor, a person who knows first aid. Some were drawn to the scene out of curiosity to see what was happening and they regarded it as one looks at a movie; they were like the spectators not the participants in a ball game. Those who did help said that it was natural to help or that they did not stop to think about reasons for helping. A few said that they would expect others to help them or their friends when they were in the same predicament. A few who had rushed to help in accidents and fires said that they enjoyed being heroic, hoped to get their names in the papers, hoped to get a reward. Of those who helped a young woman in distress, a few frankly admitted that they hoped to be able to get a date from her or her friends.

Wertheimer suggested that experimental social situations be devised to find out under what condition one does and does not react to the social fields' requirements. If milk is boiling over on the stove, will an onlooker rush to turn off the heat or remove the pot? This discussion resulted in several experiments which have been of interest to our students and have been used as classroom demonstrations and research projects. We will first describe some of the projects that were done before the war and then present the results of recent replications by ASL's graduate students.

The prewar experimental situations were as follows. One or more students wait for the experimenter in his office or in the laboratory because it was arranged by the experimenter that they come five minutes early or because the experimenter excused himself and said that he would be back in a few minutes. Sometimes one of the students was actually the experimenter's confederate who sat quietly and observed or who made suggestions or movements indicating the task to the others. At other times all the students were naive subjects. A variety of emergency situations have been used; the telephone rings incessantly, an assistant enters the room and turns on the electric fan which blows the papers off ASL's desk, or he opens a window and the draft drives the papers off the desk. Just as the students enter the room the fan goes on and the papers blow off the desk, a percolator is boiling over on a hot plate on the desk, or a foaming solution is boiling over a bunsen burner. The task involving the coffee or the foaming solution has sometimes been presented to students who came to serve as subjects in the school's chemistry laboratory. Many of the students did nothing to remedy the situation; some were unconcerned and ignored what was happening. Those who did do something usually closed the window or the electric current but did not touch the papers. Fewer students remedied the situation in the laboratory than in the office. Helpful reactions occurred most frequently when the confederate suggested that they help. When the students were questioned after the experiment, those who did not do anything to help said that it was none of their business, that it was embarrassing to touch things that did not belong to them or to have someone walk in while they were doing it, and that they did not know how to arrange the papers or how to shut off the equipment or how to handle the coffeepot or the foaming liquid. Some claimed that they did not see anything wrong or saw no need for action. A few said that they were just curious to see what would happen, to see whether another student in the room would do something about it, or whether ASL or whoever put the things there would come back before there was a real mess.

A classroom demonstration was devised in which a student dropped an armful of books and papers in the doorway of the classroom just as the class was about to enter or leave the classroom. In most cases, the student who dropped them was the only one who picked them up; the other students either stood by or pushed their way into or out of the room. When ASL asked the students why they had been delayed in entering or why they did not help the student pick up the books, some of them said nothing, or expressed annoyances, impatience, and amusement. Some said that it might have embarrassed the student who dropped the books, that it was inefficient for more than one person to pick up things in a doorway, that two people would block more of the doorway so that no one could enter, that they were on their way to another class and did not want to be late, that they did not want to mix up the student's papers and books. This demonstration was often used to motivate the students to do such things themselves. They were told to drop their books or papers in the school corridor, on the street, in the library, in the cafeteria. They were told that in some cases they should drop them when there was a crowd and in other cases when only one person or a few people were around.

Since we do not have the reports of the prewar studies we summarize the findings of the students in a 1970 class on social psychology (see table 16. 1). When a woman dropped something there was a greater tendency for a male than for a female to pick it up; a woman was less likely to pick up something dropped by either a man or another woman. Females, however, seemed to show by the way they looked that they sympathized with the person who had dropped the books or papers even though they did not help. Age also seemed to be a factor; an adult was less likely to pick up something that a child had

TABLE 16.1
Book-Dropping Experiment*

Trial	Location or situation	# bystanders Male	Female	# helped Male	Female	% helped Male	Female	Total
1	library check-out	3	2	1	0	33	0	20
2	elevator entrance	1	2	0	2	0	100	67
3	supermarket check-out	2	2	0	0	0	0	0
4	college building doorway	5	3	1	1	20	33	25
5	library check-out	0	3	0	0	0	0	0
Total		11	12	2	3	18	25	22
I	college hallway							
II	during class	1	3	1	0	100	0	25
III	class breaks	3	0	3	—	100	—	100
IV	class breaks	5	3	1	2	20	63	38
Total		0	2	—	0	—	0	0
V	paused before retrieving	9	8	5	2	55	25	41
VI	paused before retrieving	4	1	2	0	50	0	40
VII	immediately retrieved	0	2	2	0	0	0	0
VIII	immediately retrieved	2	2	2	1	100	50	75
		0	4	—	3	0	75	75
A	male experimenter of pair	10	5	4	1	40	20	33
B	female experimenter of pair	9	12	2	3	22	25	24

*Trials 1 through 5 were conducted by a male student working alone and Trials I-VIII by another male student working alone. Trial A(B) gives the totals for a pair of students working together when the male (female) dropped the books in the hallway or cafeteria.

dropped. Certain social factors such as what is customary or good manners in a certain situation facilitated or inhibited helping others. Certain expressive behavior of the person who dropped the books also seemed to influence the results. One student found that when he bent down as soon as the objects fell, people more often helped him than when he first paused, for example, when he immediately bent to retrieve the books, 75% of the bystanders in two situations helped him, compared to 0% and 40% in two other situations where he paused before retrieving the books. Studies by other students suggest that it was not just the pausing that was important but what the person who dropped the books did during the pause. Those who looked helpless seemed to invite help; those who looked ludicrous or efficient tended to get help less often.

The protocols also showed that the location in which the objects were dropped played a role. One student found that when he dropped books and papers so as to block an elevator entrance, the two female bystanders helped him pick them up and the male rushed to hold the elevator door open; when he dropped them on two occasions in the library 20% and 0% respectively helped; and when he dropped groceries at a supermarket checkout point, none of the four people (two males and two females) helped him but instead they rushed past him to check out their groceries. In general, objects were less often picked up in passageways with moving traffic, in the school corridor, in campus streets between changes of classes, or on a busy thoroughfare where many people were walking hurriedly. Less people helped when they were lined up waiting for a bus or waiting their turn at a cashier's window. People who were working in the street (telephone repairmen, ditch diggers) or students in the library were less likely to rush to help someone than people who were not occupied with tasks or their thoughts.

Personality traits of the bystanders also seemed to be factors. Some people tend to get preoccupied or narrowed down by their goals, motives, actions, thoughts, whereas others pay attention to what is going on around them. Some people are open to the world; others are closed. Some people seek to be helpful, like boy scouts trying to do a good deed. Some people want to be helpful but do not because they are timid or fearful of the consequences of getting involved or being conspicuous. The personality and appearance of the person who drops the books also played a role; a pretty girl or a handsome man generally got more help than less-attractive people. Some of the students reported that over 50 percent of the bystanders helped them, whereas others averaged less than 25 percent help. Why do some people frequently get help and others do not?

The number of bystanders also was a factor. Some students found that a lone bystander was more likely to help than were several. However, they found that if one of several bystanders helped, then others might pitch in particularly if they were acquainted with the helper. In some variations where pairs of students worked together and one bent to pick up what the other dropped, bystanders tended to be more helpful than when one student worked alone.

Two graduate students, Mrs. Christensen and Mr. Suggs, recently replicated one of the prewar studies. They worked as a team, one dropping the books and the other observing the bystanders (but not picking up the books). They alternated their roles so that each of them dropped an armful of books in the cafeteria or in the corridor when groups of students were passing by. Since the results were about similar in the two locations, they were combined. Of the total of 15 bystanders when Mr. Suggs dropped the books, 5 or 33 percent helped him (one of the five females and four of ten males). Of the total of 21 bystanders when Mrs. Christensen dropped the books, 5 or 24 percent helped (three of twelve females and two of nine males). It was possible to question only 5 of the 10 subjects who helped and 16 of the 20 who did not help. Their answers are summarized below; since there were multiple responses the percentages total over 100.

Reasons for Helping	Number	Percent
It is natural	3	60
It is kind	3	60
It is embarrassing	2	40
Felt sorry	1	20
Materials seemed of value	1	20
Courtesy	1	20

Reasons for Not Helping	Number	Percent
Someone else helped	4	25
Did not look as if he (she) needed help	4	25
Did not trust the person	3	19
Females should not help males	3	19
Women want to be liberated	2	13
Did not know her	1	6
She was not attractive	1	6
She looked as if she did not want help	1	6

The most frequent reasons for helping were that it was natural and kind to do so or that it was embarrassing to drop things. The most frequent reasons for not helping were that someone else was helping, that the person who dropped the objects did not seem to be in need of help, that they did not trust the person, that females should not help males, and that women want to be liberated (and presumably do not need chivalry from men). It could be said that the helpers had a traditional attitude and the non-helpers a modern attitude toward people. It is of interest that Mr. Suggs is a black student and Mrs. Christensen a Puerto Rican. Because of the liberal atmosphere of the campus we expected that they would be helped more than white students who conducted a similar study but the results were essentially the same.

All these book dropping situations did not have what Wertheimer would call the strong appeal of a real life emergency situation that calls for actions. Latané and Darley (1970) have recently studied real-life situations that have more appeal quality since they involve emergency life situations; some of their results seem to corroborate Wertheimer's conjecture that there are a variety of reasons that people help or do not help. From Wertheimer's point of view it is important to experiment with a variety of situations in order to find out what factors extremize helping or not helping.

More on Moral Judgment

The story which Wertheimer used to criticize Piaget's study of morality was modified and used for projects in ASL's classes. One of these projects has in recent years been used as the basis of a discussion of Piaget's work and to stimulate research in line with Wertheimer's suggestions. The stories and questions of one of the studies which we replicated recently are as follows.

Another Person Is The Victim
Part A. Mr. A had to get to a certain place in a great hurry. It was important that he get there on time. Something terrible would happen if he did not. Since he did not know how to get there, he asked a boy named John. John wanted to fool Mr. A as he did not like the man's looks. He therefore gave him the wrong directions—to take a bus that went in the opposite direction. [Watch how the child reacts to this, record spontaneous comments and, after a pause of 15 seconds say:] The man took the wrong bus but while riding he became nervous. He asked the bus driver whether the bus would get him to the place. The driver told Mr. A that he was on the wrong bus, that he should get off and take the bus that goes in the other direction. Mr. A did this and arrived in time at his destination. After a pause for comments ask: 1) What do you think of Johnny? Why? 2) What do you think of Mr. A? Why?
A few days later, John saw Mr. A walking toward him on the street. 3) What did Johnny do? Why? 4) Suppose Mr. A caught John. What would Mr. A do to John? Why? 5) What would John tell Mr. A? Why?
Part B. Mr. B, too, had to get to a certain place in a hurry. It was very important that he get there in time. Something terrible would happen if he did not. Since he did not know how to get there he asked Harry. Harry wanted to help Mr. B and told the man to take a certain bus. Mr. B sat nervously until the bus driver said, "All out, last stop." Mr. B asked the driver how to get to the address. The driver said that he had taken the wrong bus; he should have taken the bus that went in the other direction. The man arrived late at the place and something terrible happened because he was late. [Watch how subject reacts and after a pause of 15 seconds, say:] 1) What do you think of Harry? Why? 2) What do you think of Mr. B? Why?
A few days later Harry saw Mr. B walking toward him on the street. 3) What did Harry do? Why? 4) Suppose Mr. B stopped to talk to Harry. What would Mr. B do? Why? 5) What would Harry say? Why?
Part C. 1) Who is the bad boy? Why? 2) Is Harry bad? Why? (or, why is he not bad?) 3) Is John bad? Why? (or, why is he not bad?) 4) Which boy would get punished? Why? 5) Which boy should get punished? Why? 6) Did you ever do things like Johnny did? 7) Did you ever do things like Harry did? 8) Did either boy tell a lie? Which one?

The Subject is the Victim
Part A. Suppose you had to get to a certain place in a great hurry. It was very important that you get there on time. Something terrible would happen if you did not. Since you did not know how to get there, you asked John. John wanted to fool you as he did not like your looks. He therefore gave you the wrong directions to take a bus that went in the opposite direction. [Watch how the child reacts to this, record spontaneous comments and, after a pause of 15 seconds, say:]
You took the wrong bus but while riding you became nervous. You asked the bus driver whether the bus would get you to the place. The driver told you that you were on the wrong bus, that you should get off and take the bus that

goes in the other direction. You did this and arrived on time at your destination. [Watch how subject reacts, after 15 second's pause say:] 1) What would you think of John? 2) What would you do if you saw John the next day? 3) What would John do if he met you? 4) Did such a thing ever happen to you?

Part B. Suppose you had to get to a certain place in a great hurry. It was very important that you get there in time. Something terrible would happen if you did not. Since you did not know how to get there, you asked Harry. Harry wanted to help you and told you to take a certain bus. You sat nervously until the bus driver said, "All out, last stop." You asked the bus driver how to get to the address. The driver told you that you had taken the wrong bus and that you should have taken the bus that went in the other direction. You arrived very late at the place and something terrible happened because you were late. (Pause for comments, 15 secs.) 1) What would you think of Harry? 2) What would you do if you met him? 3) What would Harry do if he met you? 4) Did such a thing ever happen to you?

Part C. The same as Part C above.

Experiment 1. Since the prewar studies are not available to us, we present the results of a study conducted with the assistance of Janet A. Reuther of the 1970 Advanced Social Psychology Course at SUNY-Albany. She interviewed individually 21 children (four boys and five girls in kindergarten and six boys and six girls in second grade) who were pupils in an outer-fringe city school in the Tri-Cities area of New York State. Most children were interviewed in two sessions, one held a week after the other. In the first session some children were told the stories in the reverse order. The order of the stories (the A part before the B part or vice versa) was also varied in each session for different children. The counterbalancing was done in order to see if the order of presentation influenced the children's answers.

Generally speaking, we found that children of the same age gave very different responses. In each class some children responded in terms of intentions, other children responded on the basis of the consequences and still others responded in terms of both intentions and consequences. Moreover, some of the children were inconsistent, sometimes responding on one basis and at other times on another basis; inconsistencies occurred within each of the parts as well as between parts. Because they point to much needed research, some of the questions raised by Wertheimer about the results of the prewar study are also raised for the present study. Who are the children who judged in terms of intentions, who judged in terms of consequences, and what may be the reasons for the differences in their behavior? Did they really understand what took place? What were their attitudes and assumptions and from what kind of educational and home background did they come? How did they view the experimental situation and the tasks? What can be done to find out whether they were giving stereotyped, habituated answers or whether they were judging with understanding? In a judgment situation one may apply social standards arbitrarily and blindly, regardless of whether they refer to intentions or consequences. What can be done to open one's eyes to the requiredness of the situation and to get him to judge it in terms of its requirements and not to evaluate it arbitrarily? To label someone as good or bad does not necessarily mean that one is aware of the structure of the act, (the behavior) and its place, role, and functions in the social field in which it takes place.

We analyzed the data by studying each child's answers in order to see if they formed a pattern. We present here patterns which were determined mainly by the replies to the first five questions of Part C. If these questions were consistently answered on the basis of intentions or of consequences or of both intentions and consequences, then the responses were said to form patterns referred to as Int., Cons., and Both, respectively. They were as follows:

Questions	Patterns		
	Int.	*Cons.*	*Both*
1. Who is the bad boy?	John	Harry	Both
2. Is Harry bad?	No	Yes	Yes
3. Is John bad?	Yes	No	Yes
4. Which boy would get punished?	John	Harry	Both
5. Which boy should get punished?	John	Harry	Both

If in addition to showing the Int., Cons., or Both pattern, the child gave an answer to the eighth question which was in line with the pattern, that is, if he said that a lie was told by John or by Harry or by both boys respectively, then a plus sign was added. If the responses to only one of the first five questions in Part C deviated from the pattern, the result was called a near pattern and designated by a minus sign.

Comparison of a child's answers in the first and second interviews revealed that there were four children (two in each class) who showed the same pattern in both sessions; in each case the pattern was based on intentions. There were also three other children in the second grade who each time showed patterns or near patterns based on intentions or on both intentions and consequences: No child consistently judged on the basis of consequences alone. Moreover, no child in either session showed a pattern based only on consequences. This result is counter to Piaget's hypothesis that young children tend to judge in terms of consequences.

The following tabulation gives the numbers of patterns and near patterns under the various conditions; *none* indicates that neither a pattern nor near pattern was shown.

Class	Kindergarten				Second Grade				All Ss				Total	
Order	AB	BA	AB	BA	AB	BA	AB	BA	AB	BA	AB	BA		
Session	1	2	1	2	1	2	1	2	1	2	1	2	1	2
Victim	0	S	0	S	0	S	0	S	0	S	0	S	0	S
Int. +		2	1	1	1	2	2	2	1	4	3	3	4	7
Int.			1	1							1	1	1	1
Int. −		2			2	1				3	1		1	3
Cons. −	1		1	1			1	1			1	2	2	2
Both +	1				1		1	1	1			1	1	2
Both −		1	1	2		3	1	2	4			2	6	2
None	3				2	2			5	2			5	2
Total	5	4	4	4	5	6	6	5	10	10	10	9	20	19
Full Patterns	1	2	2	2	1	3	2	3	2	5	4	5	6	10
Near Patterns	1	2	2	2	2	1	4	2	3	3	6	4	9	7

The results did not seem to depend on whether the story about Mr. A was told before the story about Mr. B (AB order) or the other way around (BA order). They did seem to depend on whether the subject (S) or another person (O) was the victim and on whether it was the first or second session. In the first session the frequency of patterns and near patterns was greater when the subject rather than another person was depicted as the victim. Patterns and near patterns in the first session together constituted 40% and 60% of the responses in the kindergarten and second grade respectively when the man (Mr. A or Mr. B) was the victim but 100% in each case when the subject was the victim. However, this was not the case in the second session. In each class the sum of the percentages of patterns and near patterns was as large or larger in the second session than in the first session. For all subjects combined the sum was 75% in the first session and 89% in the second session; the corresponding percentages of patterns were 30% and 53%. Thus more patterns of responses were shown in the second session by each group.

Judgments based on intentions were more frequent when the victim was the subject than when it was someone else. In the first session the kindergarten children showed no patterns or near patterns based on intentions when the victim was another person, whereas these constituted 50% of their replies when the victim was the subject himself; the corresponding figures for the second-grade children were 20% and 50%. In the second session patterns and near patterns based on intentions constituted 50% of the kindergarten children's results when someone else was the victim and 100% when the subject was the victim; for the second grade the corresponding figures were 40% and 50%. These results not only show that judgments based on intentions depended on who was the victim but also show that the second-grade children did not consistently make more of these judgments than the younger children. Similar trends were found when the responses to the first five questions were considered regardless of whether or not they formed a pattern or a near pattern. For the kindergarten children, with the two sessions considered together, judgments indicative of intentions averaged 40% when the victim was someone else and 70% when it was the subject. For the second-grade children the corresponding figures were 34% and 50%. Thus these criteria also suggest that the frequencies of judgments based on intentions depended on who was the victim and were not higher for the older subjects.

In summary, patterns and near patterns constituted 14 of the 17 opportunities to form patterns by the kindergarten children and 18 of the 22 opportunities to form patterns by the second-grade children, in each case 82%. In each group, patterns based on intentions were the most frequent. Of the 14 patterns and near patterns in the kindergarten group, 8 or 57% were based on intentions, 3 were based on both intentions and consequences and 3 on consequences, each constituting 21%. Of the 18 patterns and near patterns in the second-grade group, 9 or 50% were based on intentions, 8 or 44% on both intentions and consequences, and 1 or 6% on consequences alone. Thus the older group had fewer Cons. patterns, relatively fewer Int. patterns, and more Both patterns than the kindergarten group. Of the total 32 patterns and near patterns, 17 or 53% were based on intentions, 11 or 34% on both intentions and consequences and 4 or 13% on consequences alone.

Because of the inconsistency shown by some of the children, the results depended somewhat on the particular criterion used in the analysis. For example, of the five kindergarten children tested in the first session when Mr. A or Mr. B was the victim, no one chose John in response to the first question, which asked who was the bad boy, but three chose him in response to the fourth question, which asked who would be punished, and two chose him in response to the next question, which asked who should be punished; thus their judgments based on intentions ranged from 0% to 60% depending on which question was used as the criterion. (Possibly the children did not understand the distinction between would and should.) Similarly, their judgments based on consequences ranged from 10% to 60% depending on which question was used. Of the five second-grade children who were tested in the same session, in response to question 1 four chose John and the remaining child chose Mr. A as the bad boy but possibly he meant John who misdirected Mr. A; in response to question 3 all answered affirmatively, that is, all now said that John was a bad boy. Thus their responses based on consequences ranged from 0% to 80% depending on which question was used as the criterion.

An analysis was made of the relationship of the results to personal and scholastic data and to the classroom teacher's ratings of the children's personalities. There was a tendency for the girls to show more patterns based on intentions than the boys. Are girls more person-oriented? Also, of the four children (two in each class) who showed patterns based on intentions in both sessions, three were girls. Two of these girls, both in kindergarten, received high ratings by their classroom teacher on maturity and leadership but that was not the case for the boy and girl in the second grade. There did not seem to be a consistent relationship of the results to the other rated traits, to family size, sibling order, or to achievement test scores. Further study along these lines is needed with more subjects.

One result of this study as well as of the collated data of all the laboratory reports of the students in the Advanced Psychology class was similar to the prewar results. When the subject judged the situation in which he was the victim there were more judgments in terms of intentions. Offhand this seems to be counter to Piaget's conjecture that judging in terms of consequences is a sign of egocentricity. But we do not think it is so simple a matter. Ego involvement may make one focus on consequences or on intentions. When someone steps on your toes you glare at him because of the consequences of his act but accept his apologies because of the possible consequences of bawling him out. We can also conceive of cases in which ego involvement or egocentricity leads to judging in terms of intentions. In view of this we are inclined toward Wertheimer's comment that the argument over whether intentions or consequences are more important, basic, or superior standards for ethics, is an echo of a theological and philosophical dispute in the Middle Ages. Would we say that the philosophers who had favored consequences were more egocentric than those who had favored intentions? Why focus on this issue in studying morality in children and naive people?

Experiment 2. In another study with the same stories, underprivileged children in a New York City slum were interviewed by Alice Kanouse, a psychologist working among them. (Mrs. Margaret Brown, ASL's assistant, made arrangements for the collection of the data and also helped tabulate the results.) Because of the restriction on time, only one session was held with each child during which either the child (S) or Mr. A and Mr. B (O) was depicted as the victim. The stories in which Mr. A and Mr. B were the victims were told to 14 girls and 4 boys (12 to 14 years of age) with the story about Mr. A given first. One of the boys refused to answer any questions and was not considered in the analysis. In Part A, when asked what they thought of John (who deliberately misled the man) the subjects invariably voiced negative opinions; they referred to him as thoughtless, rude, wrong, very bad, foolish, cruel, selfish, disrespectful, mean, dirty, and terrible. Some gave no reasons for their answers when they were asked but others said that it was because John fooled a man, because he did it on purpose or for fun, or because he knew that something terrible could happen to the man. In Part B, when asked what they thought about Harry (who lied unintentionally), 9 of the 14 girls and all 3 of the boys voiced negative opinions; they said that if Harry didn't know the directions he should have said so, that he should have kept his mouth shut, that he was ungrateful, wrong, not polite, etc. The others said that Harry was probably good, that he was nice, that he made a mistake but tried to help. When they were asked what they thought of Mr. A, 6 of the 14 girls and 2 of the 3 boys said that he was a nice, kind, or good man because he asked directions of a boy or because he trusted a boy. But only half as many, 3 girls and 1 boy, said such things about Mr. B (who did not get to his destination), so that they seemed to be judging partly in terms of consequences. Subjects said that Mr. B didn't know how to travel, that he should not have asked Harry, that he should have been ashamed to ask, that he should have known by himself or that he should have asked the bus driver or someone else. Fewer subjects made such comments about Mr. A. When asked what John would do when he saw Mr. A., 13 of the 17 subjects said that he would run away; six of them added that he was scared or afraid or ashamed. Only one subject said that John would apologize to Mr. A. In contrast, 7 subjects said that Harry would speak to Mr. B; most of them said that he would ask Mr. B if he got there and apologize. Of three who said that Harry would run or hide to stay out of trouble or because Mr. B might be angry, two added that he would also say that he was sorry. Some subjects said that Harry would do nothing because he did not know that anything was wrong. Thus the subjects clearly differentiated between intent and mistake when describing the boys' reactions. However, there was less differentiation in describing the reactions of Mr. A and Mr. B. Seven subjects said that Mr. A would question John to find out why he did it, two said that he would explain to John that what he did was wrong and one child said that he would just tell him what happened. Other reactions, given by one subject each, were that Mr. A would tell John's parents, would scold John, would force him to apologize, would hit him. The one subject who said that Mr. A would hit John also said that Mr. B would hit Harry. But all the others said that Mr. B would talk to Harry. Nine said that Mr. B would tell Harry what had happened, that he gave him wrong directions or that he took the wrong bus, two said that he would ask him why he gave the wrong directions. One child said that he would accept the boy's apology. Another child said that he would use bad words. None of the children mentioned the terrible thing that had happened to Mr. B as a result of the mistake.

In Part C they were asked the questions used in the previous study except for the last question about which boy had told a lie. Patterns or near patterns of responses were shown by 8 girls and by only 1 boy or by 53% of the 17 Ss. In contrast they were shown by 82% of each of the kindergarten and second-grade groups in the previous study. It seemed that the present subjects were less consistent than the younger children. They showed 6 patterns based on intentions, 2 near patterns based on intentions, and two patterns based on both intentions and consequences. As in the previous study most patterns were based on intentions. There were now fewer Both patterns than in the previous study and no patterns or near patterns based on consequences. However, answers in terms of consequences were given to some of the five questions in Part C. Of the 85 answers to these questions made by the 17 subjects, 45 were scored as intentions, 22 as both and 18 as consequences. Half of the answers scored as consequences were made to the fifth question (Which boy would get punished?). It seemed that the children had realized that in this world punishment was meted out on the basis of consequences. One girl who said that Harry would be punished had answered the preceding four questions by saying that neither boy was bad and neither one should be punished. Another girl said that both Harry and Mr. B would be punished, Harry for making him late and Mr. B for not planning ahead of time. One boy who said that Harry would be punished described John as the worst boy because he started the whole thing; perhaps because he heard the story about John first, this subject regarded John as the one who started the mischief.

The stories in which the subject was described as the victim were told to 17 boys, aged 11 to 14 years, with 9 of them receiving them in the AB order (the story of John who had malicious intent described first) and the others in the BA order. Three subjects were lenient when asked what they thought of John, saying that something must be wrong, he didn't know what he was saying, he was not to be punished. (In contrast, none of the 17 subjects who heard about Mr. A had been lenient to John.) The remaining 14 boys gave negative judgments of John; he was wrong, unfair, ignorant, unkind, stupid a fool, a boy who misbehaves, a joker, a liar, a prankster, a wrong dude, a dirty guy, a double crosser, a rat. Three of these subjects also commented on their relationship to John, saying, I would not believe him again; I don't like him; John knows that I know he is not my friend. These comments fi Wertheimer's point that the lie may affect the relationship between the lia and the one lied to.

There were varied reactions concerning what they would do when they sav

John the next day. Some would do the same thing to him or teach him a lesson or play a trick on him. One would tell him off and another would talk to him in a bad manner. Five would just talk to him and ask him why he did it or tell him that they arrived at the destination. One would look at John with a terrible face and another would ignore him and walk by without speaking. Three would use more violent methods; they would beat him up, slap him, and tell his parents, and one would kill him. When asked what John would do the next day, the most common response, given by 8 subjects was, He would laugh at me. Some children said that John would say that he fooled them or that he would tease them and two children said that John would start a fight. Only two of the 17 boys said that John would run away. In contrast, 13 of the 17 subjects who heard the story in which Mr. A was the victim said that John would run away when he saw Mr. A the next day. In short, the common reaction was that John would run away from an adult but instead of running away from a peer he would laugh at him and tease him or fight with him. Possibly John was pictured as reacting in terms of the possible consequences, since an adult might punish him but he could cope with another boy. The comments corroborate Wertheimer's ideas about the importance of the role of the interpersonal relationships in the social field. The same lie told by the same person meant different things depending on to whom it was told or the situation in which it was told. To understand the effects of the lie we have to know the structure of the interrelationship between the two persons, the liar, and the lied, since different structural relations may make for different effects.

When asked what they thought about Harry, ten subjects were lenient; he tried to help, he did the best he could, he made a mistake or an honest mistake. (Only half as many who heard about Mr. B had been lenient to Harry.) Others said that Harry was unkind, terrible, crazy, ignorant, thought of funny things, could not be trusted, and had no home training. When asked what they would do when they saw Harry the next day, five said that they would tell him what happened or tell him that he made a mistake; one boy said that he would tell him *softly*. Two said that they would shake hands with him and thank him anyway and one said that he would forgive him. One child would ask why he did it, two would do nothing, and one did not know what he would do. One boy would not trust him. Four used rather violent methods; they would slap him, kick him, and two of them would kill him. Thus there was an extreme range of reactions, with even more violent reactions than to John's behavior. The reactions were also more extreme, both in terms of forgiving and seeking revenge, than those that had been ascribed to Mr. B when he met Harry.

When asked what Harry would do when he saw them, four subjects said that he would ask what happened and three said that he would say or might say that he was sorry when he found out. One said that Harry would try to give him the right directions. Two said that Harry would do nothing and two did not know what Harry would do. One thought that Harry would not remember him. Four said that Harry might laugh at them. One thought that Harry would run but another said that he would fight. Thus, while Harry was portrayed or was seen as less belligerent in his reaction to the subjects than John, he was portrayed or was seen as more belligerent than he would be to an adult, Mr. B.

In Part C the second and third questions, which were essentially elaborations of the first question, were omitted in order to ask the subjects the following: Who is the bad boy? Who should get punished? Who would get punished? One subject, who was given the BA order, did not answer any of the questions. Six answered all three questions on the basis of intentions; four of these Ss were given the stories in the AB order and two the BA order. Two subjects answered the first two questions on the basis of intentions but in response to who would be punished, they said that it would be themselves, the travelers themselves. Such an answer to the last question was also given by two other subjects whose responses to the previous questions were that no one was the bad boy and that no one would be punished. Thus four subjects believed that they themselves would be punished by not getting to their destinations or for getting into trouble. One subject who gave the answer of nobody to the first two questions mentioned Harry in response to the last question, that is, he answered it on the basis of consequences. Three subjects, two of whom had the BA order, answered all three questions on the basis of consequences. Thus there seemed to be a slight tendency for the BA order to yield more responses in terms of consequences and fewer responses in terms of intentions than the AB order. Of the 48 possible answers to the three questions by the 16 subjects, 23 were based on intentions, 13 on consequences, 6 involved the answer of nobody, 4 referred to the subjects or travelers, two were failures to respond; there were no answers which were based on both intentions and consequences. On a percentage basis, the types of answers to these three questions were as follows when the victims were Mr. A and Mr. B (O) or the subjects (S):

Victim	O	S
Int.	51%	48%
Both	24%	0%
Cons.	20%	27%
Nobody	4%	13%

Thus when the subject was depicted as the victim, responses based on both intentions and consequences were much lower, responses based on intentions only were lightly lower, responses based on consequences were slightly higher, and responses that nobody was bad and nobody should be punished were higher than when others were described as the victims.

We do not wish to add to the noise level about Piaget's thesis of moral development but merely to open up new ways to study the problem. We have considered Wertheimer's conjecture because we think that it does just this. Wertheimer conjectured that telling lies affects the liar's interpersonal relations. We did not really test Wertheimer's conjecture. The child was asked to judge the behavior of people in a story and was questioned concerning his awareness of the consequences of the lie and the interpersonal relationship of the boy and the victim. This does not mean that in a real situation the child would really have reacted in this way. Two issues were raised by Wertheimer. First, there is the need to study in an experimental way or by naturalistic observation what happens when a person lies to another. What are the various effects that it has on their interpersonal relations and on their social field, and what factors determine the different effects: Secondly, there is the need to extend Piaget's methods to find out whether the child is aware of the structure of such acts as John's and Harry's and the place, role, and function of the acts in the social field. Does focusing on different features of the act cause a miscentering so that one does not realize its actual place, role, and function in the social field? In making a judgment one may focus on his likes, dislikes, needs, habits, or attitudes and assumptions about the person or his behavior, or on what happened in the situation. He may therefore evaluate the act in terms of what is most conspicuous to him. This may result in his being blind to certain important features of the act and its place, role, and function in the social field. Such blindness and miscentering may occur whether one judges in terms of intentions or in terms of consequences. Children may not be aware of certain consequences or intentions that adults are aware of because of their experiential backgrounds. Children of different socioeconomic or cultural backgrounds might also be aware of or ignore different consequences and intentions. If we study the history and effects of religious, political, and economic ideology in the past and present, it does not seem to show that children are more prone than adults to focus on consequences or ignore intentions.

Wertheimer pointed out that under some conditions children as well as adults may judge in terms of consequences of the acts and be blind to the intentions of the actor but under certain conditions they may judge in terms of the actor's intentions and be blind to the consequences to them, to others, and to the social field. We need to know more about the factors that bring about such blindness and what can be done to save people from it. He objected to the idea that judging in terms of intentions is a superior way of judging; people have destroyed and harmed others while intending to help them. Social, religious, and political reformers have created misery and suffering with good intentions; the way to hell is paved with good intentions, a hell to those who are the recipients of the acts. We need to study cases where good intentions lead to good as well as bad consequences and cases where bad intentions lead to good as well as bad consequences. Moreover, we need to study the consequences in terms of the short run and the long run. In conclusion, Wertheimer was not primarily interested in the problem of at what age certain kinds of judgments occur more frequently; he was not primarily interested in testing a theory of mental development. He wanted to know what factors lead adults, as well as children, to blind, arbitrary action and judgments and what factors can be introduced in the judgment situations to open their eyes so that they deal justly with the situation.

17
Evaluation

[*Over a period of six years certain experiments on social influences were discussed repeatedly in the seminars. Wertheimer not only criticized the theoretical assumptions of these studies but suggested ways to test them. Solomon E. Asch developed in detail Wertheimer's insights in his Gestalt-oriented* Social Psychology; *other members of the seminars, William Garber, Jacob Goldstein, Abraham H. Maslow, Alexander Mintz, as well as ASL, have also published reports of studies that have their origin in these seminars. But these published reports reflect only certain aspects of what was covered in the seminars. The reconstructed seminars are presented with the hope of stimulating research on the neglected aspects and of portraying the way Wertheimer dealt with these topics. We have collated the different discussions and are presenting them as if they occurred at one time, including comments, discussions, and class projects from ASL's classes which were discussed with Wertheimer.*]

In the beginning of the session Wertheimer remarked that Sherif had recently conducted an experiment on evaluation in which he gave college students a list of names of authors and asked them to rank the authors according to their greatness. A few weeks later they were given a list of prose paragraphs to rank according to literary quality; after each of these paragraphs was the name of a different author. Unknown to the students was the fact that every paragraph had been written by the same author, Robert Louis Stevenson. Sherif had placed after each paragraph the name of one of the authors whom the students had ranked before. Wertheimer asked the seminar members to predict the results. Some correctly predicted that Sherif had found that many subjects ranked the prose paragraphs in the same order as they had previously ranked the names. When he asked what the results meant, a visitor said that before we could discuss the study we needed to know the size of the correlation and whether it was significant. When someone told him that it was about .50 and that it was statistically significant, the visitor remarked that the prediction from such a correlation was too low to have much meaning. Wertheimer asked, What would the results mean if the correlation were larger? . . . Were there subjects who ranked all or most of the paragraphs in the same way as they had ranked the names? Were there subjects who ranked none or few of the paragraphs as they had ranked the names? If there were such subjects, why did they behave so differently? After a pause he asked What happens when one is given such tasks? In response to a question he said that it is important to know why a subject places a certain author or a certain paragraph in a certain rank; not just the response but the process that led to the response also has to be studied. When a student interrupted to argue that

218

group trends are sufficient in such studies, Wertheimer illustrated how the use of group trends or averages may give a false picture of what actually occurred in an experiment. When the same student said that the standard error took care of his objections, he said that such statistical devices are not substitutes for studying the extremes or the singularities of one's results. He added that the singularities might reveal more than the regularities; they might suggest reasons for the results which could be used to design experimental variations in order to get clearer and more striking results or suggest ways to extremize the phenomena under investigation.

A visitor said that Sherif's experiment was designed to test a specific hypothesis and that the results had substantiated the hypothesis. He went on to object to Wertheimer's suggestions, claiming that they had little to do with Sherif's goals. This led to a discussion of experimental design that was cut short by Wertheimer's asking, How can we understand such results; what does it mean that some people ranked the prose passages in the same way as they had ranked the authors' names? After a pause, he sharpened the issue, saying, Suppose that all of the subjects had ranked the list of named prose passages in the same order as they had ranked the names alone. How would you interpret such a finding?

Someone said that Sherif had demonstrated a well-known phenomenon about the judgment of works of art and literature. In these fields there were sacred cows whose milk was supposed to be superior to that of all other cows. When a writer is unknown, his work has no value, but the same work becomes very valuable when the author becomes famous. Wertheimer gave some examples from the history of art and music to illustrate such changes of value and asked whether they demonstrated the thesis that the same thing was arbitrarily or blindly evaluated negatively and then positively. Someone said then that the same thing may be evaluated differently because of changes in peoples' tastes and because of changes in fads and fashions which are due to publicity and to promotional activities. A college instructor said that most people judge music, art, and literature in terms of the standards of the experts. People rely on experts' judgments because they have learned to trust other people's judgment about things they themselves do not know. ASL added, we do not taste the contents of a bottle when it it labeled poison; similarly we have faith that the art experts will not fool us. He added that Cantril had stated in one of the lectures in his course Social Psychology of Everyday Life that we need to know more about the meaning of faith in peoples' daily lives and not to dismiss it because it is related to discussions in theology. Sherif's experiment might be suggestive of ways in which to study the operation of faith in the social field. A visitor noted that people are influenced by individuals who are not experts in the particular event or thing that they evaluate. For example, the prestige of Henry Ford, which is the result of his status in business, has made people agree with him when he says that we ought to maintain the Volstead Act, to abolish New Deal Legislation, and to follow certain foreign policies. People even follow his advice about farming and conservation because the prestige he has earned in one area has spread to all areas to which his name is attached.

A few students developed the thesis that because of a desire for social status some people exhibit their knowledge of music, art, and literature. They might actually have little or no understanding of the music, literature, and art and have little or no personal feelings or opinions about such subjects but they glibly mention the names of popular musicians, artists, and writers to appear to be in the know. They strut like peacocks to display signs of culture. Therefore, they belong to book clubs, buy the classics, the best sellers, and other works that receive favorable reviews. They do not even bother to read the books but merely repeat what the reviewers have written about them. A school teacher said that such activities reflect habits about literature appreciation which may have been learned in elementary school, high school, and college. Literature is taught in terms of small excerpts from poems, novels, and essays along with evaluations by experts. In order to pass courses in literature appreciation the students must memorize the names of the writers and what their textbooks or teachers have said about them. Therefore, the students learn to evaluate literature in terms of the author's status or prestige in our society; they learn the social standing of many authors and have little acquaintance with their works. She went on to say that even though people do not know much about an author's work, they are usually ready to give their judgments when asked. Why is this so? ASL suggested that a failure to answer might indicate that they are not cultured. In order not to lose status they repeat the evaluations that have been called correct by their teachers. They have been taught that Tolstoy is a greater novelist than Thackeray and that Dostoyevsky is greater than Dickens. They have learned to make a fuss over foreign authors whose novels are considered mediocre in their own countries.

A professor said that Sherif's work demonstrated experimentally what we had always known intuitively about judgment. All judgments are made in terms of a frame of reference; a thing is not inherently good or bad but is good or bad from a certain point of view. One's frame of reference determines whether something is good, bad, beautiful, or ugly. The concept of the frame of reference helps one appreciate why someone calls a certain act anti-religious, unholy, un-American, disgusting, and immoral whereas somebody else may call it religious, holy, American, tasteful, and moral. He went on to say that Sherif had applied the Gestalt principles of perception to social phenomena. Sherif's *Psychology of Social Norms* used perceptual principles which were discovered in the laboratory to explain differences in the evaluation of physical and social phenomena in daily life. When the professor said that Sherif had taken perception out of the laboratory and had extended Gestalt psychology to social behavior, Wertheimer brushed aside this statement and asked, Just what happens when someone is given the task to rank such a list of authors? What actually happens when one is asked to rank such prose passages? ASL told the class that he had been a subject in a similar study that was conducted by Hadley Cantril. He had been asked to rank a long list of artists' names; some of the artists were very familiar to him and could be readily ranked but some of the names were not well-known to him. He had first ranked all the artists whom he knew and then assigned ranks in haphazard manner to the other names. Thus the familiar artists had been ranked higher than the unfamiliar ones. He had never seen the work of some of the artists but their names had often been mentioned in his courses on art appreciation; he ranked some of these unknown famous artists higher than artists whose work he had seen. In judging the names he did not usually think of their work but of their general reputation. After the experiment he had discussed the ranking with other subjects who were in his class. Some of them had also made a list in which all known artists were placed on top and all unknowns on the bottom. There were students who had not separated the names into known and unknown artists but tried to arrange them in the order that they had learned in school or elsewhere. Some subjects had thought that it was an art appreciation test or an art aptitude test. Some of the students had not bothered to rank the names carefully at all. A few weeks later Cantril gave the class the task of ranking small colored photographs of paintings; each picture had the name of an artist under it. While looking at the photographs, ASL thought that one picture had been misnamed. When he called this to Cantril's attention, he was excused from the experiment. Later on ASL asked the other students what they had thought about the pictures. A few students said that the pictures were photographs of paintings by famous artists and that they had ranked the pictures believing that they had been drawn by the artists. Later on in the term Cantril told the class that all the paintings had actually been drawn by the same artist. The results of the study were similar to Sherif's study with the prose passages. After some students' comments, Wertheimer remarked that Sherif had not given his subjects enough evidence upon which to base their judgments. Because of personal or social reasons, they felt compelled to make a judgment. Since the paragraphs were of about the same literary quality and the main differences between them were the names, the subjects relied on the names to make their judgments. ASL said that Sherif purposely used such ambiguous evidence because in such situations social norms played a dominant role in determining one's judgment. The professor noted that Sherif was in agreement with the fundamental thesis of Gestalt psychology. There is a tendency for people to structure unstructured material; they are perceptually on the offensive to organize and structure their worlds. Had Sherif given his subjects a clear-cut situation, there would be no need to structure it and they would readily react to it as it was. When people are given a situation for which they do not have a ready frame of reference, they seek to structure it. In Sherif's study the ambiguous evidence brought about an unstructuring of the subject's mind and he had to find some way of organizing it in meaningful manner.

Wertheimer agreed that there was a tendency in man to seek meaning and structure and that this tendency could be demonstrated by placing people in unstructured situations, but the utilization of such evidence-free situations for the study of social influences led to a one-sided picture. We also have to study what happens when unambiguous clear evidence is given for judgment. The professor said that nothing dramatic would happen in such situations. ASL said that Sherif does not claim that what happens in an unstructured situation is the prototype of all social influences and of all evaluations, but that certain kinds of social influences are very pronounced in them. Sherif believes that one relies more often on the social factors of a situation when the evidence does not clearly indicate what one had to do or to say.

In the beginning of the next sessions several members of the seminar said that they agreed with Wertheimer that Sherif's results were due to the fact that the subjects were under the stress of uncertainty and therefore were forced to use the names. Nevertheless, they agreed with Sherif that the results were due to prestige. Wertheimer said that Sherif assumed that one could attach different evaluations to the same content, that evaluation was arbitrarily attached to a content. He went on to say that this was a dogma, that it had not been proven.

ASL persisted in defending Sherif's experiment, saying that he had been corresponding with his former teacher Hadley Cantril about the Sherif experiments and Wertheimer's criticisms of them. An outgrowth of the correspondence was a series of demonstrations in his Adult Education class. ASL asked his class to judge the temperature of the room one day in July. Their answers ranged from 80° to 100°. Some judged it correctly at 89° because they had read the thermometer on one of the buildings on their way to school or because 89° had been the temperature at the same time on the previous day. When he told them that the temperature was 98°, many of the students readily shifted their judgments to a higher temperature. During the five-minute class recess, he asked a few students to help him with his demonstration. They were requested to agree with him when he told the class that he was surprised to find out during recess that it was actually only 70° on a thermometer which he had borrowed from the physics department. When this was done, not one student of the class was willing to believe that it was only 70° but there was a slight shift away from the upper limit of the previous range. The students were then asked why they were willing to shift their guesses upward but not downward. A few said that 70° was a Spring or a Fall temperature but not a Summer temperature. Some said that they had felt too hot to believe that it was 70°, which was a comfortable temperature. One student remarked that saying that it was 70° did not cool him but saying that it was 98° had made him more aware that he was hot and perspiring. In the discussion that followed, the students said that they had been guided by how they felt; the temperature was not just a number, it was related to their physical condition. Some remarks seemed to indicate that the students' ideas about temperature were in terms of certain temperature ranges; 30-50 was considered cold, 60-70 cool, 80-90 hot; the temperature of the classroom was judged in terms of these ranges. ASL went on to say that the next day when he asked the students to estimate the volume of the room, their answers ranged from 8,000 to 160,000 cubic feet. When ASL then told them that it was about 19,200 cubic feet, many students refused to accept it. Therefore, he told them that the room's floor was about 40 feet by 40 feet and that the ceiling was about 12 feet from the floor. Some students then measured the room and said that these dimensions were reasonably correct. After everybody was willing to accept the measurements, ASL asked the class what could have produced the vast range of their initial answers. Some students said that they had calculated incorrectly or that they had used the wrong formulas. When asked why they had been willing to shift their judgments about temperature but not about volume, some said that it was because ASL had tried to fool them the day before—they no longer trusted or had faith in him. The discussion also revealed that the concept of volume was rather nebulous to them. They demonstrated this by their incorrect answers to examples such as these: How many sheets of paper can be placed in this room; how many reams of paper could be stacked in the room? During the discussion of their answers, someone remarked that in volume one was interpreting his perception of space in terms of a certain standard that was external to him, such as the number of cubic feet, and that they had little experience in using such a standard; but in the estimation of temperature they were judging how they felt and they had relatively more experience in using our society's standard of measuring temperture to express or to communicate such feelings.

Wertheimer remarked that no one's judgment was absolutely correct, that there was a realm of uncertainty; for example, in the area of acoustics it had been shown that if one was wrong, he was usually wrong in a certain direction; thus his estimates did not tend to be in the center of the range but nearer to one side. Was this also true for the other sense modalities? He went on to suggest that the students study different kinds of people's judgments: of temperature, size, weight, volume, velocity, length, and the distance of unusual and of ordinary things, and they should ask people to estimate the probability of the occurrence of certain uncommon and common events. Then they should use social pressure to try to bring about shifts away from the upper or lower limit or from the medium, mode, and mean of the group's estimates. Which kind of judgments were more readily changed and which were not at all changed? After a pause he said that in Sherif's study of the judgment of the Autokinetic Effect all the judgments had been within a certain range. It would be of interest to find out the relation of the range of perceived movement to the size of the room and the subject's conceptions of the dimensions of the room as well as to the subject's idea of the distance of the light from where he sat. Would subjects agree with an overheard judgment that the light moved one mile or 100 feet, when they knew that they were in a small room? Someone said that when he had suggested to some subjects in his study of the Autokinetic Effect that the light had moved 200 feet, most of them objected that it was absurd, but there were students who had agreed because the light appeared to keep on traveling rapidly for a long time in the same direction. A school teacher interjected that the understanding of what was involved in measurement and what was meant by the various standards must play a role (cf. Luchins & Luchins 1970a). Wertheimer agreed with her that the study of how one learns to use such standards and to appreciate what is involved when one uses them may further our understanding of the origin and use of social norms.

Wertheimer proposed that in the experimental situations we have been discussing people might change or correct their judgment in the direction of truth or in the direction of conformity to the socially offered standard. We need to find out what factors produce changes in either direction, to truth or to conformity. He went on to say that when people's judgments are in the direction of truth, social psychologists usually assume that the judgments have been brought about on a reasonable basis; however, when the judgments are in the direction of social conformity, social psychologists assume that they are brought about on an irrational basis, that it is a matter of suggestion or imitation. Someone interrupted to say that these assumptions reflect an ideology in which group influences are believed to be malign in nature, they overpower or weaken one's intellect. He referred to Allport's studies as typical of this point of view and concluded that Sherif also reflects this ideology. ASL objected, pointing out that Sherif does not subscribe to this thesis. Wertheimer went on to conjecture that a person usually judges within a range which he thinks is reasonable and that when he hears someone make a different judgment, it may make him reconsider the truth or validity of his judgment. In response to a student's comment he said that this is not always done merely because one wishes to conform or to repeat what the other person has said but because he is concerned about the truth of his judgment. In such cases social influences may sometime lead one to a better appreciation of the evidence and to a change in judgment.

In response to a question, Wertheimer said that he does not deny that social influences sometimes lead to blindness to the evidence but not all social influences are of this kind. The last comment evoked many objections. Some students pointed out that there were experiments in group problem solving that indicated that people did worse in group situations than when working alone, that the group produced mediocre solutions. Someone challenged these findings, saying that the results of these studies might be a function of the kinds of problems used as well as of various attitudes and assumptions of the subjects. He went on to say that these studies had been designed to support the notion that group thinking was on a lower intellectual level than individual thinking. They had been used in arguments favoring aristocracy as opposed to democracy. Another student objected to the criticism of the work of men like F. H. Allport on the basis of ideological issues; just as individualism had been glorified until recent years, the group was now (in 1938) being deified. It would be more productive to find out for which people and for what kinds of problems group thinking led to superior solutions, and for which people and problems individual thinking led to better solutions. Neither the individual nor the group was a devil or a deity. Someone remarked that Wertheimer seemed to assume that man individually and collectively was naturally good, that man naturally sought the truth, that man wanted to be just, kind, and honest, and that dishonesty and other bad behavior was brought about by special social conditions. He asked why we should not assume that man was naturally selfish and blind and did what was good and true only under certain conditions. It would make no difference, as long as one did not say that it was an invariant trait occurring under all conditions. A visitor insisted that it would make a difference. If we accepted evil and disorder and fought for an island of order and goodness in our lives, we might be doing things differently than if we denied evil and assumed that everything was *hotsy totsy*. He made a comparison with fire fighting. It was like assuming that one lived in a world that was ablaze and that he had to fight for an island that was not burning, as opposed to assuming that only under abnormal times and only occasionally there was a fire to put out. The former assumption might lead to the establishment of a full-time fire-fighting institution, whereas the latter would not. When someone said that such a pessimistic view rejected humanism and liberalism, the visitor countered that we have to forget the ideological quarrels that have centered about the various theories of what man is and face the possibility that social systems, just like natural systems, tend toward a state of chaos or disorder. The early social philosophers and social scientists had utilized Newton's mechanics to preach social doctrine that assumed that there was a natural social harmony. It was about time that social scientists realized the implications of the laws of thermodynamics and began to worry about the problems involved in identifying and controlling the factors that led to social disorder instead of assuming that all was naturally in order. He asked, What kind of social institutions and what kind of people were required to have order, and what kind of forces did we need to preserve the order we have set up?

Wertheimer brought the class back to social influences on judgment by saying, People react differently to drama critics' evaluations. Some people may say that such and such a play is a good play because the critics have said that it is a good play. Since it is fashionable to go to see well-reviewed plays they go to the theater and may even sleep through the performance. For other people, however, the critics' statements serve to open their eyes to aspects of the play which they may otherwise have not thought about or noticed. If they already have seen the play, they may go to see it again; they may even see it more than once to look for the qualities that have been pointed out by the critics. Someone said that Wertheimer was assuming that the people were capable of making up their own minds and that they sought to see or think for themselves, but how true was such an assumption? He then argued that most people are gullible and simple-minded and accept things uncritically on authority. People in a group situation are like animals in a herd; they follow the leader. Only a few people have reached a stage of mental development that precludes their imitativeness and suggestibility. Someone referred to studies that supported the thesis that people of lower intelligence were more suggestible, but another student argued that conformity was learned behavior and that even people of intelligence are imitative and suggestible. It takes brains to imitate and to accept certain suggestions.

Wertheimer remarked that discussion on social influences on behavior and thinking reflected two theses. One thesis stressed that in social situations such nonintellectual processes as prestige suggestion and imitation determined behavior. There was a tendency in social situations to do blindly what others did; to repeat blindly the behavior of others was a fundamental human attribute. Just as there was the repetition of phenomena in the physical world, so was there an analogous form of repetition in the social world [cf. Tarde's concept of imitation]. The other thesis stressed that such behavior was not due to a natural, fundamental attribute of social or personal life but that it occurred only under certain conditions. The session ended on this point.

Out-of-Class Discussions

1. Some students followed Wertheimer to the cafeteria where they expressed surprise at his criticism of Sherif's work since Sherif used concepts of Gestalt psychology. Wertheimer said that just because a study made use of Gestalt psychology's terminology did not mean that one must not criticize it. [A few years later when Wertheimer was on leave of absence Koffka was a visiting professor at the New School. Wertheimer would sometimes attend Koffka's seminars and criticize and object to his formulations despite Koffka's protests that he was in agreement with Wertheimer. When Köhler once visited and spoke at Wertheimer's seminar, Wertheimer did not attend the session. He told ASL that he has made a deal with Köhler never to attend a seminar in which Köhler presented a paper. ASL kept Wertheimer company during these visits and got the impression that Köhler did not like Wertheimer's classroom criticism, although he would engage with him in private arguments.]

Wertheimer suggested that the students replicate Sherif's study and vary the method of presenting the paragraphs. First present to people only the paragraphs with no names assigned to them, in order to see how they go about ranking them. What would happen when they were afterwards asked to rank the named paragraphs? What differences in behavior would occur now that they had the names? Moreover, after they had ranked the named paragraphs, they should be given the paragraphs again but this time they should be told that the experimenter had made a mistake, that he had assigned wrong names to the paragraphs. He asked the students to predict what would be the results and said that we need to know more about what happens in such judgment situations.

2. The following week ASL described to Wertheimer some preliminary results of ranking twenty-five descriptive paragraphs written by Dickens. Without assigning any authors, he had asked his Adult Education students what they thought about the paragraphs. Most students had made comments about the contents of the paragraphs; not one of the ten students had mentioned that one paragraph was better than another. When they were then told to rank the paragraphs, most of the students had been annoyed, perplexed, or frustrated. Some students said that they could not or would not do it; it took much urging to make them rank the paragraphs. Many students were uncertain about their rankings or made them hesitantly. When they were later given the same paragraphs with the names of American and English authors assigned to each of them, they expressed relief because the task had been simplified. Some subjects now ranked the paragraphs differently than before. When asked about the differences, a few of them said that they had guessed before but that now they were guided by the names. A few said that the names had made it easier because they could now use their knowledge of literature. When the names were changed, a few subjects rearranged the paragraphs so that the ranking was in line with their previous rank for the author. Some of them claimed that the reassigned names changed their ranking because the author's name made them see the paragraph in a new light; others said that they changed because they had not been sure the first time. Still others said that it was confusing to have to rank so many paragraphs, nor could they remember what they had done the first time.

Wertheimer suggested experimental variations in which the subjects were told to remember how they ranked the paragraphs for future use. He also suggested that fewer paragraphs should be used and that the subjects should be given repeatedly the paragraphs without names assigned, until they consistently ranked them in the same way. Only then should they be asked to rank the paragraphs with the names assigned to them. ASL tried this out in another of his adult education classes; however, because the subjects found the task disagreeable, he discontinued the study. Wertheimer also suggested other variations of the Sherif experiment in which subjects would be asked to rank the authors' names several times, with and without giving them examples from the authors' writings and with and without telling them to study selections from their work for future use. (This study was used by one of ASL's students to test the effects of his teaching literature to junior high school pupils.) Since Wertheimer said that the paragraphs were too similar in style and content, we planned studies in which the style and/or content of each paragraph was different. Descriptions and dialogues from Proust, Hamsun, Balzac, Joyce, Poe, Tolstoy, Mann, Hardy, Upton Sinclair, and Sinclair Lewis were used.

3. A few days later ASL told Wertheimer about a study that he had conducted to test Sherif's theses and went on to say that he agreed with Wertheimer that social influences on judgment took place in terms of a certain range within which the other person's statement seemed reasonable. For example, if you show someone one of the ambiguous drawings he had made for

the experiment and told him that you saw a battleship in it, the subject would not agree with you but he would agree if you said that you saw things in it that were at least partially supported by the drawings. A student who had joined the discussion said that the ranges one uses depend on one's experience. When one is very little one's father looks big, a walk around the block is a big walk, two or three pennies are a lot of money, Swiss cheese is too sharp, cigarettes are nauseating. But when one grows up, his father is smaller, a walk around the block is a short walk, three pennies is very little, and Swiss cheese and cigarettes are appetizing. In response to Wertheimer's questions, the student said that his illustrations were of two kinds of changes; the cheese and cigarettes are judged differently because of physiological changes, but the judgment of size is due to changes of a psychological nature, it is due to learning to translate one's personal judgments into society's standards of measurement. He went on to say that social influences on judgment are different when there is an external standard of measurement than when there is none. The use of such external standards like a ruler saves one from being overwhelmed by his own and other people's subjective judgment. The discussion then turned to how one develops subjective judgment scales such as pleasantness and how one learns objective scales or standards such as inches and quarts. The previous speaker said that there is a difference in the way they are learned; the former are learned informally and incidentally and the latter are learned formally and systematically. A student said that when a child says that he has walked a million blocks, we correct him by saying that he has walked ten blocks or we may try to give him an appreciation of the size of the number he has used. He went on to say that the so-called subjective ranges are not accessible for scientific analysis. Wertheimer challenged the idea that whatever cannot be studied by existing methods or does not fit existing ideas of science is to be banished from psychology. He referred the students to developments in psychophysics and probability theory where the so-called subjective factors are being studied and asked them to write to him their opinions of them.

When the discussion turned to ethical standards, Wertheimer objected to the notion that there was no objective basis for determining what was good or bad. When the students insisted that what was good was determined by the standards of the group, Wertheimer remarked that this was too sweeping a generalization. Of course, the question of what is good is sometimes answered in terms of what is required by the social situation rather than by the evidence; the group standards and the social influences are given more weight than the requirements of the object of judgment but there are also cases of judgments that are in terms of the evidence. We need to study such situations too. He added that there are social influences that blind and there are social influences that open peoples' eyes to what is required by the structure of the situation. We need to study both kinds of social influences if we are not to have a one-sided view of social influence.

On the way to the subway station ASL told Wertheimer that he had been replicating Sherif's experiments and had found that there was a certain amount of uncertainty in the subjects' judgments. Some subjects were not sure about the ranking. It was a difficult task to rank the men; it was easier to group them into classes or to say whether or not they liked them or knew their work. However, there were a few students who had had no difficulty, who had been certain and had repeated their rankings correctly on different days. Some of the subjects' responses had reflected their courses on literature and their ideologies. But, generally speaking, the results supported Sherif's thesis about the role of social norms in determining the judgment of the paragraphs. It seemed to ASL from Wertheimer's remarks that he was interpreting Sherif's results in terms of their offering support for ideological views about social behavior. He therefore told him that Sherif and Cantril believed in democracy and were humanists. Wertheimer reiterated the need to know more about what actually happened in such judgmental situations before we made generalizations. He wanted to know what kind of factors had to be introduced to make the subjects face the evidence or the object of judgment in a more direct, honest way and not to deal superficially with it. He hypothesized that Sherif's results might be related to the methods of teaching and learning literature that led students to revere names but did not make them come to grips with the authors' writings and, more generally, to an education that did not teach one to appreciate art but to repeat names and evaluations made by others; it taught one to rely on others and not to look for oneself.

Experimental Outgrowths

One of the most popular courses in the WPA Adult Education School in which ASL taught was a course in modern world literature that focused on the modern novel. Many of the students who took this course were also students in ASL's course in psychology. Because ASL used the project method of teaching, it was possible to conduct many of the experiments suggested by Wertheimer. The results of the experiments led to experimental variations which became students' term projects. Some of these experiments were later used in ASL's courses in Social Psychology at Yeshiva College and McGill University where they became projects which were carried out by the students as an integral part of the course.

1. The names of fifty European novelists, among whom were Nobel Prize winners of literature, were presented to the students. They were asked to write after the name of each author whether or not they liked his work and to state why. After they finished, they were asked to indicate how well they knew each author by putting a line through any author of whom they never had heard and by circling the name if they had heard it in their course. They were asked to write where they had heard about the authors with whom they were familiar and to list the books they had read of each of these authors. This usually took about one hour. After this the class discussed their answers. There were students who said that they liked or disliked an author even though they had read none of his work. Their comments were based on the man's reputation, his philosophy of life, or his political and socioeconomic beliefs. Some of their judgments reflected their teacher's opinions of the author and their teacher's ideological point of view, or the dominant liberal philosophy of the day. There was very little relation between the numbers of his books they had read and their liking of an author.

2. In another class the students ranked forty authors on a list that included the twenty most known and twenty least known from the previous study. A month later they ranked the names again. The well-known names were often

ranked nearly the same way both times but the unknown names were often not ranked the same way; the correlation between the two rankings was .60.

3. Twenty-five paragraphs were used that were written by authors from the first study including ten of the best known authors, ten of the least known, and five who were not known. The author's names were not assigned to the paragraphs. They were asked to indicate whether or not they liked each paragraph using a five point scale (like, more like than dislike, neutral feeling, more dislike than like, dislike) and were asked to give reasons for each rating. Some subjects judged the content of the paragraph, for example, they liked the descriptive paragraphs better than dialogues or vice versa, or they judged the ideas that were expressed. A few students judged the paragraphs in terms of their literary style and a few students recognized the book from which the paragraphs were drawn and used as the basis for their rating their opinions of the book or their attitudes toward the author, his work, or his style of writing.

4. When the same twenty-five paragraphs were given to other subjects to rank and they were asked to give the reasons for each ranking, the students had more trouble than in the previous study. However, the bases of their ranking tended to be the same as the ratings in the previous study.

The last two experiments were replicated in other classes with one change: the name of the author was assigned to each paragraph. Now the subjects found it easier to rank and to rate the paragraphs and there were fewer failures to respond than in the previous experiments. From their comments it seemed that the names directed their thinking to what they knew about the authors and their works. This is related to Wertheimer's idea that the name may arouse a background of information which the person utilizes to evaluate the paragraph.

5. When the subjects were again given the paragraphs a month later, there tended to be less changes in the rating and the ranking of those authors who were well-known to them than of those who were not known. Moreover, there was more variability in the ranking than in the rating of the paragraphs.

6. In another study we asked students to rank one hundred authors' names. One group was told that they must not leave out any name from their ranking. Another group was told that they were allowed to leave out names if they did not know the author. In still another group the subjects were told that they must not rank a man whose work they had not read. The rankings and the subsequent discussions revealed that some students in all three groups ranked men whom they did not know and whose work they had not read. They said that if a name seemed familiar or if it was a name that they had once heard or read about in their literature course, they ranked it. A few students admitted that they had guessed.

We modified this study by telling the students to cross out all names they did not know before the ranking was done. There were students who wanted to show that they were knowledgeable about literature and were reluctant to cross out names. A few ranked some authors high because they were famous even though they had personally found their work to be boring and uninteresting.

7. In another study we used biblical stories and Greek myths but interchanged the names of the people and places in them. The Adult Education students were asked to indicate which were Greek myths and which were bi-

blical stories. Some students who had rarely or never read the Bible tended to group the stories in terms of the names. After they were told which were the biblical stories and which were the Greek myths, they were asked to differentiate between the writing styles of the stories.

8. In still another study, we read to the students passages from Proust's *Swan's Way* and told them to compare the style with those of Stevenson and Joyce. A few weeks later they were given paragraphs which were taken from the works of Huxley or Hardy but were attributed to Mann, France, Proust, Hugo, Balzac, Lewis, Tolstoy, Gorky, Mark Twain, Upton Sinclair, Hamsun, Bojer, Werfel, and Wassermann. Some students challenged the authorship of the paragraphs but many did not notice anything strange or wrong about the paragraphs even though they had some knowledge of the works of all or most of the authors from their courses in literature and even though some of the paragraphs were at variance with what they knew about the authors' works.

Conclusions: All these studies give support to both Sherif's and Wertheimer's conjectures. Because of the nature of the social situation and personal factors, the subjects felt that they had to make a judgment even though they were given only a few sentences. Due to their uncertainty about the evidence, the subjects used the names as cues about the qualities of the writing and thus were able to make judgments. They were unsure about the material which they had to rank and relied on what they had learned in school about the authors. In all the demonstrations there were students who knew the writers' works, their styles of writing as well as their ideas but even among these subjects there were individuals who relied on the names. The names made them think about the work of the particular author and they then proceeded to rank the paragraph in terms of their general conception of the author's work. Although some subjects' responses were brought about by a rational process, their answers, however, were similar to those subjects who had merely ranked the names and were not at all concerned with the work of the authors. Thus the same responses were brought about by different processes, by rote memory, or on a reasonable basis. There were subjects who liked the same author or rated his name or work the same way but they did it for different reasons; here two different processes brought about the same response.

18
More on the Sherif-Type Experiment

In another seminar given two years later, Wertheimer told the class that Sherif and Cantril had in a recent study given subjects musicians' names to rank. A few weeks later they played selections and asked them to rank the musical selections. Each selection was attributed to one of the musicians whose names they had previously ranked but actually they were all written by the same music professor. Wertheimer asked the class to predict the results. A student said that the subjects probably ranked the selections in the same way as they had done the names. Wertheimer remarked that the subjects tended to rate the music in the same way as the names. Moreover, Sherif and Cantril had included a foreign name and a common American name which did not belong to any musician and the nonexistent foreign composer was ranked higher than the nonexistent American. Wertheimer asked for comments and then said that his first reaction to the study was to wonder who the subjects were. He asked the class to hazard a guess. He told the class that he was surprised to find out that they were students with considerable formal education in music. After a pause for comments he asked what kind of education produced such behavior. A visitor said that in the music appreciation tests given in school, one was often given a short musical selection and asked to identify it. In view of this the Sherif and Cantril study was a normal kind of school activity. Such music education made one revere names rather than face the structure of the music.

After a pause, Wertheimer said, When someone is given such a small musical selection he tries to get some meaning out of it. When he is told that it has been written by Beethoven or Mozart, he may ask himself from which work of Beethoven or Mozart it comes. He might succeed in relating the selection to something Mozart had composed and therefore rate it higher than another selection that he had related to another composer. He might not succeed in relating it to anything that a famous musician had written, or he might be aware that it was a meaningless or mediocre selection by the famous man but say to himself that the master must have been asleep when he wrote it or say that it was perhaps from something that he had never published and then rank the master higher than the others because of the superior quality of most of his work. Because of the social atmosphere of the school situation, some subjects might have felt ashamed to say that the material which had been given to them to judge was senseless. ASL pointed out that people give descriptions or impressions of a person on the basis of little or no information; perhaps in the Sherif studies we are witnessing the same tendency of

231

people to go beyond the evidence to make statements and judgments.

Wertheimer went on to criticize the music that had been used in the study. He sat down at the piano, played a few very short selections, and after asking the class to rank them, proceeded to analyze them. After this he played the music again and asked for another ranking, helping the students to see the difference in the structural meaning of the selections. Some students realized the structural differences but others protested that Wertheimer was assuming that music had inherent qualities. It was well-known that Americans listening to Chinese music would think that they were hearing meaningless noise and Chinese men who did not know European music might applaud the New York Philharmonic Orchestra after the musicians had tuned up their instruments. What was noise to people of one culture might be music to people of another culture and vice versa. Wertheimer objected to this thesis and told the class that during the German post-war inflation, he had made a wager of one-half million marks that it was possible to recognize and to judge correctly music of different cultures. He had won the wager. In response to a question he said that after one got over the feeling of the strangeness of the foreign music, one began to appreciate it and was able to discriminate between various musical selections such as funeral, wedding, and martial music. The students persisted in giving examples from their textbooks to prove that it was not possible to do what he had claimed. Wertheimer said that he did not mean to say that everybody who heard a strange melody would immediately grasp its meaning. If a melody were played to educated Japanese they would be cautious and nice but an open and frank reaction would reveal that they had not understood it. If someone were not acquainted with chickens or Chinese or white people, he might think that all chickens were alike and, similarly that all Chinese and white people were alike in appearance. One was overwhelmed by their common features; because one did not understand them, the differences could not be understood. He went on to say that music was composed in a certain frame of reference. If one was unfamiliar with the particular frame of reference, he would not notice the subtle differences between sounds. Years ago Europeans thought that Chinese music was bad but after awhile they found out that European music was not the only kind of music. In order to understand other kinds of music we have to understand them in terms of their cultural frames of reference. We can not understand them unless we get beneath the frame of reference.

In response to questions, Wertheimer said that social, cultural, and personality factors played a role in the judgment of music. Certain music might be popular because it fitted the times of the society. Certain needs and moods might make one prefer one kind of music to another. But this does not mean that one is incapable of facing the meaning of the structural features of the music. Wertheimer then wrote notes on the blackboard and played the music on the piano. (Since ASL was ignorant of the technical aspects of the music, he did not record it and thus cannot present Wertheimer's analysis). Wertheimer then said that he was going to play two musical selections. After he played the selections, he asked the class to write down what each selection meant. He then replayed them and asked which one was gay, which one was sad and why. He went on to improvise on the piano and asked the class to guess the moods and the social events the music portrayed. Many students judged the music correctly. Sometimes he told the class that one selection was a wedding march and the other a funeral march or that one selection represented joy and the other grief but in playing them he switched the selections around. Some students were not fooled. The rest of the session was spent in discussing with the students why some of them had been fooled and others not. He played and replayed the music during the discussion to illustrate what misled them or to make clear the music's structure (cf. Wertheimer, 1910 for a report on his research on music of primitive people).

Before dismissing the class, Wertheimer told the class about Razran's conditioning experiment in which students ate sandwiches while listening to music. The aim of the study was to see whether we can cultivate any music taste we please. Is it true that we can make people like certain music just as we teach a dog to salivate to Bach or to Beethoven? What doctrine about the nature of man is implied here?

After-Class Discussion

Some students sat in the cafeteria talking about Wertheimer's musical demonstration. Someone said that Wertheimer was assuming that the emotion, feeling, or meaning expressed was inherent within the music but many experiments on music and art had shown that there was no intrinsic meaning in music; one projected meaning into it. Someone reminded the students of the Arnheim-Wertheimer experiments on expressive movements that seemed to indicate that there was an intrinsic connection between the structure of a person's behavior and what an observer saw it express. When Wertheimer sat down a student was saying that he could not understand why Wertheimer had expected students to recognize the styles of writers and musicians. It took much training to do this. Wertheimer remarked that experience and training did play a role but that the effects of experience could be positive or negative. Certain kinds of experiences could open one's eyes to the structural features of a composer's music or an artist's work while other kinds of experience could blind one. He added that Cantril and Sherif's results might have been due to the kind of education the subjects had received. He then asked, What kind of education would lead to an awareness that all of the musical selections or all of the passages of prose were written by one person?

ASL said that it might be possible to get the subjects to face the music and not the names if the music had a physiological impact on them. Suppose two pieces were played, one gentle, quiet, and smooth but the other jarring, noisy, and erratic. Would subjects agree if their descriptions were interchanged? Someone conjectured that calling a pleasant sound unpleasant and an unpleasant sound pleasant might initially lead to a rejection of the descriptions but that the subjects could be made to agree to such descriptions if sufficient pressures were exerted. Wertheimer said, Suppose you have a two-day-old kitten and that you approach it, making a brutal or gentle movement toward it. The kitten will usually behave differently to the two kinds of movements. It gets the meaning of your gesture, of what you are doing. But some psychologists would say that we can condition the kitten to respond to the gentle movement as it does to the brutal movement, and vice versa. When someone said that an animal can be so conditioned that it will behave as though nothing has happened following an action, Wertheimer said that he would like to see psychologists actually do these things instead of arguing about whether the kitten understood the meanings of the two kinds of actions. What kind of world would make such results possible; what would the effects of such a world be on the animal?

When Wertheimer left, the students discussed his proposed conditioning experiment. Someone said there was no need to run the experiment with cats; we need only observe the social scene. In Germany, the Nazis' behavior is called heroic, brave, honest, and Christian but anti-Nazis call it brutal, dishonest, and unchristian. Nazis and their opponents see things differently because of conditioning. Many Americans saw the Moscow trials as frightful and cruel but the Stalinists saw them as just and proper. Someone remarked that such reversals were easier to accomplish in men than in kittens because men could so rationalize and intellectualize their behavior that love became hate and hate became love. The rest of the discussion focused on other historical incidents that illustrated this point. As the group parted, one student said that they had overlooked cases which did not fit the thesis; perhaps man has survived because of the overlooked cases.

Experimental Outgrowths

Wertheimer's remarks led to a series of studies in which subjects were asked which of two metal plates was warmer or gave less of a shock; which of two odors or liquids was more pleasant; which of two sounds had a nicer tone; which of two bright surfaces was less glaring. ASL's adult education students judged correctly even when told that most people responded differently. Because of the pain inflicted on the subjects the studies were discontinued (cf. Luchins and Luchins, 1966, 1967, 1970). In discussing these experiments with Wertheimer, we planned a number of studies that would not involve discomfort. A lively martial march was played to the class and the students were told to write their impressions of it. Then a very sad dirge was played and again they were asked to write their impressions. After this, the class was told that the first piece was a dirge and the second a martial march. The class protested. When ASL insisted and was backed up by a few music students who served as his confederates, many subjects would still not agree. There were, however, students who were willing to agree. When challenged by the other students, they gave very complicated explanations, for example, that the funeral march was the dirge for a fierce and bold general. When ASL reported this to Wertheimer, he suggested that special selections be composed that clearly portrayed an emotion, for example, sadness, gladness. This still has to be done.

19
Lorge's Experiment

A visitor told the class about a recent study by Irving Lorge that corroborated Sherif's work and Thorndike's learning theory. Lorge asked his subjects whether they agreed or disagreed with such a quotation as, The government should support the people and not the people the government. The same quotation was attributed to different people, to Hoover and to FDR. Lorge found that subjects who were Democrats agreed with the quotation when it was attributed to FDR but disagreed with it when it was atttributed to Hoover. Republicans agreed when it was attributed to Hoover but disagreed when it was attributed to FDR. Generally speaking, subjects agreed with a sentence when it was attributed to a leader of their party and disagreed with it when it was attributed to a member of their rival party. The visitor went on to say that the study testified to the generality of Thorndike's conception of learning; what was right was what the teacher, parent, leader, authority said was right. This led to an argument over the Law of Effect. The argument was interrupted by Wertheimer, who told the class that he was going to read two statements, one from Earl Browder and the other from FDR. He then said, Here is the statement from Browder. After he had read it he asked, Do you agree with him? Answer yes or no and give your reasons. After the class had written their answers, he said as he picked up the next paragraph, Oh, I made a mistake. The statement that I just read to you is FDR's. It is from the end of his Madison Square Garden speech in 1936. Some students expressed surprise. He continued. Do you agree with him? Answer yes or no and give your reasons. Wertheimer then asked the students who had changed their answers and those who had not to explain why they did or did not change. Those who had changed said that the statements meant a different thing when said by FDR or by Browder. Of those who had not changed some said that it was the same sentence or that it preached revolution and war and that they were against all violence; still others said that they did not agree with the views of either Browder or FDR.

The discussion returned to Lorge's experiment when someone said that it showed the importance of judging a proposition in terms of its contents or logic and not being influenced by who said it. Too often people are misled in their judgments of a proposition by the fact that they like or do not like who said it, for example, Love they neighbor as thyself is interpreted differently by some people if they know that it comes from *Leviticus* or that it comes from the *Gospels. Proclaim liberty throughout the land* is interpreted differently if one is told that it comes from *Leviticus* or that it is the inscription on the Liberty

Bell. A visitor said that the speaker is assuming that statements are isolated facts like the *pure sensa* of perception, but Gestalt psychologists have shown that things get their meanings from their places, roles, and functions in structures. No one took up the analogy to perception, instead they argued about the statistical design of Lorge's experiment.

Wertheimer asked, Did Lorge's subjects know or realize that they were judging the same sentence; did they really base their answers only on the men's names; did they agree with Jefferson because they liked him or liked Democrats and disagree with Lenin because they did not like him or the Communists? Just what were the bases for their saying yes or no? After a pause, Wertheimer remarked, Lenin once said that a little revolution every now and then is perfectly all right; like a summer cloudburst it refreshes the earth and clears the atmosphere. He asked the class to write whether or not they agreed with Lenin and to give their reasons. He then reread the same sentence but now told them that it was also once said by Jefferson. After they wrote whether or not they agreed with Jefferson and gave their reasons Wertheimer asked, Are Jefferson and Lenin saying the same thing? After a pause he said that Jefferson had spoken to cool the passions of government officials who wanted to take strong measures to punish people in Washington, Pennsylvania, who had participated in the Whiskey Rebellion, protesting a federal tax policy. He asked the students to write whether or not they now agreed with Jefferson and why. The results of the demonstration were clear. Now most students agreed with Jefferson because the meaning of the quotation had changed when they understood the circumstances under which it was uttered. The visitor said that this does not invalidate Lorge's thesis because before they were told of the historical context, students had agreed with Lenin or with Jefferson merely because they agreed with Lenin's or Jefferson's political ideology. Wertheimer replied that he does not deny that a statement is sometimes judged in terms of who said it but this does not mean that one always agrees or disagrees blindly because of one's likes or dislikes. If one knows or realizes the circumstances under which it was made he may see it in a different light. He went on to question the thesis that in all cases of social influence people reacted in the manner implied by Lorge's thesis, namely, that they focused only on who made the statement and did not take into account the situation in which it was made. In many social situations it would be stupid to act in this way. A student interjected what he thought were examples of Wertheimer's thesis, saying that in social situations the greetings *How are you?* or *How do you feel?* are not interpreted in the same way as when they are posed in a hospital by one's physician during ward rounds. The word *yes* in a telephone conversation does not mean the same thing as *yes* in courtroom testimony. The word *no* may mean *yes* in certain situations and *yes* may mean *no*. Someone argued that these were examples of special ritualized social situations. Lorge's study, however, referred to situations which involved issues of values, beliefs, and philosophy. Such situations were usually much more fluid and ambiguous and therefore people were influenced in them by prestigeful figures. He went on to present evidence of blind, irrational agreement with what one's teachers, parents, and leaders say. He then objected to Wertheimer's thesis that the same sentence means something different in terms of a person's ideology or philosophy than in his daily dealings with people in ordinary situations. The visitor objected that the discussion was overlooking what Lorge had done; Lorge was testing Thorndike's theory of learning. He went on to say that Wertheimer's classroom demonstrations could not be used as evidence against Thorndike's theory.

Wertheimer suggested that Lorge's experiment be repeated with the following modifications. Ask the subjects why they say yes or no and what is the meaning of each sentence. After they answer conduct an inquiry; show the subjects their answers and ask them why they changed if they changed; ask them why they did not change, if they did not. Also, ask them under what conditions and for what interpretations of the sentence they would and/or would not change. Wertheimer added, Ask them if they know when, why, and where each man originally made the statement; give them the information if they do not have it and see what happens to their answers.

In the next session Wertheimer read from newspaper clippings and then asked the students for comments. A student remarked that the same event had been described differently and that he could guess that one report was from the *New York Times* and the other from a Hearst newspaper. He went on to say that the schools and the press mold the minds of man so that they will have certain predictable attitudes. Wertheimer agreed that people may think about things as newspapers and teachers have taught them to think; one can predict from what some people say just what newspapers they read or the kind of education they have received. Does this mean that people do not ever judge on an objective basis, that what they say is determined by the newspapers? When the same student said that there is evidence that this is so, Wertheimer suggested that we investigate how prevalent this is and find out what are the factors that bring it about. In response to an argument he said, O.K. suppose fifty percent do it. So what? Someone said that research on social influences is actually dealing with errors in thinking due to *argumentum ad hominem;* we need to know how such errors are brought about. A visitor said that the research reflects a traditional thesis. When thinking is in terms of the laws of logic it is rational; when it is not, it is irrational. Contemporary research has accepted this thesis in its stress on such factors as suggestibility. Just because thinking does not conform to the laws of Formal Logic does not mean that it is irrational.

Wertheimer remarked, Suppose I gave you the same sentence and you first see it as Marx's and then you see it as Cantril's. Would you agree with Cantril because he is the kind of man you admire or trust as a scientist and would you not agree with it because it was said by Marx because he is not the kind of man you admire? Suppose you admire both men, Would you each time agree with the statement? A college instructor gave examples in which people agreed with statements merely because they admired the person to whom it was attributed, his profession, or ideology.

Wertheimer wrote on the blackboard, (1) thing + value (2) thing + value in it, saying that these are two theses about what takes place in evaluation. Cantril and Sherif assume the first thesis, that values are arbitrarily attached to something, blind to its structure. Is it true that all cases of evaluation are explained by thesis I? Someone pointed out that Sherif's work with the Autokinetic Effect supported thesis 1. The subjects did not question whether or not the light actually had moved when they disagreed in their judgment; they did not examine the evidence but finally agreed because of personal or social factors and not because of the nature of the evidence. The light never moved, the movement was an illusion; if they had been oriented to the evidence their disagreements would have made them suspect that the light did not move or at least that the movement was illusionary and that the different judgments were equally correct. Wertheimer said, The thesis that the light in the Autokinetic Effect does not move is an old fairytale. If you place a quiet [stationary] object on the retina it will move; vice versa is not true. The frame of reference is important; if there is none, then it [the stimulus on the retina] is labile to the least move. In response to a question, he drew the following:

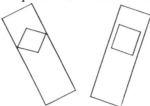

and said that the inner figure looks different because of the frame in which it is. He added that the fact that the frame of reference changes one's view of the figure does not mean that one arbitrarily sees it as he wishes.

Wertheimer brought the discussion back to the newspaper clippings when he said that they do not prove the generality of the first thesis, that there is no relation between evidence and evaluation. Newspapers do not just tell one that this or that is the correct way to think, they present some evidence to support their stories. When someone pointed out that they tell lies and half-truths, Wertheimer remarked that a German theologian had once said that even the devil has to speak some truth or else the people would not follow him. Someone remarked that Lincoln had once said that you can fool some of the people some of the time but you cannot fool all the people all the time. This statement was challenged by a student who argued that if one controls all the news media, the schools, and the police force it is possible to fool all the people all the time; this is the way of autocrats and dictators. ASL's student pointed out that there must be something in man's nature that makes him seek evidence and not do things blindly because even the Bible contains examples of God reasoning with man and pointing to evidence.

Wertheimer asked the class to comment on the use of the terms *election* and *self-determination* by FDR and by Hitler. After a pause he said, To FDR it means that you can vote without threat or violence; to Hitler it means that if you disagree with him he'll kill you. He intimidates people to vote for him, it is a criminal use of the words to avoid issues. The words *voting* and *plebiscite* mean different things in America and in Germany. In response to questions, he said that according to Koffka we have to distinguish between the geographical and the behavioral worlds of the subject when we talk about the stimulus to which he reacts; this distinction may help to explain why the subjects react differently to the same thing. One could also use Duncker's distinction between the stimulus and the situational meaning of the stimulus to account for what happens in such experiments. He went on to say that a stimulus is a part in a field and that the field determines the stimulus. In response to a student's argument that the evaluation of the stimulus does not actually change, he remarked that one may say that the standards change the meaning and therefore the content of the judgment changes. How can we go about testing this assumption?

Someone described a study in which he asked students to judge politicians and after this he gave them a fictitious report of how the group had judged them. When he asked them to judge the politicians again they now changed their judgments in terms of the group's. Wertheimer told him that he would have asked the subjects, What kind of politicians did you think of when you judged them and when you were given the group's norms? Maybe they judged the politicians in terms of what they had done. FDR and Norman Thomas were men who accomplished things of real merit and therefore they were placed in the high status group, but other men were considered to be like Tammany Hall bosses and therefore they were placed in the low status group. Someone argued that the group's norm defines the meaning of the situation and therefore all depends on it. Another student objected to the view that the standards arbitrarily changed their meanings. He went on to describe the techniques of propaganda in order to prove that people do what everybody else is doing. After a pause, Wertheimer distinguished between two kinds of propaganda, the Democratic and the Fascistic. The former deals with or tries to change facts, the latter tries to change emotions. He went on to distinguish between propaganda that blinds and propaganda that aims at enlightenment, that gives one an opportunity to think. In response to a direct question he said that we can evaluate propaganda as being good or bad on the basis of whether it is efficient or not efficient, or on the basis of whether it sheds light, lets one have a genuine reaction, clears up contents, or blinds people. Someone remarked that Wertheimer is mixing up ethics with propaganda which is a technology based on the use of scientific facts about how people behave. It seeks to predict and control behavior, therefore, it is either efficient or not efficient.

Wertheimer told these two stories. The police of Darmstadt raided the office of a deputy and found in it treasonable papers, plans for a revolution, etc. When these papers were published Hitler's press headlined on page one that it was an invention of the police; the deputy never did these things. Thus you see how the Democrats use lies to fight the Nazis. On the second page the deputy claimed that the seized papers were only plans to beat the Communists when they'd dare to rise; they were plans to fight the government if it did not fight the Communists. One of Hitler's dailies carried a daily column, *How the Government Lies*. It once carried a story about a famous socialist which was a clear lie. When Wertheimer met a Nazi leader in a checker game, he asked him, Is it true? The man said, It is not. It is a possible lie. Wertheimer then said to him, You say that the Nazis want to bring sincerity into the government. I do not understand this. The Nazi said, It's not a lie; it's propaganda. We enlighten the people to the truths of the Nazis and the lies of the Democrats. Wertheimer asked the class, What does this illustrate? A student remarked that all propaganda, whether it is to propagate a faith or a political ideology uses such statements.

In the next session a visiting college instructor brought the discussion back to Lorge's experiment when he said that Lorge's study demonstrated clearly that people judge in terms of labels. Wertheimer said, Maybe it proves that the prestige of Lenin is greater because he says what the subjects like. . . . The prestige of the statement caused the evaluation of Lenin. . . . Therefore what is proved is the other way around. . . . Lorge assumes that the stimulus (the sentence) is identical in both situations but maybe the sentence is different depending on who said it. He is interested in the question of plus or minus and not the nature of the material. After a pause he said, How about the possibility that such factors as reason, sincerity played a role? In old psychology such things were considered to play a role; Gestalt psychology is trying to bring it into psychology again. After the visitor objected to the last statement, Wertheimer illustrated the extreme opposite procedure of his conjecture by saying, Suppose a child of ten gets two letters, one from a man he knows to be good and the other from a bad man. He expects something good from one and something bad from the other. Can we say that prestige influenced his choice because he throws away the bad man's letter without opening the envelope? A wise child will not be satisfied with looking at the unopened envelope but looks into it. . . . As long as your attitude is to the closed envelope, you get Lorge's results but if you look at the contents you might get different reactions. . . . This was known by old-time logicians and philosophers. They formulated it as a formal fallacy, *argumentum ad hominem*. After a pause he said, There is the questions of confidence. Is it different from prestige? I found him reliable is not the same thing as saying that my group told me he is OK.

Wertheimer remarked, Suppose the president of the USA asked a teacher to try to influence the political opinions of his class. The teacher not only admired FDR but agreed with his opinion but he said that he enjoyed how students faced arguments even if it went against him, yet there were certain dangerous topics which he avoided. He would lose his status in his political and social group if he brought them up. Therefore he sticks to the safe topics. What does this illustrate? This shows external influence. But there are other factors too involved. What are they? After a pause he said that the thesis of external value is related to the thesis of sociological relativism. Forty years ago many people believed that there is a difference between good and bad, right and wrong; to make this differentiation is a human ability. It's one of man's characteristics, of Homo sapiens. This belief has changed due to anthropologist's finding differences in evaluation in different cultures. . . .

The finding that the same stimuli are evaluated differently does not prove the thesis of sociological relativism. The same thing under different conditions may mean a different thing. We need to find out what the behavior means in each society. Duncker (1939) has pointed this out. Many stick to the thesis of cultural relativism because they can't see another positive theory. After students' comments he said that there is a widespread belief that the old traditional axioms cannot be taken as universal axioms and that it is hard to get new axioms. However there is the start now of a new theory of value and evaluation. . . . The Sherif kind of experiment is considered to be basic to the study of social values. Wertheimer drew, $\underline{(A) \neq \text{Evaluation} (B)}$ saying, B is at-

tached to A; A and B are heterogeneous. One can attach the same attitude or value to all kinds of contents. There are such cases, where there is no inner connection between the thing and the value but even in this arbitrary situation the person's behavior can be explained as due to reasonable assumptions, for example, hearing other men's reaction may lead to intelligent thoughts on the matter, not blind imitation. After a pause he said that Sherif's and Lorge's experiments exclude the possibility of objective evaluation; we need experiments of the other extreme. He agreed that maybe it is difficult to do this because they play too little a role but we could help them play a bigger role.

In response to a student's comment Wertheimer said, There is no general trait to imitate. The task is to find out the characteristic differences between cases of imitation and no imitation, and to find the factors underlying each. After a pause he said that man is not merely shaped by drill. Man has some tendency to face issues, to be oriented to and to try to grasp objective qualities of situation and objects, and man may long for justice.

After a pause he told the class about an experiment in which he first read to a class an editorial on pacifism. Two weeks later he gave them four arguments pro and four arguments counter. After this he asked them, What will Hitler think if he sees your arguments that we'll never go to war? A few students then said, Oh, it will mean, just go ahead with your plan; it'll increase his aggressiveness. Some students reacted to them with counter-arguments and rationalizations but still others said that this experience made them see that they were not justified in their opinions. Wertheimer went on to conjecture that the experiment illustrates that miscentering of the social field may be due to field conditions. He added, Even German refugees have some opinions that are like the Nazis' because of having been exposed to the social field in Germany. The Nazis gave them solutions to all kinds of problems, therefore, they have a clear field.

The discussion returned to Lorge's and Sherif's experiment when someone said that he still believes that evaluations are fixations and stereotypes that are established by external factors. Attitudes and evaluations are determined by the prestige or the evaluations given to a person, author, object, or event by a group; social standards are given to a person by his society and thus evaluation has nothing to do with the objects themselves. Wertheimer remarked that this is similar to the accepted ideas about psychology of learning, for example, conditioning, and is similar to sociological relativism. Is it true that what you evaluate plus or minus is due to what you were taught by your group, that it depends on social approval, that social approval brings pleasure, therefore you do it? How valid is the axiom of pain-pleasure? After a pause he said that in replicating Cantril's music experiment he found groups in which the subjects protested; they did not show "the polite attitude to listen and answer." Why the difference in reactions? Maybe it depends on the kind of education of the subjects and social atmosphere in the experimental situation? Perhaps this is an investigation into the type of education and habits of certain groups but not a study of value.

He went on to say that the same thing in two places may mean two different things. Wertheimer played the same motifs and said, If it's said to be Beethoven, it is something tragic; if it's said to be Sousa, it is the start of a very amusing march. Listeners are influenced by the tragic motive, not by Beethoven. He concluded that there is an old axiom, if two people do the same thing, they may not be doing the same thing. It's hard to get it into science. Science deals with sum of stimuli but we must view a stimulus in terms of the role it plays in a situation in order to understand it. What is the reason why it was not accepted? Scientific tools to deal with this axiom were lacking.

Someone asked, Do people think in an atomistic manner? Is it right to think atomistically or is it better not to do so? Wertheimer said that in many situations, even in social influence studies, people do not think in such a way. In some cases it would be extremely stupid to do this, even though it is a scientific manner of behaving. To understand a thing, in certain conditions, you must not be piecemeal in your approach. If you do, you destroy the possibility of studying the phenomenon. In response to a question he presented two theses about consistency of judgment. I. Judgment of a sum of items in a person which are separated but unified in an external way; II. The items which are judged are related to each other in an intrinsic way. In thesis I the contents that are evaluated play no role; for example, advertisers link large or good to anything. In II however we seek the inner quality; the value is intrinsically related. In response to a student's comment he asked, What spreads when we say that prestige spreads? Is it something that is foreign to the content? Someone interrupted to say that prestige is not necessarily in the item itself. Wertheimer remarked, Before talking she was attractive but after speaking she was no longer attractive. What determined her being attractive? The various features may depend on each other; one feature may cast new light on the person, thing, or event which helps one understand the other features. . . . You look at the person or thing and have your eyes focused in a certain way; certain common qualities color your evaluations. If a person has intellectual power but is dishonest you look at his intellect as shrewdness; it now plays a different role than before you knew that he was dishonest. It's not an artificial attachment of a new label but understanding the various elements under one character quality. We do not just pile up events but build up a certain character quality that gives the impression of the thing which we esteem or desire.

20
Prestige

The session began with several remarks by Wertheimer about the widespread use of the concept of prestige in social psychology; it was used to explain leadership, mass movements, advertising, and social influences on judgment, perception, thinking, feeling, and action. Some textbooks describe prestige as a powerful force that enables its possessor to influence and control people. Prestige is an important factor in social control; the greater one's prestige, the greater one's control. Someone interjected that even casual observation reveals that it is a powerful force that enables its possessor to control people's behavior; people with prestige compel obedience and submission to their wills. He went on to say that Lorge's and Sherif's work are important contributions to the understanding of prestige and that he cannot understand Wertheimer's objections to the concept. Wertheimer replied that prestige has been defined in a recent textbook as a characteristic social attitude of a group of individuals toward persons possessing fame or status which predisposes the members of that group to the person's influence through suggestion and imitation. Prestige does not have a rational basis; it is an emotional, nonintellectual feature of man's behavior. Wertheimer asked, What doctrine of man, of society, and of the individual's relation to society does this thesis of prestige reflect? A student said that it was anti-democratic; if it was valid, democracy was not possible. The proponents of the democratic way of life believe that the masses possess common sense; if you give them the light they will do what is right. However, opponents of democracy claim that the masses are asses who are led by their emotions; they are swayed and manipulated by social elites, the people with prestige. Wertheimer added that the democrats believe that social life is based on reason, that people are reasonable, but the Fascists say that social life is devoid of reason, that man loses his intellect as he gives himself up to the irrational forces of the crowd or of the group. He went on to say, Psychologists must carefully examine the concept of prestige before putting it into textbooks because it might justify a belief in Nazism and Fascism and make people believe that democracy is not possible. Someone said that the prestige thesis should not be judged in terms of ideologies but on the basis of the facts behind the thesis. There are numerous examples in daily life which indicate that prestige has an emotional and not an intellectual basis. He argued that the doctrine was a good antidote to the rational model of man that has been advocated by the Philosophical Radicals and by contemporary liberals. Their doctrines have overstressed the reasonableness of man; man is often not really rational and social behavior is often irrational. A person behaves differently when alone and when in a social situation; when alone he

243

may be rational but in a social group he may become irrational because of the operation of prestige suggestion. A visiting professor remarked that psychologists who have used the prestige thesis have sometimes shown a bias toward individualism and liberalism or a bias against statism and socialism. LeBon, who believed in the irrationality of social behavior, favored states that stressed individualism as well as states that favored socialism. Just because one stresses the role of prestige in social life does not mean that one is a Fascist.

Wertheimer said that according to some psychologists the desire for prestige is a basic, innate characteristic of man; the desire is fundamental, all men seek prestige. It is related to man's seeking power, self-enhancement, and other egotistical behavior. There is constant competition to be first. In the struggle to get on top, to get fame, status, and reputation, some people are less successful than others. The less successful conform to and imitate the ways of life of those who are on top. Those on top do not have to be ideal characters because the prestige of their positions endows them with wisdom, virtue, and powers which they really do not have. Psychology texts are replete with examples of how people are fooled by prestigeful persons.

When he paused for comments, a college instructor said that among the Zuni Indians there is very little competition to be first but among the Kwakiutl there is extreme competitiveness for status. Even in our own society there are people who do not seek fame or fortune; they are not at all concerned about the reputations of themselves or others. It is therefore not possible to generalize that all people seek prestige; it is learned behavior and is not due to an innate tendency. ASL pointed out that sometimes little children, the weak, the poor, and even outcasts have prestige to us in the sense that we respond to suggestions or demands from them. Therefore, it is not correct to say that prestige is a powerful force of social control that is wielded only by the mighty and by people of high status; people of low status may also have prestige. Wertheimer remarked that the proponents of the prestige thesis do not deny that who has prestige varies from society to society; that in one society the humble man, the worker, the peasant may have prestige but in another society the arrogant, the capitalist, the landowner may have prestige. They claim that the drive is the same but its form of expression is determined by the society's culture.

After a pause for remarks, Wertheimer said that to other psychologists prestige is an important human attribute that occurs under certain conditions, for example, an immature child looks up to his parents, a sick man looks up to his doctor. In certain kinds of social situations mature and very intelligent individuals do what the prestigeful person does or suggests. According to this thesis, prestige is not due to a fundamental tendency but is created by special factors in the situation. To understand the behavior called prestige, we need to study the characteristics of the situations in which it comes about. We must take into account characteristic structural features of the whole situation in which the behavior takes place. When he paused for comments, students give examples of how people learned that certain persons have prestige. They used the concept of reinforcement and Freud's theory of psychosexual development to explain why certain people have prestige. Wertheimer remarked that all their examples focused on prestige as a trait of the individual and ignored the field conditions in which prestige occurred. Moreover, they were all examples of the first thesis' claim that prestige was due to irrational factors, that it was blind behavior. He asked for counter examples of this thesis, for examples that illustrate the second thesis that he presented.

Wertheimer asked whether the prestige of a movie star was the same as that of a scientific person. Was the prestige of Einstein the same as Clark Gable's; was Jean Harlow's prestige the same as Madame Curie's? When a student said that both were famous and that people looked up to both of them, Wertheimer asked him whether that was all that there was to it. ASL remarked that the advertising industry seems to differentiate between the prestige of movie stars, scientists, and athletes; they are used to sell different products and to appeal to different types of people. Although soap is a chemical, an actress or athlete and not a chemist or dermatologist is used in soap advertisements. A visitor said that perhaps the advertisers had found something out about prestige that the social psychologists did not know or did not put into their textbooks.

A visiting refugee professor said that we speak about contemporary prestigeful objects, institutions, and people as if they meant the same thing to people in the past as they do to us at present, for example, the prestige of the Catholic Church. We do not study their prestige in the context of the past and of the present social conditions but assume it to be the same$_2$ to mean the same thing. In view of the second thesis presented by Wertheimer, their prestige might have had different purposes in the past and present and affected people differently. Moreover, certain objects, institutions, and people that once had no prestige now do have prestige, and vice versa. After a pause, Wertheimer said, What determines the giving of prestige or the taking away of prestige in particular cases? Is the prestige of the Kentucky Derby winner or of Rin Tin Tin the same as the prestige of a man? Is the prestige of an institution the same as an individual's? Is the prestige of certain goods and services the same as that of a person or of an institution?

Someone remarked that in our society the person who has accumulated much property has more prestige than the person who has little or none. The prestige of the rich is seen in the way they control the economy and social political life. But, such people are not esteemed in the USSR. Thus, we see that social groups arbitrarily attach prestige to people. Someone said that this example illustrates the need to understand the situational reasons for the attachment or detachment of the prestige. He went on to say that a basic idea of our society was that if every man had a piece of land that he could call his own, he would have a base from which to operate as a free man. Another idea was that those who made or had goods would take better care of them because they were their own. A related idea is that one who could develop and offer his services wherever he wished would learn and perform them better. The ownership of private property and the free disposal of it had led to the development of our industrial society; we hold wealth in high esteem because of its role in the productivity of our society. A visiting student argued that private property was required in the capitalistic system and therefore the prestige associated with it was justified. But this prestige also blinds us to the fact that private property has also produced evils, poverty, war, and race prejudice. The student then presented the thesis of economic determinism and concluded that private property did not fit the requirements of the present-day's socialized methods of production. The prestige of private property was lower in the USSR because there a social system had been set up that fits the requirements of modern social methods of production. He concluded that prestige was not arbitrarily attached or detached but was given or taken away because of the requirements of the economic system. Some students objected to this formulation; they argued that propaganda and force were being used to make people do and believe what Stalin wanted, that Stalin was looked up to because he had power. The same holds for Hitler, Mussolini, and other dictators throughout the world; they have prestige because they hold the pistol. They argued that some elite groups use more subtle methods to gain prestige, for example, propaganda. A visitor said that by the manipulation of the mass media, public relations men build reputations for mediocre actors and actresses and make angels out of the scoundrels of the political and economic world. [ASL's Adult Education students wondered whether such creation of synthetic prestigeful figures would undermine our society. It might make people think that there were no intrinsic reasons for fame or reputation, that it depended on the subtle or direct use of force. They also pointed out that the use of public relations men to build fame and reputations might result in making people seek notoriety. Their slogan would be like that of Barnum, I do not care what people say about me as long as they talk about me. One student exclaimed, Just think what the world would be like with everybody trying to get into the limelight.]

Wertheimer remarked that the term prestige was often used as if it were a single psychological process, one simple kind of phenomenon—submission to the will of others. Maybe one reacts to so-called prestigeful people for a variety of reasons; prestige is given for many reasons. After a pause he asked for examples in which one had a feeling of nonachievement and saw someone who had what he lacked and therefore he lived or tried to live in that person's world. A college instructor said that it is well known that charwomen read the society page and that secretaries read the gossip columns about the doings of movie stars because they lack what the society women and stars have. When someone said that the behavior of the charwomen constituted an escape from life, Wertheimer admitted that this could be the case but added that we should examine what such people had done before coming under the influence of the prestigeful person. What is the effect of giving prestige on the lives of the giver and the receiver of prestige, and on the lives of those around them? After a pause he said, Consider a person, an adolescent, who looks up to a certain teacher or famous person in the social field. The adolescent sees himself expand and develop in a certain way. In such cases, prestige-giving may help the individual to grow and become a better person. ASL pointed out that in his study of adolescents there were cases of youths who looked up to the local gangsters. They too wanted to have silk shirts, a bankroll, a big car, and dames. In order to achieve this, they became the henchmen of the local gangsters. Some of them behaved like hypnotized individuals who blindly carried out what they were told to do; they were not thinking but dreaming. Someone else described how adolescent girls became prostitutes while imitating local popular girls, prestigeful dress models, or movie stars. Other examples included those in which youths tried to change their manners, beliefs, features, or ways of dress to resemble the prestigeful person with the result that they became alienated from their family, friends, race, religion, nationality, and social class.

Wertheimer said that prestige-giving could have different effects: it could result in self-criticism and self-correction; it could also result in a certain kind of focusing or centering that produces a concentric narrowing of one's visual field. In this narrowed world one may become a slave as he blindly imitates the behavior of others. There is no self-criticism; one is lost in following and conforming to the prestigeful person.

A refugee scholar suggested that Wertheimer was proposing two kinds of prestige; formative prestige, which was essentially cognitive; and emotional prestige, which coincided with the usual conception of prestige. He went on to say that in formative prestige the prestigeful person has to live up to what others see in him or else he loses his prestige, but it is still a kind of conformity. For example, the conscientious student might look up to his teachers and have a great desire to please them. In order to get their approval, he does what they do. Though the student's world might thus be broadened, he is playing a role rather than living his own life. A visitor said that the effects of the two kinds of prestige might be the same for the social field. He challenged the assumption that formative prestige led to or was a process of self-actualization whereas emotional prestige stultified and thwarted the growth of a person's potentialities. Someone said that in formative prestige one saw in the model a certain kind of person and that one had certain expectations about his behavior. If the model did not live up to these expectations, one's world could be destroyed. Thus one would be aware of what the model did. A visitor said that some people are particularly critical of their model's behavior and if the model does not live up to certain standards his prestige suffers.

ASL raised the question whether a prestigeful model's behavior could be transformed because of his awareness that he must live up to the standards which his followers set for him if he is to retain his prestige. Someone gave an example of a girl who was immoral and became moral because some of her classmates idealized her; she felt that she would lose their respect if they found out that she had clay feet. The refugee scholar said that prestige was not always a one-way affair; there was a mutual need between the follower and the leader. Wertheimer remarked that all prestige cannot be conceptualized as a thing attached to a person. In some cases it involves a systemic relationship between the prestigeful person and his worshippers. ASL's student interjected that this reminded him of sayings such as these: God needs man as man needs God; one can not be a king without a kingdom or a leader without followers. The visitor remarked that in order to maintain such a relationship the prestigeful person cannot act in too arbitrary a manner. Perhaps there develops a tacit covenant or social contract in which each has duties and privileges in order to maintain the prestige-giving and -taking relationship.

Wertheimer remarked that it sometimes happens that the prestigeful model helps a person to develop and to outstrip him. He gave as an example a teacher who was admired greatly by a pupil because of his prestige in a certain subject that the pupil wished to learn. The pupil eventually became an expert in the area in which his teacher had introduced him. Though the erstwhile pupil still had great respect for his teacher and appreciated what his teacher had done for him, the teacher no longer had in his eyes the same prestige; his knowledge and work were no longer so formidable. The prestige took a new tone as the structure of their relationship changed. A school-teacher interjected that in view of this formulation, the aim of education should be that the pupil outstrip his teacher rather than be like him. Someone said that Wertheimer's remarks raised the question of the effects of prestige on different people. Some people who have prestige in the eyes of a certain group or person try to maintain it by not letting themselves be out-stripped by their admirers or replaced by other people who are competing with them for the adulation. They do not permit or they try to prevent their followers' outstripping or leaving them. We see this in mothers who do not let their children grow up, in teachers and political leaders who do not permit change in the status quo. Someone remarked that good parents, wise teachers and leaders learn from their followers and become more adept in playing their roles. [In ASL's class the question was raised of the effect of the person's stature on his status, and the effect of his status on his stature.]

After a few remarks by students about the nature of the leadership-followership relationship, several comments were made by them about the roles of authority and suggestion in the lives of men. A student commented that there is developing a negative evaluation of all authority and of the ac-ceptance of suggestion, commands, or requests from authorities. This view may be based on the assumptions that people can make up their own minds, that no one is better than anyone else. Some of the contemporary objections to the doctrine of prestige represent objections to the idea that society must have a hierarchy of statuses. Adherents to egalitarianism do not wish to admit the existence of differences in abilities or capabilities among people. Educators, psychologists, and social workers encourage this new point of view; they claim that a democracy needs leaders, innovators, and not followers. In order to develop leaders the schools encourage each child to feel that he is as good as the next person; educators believe that this stress on equality will bring forth the best possible social world as well as create healthy per-sonalities. Psychologists, sociologists as well as educators claim that children should not be tied to tradition but be free to make their own norms in order to further the progress of mankind. Only authoritarian, anti-democratic lead-ers and educators deny each person the right to participate in the creation of the laws he must obey; a person is not bound to rules and standards made for him by others. Someone pointed out that while tradition may hold back the adventurous and creative individual, to have no tradition may lead to an abuse of those who are not creative or adventurous or not able to actualize themselves, so that tradition may protect the weak.

The session ended with Wertheimer's remarking that we must make a dis-tinction between getting lost in the world of others, merely mimicking their behavior, echoing their speech and thoughts, or developing ourselves through and by the values for which the prestigeful person stands. He added that people may have prestige because of what they have done for us, singly or in groups, in the past, in the present, or what they will do for us in the future. Before he dismissed the class, he told them that he once had listened to an opera at whose conclusion the audience applauded until the tenor, a mediocre singer, took several curtain calls. The man next to Wertheimer remarked that he should have heard the tenor twenty years ago. It was obvious that the tenor was past his prime but the audience still admired him. In fact, most of the people had come just to hear and see him. What do such cases illustrate?

What social conditions produce such behavior? What conditions produce the opposite kind of reactions to people who lose their ability? [Cantril, 1960 tells about Moochie, who was idealized by the prisoners in a Japanese prison of war camp but lost his prestige the moment they were freed. It is instructive to compare Moochie to the tenor. Do these stories reflect different doctrines of the value of a man?]

21
Later Remarks on Prestige

A few years later, in a special seminar on value, Wertheimer read excerpts from several texts on anthropology and psychology to illustrate the dominant view concerning prestige (it was similar to what has already been presented above). He challenged the theses that the seeking of prestige was a universal force, that it was irrational and that it was illogical, and that it always led to blind and arbitrary conforming or following. He went on to say that in all the textbooks' examples prestige was used as if it were one process; no distinction was made between various types of prestige. Moreover, they ignore the field conditions in which the prestige-giving occured. After a pause he commented on a recent study that concluded that one sometimes attributed to prestigeful people virtues and characteristics which they did not have and he challenged the results. He then asked, What does it mean that FDR is seen to be intelligent, good-looking, and kind by the people who hold him in esteem and that Hitler is also seen to be intelligent and good-looking by the people who hold him in esteem? Is their intelligence the same thing? Maybe intelligence means a different thing when viewed in the context of FDR and Hitler.

After a few comments by the students, he presented what he called some preliminary conjectures about prestige:

Holding one's teacher in prestige may make her look beautiful and good because she is seen as a creature of a higher order. The child has admiration for certain qualities in her and these qualities seem to be realized through her, in a real way, in the social world of the child. . . . They are what the child lacks and would like to have. . . . Self-realization may be involved here. . . . The prestigeful person, the teacher, is on a different level, in a higher world and the contrast between the child and the teacher leads to a gap. Prestige for the teacher is related to the awareness of this gap. . . . Since this attitude is based on the entire prestigeful person, her faults may be ignored or distorted. Such prestige has a precarious nature. As the child learns more and more about his teacher, her prestige may change. Prestige here is not merely a function of being gullible but it is due to the focus on a certain relationship that one has to another person. One who looks up to certain people because they have what one lacks, needs or admires, may therefore be blind to the rest of the person.

Prestige may be earned by a person by an unusual achievement or it may be due to his manifesting an unusual character or ability. It may even exist along with self-criticism and group criticism.

One may have prestige in the eyes of others because of his high ideals. If he does not live up to them, he may forfeit his prestige and may be hated for betraying their trust. There are examples in everyday life in which the person who has prestige is judged by and has to behave according to, a higher standard. In such cases there is a *noblesse oblige* principle and if he does not live up to the group's expectation of him, there is no desire to imitate him. . . . There is not merely a desire to imitate a prestigeful person but an attempt to be like that kind of person, to be similar to the ideal. The prestigeful person is admired because he represents the ideal.

When Wertheimer paused for comments, a refugee scholar remarked that this puts the problem one step behind. Prestige is attached to the achievement and the doings of the person; but why is it so? Is it because it pays off to do so, or because it is the way it has to be done? Moreover, is not the evaluation of the action of the prestigeful person a sort of S-R bond or conditioned response? Wertheimer replied that this raises the question of what is the nature of value and of how and why we evaluate. It is not adequately explained in terms of conditioned response; it is much more complicated.

A student said that such a formulation may be a person's rationalization for his gullibility, even though he may feel that he is telling the truth about why he looks up to prestigeful people. People often act unthinkingly and then give explanations. A sociology professor then made the following remarks:

Let's stick to the word prestige in a face-to-face relation and use social esteem or honor instead of the word prestige in other situations. Whether it is face to face or otherwise, we esteem certain social roles, offices, positions, and socialized behavior such as the striving for success or activity for self enrichment. At present, college professors have less esteem in the USA than in Germany; military officers are also esteemed differently in the USA than in Germany. Similarly, workers are esteemed differently in South America than in the USSR. Artisans in ancient Greece were esteemed differently than in the present-day USA. Esteem also depends on the class membership of the person; different classes esteem different things, for example, leisure, work, politics, or cultured speech. We need criteria to differentiate between prestige and esteem. . . . Prestige pertains to persons; esteem pertains to roles and institutions. When you look at the person, the giver of prestige or esteem may be distinguished with regard to his imitativeness. The esteem does not depend on the particular judge but on others. It is in the world and he joins it. He joins the other people's world where it exists. It cannot be avoided; it overwhelms him; it is less of his making. In formative prestige, the person who is selected by one person may not have prestige for others. In prestige we know the person but in esteem we do not and therefore cannot judge him so well. The chance of being inadequate is less in prestige than in esteem. I do not have to know him for esteem. There is a greater chance for manipulation and for propaganda in esteem situations because we have less possibility to check up. Therefore, we have to accept things on a hearsay basis. We cannot see *all* businessmen as plutocrats or vice versa but we can see our father called vicious or benevolent.

There are two kinds of situations: (A) situations in which there is prestige; for example, I like the fellow because he is just. (B) situations in which there is esteem; for example, I esteem rules of society that seek justice. I may have a conflict between the two situations (A and B) because I do not like the way esteem is given, I do not like the social world. I may therefore give prestige only to just people, I may refuse to esteem others. Since such behavior causes social breakdowns, I may get shot for this or suffer in other ways.

After some students reacted to the professor's formulations, Wertheimer said, The position may have prestige and the person who gets the position gets the prestige too. It is the position in the social situation and the direction in which it goes in the society that is given the prestige. . . . Maybe people do not take over the esteem without realizing the role and function and behavior that it (the position) has in the lives of people and in their world.

Someone said that a person may seek the esteemed position or the status but not have the stature for it. However, he may before or after he gets the status develop the stature because of his desire for the status. This is formative prestige. Another person may just seek status and not be at all concerned about the required stature—he just wants to be esteemed. He wants to be respected but does little to earn the respect. Suppose he achieves the status, the esteemed position, will he upset and destroy the status?

Wertheimer's closing remark was, One may not like the word prestige but if you try to view it in concrete terms, in terms of what is actually going on, then you may have to give people prestige and esteem because it may have real consequences for you. This is different than if you do it because others do it. Whether or not you esteem your boss's acts and decisions, they are important to you; it is not just conforming because others do it. . . . The question about a person who seeks and holds on to a prestigeful position in which he does not fit is a complex problem which we need to discuss at another time. [He never came back to the question. It was ASL's impression that the seminar on power would deal with it, but it did not. The question was discussed in private and personal terms with Wertheimer but this is not the proper place or time to report on what took place in these conversations.]

Out-of-Class Discussions and Experimental Outgrowths

When ASL presented Wertheimer's conjectures about prestige in his WPA Adult Education classes, the students agreed that one may look up to and imitate or follow the demands or suggestions of someone because that person is living on a higher plane and because one wishes to join him on this plane. However, because of this one may be exploited by the person on the higher plane. In the life histories which these students wrote, there were reports from girls who wanted to become intellectuals or actresses and therefore were attracted and looked up to certain men. These men exploited them sexually; when the men tired of the girls, they ignored them. While the girls were with these men, everything they had said and done seemed reasonable, required, fit, and proper; but now, in retrospect, the girls wondered how they ever could have thought or felt this way about these men. Their past behavior now seemed irrational, blind, and stupid. These girls, as well as other students, reported a variety of behavior that supported Wertheimer's thesis. They realized that some of their actions were fit for certain times and places and not for other times and places, that is, there was no generalization of the prestige to everything they did. It frequently happened that a particular feature of someone's behavior was a model for them to imitate and that they did or did not hold in prestige or admire that person because of this. Sometimes the model was aware of this and sometimes not. Sometimes other features of the model's behavior also seemed attractive but sometimes only the features rele vant to the observer's particular interest or problem were noticed. Sometimes they actively sought someone who could be a model and would help them; sometimes they just happened to meet someone, read about someone, or see in the movies someone who behaved in a certain way and they then realized that this behavior was the solution for their problem or a suggestion of what to do. Sometimes they appreciated that someone had been of help to them and they showed their appreciation by following that person or accepting his suggestions about other matters. There were a few instances when someone was imitated or when suggestions were accepted because of pity, sympathy, or because of their commitment to an ideology or because of love for or caring about the particular person. A few students reported that they had sometimes ostensibly showed that they respected, admired, held in prestige certain ideas, people, or objects in order to get their way with certain people, or to get something from people who also respected and held in prestige these people or ideas. Thus they lent them prestige because it was stylish or because it paid to do it.

When these examples were reported to Wertheimer his comments led to several studies to find out more about prestige. ASL asked his WPA Adult Education students, who ranged in age from 16 to 65 years (and later his Yeshiva College students) as well as elementary and high school students, the following questions: What is prestige? Did you ever hear the word used by people? Do you ever use the word yourself? Below the sixth grade, few children had heard of or used the word but the older subjects had heard it and had used it. The word was used in and had a variety of meanings, for example, fame, importance, reputation, stature, high regard, dignity, esteem, notability, reputation, charm, success, influence, fascination, attraction. Sometimes it was attributed to a person's past success and/or to his good character. It was also attributed to a person's shrewdness and his ability to delude, to obscure, to create an illusion as does a magician, an imposter, or a trickster; prestige was something that helped one to get away with something. They listed things such as participation in certain activities, membership in certain groups and institutions, the association with certain people, and the possession of certain traits as giving a person prestige. The results were discussed in class in the context of Wertheimer's comments about prestige, and this led to a number of class projects which investigated in greater detail to whom, to what, where, when, and why prestige was attributed, and the nature of the consequences for the giver and the receiver of prestige. Also discussed was the nature of the consequences for the social field in which prestige was manifested. In one study the students recorded every other day for two months everything they were aware of concerning the prestige phenomena. They analyzed the data every week in order to answer the above-mentioned questions. In another study the students interviewed children and adults. They started the interview by asking the subject if he had heard or had used the word prestige and asked him to give examples. Then he was asked to rank the examples and to explain why each was prestigeful. Some subjects were first asked if the examples were equally prestigeful and then they were told to rank them. They were also asked whether the object of prestige had always been prestigeful to them or to others, and what made objects gain prestige and what made them lose it. They were asked whether its influence was felt only when they were near the prestigeful object or when they were not near it as well. Also, did it influence their attitudes toward other things or objects? In still another study, subjects were asked whether they sought prestige; where when, and why; and whether they had achieved it and how they felt about it before they acquired it and now. If they had not acquired the sought-after prestige, how did they feel about it and if they no longer had the sought-after prestige, why did they not have it and how did they feel about it now? They were also asked whether the prestige in one field or aspect of life gave them or other people prestige in other aspects or in all aspects of the social field. They were asked what the prestigeful people thought about them personally and what they thought of the people who gave them prestige. Still another method used by some students to study prestige was a variation of the method ASL had used to study values. The subject was asked: What is prestigeful to you now (what do you look up to) and why? Did it always have prestige for you (did you always look up to it) and why? What had prestige for you (what did you look up to) before? Why do these things no longer have prestige? What do you think of them now? In this way, they attempted to trace what had been prestigeful for the person from childhood until the present. In a variation of this study, the students asked a subject to list his earliest recollection of prestigeful objects, for example, before the subject had gone to nursery school, to elementary school, before he had learned to read, which people, objects, events, etc., were prestigeful. In addition to these studies each student analyzed his own life history in order to find out what or who was held in prestige at different stages of his development, the changes in prestige, the effect of the changes in prestige on him and other people close to him, and why certain objects, people, events, etc. maintained their prestige and others did not. Each student also studied his life history to find out when, where, and why he had been a prestigeful person or had done something that gave him prestige. How had he felt about it and how had it affected his relations and behavior toward others? Their reports were used as a basis for a discussion of prestige which also referred to the results of other studies. What follows is a summary of the discussion.

Nearly all subjects, old as well as young with little or with much education, acknowledged that certain objects, groups, institutions, and people had appeared at one time or another as prestigeful to them; that they had identified with, imitated, admired and/or looked with awe on them. Sometimes they had envied or wanted to be with or like the prestigeful persons but sometimes they had merely respected and worshipped them with no such desire. Sometimes they had imitated certain individuals in order to achieve some personal goal or satisfaction but they did not consider them worshipful. The object of prestige might have been an older or a younger person, a person of a high or low social class or status. The person might have prestige because of clothing, money, athletic or intellectual ability, artistic or musical talents, creativity, and good looks. He might be popular with boys or girls, dance well, be entertaining, have charm or personality, be kind or tough, know his or her way around, *know the ropes,* have influence or be related to people who had influence, power, good looks, or status. He might have prestige because he was baby, had had an operation, had had an accident, had had his name in the paper because his family had been evicted from their flat, or had had a death in his family. In some of these instances, subjects were not interested in the person, thing, or the group per se but in what he or it could give them i

terms of satisfying their needs or by helping them to share the fame or notoriety the other person had achieved. Although to some people the event might
be a tragedy, disgrace, or notoriety, to them it was something of prestige.

Sometimes the giving of prestige resulted in mutual exploitation or gratification of desires. At other times the subject felt that he or she alone had been
used by or had used the object of prestige to achieve his or her goal. In some
cases the prestigeful feature was all that was noticed about the object of prestige and the giver of prestige was blind to everything else about the object of
prestige and was blind to the effect of the prestigeful person or the prestigeful characteristics on others. In other cases, the subjects were aware of the
other aspects, even the negative ones, of the objects of prestige but esteemed
them anyhow. Sometimes they made concessions to or excuses for them.
When someone pointed out the clay feet of a prestigeful person, they often
interpreted the characteristic differently because of what they admired or esteemed in him; for example, he was seen as cool and smooth rather than
cruel and indifferent, strong rather than domineering, clever rather than
shrewd, cautious rather than cunning. There was critical as well as noncritical
acceptance of the prestigeful person or object. There were instances of a wil-
lingness to disbelieve or to rationalize away what they themselves or others
saw as not fitting or improper about the prestigeful object; there were cases in
which they merely took advantage or used what was prestigeful; there were
cases in which they looked up to the person just for certain features and did
not admire and were not influenced by the other features.

The prestige was sometimes for the whole person and sometimes for a part
or aspect of him. Sometimes it started out with prestige for a part or aspect
and ended up with prestige for the whole person or vice versa. The same subject sometimes reported prestige for a whole person and his social situation as
well as prestige for a single characteristic or a talent or a feature of the same
person in a particular situation. The giving of prestige to a part of the person
sometimes produced problems for the subject because parents, teachers, and
friends held certain characteristics or the whole person in low esteem and
were concerned about the possible effects of the negative features of the object of prestige on the subject. They feared that the subject might be *star crazy*,
in love with a certain person, developing a passion for a certain sport or activity, or idealizing a certain boy or girl of the neighborhood or in school to
their own detriment. The subjects' reactions to others' criticisms often revealed the depth of their attachment to and the controlling influence exerted
by the objects of prestige on their lives.

Sometimes they esteemed the action, the idea, or the behavior of a person
even though they did not desire it for themselves. It was admirable and
seemed a proper object of prestige from a certain point of view. Sometimes, it
was because everybody in the class, school, home, or street looked up to and
imitated the prestigeful model. They therefore showed or gave prestige with
no feeling for or thought about what they were doing. Some subjects centered
on one individual or a group which possessed the prestigeful characteristic;
other subjects sought or were attracted to all groups or people whom they
met and who appeared to have the esteemed feature. This sometimes led
them to be duped or fooled because the group or person did not really have
the sought-for feature. The former kind of centering sometimes led to a narrowing of the person's interests which worked to the detriment of other in-

terpersonal ties and to the neglect of their work and obligations to school and
home. The latter kind led to a scattering of effort and a failure to develop a
living relationship with or to become involved in the world of the prestigeful
person or activity.

Some subjects' prestige was manifested only when they were in the presence
of the person or object. When they were not with the person or object, they
readily gave the prestige to someone or something else. It might be for the
same or for different reasons. Some subjects lost their esteem for a person
when he was near to them, or when he was not yet obtained or was felt to be
unobtainable. The nearness to or the acceptance by the prestigeful person or
group made him or it lose its prestige, that is, as long as the object was unobtainable, an ideal, it was prestigeful. Some subjects said that certain people
had prestige for them because of what they had heard or read about them
but that meeting them was a disappointment which resulted in the decrease
or loss of prestige.

The object of prestige was sometimes very concrete: money, looks, clothing,
ownership of a certain kind of car, a certain job or position, the attending of
a certain school, the taking of a certain course of study, belonging to a certain
church, being a member of a certain family, gang, race, nationality, or neighborhood, or the possessing of a certain physical or mental ability, skill, or
knowledge. The children as well as the adult subjects showed a great variety
of prestigeful objects in the life activities in their neighborhood and home.
The college students were less parochial in their prestige-giving but they usually gave it to a smaller range of people, objects, and institutions. This may
have been due to their commitment to the ideologies that were current in the
colleges, the economic and political doctrines, the scientific and cultural
philosophies. The Yeshiva College students, however, had the greatest variety
and the greatest number of objects and people of a prestigeful nature. This
may have been due to their religious studies, which involved the mundane
world of everyday life as well as the theoretical and practical concerns of their
religion and philosophy. The Yeshiva College subjects as well as little children
often mentioned their parents and teachers as objects of prestige but the high
school, college, and adult education students did not. The latter were often
ashamed of or looked down upon the ignorance and old-fashioned ideas of
their immigrant parents.

Many subjects reported that as little children they had looked up to people,
objects, or institutions which had also been admired by their parents or other
adults. They had esteemed what the adults esteemed. Sometimes they related
their esteem for them to what these people and institutions had done for
them or for their parents, for example, the mailman brought letters and pack-
ages, the grocer gave them·food, the plumber fixed the pipes, the janitor
kept the halls clean, the street cleaners cleaned the streets, and the policeman
protected them. Sometimes they believed that a person was esteemed merely
because he was dressed in a certain way, looked or acted in a certain way, or
was associated with a certain institution, race, nationality, religion, church
school, government agency, gang, or club. Some of the children believed that
if they dressed, looked alike, or did what these prestigeful people did, they
would have the same prestige. Therefore they acted or dressed or tried to
look like these persons; they pretended that they belonged to the race, relig
ion, or nationality of the prestigeful persons of their environment. This wa

often done in play activity with other children, alone, or with certain adults who tolerated or encouraged such playing. Such behavior sometimes increased when they moved to a new neighborhood or met new people. They also reported it as frequently occurring during puberty and adolescence. It was during such transitional periods in their lives that movie stars and characters in books, magazines, and newspapers became prestigeful models to copy. Because they sought recognition and popularity by doing what they thought had brought their models esteem, they became interested in clothing, grooming, sex, dancing, gangs, cars, smoking, dating, social and political ideologies, literature, art, dramatics, music, religion, and sports. Some said that as they grew older they continued such role-acting and pretended to be like the prestigeful people, except that now they held other people and groups in prestige, for example, instead of the mailman it was now a movie star, instead of the plumber or the grocer it was a scientist, a politican, or a labor leader. As children, they had often thought that people believed them when they pretended and they basked in the glory. They realized, however, when they grew older, that pretending or acting or wishing to be like the prestigeful person or a member of a prestigeful group did not necessarily make them prestigeful. Therefore, they sometimes stopped such role-playing but sometimes they daydreamed and tried to act or to pretend to be like them.

As children, more often than as adults, they imitated many outward features of the person whom they esteemed; for example, they walked, talked, and dressed like him or her, or they reflected what they believed to be the person's tastes, thoughts, and feelings. When they were young, they did this on the basis of what they saw but when they were older, they read as much as they could about the person and inquired about him or her in order to find out more about him. When they were young, their acts of imitating were more like mimicking behavior without a full understanding of and/or feeling for the behavior but when they were older, their feelings and thoughts were appropriate to the behavior, for example, imitating the lovemaking of a movie star.

Subjects reacted differently to prestigeful people. Some were attracted to and wanted to be near the person; they wanted the prestigeful object to notice and/or to touch them and were envious when someone else was noticed or touched. Others wanted to be helpful to and to further the prestigeful person's reputation. Still others held the prestigeful person in awe and worshipped from a distance. Some sought to learn and to advance themselves by being associated with the prestigeful person. Some did not imitate but admired and respected or used the person as an inspiration. In some cases the prestigeful figure's actual behavior or ability was not desired or even noticed. Some put the prestigeful person on a level above them, in a realm they were not allowed to or could not or should not enter. Some were not at all concerned with becoming like him but obtained a feeling of intellectual and emotional stimulation from observing and learning about what he had done or was doing. Some did not try to be as adept or skilled as the prestigeful person but appreciated the skill and products of his or her behavior; others set themselves to surpass him, to achieve as much as he had or to take his position.

A few subjects reported that they really felt no admiration or esteem for the persons to whom they gave prestige. They did it because it was stylish and proper and they did not want to show ignorance or lack of sophistication, or they did so because they did not wish to antagonize people by failing to show proper respect for the prestigeful persons.

Sometimes the person they esteemed rejected or avoided them, for example, cases of having a crush on a teacher, a boy, or a girl. In some instances they chased after the person, much to the idol's annoyance. In a few instances the prestigeful person became accessible to them and then the prestige wore off.

They often reported that they outgrew their prestige. As they obtained new knowledge, interests, and values, they looked back at their former objects of prestige and wondered how they ever could have held such a person or feature in esteem. Some even laughed and thought that the person or their previous behavior was foolish, pathetic and stupid. A few even ridiculed the person or people whom they had held in esteem. Some reported a change after a long struggle to achieve the status that the prestigeful person had; then the person lost prestige in their eyes because they changed their level of aspiration. Sometimes they became interested in other things or people and had no time for the old object of prestige. Religious ideas and patriotic ideas lost prestige because of their new philosophies and ideologies. They were often told or learned to believe that they could not hold certain persons or groups in prestige if they wanted to succeed in life or to gain the recognition of certain people and groups; therefore, they disassociated themselves from them. Sometimes the people, ideas, behavior, and things that had once been held in low esteem, or that had been ignored, became their new objects of prestige. Some reported that they changed their esteem or experience of esteem to fit the times; they secretly admired certain people and ideas but would wait until the time was propitious to express their admiration. This was done because of a fear of hurting themselves in the eyes of the general public, because of their parents or their teachers, or because they had plans to use the prestigeful idea or person when he or it became fashionable or acceptable. They would then point to their long-time association with the prestigeful idea or person.

Generally speaking, the subjects said that at present people and things were held in esteem because they would lead them to a certain desired realm of ideas, actions, feelings, or status. Some subjects reported instances in which the prestigeful person did not lead them into the world they had expected. They were disappointed and even angry at him because of this but some still held him in esteem. Others, however, reacted with resentment and disdain. Sometimes the person led them to success and they felt that they no longer needed him. Thus he lost their esteem. Others, however, still felt kindly toward the person and still esteemed him for what he had done. Some of these subjects said that their prestige was based on their personal affection, their love of the person, and not on the ideal or skill he represented. Therefore they held him in esteem even though their ideals and skills had changed.

Nearly every subject reported prestige for things and people that was merely due to the current fashion in their neighborhood or in their school. They were oriented to be in step with others, they did not want to be alone or to stand out or to be different.

In describing the cases of self-actualizing prestige, the students reported that sometimes it led to a radical change in the person's values and aspirations, with the result that he became alienated from his old way of living. He sometimes became lost in an empty world in which he could not find himself.

Yet he could not reject the prestigeful person or ideology. Although it proved unsatisfactory he kept on pursuing it in an obsessive manner. One college student's report noted that self-actualization may take different forms. One may actualize himself as a sensual creature, as an aesthete, as a scholar, or as a thief. The prestigeful object or person, therefore, can lead to immorality or to morality. This led to the question of whether certain prestigeful models were better than others for a group's or mankind's welfare and whether the synthetic creation of prestigeful models by public relations experts and by certain value-free theories of therapy and education were leading to social disintegration.

Sometimes the prestigeful object led the giver of prestige to build with the receiver of prestige a common world that helped each to actualize himself. But sometimes only one person was actualized and the other became a means for his actualization.

Some people sought ideas and embodied them in people who could never be what the giver of prestige wanted them to be. Their lives seemed to be one crush after another, one passion or fad after another as the person never lived up to their ideal. In only one case a student reported that the giver of prestige demanded that the person change so that he would live up to the prestige given to him.

Many subjects reported instances of seeking or using others as a means to solve their problems and to further their goals. They did not value others or give them prestige for this; they gave prestige only when they had to. The giving of prestige was a pragmatic business transaction. In sharp contrast to them were a few subjects who were not at all concerned with the use of the thing or person but who seemed to feel reverence, a sort of religious awe for the prestigeful person or thing, as representing something sacred. One of the Adult Education students said that one reason that so few college students reported the latter kind of prestige was because our technological world had made us look at nature and man as things to be manipulated and to be valued for what they could give us in terms of goods and services. The ancient ideas of the sacredness or holiness of nature and man were disappearing as the technological attitude was becoming all-pervasive. In view of this, he hypothesized that modern prestige was different from the prestige of the past, such as was found in the folklore and myths of our culture. Perhaps a distinction should be made between prestige that reflected sacredness and prestige that represented usefulness. These two kinds of prestige were not in contradiction to each other: consider the Biblical description of the relation of God to the Hebrews—He had not merely demanded awe and imitation of his attributes but He had also made a covenant with them in which He had promised them material goods and actual services. Worship was a duty but still it was useful. Sacredness was immanent in the mundane world of the primitive and ancient man. Science might have accelerated the destruction of the realm of the sacred but it was a realm that had already been divorced by some of the universal religions which separated the sacred from the mundane, which separated the *City of God* from the *City of Man*.

Nearly all subjects said that they had experienced the seeking of status, prestige, and self-esteem. Sometimes it was part of a general desire to rise up from a lower status, sometimes a desire to be recognized for certain physical, intellectual, and personality characteristics, a desire to obtain fame, a desire for pecuniary and other gain, to overcome a feeling of lack of or low esteem or of being powerless, of being a nobody. Many strove for or sought prestige when they became aware of the low economic and social status of their family, neighborhood, nationality, religion, or race. They had felt this especially when they had moved to a new neighborhood, gone to a new school, new class, or new job, or had met unknown people. Some reported the most intensive feeling for the need for prestige during adolescence. A few subjects reported that they had experienced striving for fame or prestige only in certain but not in other institutions; for example, in the school or in the community but not in the home. The place most frequently mentioned was the school and the goal was grades or honors. Competitive sports were more often mentioned by boys and clothes and attractiveness more often by girls. Some said that certain people more often than others made them try to get prestige. Very few said that they only rarely wanted recognition or to be looked up to. It seems from their reports and comments that desires for status or prestige were experienced when they felt that they lacked something specific; for example, money, clothes, looks, status; and when they felt a general feeling of insecurity, a desire to master or to assert themselves. A few people reported seeking power or fame in order to get even with or to prove to someone that they were somebodies or to be noticed by someone who had ignored them.

Some subjects seemed to be blind to the consequences of their striving for prestige for the social field in which they lived. They were so obsessed with getting fame that they did not care about other people or other aspects of their own lives. Others tempered their striving so that they would not hurt others or contradict their dominant values. Some went about achieving status systematically and others pursued it in a rather haphazard manner. Some felt that they were really living and expressing themselves while in pursuit of status but a few felt driven by external forces and were not happy to be seeking the prestigeful status.

Some were not content when they obtained the status that they had been seeking; it turned out to be boring and not at all fun. They seemed to be more interested in the conquering, in the process of striving, than in the object or the status itself. Others found that the status called for responsibilities and obligations that they were not willing to accept, therefore, they gave up the status or changed the situation so that they could avoid the duties it involved. Some changed their way of life in order to meet the status' responsibilities. Some subjects had a need for status for status' sake. They would do anything to be looked up to, to be a somebody. A few learned when they achieved a certain status that the status was a two-way street, that people expected prestigeful people to act in a certain way and, if one did not, one lost the prestige. Thus the obtaining of prestige sometimes resulted in the person's becoming transformed as he worked hard at maintaining his status. A few subjects felt that they had sacrificed their lives for the esteem of certain people, groups, and institutions and that the people did not fully appreciate what they had done, but others felt that in doing this, they had become part of a world-building experience in which their actions had played a crucial role and they were proud of this.

In view of these results we can agree with Wertheimer that there is a need to differentiate the variety of ways that people show and seek prestige and a need to study the structure of the field conditions in which they occur in order to determine the factors that bring them into being. We need to know what factors minimize and maximize the different kinds of phenomena as well as the effects of the giving and taking of prestige on the social field and on the persons involved. A study of the dimensions, the origins, and the effects of prestige was made by a graduate student for a master's thesis written under Wertheimer's supervision (Malamud, 1942). Wertheimer regarded this thesis' results as well as ASL's students' findings, as invalidating the generality of the traditional theses of prestige. He stressed the need to study the phenomena instead of making sweeping generalizations.

The contemporary stress on the cognitive aspects of prestige overlooks or neglects its noncognitive aspects. Possibly this may in part be due to Wertheimer's contention that the traditional thesis' stress on noncognitive factors leads to a one-sided view of the phenomenon. Wertheimer was not so concerned with whether prestige was due exclusively to cognitive or noncognitive factors as with the question of whether it was always noncognitive and whether its effects were arbitrary in nature. He saw no virtue in cognitive theories per se but was concerned with the doctrine of man and the use of the doctrine of man to shape the lives of men. [Some clinical psychology students have pointed out that Wertheimer's gap-fitting conjecture was an idealized model that would be given flesh and blood by relating it to Adler's and Sullivan's theories about the interpersonal field. Although the Gestalt psychologists may not agree with the doctrine of man implied in Freud's and Jung's theories, these theories also would be of value to flesh out Wertheimer's model.]

In the post-World War II period, we have become interested in the effects that people have on the power structure of institutions, particularly the effects of the so-called followers or powerless ones. Some of our graduate students at the University of Oregon kept records of the effects on them of the entrance of new members into their classrooms, social clubs, and families. This was done to test the dominant view that the newborn child and the newcomer to a class is shaped or molded by an inalterable family or classroom structure, that they are stamped by an unalterable die into a certain shape. This is perhaps due to the acceptance of the psychoanalytic theories of the growth of the human personality. These theorists do not describe how an infant actually affects the values, attitudes, and assumptions of his parents and siblings; instead, they tell us about a helpless creature looking up to and being influenced, if not totally overpowered, by masterful adults. What is neglected in their descriptions is the manner in which the parents and siblings are changed in the process of reacting to and acting on the infant. Similarly we are told how group membership or the joining of a group changes the person but not how the person actually affects the group. The protocols of ASL's students who were parents or teachers did not support the thesis that the parents or authority figures remain unchanged, that only the infant or the school child was changed, and that only the child felt overwhelmed, helpless, and tyrannized. The results point to a need to study the structure of the social organization before, during, and after a person or a child passes through a family, group, or institution. The procedures of systems analysis might be applied in such a study. Such studies might help psychologists move away from the idea that social influence is a kind of battle of wills or a matching of wits.

22
Imitation

In the beginning of the session someone said that some of Wertheimer's objections to the associationistic view of social influences had been disproven by the work of Miller and Dollard. The student went on to describe one of the studies. Two children had been brought into a room where there were two covered boxes. They were told that a piece of candy was in one of the boxes and that if they opened this box they would get the candy. The child who went first was the experimenter's confederate. He always chose on the basis of a prearranged signal from the experimenter and always found a piece of candy no matter which box he opened. The second child, who saw all this happen, got a piece of candy only when he chose the same box; if he chose the other box, he found that it was locked. Thus in order to get the candy he had to open the box that had been opened by the first child. The interesting feature of this experiment was that it was similar in design to experiments in which Miller and Dollard taught rats to follow other rats. Thus the same learning principles that explained the rat's learning to imitate also explained the child's learning to imitate. When Wertheimer asked the student to describe the learning principle, he said that imitative behavior was a conditioned response brought about by drive reduction. Due to drive reduction, the first rat's or child's response became the cue for the second rat's or child's response. The conditioned response learned in this situation generalized to other similar situations. Wertheimer asked the class whether such a description was adequate. Someone said that it was like saying that we could condition a child to stand when another child stood. Suppose that a child was given candy if he stood up when another child stood up, but if he sat down, he did not. Could we conclude that standing was a conditioned response? One of the visiting professors came to the defense of Miller and Dollard by describing how a child and a rat learned to imitate in terms of Hull's learning theory. Wertheimer then asked the class whether they now knew what actually took place in Miller and Dollard's experiments. After a pause, he asked the class for some of the possible reasons that the second child would or would not, on the first trial, follow the confederate. An elementary school teacher interjected that some children would not do what the other child did because they did not want to cheat. Since they had been taught not to cheat they would be reluctant to go to the same box. A visitor said that the child might think that there was but one piece of candy in the box that was chosen by the first child and therefore he would go to the other box. After the students' comments, Wertheimer remarked that Miller and Dollard had focused on the subjects' responses and had not faced the possibility that various processes might produce the same response. When the visiting professor pointed out that one could not ask a rat why it made a certain response, Wertheimer said that he appreciated this difficulty with rats but why didn't they ask their human subjects? The professor argued that children would not know what to say; even if they did speak, their reports would not be trustworthy. He went on to say that the beauty of Miller and Dollard's work was that it showed the generality of the reinforcement concept; it was a universal concept that explained the behavior of all organisms.

Wertheimer questioned the assumption that society was like their experimental situations and that all social learning in daily life was explained by such experiments. After a pause he questioned the assumption that all social behavior was forced behavior and that people act to maximize pleasure and to avoid pain. Someone protested that all we know is how things affect us. The world is a pattern of pleasure and pain; it is the only reality we know. An elementary school teacher said that Miller's thesis held for simple learning situations, for one-step problems like learning that 2+2=4. Wertheimer said that Miller could say that a complex situation was made up of a series of simple situations, that a complex problem was a series of simple one-step problems. The teacher interjected that Thorndike's method of teaching arithmetic is based on this assumption. Yet children may know all the number facts and rules but not be able to solve a problem that actually involves only one step. They know how but do not know when to add, multiply, divide, or subtract. A visitor then said that first one must learn the elementary facts of arithmetic; later on he learns to link up the facts into complex responses. He went on to say that first one only knows the individual steps, but because certain combinations are called wrong and others are called right by the teacher he learns to order the simple reactions into the socially acceptable complex patterns. The teacher protested that such learning mechanized the child, that perhaps that was why children as well as adults did not like mathematics. The visiting professor said that the success of its application could not be used to test a theory; specially designed and controlled situations had to be devised to test a theory. The teacher then asked why learning theorists tell educators the implications of their theories. If it is only a theory, why do they tell us how to teach children? Wertheimer interrupted their argument to ask whether Miller and Dollard had really studied social learning, whether certain crucial aspects of what took place in social situations had been overlooked, and whether one was allowed to generalize from such studies to everything that was learned from one's teachers, friends, or parents. Someone noted that Miller and Dollard had studied the behavior of a child or a rat at a choice point; there are similar situations in life in which one watches somebody in order to learn what to do. However, one does not blindly copy the other person's behavior but realizes from his behavior what he has to do. Social learning often depends on understanding; for example, a little child who wants to make smoke come out of his father's pipe, just like his father does, may instead put it out because he blows into it instead of sucking it. There were many examples in social life in which blindly imitating a response led to trouble or humor. He then told the story about the donkey who wanted to be petted by his master and therefore sat down on his lap, just as he had seen the dog do; instead of being petted he was beaten.

Another student said that Tarde had written that there was imitation by rote and imitation by understanding and that they produced different consequences. This difference had been ignored by Miller and Dollard in their attempt to reduce all social learning to what took place when a child was made to follow another child at a choice point. When the professor asked what was meant by understanding in rat behavior, the student pointed out that the issue was not if rats but if children learned by understanding. In defense of Miller and Dollard's work, ASL pointed out that the Einstellung experiments showed that some children learned without understanding. The teacher asked whether there were different consequences for a person who learned by rote rather than by understanding. When the professor said that much of school learning was a form of social learning in which children imitated their teachers or textbooks with little understanding, she said that this may be the reason for their slavish obedience and lack of creativity.

The discussion turned to the Gestalt psychologists' evaluation of learning by imitation. Someone remarked that since such learning involved repeating what someone else said or did instead of discovering by oneself what to do, Gestalt psychologists would be against such learning. Wertheimer pointed out that in some cases learning was helped by observation of a model's performance. The problem solving or the learning situation might be improved by the presence of a model if the model's behavior hinted at the way to proceed, if it focused one on the important features of the problem situation, set one on the right track to the solution, and made one more attentive to things not previously considered to be related to the problem situation. But, the less meaning a model's actions had, the more difficult it might be to imitate. After a pause, he added that one did not mimic everything that the model did in the problem solving situation but only those things that were relevant for the solution. He added that there were also cases where imitation did not help, where it blinded one. We need to study both kinds of cases, where it helps and does not help, in order to find out the crucial factors that are involved (cf. Luchins & Luchins, 1959, p. 332 ff).

Somebody said that imitation was an inferior type of learning, that it was utilized by immature individuals who did not possess the necessary intellectual maturity to think things through for themselves. He elaborated with examples from developmental psychology and added that people who imitated were not creative people. They were submissive, dependent people who could not think for themselves. Moreover, imitation was the kind of behavior that made one accept what authorities or leaders said or did; it was also the behavior of anti-democratic and anti-scientific people. Wertheimer objected to the negative evaluation of imitation. Certain behavior could not be learned without the aid of imitation. He referred to Koffka's (1925, 1935) and Köhler's (1925, 1929) books and said that many things which we learned were not acquired through our own discovery but by understanding the behavior of models or of instructions expressed in language. He added that Köhler had once said that he knew of no case of mere imitation without a trace of understanding of what was being done, and that the less meaning an action had the more difficult it was to imitate it. In response to an objection he said that it is possible to so arrange a situation, as in the Einstellung situation, that a person blindly repeats a response and develops a blind reliance on what others do instead of looking for himself or trying to understand why his response is or is not correct. The last comment led ASL to relate the Einstellung effects in learning to solve problems to imitative behavior, to ideo-motor suggestion and social norms (Luchins 1939; 1942 Sec. 14, Chap. 14).

Someone said that people of lower status or people who were in the dark about what to do or what was correct, would imitate those who were superior to them or who were knowledgeable, for example, dumb students would copy a bright boy's test answers or follow the advice of successful or popular students. This showed that one did not imitate just anybody's behavior; one did what prestigeful people did.

Wertheimer remarked that one often changed the behavior while repeating or imitating it; one might even do it better than the model. After a pause he said that it was very difficult to repeat exactly what someone does; it takes skill to be a mimic. He went on to suggest that we study what happens when someone tries to imitate. What aspects of the action are easy to imitate and what aspects are difficult and why?

For the rest of the session the class argued about whether imitative behavior was a function of the person or of the situation. Before dismissing the class, Wertheimer remarked that perhaps it would be advisable to study just how children learned from each other and from older and younger people in ordinary life situations. What kinds of situations produce blind, slavish imitation of what the teacher, the other child, the parents did? What were the structures of the situations in which people felt compelled to repeat and not to deviate from a model or from the instructions; what were the structures of situations where people deviated? What were the variety of ways in which people repeated when they were consciously trying to repeat; what were the changes in the structures of the action when they deviated?

After-Class Discussion

Some students followed Wertheimer into the cafeteria. When he saw them he invited them to his table. A student told Wertheimer that he was certain that most children in Miller's experiment were only interested in the candy and just repeated what the other child had done; they had no curiosity about the other child's continued success; they did not even realize that they were correct only when they did what the other child had done. Wertheimer told the student to repeat the study and to tell him the results. ASL told them that he and his adult education students had been replicating Miller and Dollard's study with kindergarten children of slum neighborhoods in Manhattan and Brooklyn. They found that some children were reluctant to repeat; they did not want to be copycats. Some even asked to go first so that they could find the candy by themselves without having to copy. Someone remarked that this suggested that some children had learned not to imitate, that imitation was a bad thing, that it was not right or that it was stupid. If this is true, then the question arises, what do children learn first, to imitate or not to imitate? Someone remarked that little children often imitate adults' behavior. At first parents encourage their children to imitate but later on they discourage it. Wertheimer suggested that we study children to find out in which situations children imitated and in which they did not, in which situations they were told to imitate and in which they were told not to imitate, in which situations they were first told to imitate and then told not to imitate, and in which they were first told not to imitate and then told to imitate.

23
More on Imitation and Social Learning

INFORMAL DISCUSSIONS

In his first report on the Einstellung experiments ASL told Wertheimer that many children seemed to be trying to repeat what had been written on the blackboard during the explanation of the illustrative problem. Some pupils even drew for each problem the jars and arrows exactly as in the illustrative problem; their diagrams were correct but they did not solve the problems by means of the diagrams. Wertheimer asked whether or not they were blindly repeating the drawing and what could be the reasons for such behavior. Perhaps it reflected the way they had learned arithmetic and/or the social atmosphere of the school (Luchins & Luchins, 1970c). An elementary school teacher who had joined the discussion said that children are always imitating adults without really understanding their actions. When they play house, doctor, cops and robbers or store, their conceptions of these roles are not similar to the adult roles. When they imitate animals they are not doing what the animal is doing. A child sees these roles from his frame of reference; he repeats what strikes his fancy. She went on to say that some children ape their parents, teachers, or other adults without even knowing it. She concluded that such behavior suggests that imitation may be instinctive. A student who had joined the discussion asked her how it was possible for one to learn insightfully the language and other cultural artifacts of a society if they were based on unconscious or blind instinctive behavior. When ASL said that instincts were not necessarily blind, that according to McDougall an instinct had cognitive as well as emotio-conative features, the previous speaker said that the usual definition of an instinct stressed its unconscious nature. When we say that something was done instinctively we mean that it was done without thinking. The teacher noted that children do not automatically repeat what ever happens around them. They repeat what is done by people with whom they identify. They learn, by rewards and punishments, to identify with certain people and not with others; similarly, they learn to make certain and not other responses. In response to Wertheimer's questions she described the psychoanalytic mechanism of identification. When the student said that she was mixing up Freud's explanation with Thorndike's, Wertheimer remarked that a popular but mistaken view is that Freud's theory is basically different from the Behaviorists' theory. The student replied that they are different; Freud's theory is based on instincts, a concept which the Behaviorists reject. Moreover, Freud's theory reflects a belief in innate ideas but the Behaviorists believe that all behavior is learned. A visitor who had joined the discussion remarked that Allport has shown that children do not learn to speak by imitating adults but because adults imitate the baby's babbling. When the student asked him how a child changed from babbling to speaking, the visitor described Allport's theory and concluded that Allport had shown that all social behavior is learned by conditioning and that Miller and Dollard's work was an extension of Allport's. These men have made it clear that imitative behavior is not an instinct but that it is learned.

The visitor added that Wertheimer's conjecture about what the children did in Miller and Dollard's study had been raised by the experimenters. They realized that on the initial trial a child might not select the same box as the first child because he thought that the candy had already been taken from that box or that it would be hidden in the other box on his turn. Miller would not object to Wertheimer's descriptions but they were not explanations of what had happened. In terms of learning theory, the first child was operating under the drive of hunger; the cue for what to do was the experimenter's instructions about the correct box and the behavior to be learned was walking to the box, opening it, and taking the candy. The taking and eating of the candy was the reward. The second child was also operating under the hunger drive but his cue about what to do was seeing the first child go to the correct box. The behavior to be learned was to go to the same box as the first child and obtain the candy, the reward for imitating the first child's behavior. Thus one learns to imitate others because it is rewarding. What the child learned was to put into a certain order the responses that he already had in his response repertoire. In the state of drive, behavior is random; one moves about until he happens to make a response that reduces the drive. In this way society edits the responses and forms them into the complex patterns needed in various life situations. A student pointed out that the visitor was assuming that a reward has to be given for a child to learn to imitate but there are many instances in which a child watches someone do something and receives no reward but later on imitates what he has seen. Why? The teacher as well as the visitor argued that such cases must involve the gratification of some motive. When Wertheimer challenged the thesis that people learn only because they are forced to learn or get rewards, the teacher said that in some cases the child identifies with adults and therefore acts as if he were they. But learning in these cases also satisfies an internal need, a need based on previous gratification of the instincts. When Wertheimer objected to the thesis that all social learning rests on the gratification of the ego or the organism, she said that she had recently heard about Sullivan's theory which postulates an empathic relation between the child and the mothering adults. At first there is an emotional contagion between the child and mother; when the mother cries the child cries, when the mother is tense or scared, the child is tense and scared. Although Sullivan says that there is from the beginning a social field and that it determines the person's behavior, he describes personality development in terms of the approval and withholding of approval by adults. The child does not personally have to experience the rewards and punishments but experiences them vicariously when he sees someone else being punished or rewarded, getting approval or disapproval. When ASL asked her how the child learns to appreciate what is happening to others, she said that it is due to empathy; from the beginning there is an empathic relationship with others. She went on to relate empathy to identification and then concluded that children learn who in the social field controls or has power over the rewards and punishments and they identify with and imitate such a person in order to get pleasure. Children also tend to imitate models that they feel are similar to themselves and thus they get a feeling of mastery and control. When Wertheimer said that this was a funny kind of mastery and control of others, the teacher said that the child may really be controlling the parent or other adult because he sees his behavior as producing the rewarding response or approval.

When the visitor again began to contrast Freud's theory with the Behaviorists', Wertheimer pointed out that Freud and the Behaviorists have much in common. Both stress that to understand a person's behavior one must find out about his earliest childhood. How true is this? He went on to say that both Freud and Hull have the same doctrine of man; in both theories drive reduction plays a central role and seeking pleasure is the goal of man. Instead of talking about the fate of the expression of the libido, Miller talks about drive reduction. When the visitor protested, Wertheimer remarked that Hull and his students are aware of similarities between Freud's and their theory and are rewriting Freud in terms of Hull's terminology in order to make psychoanalysis scientifically respectable. The visitor protested that Freud's instinct theory is a mythical idea but that Hull's concept of drive is a biological fact; there are tissue needs, the need to gratify the organism and the need to preserve the species. According to Freud, the mechanisms by which the drives are gratified are innate and universal but according to Hull the mechanisms are learned and not universal. He went on to give examples to disprove the stages of Freud's theory of psychosexual development, examples which indicated that different societies have different patterns of raising children and that there are societies where there is no *Oedipus complex*. A refugee scholar defended Freud's theory saying that Freud's instincts do not include innate mechanisms; the mechanisms are learned ways of expressing the basic drives. The ego develops out of the experiences of the organism in the course of expressing its instincts. The big difference is that Freud describes the development in dramatic everyday terms. Miller and Mowrer can be said to be rewriting the descriptions in terms of Hull's theory. Wertheimer said that he wondered whether something gets lost in such translations, and after a pause he suggested that we must consider carefully what the concept of reinforcement involves. The refugee scholar said that reinforcement is another kind of instinct concept and that Freud's drives have a foundation in the physiological functioning of the organism. Freud would not object to translating libido in terms of physiology; indeed, he believed that some day physiologists and chemists would discover the chemical basis of the libido and death instincts. He concluded that both Freud's and Hull's theories are organisms-centered theories.

Wertheimer asked, Suppose it is true that there are tissue needs. Is it right to say that rats, bacteria, and men have the same needs? He challenged the attempts to reduce all behavior to the gratification of tissue needs. When ASL argued that it is in line with the theory of evolution that man is another animal, Wertheimer remarked that such statements do not tell us much, that they are sweeping generalizations. Moreover, there is a danger in saying that man is just another animal; it is used to justify behavior in man that is not at all true of animals. Maslow, who had joined us, said that the possibility of the existence of humanoid characteristics was being overlooked by Hull. He referred to Goldstein's forthcoming book (1939) and said that man may have certain species' specific features that are due to his having a nervous system that is structured in a certain way.

Wertheimer briefly outlined some contemporary objections to the instinct doctrine; for example, the confusion due to the variety and vagueness of the definitions and the variety of lists of instincts; the thesis that they are universal, unlearned, innate and unmodified patterns of behavior of all the members of a species. He suggested that we read Lewin's (1935) criticism of the instinct concept and write him our reactions. He then brought us back to the concept of imitation. What happens in particular cases in which one imitates, mimics, tries to copy or reproduce another person's behavior; just what is repeated? What does it mean when we say that one did what he saw someone else do, that he repeated everything? What features were actually reproduced; which were not copied, which were changed and what was the direction of the change? Are there features of a task, of a situation and of a person that determine what is repeated, omitted, and changed? Does Allport's description of learning to speak really account for learning to speak? Observe little children at home, at play, at school; when, where, why do they repeat when it is required, not required? Which of the cases of imitation and non-imitation fit and do not fit the theories that have been discussed? When the visitor said that both kinds of cases can be explained by S-R learning theory, Wertheimer told us that we should see for ourselves instead of accepting it as a dogma. When the teacher protested that children do imitate, Wertheimer said that he does not deny that children's behavior resembles adults', that a child's behavior becomes more like that of the members of his family. What we have been discussing is what are the underlying processes that bring this about. After he remarked about the circularity of the definitions of reinforcement, he said that some people repeat slavishly, blindly but others do not. Why?

After he left the visitor said that Wertheimer's last question can be answered by S-R learning theorists. One's personality is a result of how one has learned to act, feel, and think. One is not born with certain patterns of behavior, feelings, and thought but learns them in a culture. In each society only certain people are trained to be innovators; most are trained to imitate. The teacher protested that he is implying that there is no free will. She went on to say that in a democracy leaders are not born into leadership positions but people compete for the positions. Since a country's leaders must be creative if it is to survive, we idealize creativity and not repetition in our school. Children are taught not to copy, not to reproduce what others do but to be original; copycats are not valued highly. ASL remarked that maybe children learn to imitate as well as not to imitate and the school teaches both kinds of behavior. Why is it that children more readily learn to imitate than to innovate? ASL went on to say that Wertheimer had once proposed that we start the study of learning by finding out in informal learning situations, what children readily learn and what they do not readily learn in the home, school, and community. In which situations must they repeat exactly what the other person does? Just what role do rewards and punishments play in these informal situations? If the person modifies the behavior, what happens to him in these situations? He also suggested we study what they learn readily, not so readily, and not at all in formal learning situations. He also suggested that we study cases in which an individual is trying to learn to do something from a model: to dance, to ride a bicycle, to type, to speak a language, to cook. Study the change of performance during the period of learning such skills. What changes occur and why? What happened when someone wanted later on to repeat what he did the first time? Wertheimer conjectured that the need or the requirement to reproduce exactly occurs only under unusual conditions. Most situations do not require slavish reproduction or blind performance but allow improvement and understanding of the responses. Even in ritualized behavior the ideal is not a robotlike performance. The teacher said that Wertheimer seems to be saying that the ideal is to behave like Homo sapiens not like machines. She agreed that it is the ideal and added that everybody pays lip service to the idea that man must be a creative, self-actualizing, autonomous creature but the moment a person deviates he gets hit on the head. Modern society puts one in a conflict situation; on the one hand you are told that imitation is bad and on the other hand it punishes you if you do not imitate.

A few weeks later students engaged Wertheimer in another discussion. ASL played the devil's advocate, saying that society is a maze and that one learns by drive reduction what to do just as a rat learns to move in a maze. Someone said that society is not a simple T-maze but a complex pattern of maze ways. Moreover, since psychologists are not even in agreement over what a rat learns in a simple T-maze, why do they talk so confidently about all cases of social learning? He went on to argue that cognitive processes play a role even in the rat's behavior, citing the work of Tolman. Wertheimer said that the issue is not settled by just saying that cognitive factors play a role. He then asked, How would you go about studying social learning in rats? Would you do what Miller did? He then suggested that animals be raised under different conditions; raise some animals in separate cages as Miller did, but raise others together in a big box and in freedom. Would they behave differently? Suppose you took a rat on a trip on a sheet of plate glass that covered a maze in which another rat or a member of his nest was running. Would he learn from him? Suppose you dragged both rats, one on top of the plate and the other in the maze, at the same time so that each followed the other, with and without reward. Would they learn? What would happen if you used little children in such situations?

The discussion changed when Wertheimer proposed that we should begin by observing the ways children perform adult roles and the way adults learn roles and also how children and adults learn fads, fashions, rules. Find out the reasons that the children and adults imitate and do not imitate these things and just what they really repeat. What are the roles of models? Maybe models point to things in the person's world that he wants to achieve. After a pause, he objected to the negative evaluation of imitation.

Wertheimer's comments suggested a preliminary study that was conducted that evening in an adult education class. The students were asked to free associate to the word *imitate*. What comes to mind when you think of the word? The answers, which were tabulated on the blackboard, were as follows: copy, follow, imitate, mock, mockingbird, parrot, polly, mimic, reproduce, repeat, mirror, reflect, echo, ape, forge, plagiarize, parody, imposter, falsehood, unoriginal, counterfeit, false, not genuine, imitation, veneer, copycat, baby, naive, follower, unimaginative, uninventive, stupid, forced, obey, robot, mechanical, school, ritual. Most of the 37 students said that all the words on the blackboard were negative or at least were not ideal ways of behaving.

When they were asked if they had ever heard imitation used as an ideal, not one student said yes. ASL then asked what was meant by the expression *Imitatio Dei, Imitation of God*. No one responded. When they were asked where the expression was used, someone remarked that it was a Catholic theological concept. He added that man was not allowed to imitate Him; man was expelled from Paradise because he tried to be like Him. Another student said that he believed that the phrase referred to man's duty to imitate God's ways of loving kindness and pity, to bestow them on others as He bestows them on us; we know of His goodness and we can follow His ways of mercy and forgiveness; man is never nearer to Him than when he is compassionate. Man can strive to be Godlike by imitating His qualities of mercy and forgiveness. Someone interjected that this is one reason that the poor and wretched of the earth are complaisant. It makes men escape the here and now and dream of pie in the sky. The previous speaker pointed out that *Imitatio Dei* has been used to arouse people to fight injustice. He added that the phrase *Be thou holy for I am holy* did not mean to the Hebrews to escape into mystical communion with Him but to strive for purity and justice in the ordinary simple acts of daily life. It was used to support the ethical precepts as well as the rituals that governed all that a person did: reverence for one's parents and teachers; consideration for the needy, the widow, the orphan, the poor, and the stranger as well as consideration for all kinds of birds and animals; prompt payment of wages and not to deprive someone of his livelihood; not to maltreat servants and slaves; honorable dealings; no tale bearing; showing no malice; loving one's neighbor; consideration to the alien; equal justice to rich and poor, native or stranger, priest, king, or layman; just measures and balances, etc. In short, *Imitatio Dei* means, "doing justly, loving mercy, and walking humbly with your God" in the minute particulars of daily life. Most of the students argued that all these were hortatory phrases that made men feel good as they went about doing what they pleased.

This discussion made ASL curious about the use of the concept of *Imitatio Dei* as a foundation of ethics. He found in the New School library a copy of Coppens' (1924) book that stated in the prefex that it is "a brief yet clear outline of the system of ethics taught in Catholic colleges, seminaries, and universities." The index did not contain *Imitatio Dei* but contained the *Golden Mean*. When Wertheimer entered, ASL told him about his students' reactions to the concept of *Imitatio Dei* and that it seems that one student may have been giving the class a sermon but not the facts because he could not find it in the book he was reading. According to the book "the glory of the infinite Creator is not only the absolutely ultimate end of man but also *the supreme direct and immediate purpose of his existence here on earth. . .*(since) morally good conduct is the fulfillment of the supreme immediate purpose of man's existence on earth, it is logical to begin our ethics by clearly demonstrating that the supreme purpose of man's existence is God's external glory and man's eternal happiness" (Ibid., 233-34). Wertheimer suggested that the answer is not to be found in books on morality but in the behavior of people. [When ASL told his students to make a study of the role of *Imitatio Dei* in the lives of people, one student went to talk to Wertheimer. Because the student was a rabbinical scholar, he raised certain questions about the relation between Gestalt theory and Judaism. Wertheimer referred him to an expert on religion, one of the local college professors who was a member of the seminar. The student neither consulted the instructor nor conducted the study. It would be of interest to study members of different religions as well as non-religious groups, to give them the classical Hebrew conception of *Imitatio Dei* as well as other views but not to tell them the source, and to ask them where, when, and how people use each of these qualities. Would they answer the list differently if they knew the source of the list of attributes? Another suggested study is to ask subjects to indicate social and political ideologies and religions that practice, that do not practice, or that are for or against each of the qualities.]

On the way to the subway ASL referred to a previous discussion in which he had told Wertheimer that to the ancient Greeks repetition was connected with the idea of causality; the continued repetition of the same sequence of events indicated that it was not accidental. Moreover, to repeat exactly was a virtue, something that only the perfect Artisan could do (cf. Luchins & Luchins, 1970c). Wertheimer said that the concept of imitation meant a different thing in the context of Platonic and Aristotelian philosophy. There it meant to strive after understanding of the nature of things, to understand its essence; it did not mean to repeat blindly but to grasp the structure of the thing and to strive to actualize the Ideal in what one was doing (cf. Collingwood, 1965). Wertheimer seemed to imply that we need not get involved in the philosophical nature of what is imitation in order to study what takes place in concrete cases of social learning.

Informal Discussion

One day some students engaged Wertheimer in a discussion on social influences. It led to one of the last informal discussions of social influences. A student told Wertheimer that Brown (1936) had pointed out that the concepts of imitation and suggestion were related to the view that society or a group is composed of atomlike individuals. These concepts often were used to explain why people affect each other but were not needed if society or a group was regarded as a field of force. Wertheimer said that a field theoretical approach was useful and added that when a proper understanding of the structure of the social field was obtained, we would be able to understand the behavior of individuals in terms of their places, roles, and functions in the social field of which they were parts. He regarded Kurt Lewin's topological psychology as one way of doing this and went on to say that we do not have enough information about people in terms of their roles and functions in social systems and that just using topological concepts would not solve this problem. [This is similar to what is being said at present about psychologists' and ecologists' attempts to use cybernetics and Information Theory (Parsegian, 1970).] A visitor said that Wertheimer's objections to the atomistic approach did not preclude the focusing on the individual person and studying a person's relations to others. His objections were relevant to the atomistic conception of society that had been used by Hobbes and the Philosophical Radicals and to the idea that man was a microcosm as depicted in Leibnitz's monadology. But they did not hold for the work of modern experimental social psychologists. The visitor said that he was beginning to feel that Wertheimer was objecting to theories. Wertheimer replied that he wanted theories to deal with what was vital in man and in society. He objected to passing off ideologies in the name of theory. The discussion turned to a recent study by ASL (see the chapter on Experimental Outgrowths).

Wertheimer raised the question of whether the conclusions from the research on social influences of the judgment of such things as lines held for natural groups. Were there important features that the experiments did not have? Someone referred to Simmel's thesis that the number of people in a group affects its functioning. A group of two people will more likely keep a secret because each person knows that only he or the other person could reveal it, but as the group increases in size, it is more difficult to know who reveals a secret. Wertheimer pointed out that in ASL's studies on social influences, two total strangers meet to serve as subjects in an experiment. What would happen if two real friends or a husband and wife or two enemies were called upon to decide which line was shorter?

Someone remarked that number *per se* was an important variable because in some preliminary studies with pairs of lines, subjects agreed with the wrong judgment when two confederates instead of one answered first and also more agreed when four confederates were used. He went on to say that this supports the thesis that learning is a monotonic function of the number of repetitions. In the social influence experiments one hears others repeat the same response to the same stimuli instead of making it himself but the experiment still fits the associationists' learning model. Someone interjected that maybe more repetitions are needed in social influence experiments to form the association because the learner does not imitate the response to the stimulus himself. He added that experiments in educational psychology show that it is better for one to discover the response to the stimulus himself; being active helps strengthen the connection between stimulus and response; because of more concentration and attention there is more effect, more drive reduction. Putting it in one's own words also makes it more personal and familiar and aids memory. ASL said that some of his experiments with children show that it is not necessary to have any confederates. It suffices to repeat the series of pictures or lines with a challenge to the subject to get 100 percent. This led to a discussion of the use of force to get conformity. Wertheimer remarked that in all of the experiments the children were forced to agree; they were not allowed to say what they had seen. Some children had been upset because they were not allowed to say what they had seen; they even cried or protested that when they said what their eyes saw they were called wrong and that when they merely repeated what the other person had said they were called right. We need to study the variety of ways that a particular individual acquiesces to various kinds of social pressures and authorities. The different ways of submitting to an authority may have different consequences for the group and for the person who submits. The social force or the authority may produce outward submission in which the person mechanically or sullenly does what he is told to do and no longer cares what happens. It may also produce hate or love, skill or stupidity, involvement or noninvolvement with the goals of the authority. One of the visiting professors said that if one submitted out of love and respect for the group or the authority, it might not mean the same thing as when he submitted because he was forced to do so by the power of the authority. A good leader, therefore, would first get people to love or to respect him and then he would do as he wished with them. A graduate student from another university said that even if one is forced to do something, one becomes used to doing it and after a while he continues doing it even when there is no longer any force. The forced behavior may even become a drive to action.

A visiting professor objected to the idea that seducing someone into doing something by kindness was different from forcing him to do it. Even those leaders who got one to follow them out of love and reason were still exerting power; it was a silk-covered mailed fist. Wertheimer objected by saying that such a formulation ignores the direction of the force in the social field and in the life of the person. A child may be restrained from doing something that might result in injury or death to him or to others; this is not the same thing as being forced to do violence to himself or to others. He asked the students to formulate what they meant by the words force and authority and went on to say that this was not just a theoretical issue. There are people at the present time who will do nothing to stop Hitler because they say that Nazism and Capitalism are equally bad, that both have violently conquered and suppressed people. How true is it that they are doing the same things? Would the results be the same if Hitler won or England won? Some students claimed that for the average person it made no difference who won the war. Others pointed out that at least for Jews and the liberals it would make a difference. The former students accused them of being warmongers. One of the college instructors pointed out that the war between Hitler and England was a sham; eventually both would attack Russia.

Someone took the class away from the political controversy by saying that the groups in the social influence experiments were different from real groups, that the experimental groups were more similar to Allport's description of a group as a collection of individuals. There was no compelling reason or binding myth that led the individuals in the experiments to see themselves as members of a group. The question then arose of how one should study social influences in real groups. ASL said that in order to interest his students in this question, he had suggested that they keep a diary of those changes that occurred in their own behavior when they joined a group and a record of the changes that occurred in their groups when new members joined them. [This procedure was in later years modified to study the structure and processes of groups that met for therapy in the New York Regional Office of the Veterans Administration (cf. Luchins, 1947, 1948).]

Wertheimer pointed out that in real groups people influenced each other but many discussions of social influence in psychology seemed to focus on a one-way traffic: influence from superiors to inferiors. This reflects an ideological point of view about the nature of social influence. It is assumed that the superior, the powerful, the mature individuals influence the inferior, the less powerful, and less mature. This is not factually correct. Another student said that the assumption that the upper echelons of the social structure do the influencing may be the reason why people want to be on top; to be on top is to be successful, to be in control of the situation and not to be influenced by anybody is the ideal in our society. This, perhaps, might be the basis for what

Adler called the drive to mastery and striving to overcome feelings of inferiority. Are Harry Stack Sullivan's notions of the ego dynamism and the desire to be the master of the interpersonal field also examples of this? Someone said that the social influence that we are studying is the influence that exists in a power struggle. It is assumed that life is a battle of wills. A student said that an outside observer might see certain people as being more or less influential or powerful than they see themselves to be. A group member might be seen as a leader or a follower by an outside observer, but he might not be seen to play such a role by himself or by his fellow group members. These remarks led to a conjecture that a group is a system of leadership-followership relations in which the leader is conceptualized as a focus from which influences flow that affect the behavior of others. The difference between what the members of the group see and what an outside observer sees may be due to different ways of conceptualizing who influences whom, or due to the fact that an outsider may get a better overview of what is going on in the group as a whole. In the formal as well as in the informal views of the group held by others or by its members, the group may be seen as a system or network of communications, of mutual aid, of persons doing and accomplishing something with no concern about who influences whom or as people exerting their wills on others. Someone remarked that all groups have a power structure and group members have to learn who bosses whom, to whom one must submit, and to whom one need not. A group is like a flock of chickens in the barnyard with a pecking order. Someone pointed out that Wertheimer had said in a lecture in his adult education course that this was the barnyard model of social behavior and had criticized it. It implied an atomistic view of the group and was related to a certain doctrine of the nature of man. According to another doctrine, man was from birth a social being, a subsystem of a cultural tradition as well as of a certain society. He was part of a subsystem of social institutions such as the family which was in turn a subpart of a society. One's behavior was determined by his place, role, and function in the subpart of the social systems of which he was a part. According to this doctrine, in order to understand a person's behavior, one must try to find out the laws of the functioning of the social systems of which this individual was a subsystem. A particular man could not be understood in terms of his individuality alone but must be viewed in terms of his culture and society. The very notion of the individual or the person was a myth of a particular culture that stressed individualism. He went on to say that two doctrines are often presented in opposition to each other: that society was nothing but the and-summation of the particular individuals that composed it; and that society had an existence above and beyond that of its parts. Then Wertheimer remarked that maybe both doctrines were not valid. Someone said that regardless of their validity both doctrines have been used by social reformers to justify their programs. Some social philosophers have regarded the popularity of the doctrine of individualism as a sign of social progress. Like Nietzsche they have claimed that it would give rise to the superman as more and more people reject the morality and traditions that developed in earlier stages of social development in which men were not conscious of themselves as individuals and were submerged in the group. But there are other social reformers, especially today, who see the doctrine of individualism as a regressive feature in human development. They see man's advancement as lying in man's changing from focusing on himself to focusing on the family, clan, tribe, nation, and ultimately, on all mankind. This would result in the realization of the interdependence and mutuality of all peoples. The stress on individualism had led to social chaos in the past century. The student went on to say that the doctrine that stressed the individual leads to social disintegration because it views persons as expressing their wills, their egotistical desires, and regards society as a battlefield in which each individual competes to get as much as he can for himself. This doctrine of individualism is reflected in the psychology of the Associationists and in Freud's theory. Someone said that the stress on the society is reflected in Adler's and in the Gestalt psychologists' theories. Gestalt psychology has stressed that the whole is more than the sum of its parts and that social influences are due to the effects of a field generated by the interacting individuals. He then noted that Gestalt Psychology's thesis that the whole is more than the sum of its parts is in line with the Nazi philosophy. When students challenged this remark by saying that the Gestalt thesis is used by Democrats and Socialists, the student argued that the Gestalt thesis runs counter to the liberalism on which democracy is based because it sets limits on the freedom of the individual. Wertheimer remarked that Gestalt psychologists did not say that the whole was *greater* than the sum of its parts but had only said that there were wholes that could not be understood by studying arbitrarily selected parts in isolation. He went on to say that the discussion about the two doctrines had often centered around ideological quarrels to the extent that what people actually said and did was a secondary issue. Wertheimer proposed that we study the effects of each doctrine on man and society, that we see how each doctrine was actually used and not to focus on the rhetoric. Did either doctrine maximize certain factors that in turn destroyed men's freedom, robbed them of their freedom to think? Did it maximize certain factors that destroyed the possibility of social living because it destroyed the necessary relations among people, groups, and nations? These were matters of every day life, not merely matters of theoretical speculation.

24
Propaganda*

Wertheimer read from the first newsletter of the Institute of Propaganda Analysis and asked the class, What do you think of it? Do you agree with the proposed method to save people from the clutches of the propagandists? Someone described how *Poison Ivy* Lee had changed the reputation of J.D. Rockefeller from that of a ruthless monopolist into a great humanitarian. He went on to argue that propagandists, publicity agents, and others are always duping the public. He referred to the recent celebration of the invention of the electric bulb by Edison as a smoke screen to hide the abuses of Consolidated Edison of New York. ASL, who had attended Cantril's lectures, referred to them as he said that propaganda was in disrepute at present because it was used to drag the USA into World War I and because Hitler had a Minister of Propaganda; but it had not always been a bad thing. Pope Gregory XV founded the *Collegio di Propaganda Fide,* its purpose was to propagate the true faith, to sow the seeds of Christianity among the heathens. Pope Gregory would be shocked were he to read the Institute's newletter. His propaganda did not aim to dupe people but to enlighten them. He had no selfish motives, he wanted to save people's souls. Cantril is aware of such uses of propaganda but at present propaganda is a menace; commercial advertisers, politicians and various social organizations seek to fool people by means of propaganda. Doob's authoritative text (1935) defines it as "the systematic attempt by an interested individual or individuals to control the attitudes of groups of individuals through the use of suggestion and consequently to control their action." Propaganda is usually planned; it is selfish and it uses suggestion and emotion but not reason because what is being proposed will not bear close scrutiny. It wants a certain response and does not consider its ethical basis. Cantril (1938) as well as Doob (1935) have illustrated how people unintentionally propagandize others because the information that they convey had been slanted by propagandists. Someone cited Ellis Freeman's *Social Psychology* when he said that arithmetic teachers unintentionally propagandize; for example, in the first 200 pages of Thorndike's arithmetic book there are 643 problems of commercial gain. When someone interjected that this is necessary because we live in a capitalistic world, ASL asked, What would happen if I put such problems as these into an arithmetic book. A family of four needs 15 dollars a week for food but receives only 5 dollars a week from Home Relief. What is the percent of undernourishment, if 15 dollars represents nourishment? In a modern war of ten million combatants there are two million casualties. What percentage of the soldiers become casualties? USA's budget is

*We have put together in this section several discussions of propaganda that arose during the sessions on social influences.

$500,000,000; $5,000,000 is allocated for a new battleship and $200,000 for education. What percentage of the budget money is used for the battleship and what percentage is used for education? Such problems would be called propaganda; educators would ban the book and would say that it is not impartial. Their action, however, would show that they have been conditioned to think of arithmetic in a certain way and to have a positive reaction to certain kinds of problems and a negative reaction to others.

Wertheimer remarked that some psychologists believe that it is possible to connect any emotion to a thing, that love or hate can be conditioned to the same thing and that there is no intrinsic connection between the emotion that is aroused and the object that arouses it. A man, like a cat or a rat, can be conditioned to approach or to run away from the same thing. This is traditional psychology's view of the matter. Cantril uses it to explain propaganda. How valid is it?

ASL said that in 1930 the *Journal of Abnormal and Social Psychology* published an article on the influence of Gestalt psychology on the study of social behavior. It pointed out that more psychologists at present accept the thesis that people seek a meaningful structured world and that their behavior can be explained by such Gestalt laws of organization as closure. Since then Cantril and Sherif have demonstrated experimentally how social norms and people's attitudes are the result of the operation of Gestalt laws of perception. Cantril believes that propaganda also can be interpreted in terms of closure; for example, the propagandist first unstructures the mind of the people so that his solution will be seen as fitting the situation's requirements. By applying the Gestalt law of objective set, Einstellung, the propagandist arranges situations in such a way that people are directed to think in the way he desires. Cantril and Sherif have shown that the same Gestalt laws that work in psychophysics also hold in attitude change and propaganda. Someone pointed out that before the advent of psychology, logicians were concerned with such logical fallacies as accent and composition and that the Gestalt laws also reflect this concern. He added that Gestalt psychology's approach to propaganda is similar to common sense and is not scientific. The question for the science of psychology is to determine whether propaganda can be explained by conditioning concepts. If it could, then it would show the generality of the laws of learning. He then went on to say that Watson has successfully been using conditioning concepts in advertising. Someone said that Watson is no longer concerned with validating conditioning concepts but in selling products. In doing this he does what is needed to sell a product. A visitor pointed out that a recent advertising campaign by Watson's agency was "a flop" because it was based on the belief that repetition was all that is needed. Wertheimer said that it is possible to use such conditioning methods; they can be made to be more successful. However, what are the consequences for man and the social field if such methods are used? It may lead to blindness to evidence, and to actions that are perhaps admirable in robots but not in men.

A visitor remarked that according to some people propaganda is good, to others it is bad, and to still others it is neutral. Bernays (1928) says that propaganda is on the side of progress, morality, religion, and science and that we overlook its good features because it is sometimes misused. However, Brown (1929) condemns all propaganda as unethical and inimical to a democratic way of life because it treats man as a tool and is manipulative. He and others believe that whoever denies a person freedom of choice violates his humanity.

Since they assume that freedom is intrinsic to man's nature, these people fight propaganda as an evil. Those who say that propaganda is neutral are people who have a job to do and they focus on getting it done. Some of these people assume that there is no absolute good or bad. The Cultural Relativists' doctrine supports what they do. The Institute of Propaganda Analysis also takes this position. Good and bad are relative terms; that which is good for one person may be bad for another. Good or bad depends on whose interests are served. Someone interjected that when one considers how often psychologists justify their manipulation of people in terms of ethics, it is a welcome relief that there are psychologists who frankly admit that they are technologists doing a job. In response to Wertheimer's objections, he said that in a free country everybody is free to use propaganda. No one can stop you from hiring publicity agents to sell your ideas and products or to build you up as a great star, scientist, or philanthropist. The people will decide for themselves whom to believe. Propaganda is democratic as long as there are free speech and free press. In Germany only one point of view is allowed but in America everybody is free to speak, to print, and to publicize his doctrine. He reiterated that propaganda is not undemocratic as long as people have free speech and free press. Wertheimer asked him whether a rich man is not in a better position to buy radio time and newspaper advertisements. But ASL pointed out that FDR defeated the Republicans twice even though they had more air time and newspaper ads as well as most newspapers' editorial support. [How valid would such arguments be for contemporary politics and commerce?]

Someone said that according to the *Prägnanz* principle people tend to organize their experience as simply and clearly as possible under the given conditions. People avoid unstructuring their minds. Therefore it is possible for someone to get to the people first and to structure their minds in terms of a certain doctrine before another point of view is presented. Just as the laws of conditioning can be used to blind people so can one use the Gestalt laws. Both can mechanize and blind people. Wertheimer agreed and said that this raises an interesting question for research. What is the effect of the order of presentation of information on the making and changing of attitudes? (Cf. Hovland et al., 1958.) He went on to object to the superficial application of the concept of closure in discussions of propaganda and attitude change. We should ask: What kind of closure, in what direction, in what field conditions, in what frame of reference, and what effects does it have on man and society?

Wertheimer brought the class back to the newsletter by saying that each month the Institute will put out a report which will analyze an act of propaganda and will try to expose the tricks that were used by the propagandist. The present newsletter describes seven methods that are used by propagandists: name calling, glittering generalities, card stacking, testimonials, bandwagon, etc. What do you think about this way to analyze propaganda? After a pause for students' comments Wertheimer said that it is a piecemeal approach. It might blind people to the actual state of affairs, it might make them so adept at debunking a statement that they will actually be misled. When someone challenged this assertion, Wertheimer told him to devise an experiment to see whether or not it is valid. Someone asked Wertheimer how he would analyze propaganda; he threw the question back to the class. A student said that in view of what had been said in a previous year's seminar, a Gestalt psychologist would clarify the working of propaganda in specific cases; he would help people realize to what it directs one's actions, feelings, and thoughts. Does it enlarge one's mental horizons and clarify issues or does it narrow and blind? Does it center one on certain details so that he gets an impression that violates the sense or meaning of the thing as it really is? Does it hide or reveal evidence? What does it do to the propagandized, what kind of person does it produce? Is there a narrowing of the person's consciousness and of his visual field so that he acts with little or no understanding of the consequences of his behavior, so that he is forced to behave in a certain way and is robbed of the possibility to think for himself?

ASL played the devil's advocate by saying that the methods of the Institute of Propaganda Analysis are easy to apply; with a little practice an elementary school child could dissect a propagandist's statement. It is much less difficult than a Gestalt analysis in which one has to use such concepts as centering, recentering, grouping, regrouping, contextual meaning, part-whole relation, *Prägnänz,* closure. Even in the analysis of the solution of a mathematical problem it is difficult to use these concepts. A visitor pointed out that the approach of Gestalt psychology involves an attitude to propaganda that is different from the Institute's, which is piecemeal whereas Gestalt psychology is holistic. The Institute's approach puts labels on words instead of trying to understand the message which they convey. It is a mechanical approach, like using an algorithm by rote. The Gestalt approach stresses understanding the structure of the message and its place, role, and function in the social field. It calls for intelligent behavior, not mechanical responses; it educates a person to think for himself. ASL argued that all education is a kind of indoctrination; one can be indoctrinated to use the Gestalt or the Institute's methods; both may lead to blind mechanical behavior. When he said that education is a virtue term, a glittering generality, Wertheimer asked whether ignorance is good and education is evil. ASL replied that ignorance is often bliss. Perhaps Lao Tzu was correct when he made statements as these: When we give up learning we have no more troubles; Discard sageness, get rid of wisdom and the people will be a hundred times better off. Lao Tzu taught that people will be happy when they remain in their primal ignorance: A wise ruler empties the peoples' minds and fills their bellies; weakens their will and strengthens their bones. He constantly keeps the people without knowledge and without desire. When there are those who have knowledge, he sees to it that they dare not act. When he thus enforces nonaction, good order is universal. Someone observed that perhaps Lao Tzu is wiser than the Biblical Deity who commanded that His law be studied day and night and who stressed the virtue of dialogue and even controversies in the name of heaven. The session ended at this point.

After-Class Discussion

ASL walked out with Wertheimer and told him that he had written a few years ago a paper on education and indoctrination for George Counts of Columbia. When he handed him the first page, Wertheimer read it and asked, Do you really believe this? (What Wertheimer read was as follows: Educators accept the thesis that man is a cultural product, a reflection of a certain society's conditioning. Yet the same educators claim that teachers must not present any biases, that they must present the truth concerning all sides of any issue, that they must not make a choice of what should be taught but must passively pass on all the ideas and knowledge of our culture. If one does not do this, one becomes an indoctrinator and education becomes propaganda . . . and thwarts the development of the child's personality. . . . If man is a cultural product his mind is a result of his interaction with a certain society. His needs, desires, values, his very thoughts and the very ideas about himself and his physical world are due to the social norms which have become interiorized in him. The entire process of education is the socializing of an organism's general biological needs into a specific kind of human being. Education is a form of indoctrination; it does not create a free spirit who will do things because of his free will and choice. His choices are society's choices; he pleases to do what society taught him to please. When Johnny comes to school, he is not taught all the bad and good points of all the existing and obsolete alphabets and then asked to take his choice. Nor is Johnny taught various cultures' concepts for denoting the phenomena of the environment and by his own free will decides to call X a cat. Not only has Johnny been bombarded by the English language from the moment he was born but without being consulted he was brought into a particular culture, a particular class, and a particular family. He is later on sent to a certain school building where he is regimented in a certain manner. His self expression is thwarted while he is forced to learn the three R's, history, geography as well as such frills of culture as music and drawing. The educators made the choices, not Johnny. Some would defend the educators by saying that we have to present to Johnny the tools and knowledges which will aid him in adjusting to society. If he is to live in America he must know its traditions, language, ideals, and its standards of judgment.)

ASL told Wertheimer that one of his education professors had defined education as the process of stuffing nine gallons of slop into five-gallon pigs. He went on to defend his paper's thesis that all education is propaganda, saying that an infant is not born with a spare diaper and diaper pin. He is malleable matter that a society shapes into its image. It is true that there are constraints in the biological makeup of the infant which may set limits to what the society can do to it; but it can decide that if the infant does not live up to certain standards it should perish. It could do this intentionally as in ancient Sparta or unintentionally by the sheer impact of the ways the adults treat the infant. It is a matter of chance that X is born a blond Jew instead of a blond German and is regarded as subhuman or human, is killed or does the killing. He concluded that one is what he is because of the tradition into which he is born. Education is the process of introducing a biological organism to a certain society's traditions. Another student who had joined the discussion said that it had been proved that man is a cultural product. Wertheimer asked whether there were any characteristics that all humans share. He remarked that people differ with regard to physical features but they also have certain species' specific physical characteristics. He asked, Do they also have certain common mental characteristics? ASL said that according to Aristotle and Plato man had certain common characteristics and that it was his duty to actualize these potentialities. Plato is reported to have said that men who do not actualize their intellectual souls are reborn as women. Plato in the *Republic* describes a program of education that will make one see the True, the Beautiful, and the Good—the Eternal Verities that the soul knew before it was put into the body. But present-day psychologists do not believe this; they know that there are no souls and that people have no minds. A student remarked that a good Buddhist, Catholic, or Jew may think that when he fasts he elevates his soul but a biologist knows that he is merely starving himself. All the talk of psychic expansion, widening or broadening of people's mental horizons assumes that there is a mind or soul in man that is seeking a relation with the cosmos. But men have no souls. Wertheimer asked whether the aim of education was to create robots. Even drill masters do not want a child to grow up into a robot. They hope that the child will be able to be productive, will develop traits which are characteristic of Homo sapiens. The student objected to the assumption that there are such characteristics; so far psychologists have not found them. We now know that people from different cultures regard themselves as uniquely human and do not consider people of other cultures as human. That is why they can readily kill them or enslave them. ASL argued that modern society has the techniques to turn its members into robots as described in Huxley's *Brave New World*. Man seems to want to become a robot. Wertheimer agreed that a society can be organized to create robots, but even such a society will need some people who can think or who at least will need to be educated instead of indoctrinated.

Propaganda Continued

Wertheimer started the next session by presenting the results of a Gallup Poll that showed that with the increase of the success of Hitler there was an increase in the number of people who favored the USA going to war with Germany. A visitor reported that he had heard that FDR had not really been sick when he delayed declaring a state of national emergency. He delayed because he felt that the people were not yet ready for it. A good leader knows that he needs evidence and that he cannot depend on emotional appeals. Even in advertising it is best when you can show that your product has some real intrinsic worth. The visitor went on to say that recent discussions of propaganda focus only on the use of emotional appeals but evidence also plays a role. ASL told the class that a few years ago a study had been conducted to test what was more effective in getting votes: a factual or an emotional appeal. Two districts in Pennsylvania were chosen; in one district the Socialist Party's candidate used an emotional appeal and in the other the same candidate used reason and facts. He got more votes where he had used an emotional appeal. A student pointed out that the reason Fascism and Nazism have been more successful than the Democratic and Socialistic parties is that the former have used emotional appeals. The liberals and radicals are committed to reason and to science; therefore they reason with people and use scientifically valid concepts. The Fascists and Nazis stir up emotions and defend traditional institutions and values. Perhaps we ought to realize what Freud and Pareto have been saying for a long time: man is an emotio conative creature. This led to a controversy about whether it is better to appeal to people's emotions than to present evidence when attempting to persuade them. Some students said that people are very susceptible to appeal that are in line with their beliefs and desires. They see and hear only the evidence that is in line with their beliefs and values and do not notice the evidence that contradicts them. Wertheimer asked, How valid is it that men are like resonating tuning forks? A visitor replied that in addition to being tuned-in to pick up certain facts they actively defend themselves against facts that go against their beliefs. Someone remarked that emotional appeals have only temporary effects. Once their feelings are cooled, people realize that they have been fooled if nothing has been done. People can be fooled temporarily but in the long run the facts win out. Lincoln once said that you can fool some of the people some of the time but you cannot fool most of the people most of the time. ASL said that there is some evidence in daily life that shows that facts may produce temporary changes in attitudes; for example, a recent study showed that immediately after *The Birth of a Nation* was seen there were changes on Thurston's attitude scale but a few months later the viewers showed no effect; the change in attitude had been temporary (cf. Luchins & Luchins, 1970d).

Wertheimer made the following summary remarks: If one tries to understand what usually goes on in propaganda, one finds at minimum two different kinds of phenomena. Phenomena I: People lack knowledge, do not know what to do, are blind, are misdirected, are blindly directed. The propagandist opens their eyes, strengthens their wills and emotions in such a manner that they gain insight into the things and problems facing them. Phenomena II: The propagandist tries to impose or does impose his ideas on people with no regard to what they would do if they were informed and decided for themselves what to do. The propagandist enforces on them a certain goal or view, resulting in a narrowing of their mental fields. The people become objects to be pushed around; this is accomplished because they are robbed of the preconditions for insight and understanding in their behavior. After a pause, Wertheimer asked, Can anyone be blind to the structure of these two types of propaganda? Do Types I and II really have at their bases the same psychological mechanisms?

Someone remarked that propaganda is used in times of war to strengthen one's own country and to weaken the enemy. In response to a student's question Wertheimer said that there was propaganda by pacifists in World War I who sought to make peace. This was not propaganda to blind the eyes of people. He added after a pause that because of the existence of propaganda of Type II we assume that propaganda is always biased, always blind. Such claims do not differentiate between appeals to emotions and reason. A student argued that the propaganda of pacifists can be like Type II because it blinds people to the facts; for example, the Oxford Pledge Movement has kept people from fighting Hitler; Churchill has been called a warmonger because he wants to stop Hitler's expansion; American pacifists have said that FDR is fooling the public and is trying to drag us into a war with Germany because he does not like their political philosophy. If you agree with these propagandists you will say that it is the reasonable, helpful, and informative Type I; if you do not, you will say that it is Type II.

Wertheimer remarked that in dealing with the evaluation of propaganda, psychologists have said that the evaluation is always biased. But is this so? Someone said that in Type I the emphasis is on understanding and on reason but in Type II the emphasis is on emotions. The former is cognitive and the latter is noncognitive. Wertheimer rejected this distinction as too simple. Type I can be brought about by reasonable, assumptions and Type I can be brought about by feelings and emotions. One of the refugee professors described the methods used by the Nazis to induce countries to surrender without fighting. At home they use vituperation and report atrocity stories about the enemy, but to the enemy they pretend that everybody among them is not their (the Nazis') enemy. They tell the enemy that they do not use violence; violence is used only when it is necessary to achieve certain ends, when absolutely needed. They also tell the enemy that they (the enemy) cannot win the war, that the odds are against them, that they are too weak. They also attack the enemy's confidence in victory by telling the enemy that they are divided but that the Nazis are not. They prevent a proper understanding of the issues by telling the enemy that they have internal enemies and that the Nazis are their real friends who will treat them well if they do not fight. They point out that nonpolitical values are most important. Nazis attack the other people's convictions of their right to victory by stressing that they themselves are just. After a pause he said that it is significant that Germany has a Ministry of Propaganda and England has a Ministry of Information. Someone interjected that he wondered whether the USA would call it The Truth Bureau or True Information Service and asked whether this means that the USA and England use Type I propaganda. Wertheimer said that giving people *mere* information, piecemeal facts, does not make it Type I because facts can be presented in a misleading way. After a pause he added that you must understand the particular act of propaganda in relation to the social situations in which it occurs. If you do not, you take the flesh and blood out of it. He reiterated that Type II propaganda tries to keep people from thinking, from acting as humans with rights; but Type I tries to let them function as people who stand on their own feet and are free. It deals with people as equals and is willing to be challenged.

Someone interrupted to ask whether all education is indoctrination. Wertheimer answered that this is believed by many. How factual is it? It is one thing to teach physics to enlarge the student's knowledge and another to speak to the class in order to try to develop a certain social movement in a certain definite direction. When Wertheimer said that the purpose of education is to open the students' eyes, ASL pointed out that Counts, Rugg, and other educators claim that the role of the school is to change the social order. A college professor said that this is a dangerous viewpoint. He recalled how students in his college classes would interrupt lectures to ask for the Marxian point of view; they even did it in chemistry and physics lectures. A refugee said that the Nazi students did the same thing in German universities. They would attack the teachers for being Communists, Jews, Liberals, etc. and for teaching things that were not correct or were divorced from life.

ASL then reported that recently he was asked to take over a WPA Adult Education class in which the students had protested against their teachers; three different teachers had failed to satisfy them. It was found out that the class was composed mainly of American Nazis. ASL took over the class and was rather successful with them because he looked to them like the stereotype of an Aryan whereas the previous teachers looked Jewish even though some of them were not. He got their attention by telling them he would teach them about important things, about Christianity and race theory. He taught them the Nazis' race theory for three weeks and then told them that the Nazis were struggling to save mankind and to preserve Christianity. During this time few students complained to the Board of Education that ASL was a Nazi. But when ASL compared the Sermon on the Mount with one of Hitler's sword-rattling speeches nearly all students walked out. They picketed the building and complained that he was a Communist. (See Luchins, 1944 for a report of what happened.) ASL asked the seminar members, How can you open people's eyes when they see and do not understand or when they refuse to see and to understand?

Someone said that American students are apolitical. He contrasted them with South American students and said that in South America the universities are headquarters of revolutionary movements but in America students swallow goldfish, drink booze, whore, and gamble to show their power. American students have not realized that they are in a very strategic position, that they could paralyze the university and even society if they wanted to. The session ended with examples of youth movements in Russia, France, Italy, and Germany that were the dynamos of revolutionary movements. A visitor said that youth has been a fertile field for the propagandists who seek to start social movements of various kinds.

After-Class Discussion

On the way to the subway ASL told Wertheimer that most of the college instructors in the seminar are opposed to the draft and to getting involved in the war and yet he, Wertheimer, and the German refugees who are not Stalinists are in favor of the war. How is it possible that in spite of all the discussions in the seminars during the past few years the college instructors have not had their eyes opened to the situation as it really is? When he said that they are blinded by their ideologies, ASL told him that maybe these seminar members can say that he is blind and not that they are blind. The talk turned to Wilkie's campaign speeches in which FDR was being tarred as a warmonger. Wertheimer expressed concern and said that some refugees are worried, they even feel that they will have to leave the country if FDR loses the election.

25
Experimental Outgrowths: Social Influences

The Defense of Sherif's Pioneering Studies

Wertheimer's criticism of Sherif's work in the seminar on methodology in the social sciences provoked ASL to defend Sherif's and Cantril's work on social influences on perception and judgment (cf. *Wertheimer's Seminars Revisited: Problem Solving and Thinking*, Vol. 3). The defense was in the form of an experiment with a series of pictures that started out with an ambiguous drawing and in subsequent drawings gradually developed into a picture of a bottle (AB series). When children were given the AB series beginning with the ambiguous picture, they usually saw the bottle one or two drawings earlier than did those children who were first given a series of pictures (henceforth called the FA series) which started out with the profile of a face but in subsequent pictures the face deteriorated into an ambiguous picture that was similar to the first picture of the AB series. Moreover, the subjects who started out with the FA series persisted in seeing a face in pictures of the AB series in which the children who had been given only the AB series did not see a face, that is, they had become set in the FA series to seeing a face and were blinded to an obvious picture in the drawings of the AB series.

Among the experiments conducted to extremize the set, the Einstellung effect, in the series of pictures, were experiments in which various instructions or social factors were used. In one experiment a pair of children was shown the pictures of the AB series. One child of the pair was the experimenter's confederate and, in accordance with previous instructions, he always responded first, saying that he saw a face. The naive subjects of the pairs were influenced by the confederate's response; they saw a face and did not see the bottle in pictures in which subjects who judged alone did not see a face but did see the bottle. Their answers were similar to those made by subjects who had been given the FA series before the AB series. This indicated to us that social factors could produce blindness to distinctive features of the drawing just as repetition produced Einstellung effects in problem solving. We found that when the confederate and the naive subject were first given the FA series and then the AB series, even more naive subjects reported seeing the face and did not report seeing the bottle. And when the experimenter said that the confederate's response was correct, still more subjects reported seeing the face and fewer reported seeing the bottle. These results suggested that through the introduction of more forces in the social situation it was possible to increase agreement with an overheard response and blindness to a dominant feature of the drawing.

It did not seem to be just a matter of reinforcement because when the confederate said that he saw a battleship, there was very little influence; the confederate's response had to have some basis in the drawing. However, more agreement with the confederate's incorrect response was obtained when the experimenter called the confederate's incorrect response correct and when, in addition, he told the confederate that he had 100% and told the naive subject that he would be shown the pictures again to see if he too could get 100%. These results suggested that with still more social pressure we might be able to get children to focus on the social influences and to ignore the evidence. We therefore planned experiments to extremize wrong responses when the confederate gave incorrect answers and when he gave correct answers. (The strength of a factor was gauged by the picture in the series in which subjects gave the desired response.) It was possible to get 60% agreement with the confederate's answers in the last picture of the AB series by saying to the children after the entire series was presented that the confederate had 100% and that the naive subject had a percentage based on the number of times that he had given the same response as the confederate and to urge him to get 100% next time. It was not as easy to get the naive subject to disagree with the confederate when he gave the correct answer and the experimenter called him wrong and told him that he had 0%. The children protested, cried, or became so tense that the experiment was terminated. When Wertheimer was shown the results he was surprised at the ease with which the children could be intimidated and made to disregard the evidence. He attributed it to the social atmosphere of the classroom and to the children's assumption that the experiment was a test and that on tests the teacher decides what is correct.

The experiments on social influences were conducted at the same time and in the same manner as the problem-solving research (Luchins & Luchins, 1970c pp., 11-12) except that we never stopped to organize the experimental data for a monograph as was done for the Einstellung effects (Luchins, 1942). Moreover, Wertheimer made so many suggestions for experimental variations that our concern was more with doing research than formulating the results for publication. ASL's joining the U.S. Army interrupted the research. The employment situation on his return to civilian life made it impossible to complete the projects that had been planned with Wertheimer. What follows is a summary of some of the work that had already been completed in the prewar years as well as replications and extensions of the earlier work with the help of ASL's undergraduate students. It is an informal report reflecting our thinking when the research was originally undertaken. We hope that it will raise new questions for research and thus further extend the seminal ideas of Wertheimer's seminars.

1. Wertheimer asked, What would be the effects of learning to agree with someone in several ambiguous pictures (from different series of pictures) on seeing the gradually emerging bottle in the AB series of pictures? Ten ambiguous pictures, which were different from the first picture of the AB series, were presented to a pair of children; the first child of the pair was the experimenter's confederate and said that he saw a face in all the pictures. Some subjects readily agreed with the confederate in all ten pictures. In order to obtain 100% agreement we told the confederate that he had 100% on the test and told the subject that we would readminister the test until he too

would also have 100%. In this way it was possible to train the second child to agree in all ambiguous pictures with the confederate. When the second child received 100% the experimenter said that the series would now be given once more in order to see if they could both get 100% again. This time the AB series of pictures was added after the ten ambiguous pictures. Many children kept on reporting in the AB series what the confederate had said and did not report the bottle until the third from the last picture of the AB series.

We wondered what would happen if ten unambiguous pictures were used and the confederate made incorrect or correct responses. It was very difficult for us to get 100% agreement when the confederate reported something that did not appear to be in the picture but there were children who after the third representation of the ten pictures began to repeat the confederate's responses. Some children repeated the confederate's wrong response in the AB series but some saw the bottle earlier in the series than when the confederate gave correct responses. Wertheimer suggested that the AB series be used as the training pictures and the ten pictures be used as test pictures. He asked, Would it reduce the influence of the first child's reports when the AB series was given after the subject had attained 100% in the earlier pictures? It did not do so in many cases. Therefore Wertheimer asked, What can be done to make it more effective? Why not try the method that had been used to prevent Einstellung effects in problem solving? (Cf. Luchins, 1942.)

2. We decided to focus on these questions: If after hearing someone else describe a picture, an individual is asked to describe it, will the overheard response influence what he sees? Will this influence take the direction of focusing the individual on seeing what the other person described? Will it, perhaps, cause him to overlook certain prominent structural features of the drawing? Will the influence differ for designs of various degrees of structural clarity? A series of twelve pictures (a modified AB series) was presented one at a time to children; they were asked to describe what they saw. About 50% of the children said that they saw a face or part of a face in the first ambiguous picture of the new AB series. After the fifth picture about 10% reported a face but now about 90% saw a bottle in each drawing. Experimental variations were conducted to increase and decrease the reporting of the bottle and the face when the subject overheard the confederate's report that he saw a bottle or a face. When the confederate said that he saw a face, there was an increase in the seeing of faces and a decrease in the reporting of bottles in the drawing. When the confederate said that he saw a battleship or an automobile, however, there was less influence. However some subjects just repeated what the confederate said; they were oriented to what he said and did not seem at all concerned with the object of judgment. But, other subjects did not blindly repeat what the confederate had reported. They examined the drawings and looked in them for the object that the confederate had reported. When a characteristic of the drawing that was compatible with the confederate's statement was found, it became for some subjects the prominent or sole feature of the drawing to which they paid attention; they, therefore, overlooked other and more dominant features of the drawing. Thus, whether or not they agreed with the confederate depended to some extent on the content of the drawing. For such a subject to agree with the confederate, the drawing had to possess some characteristic of the description or have the possibility of being organized in line with it. These subjects focused on the obje-

of judgment and would not be deflected by the social factors of the situation. They were evidence-oriented in contrast to the subjects who focused on the social factors and were blind to the nature of the evidence given to judge. Similar results were obtained in experiments without the use of confederates by giving the subject private, prior experiences that set him to see a face, for example, he was told to look for a face and the experimenter called his response correct when he said that he saw a face, or he was given profiles or other drawings of faces or the whole series FA immediately prior to series AB. Wertheimer pointed out that these results do not disprove the role of social influences on perception or judgment because certain social factors were embodied in the experimental design; the experimenter had arranged the subject's previous experience so that the desired response occurred in the AB series.

3. The results indicated that some of the pictures gave rise to a certain range of responses; therefore, Wertheimer suggested that some of the ambiguous pictures be shown to many individuals of various ages and backgrounds in order to obtain information about what people saw in each picture. Were there certain features or things that would be seen by all people regardless of age, educational level, and socioeconomic background? Were there certain things that would be seen by only some of these subjects and not by others? What would happen if someone overheard a response that was typical or atypical for all groups of subjects or only for his or another group? Would he agree with the overheard responses that were atypical for the groups of which he was a member? We collected responses to several ambiguous pictures but the data was not systematically studied because ASL left for the army; the study still needs to be done. In order to stimulate interest we shall mention some trends that were found. Preliminary analysis of the data had indicated that there was a greater variety of responses when the subjects were told to guess, and/or were told that there was no correct answer than when they were told to trace what they saw and not to guess and that certain things were seen by most people and that these things were the correct answers. We also found that social influences were somewhat greater when a response made by the confederate was typical of or within the range of responses that the subject had previously made to the drawing or was similar to the responses of people from his background. The subject's knowledge or acquaintance with what the confederate said also influenced his agreement, for example, when the confederate said that a picture reminded him of a certain slide in his bacteriology course or another object with which the subject was unfamiliar there was less influence. We had expected that the responses would be more similar for those pictures in which there were organizational features that implied a grouping of the stimuli in a certain way (cf. Wertheimer's principles of organization in Ellis, 1938). This thesis was validated with those subjects who were oriented toward the drawings' structural features instead of just looking at them in terms of their past experience or repeating what a confederate said. We also found that the way the subject looked at the pictures played a role in determining what he saw. Some subjects of each age level focused only on parts of the drawing or had an analytical attitude but others surveyed the drawing as a whole in order to understand it; the former were more influenced than the latter (cf. Wertheimer 1905, Arnheim, 1928). Generally speaking, attitudes toward, assumptions

about, and approaches to such perceptual tasks as well as ideas associated with them, influenced the subject's sensitivity to the pictures' structural features. In view of this, Wertheimer suggested that a complex drawing be used in which the structural features were more evident even though the pictures were still ambiguous. He poined out that our pictures were unclear, complex as well as ambiguous. This led to a discussion of the nature of the stimulus field in such studies (Luchins, 1950, 1955a). He also suggested that more lifelike things be used; for example, what effect would social influences have on the description of real people, of ordinary scenes and events? Would someone agree when someone else said that he saw a mountain in Central Park or a man on top of a church's steeple? Why not adapt the *Aussage* (testimony) experiments for experiments on social influences of perception? We went on to plan experiments on the role of social influences on the descriptions that he had used as demonstrations in the problem-solving seminars (cf. Luchins & Luchins, Vol. 2, 161, 277ff; Vol. 3, 215-226, 373 ff., 396 ff). [Many of Wertheimer's demonstrations could be used to test his conjectures about the amount of force needed to make someone respond in a prostructural or counter-structural manner.] Wertheimer's suggestion led to the construction of a series of paragraphs that described a youth in different situations: the first paragraph described rather extroverted behavior and the last paragraph described rather introverted behavior. The first to the sixth paragraphs described respectively less and less extrovertive behavior; the sixth paragraph described rather average or neutral behavior. From paragraph 6 to 12 the descriptions became more introverted. These paragraphs were used in experiments similar to those with the series of pictures in order to extremize agreement and disagreement with the confederate's correct or incorrect judgment (Luchins & Luchins, 1961, 1963, 1965 report on similar studies.)

4. Experiments were conducted to see the effects of previous experience with ambiguous as well as unambiguous perceptual stimuli under various social conditions (cf. Luchins, 1955a, Luchins & Luchins, 1955a). Generally speaking, we found that hearing another person's response called correct or giving the subject previous experience with the socially offered descriptions resulted in the increased effectiveness of the social influences. Moreover, when some subjects were retested alone, some days later, they gave the same response as in the experimental session. Features of the results raised the question of what is meant by an ambiguous stimulus and did not support the thesis that social influences are always greater when the stimuli are ambiguous.

5. Studies were conducted in which the confederate's responses were always in line with, or always were counter to the structure of the series of drawings, or in which the confederates' responses were correct in one half but incorrect in the other half of the series. After such experiences, the subjects were given a series of pictures in which the confederate was either always wrong or right. This study was replicated at McGill University in 1952 with the assistance of Miss Lamprecht and will be summarized in another section.

6. Wertheimer once suggested that the material used in the Einstellung experiment be used to study social influence; therefore, experiments were devised using word blocks, anagrams, mazes, and the water-measuring problems of the Einstellung tests (Luchins and Luchins, 1959, Chapter 22). This early work with Wertheimer suggested several studies in the area of clinical

psychology, for example, social influences on responses to the Rorschach Test (Luchins, 1947a), psychodiagnostics, and psychotherapy (Luchins, 1947b, 1953, 1959). Some of these studies investigated, among other things, the role of social influences on perception in everyday life and in clinical situations with the aim of obtaining veridical perception. Such situations must be studied, Wertheimer said, in order to avoid a one-sided view of the role of social influences. He also observed that most of the research in this area had dealt with the negative effects of social influences. Although social influences may blind and may make people act uncritically there are also cases where they open one's eyes and make one deal intelligently and critically in judgment situations.

7. Wertheimer once remarked that there was something deceitful in our experiments because the confederate gave the wrong answer and the experimenter called him correct and even said that he had 100% on a test of visual acuity. We therefore made experimental variations in which we set the subjects by means of an Einstellung to respond in a certain way. In one study two children, who sat at opposite ends of a large table, were tested at the same time. They were given the same instructions except that unknown to them they were given different series of problems. One subject had been given a series of water-measuring problems that could be solved by B-A-2C (E method) and another child had been given a series that could be solved by A+C (D method). After eight problems we gave them the same critical test problem in order to see whether they had developed a set for B-A-2C and A+C respectively. If they did, we told them to sit next to each other and said that from now on when they were given a problem they should work together on it. A problem, written on a card similar to the other cards, was then placed before both of them. In ten pairs of subjects the child who had developed an E-set was asked to solve the problem first while the other child listened; after this, the other child was asked to solve it. In ten other pairs, the child who had developed a D-set answered first. When the E-set subjects of the experiment answered first, all of them gave the E solution in C_1 (the first critical) but when they heard the other subject give the D solution, six of the ten subjects changed their answers to the D solution. In no case did a D-set subject change to an E solution when he overheard it. In the variation in which the D-set subjects went first, they all gave a D solution and some of the E-set subjects gave a D and not an E solution. We conducted experimental variations to maximize the giving of E solutions. In one variation, the ten pairs of subjects were told to generalize a rule while working on the problems and they were also told to see if they could use it later on. Again not one of the D-set subjects changed to the E solution. However, less E-set subjects changed to the D method than in the previous study. All E-set subjects used the E method in C_1 and two failed to solve number 9 because they insisted that the rule must work; six E-set subjects who had used the D method in number 9 went back to the E method in C_3 and C_4; they were glad that they could use the rule again. In variations in which we used a key to mark the papers and said that the E-set subjects had 100% it was possible within five repetitions of the series of critical problems to get 100% E solutions. But, when we said that the D-set subjects had 100%, it was possible to get 100% with two repetitions of the series of criticals. These results support Wertheimer's conjecture that the more arbitrary the response the more force is needed to get it to be made.

We conducted variations in which pairs or trios of subjects solved the E problems. In one of these experiments two subjects worked together and generalized a rule which worked in the critical problems. Before the first critical was given to them, a naive subject or a confederate entered the room and was asked to solve the criticals before the group solved it (or after the group solved it). Generally speaking, when the naive individual went first he gave a D solution and objected to being told that the E method was the rule, but some did "obey the rule" and changed to the E method. More subjects agreed with the confederate when he suggested a D solution than when the group had generalized the D method and the confederate suggested the E method. However, when the confederate's answer was supported by the experimenter's verdict it was possible to get such subjects to change their rule and give E or D solutions. This indicates that agreement can be obtained in a group by a minority if it has the power to obtain conformity (cf. Luchins & Luchins, 1959, 536-568).

Discussion of these experiments led to such questions as these: What would happen if each of three subjects was given a card containing a different jar of the problem and they were told to obtain the required amount of water by means of the jars given to them? What would happen if the set and test problems were presented in this manner? Would the subjects realize that they must cooperate in order to solve each problem? What factors would help or keep them from cooperating? What happens when the problem is solvable by the use of only two of the jars? Does a different group structure develop when the same subjects get the A, B, and C jars respectively in each problem than when the assignment of problem to subject is varied? What happens when there are four subjects and a superfluous jar in each problem (one unnecessary for the solution) is assigned always to the same subject or is varied among different subjects?

An interesting feature of these experiments was that a group member had a means or asset (one jar) which by itself was inadequate to solve the problem but which could lead to a solution when combined with some or all of the group members' assets. In these experiments a variety of group processes and structures emerged out of the attempts to combine their means to solve the problems. Wertheimer had been critical of a one-sided approach to social influences on problem solving (Dashiell, in Murchison, 1935) because the nature of the problem did not require cooperation; the same problem could be solved in a group or alone. How about problems that could be solved only when people pooled their assets? We need to study situations where the structure of the social field is pro and counter to the structure of the problem, where personality and social factors center one on or blind one to the requirements of the problem. We have made some attempts in this direction (cf. Luchins & Luchins, 1969).

Wertheimer's Theses. Some of the results of the experiments of the previous section do not support Wertheimer's conjecture that if subjects were given evidence on which to make their judgments, the results would be different than those obtained by Sherif and Cantril. In the experiments with the above-mentioned series of pictures it became apparent that the introduction of evidence did not always minimize social influences. Moreover, subjects could be made to say whatever the confederates said, even though the responses were counter to the evidence. While discussing these experiments Wertheimer made the following formulation: What occurs in these experiments may be described as a clash between two tendencies: the tendency to be guided by what the confederate says; the tendency to be guided by the structural features of the drawings. It is of interest both for theoretical and for practical reasons to determine how to strengthen each of these tendencies, to investigate under what personal, attitudinal, and social conditions an individual is or is not influenced and to determine how to organize objects in the social field so that one will or will not be blind to the evidence. [Some of the work done with Wertheimer had been described elsewhere (Luchins, 1945; Luchins & Luchins 1970a). Other questions which he raised in discussing these experiments have been presented in Luchins, 1950, and in a report on the influence on perception of previous experiences with ambiguous and unambiguous pictures as well as in a report on the effects of previous experience with ambiguous and unambiguous pictures under various social influences (Luchins & Luchins, 1955a, 1955b). Luchins & Luchins, 1959, chapter 22 contains reports which stemmed from the discussions of the above described experiments.] Just as in the work with the water jars, many experiments were planned, some were conducted systematically, others were started and never completed, and still others were never even undertaken. The following survey is presented to show the numerous ideas that flowed from a discussion with Wertheimer. He had a remarkable ability to see various possibilities to test theoretical and practical problems while discussing a simple demonstration or experiment.

Wertheimer wanted to know what would happen if the evidence was simpler and clearer. Therefore we made a series of 16 pairs of parallel lines; each pair was perpendicular to the bottom side of a small square and was drawn on a small card ($2'' \times 3''$). In the first card both lines were one inch long but in successive cards only one line of the pair was one inch long and the other line was 1/16 of an inch shorter than the (shorter) line of the preceding card. Thus the series started out with both lines being equal but ended with one line being one inch and the other 1/16 of an inch. We tried out the series on sixth-grade children of a Brooklyn slum. Two children were tested at a time; they were told that the Board of Education was making a new intelligence test and that we were going to try out on them the visual acuity sub-test. In order to put them at ease they were told how tests were standardized and that they were helping us standardize a new test. When each child answered so that only the experimenter could hear him, there were some errors on the judgment of the first card although most children said that both lines on this card were equal; there were some errors on the second card, very few errors on the third card, and no errors thereafter. But, in the experiments in which the child who answered first was the experimenter's confederate the results were different. The confederate always responded outloud so that the other child could hear him. When the confederate gave wrong answers about one-third of the subjects agreed with him in the first card where the lines were equal and in the second card. A few agreed with him in the third, fourth, and fifth cards but no one agreed with him thereafter. When the confederate answered correctly a few children gave incorrect answers in the first few cards but correct answers thereafter.

In an experimental variation in which the experimenter said after both had judged a card that the confederate was correct and the naive subject was called correct only if he too gave the confederate's wrong answer, a third of the subjects gave wrong answers to cards 2, 3, 4, 5 and a few agreed with his wrong answers until the eighth card. After the entire series was judged, the experimenter told the confederate that he had 100% and told the subject that the test would be readministered so that he too could get 100%. After the third administration of the entire series of line segments there was 100% agreement on the first three cards; about half of the subjects agreed in all the cards until the eighth and about a third agreed in all the cards of the series.

When these results were shown to Wertheimer he asked, Why did the children in the second experiment give wrong answers when the confederate answered correctly? ASL replied that the children seemed reluctant to give the same answer as the first child because it would be cheating. It was a strange test because they had to answer after they had already heard someone else give the answer. Wertheimer then asked, Why did the children agree with the wrong answers in the first experiment; weren't they afraid of cheating? He went on to say that we need to know more about the children's attitudes and assumptions and just how children regard such a task. He then pointed out that in the third and fourth variations some children were readily affected by the social forces in the situation that demanded wrong answers but other pupils faced the evidence. He suggested that we find out more about these two groups of children. What attitudes and assumptions did they have about the test that might explain the differences in responding? ASL never found this out, because the experiments were never replicated. Instead he continued making variations of the experiment in order to obtain 100% and 0% agreement with the confederate's judgments in all of the pairs of lines of the series when the confederate gave objectively wrong answers and when he gave objectively correct answers. In some experiments we changed the drawings on each card; the two line segments radiated out of the square so that each made an angular space with the side of the box, for example, . Because the experiment took too long, we shortened the series to five pairs of lines and used a series in which the lines radiated out at different angles. One line of each pair was one inch long but the other line was 15/16, 14/16, 12/16, 10/16, and 8/16 of an inch in cards 1 to 5, respectively. When a survey of the experiments was presented to Wertheimer he noticed that certain experiments showed an interesting trend and suggested that these experiments be presented to the seminar for discussion. The following is the summary we presented in the seminar.

The Confederate Gives Correct Answers.

In the initial experiment 50, 80, 100, 100, 100% of the children gave correct judgments when they answered after hearing the confederate respond but when the confederate left the room and the series was readministered they all judged the lines correctly. A few children were surprised to learn that they had judged the lines incorrectly the first time; these children had been visibly nervous during the experiment; the other children said that they gave a different answer before because they did not want to copy or cheat.

A. Attempts to Increase Agreement with the Confederates' Correct Answers.

When the experimenter confirmed the confederates' correct answers there were 80, 100, 100, 100, 100% correct answers to cards 1-5, respectively. When a series of five pairs of parallel line segments that were 1/16 of an inch apart was used, there were 95, 100, 100, 100, 100% correct answers in cards 1-5, respectively. When the children were given a strip of cardboard and shown, on an illustrative card, how to use it to compare the lines of the usual series of five pairs of lines, not one subject gave a wrong judgment. In this experiment all the children answered with no hesitancy and they did not seem to be disturbed by the confederate's answers.

B. Attempts to Decrease Agreement with the Confederates' Correct Answers.

The naive subjects as well as the confederates became so tense and tearful during these experiments that it was decided not to go on with them. But these variations worked well with college students (cf. Luchins & Luchins, 1955c).

The Confederate Gives False Answers.

In the initial experiment the confederate selected the objectively incorrect answers; there was 23, 23, 15, 15, 23% agreement with him in cards 1-5, respectively. In the retrial, when the child judged alone, there were no incorrect answers. Whether or not they agreed with the confederate's wrong answer, they were somewhat worried and ill at ease by his consistent and confident selection of the longer line. Some tried to find some reasonable explanation for his behavior, for example, that the assigned test was to select the longer line or that the sides of the box or the angle formed by the lines made the longer line look shorter. [It is interesting that fewer children in this and subsequent experiments were concerned with the possibility that they would be cheating if they agreed with the confederate. Did the strange behavior of the confederate create a different social atmosphere in these experiments than in the experiments in which the confederate gave correct responses?]

A. Attempts to Increase Agreement with the Confederate's False Answers.

The variations that increased agreement with the confederate's wrong answers (yielding at least 50% agreement in the fourth and fifth cards) were as follows: In one variation, after both children had judged a card, the confederate's answer was called right and the subject's answer was called wrong unless he had agreed with the confederate. In another variation, a series of fifteen cards, in which both lines were equal, was given over and over again until the subject agreed in every card with the confederate's choices; then the series was repeated once more but unknown to the naive subject the usual five cards were added at the end of the series. In still another variation the usual five cards were preceded by a series of 20 cards. In the first card of this series the difference between the two lines was one inch but in each succeeding card the difference decreased until in the last card the lines were equal. The confederate selected the objectively shorter line of each of the twenty cards but when the usual five cards were presented, he selected what was actually the longer line but said that it was shorter. Complete agreement with the confederate's wrong answers was obtained by repeatedly presenting the usual five cards and each time telling the confederate that he had 100% and basing the subject's score on the test on the number of times that he had agreed with the confederate. Before the series was readministered the subject was urged to get 100% on the easy test. [Wertheimer conjectured that the results of the last experiment may reflect the effects of the children's schooling and asked, Would this procedure work with children who were not grade-conscious? The other methods, he pointed out, were in line with what could be expected from what was known about Einstellung effects. He suggested that we use the method that had maximized the Einstellung effects to increase agreement with the confederate, for example, to tell the subjects to generalize a rule or a principle or give them more practice to repeat the overheard response or create speed-test tension.]

B. Attempts to Decrease Agreement with the Confederate's False Answer.

When the series of pairs of parallel lines were used there was 10, 10, 10, 30, 30 % agreement with the confederate in cards 1-5, respectively. This method was not successful in eliminating agreement because the clarity of the differences between the lines and the consistent and obviously wrong answers of the confederate led to hypotheses to justify giving the wrong answers. When they were given strips of cardboard and taught how to measure the lines there was only 20, 10, 10, 0, 0 % agreement with the confederate in cards 1-5, respectively. In another variation, the child was given these means to measure and also told that it sometimes happens on oral tests that a child knows the correct answer but when called upon to recite he overhears someone and changes his mind and gives the wrong answer. We asked the child, Why does this happen? After waiting for him to answer, we said, Sometimes it is because the boy or girl is not so sure. In this test I want you to be sure of what to say; therefore, I am going to show you how to measure the lines. In this experiment all the subjects disagreed with the confederate. They gazed at him with astonishment, amusement or pity and even offered to show him how to measure. Because of the effects on the subjects and the confederates, we had to discontinue the experiments in which the experimenter said that the confederate's correct answer was wrong and in which he was given a score of zero in the foretraining series of cards and in the readministration of the usual five cards with the challenge to get 100 % issued to both the confederate and the subject.

While ASL read this summary, Wertheimer wrote on the blackboard a table of the results. He then asked the class what the results meant. ASL remarked that it shows that it might be possible to get a child to say whatever one wants him to say. Wertheimer asked, When was it easy to get agreement and when was it difficult? After a pause for comments, he pointed out that it was relatively easier to get agreement with the confederates' judgments when they were true than when they were false. Special factors had to be introduced to force the child to give the socially approved but false response. He asked the class to comment on the various methods that had been used to obtain agreement and disagreement with true and false judgments. ASL said that the most efficient methods to obtain agreement with the social forces involved approval and disapproval. Thus it shows that Thorndike's learning theory holds for social psychology (Thorndike, 1935). Someone pointed out that it illustrates how such learning methods may be used to blind people to the evidence and to accept what the authority or majority tells them. It brings about blind obedience to authority. Wertheimer asked whether the results might be due to the fact that the subjects were children. Would the methods work with college students and naive adults? A visiting professor said that the damage done to children by such experiments outweighed the value of the results. She went on to say that the stimulus' meaning changed; that the experimenter changed the meaning of short and long. The experimenter forced compliance; the child had to say whatever the other child said because the experimenter said that it was correct. Some seminar members were surprised by the forceful way Wertheimer defended the results of the experiment because the results were counter to many of the things that he had said about social influences on judgment.

A few weeks later Wertheimer told ASL that a member of the seminar had obtained different results in a replication of the study in Brooklyn College. Wertheimer proposed that ASL hold up publication of his findings so that both reports could be published at the same time. For reasons unknown to ASL, a few years later Wertheimer told him that it had been decided that ASL publish first. Wertheimer helped write the report of the results (Luchins, 1945a); in the discussions during the writing of the report Wertheimer stressed that the experiments involved the problem of the interplay of external factors (attitude, interpretations) and the evidence presented for judgment. Future research should be directed at strengthening the operation of the role of the evidence as well as the role of the external factors. In discussing the relative ineffectiveness of the experiments in which we used more than one confederate, he pointed out the need to study the relationship of the subject to the confederate and to the social atmosphere of the experimental situation. We need to know more about the subject's attitudes toward and his assumptions about the other child who constantly gives wrong answers. Perhaps the experimenter's right-wrong verdicts were more effective because of the children's reliance on their teachers to tell them what was right or because they felt that they had to pass the test. We might not get the same results if the experiments were conducted in a non-school setting or in progressive schools where there was a different kind of teacher-pupil relationship and social atmosphere. In helping to write up the report as well as in discussing the experiments that were not included in it, Wertheimer stressed the need to get a fuller picture of what actually takes place in such judgment situations. What follows is a survey of what has been or still needs to be done. It is presented in the informal way in which the problems were raised. We hope it will stimulate research along the lines Wertheimer had suggested.

The literature on social influences is replete with assertions that imply a negative relation between social influence with age, education, intelligence, and social status. Wertheimer pointed out that some aspects of our investigation seemed to support these hypotheses. Therefore, wide varieties of populations need to be studied in order to find out how different kinds of subjects react in such experimental situations. Would they differ in terms of where in the series of cards they agreed or disagreed; would they agree and disagree for different reasons; would the methods that minimized and maximized agreement with correct or incorrect judgments work only for certain populations and not for others? Which methods are effective for all populations? We are at present in no position to answer these questions because of a lack of systematic study. [Some preliminary studies showed that in some schools and in some social situations outside of the school, college students were more readily influenced than children. We also found that certain groups of children were less influenced than college subjects when the same methods were used. Attitudes and assumptions that are related to the social atmosphere of the school played an important role in determining how the subject reacted; they seemed to be more crucial than sheer age of the subjects. These results support Wertheimer's hypotheses about the important role of field conditions.]

Wertheimer remarked that instead of arguing whether or not certain people were more or less susceptible to social influences, it might be of value to observe a person's behavior in different situations. Therefore, ASL had asked his Adult Education students (and later on patients and personnel of US Army Hospitals) to record three times a day all instances in which they were influenced by or in which they influenced others. In one class project some students selected a patient in a ward, a child in a school or in the neighborhood, or a college student on the campus and observed him several times a day for a month. They recorded all the times that they saw the person being influenced by or influencing others. Other students kept such a record about themselves. Each student wrote a report in terms of who, what, when, where, how, and why the influences occurred. The students rarely reported that they or their subjects never influenced somebody. Their results also indicated that there were certain places, formal as well as informal situations, in which they were more often influenced and others in which they more often did the influencing. The question of whether one influences more than he was influenced seemed to be a function of the personality of the individual as well as of the social situation.

Wertheimer proposed that a variety of evidence be used for judgment; therefore, instead of giving subjects lengths of lines to judge we asked in different experiments which of two figures was more like a circle, a straight line, or a square, which of two figures was larger, which of a pair of spots of light was brighter, had less glare, or was more like a certain color. We used auditory as well as visual stimuli, asking which was the louder of two sounds, which was of longer duration and of higher pitch. Tactile stimuli were also used; subjects were asked which of two objects was rougher or smoother. Kinesthetic stimuli were used, for example, to select which of two weights was lighter or heavier. Olfactory and gustatory stimuli were also used, for example, to select which of two liquids or solids smelled or tasted more pleasant; which was more sweet or more bitter. Subjects were asked which of two metal plates was cooler or warmer or which gave them a greater shock. Instead of the line segments, we used pairs of pictures to judge, asking which had better balance, symmetry, color, or design; which had pleasanter content or which expressed more quietude or violence. We also used descriptions of people, asking who was more extroverted or more friendly (cf. Luchins and Luchins, 1961c, 1963). In recent years we have been using a variety of stimuli that are related to the daily lives of our subjects, asking which budget is more unbalanced, which problem is correctly solved, what skirt is longer, who is better dressed, smarter, or more good looking, who is kinder, who is more sexy or athletic looking, and which statement is more in accord with a certain ideological position: integration, anti-communism, anti-semitism, or racism. (It may not be out of place to mention here that a systematic study of social influences on the autokinetic effect was started with Wertheimer and continued by ASL and his students. Luchins & Luchins, 1969a, surveys these studies.)

Social influences were not as easily obtained with all the evidence. Stimuli sensed through the so-called lower senses, glaring lights, jarring noises, odors, weight, and taste, as well as other stimuli that have a physiological impact on the subject, are not so readily affected by overhearing wrong judgments that are made by an authority or a prestigious group. However, it is possible to train the subject to gradually adapt to or to intellectualize the physiological impact so that he does not react to it, for example, when the stimulus or the event is put into the context of a fraternity's initiation ceremony. Generally speaking, these results indicate that social influences are greater when the subject deals with the evidence in terms of socially learned concepts or ideas. A line segment is more of a social artifact than the pleasantness or unpleasantness of an odor or the pressure or the muscle tension of a weight (Luchins & Luchins, 1967a, 1967b). In one way our results are related to Janet's ideas about suggestion. He pointed out that the suggestible person reacts to the demands of others without first weighing or considering the consequences of the action, that suggestion is due to inadequacy in or to a breakdown of the rational or judgmental processes, thus reflecting the general thesis that social influences are irrational in nature. However, our results show that the so-called primitive reactions or unreflective judgments may sometimes lead to veridical judgments despite the social forces, and that sophisticated, reflective reactions may give rationalizations for non-veridical judgments. This fits Wertheimer's conjecture about the behavior of naive individuals. Our results can be interpreted to mean that individuals operating on a level that Piaget calls egocentric, that Lewin refers to as primitive Gestalten, and that Goldstein and Werner call concrete-mindedness may reject social forces that try to deflect them from the evidence; they stick to the evidence and will not be moved to tell lies. Perhaps to be naive is not necessarily a bad thing. Our results indicate that functioning on the so-called higher levels of mental development does not necessarily lead one to tell the truth and that the so-called lower levels of mental functioning might at certain times lead one to the truth.

Perhaps the so-called lower senses require stronger social forces in order to be affected by social pressure. Therefore, several studies recently have been undertaken in which the need to follow the majority, the confederate, or the authority was related to the subject's status in school. In one study the subjects were tested by their chemistry teacher and the experiment was part of a class chemistry project (see report at the end of this chapter).

Wertheimer suggested that the experimental set up itself may contribute to the results. He suggested that we vary the set up as we did in the Einstellung experiments. The following are variations that were outgrowths of this suggestion. Much more remains to be done.

1. In all the studies with the series of lines, the evidence was presented in one order, from the ambiguous stimulus to the clear stimulus. Would the social influences be as effective if the evidence were given in the reverse order? Generally speaking, there were now fewer wrong judgments in all cards except the last, the most ambiguous card. The subjects were unhappy to disagree repeatedly with the confederates and were glad at the end that finally they could agree with him (Luchins & Luchins, 1963c).

2. In all the studies with line segments the confederate went first. What would happen if he went after the subject? Such a variation would make it possible to test whether the subject made his response on a reasonable basis when he agreed with the confederate, because the subject would have to know the basis of the confederate's response in order to be able to give it before the confederate judged a card. Many subjects were able to agree with the confederate and get 100% on the second readministration of the five cards because they had realized the basis on which the confederate was called correct or incorrect. In these experiments the subject not only had to be oriented to agree or disagree with the confederate but also had to discover the basis of the

confederate's response in order to be correct. It was difficult for the subject to get 100%, that is, to agree with the confederate, when the confederate's responses were arbitrary, when there was no reasonable basis for his response (Luchins and Luchins, 1963a).

3. In order to see what would happen if the subjects measured the lines, we gave college students rulers. Engineering students generally refused to agree with the confederate's wrong answers but the female fine arts students sometimes juggled their rulers so that they could pretend that they were giving correct answers in order to get 100% (Luchins & Luchins, 1963b). Thus, those subjects who considered themselves to be experts in measuring refused to agree.

4. The experiments were also replicated using pairs of subjects in which the confederate was a child and the subject a college student. Generally speaking, the college students were less often influenced by the child confederate than vice versa. However, the results of the college subjects were within the lower range obtained in experiments when college students served as confederates for children. Also when the experiment was administered to airline pilots in the airport, with other airline personnel serving as confederates, few agreed with incorrect judgments. When the confederate was a female, male subjects tended to follow her more readily than did female subjects; female subjects tended to follow male confederates more readily; but males followed males just as well as they followed female. Subjects tended under certain conditions to be more influenced by an authority than by a majority (Luchins and Luchins, 1961a).

5. There are many life situations in which the object of judgment is dynamic; it changes in time. In such situations one may have to take into account the future conditions of the object he is judging at present, that is, the present judgment of an object has to be based not on its present appearance but on what it would look like in the future. Therefore, we gave a subject drawings to judge from a distance. A drawing was exposed in an aperture in a box. The subject stood several feet away and was told that after he judged it, it would be handed to him so that he could check his judgment. In one study, fifteen cards, each containing various geometric designs, were exposed one at a time for five seconds at a distance of five feet from the subject who was asked to make a judgment, for example, about the relative length of two line segments or the size or the shape of a plane figure. The subject was told that after its exposure the card would be handed to him for observation and measurement; but what was handed to him was actually a card from an obverse series which was superficially similar in appearance to the exposed card but differed from it with regard to the aspect under judgment, for example, the length of the two line segments was reversed so that an answer which was correct for the initial card was incorrect for the obverse card. Various social influences were introduced to maximize agreement and disagreement with a confederate who gave correct or incorrect judgments before the subject answered. The subjects learned to judge in terms of how the evidence would appear later when it was in their hands instead of the way in which it first appeared in the aperture (Luchins & Luchins, 1961). A study was made without the use of confederates but in which the cards were repeated over and over again to get the subject to report, while the card was still in the aperture, the judgment he would make later when the card was in his hand. Some subjects

developed a set to report the opposite of what they saw in the aperture so that when the experimenter handed them the card which was in the aperture instead of the obverse card, they needed two to three runs of the series to learn to report what they saw in the aperture instead of what they thought it would be later when handed to them. In discussing this study with Wertheimer we planned to modify it to study the role of experience in creating veridical and illusionary percepts.

6. Wertheimer once asked, What would happen if there were consequences for wrong judgments? Therefore the subject was first asked to select which one of a pair of cut-outs (pieces of cardboard) was smaller and was pressured by the usual methods to give incorrect answers. After this, he was told that if he had chosen correctly the pieces would fit the gaps in a house which was then given to him to complete. Subjects who had agreed with the wrong judgments failed to complete the house. Immediately after this negative consequence for agreeing with the social influences the same procedure was used in order to obtain wrong judgments in the usual series of pairs of line segments. There was no sharp decrease in wrong answers even though agreeing with the same confederate had previously led to bad consequences. When subjects were asked after the experiment why they had agreed with the confederate the second time, their answers indicated that they were concerned with passing the test, that the anxiety and pressure to get 100% made them think of nothing else but the immediate reward (Luchins & Luchins, 1966a). Since the consequences for wrong or right choices in the previous study were not immediate, the experiment was modified. The subject had to select the member of a pair of cut-outs that fitted a form board (Luchins & Luchins, 1967b). Subjects tended to fit into the hole the piece that the majority or the experimenter called right. They judged in terms of the social pressure and not in terms of the requirements of the hole in the form board and they interpreted the word fit in a manner to rationalize choosing that piece which was called correct by the majority or the experimenter. We therefore clarified, by means of previous experience, what was meant by the word *fit*. Now subjects gave correct answers; they resisted the social pressure to select the wrong pieces. This result is in line with Wertheimer's conjecture about the role of clarification in problem solving and judgment (Luchins & Luchins, 1970c).

7. In life people are motivated to tell the truth and to resist social pressures to tell lies. We therefore have been conducting studies in which subjects are motivated to tell the truth. In one study ASL's general psychology students were told that they would be given a laboratory test in which we were going to test some principles of scientific methodology, among them the duty of scientists to tell what they saw and not to be influenced by social pressure to say what others say. The various procedures were not effective (Luchins & Luchins, 1968). It seems that the test tension atmosphere created by the experiment focused the subjects on giving the response that was called correct rather than on judging the lines. When they were told in class that they had not told the truth and would lose 10% on the first examination they asked for another chance, which they were given. Some of the subjects again fell victims to the social influence. In comparing the results obtained in this group with those obtained from a college group studied about twenty-five years ago, we found that the recent class was more influenced. This led to an analysis of all studies made since we had undertaken this research in 1937. The trend of

results seems to indicate that present-day students are more readily influenced by the right-wrong verdicts and by being told that they have 0% or 100% on a test than the 1937-1950 groups of college students. Replication of these studies by ASL's assistant, Michael Golemba, and by Hubert Dolzeal, a student in one of ASL's undergraduate courses, yielded essentially the same results. This may reflect the present-day attitude toward tests; namely that there is no objectively correct answer, that the key determines what is correct and that a passing grade is determined by the normal curve. Would the results be different among the present-day students who lead campus revolts?

8. In order to reduce wrong judgments of the line segments, the subject was connected to a lie detector and was told that if he did not tell the truth he would get a slight shock in his forefinger. Now social influences were minimized; few subjects gave wrong answers (Luchins & Luchins, 1970d). We varied this procedure; two subjects, either a confederate and a naive subject or two naive subjects, were tested together and were told that one of them would judge the lines and that the other one would be wired to the lie detector. They were told that if the subject who judged the lines did not tell the truth, the person attached to the lie detector would get a shock. In some variations they were also told that after this experiment the student who had been attached to the lie detector would judge the lines and the previous judge would be attached to the lie detector. The three replications of these experiments have shown consistent results. Agreement with wrong answers was not minimized but was less than in the usual experiments. Some subjects who gave wrong answers went so far as to apologize when the other person received a shock, saying that they were sorry but they wanted to get 100%. Do these studies support the hypothesis that veridical judgments in social situations occur when there is a physiological impact on the subject for judging incorrectly? (See reports at end of this chapter.)

9. In all the studies on social influences that we have conducted as well as in most of the studies in the literature, the experimental situation is in some respects an atypical social situation; an unyielding authority or a group exerts its power on others. The confederate's and the experimenter's verdicts are arbitrary because they have decided in advance never to change their judgment. See end of chapter for experiments without confederates. Here we will describe a class room experiment that we have sometimes used as a basis for a discussion of social influences.

In experiments conducted by ASL's classes at the University of Oregon, some students were given a sheet of paper on which was drawn a line segment and they were asked to report out loud whether their line was bigger than a standard line drawn on the blackboard. In other classes students were given different descriptive paragraphs about a person named Jim and were asked to produce six adjectives that best described him. In all these studies the subjects did not know that they had each been given different lines or different paragraphs. In these studies there was no confederate. The subjects at first disagreed because they had been given different evidence. Often many subjects argued about their differences and tried to reach a decision without comparing their evidence. When the majority won out, ASL introduced factors that directed them to the evidence. When they discovered that they had different evidence, they understood why they had disagreed and now readily agreed on the correct line. When they had descriptive paragraphs, word blocks, pictures, or problems that had only one correct answer, they agreed; if more than one answer was possible, they often agreed on both or agreed that one answer was better than the other. It was possible to get the subjects not to agree in terms of the evidence by telling them before the experiment that the purpose of the test was to see how persistent they were, especially when such persistence was related to a high mark on a test.

Concluding Remark.

After thirty years of research we are led to conclude that it is difficult for people to stick to the evidence in the face of social forces and that it is relatively easy to get intelligent people to give nonveridical judgments. This is not a new finding. It was known by the compilers of ancient codes of law, for example, the Talmud, that personality factors, social status, and social conditions affect judgment and blind judges to the evidence. Therefore, various juridical procedures have been proposed in these codes to prevent this. Wertheimer was aware of the difficulties as well as of the importance of obtaining true judgments in courtroom testimony; his PhD thesis and some of his early research and publications dealt with methods of increasing the veracity of witnesses. We shall refrain from speculating about the reasons why he never related this research to the results we had obtained when he was helping us write our reports.

Our results indicate that Wertheimer was correct; social influences are more complex than in the usual discussions of the concepts of suggestion, imitation, and prestige and even more complex than the formulations given by the members of Wertheimer's seminars in their publications. While working on the formal report of the first study (1944) with Wertheimer, we were struck by the fact that the various hypotheses that had been formulated to explain the effect of Einstellung in learning by repetition could also be used as hypotheses to explain social influences. We could substitute the phrase, "what someone else said" for "repetition" and the list of hypotheses could be used to describe the variety of factors that seemed to play a role. Wertheimer suggested that we examine the experiments in light of the list of these hypotheses and think of ways of deciding experimentally which were crucial explanations (Luchins, 1942; Luchins & Luchins, 1970c) When we were working on the concluding remarks of the monograph on the Einstellung effects, we often used the same formulations for the social influences experiments. It is mentioned here because it may have influenced the way we went about studying social influences. We focused on extremizing the phenomena which we found in our first investigation instead of theorizing about conformity. In this way our work differs from other work which was also an outgrowth of Wertheimer's seminars. It could be said that two streams of research followed from Wertheimer's criticism of Sherif's work: one focused on extremizing the various phenomena and the other sought to demonstrate certain theoretical issues that were said to have been overlooked by Sherif. The latter stream of research is well known and is often considered to be the Gestalt approach to the problem. The other stream is relatively less well known and may not be considered to reflect the Gestalt point of view even though the first reports were written under Wertheimer's supervision. Our experience with him leads us to believe that Wertheimer was more phenomenon- or problem-centered and much more critical of the application of his theories to the results than were most people working in the Gestalt tradition. He wanted the data to speak for itself in the reports we wrote under his supervision. On the one hand, some of our methods of extremizing the results are similar to Thorndike (1935) and the methods used by social psychologists who are working in an S-R tradition; in fact we found that reinforcement is a powerful method to obtain conformity, or as Wertheimer would say, powerful in producing blindness to the evidence. On the other hand, an S-R learning theorist, Carl Hovland, with whom we were associated between 1952 and 1960, often suggested that the methods used in the paper we wrote with Wertheimer's help (Luchins, 1944) be used in our studies of attitude change.

In the post-World War II era, various cognitive models have been constructed to explain social influences; they have replaced the popularity of the associationistic models that Wertheimer so often criticized. However we believe that Wertheimer would not deny that many of the results of our investigations on social influence can be explained by the associationistic models. He once remarked that some of the results of the initial experiments (1942, 1944) could be readily explained by the associationists. He noted that it could be argued with some justification that the blind repetition of another person's behavior that results from reasonable assumptions amounts to the same thing as blindly repeating another person's responses; repetition is repetition and one need not concern himself with the processes that bring it about. However, Wertheimer believed that there might be differences in the kind of person that was produced when his behavior was molded by rewards and punishments than when his behavior was brought about on a reasonable basis. The experiments on social learning seem to support this. We agree with him that what is involved is a difference in doctrines of what is man and not just a learning theory (cf. Luchins & Luchins, 1970c).

Social Influences on Nonvisual Tasks: Odors

We have pointed out before that many studies of social influences on perception and judgment utilize visual stimuli as evidence and yet draw generalizations concerning the entire realm of perception and judgment. Such generalizations may be valid for much of man's perceptual and judgmental behavior because of the dominant role that vision plays in his life. But men also make judgments about pain, pressure, warmth, coldness, smell, taste, etc. which involve the chemical, cutaneous and kinesthetic senses, the so-called lower senses. They also make judgments about sounds which involve the auditory sense. Are the factors which are effective in producing social influences on the perception of judgments of visual stimuli also effective in influencing the judgment and perception of evidence that involves the other sense modalities? Wertheimer raised this question and suggested the study of a wide range of stimuli in order to discover which factors operate in all modalities, which operate most effectively in one modality, which produce transfer effects from one modality to another and which do not. We started research in line with these suggestions but discontinued it because of the noxious nature of the stimuli. In recent years we have resumed research in this area.

We have reported elsewhere (Luchins, 1967a) on experiments in which Ss were given the task to select the more pleasant of two odors. Ss usually selected the objectively more pleasant odor and not the one that was socially evaluated as more pleasant; they judged on the basis of the impact of the odors on the sensorium and not in terms of the social evaluation of the odor. In these studies, the Ss' transactions with the object of judgment often resulted in an unpleasant experience, pain or disgust. The results may have been due to the noxious nature of the evidence. Therefore other studies were conducted in which the task was to select the heavier of two weights in a pair, for example, the weights in ounces of five successive pairs were ½ and 1, ½ and 2, 1 and 4, 2 and 8, and 4 and 16 ounces respectively. The social influences that had been effective in producing nonveridical judgments when the line segments were used were generally ineffective with the weights or the odors. It seemed that Ss reacted not to the social influences but to the physiological impact of the stimuli.

Since the situation in which the judgments are made may play a role in determining the effectiveness of the social influences, we asked a high school chemistry teacher to replicate the odor studies during his class' laboratory session. Perhaps the students would take more seriously being called wrong and failing a test than did our college students who knew that it was just another experiment. Thus, in order to enhance the social pressures to make incorrect judgments of odors, the experiments were administered by the teacher to high school students as laboratory tests of ability to detect chemical odors. There were five pairs of test tubes which contained ammonium hydroxide solutions; the molar strength and the difference between solutions increased monotonically from the first to the fifth pair. The task was to select the more pleasant odor, that is, the more pleasant smelling of the solutions in each pair of test tubes.

As in the previous study (Luchins, 1967), the experiment was administered to two individuals at a time; one of them was a naive S and the other was E's preinstructed confederate. There were 21 naive Ss, 13 boys and eight girls, 15 to 18 years of age, with a mean of 16.2 years. The confederate, a fellow classmate of the same sex as S, always judged first. After pretending to inhale the odors, he stated his choice and passed both test tubes to S, who then made his choice. In Experiment 1, in accordance with E's instructions prior to the experiment, the confederate consistently chose the solution of greater molar strength as more pleasant, making nonveridical judgments. After the five pairs of odors were judged by the confederate and S, E announced that the confederate had 100% on the test and gave S as his score the percentage of times that he had given the same answer as the confederate. In Experiment 2, however, the confederate always chose the weaker of the two solutions, making veridical judgments. After the five pairs had been judged, E said that the confederate had zero percent on the test and gave S as his score the percentage of times that he had disagreed with the confederate. Thus in both experiments E scored nonveridical choices as right and veridical choices as wrong, but did not reveal the basis for the scores. After announcing the scores, E said that they would be given another chance on the test. In this manner the series was administered five times, with scores announced after each trial. After the fifth trial, the confederate left the room and S alone was given a retrial.

Many Ss asked to be excused from the experiment because the odors were too unpleasant and produced coughing, choking, and excessive tearing of the eyes. They were, however, persuaded to participate in the first three trials but some of them were excused thereafter. Because of this, 13 of the 21 Ss did not complete all five trials. This is in contrast to what happened in the previous study where only one of the 20 college Ss did not complete all the trials, although they too found the odors to be noxious. The high school Ss actually sniffed, often inhaling deeply, but the college Ss usually passed the solutions under their noses without inhaling, after the first trial. Thus the high school Ss apparently experienced more discomfort but they made relatively more nonveridical judgments on each trial than the college Ss. The following table presents the percentages of nonveridical responses to each pair of solutions made by the high school Ss who participated in a trial. For purposes of comparison we use the third trial, the last one in which all the high school Ss participated. (The results for the college Ss remained unchanged from the third through the fifth trials.)

TABLE 25.1
Percentages of Incorrect Responses to Pairs of Odors

Experiment 1

Confederate's Incorrect
Responses Confirmed
Odoriferous Solutions

Experiment 2

Confederate's Correct
Responses Infirmed
Odoriferous Solutions

Trials	Ss	1	2	3	4	5	Mean		Ss	1	2	3	4	5	Mean
1st	11	73	18	9	0	0	20		10	10	0	0	0	0	2
2nd	11	82	73	26	0	0	36		10	70	30	0	0	0	20
3rd	11	73	46	0	0	0	24		10	60	30	0	0	0	18
4th	8	75	37	0	0	0	22		7	45	0	0	0	0	9
5th	5	100	20	0	0	0	24		3	67	0	0	0	0	13
Mean		81	39	7	0	0	25			50	12	0	0	0	12
Retrial	8	13	0	0	0	0	3		4	0	0	0	0	0	0

In Experiment 1 (where E confirmed the confederate's incorrect responses) on the third trial the eleven high school Ss gave 73, 46, 0,0, and 0% nonveridical judgments of the five pairs of odors respectively, with a mean of 24%. In contrast, on the third trial the ten college Ss of our previous study gave 20, 10, 0, 0, and 0% nonveridical judgments respectively, with a mean of 6%. Incorrect judgments were 53% higher for the high school Ss than for the college Ss on the first pair of odors and 36% higher on the second pair; the first difference was statistically significant at the .01 level of confidence (t=2.88) and the second approached statistical significance at the .05 level (t=2.02). Thus the increased social pressures were effective for the first two pairs of chemical solutions but not for the last three pairs where the solutions were stronger and the differences between the odors were more marked. Although the level of nonveridical responses was higher than for the college Ss in our previous study, it was not as high as that shown by comparable Ss who judged lengths of line segments (Luchins, 1966). For example, 10 college Ss who judged a series of pairs of line segments made 80, 60, 60, 30, and 30% nonveridical judgments respectively, with a mean of 52%, when E confirmed the confederate's incorrect choices. There were incorrect judgments even when the difference between the lengths of the lines was clear-cut (for example, one-half inch difference in the last pair whereas there were no incorrect judgments for the later pairs of odors.

In Experiment 2 (where E infirmed the confederate's correct choices), on the third trial the high school Ss had 60, 30, 0, 0, and 0% nonveridical responses respectively, with a mean of 18%. In contrast, ten college Ss of our previous study had 10, 0, 0, 0, and 0% respectively, with a mean of 2%. Nonveridical responses were now 50% higher for the first pair of odors, which was statistically significant at the .01 level (t=2.75) and 30% higher for the second pair of odors, which was statistically significant at the .05 level (t=2.07). Again the social pressures were effective for the earlier pairs of odors but not for the last three pairs. There were again fewer incorrect responses than when line segments were judged. For example, 15 college Ss had given 60, 60, 40, 33, and 33% incorrect responses respectively, with a mean of 45% to the line segments.

In both Experiments 1 and 2 the percentage of incorrect responses decreased monotonically on each trial for successive pairs of odors which suggests that the social forces were less effective as the evidence became stronger. In each experiment, the largest mean frequency of nonveridical choices occurred on the second trial, following E's first announcement of the test scores; this apparently had more dramatic effects than the subsequent announcements. In Experiment 2 the frequency of incorrect responses was lower than (or equal to) the frequency in Experiment 1 for each pair, and each trial; for example, for the first pair of odors, incorrect responses ranged from 73 to 100% with a mean of 81% in Experiment 1 but from 10 to 70% with a mean of 50% in Experiment 2; note that the ranges do not overlap. The mean for the five trials was 25% in Experiment 1 and 12% in Experiment 2. These findings are not surprising since both the confederate and E were aligned against the evidence in Experiment 1 but only E opposed it in Experiment 2.

On the retrial, given to S only, there was only one incorrect choice and it occurred for the first pair in Experiment 1. Thus, with the social pressures removed, veridical judgments prevailed. In contrast, the retrial with the line segments yielded considerable nonveridical responses. For example, on a retrial which followed a trial with the procedure of Experiment 1, 10 college Ss gave 50, 60, 30, 30, and 30% incorrect responses with a mean of 40% for the line segments.

In Experiment 2 Ss appeared more at ease than in Experiment 1. They seemed to get support from the fact that the confederate gave veridical judgments. It emboldened some Ss to challenge E's scoring. On the whole, however, overt protests against E, the confederate, and the experiment were less frequent than in the study with college Ss.

The confederate was usually an individual who had served as an S and then was told about the experiment and asked if he would be a confederate. The Ss, whether or not they had been excused from some of the trials because of physical discomfort, were usually willing to serve as confederates; they said that it would be fun and that they were curious to see what would happen. Apparently they did not object to helping someone else suffer physical discomfort. Their behavior is somewhat similar to that found by Milgram (1965) in his study of obedience, and in our preliminary study with electric shock and the line segments in which Ss gave nonveridical responses, scored as right by E, even though they knew such responses would result in the other individual receiving electric shocks.

Lie Detector Experiments

Motivation to tell the truth. In the course of our research to strengthen motivational factors to tell the truth we conducted several studies (Luchins & Luchins, 1970) in which a lie detector (actually a Harvard Inductorium which had been adapted for use in the experiment) was used to administer a mild electric shock to the subject whenever he gave a nonveridical response. After the usual introduction to the line segment judgment experiment as a test of visual acuity, a college student, who had been told to select the shorter of the two lines on each card, was given the following additional instructions as motivation for telling the truth:

It is very important that you tell the truth, that you report exactly what you see. Therefore, you are being attached to this lie detector. If you do not tell the truth, you will feel a stinging sensation in your finger. This sensation is to alert you to the fact that you are not reporting which of the two lines is the shorter. Whenever you do not report what you see, you will get a stinging sensation.

Each of the following four experimental variations were administered to 20 college Ss.:

a. E confirms the incorrect responses of three confederates. The three confederates gave nonveridical responses which E scored as right. On every trial the confederates each received a score of 100 % and S's score was based on the percentage of times that he had agreed with the confederates.
b. E confirms the incorrect responses of one confederate. The procedure was the same except that there was only one confederate.
c. E infirms the correct responses of three confederates. The three confederates gave veridical responses which E scored as wrong. On every trial the confederates each received a score of zero percent and S's score was based on the percentage of times that he had disagreed with the confederates.
d. E infirms the correct responses of one confederate. The procedure was the same except that there was only one confederate.

In each of the four experiments there was a marked decrease in nonveridical judgments compared to previous experiments without the "lie detector" and without shocks which had been administered to 10 or 15 Ss each. The average of nonveridical responses for the five trials now ranged from 6 to 16% for the four variations whereas they had ranged from 40 to 60% for the previous experiments. For purposes of comparison, we use results on the third trial. When E confirmed the incorrect responses of three confederates, on this trial nonveridical choices were now 25, 10, 10, 10, and 10% on cards one through five, respectively, with a mean of 13% in contrast to 100, 40, 40, 60, and 60% with a mean of 60% in the previous study. Where there was only one confederate whose incorrect responses were confirmed by E, on the third trial there were now 20, 5, 5, 5, and 5% incorrect answers with a mean of 8% in contrast to 80, 60, 60, 30, and 30% with a mean of 52% made in the previous study. When E infirmed the correct responses of three confederates, there were now 50, 30, 15, 10, and 0% incorrect responses with a mean of 21% compared with 60, 60, 40, 20, and 20% with a mean of 40% in the previous study. When one confederate's correct responses were infirmed, there were now 35% incorrect responses on the first card but none thereafter so that the mean was 7% in contrast with 60, 60, 40, 33, and 33% with a mean of 45% in the previous study.

These results might be related to the fact that nonveridical answers led to shocks which had physiological impact on S (cf. studies in which odors and weights yielded fewer nonveridical responses than judgments of the lines). We decided to vary the procedure by having the physiological impact on someone other than the S who judged the lines. The experiment was administered to three individuals at one time. After they had been given the same instructions and told about the lie detector, one of them was attached to it and the naive S was told that whenever he judged incorrectly the other person would get a shock, which would be a signal to him that he was not making veridical judgments. The person who was attached to the electrodes was the experimenter's confederate who winced and cried out "ouch" whenever he got a shock. (In some variations there were two naive Ss who flipped a coin to decide who would judge and who would be attached to the lie detector.) The third person was also a confederate who responded to each card before S did. When E confirmed the confederate's incorrect responses, 10 college Ss gave 30% nonveridical responses. Although it was less than in the usual experiment, it was more than in the experiment in which S himself received a shock. When E infirmed the confederate's correct answer, 10 college Ss gave 20% nonveridical responses. Thus again there were fewer nonveridical responses than usual but more than when S himself got the shock. Both variations have been replicated several times at SUNY-Albany with the same trend of results. In both variations there were Ss who apologized to the person who was being shocked saying that they were sorry but they wanted 100%. A few protested to E that the lie detector was at variance with the test scores; some said that something was fishy or even threatened to quit. Some said that they would not give wrong answers in order to get 100% or would not let the other person get shocked at their expense; a few sometimes appealed to the fact that the other person was not receiving shocks as evidence of the truth of their answer. These Ss seemed to be cooperating with the person who was attached to the electrodes. A few, however, did not seem at all concerned with the evidence or with what happened to the other person because they were interested in getting 100%. There were also varied reactions to the confederate who was judging the cards first. Thus there were a variety of attitudes and assumptions about the experiment, about the experimenter, about the person attached to the electrodes, and about the person who answered first.

In order to obtain more information about the attitudes and assumptions of the Ss, we have conducted several variations. In one variation, it was announced at the onset of the experiment that the roles of the S who judged the cards and the person who was attached to the electrodes would subsequently be interchanged. Thus S was given an anticipatory warning that he might later be receiving shocks if the other person gave nonveridical responses. Of particular interest were the reactions when there were two naive Ss. A few Ss balked and quit when it was their turn to be attached to the electrodes, for example, because they did not want to get shocked; a few who had been attached also quit because they did not want to tell lies in order to get 100% or because they did not want to give shocks to the other person or because they thought that the other students were in E's confidence. Some, however, seemed eager to get revenge for the shocks they had endured. Some thought that it was a test of tolerance of pain, of forebearance, and seemed to be ashamed to tell E that they did not want to take their turn at the electrodes. Some gave wrong answers occasionally in order to test various hypotheses even though it meant that the other person would get shocked.

In some variations we changed the scoring scheme after the S who had judged changed places with the S who had been attached to the electrodes. Some told us or complained that the scoring had been changed. A few seemed disappointed that to get 100% they did not have to give answers which made the other person receive shocks but others seemed relieved that they were not in the predicament of having to decide between passing the test and avoiding hurting someone. A few Ss seemed not to be aware that the scoring had changed.

Motivation to tell lies. What would happen if shocks were administered when veridical responses were given, that is, if the shocks were used to motivate to tell lies? Several variations were conducted with the assistance of three SUNY-Albany students, Gerard R. Brophy, Allan Edgar Gehring, and Harold S. Williams. Each experiment was administered to three individuals at a time, a confederate who responded first, a naive S who responded after him, and another person (either another naive S or a confederate) who was attached to the electrodes. The instructions and scoring were as in the usual experiments. In particular, although the instructions were that a shock would be administered when the truth was not told, actually shocks were given when veridical responses were made. Half of the Ss were told that they would subsequently change places with the person attached to the electrodes, that is, they had an anticipatory warning of the possibility of receiving shocks themselves (but actually this phase was not usually carried out).

Table 25.2 surveys the percentages of nonverdical responses when the person attached to the electrodes was a naive S and E confirmed the confederate's incorrect responses (Experiment 1), when the person attached to the electrodes was a confederate and E confirmed the other confederate's incorrect responses (Experiment 2) or infirmed the other confederate's correct responses (Experiment 3). Under each of these conditions and regardless of whether or not S received the anticipatory warning, there were as many or more nonverdical responses than when a shock was given for such responses to S himself or to the other person. However, there were fewer nonveridical responses than in the usual experiment where no shocks were given. In other words, there were more veridical responses than in the usual experiments in which subjects were not shocked in order to motivate them to tell the truth. This is a somewhat surprising result; the shocks for veridical responses might have been expected to decrease such responses. It seemed that Ss were more willing to tell the truth when someone was hurt as a consequence than when they had only a high score to gain. Some Ss seemed to reflect a feeling of righteousness, that they would tell the truth even though it hurt people or disturbed the situation. It would have been of interest to use them as subjects in which they get shocked for telling untruths. Are we dealing here with a genuine desire to be truthful or with an attitude to tell the truth if it does not hurt them? The experiments need to be replicated with more attention paid to the attitudes and assumptions of the subject as well as to study the effects of the introduction of other factors, for example, infirming correct responses with two naive Ss and infirming as well as confirming responses when more than one confederate responds before S. In a preliminary study in which two

TABLE 25.2
Percentages of Incorrect Responses with the
Lie Detector

	Trials	Antici pation	Cards 1	2	3	4	5	Mean
Experiment 1	1	yes	7	0	0	0	0	1
confirming	2	no	0	0	0	0	0	0
incorrect	3	yes	43	21	7	21	7	20
responses	4	no	40	13	0	0	0	11
with 2	5	yes	57	36	14	14	14	27
naive Ss	Mean	no	53	13	0	0	0	13
		yes	80	57	14	21	7	36
		no	40	27	13	20	13	23
		yes	80	57	28	36	28	46
		no	40	33	20	20	13	25
		yes	53	34	16	18	11	26
		no	35	17	7	8	5	15
Experiment 2	1	yes	0	0	0	0	0	0
confirming	2	no	10	0	0	0	0	2
incorrect	3	yes	10	10	0	0	0	4
responses	4	no	40	20	0	10	0	14
with a	5	yes	30	10	20	10	10	16
confederate	Mean	no	40	30	20	30	20	28
and a naive S		yes	30	20	20	10	10	18
		no	40	30	30	20	20	28
		yes	30	30	20	20	20	24
		no	40	30	30	20	30	30
		yes	20	14	12	8	8	12
		no	34	22	16	16	14	20
Experiment 3	1	yes	0	0	0	0	0	0
infirming	2	no	0	0	31	8	8	9
correct	3	yes	8	39	15	31	23	23
responses	4	no	8	31	31	39	31	28
with a	5	yes	31	31	31	31	46	34
confederate	Mean	no	39	46	54	46	46	46
and a naive S		yes	31	39	54	39	46	42
		no	70	54	54	46	54	56
		yes	39	46	46	39	39	42
		no	70	54	62	54	62	60
		yes	22	31	29	28	31	28
		no	37	37	46	39	40	40

confederates answered correctly before S, and E infirmed their responses, but did not tell S that he would subsequently be attached to the electrodes, five college Ss averaged 27% nonveridical responses and 73% veridical responses when shocks were given for the latter compared to about 60% veridical responses under similar conditions when there were no shocks. Table 25.2 also shows that those Ss who received the warning that they would subsequently be attached to the lie detector gave more nonveridical responses on every trial than the Ss who did not receive the warning in Experiment 1 whereas the reverse was the case in Experiments 2 and 3. Again more research is needed to see if similar trends are obtained.

In Experiments 2 and 3 the previous naive S was used to play the role of the person being shocked. The first S in each experiment was given special instructions about how to play the role. After the experiment each S was asked questions to get his reactions to the experiment. In particular they were asked how they felt about the other person, who was a classmate, getting a shock. The reactions were very varied as illustrated by the answers given in Experiment 3.

It seems necessary for theoretical reasons to investigate the basic differences in the attitudes of the subjects who do and do not make nonveridical judgments in the lie detector experiments. It is no less important to study what are the actual social and educational conditions which favor or disfavor telling the truth in the different setups. Wertheimer conjectured that there is an urge in man to tell the truth and that it is too readily destroyed by certain kinds of education and social fields. We hope that these experiments as well as the other ones in this chapter will motivate the reader to test Wertheimer's conjecture, which was to him not a theoretical issue but was related to what is man and what is man's relation to the social and physical world.

Studies without Confederates: Word Blocks

Wertheimer objected to the use of a confederate. There was something deceitful and arbitrary about the procedure; the naive subject might think that the other person was actually reporting what he saw instead of saying what the experimenter had told him to report. Wertheimer suggested that experiments be devised in which two or more subjects were set by previous experiences to respond differently. Suppose one subject had developed an Einstellung to solve a series of anagrams (Luchins, 1942) in the E way and the other subject had developed an Einstellung in another series to solve anagrams in the D way. What would happen if they were then brought together and heard each other solve a series of anagrams that could be solved by the E and the D way? Would a subject who had developed a set to use the E method change to the D method, would the other subject change, or would each subject give both solutions? What would happen when they were given a series of anagrams that could be solved only in the D or E way? Wertheimer also suggested that the water-jar measuring problems and the mazes be used in the same way (Luchins, 1942). Would the results be different? During a discussion of the results of these studies with Wertheimer, another kind of task was suggested, namely, a series of squares composed of alphabet letters. These are referred to as word blocks because they were called the *World Block Test* in the Luchins

1950 Einstellung Tests of Rigidity of Behavior. We have reported elsewhere the results of some of these studies that were outgrowths of Wertheimer's suggestions (Luchins & Luchins, 1959, 548ff). Since these procedures have been used as laboratory exercises in ASL's Advanced Social Psychology classes, we now present some recent replications of these studies.

Word blocks were used, each of which consisted of 25 alphabet letters arranged on a card in a five-by-five array. The various kinds of series of arrays were as follows:

Series A (ten cards). Each block contained a word which was read diagonally from the top right to the bottom left.

Series A¹ (ten cards). Each block contained a word read diagonally from the top left to the bottom right. Corresponding cards of Series A and A¹ contained the same words; for example, the fifth card of each of Series A and A¹ contained the word *paper*.

Series B (five cards). Each array contained two words, one running along the diagonal from the top right to the bottom left, and the other along the diagonal from the top left to the bottom right; these were the directions of reading the words in Series A and A¹ respectively. For example, in Card 5 of Series B the two words were *groan* and *grove*.

Series C (five cards). Along the diagonal from the top right to the bottom left was the same word that was on this diagonal in the corresponding card of Series B. The word along the other diagonal was destroyed by altering one or two letters. These were the only differences between the arrays in Series B and Series C. For example, in Card 5 of Series C, as in the same card of Series B, the word was *groan;* the non-word *groxw* replaced *grove*.

Series C¹ (five cards). This series was the counterpart of Series C in that it preserved the other words of Series B. Thus, each array contained, along the diagonal from the top left to the bottom right, the same word that was on this diagonal in the corresponding card of Series B. The word along the other diagonal was destroyed by altering one or two letters; these were the only changes made in the blocks of Series B. For example, in Card 5 of Series C¹ the word was *grove;* the non-word *gzoyn* replaced *groan*.

Series D (five cards). Each array contained three words, one along the diagonal from top right to bottom left, another along the diagonal from top left to bottom right, and a third along the horizontal middle row from left to right, for example, in Card 5 these words were *cream, opera,* and *green,* respectively.

The words in the various series were as follows:

Series A (↙)	Series A¹ (↘)	Series B (↙ and ↘)	
1. SMILE	6. WOMAN	1. CHAIN	BLAME
2. BLACK	7. WITCH	2. TOOTH	DROVE
3. TIGER	8. STAMP	3. GRAND	CHASE
4. TABLE	9. STORE	4. BRING	FRIED
5. PAPER	10. PROVE	5. GROAN	GROVE

Series C (⬈) Series C¹ (⬊)   Series D   (⬈ and ⬇ and→)

1. CHAIN	1. BLAME	1. FORCE	NURSE	GIRLS
2. TOOTH	2. DROVE	2. BEGIN	NIGHT	PAGES
3. GRAND	3. CHASE	3. GRANT	STARE	BRAIN
4. BRING	4. FRIED	4. CREED	PLEAD	SHEEP
5. GROAN	5. GROVE	5. CREAM	OPERA	GREEN

The fifth blocks in Series A, A¹, B, C, C¹, and D respectively were as follows:

KRODP	PDORK	GPSOG
LBEAA	AAEBL	FRTRS
ASPEI	IEPSA	MOOPX
DERAO	OARED	TAVVG
RSURD	DRUSR	NREPE

A-5   A¹-5   B-5

GPSOG	GPSOG	OACJC
FRTRS	FRTZS	CPZRB
MOOPX	MOOPX	GREEN
TAVXG	TYVVG	GAKRJ
NREPW	NREPE	MNIMA

C-5   C¹-5   D-5

The word blocks were administered to a pair of subjects who were seated on opposite sides of a table, with a partition between them. The experimenter pointed to one of them (S_1) and said that he would always go first; the other subject (S_2) would answer after him. The subjects were told to raise their hands when they were ready and not to call out any answers until they were asked for them. For each card, after both had raised their hands, the experimenter first asked S_1 for his answer and then S_2 for his answer.

Series A was given to S_1 and Series A¹ to S_2. The experimenter said: Look at the first card in your pack. There is a word there among all those letters. Let's see if you can find it. Help was given when necessary, that is, when S_1 (S_2) could not find a word in Series A (A¹). After the tenth card, the experimenter said, Lets go through these cards again and see if you can get 100 percent. Series A and A¹ were then given again in the same manner. On completion the experimenter said, I want you to do it again and I will time you to see how well you know it. You will be given credit for quick work. The experimenter timed the subjects while they went through Series A or A¹ for the third time.

After this, the experimenter said: In order to save time, you are now both going to use the same card. First I will give the card to you (S_1) and, after you answer, you (S_1) give it to him (S_2). Some of the pairs were also told, When you answer, I want you to remember to use what you have learned before. These subjects will be referred to as the instructed pairs. The B series was then presented, followed by the C series, the C¹ series, and then the D series. One card was given at a time, with S_1 responding aloud to it before S_2 did. After the last card, the experimenter announced a score for each subject. The method of determining the score will be given later. It depended essentially on how many times the orientation of the A series was used. After S_2 was given his score, he was told: We're going to do it another time in order to give you another chance to do as well as he (S_1) did. Try your best. Series B, C, C^1, and D were then administered to both subjects in the same manner as before. After the announcement of the scores, S_2 was again challenged to do better and Series B to D were readministered for a total of two to four trials. After all trials were completed, each subject was asked why he had answered as he did and if his partner's answers influenced him in any way and why.

Experiment 1 was administered with the cooperation of Barbara Quint, a student in ASL's social psychology class, to 20 pairs of sixth-grade children from a suburban Albany elementary school. Members of a pair were matched for sex and for scores on the Iowa Test of Basic Skills. The subjects were selected so that a pair of boys and a pair of girls had scores on the national norms in this test in each of the following ranges; the low 50s (50-54), the high 50s (55-59), the low 60s, the high 60s, etc., until the high 90s. One pair in each range (a male pair in the low 50s, a female pair in the high 50s and so on alternately) received the additional instructions to remember to use what they had learned.

In Experiment 1, the subject's scores were determined by considering a response to be correct only if it included a word that followed the orientation of Series A. Since Series B, C, and D allowed such responses but Series C^1 did not, the maximum possible score was 75 percent; this was attained if the subject reported a word that was in line with the orientation of Series A (possibly along with other words) whenever it occurred.

The percentages of responses in the B and D series are given in Table 25.3. *Set* refers to the orientation that was used by the given S in the learning series; *shift* refers to a response in line with the orientation that the other S had used in the learning series; *both* refers to a response in which both diagonal words were given; *other* denotes non-diagonal words (which were possible in some cards); *agreement* refers to a response in which the child used the other subject's learned orientation to a card and the latter also used this orientation. For example, Table 25.3 shows that on Trial 1 of Series B (where both diagonal words were possible), in the non-instructed group the S_1 members agreed with 40% of the S_2 members' replies to a card, both giving the response for which S_2 had been set, and that the S_2 members agreed with 10% of the S_1 members' replies to a card, both giving the response for which S_1 had been set. The table shows that the main trend of the results in the B series were as follows: On Trial I most children gave the orientation which they had used in the learning cards (set responses). By Trial III set responses had decreased and there was an increase in shifts to the orientation which the other child had learned (shift responses). In the non-instructed pairs, on each trial S_2 (the second child to respond) gave more set solutions, fewer shifts, fewer cases of agreement with the other child's orientation when the latter used it, more reports of both diagonal words, and fewer other responses than did S_1, (the first child to respond). On the average, S_2 showed 14% more set responses, 26% fewer shift responses, 17% fewer agreements, about three times as many both responses and about one third as many other responses as did S_1. In the instructed pairs, S_2 also gave more set responses, fewer shifts, and fewer agreements than did S_1. No child in the instructed pairs gave both diagonal responses or non-diagonal responses to any of the B cards.

In the C and C^1 series most children gave answers even though it meant abandoning the set orientation. Their experiences here may have affected

TABLE 25.3
Percentages of Responses in Experiments 1 and 1

Series	Group	Trial	Set S₁	S₂	Shift S₁	S₂	Both S₁	S₂	Other S₁	S₂	Agreement S₁	S₂
B	Non-instructed	I	54	78	46	16	0	4	0	0	10	40
		II	38	52	52	20	10	28	28	8	32	50
		III	34	38	48	34	10	28	28	10	42	46
		Mean	42	56	49	23	7	20	19	6	28	45
	Instructed	I	84	64	16	36	0	0	0	0	30	10
		II	40	68	60	32	0	0	0	0	20	46
		III	50	58	50	42	0	0	0	0	20	30
		Mean	58	63	42	37	0	0	0	0	23	29
D	Non instructed	I	16	50	58	18	24	26	22	36	26	64
		II	22	42	48	24	28	30	38	38	30	50
		III	24	36	38	28	28	28	42	42	34	44
		Mean	21	43	48	23	27	28	34	39	30	53
	Instructed	I	26	66	70	30	0	0	4	4	18	58
		II	28	62	68	36	0	0	4	4	12	44
		III	42	31	54	32	0	0	6	6	26	44
		Mean	32	53	64	33	0	0	5	5	19	49
B	Non instructed learning orientation interchanged	I	76	36	20	64	0	0	4	0		12
		II	66	48	30	48	0	0	4	4		18
		Mean	71	42	20	64	0	0	4	2		15
D	Non-instructed learning orientation interchanged	I	35	52	35	28	4	0	26	20	12	16
		II	42	34	38	28	2	0	18	38	6	10
		Mean	38	43	37	28	3	0	22	29	9	13

their responses to the subsequent D series where set responses tended to be less frequent than in the B series. Both diagonal and non-diagonal responses were higher in the D series than in the B series for the noninstructed pairs. The instructed pairs never gave both diagonal words and gave few non-diagonal words to the D series. There were no consistent trends with regard to shifts and agreements. Again there were more set responses and fewer both and other responses for the instructed pairs than for the non-instructed pairs. Also, again S₂ tended to give more set solutions, fewer shifts, and fewer agreements than S₁.

In short, despite the announcement of scores which favored S₁'s set orientation in both the B and D series, the S₂ subjects showed a greater tendency to adhere to the set orientation and less tendency to shift or to agree with the other child's orientation than did S₁. One reason for this result may be that the orientation learned by S₂ was a more natural one since English is read from left to right. It is also possible that the second child was reluctant to copy the overheard response, perhaps because it might be interpreted as cheating; or maybe S_2 did not understand the basis of the scoring or did not want to appear to be influenced by it. The study's finding that the instructed pairs tended to give more set responses and fewer agreement than the non-instructed pairs suggest that the subjects adhered to the instructions to use what had been learned before. However, the instructions did not consistently influence shift responses.

Although the numbers of subjects were small, there seemed to be no consistent relation between responses to the word blocks and scores on the Iowa Test of Basic Skills.

Experiment 1[1] was administered (with the cooperation of another student of ASL's social psychology class, Anne Brannon) to ten pairs of students at the State University of New York at Albany. The procedure differed from that in Experiment 1 in several respects: the learning orientations of S_1 and S_2 were interchanged so that S_1 learned the diagonal word read in the direction from left to right, the direction in reading English, whereas S_2 learned the diagonal word read from right to left; there were only two trials; and to facilitate scoring each S was told to give only one answer to each word block. The pairs were not instructed, that is, they were not told to remember to use what they had learned before in the subsequent series. Table 25.3 shows that, unlike what happened in Experiment 1, in Series B S_2 showed a greater tendency to shift and less tendency to adhere to the set solution than did S_1. Thus on the first trial S_2 showed 64% shift to the overheard response and 54% agreement with S_1 when he used his learned orientation. In contrast, on this trial S_1 showed only 20% shift and only 12% agreement with S_2 when he used his learned response. The same trend was found on the second trial, although it was less marked, with somewhat more convergence of the responses. Now S_2 showed 48% shift and 32% agreement whereas S_1 showed 30% shift and 18% agreement. In Series D, however, the trend was the same as that found throughout Experiment 1, namely, S_2 had less tendency to shift and to agree with the other's response and more tendency to use the set orientation than did S_1. These findings suggest that the results may be functions of the nature and familiarity of the learned orientation as well as the nature of the test series. That college students were used in Experiment 1[1] and children in Experiment 1 may also have been a factor. (Other experiments on the interchange of the learned orientations are planned with various kinds of subjects.)

In Experiment 1[1], as in Experiment 1, there were more other responses in Series D, where a horizontal word was present in each block, than in Series B. Although the instructions in Experiment 1[1] were to give only one word per block, a few Ss gave two words (and one S gave all three words in some of the cards of Series D). However, other responses and both responses were less frequent than for the non-instructed pairs of Experiment 1.

Of the ten pairs in Experiment 1[1], four were composed of females, four of males, and two pairs consisted of a male and female. There seemed to be a greater tendency for one of the Ss to agree with the other in pairs of females than in pairs of males. Moreover, a female tended to agree with a male more than with a female. An example is one pair where S_1 was a male and S_2 a female. S_1 consistently adhered to his learned orientation whenever it led to a word; S_2 agreed with his response in every card of Set B on both trials and in the first four cards of Series D on Trial I but thereafter she gave the horizontal word. She also agreed with him in Series C and C^1. She did not seem to see a diagonal word in her learned orientation in Series B or D and later said,

"I only saw the word he said." When she was shown such a word, she exclaimed, "Oh, there's a word in the other diagonal." Possibly cultural factors were involved. More intensive study of male-female patterns in subjects of various ages would seem to be in order.

Experiment 2 was administered (with the cooperation of another student of ASL's social psychology class, Robert W. Meschanic) to 30 pairs of students of the State University of New York at New Paltz, 15 pairs of males and 15 pairs of females. Eight of the male pairs and seven of the female pairs received the additional instructions to try to remember to use what they had learned. The procedure was that used in Experiment 1 (so that Series A was given to S_1 and Series A^1 to S_2) except that the basis for scoring was changed. Since a word in line with the orientation of Series A was not possible in Series C^1, in the latter series only a word was considered correct if it was in line with the orientation of Series A^1 (the top left to the bottom right diagonal). If a subject gave these responses to the five cards of Series C^1 and a word in accord with the orientation of Series A (possibly with other words) to each of the cards in Series B, C, and D, he attained a score of 100 percent.

TABLE 25.4
Percentages of Responses in Experiment 2

Series	Responses		Set		Shift		Other		Agreement	
	Group	Trial	S_1	S_2	S_1	S_2	S_1	S_2	S_1	S_2
B	Non-instructed	I	50	62	48	37	1	1	38	25
		II	63	70	36	29	0	1	29	23
		III	55	36	45	64	0	0	25	44
		IV	80	32	21	68	0	0	1	49
		Mean	62	50	38	50	0.3	0.5	23	35
	Instructed	I	35	84	63	16	3	'0	47	4
		II	59	63	38	37	4	0	24	23
		III	75	31	21	67	4	3	8	47
			83	31	14	67	3	1	14	67
		Mean	63	52	34	47	4	1	23	35
D	Non-instructed	I	36	56	51	29	13	13	37	17
		II	67	39	31	43	3	19	7	25
		III	52	33	29	57	19	9	5	40
		IV	80	19	7	54	13	27	4	48
		Mean	59	37	30	46	12	17	13	32
	Instructed	I	25	51	49	29	21	20	29	15
		II	59	33	23	52	19	14	11	32
		III	72	33	17	56	11	11	4	48
		IV	75	7	1	63	24	31	0	60
		Mean	58	31	22	50	19	19	11	39

The percentages of responses in Experiment 2 are given in Table 25.4. There were so few cases where both diagonal words were given to a card that the column is not included in the table. Unlike what happened in Experiment

1, S_2 now showed more set responses, fewer shifts, and more cases of agreement than did S_1. This was similar to what happened on the first trial of Series B in Experiment 1[1] (which like the present experiment used college Ss). Unlike what happened in either Experiment 1 or 1[1], set responses tended to increase for S_1 and to decrease for S_2 on successive trials. Also, there were now no consistent differences between the non-instructed and instructed pairs or between the B and D series, except for an increase in non-diagonal words in the latter.

It seemed that the scores (which allowed a maximum of 100% rather than 75% as in Experiment 1) were more effective than for the children. This is seen in S_1's tendency to adhere to his set orientation that was scored as correct and in S_2's tendency to shift to the other orientation and to agree with S_1. Most subjects seemed to realize that the score reflected what the experimenter wanted and seemed to want to please him by conforming. Some subjects, however, thought that the scoring was fictitious and continued with their set orientation or sought for new words. Some of these subjects tried so hard to find words different from their partners that they reported nonexistent words, for example, *chair* for *chain* or *chain* for *chazn*. Several words were found in C and C[1] series that proofreaders had failed to notice when the blocks were typed for the study.

It would be of interest to use the procedure and scoring basis of Experiment 2 with children and that of Experiment 1 with college students to see how the results compare. Particular attention should be paid to the subjects' attitudes to and assumptions about the experimenter, the instructions, and the scoring of their responses.

Experiment 3 was administered (with the assistance of another student of the social psychology class, Jerry M. Trimble) to 28 pairs of students residing in one of the men's residence halls at the State University of New York at Albany. The subjects were between 18 and 24 years of age. The procedure and the scoring basis were the same as in Experiment 2. The pairs of subjects were divided into three groups: 14 pairs of subjects with S_1 (the first responder) designated as aggressive and S_2 (the second responder) designated as nonaggressive; 7 pairs of subjects with both S_1 and S_2 designated as aggressive; 7 pairs of subjects with S_1 designated as nonaggressive and S_2 as aggressive. The criteria for determining if a subject was aggressive or non-aggressive were as follows. The head resident director, the assistant resident director, and each of ten resident assistants were asked to compile independently a list of all those men in the residence hall who were aggressive and another list of those who were nonaggressive; a subject designated as aggressive had to appear on at least four aggressive lists and on none of the nonaggressive lists. A subject designated as nonaggressive had to appear on at least four nonaggressive lists and on none of the aggressive lists. Every pair of subjects received the additional instructions to remember to use what they had learned. The results are given in Table 25.5.

When S_1 and S_2 were both rated as aggressive (7 pairs) in Series B, S_2 showed more set responses on every trial (100% set responses on two trials and an average of 96%) and no shift or agreement with S_2. On the average when both members were aggressive, S_2 had 27% more set, 32% more shift, and 23% more agreement than did S_1. A similar trend was found for these pairs in Series D, although some of the differences were not so striking. In

Series D S_2 averaged 76% set solutions, 11% more than S_1; 10% shift, 23% less than S_1; and 3% agreement, 24% less than S_1. It seemed that when both Ss were aggressive, S_2 showed more reluctance to shift or to agree with the overheard response or to be influenced by the score. Thus S_2 showed more adherence to the instructions.

The results were quite different when S_1 was rated as aggressive and S_2 as nonaggressive (14 pairs). In Series B as well as in Series D, the nonaggressive member showed less set responses than and more shift and agreement than the aggressive one. On the whole, in the B series the nonaggressive member showed 20% less set, 14% more shift, and 26% more agreement than the aggressive member of the pair; in Series D the corresponding differences were 10, 17, and 15% respectively. Compared to S_2 of the pairs where both members were aggressive, the nonaggressive S_2 showed fewer set solutions, averaging 46% less set responses, 46% more shift, and 35% more agreement in Series B and 33% less set, 37% more shift, and 32% more agreement in Series D.

When S_1 was rated as nonaggressive and S_2 as aggressive (7 pairs) there were few differences in responses between the two Ss in either Series B or D. S_2 gave only slightly more set responses and slightly less shift and agreement than S_1.

In short, the results seemed to depend strongly on whether the student was rated as aggressive or nonaggressive and on whether the aggressive student was the first or the second to respond. Other experiments should be conducted with pairs of Ss who have both been rated as nonaggressive and in which only one or no member of the pair was instructed to try to use what had been learned in the A or A^1 series. Other variations are also needed to see what could be done to extremize social influences among aggressive and nonaggressive Ss. It would be of interest to see what happens if one member, for example, the nonaggressive S, is preinstructed by the experimenter as to what responses to give, that is, he is the experimenter's confederate.

The results obtained when an aggressive S answered before a nonaggressive S come closest to the strong social influences which we obtained in experiments in which one member of the pair was a confederate. In one prewar study the word blocks were repeatedly administered to a confederate who responded first and to a naive subject (both were sixth grade children) with the challenge to get 100%; the confederate's response was always judged by the experimenter as correct. On the third trial, over two-thirds of the naive S agreed with whatever word the confederate gave and about one-third agreed even when he gave a non-word. There was some resemblance between the aggressive first responder of the previous study and the prewar study with confederates. Both seemed sure of their responses, both seemed not to be influenced by the other person, and both influenced the other member of the pair. Possibly they are like "the haughty youth who speaks the truth" because he has learned it pays. The results suggest that an unyielding person, even when he is stubbornly wrong, may influence others' responses.

Aside from the cases with the aggressive Ss, we found considerably less of one-sided social influence with pairs of naive individuals than with a confederate. There seemed to be mutual influences, sometimes the first responder

TABLE 25.5
Percentages of Responses in Experiment 3

Series	Group S₁	S₂	Trial	Set S₁	S₂	Shift S₁	S₂	Other S₁	S₂	Agreement S₁	S₂
B	aggressive	aggressive	I	75	100	25	0	0	0	17	0
			II	57	92	43	0	0	6	34	0
			III	78	100	20	0	3	0	17	0
			IV	58	94	40	0	3	3	25	0
			Mean	67	96	32	0	2	2	23	0
	aggressive	nonaggressive	I	64	69	36	31	0	6	0	30
			II	72	59	28	40	0	1	14	27
			III	62	46	35	52	3	2	21	28
			IV	83	26	15	59	2	2	0	56
			Mean	70	50	28	46	1	3	9	35
	nonaggressive	aggressive	I	60	86	40	14	0	0	31	6
			II	83	91	17	8	0	0	14	6
			III	83	84	11	11	6	3	6	6
			IV	94	86	6	14	0	0	3	11
			Mean	80	87	19	12	2	1	13	7

Series	Group S₁	S₂	Responses Trial	Set S₁	S₂	Shift S₁	S₂	Other S₁	S₂	Agreement S₁	S₂
D	aggressive	aggressive	I	37	66	14	39	22	17	40	6
			II	57	69	8	20	22	21	8	0
			III	72	83	3	20	8	14	20	3
			IV	53	86	14	37	8	0	31	3
			Mean	55	76	10	29	15	13	27	3
	aggressive	nonaggressive	I	41	53	44	53	6	7	34	31
			II	51	53	46	41	7	11	23	37
			III	63	46	46	22	16	11	17	35
			IV	56	21	69	21	23	9	6	37
			Mean	53	43	51	34	13	10	20	35
	nonaggressive	aggressive	I	48	46	28	46	6	25	20	20
			II	44	69	22	20	25	8	17	14
			III	69	66	20	20	14	14	8	8
			IV	66	54	31	20	14	17	14	8
			Mean	54	59	25	27	15	16	15	13

shifted, sometimes the second responder shifted and sometimes they gave both responses or made new responses. There were some cases where the social influence did not work in the direction of making one blind or gullible but where the other person's response seemed to open his eyes to new possibilities, for example, some of the children asked to see a card again after overhearing the other child's response and were surprised and apparently genuinely pleased to find in it the overlooked word; cf. Wertheimer's discussion of the role of the drama critic in opening one's eyes to overlooked nuances of a play. Wertheimer did not deny that in life there are situations in which someone deliberately tries to influence people's judgment and will not change his own judgment. Just as we get a one-sided view of social influences by using evidence free situations, it gives a one-sided view to study social influences by using unyielding confederates. Perhaps it is not allowed to generalize from such situations to those social judgment situations in which there is a give and take between two individuals. In view of Wertheimer's comments it may be advisable to reconsider the generality and realm of applicability of the conclusions about social influences in the literature (including those which we have made) because many of them are based on studies which involved confederates. Their conclusions should be limited to situations where there is an aggressive, stubborn, or unyielding person, or where the social influences are intended to mislead, to blind, to develop in others a concentric narrowing of the visual field (CNVF).

Studies without Confederates: Pictures

Social judgment experiments without a confederate were also conducted with series of pictures. A 1967 replication of one of the prewar studies with the assistance of William J. Purdy, a student in ASL's Advanced Social Psychology class at SUNY-Albany, used the sailor-goblet pictures of the Luchins rigidity manual (1950). The pictures were administered to 35 pairs of children; 62 Ss were school children ranging from kindergarten to fourth grade and the remainder were pre-school children. The members of a pair were approximately equal in age and, in the case of the school children, in grade, academic ability, and popularity, according to their teachers' judgments.

The two Ss sat at either end of a table with a shield placed between them. The experimenter told them: I am going to show each of you some pictures. Your job is to tell me what you see in the pictures. Do not use your imagination. Give your answer in one or two words. Whisper your answer into my ear so the other person cannot hear.

The S to the left of E, S_1, was shown a series of eleven pictures which began with the picture of a face (a French sailor in a beret) that gradually changed in successive pictures until by the last card there emerged two figurines surrounding a goblet that also had some facial features. The other S, S_2, was shown a series of eleven pictures which began with a goblet and gradually changed in successive cards so that the last picture was the same as the final picture in the series given to S_1. E presented the first picture to S_1 and asked him what he saw. No matter what answer was made E emphasized its correctness by saying: That is right, very good. A similar procedure was followed for the first picture shown to S_2. When the second picture was presented to S₁, E asked him if he could see in it the same thing he had seen in Card 1; for example, if he had reported a face, E asked him if he could see a face in Card 2. The response was called correct if it was essentially what he had reported in the first card, with adjectives ignored and synonyms accepted. If not, S₁ was told: That is not right. See if you can do better next time. Similarly, S₂ was asked if he could see in the second picture what he had previously reported (for example, a goblet or glass) and was called correct only if he did so. In this manner all the eleven pictures in the learning series were presented to each S and a score announced. If both Ss made correct responses throughout, the learning phase was terminated; if not, the series were readministered, for a maximum of five trials, until correct responses were achieved, that is, until each S reported throughout the percept by which he was set by the initial picture.

The test cards consisted of five ambiguous pictures, the first of which was similar to the eleventh card of the learning series except for some additional curlicues. The figurines gradually disappeared until by the fifth card there was mainly a goblet with some facial features and curlicues. Beginning with the first test card, E took down the shield and said that the Ss were now so good in their observations that to save time they would be shown the same pictures. S₁ was shown the first test picture and told to give his answer aloud and then S₂ was shown the same picture and told to answer aloud. After the fifth card a score was given to each S, the basis of which differed in different variations. If both Ss had perfect scores the experiment was terminated; if not, the test cards were readministered, for a maximum of five trials, until both obtained 100%.

In Experiment 1 each S was considered correct in a test picture if he reported the percept for which he had been set in the learning phase, for example, face for S₁ and goblet for S₂. In Experiment 2 the same criterion was used and, in addition, prior to each trial, each S was told to try to see what he had seen on the earlier eleven pictures. In Experiment 3 any response to a test card given by S₁ was considered correct and S₂ was called correct only if he too gave this response. In Experiment 4 whatever response S₂ gave to a test picture was considered correct and S₁ was called correct only if he made the same response. The scores announced after each test series were based on the number of correct responses; for example, in Experiment 4 S₂ was told that he did very well and had gotten all of them right which was 100%, while S₁ was told that he did well or poorly and was given a score which depended on how often he had made the same response as S₂. Experiment 1 was conducted with ten pairs of children, Experiment 2 with five pairs, Experiment 3 with ten pairs, and Experiment 4 with ten pairs.

On the first trial of the learning series, 27 of the 35 Ss continued giving to all eleven pictures essentially the same response which they had made to the initial picture, and thus attained 100%. Seven other Ss did so on the second trial and only one required all five trials. In short, the Ss were readily set to repeat their initial response throughout the learning series, requiring on the average only one or two trials.

TABLE 25.6
Percentages of Responses to Test Pictures

Exp. Condition			Set		Shift		Both		Other		Attained Criterion	
			S_1	S_2	S_1	S_2	S_1	S_2	S_1	S_2	S_1	S_2
1	Learned response correct	First Trial	60	64	8	18	12	10	20	8	50	40
		Final Trial	52	74	12	12	14	6	22	8	50	70
10Ss (17.5)		Mean Responses	31	67	30	17	11	10	28	6	50	5
2	Learned response correct	First Trial	68	88	12	0	16	4	4	0	60	80
	plus instructions	Final Trial	100	80	0	20	0	0	0	0	100	80
	(10.0)	Mean Responses	84	42	6	50	6	8	4	0	80	80
3	S_1's response correct	First Trial	80	40	2	32	0	2	18	26	100	30
		Final Trial	72	22	6	56	0	0	22	22	100	100
	(13.0)	Mean Responses	66	28	2	33	0	1	10	38	100	65
4	S_2's response correct	First Trial	100	50	0	20	0	20	0	12	20	100
		Final Trial	22	20	10	20	60	50	32	10	90	100
10Ss (12.5)		Mean Responses	56	43	4	8	32	34	8	15	55	100

Table 25.6 summarizes the results in the test series. In Experiment 1 all ten S_1 children repeated the set response to the first picture presented in the test series and eight of the ten S_2 children did so. On the first test trial, 100% was attained by five S_1 and by four S_2 children. But none of the remaining S_1 children scored 100% on any of the remaining trials. Of the S_2 children three more scored 100% on the second trial and one more on the fourth trial. Thus the criterion for correct responses (in this case the set response) was attained by 50% of the first responders and by 70% of the second responders. There was a total of 35 trials on which the five test pictures were shown so that the S_1 members and likewise the S_2 members had a total of 175 opportunities to respond in the test phase or an average of 17.5 responses. The set response constituted about one-third of S_1s' total responses and about two thirds of S_2s' total responses. The remaining responses were shifts to the other member's learned percept, replies which had features of both percepts, or other percepts, for example, the figurines. In each of these categories S_1 tended to have a higher frequency than S_2, for example, 28% of the S_1s' replies were other percepts, usually the figurines, whereas this was the case for only 6% of the S_2s' replies. Thus there seemed to be mutual influence, but with the second responder more likely to adhere to the percept he learned.

The instructions in Experiment 2 to try to see in the test pictures what was seen in the learning phase apparently increased set responses. Such responses were given throughout the first test trial by three of the five S_1 members and by four of the five S_2 members and throughout the second test trial by the remaining S_1 members. One S_2 member consistently repeated S_1's response

(S₁'s learned percept) in all five trials. On the whole, compared to Experiment 1 there was an increase in set responses and a decrease in both percepts and in other percepts; for example, only 4% of the S_1s' replies and none of the S_2s' replies referred to other percepts such as the figurines.

In Experiment 3 any response S_1 gave to a test card was considered correct so this member automatically scored 100%. This score was attained by three S_2 members on the first trial, by one on the second trial, by four on the third trial, and by one each on the fourth and fifth trials. Of the 10 S_1 children, seven consistently gave the set response. The others occasionally gave S_2's percept or another percept. In two pairs, the other percept had first been mentioned by S_2, then picked up by S_1 and subsequently repeated by S_2. Thus, on the final trial, about one-quarter of S_2's replies were set responses, about one-half were shifts to S_1's learned percept, and about one-quarter were other responses. While set responses were lower for S_2 than in Experiments 1 and 2, they were not consistently higher for S_1 than in these experiments. Some S_1 children seemed to feel uncomfortable upon being called right and hearing the other child called wrong when each repeated what he had learned. Perhaps this accounts for the relatively large percentages of other percepts, which constituted about one-third of the total responses.

In Experiment 4, where S_2's response was always correct, only two S_1 children attained the criterion in the first trial but in these pairs S_2 had shifted to S_1's learned response. Three other S_1 children attained 100% on the second trial but S_2 had in these pairs been given both percepts and S_1 had also done so. Four more S_1 children scored 100% on the third trial; in two pairs S_2 had given both percepts and in another pair he had named another percept so that in only one of these pair did S_2 consistently adhere to the set response. One S_1 member never attained 100% in five trials; although the S_2 member consistently adhered to his percept, S_1 never shifted to this percept but gave his own set response on the first three test trials and for two pictures on the fourth trial; thereafter he named both percepts. Thus while apparent conformity was obtained in 90% of the cases, actually there was considerable mutual influence and compromise in the form of both percepts, which accounted for more than half of the responses on the final trial and for about one-third of the total responses. There were considerably more cases where both percepts were named than in the preceding experiments. On the other hand, other percepts, such as the figurines, were less frequent than in Experiments 1 and 3.

It would be of interest to replicate the experiments as well as to vary them by interchanging the learning series received by S_1 and S_2. In particular, how would this affect the results in Experiments 3 and 4? We found striking differences in results between these two experiments but it is not clear if these were due to the first or second responder's percepts being considered correct or to the differences in the set percepts.

On the whole, in comparison with experiments which used a confederate who replied first and gave one percept (for example, face or goblet) throughout the test pictures, which was scored as correct, there were now fewer shifts to the overheard percept and somewhat more both responses (in Experiment 4) and more other responses (in Experiment 3). However, other responses were not as frequent in any of the experiments as they were when the test pictures were shown to Ss who had not seen the learning pictures and who did not overhear another's responses. In short, two naive Ss sometimes became aware of each others' percepts but ignored still other percepts.

One aspect of this study raises an interesting problem that has been overlooked by investigators who have focused on the question of who conforms or yields or if individuals compromise in the judgment situation. Some Ss in the present study saw both percepts, the face and goblet, but overlooked another percept, the figurines, that was often seen by individuals who were given the test pictures only. These results are similar to those in prewar preliminary experiments conducted with mazes, water-jar problems, anagrams, and word blocks. Some naive pairs of Ss influenced each other to the extent that they each reported what the other saw in the test problems but they overlooked other possibilities. When they were set for two different indirect paths to a goal in a maze, they agreed that both paths were possible but they did not notice the direct path; when they were set for the B-A-2C and the A-C methods of solving water-jar problems, they did not see the one-jar solutions; when they were set for two different ways of finding a hidden word in an anagram, they did not see a word that was written in the ordinary manner; when they were set to read the word blocks along different diagonals, they did not see a word written along the horizontal. Ss who did not agree, that is, did not yield or compromise but stuck to the set that they had learned also were blind to the direct methods. It could be said that in all these experiments the Ss were focused on the social situation or on what they had learned before and they did not freely face the evidence.

When these results and similar results were discussed with Wertheimer, he made the point that we have to find out what attitudes and assumptions, what social influences, what methods of teaching and testing can save people from blindness to the evidence, can open their eyes and make them react in a productive manner in terms of the requirements of the judgment situation. People can be made to focus on the evidence or to focus on their ego needs or the needs of the social situation. If each of two Ss agrees to see or say what the other judges to be the case or to give both percepts, it may not be less blinding with regard to seeing what is in the evidence than if each sticks to his own judgment. Sticking to one's own point of view or agreeing to see the evidence from the other's point of view or seeing it from the other's as well as from one's own point of view may be equally blinding because in all these cases the individual may be focusing on social or personal factors and not focusing on the material given for judgment.

Wertheimer believed that there are certain kinds of social and educational conditions which teach people to be evidence-oriented so that regardless of personal or social needs they will react to the requirements of the evidence. This belief may be regarded as raising metaphysical questions about reality and may be dismissed by some contemporary phenomenologists as naive. However, Wertheimer would have considered that their sophisticated thesis endangers science because science is based on the assumption that there is truth and that man can find it. In restrospect it seems to us that Wertheimer's main criticism of Sherif and Cantril's work is that it would make people believe that there is no truth, that everything is opinion. This point of view would make possible Hitler or any other kind of tyranny. However, the work on social influences from the cognitive point of view, which Wertheimer's seminars fostered, has been used to support the very thesis that he was attacking. Therefore it seems that the initial reaction which he raised to the Sherif and Cantril work has not been adequately met. There is need for research to discover the factors that orient a person to the evidence and yet at the same time do not make him lose his sociality and individuality. This point will be taken up again in the next volume in which Wertheimer discusses group behavior.

Recent replications of social influence experiments using anagrams, water-jar measuring problems, and mazes have consistently yielded some interesting trends which are related to Wertheimer's conjectures about the differences between perception and thinking in problem solving (Luchins & Luchins, 1970b) and to his thesis about the role of the evidence in judgment. They are summarized here to stimulate research.

Two Ss worked independently at different ends of a long table. One solved a series of water-jar problems which could all be solved by the B-A-2C method (E method) and the other solved a series of problems that could all be solved by the A-C method or all by the A+C method or all by just filling one jar (D methods). After each S had developed a set to use his method, as indicated by his use of it in a critical problem that could be solved in various ways, both Ss were told, as in the experiments with the word blocks, to work on the same problems. In some pairs, the E member always responded first and in other pairs the D member always responded first in order to see who would shift to whom. Few D members shifted to the E method; more often the shift was from E to D regardless of who went first. Usually the shift to the D method increased after the extinction problem which was not solvable by the E method. The attitudes and assumptions of the Ss played a role in determining whether they would shift, for example, Ss who generalized a rule or made the assumption that the problems were all members of a certain class tended not to shift. Variations have been conducted in which Ss were told to generalize a rule or to find the principle that solves this type of problem. In these variations there was less shift and some Ss remarked that they were using the rules that they had learned. A few Ss, however, began to doubt the rule. Generally speaking, the Ss seemed to be more interested in practicing or using a rule than in facing the problem in the most productive manner.

When anagrams were used (Luchins, 1942) the results were similar, for example, there was more shift from E to D than vice versa. However, more Ss shifted in the anagrams than in the water-jar problems. A factor that might have contributed to the results was that the D method was the ordinary way to read whereas the E method consisted of cancelling every other letter to find the word, for example, in the anagrams TSINGREUR and CBALM-VEAL, the E solutions were *tiger* and *camel*, respectively and the D solutions were *sing* and *balm* or *veal*, respectively.

When the mazes (Luchins, 1942) were used, more Ss

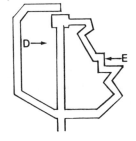

who had been set in the E way shifted to the D way than in any of the other experiments. Some who had at first used the E method asked to do the mazes over again and expressed how blind they had been. Even in the variations in which we asked the Ss to try to use what they did before or to consider that they were learning a general rule, many Ss shifted from the E to the D way.

In discussing the prewar studies with Wertheimer, ASL told him that it is possible to create working conditions or to develop attitudes and assumptions in a person so that he insists that he is correct, that his method is the method to solve the problems, mazes, and anagrams and that even in the experimental extinction problems in which his method did not work, he might argue that it must work. Wertheimer did not deny that this is possible but doubted that it would be as easy as ASL said that it was. It would seem that Wertheimer was correct; however, further research along these lines is needed.

Studies without Confederate: Problem Solving

Some of the studies of social influences without a confederate which used the water-jar problems were recently replicated with the assistance of Anthony Gribin, ASL's student at SUNY-Albany. In order to stimulate research we present the results of one of these studies. The experimenter, who sat at a table with two Ss, first solved two illustrative problems. Given jars with capacities of 17 quarts and 2 quarts, respectively, obtain 11 quarts of water; the solution illustrated verbally was $17-2-2-2=11$. Given jars with capacities of 17, 43, and 3 quarts, respectively, obtain 20 quarts; the solutions illustrated verbally were $43-17-3-3=20$ and $17+3$. These solutions are referred to as the $B-A-2C$ or E (Einstellung) method and the $A+C$ or D (direct) method, respectively. In Part I of the experiment each S was given a card which contained ten problems. For one S, SE, the first eight problems were E problems, each solvable by $B-A-2C$. For the other S, SC, the first eight problems were critical problems, each solvable by both $B-A-2C$ and either $A+C$ or $A-C$. The ninth and tenth problems, which were the same for both Ss, were critical problems, solvably by $B-A-2C$ and by $A-C$ or $A+C$, respectively. In Part II the Ss were seated closer together and the same card was shown to both, each card containing one problem. In this manner they were presented with Problems 11 and 12, two critical problems, solvable by $B-A-2C$ and $A-C$, Problems 13 and 14, two extinction problems, solvable only by $A-C$, and Problems 15 and 16, two criticals, solvable by $B-A-2C$ and by $A+C$.

When the experiment was administered to ten pairs of college Ss, aged 18 to 23, the percentages of E $(B-A-2C)$ and D$(A-C$ or $A+C)$ responses were as follows:

	Problems in Part I								Problems in Part II					
	1		2-8		9		10		11-12		13-14		15-16	
	SE	SC	SE	SC	SE	SC	SE	SC	SE	SC	SE	SC	SE	SC
E	80	40	100	10	60	0	20	0	15	0	0	0·	0	0
D	0	60	0	90	40	100	80	100	85	.100	100	100	100	100

Two SE members failed to solve the first problem and the experimenter then showed them the solution. The first problem given to the SC members yielded 60% D and 40% E responses. In subsequent problems D solutions increased for the SC members and accounted for 90% of their solutions of Problems 2-8 and for 100% of their solutions of the subsequent problems. The SE members showed 100% E responses to Problems 2-8 but thereafter such responses decreased monotonically. In the first critical problem they gave 60% E and 40% D responses and in the next critical problem only 20% E and 80% D responses. In the first two problems of Part II they made 15% E and 85% D responses and subsequently they gave only D responses.

Thus there was a slight set-inducing effect of the first eight E problems. But there was far less Einstellung effect than in previous experiments in which S worked alone or was tested with a confederate (cf. Luchins, 1939, 1942, Luchins & Luchins, 1959). Possible reasons for the present results are comments of the SC members which may have alerted the SE members to direct responses. For example, during Part I SC members made the following comments aloud: These problems are easy; I'll do it the easy way; I'm glad that I caught on to the easier way; The easier way is the faster way; Shall I do the rest the fast way? Moreover, in Part II the Ss were able to see each others' papers and solutions and one SC member showed SE the direct method.

During Part I a total of eleven comments were made by the ten SC members whereas the ten SE members made only seven comments. Most of these were with reference to the ninth and/or tenth problems, the first critical problems, for example, I'll do these a better way if you don't mind; This last problem can be done by simple addition; Problems 9 and 10 have an easier method. Other SE members' comments in Part I referred to the common method (Once you get the knack of it, it's easy; There's a system to this madness, isn't there?), to the speed of working (Am I going too slowly?), or asked for the purpose of the experiment. In Part II, unlike Part I, comments were somewhat more frequent by SE members and usually referred to their discovery of the direct method.

After the experiment each S was asked if he had been influenced by the other member. Three SE members admitted that they were influenced; two of them had not given any direct solution in Part I. Of the seven SE members who claimed not to have been influenced, all had given at least one direct solution in Part I. Two of the SE members who claimed not to have been influenced did say that they looked at SC's paper. Thus five of the ten SE members either admitted being influenced or looking at SC's paper. In contrast, only one SC member said that she looked at SE's paper and another said that they might have influenced each other even though they did not look at one another's paper but other than this no SC member admitted being influenced by the SE's responses. In general, the SC members were more confident of their work and several commented on SE's apparent lack of confidence. (See Table 25.7, which summarizes answers to the question on influence, particulary Pairs 1, 2, 3, 5, 8, 9; Pairs 4 and 6 are exceptions to the trend which was also found in earlier experiments.)

TABLE 25.7

Responses to Question on Influence by Other Member

SE

SC

Pair

1. (Male, D beginning with Problem 10) I glanced over at her paper several times; I wasn't really helped by her answers.

2. (Male, failed Problem 1, D beginning with Problem 12) He looked sure of himself all the time and his answers were always correct. I was influenced by him.

3. (Male, D beginning with Problem 10) I was not influenced by him but I looked over to check my answers.

4. (Male, D beginning with Problem 9) I wasn't influenced by her. These were easy problems.

5. (Male, failed Problem 1, D beginning with Problem 10) Yes, What can I say really? The problems we both did together were the same except they were easier than the first few. I did look over on his scratch paper because I felt stupid in not being able to do some in beginning. So when we worked together I just checked with him to make sure.

6. (Male, D beginning with Problem 9 where he comments about a better way) No, not at all.

7. (Female, D beginning with Problem 10 where she comments about simple addition. In Part II comments that problems are much easier now.) No, I did them all by myself.

8. (Female, D beginning with Problem 13, the first extinction task) She helped me see the light. I was stuck on two problems [extinction tasks] so I looked at her paper and took her advice. It was an easier way.

(Female, D except in Problems 3 and 8, seemed annoyed when SE looked at her paper in Part II) No, not at all. I can do this project myself.

(Male, all D) I didn't need any help from him. All my problems looked the same. He didn't know what he was doing most of the time.

(Male, D except in Problem 8) I was not influenced by him at all.

(Female, all D) I wasn't influenced by him and he didn't look at my paper so I guess I didn't help him either.

(Male, D beginning with Problem 2) I was not influenced by him. He didn't work too well and looked over at me several times. Once you find out the easier method of solving these problems, they go fast.

(Male, D except for Problem 3) I guess we both influenced each other even though we didn't look at our papers. I heard him say that there is a better way to do the problems so I tried to do them in the fastest and most direct way. Wasn't that right of me?

(Female, D beginning with Problem 3 where she comments that she was stupid before and is glad she caught on to the easier way) I looked at her paper because she was always done before me. I would have been correct anyway in my answers because they were easy once I saw the easier method.

(Female, D except for Problem 3; looked at A's paper after Problem 12 and said: My way is easier, less work). No, but I told her she was doing it the long way. I did that in my third problem but the rest I did in the easier way of adding or subtracting.

9. (Male, D beginning with Problem 9 writes answers to early problems slowly, erases, and asks if going too slowly). No, I was too busy doing the problems. I'm pretty slow in math.

10. (Male, D beginning with Problem 9) I was not influenced because my problems were right.

(Male, all D, works quickly and seems self-assured) I didn't pay attention to his work. He didn't seem too confident. My problems were easy anyway.
(D except in Problems 1 and in 3 where he asks about fast way) No, I got the hang of it after a while by myself. What are we doing here anyway?

The student wondered whether age was a factor in the results (cf. the discussion of the relation between age and Einstellung effect in Luchins, 1942, and Luchins & Luchins, 1959). Gribin therefore administered the experiment to four pairs of students at SUNY-Albany who ranged in age from 30 to 44. Their percentages of E and D responses were as follows:

		Problems in Part I							Problems in Part II					
	1		2-8		9		10			11-12		13-14		15-16
	S E	S C	S E	S C	S E	S C	S E	S C		S E	S C	S E	S C	S E	S C
E	100	50	100	11	100	0	25	0		50	0	0	0	0	0
D	0	50	0	89	0	100	75	100		50	100	100	100	100	100

Now there were no failures to respond. The SE members showed somewhat more E responses of the critical problems than had the corresponding members in the younger college pairs, for example, 100% E of the first critical compared to 60%, 50% E of the first two problems in Part II compared to 15% for the younger Ss. Results for the SC members were similar to those obtained with younger college Ss. It is of interest to conduct the experiment with more Ss and with a wider range of ages.

Concluding Remark

We have presented some of the work that we and our students have completed in order to illustrate Wertheimer's approach to the problem of social influence. His comments led to concrete research in order to fully understand what takes place in evaluation and social influences. He was against the sweeping generalizations of the 1930s and did not offer other ones. Instead he suggested a new approach to the phenomena. We hope that what has been presented will help those who seek theoretical clarification as well as research suggestions.

26
Experimental Outgrowths: Social Learning

In an after-class discussion someone told Wertheimer that Miller and Dollard would agree with Wertheimer's conjectures that the second child may have imitated the first because of various kinds of assumptions or reasons. However, they could say that they were not concerned with these factors because they were not theoretically significant. They had made certain predictions to test their learning theory and the results of their experiments proved their thesis. When a philosophy major pointed out that experimental findings do not necessarily validate a theory, the student asserted that science would not be possible if we did not abide by the outcomes of experiments. The philosophy major then referred to a controversy in which Fermat had refused to accept Descartes' experimental proof of a law of refraction. Fermat had argued that the results may be misleading, that even the most acute observer could be deceived by them, and therefore the results do not settle the matter. The same student then said that metaphysical assumptions or logical arguments do not overrule experimental results. Wertheimer said that Descartes had a mechanical view of nature and that Fermat had a teleological view. According to the Cartesians, nature operated in terms of a principle of economy and there was no need for Fermat's assumptions. The philosophy major said that Fermat was questioning the dogma that observational equivalence entails theoretical equivalence. One must not think that one's results settle theoretical issues; there is always a possibility for a fresh attack, for another look at the problem. A mathematics major pointed out that Gauss had once measured the angles of a triangle and concluded that his measurements were compatible with the predictions from Euclidian as well as non-Euclidian geometries; that the sum of the angles of a triangle could be equal to, less than, or more than 180 degrees, illustrates the principle of experimental equivalence (cf. Luchins & Luchins, 1952, 1959). Someone brought the discussion back to social learning by saying that he objected to Wertheimer's *posteriori* speculation about what had happened in Miller's investigation. Wertheimer said that he was not suggesting that we only speculate about what Miller's subjects did but that he had been pointing out possibilities for research. Why not repeat the experiment and see for yourselves what happens?

The next day ASL told his Adult Education students about this discussion and planned with them to replicate or modify the experiment. If they did not have available the boxes that they could use, ASL told them that they could hide the candy in a table or desk drawer. Using a pair of identical tin boxes which could be closed with a key, ASL replicated the experiment with fifth-grade children of a Brooklyn slum's elementary school. Records were kept of expressive movements and comments. After both children had made their choices, each child was taken aside and asked why he had selected the box. The naive subjects sometimes spontaneously made comments during the experiment saying that they wanted to go first. Their behavior during the experiment showed some hesitancy and reluctance to copy or to follow. This was perhaps due to the fact that the experiment was conducted in a school situation and was regarded as a test; they did not want to appear to be cheating or copying. A few children asked whether they could go first so that their choices would not be regarded as copying. The subjects' answers to the experimenter's questions indicated a variety of reasons for not choosing the same box as the first child: they did not want to copy, they wanted to find the candy themselves, they picked the other box because the first child had taken the only piece of candy in it, there was candy in both boxes, the experimenter would fool them and not put candy in the same box, they expected alternation schemes of various kinds. A few children said that they picked the same box because the experimenter would expect them to think that he would alternate and therefore he would try to fool them by hiding the candy in the same box. A few chose the same box because they assumed that the other box was locked and that the candy was in the unlocked box or that it was the box where the experimenter had put all the candy. A few did what the first child did because they thought that they were working as a team to find the candy. Some children frankly or with some embarrassment admitted that they went where the other child went simply because he had found the candy there. Some children could not or would not give any reasons for their choices. After the experiment the naive subjects were told that the first child was a confederate and that the purpose of the experiment was to see whether they would follow him. Some were surprised that the experimenter had tried to make them follow but they usually thought that it was a clever trick and readily agreed to be the confederate with the next child who came to take the test. When ASL described these results in his Adult Education class, the students reported similar findings except that more of their subjects imitated the confederate on the first trial. The students hypothesized that this was due to friendship or other interpersonal relations that existed between the members of the pairs of subjects they studied. ASL pointed out that they had not conducted their experiments in a school; in school one is not supposed to copy, therefore he found less following. He asked them to suggest variations in which there would be less copying in non-school situations and more copying in school situations. He also asked them for variations to increase and decrease the subjects' assumptions that it was similar to a gambling game, that two pieces of candy were in one box, that one piece of candy was in each of the boxes, and that one must be self-reliant and not a copycat.

In discussing these results with Wertheimer he noted that some subjects behaved blindly but others did not. When ASL said that the former acted in terms of Miller's theory, Wertheimer said that it was not merely a question of whose theory was correct; different doctrines of man were involved. There are schools where children are taught to do things blindly, to follow unthinkingly what others do. What are the consequences for the person and the social field when one learns to follow blindly? When ASL wondered whether this was an objection to Miller's thesis, Wertheimer said that when he had told

Hull about the blinding effects in the Einstellung experiments, Hull had said that he was raising an ethical, not a scientific question. Wertheimer changed the subject when he inquired about one of ASL's experiments on social influences. While ASL was telling him about the experiment on the judgment of line segments, Wertheimer's questions gave him the idea of changing it into the following experiment on social learning which was conducted the next day. A pair of sixth-grade elementary school children were shown a paper-and-pencil maze in the form of a drawing of a house that had two paths leading to the front door; one path was a straight one and the other a zigzag (Luchins, 1942). They were asked which path they would use to get to the house. After both children indicated their choices, the experimenter put a wooden block on one of the paths and told each child to go again and to make sure that he did not select the blocked path. After they both made their choices, he told them that he was now going to make the task a little harder; he would not put a block of wood in the path but would block one of the paths in his mind. Their task was to select the path that was unblocked. They were told that if they paid attention to when they were called right and when they were called wrong, they would be able to discover the basis for the mental blocking of the paths and would be able to select the unblocked path each time. After both children had made their choices, the first child was told that he was correct; the second child was called correct only if he selected the same path chosen by the first child. The latter was actually the experimenter's confederate who had answered on the basis of prearranged signals from the experimenter. The confederate always went first and was always called correct. After several trials, the confederate whispered in the experimenter's ear, who then said out loud that he had discovered the scheme and that they would continue with the experiment until the other child also discovered it. After the second child guessed correctly in ten successive trials, he was asked what was the basis of his choices, if he had not spontaneously reported it. Then the experimenter told the children that he was now going to use another scheme to decide which road was to be blocked. After the naive child had guessed correctly in ten successive trials he was again asked what was the scheme. Two schemes were used in each sub part of the experiment: (A) the confederate answered on a random basis and was always called correct, (B) the confederate always chose the shorter path and was always called correct. Forty-two sixth-grade children from a school in a Brooklyn slum first learned scheme A and then scheme B and forty-two other sixth-grade children in the same school first learned scheme B and then scheme A. The results were striking. It took many more trials to learn scheme A than Scheme B regardless of the order. Some children did not learn scheme A even after 200 trials. Thus the results indicated that it was much easier to learn to follow when the model's response had a reasonable basis than when the model's behavior was arbitrary. Moreover, those subjects who first learned scheme A had more difficulty in learning scheme B than did those for whom it was the initial scheme. Learning to follow first in B did not interfere with or slightly facilitated the learning of scheme A. Thus learning to follow blindly interfered with learning a relatively simple scheme but not vice versa. ASL sent Wertheimer a detailed report of these experiments with a letter about certain troublesome findings. Wertheimer returned the report the next time the seminar met. He had marked it up with his characteristic editorial corrections.

It also contained the following comments. There was a need to conduct control experiments for A as well as for B. ASL conducted an experimental variation of the AB design in which the stooge kept quiet in the second half of the experiment. Wertheimer suggested experiments where the stooge kept quiet in the A or the B part of the AB set up or of the BA set up. He wrote that in A one had to learn from the confederate's changing responses but in B the correct response was based on the confederate's constant response to a constant feature of the maze. A was not merely different from B but more complex. Therefore he suggested the use of alternation schemes. He also noted that scheme A was a mean task because the instructions implied an objective plan behind the confederate's response. It was possible to see the plan readily in B but not in A. Perhaps the child did not follow in A because he did not want to act arbitrarily, did not want to follow blindly. He might have thought that the first child's response was based on a plan and he tried to discover it. He might have thought that it was a nonsensical thing or unjust that the other child was right no matter what path he chose. Wertheimer conjectured that scheme A was learned faster when it came after B because the subjects had already practiced in B to guess a scheme. Maybe to have an easier task first and then a harder one is more efficient for learning of the second task.

When ASL next visited Wertheimer's home to plan research, Wertheimer made the following observations. Generally speaking, as long as we do not know about the range of results in different groups, in different times, places, etc. the differences in results do not mean much. Maybe they are due to chance, to repetition, to the instructions, etc. He then took up the questions raised in ASL's letter. Maybe it is easier to learn scheme B than A because it is a matter of a simple, constant basis for choosing versus a materially complex changing one. The instructions and the whole setup block the learning in A. This seems clear: after the subject has to realize such a fantastic complicated scheme as A, he is not prepared, he does not expect to be faced with such a simple one as B. You have compared B, which is a very simple and constant scheme, with A, which is very complex and changing. You should also compare A with some scheme that is comparably complex, for example, alternating responses, or even more complex than A. Also consider that instead of a stooge there might be some internal scheme related to the individual's own previous judgment, for example, the opposite of his previous task or the task before the last is considered correct. These remarks led to a discussion of different kinds of alternation patterns, such as, in A the stooge chooses at random but in B he alternates from left to right or on the basis of a more complex pattern, such as RRLLRL; in A he uses a complex alteration scheme and in B he uses a less-complex one; in A he chooses at random and in B he uses as cues for his choices the ringing of a buzzer or the dimming of the room's lights. Wertheimer suggested that we compare the learning of the various tasks with and without a confederate in both or in one of the tasks. What would happen if neither subject was a confederate and the correct response was a pattern of alternation that was based on the first or second child's choice on the first trial? He went on to ask, Why use such a senseless figure as the house with the two paths leading to it? Why not use a simple ambiguous figure, a checkerboard maze, or a more complex maze? What is the effect of having to learn paths whose structure is not so clear or outstanding? Vary your instructions or give previous experience to focus the child on the maze, on the confederate, on getting a good mark, etc. The present tasks are far removed from real life. Why not use more lifelike situations? As it stands, the experiment does not prove much of anything about issues in social psychology. [Despite this initial negative opinion, he continued to suggest experimental variations and, when shown the survey of their results, he became quite interested.]

Later he related the experiments on social influences to Einstellung experiments by suggesting that we compare the use of various Einstellung tasks with and without a confederate. This came about when ASL referred to an Einstellung variation in which the subjects were given a series of variable problems that could be solved by using one, two, or three jars (Luchins, 1942, 64-67). Some subjects solved the entire series by always using one jar whereas other subjects always used the three jars. Usually the subjects who used only one jar were able to solve subsequent problems whose solution required one, two, or three jars whereas the subjects who had always used three jars were not able to solve problems that called for different solutions. Thus becoming habituated to the simple method was less blinding (Luchins & Luchins, 1959, Chap. 16). Wertheimer's suggestions led to variations of the Einstellung experiment in which a confederate's E response was used instead of the set-creating tasks. It was found that subjects did not use the obvious solutions to series of water-jar problems, mazes, and anagrams and even failed to solve them because they repeated the confederate's response. It was also possible to maximize Einstellung effects by setting the subjects by previous experiences or by special instructions that focused them on following the confederate. Since the same blinding effect could be obtained without the confederate, Wertheimer asked whether this meant that nonsocial factors could produce the same effects as social factors. If so, which was more influential in producing Einstellung? When Wertheimer asked whether a confederate could be used to save subjects from Einstellung effects, experiments were conducted in which the confederate used the direct method. In some variations there were less Einstellung effects than usual. This led to a series of experiments in which the influence of the confederate was pitted against the influence of repetition and generalization of the E method to produce or to prevent Einstellung effect or to bring about recovery from it. Wertheimer then suggested that social and nonsocial factors be pitted against each other in various ways in order to test their strength under different conditions. He also pointed out that our nonsocial factors were social insofar as the experimenter had arranged the subject's experience in order to obtain a certain response. These experiments suggested variations for the Einstellung study as well as experiments on social influences on learning, perception, and judgment. We planned to publish them in a monograph similar to the one on Einstellung effect in problem solving. Since ASL was planning to join the Army he made a survey of the experimental findings and sent them to Wertheimer, who reorganized the survey and pointed out the need for one variation in order to obtain a crucial decision for Gestalt theory. He suggested that the data and survey be left with him so that the study could be completed after the war either by ASL or by him if necessary. Ironically, Wertheimer died in 1943. The data and the survey were not available on ASL's return in 1947 and he could not recall Wertheimer's crucial decision. The following is an attempt to reconstruct the way the research was originally done, and Wertheimer's comments on the experiments and the results.

One series of experiments (cf. Luchins & Luchins, 1961a) involved learning various alternation schemes with and without a confederate. Several studies focused on whether different social atmospheres, attitudes, assumptions, interpersonal relations, and experiences would produce different effects on the processes underlying the act of imitation and would have different consequences in subsequent learning situations, for example, would learning to follow a model blindly interfere when one had to learn a principle alone or from a model? Would learning principles from a model interfere with learning to follow the model blindly? The results in general supported Wertheimer's conjecture that subjects would give the same response as the confederate because of a variety of reasons. Some subjects followed him because they wanted to be right and were not at all concerned about the scheme; others followed him in order to be right but did this with the hope of eventually discovering the scheme; and still others followed because they realized that the experimenter or the test required that they use the same path as the confederate. Wertheimer asked whether the consequences for the person and the social field are the same or different when one repeats a model's response because he understands the principle or follows blindly because it is stylish or is called right. In some experimental variations many subjects followed blindly but in others they did not. When ASL said that aspects of the results indicate that there is a natural tendency to be oriented to others for clues about what to do, Wertheimer said that postulating a tendency is not enough; we have to study the field conditions that extremize it. He went on to say that discussions of imitation use the same term to denote both a process and the outcome of a process. Is it true that depending on what one assumes to be the process of imitation, one might do different things to control it? Do teachers, parents, and others who want individuals to learn from them do different things when they believe that such and such is the process? What would happen if we trained someone to believe that a certain principle was the basic one underlying social learning and we gave him the task to devise a method of how to instruct someone to perform a certain action or to solve a certain problem?

When ASL pointed out that in nearly all experiments learning was very difficult when the confederate chose at random or used a very complicated scheme, Wertheimer raised the question of the relation of the model and the nature of the task's structure in learning. You can force one to imitate the model. Suppose it is a very senseless or mean thing; what would the subject do, in comparison to a situation in which it is a sensible or reasonable thing to do? In both tasks you may get compliance because of your power but is it the same? In what kind of tasks do you need more force to get compliance? He went on to say that if the behavior is senseless, following may mean a different thing to the person and the social field than when it is sensible. He added that a model can be used to clarify or hide the structure. He referred to the barbaric method of teaching area (Luchins & Luchins, 1970a) and suggested new experiments using school subject matter in which children were forced to follow blindly whatever the teacher did. What factors would make the subject comply and what factors would make him revolt? He noted that in some experimental variations the blind imitation tasks seemed to be most difficult to learn and therefore produced a social atmosphere similar to that in the speed-test-tension Einstellung experiments. But even in these conditions there were individuals who refused to follow blindly. What are the possible reasons for their behavior? Is it because there is a tendency in man not to do things blindly? When ASL argued that it is possible to make anyone act blindly, Wertheimer said that it is possible but what does it mean for man and for society when it is done?

After this discussion a series of experiments were conducted in which two or more naive subjects were tested together. The various tasks that had been used in the experiments with confederates were now used to see how they would be learned when the first person was an unintentional model, that is, the first person did not know that his response was the basis of the scheme according to which a response was judged to be correct, for example, whatever path was selected by the first person was called correct and the second person had to select that path in order to be correct, or the alternation scheme was based on the first person's response (cf. Luchins & Luchins, 1961b). The subject of each pair who was the unintentional model needed more trials to learn the scheme because he did not realize that his behavior was the cue for the correct response. Again the tasks which required sheer imitation, or in which the scheme was not clear, proved most difficult to learn. In experiments with a confederate, the model facilitated the solution of a task only when his responses aided the naive subject to discover the principle. In the tasks in which it was difficult to find the principle, learning was facilitated more by the intentional model's behavior than by the unintentional model. When these experiments were discussed with Wertheimer, he raised the question of whether conditions could be created where unintentional models would produce better learning than intentional models. Also, what could be done so that the first person would discover the scheme before the second one or that both would discover it at the same time or neither of them would discover it? Some experiments were planned in which the subject had an egocentric point of view because of previous experience or in which he had been set by previous experiences to think or not to think of his behavior as influencing or as being a determinant of what was called right in the situation.

In a discussion of the experiments, Wertheimer remarked that social learning could blind one to the structure, could turn one into a robot so that one repeated what others did or said. That it was not natural for man to behave this way was seen in the amount of force that we needed to make people to conform and to keep them from deviating from the stereotyped patterns of behavior. An outgrowth of this discussion was to organize groups in which children had to play games that consisted of blindly doing parts of tasks which had been arbitrarily divided into a series of steps. Each step had to be carried out in a definite way and the subjects could not get a survey of the whole tasks. The experiments were stopped because the children became upset. When ASL conducted this study with youths in his neighborhood who volunteered to help him, they avoided him after the first session. When he asked some of them what they thought about the experiment they said that i reminded them of Charlie Chaplin in *Modern Times* and that they had beer annoyed at the insistence to repeat exactly something that made no sense Then ASL described to them the Taylor method of increasing efficienc (after Frederick W. Taylor, the "father of scientific management") and tol them that he (ASL) had made·a time and motion study of a certain act and had given it to them to learn. They said that it was not the same thing because in a factory one got paid or one feared that he would be fired if he did not do as told. Moreover, some workers did quit if the job was too confusing or senseless.

Wertheimer did not think that it was necessary to be so cruel to test his conjectures. He suggested that we go to schools and observe the learning of senseless things which are learned by rewards and punishments. Maybe children hated arithmetic because it was taught like lists of nonsense syllables. This discussion led to an experiment in which algebra problems were divided into a series of minute steps. A child who had no knowledge of algebra was told to write each algebraic symbol that the experimenter wrote on the blackboard. The child wrote on a sheet of paper that was covered except for the place where he had to copy. The same procedure was used with college students who knew algebra. Some students and most elementary school children were content to write the symbols one by one. However, some varied the writing of the symbols or made mistakes when they became used to the task. A few elementary school children and some college students asked to see everything that they had written and wanted to know what it was all about. When ASL stepped out of the room some of these subjects uncovered their papers to see what they had accomplished. When ASL returned he uncovered the papers for those who had not done so themselves. Some college students but few of the elementary school pupils then realized that they had been solving an algebra problem. However, most subjects were not at all curious about the problem. Only a few studied it to find out whether their work was correct. This experimental set up was varied. Instead of algebra problems we jumbled sentences or parts of a picture and presented the bits one at a time, never allowing the subject to get an overview. The results were the same.

After the war we became interested in what would happen if a subject was made to work like a Turing Machine, that is, what would happen when he was given the operations one at a time and made them on the roll of paper on which he was told to write without being told what it was all about. Some subjects agreed to do this when they were told that they were imitating a calculator but otherwise they soon quit. However, while they were doing it, they invented stories or made assumptions about what it meant; some tried to guess what the next step would be. More recently we conducted experiments in which we broke up the Einstellung problems into separate numbers or into a series of single steps and the model and/or subjects operated in terms of an algorithm or heuristic (cf. Luchins & Luchins, 1970c). The aim of these experiments was to find out whether the subjects would readily act like robots, would engage in what Wertheimer had called *crippled doing*. Our results indicate that under certain conditions people would perform in this way but various attitudes and assumptions were made by the subject to make the task tolerable. Some subjects got bored or quit when they had to do over and over the same senseless tasks but they tolerated more repetitions if a variety of tasks was used. This raised the question of whether people sought novelty and new experience but not meaning. When ASL once told Wertheimer that as long as the tasks are changed subjects do not object to acting like robots, he said that this is due to the effects of their education and that there are forces in the social field that require men to act in a robotlike manner and even make them enjoy it. The job of the psychologist is not just to help create such behavior but to discover methods that prevent or bring about recovery from such blind behavior.

Wertheimer conjectured that one effect of repeating what someone else did or what one did before is the development of a concentric narrowing of one's visual field. One repeats the act and is blind to its place, role, and function in the social situation. In order to test these conjectures several life situations were used in which subjects had to perform a role exactly like the model; the behavior had to correspond move by move to the model's. Except for the subjects who were interested in mimicking or acting, nearly all objected to the task. Immediately after the experiment or on the next day they were asked to describe the room in which the experiment had been conducted. They described less things and were less accurate than control group subjects who did not have to mimic the role.

Because of Wertheimer's suggestions we decided to use different tasks. A checkerboard maze was drawn on a large sheet of cardboard. Each checkerboard box had a drawing of an object which was common or uncommon, liked or disliked. A subject was asked to draw with a blue pencil a path from the starting point to the goal. Then he was asked to recall the different drawings that he had seen in the maze. Another subject was given the traced maze and was told that his task was to retrace with a red pencil the blue-penciled path and that he must be careful not to deviate from the blue path. After he had finished he too was asked to describe the drawings in the maze. The subjects who had retraced another's path recalled less symbols and objects than the subjects who had traced freely. The experiment was varied to increase and decrease the seeing of the drawings. Different pictures were used, of neutral, well-known, and unknown objects which were in line with or against the subject's ideology. The use of drawings that were in line with the needs or values of the subjects did not always increase the seeing of the drawings. Although the results supported Wertheimer's conjecture about the narrowed visual field during slavish repetition, he raised several objections and suggested that we alert the subjects to the fact that they would have to recall later what they see in the maze. He also suggested that we conduct the experiment with subjects whose values and needs were aroused before or during the experiment. Other suggestions were that we change the size of the maze, use a floor maze, use different rooms in a house, and ask the subject to find various familiar and unfamiliar things in them when moving freely or following a leader (cf. Luchins & Luchins, 1962).

Wertheimer once remarked that the school and the home are places where children and adults learn either in an informal or in a formal way knowledge and skills that are needed in life. Why is it that some parents and teachers and some demonstrations and illustrations are better than others for this purpose? He questioned the assumption that it is all a matter of reinforcement; maybe reinforcement is needed when the acts have an and-summative structure. He added that he would begin the investigation of social learning by finding out what is easy and what is difficult to learn in the classroom, home, and shop. Are such tasks structurally different and how much repetition or force is needed to learn them? What role do social conditions and methods of instruction play in revealing or concealing the structure? Perhaps rewards and punishment are needed because the material is presented as an and-summative collection of acts. Perhaps conditioning is effective where nature is plastic and allows any rearrangement of behavior.

Learning A Role

ASL adapted for the study of social behavior the experiments that he had conducted to test Wertheimer's conjectures about trial and error learning (cf. Luchins & Luchins, 1970a). In discussing the results, Wertheimer remarked that a model's responses were helpful if the subject was aware that the model was doing the correct thing or had the means to reach the goal or when the model's behavior focused the subject on the significant features of the situation. The model confused the subject if the latter could see no reasonable basis for the behavior or if the model did things which were unrelated to the task. The discussion led to the use of a variety of tasks, for example, calisthenics, geometrical proofs and constructions, and ritualistic roles (Luchins & Luchins, 1966). One of the ritualistic roles that has been studied intensively was devised in the following manner. Preliminary experiments were conducted in which students were told to take one of the books from the bookcase and to place it on the table. Sometimes they were told to assume that they were actors selecting a certain book from the bookcase and carrying it in a certain way to a certain part of the table. On the basis of these preliminary studies, we composed a role containing movements that were frequently and infrequently made by the subjects. The role was as follows. While facing the bookcase which contained only three books on its top shelf, the subject had to take the middle book with his right hand, transfer it to his left hand, make an about-face, walk counterclockwise in six steps around the table to the corner of the table nearest the bookshelf, and place the book on this corner so that its cut pages were aligned with the edges of the table. The table was two feet away from and parallel to the bookcase. It jutted out from the side of the bookcase so that the subject, after making the about face, would be at the corner of the table on which the book was to be put. As is seen in the figure below, the subject was actually at the goal position but had to walk away from

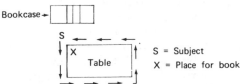

it. The role included actions that were sensible, direct, and related to the goal as well as actions that were senseless, indirect, and irrelevant to the attainment of the final goal. For scoring purposes the role was divided into six parts: (1) selecting the middle book, (2) taking it with the right hand, transferring it to the left hand, and then making an about-face, (3) walking counterclockwise around the table, (4) doing it in six steps, (5) putting the book on the corner nearest to the bookcase, (6) placing the book so that the cut pages were aligned with the edges of the table. To walk around the table in six steps usually required walking with a stride of 30 inches. Since this was generally difficult for females, they were permitted either six or seven steps.

The experiment was conducted in several ways. Some Ss were required to learn the role by themselves and others to learn it after first watching a preinstructed model perform. We have reported elsewhere sixteen experimental variations (Luchins & Luchins, 1966, 1970a). What follows is a summary of the project. In all the experiments the task was to learn to perform the above described role on five successive trials. In Experiments I through IV, each of which was conducted with 20 college Ss, a maximum of 150 trials was allowed. In Experiment I, after each trial the subject was informed whether the entire role was performed correctly. In Experiment II he was told which part of the role had been performed correctly. In neither of these experiments did any of the Ss learn the role. Each of these experiments were modified by having a preinstructed model respond before the S. In Experiment III where the S and the model were given the instructions of the first experiment, every subject reached the learning criterion by the fortieth trial. In Experiment IV, which was similar to Experiment III except that the subject was told to observe the model, every S reached it by the twentieth trial. The average time in each of the Experiments I and II was more than one hour longer than the average time in each of Experiments III and IV. The third and fourth part of the role were most difficult to learn; the first and fifth parts were most readily learned. Although the experiments supported Wertheimer's conjectures, he suggested that they be repeated with some pairs of children and with subjects of different ages and educational backgrounds. He also stressed the need to study the attitudes and assumptions of the subjects. The investigation raised many questions which we tried to answer experimentally. What would happen if the subject had first practiced alone the parts of the role? When this was done we found that some children learned the role more readily when they were later given the tasks of Experiments III and IV. This was particularly so in Experiment IV; as soon as they saw the model enact the role they enacted it correctly. We varied this experiment by having the model present the parts of the role in different orders. In some of these variations the subjects did worse than those who had no model, suggesting that the order in which the model gave information was important. Variations were conducted in which the model did things that were extraneous to the role although he performed each step of the role correctly and in the proper order; for example, he grimaced, looked around the room, paused in thought, or looked for cues from the experimenter. In these variations some subjects were confused and needed more trials to learn the role. This usually happened with the procedure of Experiment IV. In each of the variations some subjects were so intent on repeating what the model did that they were not aware that he was enacting the parts of the role that they had practiced before. The same experiment was varied as follows. Instead of the six steps, the role was cut up into more subparts, for example, the role was subdivided into 15 steps; and in the extreme case, every hand and face movement was spelled out. In these variations the subjects did not learn the role as well as in Experiments III and IV. They protested that it was an impossible task and were not at all aware that the bits of behavior were parts of the role that they had practiced before. These variations need to be repeated; they are relevant to Wertheimer's discussion of the consequences of focusing on details (Luchins & Luchins, 1970b).

The first four experiments were varied in several ways. In addition to using a model we told the subject after each trial those parts which he had performed correctly or those parts which he had done incorrectly. They learned more rapidly when they were told what they had done incorrectly. In order to test whether the results with a model were due primarily to the unvarying behavior of the model and were not due to the experimenter's verdict, the experimenter did not say that the model's performance was correct. Learning was now not as good as in Experiments III and IV. In order to overcome the reluctance to follow the model, the experiment was put into the context of a social situation in which imitation was proper, for example, a test to evaluate one's ability to mimic behavior or to act. When we used subjects who were friends of the model it sometimes happened that learning was worse than when the model was unknown; they seemed to be embarrassed when they had to copy their friend's behavior. We used models who acted in a stiff, military manner, or in a relaxed manner; in the former cases, more trials were needed to learn the role. We varied the sureness of the model's movements; this did not seem to affect the results decisively. Experiments were also conducted in which the model and the naive subject were together in the room for a few minutes before the experimenter entered; they had a discussion in which the model was critical of a known political and social belief of the subject or of the subject himself or was very agreeable; in the latter cases, subjects sometimes learned better than in the former.

We also compared learning the role by means of a written script instead of a model. Before each trial the subject read the entire script. Some learned the role better this way but others learned it worse than in Experiment IV. This raised the question of different ways to learn the role from a script; for example, reading each step and then performing it, reading the entire role before doing it, or memorizing the role before doing it. These experiments led to the question whether it was more efficient to repeat the model's behavior step by step while the model was enacting the role or watching the model do the whole role before repeating it. The question was also raised whether it was best to give the right-wrong verdict while the subject performed a correct move of a subpart, after each subpart, or after the entire role. The first procedure seemed to be the worst. In discussions of these experiments with Wertheimer his remarks were similar to those he made in the discussions of the Einstellung experiments; therefore, the reader is referred to Luchins, 1942 and Luchins & Luchins, 1970c. *Role Learning by Pairs of Naive Subjects.*

What would happen if two naive subjects neither of them confederates, had to learn the above-described complex role? Generally speaking, when the pairs were set by the instructions to cooperate, the role was learned better than when the members were set to work independently. Moreover, little children learned the role better than college students. Recently Leonard Ochs assisted us to replicate the study as part of an investigation of the cues that maximize the learning of social roles by pairs of naive subjects. What follows is based on the results he obtained with ten pairs of female college students. The study was conducted in a small room (6 by 10 feet) that contained a bookcase with three books in it and a long table (2 by 6 feet). The pair of Ss were told:

> I am interested in how people learn to play roles. This is not a test of any kind. Suppose this is a stage and you are actresses who have to perform a certain role. You can learn from trying to enact it because I shall tell you if you have performed it correctly. The script for the role requires that you take one of the three books in that bookcase and put it on one of the corners of this table in a certain way. There is a definite

number of actions you must perform in order to be correct. Feel free to ask questions or to comment on anything that comes to mind while performing in the experiment. I will try to answer all your questions if I can. Don't forget, there is a correct way to do it. I will record what you say so we will be able to talk about what happened afterward.

After the pair of Ss had been told to face the bookcase and the instructions repeated, they were told that they had a certain number of trials in which to learn the role, and that they would be informed when they completed these trials. The role, or a part of it, was considered to be correct if it was performed correctly by either members of the pair or by both members; if a part was performed incorrectly by both members, it was scored as an error for that part. A maximum of 100 trials was allowed. In Experiment I the pair of Ss was told after each trial whether or not the entire role had been performed correctly, for example, You did not play the entire role correctly; try again. In Experiment II all the instructions were the same except that the pair was now told after each trial which parts of the role had been played correctly, for example, You did not play the entire role correctly but you played these parts correctly; you selected the correct book and you placed it on the correct corner; try again.

Almost invariably the subjects of both experiments asked whether they should play the role together or separately. The experimenter told them that it did not matter how they went about learning it; the important thing was that they learn it. When the Ss persisted, they were told that they might work alone or cooperatively. In some pairs the members performed the role simultaneously and in others sequentially, that is, they alternated the role playing, while one acted the other watched, or each member attempted to enact the role when she thought of something to do.

Since in Experiment II the Ss were given information about the parts of the role that had been learned correctly, it could be predicted (on the basis of Gestalt principles or on the basis of concepts of reinforcement or attention) that the role would be learned better than in Experiment I. This expectation was supported by the results; no pair in Experiment I learned the entire role in 100 trials whereas every pair in Experiment II learned it. Table 26.1 presents the number of trials on which the 10 pairs of Ss of Experiment II reached the

TABLE 26.1
Number of Trials

Pair No.	Entire Role	Parts					
		1	2	3	4	5	6
1	31	18	19	20	31	3	4
2	55	3	7	55	26	11	17
3	44	33	28	36	44	1	34
4	31	4	15	31	16	10	13
5	11	2	8	8	11	7	1
6	20	10	20	20	20	2	9
7	19	10	19	15	17	10	5
8	40	5	40	23	37	23	10
9	54	21	32	44	54	6	1
10	19	3	11	12	19	1	4
Mean	32	11	20	26	28	7	10

learning criterion of five successive correct performances for the entire role and for each part of the role. We see that all the Ss in Experiment II learned the role by the fiftieth trial and one pair learned it by the eleventh trial; on the average 32 trials were needed.

The number of errors for each part of the role are presented in Table 26.2. In every part there were more errors in Experiment I than in Experiment II; on the average there were six times as many errors.

TABLE 26.2
Number of Errors

Exp.	N	Parts						TOTAL	Mean
		1	2	3	4	5	6		
I	10	695	1010	998	999	875	880	5447	908
II	10	89	192	219	263	65	72	900	150

The Ss of Experiment I made a total of 5,447 errors in contrast to the Ss of Experiment II who made 900 errors. It seems that learning of the role was facilitated by feedback. We also see that Parts 1, 5, and 6 of the role were not only learned better than the other parts but were also usually the first parts enacted by the Ss. It will be recalled that the previous section contained experiments similar to this study's experiments except that only one naive S performed rather than a pair. In the previous section's Experiment I, no S learned the role and the mean number of errors were 2,565 in contrast to 908 in the present Experiment I. In the previous section's Experiment II no S learned the role and the mean number of errors was 1,172 whereas every S learned the role in the present Experiment II and the mean number of errors was 150. Thus pairs of naive Ss learned better than did one naive S in comparable experiments. However, the pairs in the present experiment made more errors than did the Ss in the previous Experiments III and IV who watched a model perform the role and who averaged 97 and 60 errors respectively in learning the role.

Table 26.3 presents the percentages of errors in the first five trials and in the last five trials for each part and for the entire role.

TABLE 26.3
Percentages of Errors

Exp.	N	Trials	1	2	3	4	5	6	Mean
I	10	First Five	80	100	100	100	94	94	94
		Last Five	74	100	100	100	82	74	88
		Decrease Parts	6	0	0	0	12	20	6
II		First Five	67	100	100	100	52	60	80
		Last Five	0	24	18	60	0	0	17
		Decrease	67	76	82	40	52	60	63

In Experiment I, the last five trials were the ninty-fifth through one hundredths trials; in Experiment II they were the five trials prior to the attainment of the learning criterion. In Experiment I, errors were usually only slightly less frequent in the last five trials than in the first five, suggesting that learning did not improve very much; however, in Experiment II errors were less frequent for every part in the last five trials than in the first five. The decreases in errors ranged from 0 to 20% with an average of 6% in Experiment I and from 40 to 82% with an average of 63% in Experiment II. In the experiments of the previous section the decreases in errors ranged from 1 to 8% in Experiment I, from 20 to 72% in Experiment II, from 33 to 95% in Experiment III, and from 21 to 93% in Experiment IV, the mean decreases being 1, 48, 58, and 48%, respectively. When the total numbers of errors were plotted for successive blocks of five trials in the previous section's experiments, the difference in numbers of errors between the two variations tended to get larger in successive blocks. The curve of best fit was a horizontal line in Experiment I; it was a broken line in Experiment II, with some steps having downward and others upward slope; and it was a monotonically decreasing broken line in the experiments with the model. The curve of best fit of the present Experiment II's results was closer to the latter curve, that is, to the curve obtained in the previous section's variations with a model.

In terms of Wertheimer's conjecture about the role of the clarity of requiredness of the learning situation, we might expect that the Ss would learn to select the proper book (Part I), to place it on the proper corner of the table (Part 5) and perhaps to place it in the proper position (Part 6), since the initial instructions directed them to take one of the books and to put it on one of the corners of the table, placing it in a certain position. We might also expect that they would have more difficulty in learning the remaining parts because nothing was said about them and they were quite arbitrary and irrelevant to the role. Hence, we would expect the subject to encounter more difficulties in learning Part 2, which entails making an about-face after switching the book from the right to the left hand; Part 3, which requires that he walk around the table in a counterclockwise manner; and Part 4, which stipulates the number of steps in which this should be done. In an earlier repor (Luchins & Luchins, 1966, p. 180), we had predicted that Part 3 would be learned more readily than Parts 2 and 4 since it involved relatively fewer al ternatives. This turned out not to be the case in some variations. Furthe analysis of the role indicated that Part 3 was not as simple or natural as i might seem at first glance, since the instructions did not refer to walking an since the subject was already at the correct corner so that to walk around th table and back to this corner called for a detour. Without getting involved i the relative difficulties of Parts 2, 3, 4 or of Parts 1, 5, 6, we predict that th latter would tend to be learned more readily than the former. The resul support this prediction. Table 26.1 shows that on the average the learnin criterion for Parts 1 through 6 respectively was attained on trial number 1 20, 26, 28, 7, and 10. Thus the rank order of the parts, from the least di ficult to the most difficult, based on the trials on which the learning criteric was attained, was as follows in Experiment II: 5, 6, 1, 2, 3, 4. As predicte the parts that were required by the role were learned more readily than th parts that were not required. Moreover, there was also some support for t prediction in Experiment I where the learning criterion was attained by sor pairs for Parts 1, 5, and 6 but never for the other parts of the role. Typically, there were blocks of five or more successive correct performances of a part interrupted by errors. Such a pattern of responses was shown in Experiment I by five pairs of Ss for Part 5 and by two pairs for Part 6 (with only one pair of subjects learning all three parts). Such intermittent learning was shown in Experiment II by three pairs of Ss for Part 5 and by two pairs for Part 6.

The rank orders of the parts, based on the numbers of errors (Table 26.2), from the least errors to the most, were as follows: Parts 1, 5, 6, 3, 4, 2 in Experiment I; Parts 5, 6, 1, 2, 3, 4 in Experiment II. Again the results were in line with predictions. While the relative ranks were permuted within each subset for the two variations, in each case the subset consisting of Parts 1, 5, and 6 preceded the subset consisting of Parts 2, 3, and 4, that is, the former parts had lower ranks, indicating less difficulty.

Qualitative data were obtained from observations of the Ss and recording of their comments during the experiments, from their written responses to a questionnaire distributed after the experiment and from questions answered after the questionnaire was collected. The questionnaire contained the following: What do you think are the various parts of the role? How did you decide to use or cooperate with your partner? How did you feel when you failed or continued to fail? What were your feelings toward your partner? How did these feelings change when you failed; continued to fail, or succeeded? In the interview the S was asked questions about what hindered her and what helped her in learning the role; the effects of the experimenter's remarks; whether the remarks could have been more helpful or more hindering, and if so, how; what gave her useful ideas; how she acted during the experiment. The qualitative data provide clues to why naive pairs tended to learn better than one person alone and why learning was better in Experiment II than in Experiment I.

The most frequent comments during the sessions were requests for information, almost double the number of all other comments. Next in frequency were descriptions made by one partner to the other of her actions, movements, feelings, etc. Somewhat less frequent was the stating of hypotheses to each other. Leonard Ochs has conjectured the talking to each other may be an important reason for the difference in results between a pair working together and an S working alone.

As in the experiments of the previous section, expressions of frustration, confusion, anger, feelings of stupidity, and a sense of lacking clarity and direction were made by subjects in both variations but less often in Experiment II than in Experiment I. However, the Ss seemed to be more optimistic than those of the previous section's experiments. The fact that a maximum of only 100 trials was now required and not 150 trials as in the other studies may have contributed to their optimism. In Experiment I more Ss said that it was an impossible task than in Experiment II, in which they often remarked that they were in it together and that there must be a way to learn it. The answers to the questionnaire also suggest that the use the members of a pair made of each other's behavior tended to vary with the kind of feedback they were given. (A possible experimental variation of the present and previous section's experiments would be for the experimenter to feedback descriptions of the Ss' actions to them and to ask them to offer hypotheses.) In Experiment I Ss' remarks tended to be vague or to consist of comments about minute details.

In Experiment II, the Ss tended to see each other as trouble shooters, as idea generators who suggested plans of actions to each other which had not yet been tried. In response to the written questions concerning the learning of the role's parts, Ss of Experiment I tended to repeat the instructions given to them in the beginning of the experiment; Ss of Experiment II mentioned more often the unprescribed parts of the role, Parts 2, 3, and 4. Ss of Experiment II generally knew what was expected of them; however, they tended to subdivide the role into more parts or into larger units than the role called for.

In the interview, Ss of Experiment I said that the experimenter's remarks hindered them, that more specific information would have been helpful. Ss in Experiment II said that less feedback or vaguer information would have hinded them and that more specific information or a model to observe would have been most helpful. In response to the question of what was useful, one S in Experiment I said that she stopped trying to figure out what to do. Instead she watched the experimenter's reactions to her partner's actions and thus was able to obtain cues which the experimenter was unaware of giving. Because he tended to avert his eyes or look away when something was done incorrectly, she succeeded in learning the parts of the role suggested by the initial instructions. This pair reached the learning criterion for Parts 1, 5, and 6; they learned more parts than any other pair of Experiment I. Responses to the question about how they had acted during the experiment revealed that Ss differed in the emphasis they had placed on following the instructions. Some followed them literally and attempted to be actresses. They were concerned with facial expressions and gestures and they emphasized the aspects of the instructions which referred to a stage, to actresses, to performing a role, and to the script for the role; this misled them. Another misleading aspect was that Ss usually thought that they were being given all the information that was needed because they had been told initially, I shall tell you if you have performed it correctly. This emphasis on verbal information from the experimenter, might have blinded some Ss to other possible cues; for example, the experimenter's shifting attention and voice inflections. Perhaps it even led to inefficient observation of each other's behavior. A related misleading aspect was that the instructions suggested a three-part role. This might explain some Ss' readiness to quit after discovering Parts 1, 5, and 6; they were surprised that there was more to learn, that they had not been performing the role correctly.

In conclusion, two heads seemed to be better than one for learning this complex role, especially when there was feedback. The members of a pair depended on each other and contributed to attempts to solve the task. With vague information, they validated each other's feelings of despair or hope with specific information, they stimulated each other to vary their points o view and try various actions. Thus the group structure seemed to diffe under different feedback conditions. The characteristic reaction in Experi ment I was, We're in this hopeless situation together. The characteristic reac tion in Experiment II was, We are useful to each other; let's try this or tha Thus the group structure that developed depended in part on the require ments and resources of the situation. The dramatic differences in results be ween Experiments I and II suggest that learning the role may hinge in pa upon receiving some kind of specific information regarding one's perfo mance so that it can be evaluated and modified. Specific feedback which w pro-structural to the subjects' actions, seemed to clarify the nature of the task as well as reduce tension and allay frustrations. The overall rejection in Experiment I of their performance tended to leave subjects confused as to what they had done right or wrong.

There seemed to be direct relationships between how clearly the parts of the role were stated in the instructions and how soon they were attempted and learned and between how clearly information was given to Ss about their performances and how quickly a part was mastered and new parts attempted. The rank orders of difficulty in learning the parts, gauged both by the trials on which the learning criterion was attained and by the number of errors, were consistent with the expectation that the parts which were required by the description of the role would be easier to learn than those that were not stipulated or relevant. Finally, it is important for social psychologists to investige the learning of the unprescribed parts of various social roles because the informal components of a social role are sometimes more important than the formal and prescribed parts for a person's success in a position. Moreover, parts of social roles may be covert and not explicitly stated. One task is to discover ways of making the covert requirements integral parts of a role's overt structure; still another task is to discover ways of sensitizing individuals to the covert demands of social roles.

Other Experiments on Role Learning

In a discussion of the prewar studies, Wertheimer once asked, What happens after a time duration; what changes occur in the role; in what direction are the changes? Do the subjects forget the arbitrary unnecessary parts; do they add new features; what do the new features or changes mean in terms of the act's structure and in terms of the social situation in which the role is enacted? What can be done in the learning period so that they change or do not change the role to make it better and more sensible? What can be done to the subjects before the experiment to increase the likelihood that there will be changes in a sensible and in a senseless direction? Soon after the experiment we retested children of the prewar studies who had learned the ritualized role. The results indicated that the pairs who learned the role varied less than those who learned it alone; the latter tended to leave out more of the arbitrary parts of the role. Wertheimer asked, How valid are these results and what are the crucial factors that produce these results? This still has to be studied. Wertheimer conjectured that the degree of naturalness of the part of the role determines what changes occur in it. In view of this, the arbitrary parts of the role should be forgotten quicker than the parts that are more natural and required for the role. Therefore, would the pattern of foot and hand movements in an arbitrary role change in time differently than in a sensible part? This too needs to be studied.

Wertheimer proposed that we create roles that have more intrinsic structures, where one step leads to another because of an underlying principle (cf. Ellis, 1938, p. 79). As long as the subject is not clear about the principle that governs the series of actions he may repeat blindly but when he learns the principle of a role he may vary the parts in a more sensible way. He gave as an example the proof of a theorem in which a person who knows the structure may make changes which do not spoil the structure, whereas someone who does not know or understand the structure repeats everything slavishly; if he leaves out things he does it stupidly and arbitrarily (cf. Wertheimer's distinction between good and bad errors in Luchins & Luchins, 1970c). The discussion led to several studies in which concepts of mathematics and physics were taught. One experiment adapted Wertheimer's demonstrations of a tuning fork (Luchins & Luchins, 1970b). The subjects were told to watch the experimenter who then put the tines of a fork over a tumbler that was half-filled with water. The experimenter carefully pressed the tines to start them vibrating. When the sound was no longer audible, he removed the fork from the top of the glass and put his hand on the table so that the fork's stem touched the tabletop. The subject was told to listen; he heard a musical sound. He was then told, Now you do it. After the subject learned to make the sound by repeating everything the experimenter had done, he was given an explanation for the occurrence of the sound. To help ensure his understanding, he was also asked to read a passage from a physics textbook which explained and illustrated the principle. After this he was again told to make the sound. Many subjects still repeated the ritual they had learned even though they now knew that the glass of water was not necessary, that the sound had occurred because the tabletop had served as a sounding board when the fork's stem was pressed on the table. We turn now to variations of this experiment.

Learning a Role Involving a Principle

The tuning fork experiments were suggested by an informal demonstration that Wertheimer had made while he and some students were seated in the school's cafeteria. He had taken a glass that was full of water, emptied half of it and placed it in front of him on the table. He then picked up a fork, poised it over the glass and squeezed its tines, producing a musical sound. When no one could hear the sound any longer, he pointed to the glass with his left forefinger while he put on the table his right hand that held the fork. Suddenly everyone heard the sound again. He told the students, Now you do it but they were unable to duplicate the demonstration, that is, they failed to produce the second sound. When Wertheimer asked one of the students why he could not do it, he replied that he was not able to get the sound to come out of the glass. Wertheimer laughed, picked up the fork, and pressed its tines. When the sound could no longer be heard, he pressed the fork's stem on the table and the sound was now heard again. He pointed out that the sound had been heard the second time because the fork's stem was placed in contact with the table, which served as a sounding board. The sound had never come out of the glass; the glass, the water, the poising of the tines over the water, and the pointing to the glass were all hocus pocus intended to confuse the students. This demonstration and variations of it have been repeatedly used in ASL's classes and have been the basis of several classroom projects with different students doing different variations. Among the factors varied were the following: the ages of the subjects (from four-year-old children to adults); the instructions; the number and kind of irrelevant steps, that is, steps irrelevant to producing the second sound; the stress on the glass or on the contact with the table; the number of times the demonstration was repeated; the concern with exact reproduction of all the steps in the demonstration or with only those needed for producing the second sound; the number of trials and the number of days on which they were held; the nature of the information given concerning the function of a sounding board and whether the information was given before or after the subject attempted the demonstration. We report here on some experiments which were recently conducted with the assistance of students in ASL's social psychology class: Michael Arcuri, Steven L. Benson, Anne deRamus Brown, Norman Goldman, Marita McAteer, and Robert W. Meshanic. All the experiments were individually administered, with S and the experimenter (E) seated on opposite sides of a table or a desk. On the table or the desk were displayed a glass or tumbler half-filled with water and a fork, both of which were near E at the beginning of the session. A silver-plated dinner fork was used in most experiments but in actual tuning fork was used in one variation. In Experiments I through III the role was demonstrated just once by E and then S was asked to do it; a correct performance required only that he squeeze the work's tines to produce the sound and touch the fork's handle to the top of the table or desk in order to magnify or reproduce the sound. In the remaining experiments the role was demonstrated by E whenever S made an error; a correct performance required that S duplicate the entire demonstrated role, that is, that he perform all the parts of the role and do them in the proper sequence.

Experiment I. This experiment was administered to children, five boys and five girls, aged 5 to 11 years, from kindergarten to fifth grade. It was also administered to 20 college undergraduate students. Half of them had had a physics course either in college or in high school and are said to constitute Group P and the remaining college Ss are referred to as Group NP. Although the concern was with the production and intensification of the sound, the initial instructions were deliberately made vague so that they might be interpreted to refer either to this task or to the duplication of the entire role that had been performed by E. The initial instructions were as follows, Your task is to learn to do what I am going to show you; watch me. E then performed the following parts of the role:

1. E picked up the fork with his right hand so that approximately one-quarter to one-half inch of the handle protruded upward from his hands. He gripped the handle with four fingers.

2. Placing both hands and the fork approximately one or two inches over the glass, with the fork's tines pointing downward into the glass, E made two or three adjusting movements over the glass as if trying to achieve the correct position of the fork in relation to the glass and water.

3. With the fork still pointing downward into the glass, E squeezed the fork's tines with the fingers of his left hand so as to produce audible vibrations.

4. E moved the fork away from the glass and waited until the vibrations were almost completely inaudible.

5. E then pointed the forefinger of his left hand at the glass.

6. While performing Part 5, E simultaneously placed his right hand down on the table top so that the protruding end of the fork handle made firm contact with the tabletop.

As the sound of the vibrations again became audible or became intensified, E, still pointing to the glass, said to S, Hear it; now you do it. A maximum of 30 trials were allowed during which E did not give the demonstration again. The trials were terminated when S gave a correct performance of the task which required that he do at least the following: squeeze the fork's tines, producing a sound, and then touch the fork's handle to the tabletop. Thus the task involved Parts 3 and 6. Although the trials were terminated if the task was performed correctly, regardless of whether or not the other parts were performed, we were interested in which parts were done and in whether the role, which required all six parts, was performed.

Table 26.4 summarizes the quantitative results for the 10 children and for the 20 college subjects. Table 26.5 fractionizes the results for the college subjects according to whether or not they ever had taken a physics course either in high school or in college. For purposes of analysis of the results, S was assigned a score of 30 if he never performed a part correctly. An error was considered to occur whenever a part was omitted or was performed incorrectly or out of sequence. For example, a child performed Parts 1, 3, 4, 6, in that order on Trial 1; since the task was performed, the trials were terminated. The child was said to have done these parts and the task correctly on Trial 1 without errors. She was considered to be incorrect on Parts 2 and 5 and assigned a score of 30 for each of these; this score was used as the number of errors for Part 2 and for Part 5 and as the number of the first correct trial for these parts. The errors for the task were the sum of the errors in Parts 3 and 6 and the errors for the role were the sum of the errors in all six parts.

TABLE 26.4
Results in Experiment I for Children and College Students*

			1	2	3	4	5	Task	
									PARTS
Children	10	% Ss correct at least once	100	90	100	100	90	100	100	8⬤
		% Ss correct on Trial 1	100	90	100	100	90	60	60	5⬤
Trials: Range	1-15	First correct trials: Range	1	1	1	1	1	1-15	1-15	1-1⬤
Mean	3.8	Mean for correct Ss	1	1	1	1	1	3.8	3.8	3.⬤
		Mean for all Ss	1	3.9	1	1	3.9	3.8	3.8	6.⬤
		% Ss incorrect at least once	10	30	0	5	20	40	40	5⬤
		No. of errors: Range	0-4	0-30	0	0-7	0-30	0-14	0-14	0-6⬤
		Mean for incorrect Ss	4	14.0	0	7.0	17.0	7.0	7.0	21.⬤
		Mean for all Ss	0.4	4.2	0	0.4	3.4	2.8	2.8	10.⬤
College	20	% Ss correct at least once	100	90	100	90	100	40	35	2⬤
		% Ss correct on Trial 1	65	65	100	25	100	10	10	
Trials: Range	1-30	First correct trials: Range	1-24	1-18	1	1-26	1	1-25	1-25	1-⬤
Mean	22.8	Mean for correct Ss	3.7	4.0	1	9.5	1	9.3	8.0	6⬤
		Mean for all Ss	3.7	6.6	1	11.5	1	21.7	22.3	25⬤
		% Ss incorrect at least once	80	90	20	85	0	90	90	⬤
		No. of errors: Range	0-28	0-30	0-4	0-30	0	0-30	0-36	0-1⬤
		Mean for incorrect Ss	12.3	15.8	1.8	16.9	0	24.3	24.9	67⬤
		Mean for all Ss	9.9	14.3	0.4	14.4	0	21.9	22.3	6⬤

*The maximum number of trials was 30; a score of 30 was assigned to S for a part if he never performed the part correctly; the task involved Parts 3 and 6; the role involved all six parts.

A striking feature of the results was that children performed much bett⬤

than the college students; this was the case whether or not the latter had studied physics. Does this result support Wertheimer's conjectures about how naive individuals learn (cf. Luchins & Luchins, 1970)? Whatever the reasons might be, relatively more of the children than of the college students correctly performed the task; they required fewer trials and made fewer errors. Table 26.4 shows that 100 percent of the children but only 35 percent of the college students performed the task correctly. For the children the number of trials ranged from 1 to 15 and averaged less than 4. For the college students who performed the task correctly the number of trials ranged from 1 to 25 and averaged 8; for all the college students the trials ranged from 1 to 30 and averaged over 22. Moreover, 60% of the children (three boys and three girls) performed the task correctly on the first trial but this was the case for only 10% of the college students (two students, one of them had taken a physics course). Furthermore, 80% of the children (four boys and four girls) performed the entire role; they took from 1 to 6 trials and averaged about 2 tri-

TABLE 26.5
Results in Experiment 1 for College Students with or without Physics Course

	#		1	2	3	4	5	6	Task	Role
						PARTS OF ROLE				
College S	10	% Ss correct at least once	100	100	100	90	100	30	30	30
physics,		% Ss correct on Trial 1	60	50	100	10	100	10	10	10
Group P		First correct trial: Range	1-24	1-18	1	1-26	1	1-19	1-19	1-19
		Mean for correct Ss	5.6	6.4	1	13.0	1	8.3	8.3	8.3
Trials: Range 1-30		Mean for all Ss	5.6	6.4	1	14.7	1	23.5	23.5	23.5
		% Ss incorrect at least once	80	90	0	90	0	90	90	90
Mean	24.5	No. of errors: Range	0-28	0-29	0	0-30	0	0-30	0-30	0-101
		Mean for incorrect Ss	14.4	16.7	0	19.1	0	25.8	25.8	74.4
		Mean for all Ss	11.5	15.0	0	17.2	0	23.2	23.2	66.9
College,	10	% Ss correct at least once	100	80	100	90	100	50	40	10
no physics		% Ss correct on Trial 1	70	80	100	40	100	10	10	10
Group NP		First correct trial: Range	1-4	1	1	1-19	1	1-25	1-25	1
		Mean for correct Ss	1.8	1	1	5.9	1	9.8	7.8	1
Trials: Range 1-30		Mean for all Ss	1.8	6.8	1	8.3	1	19.9	21.1	27.1
		% Ss incorrect at least once	80	90	10	80	40	90	90	90
Mean	21.1	No. of errors: Range	0-20	0-30	0-7	0-25	0-4	0-30	0-36	0-98
		Mean for incorrect Ss	10.3	15.0	7.0	12.8	1.8	22.9	23.7	61.3
		Mean for all Ss	8.2	13.5	0.7	11.5	0.7	20.6	21.3	55.2

als. For 50% of the children (three boys and two girls) the entire role was performed correctly on the first trial. In contrast, only 20% of the college students (four students, three of whom had studied physics) performed the entire role correctly and only two of them (one in Group P and one in Group NP) performed it on the first trial. The children made fewer errors than the college students; the children's total number of errors for all the parts of the role ranged from 0 to 60 and averaged about 11 errors per child or about two errors per part. The college students' total number of errors for all the parts of the role ranged from 0 to 101 and averaged about 60 errors per student or about 10 errors per part.

The most difficult part of the role for the college students, as gauged by the fact that it was most often omitted and was usually the last part to be performed correctly, was Part 6, which involved touching the fork's handle to the tabletop. Another relatively difficult part for both the children and the college students was Part 2, which involved the hand movements over the glass and which was not essential to the task. The easiest parts of the role for the college students, performed correctly by everyone of them on Trial 1, were Part 3, squeezing the fork's tines to produce a sound, and Part 5, pointing to the glass (which E had done simultaneously with Part 6 but which most college students did without performing Part 6). Yet Part 5 was relatively difficult for the children; it was omitted entirely by one child who did the task correctly on Trial 1 and it was omitted by another child on the sixth through the ninth trials. The rank orders of the parts of the role, arranged in order of increasing difficulty as based on various means for all Ss in a group were as follows, where parentheses denote a tie in rank.

Children, first correct trial:	(1,3,4),6,(2,5)
Children, number of errors:	(3,4),1,6,5,2
College Ss, first correct trial:	(3,5),1,2,4,6
College Ss, number of errors:	(3,5),1,2,4,6
College Ss, Group P, first correct trial:	(3,5),1,2,4,6
College Ss, Group NP, first correct trial:	(3,5)1,2,4,6
College Ss, Group P, number of errors:	(3,5),1,2,4,6
College Ss, Group NP, number of errors:	(3,5)1,2,4,6
	(3,5),1,4,2,6

Thus for the children, Parts 2 and 5, which were not essential to the role, were less often performed correctly than Part 6, and all these parts were relatively more difficult than Parts 1, 3, and 4. For the college students, consistently Parts 3 and 5 were tied for first place as the least difficult and Part 6 was the most difficult. Except for an interchange in the relative order of Parts 2 and 4 in the last listing, the rank order was the same for the various groups of college students no matter which criterion was used to gauge relative difficulty for the parts of the role.

Table 26.5 shows that more Ss who had a physics course (Group P) performed the role. However, more of those who had not taken such a course (Group NP) performed the task, and, moreover, they did so on an earlier trial. Furthermore, the numbers of errors tended to be lower for Group NP.

In summary, the children learned faster than the college students; the children's performances showed no sex differences and there were no consistent differences between the college students who had taken a physics course and those who had not. The results seem to be in line with Wertheimer's conjectures that naive individuals would do as well or better than sophisticated individuals.

After the last trial, each subject was asked a series of questions: What make the sound? Where does the sound come from? What did you concentrate or before you started to perform? What did you concentrate on while you wer performing? Those who had performed the task were asked how they ha known what to do; the others were asked why they thought that they ha failed. There were no consistent differences in responses between the chi dren and the college students. While 40% of the children correctly mentioned the table in response to the question of what makes the sound or where the sound comes from, only 20% of the Ss in each college group did so. Answers to these two questions which mentioned the glass or the water were given more frequently by the college Ss, particularly those who had not had a physics course, than by the children. In each group, the most frequent answers to these two questions referred to the fork or vibrations from the fork. Most Ss in each group said that they concentrated on E's fingers before they started to perform. There was a variety of answers to what they concentrated on while performing: their own fingers or hands, trying to make the sound, the fork, the fork touching the table, the glass, the water, etc. When asked how they knew how to perform the task, of the Ss in Group P one said that he thought of a tuning fork, another said that he remembered doing something similar in his physics class, and the third said that he watched what E did. Of the Ss in Group NP, two said that they had watched what E did and two others admitted that they had accidently hit the table with the fork. Seven of the children said that they were successful because they had watched E and the remaining three said that it came about by accident. When asked why they had failed, one S in each college group said that it was because he did not know or did not remember physics and the others attributed it to not having watched E closely enough.

The next question asked each S whether the glass was necessary. Relatively more of the college Ss than the children said that it was. If S said that the glass was necessary, E picked up the fork, squeezed the tines, and pointed to the glass with one hand as he touched the fork to the tabletop with the other hand, thus omitting both Part 2, which involved the adjusting movements over the glass, and Part 4, which involved moving away from the glass. If S still said that the glass was necessary E picked up the fork as before, squeezed the tines, and then touched the fork to the tabletop; thus he completely ignored the glass and omitted Parts 2, 4, and 5. After this question, and then again after the demonstrations, S was asked to perform once more. If S still did not perform the task, he was asked to read a paragraph on the physics of sound (which will be described below) and then again asked to perform. Of the seven college students who had taken a physics course and had previously not performed the task, three were now successful, one after answering no to the question about the glass and the others after watching E's new demonstrations. The remaining four students in Group P did not succeed in performing the task correctly even after reading the paragraph. Of the six college students who had not taken a physics course and who had previously failed to perform the task, two were now successful, one after watching E's new demonstrations and the other after reading the paragraph. Thus there were four Ss in each college group who did not succeed in performing the task even after the various hints were given. In other words, by the end of the experiment 60% of each of Groups P and NP had performed the task.

Experiment 1A. The paragraph on the physics of sound which was used as a hint for some Ss in the previous experiment was in this experiment shown to each of 20 college Ss before any demonstration was given by E. Half of the Ss had taken a course in physics either in high school or in college and are said to constitute Group P. The paragraph, which was mimeographed, with the underlining as shown, read as follows:

Sound is our internal representation of a physical phenomenon consisting of vibratory waves transmitted through solid, liquid, or gaseous materials. For a given speed and strength of vibration, the loudness of the sound we hear will often depend upon the size of the object vibrating. *For example, if a small vibrating object is placed in contact with a large object so that the large object vibrates also, the sound produced will be larger than that produced by the small body alone.* This is the principle of the sounding-board of a musical instrument; *thus the small strings of a violin produce a large sound because they set the wood of the instrument's body vibrating.*

After the paragraph was read by S, the procedure was the same as in Experiment 1. E demonstrated the role and allowed a maximum of 30 trials for S to perform the task. The results, which are summarized in Table 26.6, show that those who had a physics course performed better than the other Ss. The mean number of trials was 17 for Group P compared to 25 for Group NP. Five of those in Group P performed the task and they averaged about five trials while three of those in Group NP performed it and they averaged about 12 trials. The mean number of errors was 47 for the Ss in Group P but 59 for the others. Moreover, comparison of Tables 26.5 and 26.6 reveals that the present Group P did better than the corresponding group in Experiment 1 whereas this was not the case for Group NP, for example, the present Group P averaged about 7 trials less and about 20 errors less for the role than the previous Group P, whereas the present Group NP averaged about 3 trials more and about four errors more for the role than the previous Group NP. It seems that reading the paragraph on the physics of sound before the demonstration helped those Ss who had a physics course but not the other Ss, perhaps be-

TABLE 26.6
Results in Experiment 1A for College Students with or without Physics Course

	#		PARTS OF ROLE 1	2	3	4	5	6
College Ss,	10	% Ss correct at least once	100	90	100	90	100	50
physics,		% Ss correct on Trial 1	50	90	100	60	100	30
Group P		First correct trial: Range	1-7	1	1	1-23	1	1-15
1		Mean for correct Ss	3.5	1	1	4.6	1	4.6
Trials: Range 1-30		Mean for all Ss	3.5	3.9	1	7.1	1	17.3
Mean	17.3	% Ss incorrect at least once	60	80	0	0-30	40	80
		No. of errors: Range	·0-27	0-28	0	20.0	0-5	0-30
		Mean for incorrect Ss	14.1	11.1	0	12.0	2.3	21.0
		Mean for all Ss	8.5	8.9	0		0.9	16.8
College Ss,	10	% Ss correct at least once	100	80	100	100	100	
no physics		% Ss correct on Trial 1	70	70	100	50	100	
Group NP		First correct trial: Range	1-14	1-17	1	1-26	1	
		Mean for correct Ss	3.3	3.0	1	8.5	1	
Trials: Range 1-30		Mean for all Ss	3.3	8.4	1	8.5	1	
Mean	24.8	% Ss incorrect at least once	100	80	0	100	10	
		No. of errors: Range	1-13	0-30	0	1-29	0-2	
		Mean for incorrect Ss	7.5	16.8	0	13.5	2	
		Mean for all Ss	7.5	13.4	0	13.5	0.2	

cause the latter either could not understand or could not apply the paragraph. Neither group performed as well as did the children in Experiment 1.

In response to the questions after the trials, which were the same as in Experiment 1, some Ss referred to the paragraph when they were asked what they had concentrated on before or while performing and some said that they looked for a scientific principle. Of the five Ss in Group P who had performed the role, two attributed their success to applying the paragraph; the other successful Ss in this group and the three successful Ss in Group NP said that they learned from watching E. The question about whether the glass was necessary was answered negatively by 40% of Group P and by 14% of Group NP. After E's new demonstrations two more Ss in each group performed successfully. Thus by the end of the experiment, 80% of those who had studied physics and 60% of the other Ss performed the task, compared to 60% of each group in Experiment 1. The rank orders of the parts of the role, arranged from the least to the most difficult as gauged by various criteria, were as follows for all the Ss in a group:

Group P, first correct trial:	(3,5),1,2,4,6
Group NP, first correct trial:	(3,5),1,2,4,6
Group P, number of errors:	3,5,1,2,4,6

The rank orders were the same as those found in Experiment 1, except that Parts 3 and 5 now were not tied for rank when the number of errors was the criterion.

Experiment 1B. This variation was also administered to 20 college Ss, half of whom had taken a physics course. The procedure was the same as Experiment 1 except that if S performed the task or the role, he was immediately given the paragraph on sound to read and then told to perform it again. It was found that Ss tended to leave out more of the parts that were irrelevant to the task of producing the second sound after reading the paragraph. For the remaining Ss the procedure was as in Experiment 1. By the end of the experiment, 60% of each of Group P and Group NP had performed the task. The same trends were found in Experiment 1.

Experiments 2, 2A, and 2B. The procedure in these experiments was the same as in Experiments 1, 1A, and 1B respectively. However, in order to lessen the possibility that the performance of the task resulted from accidental touching of the fork to the table, a new learning criterion was adopted (but was not revealed to the Ss): the task had to be performed correctly on five successive trials. The trials were terminated after the learning criterion was attained or after the maximum of 30 trials, whichever came sooner. The Ss were 60 college students, about half of whom were physics majors. We were interested in whether there would be more striking differences between their results and those of non-physics majors than there had been in the previous experiments between the students who had taken or had not taken a physics course. In each experiment, the physics majors are said to constitute Group P and the non-physics majors, regardless of whether or not they ever had a course in physics, are said to constitute Group NP.

There were one or two Ss in each experiment who quit even though they had not attained the learning criterion. In some of these cases, the S had performed the task correctly once (which would have sufficed in the previous experiments) or even more times but not on five successive trials. In a few cases, however, S quit when he had never performed the task correctly; for purposes of analysis of results such an S was given a score of 30 for each part. Although E attributed the refusal to continue to embarrassment or boredom, one wonders whether E (a male student) might have manifested impatience as the trials continued. The E in the previous experiments was a female student who encountered no cases of Ss quiting before the experiment was supposed to terminate.

TABLE 26.7
Results in Experiments 2, 2A, and 2B

	EXP. 2		EXP. 2A		EXP. 2B	
	Group P	Group NP	Group P	Group NP	Group P	Group NP
Number of Ss	8	12	10	10	9	11
Range of trials	5-30	5-30	5-30	5-30	5-30	5-30
Mean number of trials	14.4	13.3	13.9	13.7	18.1	16.5
% performed task at least once	63	75	90	80	67	73
% performed task on Trial 1	63	67	40	40	22	40
% learned task	63	67	80	80	67	64
% performed role	11	0	20	10	22	18
First correct trial for task: Range	1	1-10	1-26	1-17	1-23	1-13
Mean for correct Ss	1	2.3	6	5.6	8.0	4.9
Mean for all Ss	11.8	10.8	5.4	4.5	13.8	12.7
% Ss incorrect at least once	100	100	80	100	89	100
Number of errors	0-119	0-163	0-147	0-120	0-193	1-151
Mean for incorrect Ss	58.4	64.5	67.6	65.3	63.8	61.8
Mean for all Ss	58.4	64.5	54.1	52.2	56.7	61.8

In comparison with the college Ss of the previous experiments, there were fewer trials on the average, more subjects who performed the task, and more who did it on Trial 1. (However, the performances were not as good as that shown by the children in Experiment 1.) Performance and learning of the role were as infrequent as that shown by college Ss in the previous experiments and there were relatively more errors. At most one or two Ss in each of Groups P and NP performed the role even once. Most frequently omitted was Part 2, the adjusting hand movements over the glass, which was omitted by 16, 14, and 14 out of the 20 Ss in each of Experiments 2, 2A, and 2B, respectively. Part 6, which was next in frequency of omission, had been most frequently omitted in Experiment 1 and its variations. Possibly differences in the way in which the two Es performed the role might have brought about these results.

Table 26.7 summarizes the results in Experiment 2 and its variations. As in Experiment 1, Variation A, where the paragraph on sound was read prior to any demonstration, yielded the largest percentage of Ss who performed the task correctly at least once: 85% compared to 60 and 70% in Experiments 2 and 2B, respectively. Moreover, more Ss in Experiment 2A learned the task, that is, performed it on five consecutive trials: 80% compared to about 65% in each of Experiments 2 and 2B.

There was a slight tendency for the physics majors to do slightly better than the non-physics majors, for example, 5 of the 27 physics majors performed the role compared to 3 of the 30 non-physics majors. But there were no consistent differences between the two groups. Moreover, the non-physics majors who had taken a physics course did not do much better than those who had not taken such a course; for example, 5, 4, and 8 non-physics majors in Experiments 2, 2A, and 2B, respectively, had taken at least one physics course and 80, 75, and 63% of them learned the task compared to 55, 83, and 67% of the remaining non-physics majors. Moreover, there were no consistent sex differences although on the whole more of the males than the females learned the task; the task was learned by 64% of the 14 male Ss and 67% of the 6 female Ss in Experiment 2, by 86% of the 14 males and 67% of the 6 females in Experiment 2A, and by 73% of the 15 males and 40% of the 5 females in Experiment 2B.

In response to the questions, fewer Ss in Variation A than in the other experiments said that the glass was necessary: 15% compared to 40 and 30% in Experiments 2 and 2B respectively. Moreover, after all Ss had read the paragraph on sound and they were asked to perform again, more Ss in Variation A omitted the irrelevant parts of the role; 55% compared to 35% in each of Experiments 2 and 2B. It seemed that when Ss were given relevant information at the onset they made some attempts to analyze their performance in terms of the information. However, after they had seen the demonstration and attempted the performance, the presentation of relevant information was not as likely to influence them.

Other Studies. In another social psychology class every student of a class of 26 conducted Experiment I with a child and an adult. The Ss were tested once a week for ten successive weeks in order to see whether "you remembered how to do it." After this the principle of the sounding board was explained to them, with the glass of water and the fork used as an example. They were then again tested "to see if you remembered how to do it." Most of the subjects did it exactly as before, because it was the role they had learned even though they now knew what produced the second sound. These results are different from a prewar study by ASL in which college students who learned the principle refused to use the glass of water, saying that it was irrelevant or unnecessary for producing the second sound. Even now some subjects had refused to use the glass. What are the attitudes and assumptions that differentiate between those who do and do not use the glass after they learn about the physics of the sound? Moreover, what kind of social atmospheres would lead to one or the other kind of behavior? Such research might be of value in understanding why people persist in performing rituals even though they know the crucial factors that produce the effects.

Influences of Goals and Methods

Some social roles are complexes of methods as well as goals, that is, they are certain means to achieve a particular goal. The question may be asked, What happens when some people focus on the goal and others focus on the means to achieve it when they are working together? The Einstellung experiments suggest ways of dealing with this question. What would happen if set-inducing problems were used in which the volume to be obtained was the same in every problem? Would subjects develop a set for a goal and how would this goal set compare with the effect of the usual method set? To answer such questions we conducted four experimental variations in which the usual set-inducing problems were replaced by nine new problems: (A) Each problem was solved by the same method and in each problem the same amount of water had to be obtained, (B) each problem was solved by the same method but a different amount of water had to be measured, (C) the method was different but the amount of water to be measured was the same in each problem, (D) the method to be used as well as the amount of water to be obtained was different in each problem. After these problems, each group received a critical problem which was solvable by both the $B-A-2C$ and the $A+C$ methods; for the two groups which had received problems with a fixed goal of 7 quarts the goal was also 7 quarts in this critical problem. After the critical problem, all groups received the same series of incomplete problems, incomplete in the sense that it was up to the subject to stipulate the volume to be obtained and then to solve the problem. The incomplete problems were: 30, 67, 15, get. . .quarts; 32, 83, 22, get. . .quarts; 22, 59, 15, get. . .quarts; 20, 60, 13 get. . .quarts. In the first three problems the $B-A-2C$ procedure leads to 7 quarts while in the fourth problem this method does not lead to 7 quarts but to 14 quarts. The first three problems can be called criticals in so far as they are compatible with both the fixed goal and fixed method while the fourth problem may be described as a kind of extinction problem since it is not simultaneously compatible with both the fixed method and the fixed goal (Luchins & Luchins, 1959, Chap. 17). In line with Wertheimer's suggestions about social influences, two subjects were told that we would give them problems to solve. Unknown to them, they were given different series of problems to solve; one subject was given the nine problems in which the method was always the same and the other subject was given nine problems in which the goal was always different. After this, a critical incomplete problem was given in order to see whether the subject had become set for a method or a goal. Then they were told that they would work together on the same problems and they were given the incomplete problems. More subjects who were goal-set agreed to completions of the problem by the method proposed by the subject who was method-set, than the other way around, that is, they more often changed their goal-set in order to make the problem compatible with the proposed method. We varied the experiment using confederates and previous instructions in order to obtain agreement to change the method or to change the goal. Generally speaking, it was easier to get subjects to adhere to a method than to a goal.

How general are these results and what are the factors that extremize them? These results are related to one of Wertheimer's conjectures of *crippled doing*, being narrowed down by habits, goals, or motives so that one is blind to the structure of the situation and its relationship to the social field in which it takes place. Suppose a certain quantity of water was required and the method would yield less than was needed? Would the subject persist in using the $B-A-2C$ method if it did not yield the required amount of water and would the goal-set subject agree with him? These questions have been related by some of our students to the social problem of conflict over means and ends.

27
Experimental Outgrowths: Imitation

ASL introduced the topics of social influence in one of his WPA Adult Education classes by asking what is meant by the word imitation. After the students wrote their answers, they were asked for illustrations of imitation and explanations of how and why people imitate. Their answers were tallied by a student and were presented to the class for discussion. The following is an example of a survey in a class of 27 students. To the question, What is meant by the word *imitation,* the following answers were given: A false version of the original; something not real; not as good as the real thing; unreal; pretense; an act of duplicity; ability to do what others do; doing what is done by a living being, man or anim'al; to copy movements or acts of others; to capture characteristics of another's behavior; to mimic; to pantomime; to jest; to ridicule; to emulate; to copy; or to repeat others' ideas, standards or actions; to do something someone else does; to duplicate; to pattern one's behavior after another; to reenact others' behavior; to adopt a trait of someone; to talk like someone; to pretend; to impersonate; to replicate.

They gave various illustrations of imitation, sometimes repeating what they had written before. Some gave examples of children who imitate their parents' or other adults' actions, pick up their verbal expression, and use their mannerism. Some described children as well as adults who imitate someone's actions, body movement, speech, table manners, manner of dress, and manner of walking. Examples of learning by imitation were learning to knit, to dance, to act, to make love after seeing it in the movies. Other examples they gave of imitation were to copy a model, to copy a fad or the latest fashions, to use actions of one's teacher or boss, to pretend that one is some other person. To the questions of why and when people imitate, they gave various answers. A person imitates because he thinks it may be of benefit to him, because he wants to be admired, to be accepted, to get ahead, and because he thinks that imitating certain behavior may win others' admiration, acceptance, or approval. A person may imitate when he wants to compliment or humor the person who is being imitated, to share in his power or status, or to make fun of the imitated person. He may imitate to tell a story or to make a point. He may imitate an action which he does not understand, which he is not able to do by himself without imitation, or which is not natural to him. He may imitate when he feels insecure or uncomfortable. Over two-thirds of the class wrote that little children imitate more often than adults and that people who are insecure in their position or place in society or in a group do it more often than those who are secure. Some wrote that nearly everybody imitates at times because of the need to conform to conventions. They listed a variety of places where acts of imitation occur: school, home, place of work, and social situations. No mention was made about imitation when one repeats a demonstration given in a teaching-learning situation. When this was called to their attention they said that you do not learn knowledge by imitation. Although you may imitate the teacher's expression and tone of voice, you do not imitate your teacher's lesson. A student gave this example with which the class agreed; when a teacher says $2+2=4$ and you thereafter say $2+2=4$, you are not imitating her if you understand what it means. When ASL pointed out that most of the comments and examples were of a negative nature, they not only agreed but went on to say that when people imitate natural things what they produce is not as good as the real thing, for example, imitation pearls, imitation leather. But, people are always doing it in the economic field; it is an extension of imitating traits and characteristics of people.

The class discussion led to several projects which the students found instructive and which proved of value as bases of discussions of imitation. In one project, the students kept a record for several days of all instances of imitation which they noticed. They kept diaries in which they recorded such entries immediately after witnessing or engaging in an act of imitation or three times daily. The diaries were then analyzed to find out who imitated, who or what was imitated and why, where and when the acts took place. They were alerted to record the consequence of the act for the person and others; and whether everything was imitated or only aspects of what the other person did, and why. Each of the 27 students handed in a diary with at least ten entries. A group of students volunteered to make a content analysis of the diaries and to bring their results to class for discussion. Based on the contents of the diaries, they tallied items under the heading of who did the imitating, who was imitated, why one imitated, what gestures he imitated, what was the effect of the imitation on the person who did it, on the person who was being imitated, on other people in the situation, where was it done, what time of day it was done, etc. Many of the examples described children who copied older children, adults', animal sounds, or sounds of nature and man-made artifacts such as guns and locomotives. Frequently the examples involved children or naive adults who repeated or tried to repeat what was done by older children or adults whom they admired or feared, for example, copying mannerisms and expressions of teachers, parents, policemen, firemen, actresses, actors, or bigger boys and girls. Sometimes their behavior seemed ludicrous or brought scoldings and punishment because the actions they repeated were peripheral, out of context, or violated social norms. Although there were some cases in which parents or teachers encouraged imitation, there were relatively few cases in which learning was advanced by imitation. In short, imitation was more often something bad, stupid, or funny. Sometimes just peripheral or superficial aspects of another person's behavior were imitated with and without knowledge that the behavior was not the same.

In another class where students were told to keep records of imitative acts performed by others or by themselves, few reports were handed in. But after ASL presented the theory that life was a theater in which people played a variety of roles and that a person was a role player, the students became interested in keeping journals. The students' reports were collated by a volunteer and presented for class discussion. The survey suggested that everybody imitated or played roles. Children spent more time than adults in playing roles in which they imitated or reenacted what someone else or an animal did. Some of the role playing was due to the fact that parents and teachers asked for and encouraged it as part of the process of education. Generally speaking, little children blindly imitated or did so with less understanding and more frequently than adults. Adults seemed to have their own reasons for imitating or playing a role. Adults as well as children tended to imitate people whom they admired, who seemed to be leading an exciting life or doing things of value or interest. The imitation was usually not a mere replication of what the other person did; there were elaborations and changes in the acting; parts imitated seemed to fit in with the need to understand things. Some acts became caricatures; some were stark examples of the values or social norms of their adult world. Where imitation or copying was demanded there was often difficulty in complying with the demand. The repetition of the act sometimes led to boredom; they tired of it, were disappointed, or surprised by the outcomes. Sometimes they seemed to know that they were pretending or imitating and sometimes they were not at all aware of it until it was called to their attention. Sometimes they were aware that they were pretending but they were not aware that they were not really doing the act the way it originally was done. The report led to several projects aimed at answering these questions: Why do people imitate, what personality factors and social factors bring it about? Just what is repeated? What personality and social factors compel one to repeat automatically and rob one of the freedom to act intelligently? What factors lead to intelligent repetition? What are the consequences of imitating by rote and imitating by understanding?

On the bases of interviews of some people whose behavior they had recorded and upon reflection of their own imitative behavior, the students made a survey of the reasons for imitation. Their list was as follows: to get attention or recognition; to get control or have power over people or things; to be a somebody; because of love or identification with someone; because of curiosity to see what it feels like to do what someone else does or to be like that person; it caught their fancy; it stood out like something unusual, exciting, great; it implied a promise of reward; a desire to know or be like that person; because they were told by parent, teacher, other children, and·mass media to do it; to humor someone along; to help them; to be of use; to be a participant in that person's world. When ASL asked them to rank what was most often the reason, they concluded that it was fitting into a group, learning what was required to get along and to obtain approval of others. When ASL asked Wertheimer whether this does not prove that Miller and Dollard were correct, he said that it is advisable to focus on the specific attitudes, assumptions, and social atmospheres that bring about imitation instead of accepting their explanation.

The school and home most often were the places where they were encouraged to imitate, for example, to take after someone, to play house, fireman, farmer, policeman, storekeeper, to act out the roles of religious and historical characters. Certain individuals were pointed out to them as paragons after whom they should mold their morals, manners, speech, expressions, behavior, dress, and grooming; others as examples of what not to be like. It is surprising that no one listed the lessons given by their teachers and the examples in the text books or the role requirements of their jobs as demanding imitative behavior.

Sometimes they imitated for a known purpose, at other times they did it unknowingly—the cases of unconscious imitation seemed to be brought about by the structure of the situation in which they had learned to rely on others. They more often wanted to achieve the goal of the other person's behavior and not merely to repeat his behavior. Sometimes they pretended to be interested in a certain role or in repeating what others did because they did not want to appear to be different, to be naive, asociable, or to spoil the fun, to be uncooperative, to hurt someone's feelings. They sometimes imitated even though they thought it was stupid and foolish but felt that it was necessary to achieve their goals. A few students said that they were so concerned about not being out of step that they readily learned to do what was required in the situation even though they did not really want to do it. This was particularly so of behavior in dating, in school, and in office politics. This raised the questions of why some people have a greater need to imitate, to reflect in their behavior the behavior of people around them, and why other people have little of this need and act their own way, feeling free to behave as they wish. Is it a temperamental difference, or is it merely that some people have learned to imitate more generally than others? Wertheimer conjectured that one possible reason for some of these cases of imitation is that the subject has an empty life.

These examples of imitation and role playing contained cases which showed that even little children often know the difference between pretending to be someone and really being someone. A little boy whose family had just moved to a new house played carpenter and would not let his mother call him by his name. He called her lady and asked her to tell him what needed to be repaired. About an hour later he asked her, Lady where is your bathroom? She pointed it out to him. He thanked her and walked in. A few seconds later he called, Lady, please pick me up, the toilet is too high. A little girl whose mother had gone shopping, was busy playing mother and bossing her little brothers and sisters with more vigor than her mother. When her mother returned she talked to her mother as one woman to another. She became furious when her mother called her by her name. Suddenly the doorbell rang and she said, Mother, someone is at the door for you. There were many examples where children were pretending to play a role and seemed to be lost in the role but at a point in their playing they were aware of an area that was a part of the role as played by the adults and not by them. This led to a study in which individuals from the age of 2 to 50 were questioned to find out where the differences lie between a real mother and a child playing the role of mother, a real general and a private playing the role of general, a real teacher and a child playing the role of teacher, a real fireman and a boy playing the role of fireman, a horse and a child playing the role of a horse, an actress and actor making love and two little children reenacting the scene.

The following answers were given when subjects were asked, What is the difference between a mother and a girl playing the role of mother? The child is pretending, making believe or playing, the mother has responsibilities, there are physical differences, the girl is imitating a future role, the mother acts due to instinct, the mother really has a child, the mother had more experience, the child can stop playing the role but the mother can't, the mother is older, the child is younger, the child is imagining, the mother is a mother in both body and mind, they do different things, the mother is not playing, the mother is in the actual role but the child is playing, it's only real in the child's experience, it's the difference between fantasy and reality, the child can't give mother love, the child wouldn't know how to act in various household or social situations, the child's role has missing aspects, the real mother's role is a necessity, mothers provide guidance, mothers are legally sanctioned, mothers provide sustenance, the total family does not exist for the child, the child does not have to worry about paying bills, the child has no husband-wife relations, mothers have more skill and knowledge, the motivation is different, mothers are not aware that they are playing a role, mothers have real love for children but children pretend love, the child can stop playing when she pleases, the child feels it's a better position than it really is, the child admires and wants to be like the mother, the child does what she interprets about the role, there is little difference.

These are the answers given to the question, What is the difference between a horse and a child who is playing that he is a horse? There are physical bigger and stronger, the child is daydreaming, the child is pretending, it's fantasy, it's an escape, firemen are real, there is a real fire and not an imaginary fire for firemen, firemen use real fire engines, firemen put out real fires, the child's fire house and engine are imaginary, firemen save real people and not imaginary people, firemen sleep in the firehouse, firemen have to help people while the child does not, firemen can't stop playing but children can, firemen are not afraid of smoke, firemen have to walk into fires to save women and children, children are not able to be firemen, the child wishes to be a fireman, you need to go to school and get trained to be a fireman, firemen wear uniforms, firemen can open the fire alarm box, firemen can open the hydrants and connect hoses to hydrants, firemen have big ladders, can scale walls, climb ladders, firemen have axes, helmets, firemen stop traffic when they drive by, firemen take tests to get the position, firemen get paid, firemen are city employees, firemen could arrest you for making fires, they can arrest you if you touch the fire alarm box, firemen have fire dogs.

These are the answers given to the question, What is the difference between a horse and a child who is playing that he is a horse? There are physical differences, the boy is pretending, the horse is real, the boy is imitating a horse, they are two different species, the boy wants to be free like a horse, the child can't become a horse, the horse has four legs, their intellect and instincts differ, the horse is an animal, the child can't act like a horse, reality versus fantasy, the child is having a fantasy, the child is imagining, the horse can't stop being a horse, a horse is a horse, the boy needs psychoanalysis, the boy is escaping reality, the horse's role is in accordance with his nature but the child is playing a role, playing for enjoyment, the role is different, the child does not realize the hardships a horse has, the boy is interpreting a horse, it's a game to the child, horses can't play a child, there are facial differences, the child is a horse only in his mind, the child is identifying with a horse, there is no difference.

These answers were given to the question, What is the difference between a general and a · private in the army who is playing the role of a general at a Christmas party? The general earned the rank, the general is older and has ability, the general's authority is genuine, the private has lower rank, it's wishful thinking for the private, they have different uniforms, different places of residence, different social life, different responsibilities and privileges, the private is imitating, the private is insecure and is pretending, the private does not know the work, the private is playing a higher or exaggerated role, it is reality versus fantasy, the private is envious, the private can stop the role, there is no difference, the private lacks ability, the private makes believe, the behavior is different, their thoughts differ, the private holds a grudge against the army, the private is an impostor or a fake, the private does not have the power, their goals differ, the general is more important, the private is not as high in rank, the general is playing a real role, the army's opinion makes the difference, the general's role is permanent, there is a salary difference.

When ASL showed the survey of the various kinds of answers his students had obtained in their interviews, Wertheimer wondered whether the results were due to the way the subjects were questioned. Why weren't they asked other questions to find out what were their conceptions of the nature of the structures of the act; did they understand the consequences of the act in the social field, for example, for the child and mother? When ASL gave him a sample of the protocols he wondered why some subjects had focused on purpose, others on motives, and still others merely described peripheral features of the actors or behavior. What can be done to find out if these details were all that they knew about the role? The survey shows that the children said that the big difference between a girl playing a mother and a real mother lies in physical features. If the girl were as big as an adult would she become a real mother to the children and would a small-sized woman not be a real mother because she was smaller than a girl? When ASL said that the subjects might then use age as the real difference, Wertheimer said that in some places in the U.S.A. eleven-year-old and even younger girls get married and are step-mothers or even mothers of their own children. Why not ask other kinds of questions or present counter examples to the various characteristics given, until the subject will be able to realize what the crucial differences are between the real mother and a girl playing the role? He went on to point out another interesting result; the children seemed to have more information about the job requirements of firemen than of the role of mother. Why? Why did the adults and the children focus on the job requirements of these roles but not of the other roles? He went on to ask why there were numerous statements by the adults that the child pretended, daydreamed, made believe; don't adults do such things? There are mothers who play at being mothers, who pretend that they are mothers, who play the social stereotypes of the role and are blind to the consequences of their actions in the social field, blind to the effect of what it does to them and to others. He again said that we need to study the structure of the roles. A role is not an and-summation of responses or acts; it has a certain place and function in the social field; the role's requirements are related to the structure of the social field. The role may have a certain meaning in the actor's life. Why not study such things? He went on to suggest that situations be contrived to study the roles. Instead of asking questions give them the problems of becoming aware of or distinguishing between playing, pretending, and really doing what is required. How can we make one who does not see the requiredness become aware of it? What factors in the social field blind one to the requiredness and make one act in terms of the stereotype of the role? What does it do to a person if he is drilled to play a certain role blindly and what consequences does it have for the social field?

ASL has presented to his classes the various questions raised by Wertheimer. He has also presented in some of his classes the survey of the answers obtained in the prewar study to the questions on role playing and asked them what they think of the answers. Which are the essential and which are unessential features of the role: Why? What is missing? Why? Such questions have proven of value to stimulate the discussion of role-playing behavior in our undergraduate psychology classes and have led some of the classes to undertake research projects. In 1959 ASL's students in the course on Adolescence undertook as a class project to ask children between the ages of 5 and 7, 12 and 15, college students, and adults the question that had been used by his Adult Education Class. There were 40 subjects in each age group for a total of 160 subjects. The results were collated and tabulated for class discussion.

What is the difference between a general and a private playing the role of a general?

	5-7	12-15	College	Adult
Private is pretending, daydreaming, or not realistic	22	0	26	12
General gives orders, private follows orders	6	4	0	2
Job or rank difference, including authority and responsibility	17	31	18	30
Private admires and wants benefits of general	6	17	22	16
Private is not really a general	11	6	4	4
Experience and training differences	2	19	13	19
Private lacks ability to be a general	2	2	0	2
Physical differences (uniforms, residences, etc.)	11	9	7	2
Don't know, not sure	20	0	0	4
Miscellaneous	3	14	10	9

What is the difference between a horse and a child playing the role of a horse?

	5-7	12-15	College	Adult
Child is pretending, unrealistic; horse is real	23	17	28	22
Boy wants to be a horse	8	9	20	7
Boy is incapable of being a horse	3	6	0	2
Horse is a lower animal, child is human	15	20	15	23
Horse is not capable of anything human because of intelligence; boy has intelligence	0	6	7	8
Child is mentally disturbed	0	4	13	7
Physical difference	45	32	13	22
Miscellaneous	6	6	4	9

What is the difference between a mother and a girl playing the role of a mother?

	5-7	12-15	College	Adult
Girl is pretending, mother is not	20	24	22	26
Mother has a child, girl does not	10	4	5	4
Mother's job is real with duties and responsibilities, child's is not	16	25	30	21
Girl is preparing to be a mother and copies her	0	6	12	15
Girl is unable to be a real mother	4	6	10	4
Physical differences	40	22	8	23
Miscellaneous	10	13	13	17

What is the difference between a fireman and a boy playing the role of a fireman?

	5-7	12-15	College	Adult
Boy is pretending, daydreaming; fireman is real	31	13	24	22
Job and duty difference	22	26	28	25
Equipment difference	17	0	0	0
Training and experience difference	2	9	7	5
Boy wishes to be a fireman	6	9	17	10
Boy unable to be a fireman; fireman is capable	11	8	0	0
Responsibility difference	0	11	9	20
Physical difference	4	11	4	0
Miscellaneous	7	13	21	10

They are presented in the following tabulation in order to stimulate discussion and perhaps lead to research suggested by Wertheimer. Of interest are the differences in the results for the various roles. In order to let the results speak for themselves we refrain from comments. We shall, however, refer to these results in the monograph on perception when Wertheimer's conjectures about appearance and reality will be presented.

During the discussion about the difference in role playing by a child and an adult, Wertheimer pointed out that in peasant societies the audience sometimes gets carried away and rushes on to the stage to save the heroine or to attack the villain in the play. Children too sometimes do such things. He then told a story about a little boy who was playing horses and riders. When it began to rain all the children ran home except one child who was playing as a horse. He began to cry. When a man asked him why he was crying he sobbed that he and his friends were playing horses and riders and that he was a horse. When it began to rain his friends ran away and forgot to take him to the stall. That evening ASL told his class, You are walking down the street during a rain storm and find a little boy crying in the middle of the street. You ask him why he's crying, to which he replies: My friends and I were playing horses and riders. I am a horse. When the rain started my rider ran away and didn't bring me back to the stable. A. What would be your first reaction? Why? B. What would you tell the child? Why? After they answered and their responses were discussed, they planned to give this question to children between the ages of 5-7, 12-15, college students, and adults. A summary of their answers has been used to stimulate discussion of appearance and reality. It is of interest for the reader to group the answers according to ages in terms of current theories and then to question subjects of the different ages to see if the answers are similar.

To part A of the question, these responses were given: the boy should go inside, he is crying because his friends left him, the boy is confused, the boy is not in contact with reality, he isn't concerned with the rain and just wants to play, the boy became frustrated, the child is still in the role of a horse, has an overactive imagination, is very emotionally involved, he's a good actor, the boy really believes the story, he's crazy, he got carried away, he took the game too seriously, the boy lost his playmates, he's playing a game, the boy is insecure, it's a typical child's fantasy world, it's time for him to distinguish what's real, take him home and tell him it's the stable, I'd be amused and laugh, children forget their real roles, pity the child, get him to a safe, dry place, ask where the stable is and take him there, he was more serious about the game than his friends, the boy seems lost, feel sorry for him because he didn't realize the game was over, kids move back and forth readily from the real to the unreal, he's ignoring reality and should stop, if he's lost help him.

The following responses were given to part B of the question: take him to the stable, he's not distinguishing reality, tell him his rider will return, tell him to go to the stable, ride him home, tell his mother, humor him, get him to stop crying and take him to a dry place, ask for an explanation, tell him horses can find shelter, take him to the stable, take him home and tell him it's the stable, tell him to go home, tell him the rider had a good reason for leaving, comfort him, tell him he's not a horse and the game's over, assume he's lost, take him home, I'd ride him home, help make him become aware of himself again, humor him because he's a child (but wouldn't humor adults), tell him he should have gone with his friends, his friends are boys so he should be one too so he'll have playmates, tell him to go home so he won't catch cold, don't think it would do any good to tell him to stop, ask him where he lives, tell him the rain won't hurt him and take him home, tell him there's a barn near his owner's house, tell him the imagination doesn't work all the time and he should stop, tell him people aren't afraid of rain and horses shouldn't be, tell him he's not a horse and if he kept thinking he is it might become permanent, reason on his level, tell him to stop crying, horses and people get sick from the rain, tell him to resume the game after the rain stops, tell him he'll see his friends tomorrow.

The next day the class asked the following question of individuals of the same age groups: A man on the street stops you and says, Please save me from the people who are dragging me away. He talks in a well-modulated, usual tone of voice and looks like an average man. You look and see no people; the man insists that the people are there and begs you to help him. A. What would be your first reaction? Why? B. How are you sure what you see is correct? C. How are you sure what he sees is wrong?

The reactions to part A were as follows: the man is crazy, it could possibly happen, he's telling the truth, he needs help, he's drunk, he's lying, he's playing a trick, he thinks he sees people, I don't know, he's paranoid, he's having a hallucination, I feel sorry for him, it's difficult to know if he's lying, if the people aren't there then he's imagining it, it's quite an unusual story, I'd be frightened, he's a dreamer, he's in a trance, it's quite common, there's something wrong, he's in trouble, it's a joke, I wouldn't help him, I'd be suspicious, maybe he's a drug addict, I think it's candid camera, I'd be startled, puzzled, scared, I'd look for people, it's a thief trying a new angle, I'd ask him to prove the story, help him, listen, elicit information, gain confidence, make an appeal to his reason, I'd avoid him, I'd check or look for myself, I don't think you could help him, I'd refer him to a specialist, I'd agree with him. In addition, some Ss responded with a blank stare or laughter but not verbally.

The answers to part B were as follows: determine the truth of the story, call the police, take him to a hospital or psychiatrist, try to help him, tell my father or mother, run away fast, walk away, wouldn't help him, avoid him, ignore him, call my brother for help, call someone else, stay with him until the situation is determined, ask him questions about the people, ask him questions about himself, smell his breath, ask him to have a drink, humor him, reassure him, I don't know, calm him, call a priest, tell him he's not being followed, look to see if he's being followed, take him home, examine how he was dressed, pretend to help him, don't upset him, ask him to prove it to me, believe he's crazy, stay and watch with amusement, I'm not able to help him.

The answer to part C were as follows: not sure, he may really be in danger, I don't see anyone, he's wrong because I'm right, I know what I see, if the people were there, he wouldn't be calm emotionally, I value his ideas as much as mine, I'd get others' opinions if the story sounded too far out, I'd judge by my sensory reactions, I don't think he saw it, he's not wrong just because I didn't see it, I'd assume he's wrong, I just know he's wrong, I'd assume he's crazy and I can't be wrong, most likely he's wrong, if he talked logically I might believe him, my judgment against his, what a person believes is reality, no evidence that he's right, lack of group agreement, he's mentally ill, hallucinating, there is a logical basis for my response, I'd believe him, I'd say he's right, I'd appeal to his past experience, something is physically wrong with him, it's an example of the frame-of-reference concept, it's non-correspondence with reality, I haven't seen such strange things in the past, I'm not crazy or drunk, he's drunk.

The students were told a few weeks later to ask the same subjects this question: Have you ever had experiences when you heard or saw something that was not really there? A. What were they? Describe your mood and the situation. B. How were you sure they were not real?

The answer to part A were as follows: I'd seen things or heard things, déjà vu, heard sounds when alone, thought I had met someone before, rumors, gossip, talking to someone, thinking I spoke to them before, visions or dreams that eventually happen, smelling food when hungry, thinking someone is following me, hearing or seeing things at night when alone, when alone at night I thought someone was in my room, I get the feeling that people are talking about me, after the death of someone close I thought I heard him calling, premonitions about the future, misinterpreted shadows, feel a draft while watching mysteries, feelings which later proved untrue, propaganda, feel bugs crawling on me when someone mentions them, dream I'm falling through space, when walking blindfolded feel as though I'd fall off something, imaginary playmates as a child, illusions and figments of imagination, hearing or seeing things when scared, seen things when others were present.

The answers to part B were as follows: sight, sudden realization, insight, logical reasoning, confidence in self-perceptions, through the senses, memory of prior experiences, touch, recurrence, closer examination, impermanency, rationalized, it was my imagination, asked someone else, not sure at the time, by virtue of a known facts it was impossible, looked again, checked with other sense data, further hearing, awoke from the dream.

While discussing the students' results, Wertheimer suggested that the subjects be asked the following question: A Chinese man awoke out of a deep sleep and told his family: I dreamed I was a butterfly. How can I be sure that I am a man who dreamed he was a butterfly? Or am I a butterfly dreaming that I am a man? A. What would be your first reaction? What would you do? Why? B. Imagine you were asked the question by your father: (1) What would be your first reaction? Why? (2) What would you answer him? (3) What proof would you suggest if you had to prove it to him?

The answers to part A of the question were as follows: look in mirror, try to fly, try to walk, butterflies can't walk, it's just a dream, can't be a butterfly can't be in touch with reality, can't be positive, consciousness different, compare physical characteristics, society and environment are different metamorphoses, intellect, he's a man, butterflies can't dream, he can't fly can't prove he's a man, this is silly, I don't know, it's an absurd question, when asleep one can't control thought, butterflies can't think, he's very intelligent, dreams have meaning, he's crazy, I'd laugh, Chinese are mystical, creative man, maybe he is a butterfly, he's kidding, I'd be astonished, he's drunk, pinch him to feel pain, it's his imagination, man has memory, ask others, he can be anything he wants, consensual validation, examine his past experience, the life spans differ, he does human activities. I can see he's a man, ask him more questions, it's a serious problem, get help, use shock, fright.

The answers to part B (1) were as follows: maybe you are a butterfly, you're not a butterfly, look in the mirror, can't be sure, he needs a doctor, butterflies can't talk, you're a man, not similar physically, butterflies can't dream, the man is crazy, it's a bad dream, a nightmare, ask him to fly, send him to a psychiatrist, he doesn't have the physical properties of a butterfly, this is silly, he's not very intelligent, he's escaping from reality, it's only in his mind, it's just a dream, I don't know, there is no way of proving it, this is impossible, he's kidding, too strange for this to be dreamed, when asleep there is no control over thoughts, check his family, his eyes are deceiving him, man has an intellect, butterflies don't have imagination or reason, he's confused, he can't be both, so he's a man, it's imagination, everything exists in the mind.

The answers to part B (2) were as follows: he has man's physical features, I'd tell him he's a man, he can't know, he can't be sure, butterflies can't dream, he needs sleep, dreams mean something, I don't know, maybe he's crazy, he had a bad dream, tell him to stop joking, I'm human so he must be, tell him to see a psychiatrist, go along with him, tell him to fly away, ask him why he is worried, discuss reality and dreams with him, it's just a dream, tell him to pinch himself, we all question existence, give him confidence in truths via reading and listening, appeal to his rational quality, he should have confidence in his perceptions, compare abilities of men and animals, find out why he dreamed it, tell him to look in a mirror, ask him if he's crazy, tell him if he's a butterfly then so am I, tell him to forget it.

The answers to part B (3) were as follows: look in the mirror, try to fly, he doesn't look like a butterfly, point out physical differences, show him a butterfly and compare, butterflies can't talk, physical comparisons, butterflies can't think, it's a dream, pinch him, men live longer than butterflies, analyze his memories, tell him he's a man, go to a psychiatrist, make a survey of people, examine family relations, don't know of a proof, reason logically, his life is different from a butterfly, ask other people, I'm not a butterfly and I am his child, tell him it's a dream, look up the definition of a butterfly, have him prove he's a butterfly, he is joking, no proof is needed, dreams are illogical, butterflies can't dream, wouldn't try to prove it, confidence in self-perceptions, animals are irrational, he has the rational qualities of a man, visual proof.

Wertheimer suggested that they also be asked this question: How do you know that a thing (A), person (B), or experience (C) actually exists?

The answers to (A) were as follows: if it exists in the mind it's real, touch, concentrate, can't be sure, further inquiry, sight, if past experience isn't consistent, we've been told things are real, through the senses, learning, if you believe it then it is, if it leaves evidence, logical deduction, reasoning, if someone else experiences it, I feel that it exists (sixth sense), hearing, if it functioned properly, if it exists in relation to you and affects the things around you, it depends on experience, depends on how you perceive it, comparison and investigation, smell, taste, usefulness, if it can be described, if it has form or shape or takes up space, it's tangible, it's a constant thing, experimental tests, if it exists in more than one sense.

The answers to (B) were as follows: if you communicate with the person, through the senses, can't be sure, if you believe the person exists, logical experience, reasoning, consensual validation, if I feel he exists (sixth sense), sight, touch, hearing, memory of experiences, accept the fact that people are real, investigation, if he affects me, smell, can outline his physical properties, exists in my mind, historians, newspapers, photographs.

The answers to (C) were as follows: can't be sure, if past experience isn't inconsistent, through the senses, if you believe it exists, if it leaves evidence, logical explanation, reasoning, if someone else experiences it, if I feel it exists (sixth sense), sight, by going through the experience, if it affects my life in some describable way, memories of them, through perception and participation, subjective experience is real, photographs, family albums, reading about it, only if it happens to me, hearing, touch, taste, when it occurs it's real, if there is sensory stimulation it exists, exists only in the mind, past experiences seem unreal.

The project ended with the class asking subjects of the four different age groups these questions. What is real? After they answered, they were asked to give examples of what is real. The next day they were asked, What is unreal? After they answered they were asked to give examples. In the same way, on a different day, they asked the following questions: Have you ever experienced anything which, at the time, seemed real and later became unreal? Give examples. Have you ever experienced anything which, at the time, seemed unreal and later became real? Give examples. What is the difference between a lie and the truth? Give examples. What is the difference between mimicking an act and the act, between pretending and not pretending, between wanting to be taken seriously and not wanting to be taken seriously, between imitating with and without the realization that you are doing so. Since these questions have proven of value to introduce the general psychology student to the topic of perception, the results of these and other studies related to the questions of what is reality, the difference between appearance and reality, and illusionary and veridical perception will be presented in the monograph on perception to illustrate Wertheimer's discussion of the differences between appearance and reality (cf. Brandt and Metzger, 1969).

SUNY Studies: On The Meaning of Imitation

It will be recalled that outgrowths of the discussion of imitation in the seminars were studies of the meaning of the word imitation and *Imitatio Dei*. Recently these studies were replicated with the assistance of ASL's research and teaching assistant, David Houston. The data are presented in detail to stimulate research.

1. Twenty-six students in a course on guidance and counseling were given a questionnaire which contained these questions: What does the word *imitation* mean? Why do people imitate? When do people imitate? Is imitation the same as (or different from) invention, creativity, intelligence, mimicry?

What does imitation mean? Twenty-eight responses were made to this question; half of the answers referred to acting out a situation or expressing or reflecting another's looks or actions or traits, e.g., trying to reenact a person' or thing's typical behavior, to pattern something in the image of something else, to adopt another's behavior trait, to try to do something the same as another person does, to reflect another's ideas or actions, to use accepted standards, to attempt to capture the characteristics of another person's or thing's behavior and reproduce it in one's own behavior. Closely related to these answers were 32% of the responses which referred to mimicking or copying or duplicating; for example, to mimic or copy, the act of duplication, a copy. The remaining 18% of the responses stressed the falseness or unrealness of imitation; for example, to pretend you are something else which is not the real thing, not real, unreal, false, false version of the original, not as good as the real thing.

Why do people imitate? There were 41 responses to this question. The largest category, 35% of the responses, referred to imitation as the manifestation of the desire for acceptance by one's fellow men or because one felt insecure or wanted to advance socially; for example, people imitate in order to conform and be accepted by others, to act in a desired or accepted way, to advance their social status, to feel needed, some imitate because they do not feel safe enough to venture out and act as they feel, to find acceptance by becoming like one who is accepted or admired, for security, to improve, to be accepted by the majority of the crowd, because they feel more accepted if they imitate, to be a member of a group. Related to this category were 17% of the responses which centered around the idea of imitation because of admiration; for example, a way of showing your admiration for someone else, because they admire something in what they imitate, because they approve of what the other person is doing, they do it to compliment, because they value that which they are imitating, to emulate. About 24% of the responses referred to imitation to attract attention, to be funny, or to get laughs; for example, at parties people imitate famous people for a few laughs, to be funny, to jest, a way of entertaining, to attract attention, to caricature. The remaining 24% of the responses, made by one or two people each, were such reasons for imitation as to learn, to be understood, to criticize, to be sarcastic, and unintentional imitation.

When do people imitate? The 35 responses elicited by this question were similar to the answers to the previous question. The largest category, which paralleled the largest category in response to the previous question, constituted 29% of the responses and referred to the need for security or to be accepted or to improve oneself socially; for example, people imitate when they need to have security, when they feel insecure in their own attributes, when they are unsure of how to behave they use others as their models, a dependent or insecure child may pattern his behavior after his older brother or sister, people imitate when they are uncomfortable doing nothing or being themselves, when they want to be admitted to a group or to feel wanted, to preserve or improve their image. About 15% of the responses referred to admiration of others; for example, when they wish to take on the good characteristics of another person's behavior in order to win the same rewards, if a person works with someone he admires he will imitate him in hopes that the other will bestow his approval on him, a person will imitate the manner of a famous person in hopes that some of the glory will rub off on him. About 15% of the responses referred to situations in which one wanted to get attention or to be funny or to get laughs; for example, at a party or when in the eyes of the public, at parties many people imitate famous people for a few laughs, to get laughs, as part of their act, as entertainment, when they are in a good mood. About 15% referred to situations in which one wished to mock or insult or ridicule someone; for example, a pupil mocking a teacher by using the teacher's voice and gestures, many do imitations to confuse others, when they wish to ridicule or to insult someone else, to caricature, when they are mad at someone. About 12% mentioned situations in which one imitated to make a point or to tell a story or for instructional purposes, such as, during instructions for games, when playing with children, to tell a story. Three responses (9%) were that people imitate all the time or most of the time. One of these Ss added that almost everything a person does is learned through imitation and two of them said that people imitate when other people are nearby or whenever it's convenient. The remaining 9% of the responses varied: a hunter imitates animals' voices to attract them, a man may imitate a bird with his hands, some actors do imitations for a living.

Responses to the last question showed that 15, 19, 35, and 65% respectively regarded imitation as being the same as, and 73, 65, 54, and 27% respectively regarded it as being different from invention, creativity, intelligence, and mimicry. The remainder were failures to respond or ambiguous answers, for example, imitation is different from creativity except possibly for creative imitations. In short, imitation was considered to be the same as mimicry by about two-thirds of the Ss, about one-third considered it to be the same as intelligence and less than one-fifth considered it to be the same as invention or creativity. Otherwise expressed, imitation was considered to be different from invention by about three-quarters of the Ss, different from creativity by about two-thirds, different from intelligence by over one-half, and different from mimicry by only about one-quarter.

Generally speaking the results are similar to the prewar study; imitation is still often associated with repetitive, reproductive behavior. The answers to the first three questions did not contain as many spontaneous references to the notion that it is a lower-level type of behavior. It was only in the last question in which they were directly asked about the relation that most subjects said that it was not similar to intelligence and creativity. However, the numbers of subjects who equated it with intelligence and creativity are in marked contrast with the prewar study in which nearly no one responded in this way. Is this due to the educational background of the students in which the importance of role playing and adjustment to social values are taught? Perhaps it also reflects the change in our society from a stress on individualism to a stress on sociality. It would be of interest to repeat this study using interviews in order to find out the reasons for their answers as well as to ask them how they think college students would have answered these questions in 1938. What would their reactions be when they were told that no one in 1938 equated imitation with intelligence and creativity but now about one-third and one-fifth respectively did so? What has changed; the meaning of imitation or of intelligence and creativity?

2. Sixteen college students were asked, What does *Imitatio Dei* (imitation of God) mean? Give examples of what it means. One S said, "Don't know," another wrote a question mark, and still another left the space blank. The answers given by the 13 respondents (two of whom gave no examples) were somewhat vague and suggested that most Ss did not actually know what the concept meant. The answers could be roughly divided as follows: a positive view which accounted for 46% of the responses and which emphasized the good qualities and virtues of the concept; a negative view which accounted for

31% of the responses and which stressed the theme of power over others assumed by those who seek to imitate God; and the remaining 23% which were neutral.

Responses characterized as the positive view were as follows: *Imitatio Dei* is an impossibility to attain, one can only attempt to follow His commands, for example, one who follows the ten commandments; living a good moral life, for example, act charitably; being Christian or acting as we believe a true follower of God would, for example, study the life of Christ and imitate his virtues in our everyday lives; living your life as much like God would live His were he alive today, for example, love your neighbor, be charitable to all, patterning one's life after the life of Christ, for example, being kind, merciful, honest, understanding; trying to do only what is sanctioned by society as the good Christian things, for example, charity toward fellowmen (cf. the earlier *Imitatio Dei* study).

Responses characterized as the negative view were as follows: it means someone who thinks he is all-powerful, omnipotent, and indestructible, "God on earth," for example, DeGaulle at times, maybe Hitler; someone who wishes to be all-powerful, to wield power, such as a political boss; a person who must have complete authority, who is never wrong; man has the capacity to be a god *(Capax Dei)* usually interpreted in the discrete sense that man is made in the image and likeness of God but one could go further and say that many times man channels the desire into secular things such as political power, aggrandizement of money or territory; when a person puts himself above others he is assuming a godly state based upon an imitation of what he thinks God is, for example, people in high positions who look down upon subordinates.

Responses characterized as neutral were the following: trying to do those things which are godlike—a person imitating God based on his perception of what God is or what God would do in a given situation; playing the role of God, being all-knowing; means something material, something having substance here on earth, that people can use for association with God in a sense, for example, church, clergy, religious symbols. [The section on value described the answers that these subjects gave to other questions that were asked in the same study.]

Outcomes of the Discussion of Lorge's Experiments

Wertheimer's criticism of Lorge's experiments in one of the seminars led to a replication of it with Wertheimer's suggestions. Although the results were in line with his conjectures he was not content, for example, he wanted to know more about the attitudes and assumptions of the subjects who changed and did not change when the sentences were attributed to different people, what knowledge they had about the people who made the statements, what their understanding was of the statements themselves and what could be done to make them realize the place, role, and function of the statement in the social situation in which it was uttered. In order to stimulate research on these and other issues we describe some modifications of the Lorge experiment.

1. With the assistance of Spencer Rathus, a student in ASL's Advanced Social Psychology class, a modified version of Lorge's experiment was conducted with 150 graduate students who were tested individually or in groups of two or three. A statement was read and attributed to a particular famous individual. Each S was asked to write whether he agreed or disagreed with the

statement and to give his reasons. He was asked not to discuss the study with anyone. One day later S was approached on an individual basis and told that a mistake had been made and that the statement had actually been made by another famous person in another context. He was asked whether he still agreed or disagreed with it and to state his reasons. The experimenter offered to read S's first response back to him but most Ss stated that this was not necessary; usually they said that they remembered their responses but in some cases they said only that their responses had not changed. An S is said to belong to one of Groups 1 through 6 depending on the statement he heard, the persons to whom it was attributed, and the order in which it was attributed to them. There were 25 Ss in each group.

The Ss in Groups 1 and 2 heard the following statement: *I hold that a little revolution now and then is a good thing. Like a summer cloudburst it refreshes the earth and clears the atmosphere.* Group 1 was first told that the statement had been made by Stokely Carmichael at a black power rally. One day later they were told that the statement had been said by Thomas Jefferson concerning the Whiskey Rebellion; a group of Pennsylvanians had rebelled because of an excise tax that had been levied and Jefferson had intervened on their behalf when the congress was about to institute repressive measures against the rebels. For Group 2 the order was reversed, that is, the statement was first attributed to Thomas Jefferson in the context of the Whiskey Rebellion and later it was said that it was made by Stokely Carmichael at a black power rally.

Groups 3 and 4 were read the following statement: *Pressure groups with self-seeking aims have too long had their way in the congress of these United States. We must decide what is right for the nation, not who is right, and then stick to it.* Group 3 was first told that it had been said by George Wallace in reference to black pressure groups. Later they were informed that the statement had been made by Martin Luther King, Jr., concerning the white Southern voting bloc and auxiliary pressure groups. The order was reversed for Group 4.

Groups 5 and 6 were read the following statement: *Man is a creature of instincts and drives. For all his cleverness and his art, it sometimes seems that his sole purpose in life is the gratification of his blackest urges.* Group 5 was first told that the statement had been formulated by Sigmund Freud when he was delving into the mysteries of the id and of the pleasure principle. Later they were informed that it was said by Jesus when he came across the money-lenders in the temple in Jerusalem. The order was reversed for Group 6. (About one-quarter of the Ss in each group expressed some doubts or skepticism about whether the statement had been made by Jesus.)

Tables 27.1 and 27.2 summarize the quantitative responses in each group. Situation A refers to the first time the statement was read and Situation B to the next time when another name and context were mentioned. When the statement on revolution was initially attributed to Stokely Carmichael, 13 Ss in Group 1 or 52% of the 25 Ss agreed with it. When it was subsequently attributed to Jefferson, all these 13 Ss still agreed and 9 of the 12 who had disagreed with the statement now agreed with it. Thus in Group 1 100% of those who agreed before also agreed the second time and 75% of those who disagreed before now agreed. Hence 22 Ss or 88% agreed with the Jefferson-revolution statement. In Group 2 where the statement was initially linked to Jefferson, 21 Ss or 84% agreed with it. Subsequently when it was attributed to Carmichael, only 11 of these 21 agreed. And the four Ss who disagreed at first still disagreed. Thus only 11 Ss or 44% agreed with the Carmichael-revolution statement. In short, of the 50 Ss who heard the statement about a little revolution, 43 Ss or 86% agreed when it was attributed to Jefferson and only 24 Ss or 48% agreed when it was attributed to Carmichael. All Ss who

TABLE 27.1
Numbers of Ss Who Showed Various Response Patterns

Situations A—B	Groups 1	2	3	4	5	6	Total
Agree-Agree	13	11	9	11	6	11	61
Agree-Disagree	0	10	2	7	3	4	26
Disagree-Agree	9	0	6	2	6	1	24
Disagree-Disagree	3	4	8	5	10	9	39

TABLE 27.2
Percentages of Agreement

Situation	Ss	1	2	3	4	5	Means
A	All	52	84	44	72	36	
	All	88	44	60	52	48	
B	Agreed before	100	52	82	61	67	
	Disagreed before	75	0	43	29	38	

Means	Jefferson		King 66	Jesus 54	69
	Carmichael		Wallace 48	Freud 42	46

agreed with the Carmichael statement also agreed with the Jefferson statement. And all Ss who disagreed with the Jefferson statement also disagreed with the Carmichael statement. Thus there were 24 Ss or 48% who agreed both times, 7 Ss or 14% who disagreed both times, and 19 Ss or 38% who shifted from agreement to disagreement or the other way around when the statement was attributed to different authors.

The trends of results found for Groups 1 and 2 were also found, although not so marked, for Groups 3 and 4 who heard the statement about pressure groups. When the statement was initially attributed to George Wallace in reference to black pressure groups, 11 Ss in Group 3 or 44% agreed with him. When it was attributed to Martin Luther King, Jr. concerning the White Southern voting bloc and auxiliary pressure groups, 9 of these 11 Ss still agreed and 6 of the 14 who had at first disagreed now agreed with the statement. Thus 82% of those who agreed before agreed also the second time and 43% of those who disagreed before agreed subsequently. Hence 15 Ss or 60% of Group 3 agreed with the pressure group statement when it was attributed to King. In Group 4 where the statement was initially linked to King, 18 Ss or 72% agreed with it. Subsequently, when it was attributed to Wallace, 11 of these 18 Ss agreed with it and 2 of the 7 Ss who had initially disagreed now agreed with it. Thus 13 Ss or 52% agreed when the statement was attributed to Wallace. In short, of the 50 Ss who heard the statement about pressure groups, 33 or 66% agreed when it was attributed to King and 24 or 48% agreed when it was linked to Wallace. Of the 24 Ss who agreed with Wallace, 20 or 83% also agreed with King and of the 17 Ss who disagreed with King, 13 or 77% also disagreed with Wallace. Of the 50 Ss, 20 or 40% agreed with the statement both times, 13 Ss or 26% disagreed both times, and 17 Ss or 34% shifted when the author was changed.

In Group 5 where the statement on the gratification of man's blackest urges was first attributed to Freud, 9 Ss or 36% agreed. When it was subsequently attributed to Jesus, 6 of these 9 Ss still agreed and 6 of the 16 who had previously disagreed now agreed. Thus 67% of those who had agreed before still agreed and 38% of those who had disagreed before agreed subsequently. Thus 12 Ss or 48% agreed when the statement was linked to Jesus. In Group 6 where the statement was initially attributed to Jesus, 15 Ss or 60% agreed. Subsequently, when Freud was said to have made the statement, 11 of these 15 still agreed and only one person changed from disagreement to agreement. Thus 12 Ss or 48% agreed with the statement the second time. In short, of the 50 Ss who heard the statement about the gratification of man's blackest urges, 27 Ss or 54% agreed when it was attributed to Jesus and 21 or 42% agreed when it was attributed to Freud. Of the 21 Ss who agreed with Freud, 17 or 81% also agreed with Jesus. Of the 23 Ss who disagreed with Jesus, 19 or 83% also disagreed with Freud. There were 17 Ss or 34% who agreed both times, 19 Ss or 38% who disagreed both times, and 14 Ss or 28% who shifted from agreement to disagreement or the other way around.

It could be said that Jefferson was more prestigeful than Carmichael, King more than Wallace, and Jesus more than Freud. On the average there was 69% agreement with the statement when it was linked to a more prestigeful person and 46% agreement when it was linked to a less prestigeful person. For every statement there was more agreement initially with the statement when it was attributed to the more prestigeful person, the differences ranging from 24 to 32% and averaging 28%. Subsequently there was a shift toward more agreement with the more prestigeful person, the increases ranging from 12 to 36% and averaging 21% and a shift toward less agreement with the less prestigeful person, the decreases ranging from 12 to 40% and averaging 24%. And, for every statement, most Ss who agreed with the less prestigeful person also agreed with the more prestigeful one. Of those who had agreed with the less prestigeful person from 67 to 100% with a mean of 83% subsequently also agreed with the more prestigeful. In addition, from 38 to 75% with an average of 52% of those who had disagreed before subsequently agreed with the more prestigeful person. From 52 to 63% with a mean of 59% of those who had agreed with the more prestigeful person also agreed with the less prestigeful while from 0 to 29% with a mean of only 13% shifted from disagreement with the more prestigeful person to agreement with the less prestigeful. In short, there tended to be more agreement initially and subsequently with the more prestigeful person.

Offhand these results may seem to fit Lorge's findings that the name linked to a statement affected the responses to it. They may also seem to be in keeping with Thorndike's associationistic explanation, namely, that when something is associated to a person we like, we react favorably to it whereas when it is associated to a person we do not like, we react unfavorably to it. It may seem that what is involved is the halo-effect or prestige-suggestion with feelings toward the alleged author of the statement affecting reactions to the statement. However, in line with Wertheimer's suggestions, the Ss had been asked why they agreed or disagreed. The reasons they gave do not support an associationistic explanation or one based mainly on halo-effect or prestige-suggestion. The answers suggest that many Ss were responding to the meaning of the statement in different contexts and not only to the authors. This seemed to be the case for eight of the nine Ss in Group 1 who had disagreed with Carmichael but subsequently agreed with Jefferson. They consistently adhered to a belief or principle which led them to disagree with Carmichael's kind of revolution but to agree with Jefferson's. For example, S3 believed that a revolution should be held for a specific purpose and not merely to clear the air, therefore, he disagreed with Carmichael because his revolutions had the latter intention but he agreed with Jefferson because the Whiskey Rebellion had a specific purpose; S6 thought that revolutions should have significant social motivation and that the Whiskey Rebellion had been more significantly motivated; S13 thought that the Whiskey Rebellion had been a small-scale revolution that prevented a larger one whereas Carmichael's reasons for a revolution were arbitrary; S14 said that the revolution Carmichael wanted was not for the good of the people whereas there was a positive end-goal to the Whiskey Rebellion; S20 said that negative demonstration is not refreshing but an inhibitor of progress whereas the Whiskey Rebellion, like the Revolutionary War, was for progress. S20 seemed inconsistent, disagreeing with Carmichael because he is an activist who believes that the blacks should rebel against our society to gain their ends, but agreeing with Jefferson because he was also involved in a revolutionary atmosphere, and concluding that he thinks both were right.

Reasons for agreement (or disagreement) on both occasions in Group 1 were also revealing. S19, who agreed twice said that he hates Carmichael but the statement itself is good since a little revolution checks stagnation. And S20 who also agreed twice, pointed out that he believes in political change and is basically a revolutionary who has little use for Jefferson, a slave owner. Most subjects in Group 1 who agreed (or who disagreed) on both occasions gave the same reason or reservation twice. Thus S4 agreed twice provided it was peaceful revolution each time. And S1 disagreed twice because you can clear the air with more peaceful means.

Similar trends were found in Group 2. All ten Ss who agreed with Jefferson but subsequently disagreed with Carmichael seemed to be responding to the different implications of the statement when spoken by one man or the other. S1 said initially that the degree of dissent is the controlling factor and the next day he said that Carmichael's type of dissent, with people getting killed and things being burned, goes much too far; S3 said that Carmichael's statement was a perversion of the Jeffersonian ideal since anyone can use the words but Carmichael's group's goals are only for themselves; S4 reasoned that a little revolution may make others aware of certain problems but disagreed with Carmichael that bringing about such awareness should include bloodshed or looting. Similarly, S7 considered Carmichael's revolution as destructive, S10 considered it lawless, S16 could not go along with his means, S17 thought that Carmichael was talking about devastation and not revolution, S20 said that Carmichael's type of revolution does not lead to progress but leads to more hatred and riots, S21 thought Carmichael's brand of revolution was too destructive, and S25 said that this was the type of revolution we wanted to avoid.

Reasons for agreement on both occasion in Group 2 were quite varied. Of 11 Ss who agreed twice, one merely said that he didn't think he should change his answer and another said that he supposes he should stick to the statement no matter who said it, but if it had been done the other way, with Carmichael first and then Jefferson, he probably would have disagreed, at least with Carmichael. Most of the others gave some reservations or qualifications for their agreement with Carmichael. S2 said that he still has to agree but black power should be economic and in demonstrations only; S6 said that he didn't think Carmichael was talking about a little revolution; S8 wondered whether what he and Carmichael meant by a little revolution were the same; S12 agreed in principle but not if black power includes looting, fighting, and bloodshed. S13 (who called the experimenter a tricky devil) agreed, but with the qualification that revolution doesn't involve violence; and S19 agreed if Carmichael meant radical change but would disagree if he meant blowing everything up. Some who agreed with Carmichael claimed that Negroes have no alternative but to use violent means in revolution.

All four Ss in Group 2 who disagreed with the statement regardless of who said it seemed to be responding to its meaning or lack of meaning. S4 claimed that the statement didn't say anything and wanted to know what was meant by a little revolution now and then; S18 insisted that one must seek change through peaceful means; S22 thought that the statement was too flippant and poetic and ignored the fact that real live people get killed in revolutions; and S23 asked whether Vietnam wasn't once a little revolution and whether the atmosphere was any clearer.

In Group 3 also most Ss seemed to respond on the basis of different interpretations of the same statement when it was made by different individuals. For example, of the six Ss who disagreed with Wallace but later agreed with King, S9 said that King's pressure group was right but Wallace's was not; S11 said that pressure groups might be necessary but white Southern pressure groups did not meet the needs of the nation; S17 claimed that the same thing meant one thing when said by Wallace and another when said by King, that Wallace used the statement to continue discrimination whereas King used it to gain justice; and S22 said that he would have agreed with the statement if it was not made by George Wallace, that the idea was fine but Wallace only wanted to use it to promote segregation. Sometimes the same reason was given for maintaining agreement as for shifting. For example, S4 and S6 both agreed with Wallace on the grounds that what is good for the people in general is more important than specific pressure groups; S4 subsequently said that he agreed with King for the same reason but said that King didn't care about the principle or about all the people but only about the Negroes; S6 subsequently disagreed with King, saying that he still agreed with the idea although King was not interested in the welfare of all the people but only in one group's welfare.

Disagreement both times occurred for a variety of reasons. For example, S15 said initially that he's against the whole idea, that you can't separate what is right from who is right, and he disagreed again for the same reason but admitted that if he had been told at first that it was said by King he would have agreed because it probably wouldn't have made him look for a reason to disagree. That the statement was so vague and general as to be dangerous was

S2's reason for disagreeing both times; the second day he noted that it doesn't matter who said it.

In Group 4 most of the seven Ss who agreed with King and then disagreed with Wallace referred to differences in the two men's philosophies or purposes. S3 agreed with King because what is best is most important but disagreed with Wallace because of what Wallace thinks is right for the nation, adding that he knows how to say things that sound reasonable on the surface but in such a way that the racists know what he really means by them. S6 thought that King represents the views of the true majority but Wallace does not. S11 first said that issues should be considered and not personalities; he disagreed subsequently because Wallace didn't mean that we should consider issues but meant that people should stop doing what he thought was giving in to black people. S14 agreed with King but said that if we elected the wrong people he would be very afraid to have them decide what is right; the next day he noted that if Wallace made the statement he would disagree and would really want to know who would decide what is right. S17 shifted to disagreement noting that he wouldn't agree with Wallace if he said that two and two were four because there'd be something racist in it. S18 agreed with King cautioning that while it sounds reasonable there is a dangerous implication that there is some totally objective way of deciding what is right; in disagreeing with Wallace he noted that he shouldn't be swayed by who says it but he knows that Wallace thinks that only white Southerners know what's right. While agreeing with King, S20 warned that this is one of the political slogans that anybody, no matter what his political position, can twist around to push his own thing, but, how can you argue with it the way it's said? Nevertheless, he disagreed subsequently claiming that this was just what he meant, that it could have been said by either King or Wallace to push his own thing, but since Wallace would push racism, he had to disagree.

There were only two Ss in Group 4 who shifted from disagreement with King to agreement with Wallace. For example, S23 disagreed at first because King meant that there's something left we haven't yet given to Negroes; subsequently, after asking whether the experimenter was sure it was Wallace, he agreed.

Some of the Ss in Group 4 who agreed both times recognized that the statements would be made for different reasons by the two men. For example, S1 noted that the statement was still true although Wallace would use it for racist purposes and then added that he would have disagreed if he had known it was Wallace who said it. Similarly, S22 agreed initially saying that the validity of an idea or a political program should not depend on who said it and subsequently he agreed because he had made his bed and had to lie in it but added that he might not have agreed if he hadn't been told that King said it. S2 agreed initially because to have the interests of the majority at heart is crucial and he agreed subsequently, noting that it doesn't matter who said it but that Wallace and King would have different reasons. Similarly, S7 agreed twice but noted that Wallace wouldn't use it the way King did. And S13 agreed both times although he said that he didn't like the implications of the statement when made by Wallace. In contrast, S3 said that it makes no difference who said it and that he was asked to agree or disagree with the statement and not with the author. Similarly, S9 said that the statement is the same no matter who made it.

There were also varied reasons for disagreeing both times. For example, S8 said initially that it's a stupid statement involving the assumption that some men know what is right, and later he noted that if Wallace said it, it's even more stupid and he doubts whether Wallace knows what is right. Similarly, S10 disagreed with Wallace for two reasons, the one he had given before and just because Wallace said it.

When the statement that man is a creature of instincts and drives whose sole purpose seems to be to gratify his blackest urges was attributed to Jesus, about one-fifth of the Ss in each of Group 5 and 6 expressed surprise or disbelief or said that it sounds too pessimistic for Jesus and a similar number said that Jesus must have been disappointed or angry or upset to have said it. A few Ss said that they could understand why Jesus said it. Most Ss made no mention of the incongruity between the alleged source and the use of such modern psychological terms as drives and instincts.

In Group 5 most of the Ss who disagreed once and agreed another time appealed to the speaker's mood or to the circumstances under which the statement was made or to the underlying beliefs. For example, S10 disagreed with Freud because he wouldn't buy all that subconscious stuff about the real reasons we do things; he agreed the next day, noting that Jesus said it because he was disappointed with what the money-lenders were doing but he didn't think they were doing it because of the id or ego. Similarly S16 disagreed at first, saying that man is basically good even though he may resort to evil to satisfy his needs; the next day he agreed, noting that Jesus was disappointed when he said this but he knew that men were basically good whereas Freud thought that they were basically bad. S27 rejected the statement initially as too pessimistic and one-sided but subsequently agreed with Jesus, saying that history has shown that men respond more to power than ideals. A Catholic who did not like to discuss religion, he refused to elaborate on his answers or to discuss whether his reasons were inconsistent. On the other hand, S18 agreed at first because the statement seemed true from experience—man has to learn to control his basic instincts and drives; he disagreed subsequently, saying that Jesus was probably talking about original sin and he doesn't believe in original sin. S24 agreed initially because Freud studied man's inner self and strivings and discovered the real reasons we do things, which aren't noble by a long shot; she disagreed subsequently saying only, It doesn't seem right, it just doesn't seem right. A Catholic, she may have been doubting the alleged authorship. However, other Ss who questioned the authorship nonetheless agreed with the statement. For example, S3 said initially that no matter how much you rationalize, you are what you are and sometimes you do things you can't explain in any other way; the next day he said that it doesn't really sound like something Jesus would say but it doesn't change his opinion. S21 agreed with the statement initially because the voluminous amount of crime seems to prove this; he agreed subsequently, saying, I still feel the same way for the reason I said although, to be honest with you, I don't think Jesus said that. S4 agreed initially saying that people like to kid themselves about the reasons they do things and like to think they're noble; subsequently he agreed, noting that he still feels the same and who said it doesn't matter.

Among the ten Ss of Group 5 who disagreed both times were some who gave the same reason each time. For example, S1 said initially that he believes to some extent in instincts but not as the prime motivation in life and subsequently he said that he still disagreed for the same reason. S17 disagreed because gratification is not man's sole purpose in life and he said the reason for his subsequent disagreement was exactly the same. S19 disagreed initially saying that he saw man as basically good, not as one working for his blackest urgest; disagreeing the next day he said that he still feels the same way, adding that this is not typical of Jesus and he must have been very upset. S9 disagreed initially because cleverness and art are not pertinent to Freud's concept; disagreeing again he was one of the few Ss who explicitly referred to the incongruity in terminology, saying: It doesn't make sense. Jesus would have to have been thinking of devils as instincts and drives and he had the idea there was a soul too. Are you sure this was said by Jesus? More succinct and emphatic was S15 who disagreed both times saying initially that to control black urges can also be gratifying at times, and subsequently that Christ would never say anything like that. Wavering between agreement and disagreement on the second day was shown by S12, who had initially disagreed because gratification is largely social and good adjustment or happiness is usually achieved when a person is accepted by his social environment; the next day he disagreed but in giving his reason said: I don't know. It's hard to say. I mean I know how Jesus felt and I suppose I would agree with him if I didn't think about it, but I think what I said before is right, too.

In Group 6 the four Ss who agreed when the statement was attributed to Jesus but disagreed subsequently seemed to be responding on the basis of prestige and the feeling tone of the statement in the context of its purported authorship. For example, S1 said that it's pessimistic for Jesus but there are times when things look that way; yet he disagreed when it was linked to Freud saying that sometimes men live for other people's gratification. S15 agreed, saying that it sounds very pessimistic but Jesus said it so it's probably not that pessimistic because Jesus said that men could be saved if they believed in him and so it can't be as bad as it seems. Yet the next day he said: No, I don't agree, It's too black. I can understand why Freud was bitter. He was Jewish, right? So he was bitter, but things aren't that black. S4 agreed but said, I know that Jesus didn't really feel that way; he disagreed later because Freud completely ignored that conscious goals were what the person really wanted and he believed that man was not intrinsically social or decent but was just rationalizing. When the statement was attributed to Jesus, S11 asked, In all honesty, who am I to disagree? The next day he disagreed, saying, To tell you the truth, I'm glad Jesus didn't say it. It's too pessimistic.

Only one S in Group 6 disagreed with Jesus and then agreed with Freud. S17 disagreed because it was said by Jesus, adding that he himself does not believe in original sin; he agreed later, because he considered that Freud was speaking scientifically, not religiously, and man has instincts for aggression and dominance. Questioning revealed that this S was Jewish and had taken some psychology courses in New York City which had a strong psychoanalytic orientation.

The eleven Ss who agreed both times did so for a variety of reasons. For example, S3 claimed that it's a law of nature that biological drives must be satisfied before other drives and gave Maslow as a reference. Later he noted, I still feel the same way and it doesn't matter who said it but it does sound more like Freud than Christ. The first day S5 commented, Oh, I agree, self-gratification is most satisfying. The next day he said, Oh sure, that sounds like Freud—same reason. S7 agreed because men by their very nature try to satisfy primitive instincts and drives and agreed subsequently for the same reason, no difference. Similarly, S9 said initially that although the environment influences us, essentially we all try to gratify our wants and needs, and later he commented, It's still true. I don't like it, but It's true. S19 said at first, It sometimes looks that way—I would have said 'undecided' if that was allowed. The next day he said, I shouldn't change my mind because of who said it. S6 didn't really think Jesus would say that but agreed because altruism is not possible and anyone who denies this is kidding himself; later he asked, Why should I change my mind? I don't give a damn who said it. S20 was even more adamant, saying: I'm sure Jesus didn't say but should I play along with you? Okay, people like to kid themselves but they never do anything that isn't self-gratifying. Later he said, I told you that Jesus didn't say that; I still agree and my reason is the same. S23 agreed saying the statement is true of man in isolation but cultures and societies can temper or suppress the hedonistic outlook; when it was attributed to Freud he said, I didn't think that sounded like Jesus, but it doesn't matter—my reason is still the same.

Of the nine Ss who disagreed both times few mentioned any doubts about the authorship of the statements. Five Ss gave essentially the same reason for disagreeing both times. For example, each time S10 noted that there is progress because man's instincts for doing good outweigh his instincts for doing bad; S11 said that both black and white urges propel men's actions; S18 said that it's a one-sided view because men can build things up as well as rip them down. Initially S14 said that while man tries to satisfy his urges, not all of them are necessarily black; disagreeing again the next day he said: My reason is the same. I knew Jesus wouldn't say that—he wouldn't say 'blackest.' He loved men.

In short, a variety of reasons were given for disagreeing both times, for agreeing both times, and for shifting. Sometimes the same reason was given for agreement as for disagreement or for shifting. While prestige-suggestion might have accounted for some responses, there also seemed to be some tendency to take into account the different meaning of the statements in the context in which they occurred or in the light of what was known about the author and his philosophy.

In Wertheimer's discussion of the Lorge experiment he implied that it is possible to open people's eyes to the evidence on which the statement is based and to make decisions in terms of the evidence rather than reacting in terms of their likes or dislikes or their attitudes toward the person who made the statement. This had not yet been clearly established. To show, as the present variation did, that the meaning of the statement may change when it is attributed to one or another person does not meet the main thrust of Wertheimer's criticisms or suggestion. He stressed the need to make people aware of the evidence on which judgments are made and not to judge superficially or blindly or in terms of habituated responses. But it has been difficult for us or our students to devise experimental variations which would maximize the former kinds of judgments or minimize the latter kind of judgments. One variation which we have tried and which remains to be conducted on a large scale is the following. S is first given a statement (for example about a little revolution now and then) and asked if he agrees or disagrees with it and why; then he is told who said it (for example, Jefferson) and is again questioned concerning agreement or disagreement and asked for his reasons; then the circumstances or context in which the statement was made are described and discussed and he is again asked if he agrees or disagrees and why; and finally attempts are made to change his answer. One could also adapt this variation to the present study in which the statement is attributed to a contemporary person. For example, if Ss were told that Carmichael had made the statement to cool the passions of people who were about to start a riot, would they agree with the statement whether or not they liked him or his policies or the recent upsurgence of black power? The connection with Carmichael could be made before or after S was told that Jefferson had made the statement in an effort to cool the senators who wanted to send an army to Washington, Pennsylvania to quell the Whiskey Rebellion; or new Ss might be used each time. Also needed is research to develop methods which will lead people to seek to find the evidence on which a statement is based before they agree or disagree with it. In order to study whether Ss focus on the role and function of the statement in the situation in which it was made, rather than on the prestige of the person who made the statement, it may be advisable to use actual historical statements and situations.

Application of Principles

In 1938 ASL replicated Wertheimer's variation of the Lorge experiment with the aim of developing it into a thesis at the New School. In the course of discussing the results with Wertheimer, we wondered what would happen if subjects were given a description of a social conflict involving the application of a norm or principle. Would the subject side with the people in the conflict who were members of groups to which he belonged or with whose views he agreed? We planned to compare the application of the norms or principles when they were presented in the context of the subject's ingroups and outgroups. The kinds of social conflicts which we had in mind involved pairing events such as the following. The police in a certain town in Germany broke up a meeting which was protesting the Nurenberg laws. The American Bund rally was attacked by rowdies or the Communist Party rally was attacked by rowdies. After a few preliminary studies in which it was found that college students did react in terms of their commitment to the ideology of the groups involved, we varied the study. The subjects were first asked to rank a series of principles in terms of their importance, for example, freedom of speech, religion, separation of church and state, equality before the law. After this, they were asked to indicate on a seven-point scale how firmly or flexibly they would apply each principle in a concrete case (the case was not specified). A few weeks later they were given situations which involved the application of the principles in their ingroups and another week later, situations which involved the application of the same principles in their outgroups. In one variation they were first asked to react freely and then they were asked to specify the principle which was involved and to indicate on the same seven-point scale how rigorously they would apply it in the particular case. In another study we indicated the principle that was involved (it was one of the principles that they had ranked and rated before) and asked them to rate how rigorously they would apply it in the specific case. After this they were again given the same principles to rank and to rate. A few weeks later we interviewed each subject. He was shown all his answers and asked to comment on them. Then he was asked why he varied or did not vary in the application and the ranking of the principles or why he did not see that the principle was involved in the situation. It was found that subjects reacted differently to principles which they had ranked important to them than to principles which they ranked as unimportant. Moreover, when subjects were asked to specify the principles, some did not name the same principle which they were subsequently given. When the principle was given, subjects tended to apply it more flexibly or leniently when the particular instance involved their ingroups than when it involved their outgroups. They explained their different responses by saying that the situations called for different applications or that the same principle really did not hold for the ingroup as for the outgroup.

In 1952, when we became associated with the Yale Attitude and Communication Project, we modified the procedure to study how people react to and reconcile their contradictory judgments of social situations. Experimental variations were conducted at McGill University, the University of Oregon, Northwest Christian College, the University of Miami, and SUNY-Albany. A surprising result was that the Northwest Christian College students were the most consistent subjects and tended to rate a principle the same way each time, consistently showing much tolerance. When the results were told to a colleague, he remarked, What would you say if they were Nazis and rated principles the same way? Superficially his remark may seem similar to Wertheimer's comment that some subjects rated a principle the same way because they focused on it in terms of their ideology and were blind to the situation, for example, civil liberalitarians who would apply the principle of freedom of speech in the same way to the Bund, the Republicans, the Democrats, and the Communists, because they believed in unqualified freedom of speech. Wertheimer pointed out the need to study the effects on the person's attitude to the principle when he became aware of the fact that it played a different place, role, and function in one situation than in another. In order to stimulate research on this problem, we are presenting in detail the results of several studies which involved rating of principles in general as well as in various contexts. The studies used the following five-point rating scale to indicate the rigor or flexibility with which a principle should be applied:

a. No exceptions should ever be made in application of the principle.
b. Sometimes exceptions should be made in application of the principle.
c. Exceptions as often as no exceptions should be made in application of the principle.
d. Often exceptions should be made in application of the principle.
e. Always exceptions should be made in application of the principle.

The nine principles rated in this way were the following:

1. There should be segregation between Negroes and Whites.
2. In countries where there is separation of Church and State, government-supported schools should not participate in religious activities.
3. Minority groups should be given complete freedom to practice their religion.
4. Man is related to the animal kingdom and is not of special creation.
5. Anyone who believes that his religion is the true religion has a right to convert others.

6. Any duly established government has the legal right to protect itself from subversive activities.
7. Civil servants should not accept gifts from manufacturers because it may obligate them.
8. In the eyes of the law women should be given complete freedom concerning hours, wages, and type of work.
9. Lincoln believed in freedom of race, color, and creed.

Later the subjects rated each of the following nine statements on the five-point scale given above. The statements consisted of contextual situations which embodied each of the nine principles successively.

1. The school authorities of the University of Alabama have refused a Negro woman admission to the campus claiming that segregation is a basic principle of their constitution.
   The principle of this case is that there should be segregation between Negroes and Whites. To what degree do you think this principle should be applied? a. No exceptions. . .b, c, d, to e. Always exceptions. . . .
2. A Christian child, whose parents live in a Mohammedan country, has to attend, by law, the secular school of the country. During the month of Ramadon and several other times the children have pageants pertaining to the Mohammedan religious event. Songs which are Mohammedan prayers are taught. The child's parents organized protests since they were taught these prayers. The small minority of Christians said it was wrong that a secular public school should expose their children to such religious activities.
In countries where there is separation of church and state, government-supported schools should not participate in religious activities. To what extent do you think this principle should be applied? a. No exceptions . . . b, c, d, to e. Always exceptions. . . .
3. A Protestant sect here protested the persecution of their missionaries in Madrid. In Catholic Spain it is forbidden for anyone but Catholics to do missionary work. The Protestants may conduct services but it must be for Protestants only.
The principle in the above is that minority groups should be given complete freedom to practice their religion. To what degree do you think this should be applied? a. No exceptions . . . b, c, d, to 3. Always exceptions. . . .
4. According to Darwin and other evolutionists, man was not created spontaneously or separately at one time in history, but man evolved during the course of history of living creatures as one form of animal emerged out of another. It is assumed that there is a common ancestor for man and some animal species; for example, the great apes. Man, as well as other species, evolved out of the evolutionary process which, according to Darwin, is a constant struggle for survival of the fittest, elimination of the unfit, and change by mutation.
How strongly do you accept the theory of evolution in the above paragraph? a. No exceptions . . . b, c, d, to e. Always exceptions. . . .
5. Mohammedan India is considering passing a law prohibiting the converting activities of Christian Missionaries in their country because of the fighting and rioting it causes. The riots are usually protests against the missionaries. The rioters claim it is wrong for the Christian Missionaries to come and tell them that their religion is wrong.
Anyone who believes that his religion is the true religion has a right to convert others. To what extent do you think this principle should apply? a. No exceptions . . . b, c, d, to e. Always exceptions. . . .
6. It is illegal in Russia to belong to a party that aims at the overthrow of the

government. Members of anti-communist parties are continuously being sorted out of the government employment and are even jailed. Some have even been executed as traitors because of belonging to a party which had, as its aims, the overthrow of the Communist regime in Russia.

Any duly established government has the right to protect itself from subversive activities. To what extent do you agree with this principle? a. No exceptions . . . b, c, d, to e. Always exceptions. . . .

7. In the Truman administration it was discovered that several civil service employees, for example, inspectors of products which were brought by the government, had received gifts from the manufacturers. Some had received deep-freezers and their wives were given fur coats. Investigation by Senate committees as well as the newspapers implied that these individuals were acting unethically because they received gifts from the manufacturers from whom the government made purchases. Some were dismissed from the civil service on these charges.

Civil servants should not accept gifts from manufacturers because it may obligate them. To what degree do you think this principle should be applied? a. No exceptions . . . b, c, d, to e. Always exceptions. . . .

8. In Russia women have equal rights, according to law, in every respect with men. In order to demonstrate this, the government usually shows pictures, in other countries, which show women and men working in all kinds of work. Women even work as street cleaners, ditch diggers, stevedores, construction workers, as well as physicians and lawyers, etc. There is no legislation which stipulates the kind of work or the hours or pay for women, thus implying no difference between men and woman.

The principle of this case is that in the eyes of the law women should be given complete freedom concerning hours, wages, and type of work. To what degree do you think this principle should be applied? a. No exceptions . . . b, c, d, to e. Always exceptions. . . .

9. Lincoln said, "forescore and seven years ago our fathers brought forth on this continent a new nation, conceived in liberty, and dedicated to the proposition that all men are created equal. Now we are engaged in a great civil war, testing whether that nation, or any nation so conceived and so dedicated, can long endure. We are met on a great battlefield of that war. We have come to dedicate a portion of that field, as a final resting place for those who here gave their lives that that nation might live. It is altogether fitting and proper that we should do this. But, in a larger sense, we cannot dedicate—we cannot consecrate—we cannot hallow—this ground. The brave men, living and dead who struggled here have consecrated it far above our poor power to add or detract. The world will little note nor long remember what we say here, but it can never forget what they did here. It is for the living rather, to be dedicated here to the unfinished work which they who fought here have thus far so nobly advanced. It is rather for us to be here dedicated to the great task remaining before us, that we here highly resolve that these dead shall not have died in vain—that this nation under God, shall have a new birth of freedom—and that government of the people, by the people, for the people, shall not perish from the earth."

Lincoln believed in freedom of race, color, and creed. To what extent do you agree with this statement? a. No exceptions . . . b, c, d, to e. Always exceptions. . . .

10. At a fishbowl mixer at the University of Oregon a white boy cut in on a Negro boy who was dancing with a white girl. There were 30 other white girls who were waiting for partners. The Negro later continued dancing with the girl. Moreover, he asked the white girl for a date which she gave him.

Several white students spoke to the girl about her going out with the Negro. She was threatened with expulsion from her sorority.

The principle in this case is that there should be segregation between Negroes and whites. To what degree do you think this principle should be applied? a. No exceptions . . . b, c, d, to e. Always exceptions. . . .

11. A Mohammedan Priest in Brooklyn protested against the religious activities in the public school in his neighborhood during the month of December when they taught Christmas carols and Christian hymns. The parents of the children of Mohammedan faith also protested. The small minority of Mohammedans said it was wrong that a secular public school should expose their children to such religious activities.

In countries where there is separation of church and state, government-supported schools should not participate in religious activities. To what extent do you think this principle should be applied? a. No exceptions . . . b, c, d, to e. Always exceptions. . . .

12. Catholics have protested to the U.S. government against the persecution of their church members in some of the strongly Protestant countries. These countries allow the Catholics to meet in their churches but will not tolerate any Catholic missionary work there.

The principle in the above is that minority groups should be given complete freedom to practice their religion. To what degree do you think this should be applied? a. No exceptions . . . b, c, d, to e. Always exceptions. . . .

13. According to the Biblical description of the creation of man, God first created all the plants and animals in the world and after the creation of all these things the world was incomplete. He then decided to create a man. God fashioned out of clay a man in His own image; that is, the image of God, and breathed life into him. He set this man in the Garden of Eden to take care of it and to have dominion over the animals and all of those in the sea and the water and on the earth.

How strongly do you accept the theory of evolution in the above paragraph? a. No exceptions . . . b, c, d, to e. Always exceptions. . . .

14. Several years ago there were a number of riots in Quebec because of the activities of a Mohammedan Religious Mission which was seeking to convert Christians to Mohammedanism in that community. The people demanded that a law be passed prohibiting the missionary work.

Anyone who believes that his religion is the true religion has a right to convert others. To what extent do you think this principle should apply? a. No exceptions . . . b, c, d, to e. Always exceptions. . . .

15. It is illegal, in the United States, to belong to a party which aims at the overthrow of its government. Members, for example, of the Communist Party are continuously being sorted out of government employment and even brought to trial and convicted. There is an example of two Communists who were executed because of such activity.

Any duly established government has the legal right to protect itself from subversive activities. To what degree do you agree with this principle? a. No exceptions . . . b, c, d, to e. Always exceptions. . . .

16. In the Eisenhower Administration, a Senate investigation revealed that some top officials were passing on the government contracts for corporations which gave them gifts while they were working for the government. The newspapers as well as some of the Senators implied that these individuals were acting unethically. Some of these officials were dismissed from government employment on these charges.

Civil servants should not accept gifts from manufacturers because it may obligate them. To what degree do you think this principle should be applied? a. No exceptions . . . b, c, d, to e. Always exceptions. . . .

17. In the United States many women's organizations wish to have a Constitutional Amendment passed which would guarantee women equal rights with men in every respect. Pointing out the unequal treatment of men and women, they point to states where there are laws restricting the work of women; for example, in mines and factories or having minimum wage and hour laws for women and children. These women feel that as long as the states have these laws there is a fundamental discrimination policy. They feel that women should not be considered different from men in the eyes of the law as to what work she could or should do, how long she should work, how she should work, and at what price she should work. They want equal rights and no legislation which would discriminate in any way between sexes.

The principle of this case is that in the eyes of the law, women should be given complete freedom concerning hours, wages, and type of work. To what degree do you think this principle should be applied? a. No exceptions . . . b, c, d, to e. Always exceptions. . . .

18. Lincoln once said, "I will say then, that I am not, nor ever have been in favor of bringing about in any way the social and political equality of the white races, that I am not, nor ever have been in favor of making votors or jurors of Negroes, nor of qualifying them to hold office, nor to intermarry with white people, and I will say in addition to this that there is a physical difference between the white and black races which I believe will forever forbid the two races living together on terms of social and political equality, and inasmuch as they cannot so live, while they do remain together there must be the position of superior and inferior, and I as much as any man, am in favor of having the superior position assigned to the white man.

I have urged the colonization of the Negroes, and I shall continue. My Emancipation Proclamation was linked with this plan. There is no room for two distinct races of white man in America, much less two different races of whites and blacks. I can conceive of no greater calamity than the assimilation of the Negro into our social and political life as our equal. Within twenty years we can peacefully colonize the Negro and give him our language, literature, religion, and system of government under conditions in which he can rise to the full measure of manhood. That he can never do here. We can never attain the ideal union our fathers dreamed of with millions of alien, inferior races among us, whose assimilation is neither possible nor desirable."

Lincoln believed in freedom of race, color, and creed. To what extent do you agree with this statement? a. No exceptions . . . b, c, d, to e. Always exceptions. . . .

In short, both sets of contextual situations embodied Principles 1 through 9 successively. The second set of contextual situations was similar to the first set of situations except that in the second set usually the conditions and central characters were reversed. The contexts did not necessarily reflect the subjects' ingroups or outgroups. One reason for this was that if a succession of situations involved the subject's ingroup (or outgroup) it might arouse his suspicion or set him to answer in a certain manner. Another reason was that it was difficult to know the ingroups and outgroups in advance, particularly when the experiments were group-administered. However, for most of the subjects rigorous applications of the principles seemed to favor their ingroups more in the first series of contextual situations listed above than in the second series, for example, rigorous application of Principles 2 and 5 favored Christians in the first context but favored Mohammedans in the second context.

In addition to rating the principles and situations, some of the subjects were interviewed and were asked to give reasons for inconsistent ratings. A major interest was to discover why subjects were inconsistent in the application of principles and how they reconciled their inconsistencies and phenomenal con-tradictions. Background variables, such as religion, party affiliation, and geog-raphical region of upbringing, were obtained for some subjects.

We are indebted to Arthur L. Maer, then a student at the University of Miami, for assistance in conducting several of the experiments and helping to compile the data. Unless otherwise stated, we conducted the experiments at the University of Miami.

Experiment 1. The experiment was group administered in 1960 to two classes at the University of Miami with a total of 100 students. Each class first rated the principles in general or in the abstract. One week later one class rated the principles in the first context, followed immediately by rating them in the sec-ond context. In the other class there was a one-week interval between the rat-ings in the two contexts. The results of the two classes showed no significant differences and were therefore combined. From the two classes 50 subjects were selected at random for more detailed analysis of results. Their ages ranged from 18 to 40 and their majors included psychology, art, history, ac-counting, marketing, nursing, etc. Neither age nor major subject seemed to be a significant factor in determining the results. Most Ss recognized and com-mented on the similarities of the principles in the different contexts, for ex-ample, saying that they were the same principles with different stories or in different concrete situations.

TABLE 27.3

Percentages of Ss Who Gave Various Ratings of the Principles in Experiment 1

Principles

Situation	Ratings	1	2	3	4	5	6	7	8	9	Mean
Abstract	a	12	32	32	12	26	64	28	42	60	34
P	b	38	38	38	16	20	22	52	24	22	30
	c	6	8	10	24	12	2	14	12	10	11
	d	6	14	6	12	16	2	4	12	4	8
	e	36	8	14	36	24	8	2	8	2	15
	a	22	44	50	18	18	54	50	26	62	38
First	b	24	36	20	40	32	24	40	42	22	31
Context	c	10	4	6	14	12	10	6	8	10	9
QI	d	6	8	12	8	12	6	4	8	4	8
	e	26	8	12	20	26	4	0	16	2	13
	a	20	42	42	20	18	68	48	36	64	40
Second	b	42	44	42	30	40	28	48	40	22	37
Context	c	8	8	8	26	8	4	2	14	6	9
QII	d	12	4	8	4	16	0	0	6	4	6
	e	16	2	0	18	18	0	2	4	4	7

Table 27.3 gives the percentages of the 50 Ss who gave various ratings, from a (no exceptions) to e (always exceptions) to the principles in abstract (P), in the first context (QI) and in the second context (QII). The results seemed to depend on the particular principles, on the particular ratings, and on the context. Thus Principle 9 (Lincoln's beliefs) was rated *a* by 60% or

more and *e* by 4% or less; in contrast, Principle 1 (there should be segregation) was rated as *a* by less than 22% and as *e* by as many as 36%. Whereas 36% gave an *e* rating to Principle 1 and to Principle 4 (evolution) in the abstract, 18% or less did so in the second context. In each task, ratings of *a* (no exceptions) tended to predominate, with ratings of *b* (sometimes exceptions) next; together they accounted for from two-thirds to three-quarters of the ratings. For all the tasks combined themeans were 37, 33, 10, 7, and 12% respectively for ratings *a* through *e*. Only 2% of the Ss failed to rate the principles in the abstract and only 1% failed to rate them in each of the contextual situations.

An individual's shift in rating from one task to the other was also determined. For this purpose, scores of 1 through 5 were assigned to the ratings of *a* through *e* respectively. Absolute deviation scores were then obtained by taking the absolute value of the differences between successive ratings of a principle. For example, if S rated Principle 1 as *a* in one context and as *b* in the other context, his absolute deviation score for this principle was 1 for the comparison of the two contexts, QI, QII; if he rated it as *c* in one context and as *e* in the other context his absolute deviation score was 2. In general, the absolute deviation score measured the extent (but not the direction) of the

TABLE 27.4
Percentages of Absolute Deviation
Scores in Comparison of Two Contexts of Experiment 1

Comparison	Absolute Deviations	1	2	3	4	5	6	7	8	9	Mean
	1										
	2		32	26	8	30	16	16	14	14	19
	3	18	6	6	22	12	0	4	2	10	8
QI QII	4	10	2	8	10	6	4	4	10	2	7
	Total	20	6	4	10	4	4	0	6	0	5
		8	46	44	50	52	24	24	32	26	39
	Weighed	56	7	8	12	9	4	4	8	4	8
	Mean	13									

individual's change in rating for a given principle in the two contexts. Table 27.4 lists the percentages of the 50 Ss who showed various absolute deviation scores in the comparison of the two contexts. For example, for Principle 1, 18% showed an absolute deviation score of 1, 10% of 2, 20%, of 3, 8% of 4, and 0% of 5 so that a total of 56% deviated on this principle while the remaining 44% gave the same rating to it in the two contexts, that is, they had a deviation of zero. The largest percentage of Ss shifted for Principle 1 (segregation) while less than half as many shifted for Principles 6, 7, or 9. On the average, 39% of the Ss were inconsistent in their ratings of a principle in the two contexts, with over half of these shifts involving only one letter change, that is, a shift of one unit. The weighed means were obtained by multiplying the percentages that shifted by the amount of the shift. The largest weighed mean occurred for Principle 1 with that for Principle 4 (evolution) a close second.

Experiment 2. This experiment, which was administered to 89 college students at the University of Miami, used the same procedure as in Experiment 1 except that there was a two-day interval between successive rating tasks. Recently Ilze Melkis, a graduate student in sociology at SUNY-Albany, put the data through a computer program for statistical analysis.

As in Experiment 1, scores of 1 through 5 were assigned to ratings of *a* through *e* respectively. Comparisons were made of each S's ratings of a principle not only in the two contexts but also of his rating of a principle in abstract with his rating of it in the first context and in the second context. If S gave a different rating for a principle in any of the three rating tasks, he was considered to be inconsistent for that principle. There were two Ss out of the 89 who were consistent in each principle, that is, who gave the same rating to the principle in the abstract as in the two contextual situations. At the other extreme there was one S who was inconsistent in all nine principles. The numbers and percentages of Ss who were inconsistent on various numbers of principles were as follows:

Numbers of Inconsistent Principles

	Zero	One	Two	Three	Four	Five	Six	Seven	Eight	Nine
# Ss:	2	4	5	13	10	11	21	11	11	1
% Ss:	2	5	6	15	11	12	24	12	12	1

The median and mean occurred at five inconsistent principles and the mode at six principles. Thus about half of the Ss were inconsistent in rating over half of the nine principles.

For each principle Table 27.5 gives the percentages of Ss who were inconsistent in the various comparisons as well as the percentages who were inconsistent in two or three of the comparisons. (It was not possible to be inconsistent in only one comparison since a deviation would be reflected in at least two comparisons.) For example, the table shows that for Principle 1 (segregation) 38% of the 89 Ss were inconsistent in two cases and 17% were inconsistent in all three cases so that a total of 55% were inconsistent in two or three cases. The most inconsistency was shown on Principle 4 (evolution) for which 66% were inconsistent in two comparisons and another 23% inconsistent in three comparisons so that a total of 89% were inconsistent for this principle. Principle 5 (religious conversion) yielded the next highest frequency of inconsistent Ss, with 58% inconsistent on it in two or three comparisons. The least inconsistency occurred on Principle 7 (bribery) with 39% inconsistent on it in two or three comparisons. Table 27.5 also shows that for each principle the highest percentage of inconsistent Ss occurred when the initial rating of the principle was compared to its rating in the second context. Indeed, for every principle with the exception of Principle 8 (work equality for women) the frequency of inconsistency increased from PQ_I to $Q_I Q_{II}$ to PQ_{II}; that is, inconsistency increased in successive rating tasks. One wonders whether the results were influenced by the fact that there were more outgroup situations in the second context.

Correlation coefficients were obtained for each of the nine principles by correlating its ratings in the abstract and in the two contexts. The correlation coefficients, which are also shown in Table 27.5, ranged from $-.43$ to $.69$ and averaged $.42$. Since perfect consistency in the ratings would have yielded cor-

TABLE 27.5

Meaures of Inconsistency in Experiment 2

Measure	Comparison	1	2	3	4	5	6	7	8	9	Means
% Inconsistent	PQI	37	30	31	43	38	38	21	34	29	33
Ss	QIQII	40	37	33	76	42	40	29	42	39	42
	PQII	49	40	38	80	51	43	34	40	44	47
	2 cases	38	37	43	66	45	47	34	43	46	44
	3 cases	17	11	5	23	13	9	5	10	7	11
	2 or 3 cases	55	48	48	89	58	56	39	53	53	55
Correlation Coefficients	PQI	.58	.43	.49	.61	.60	.31	.69	.51	.49	.52
	QIQII	.65	.46	.40	−.43	.48	.34	.51	.48	.44	.37
	PQII	.57	.48	.41	−.29	.45	.43	.50	.47	.30	.37
Mean Absolute Deviations	PQI	.73	.65	.56	.84	.73	.76	.38	.61	.53	.64
All Ss	QIQII	.70	.62	.62	2.12	.87	.73	.48	.69	.65	.83
	PQII	.84	.73	.84	2.09	1.06	.69	.57	.66	.75	.91
Mean Absolute Deviations	PQI	1.97	2.15	1.79	1.97	1.91	2.00	1.79	1.80	1.81	1.91
	QIQII	1.72	1.67	1.90	2.74	2.08	1.81	1.65	1.65	1.66	1.87
Inconsistent Ss	PQII	1.70	1.81	2.21	2.62	2.09	1.61	1.70	1.64	1.72	1.90

relations of 1.00, these fairly low correlations point to inconsistency in the ratings. On the average, the correlation coefficients were .52 for the principle in abstract and the first context (PQI) and .37 for the principle in abstract and the second context (PQII) as well as for the two contexts (QIQII); these findings also suggest that consistency decreased monotonically in subsequent tasks. Relatively high correlations were found for Principle 1 (segregation) and Principle 7 (bribery). Principle 4 (evolution) received the most variable and inconsistent correlations and the only negative ones. Other low correlations occurred for Principle 6 (subversive activities) and Principle 9 (Lincoln's beliefs).

An absolute deviation score was assigned to each S by summing his absolute deviations for the various principles. These absolute deviation scores ranged from zero (for the two Ss who were consistent throughout) to 48 for two Ss who were inconsistent in eight or nine principles. Both the mean and the median absolute deviation scores were 21. For each comparison a mean absolute deviation score was obtained by taking the sum of the absolute values of the deviation scores and dividing either by the number of Ss (which yielded the mean deviation for all Ss) or by the number of Ss who actually shifted in that comparison, that is, omitting those Ss who had a zero deviation score for that comparison (which yielded the mean deviation for inconsistent Ss). Table 27.5 shows that the absolute deviation for all Ss ranged from .38 (for Principle 7, PQI) to 2.12 (for Principle 4, QI QII). For the inconsistent Ss they ranged from 1.61 (for Principle 6, PQI) to 2.74 (for Principle 4, QIQII). On the average, the mean deviations for PQI, QI QII, and PQII were .64, .83, and .91 for all Ss and 1.91, 1.87 and 1.90 for inconsistent Ss respectively. In short, the mean absolute deviation was about one unit when zero changes were included and about two units when they were excluded.

In addition to the absolute deviation for each comparison a signed deviation was used to denote the extent and direction of an S's change in the rating of a principle. For example, if S rated a principle as a (1) in the abstract, as e (5) in the first context, and as c (3) in the second context, his signed deviation for

TABLE 27.6
Percentages of Initial Ratings
and Shifts for Various Religious Groups
in Experiment 2
Principles

Group	N	Rating	1	2	3	4	5	6	7	8	9	Mean	% Shifted
All Ss	51	a	22	20	37	27	14	43	37	29	49	31	44
		b	37	55	45	14	22	35	47	47	37	38	43
		c	2	6	4	8	10	4	4	12	6	6	79
		d	16	14	6	12	10	8	2	4	2	8	84
		e	24	6	8	39	45	10	10	8	6	17	57
Protestant	19	a	26	21	42	37	5	37	42	26	53	32	44
		b	47	47	42	16	37	37	47	47	42	40	34
		c	5	5	5	0	11	0	0	16	0	5	87
		d	11	21	0	11	11	5	5	0	5	8	100
		e	11	5	11	37	37	21	5	11	0	15	74
Catholic	16	a	19	13	38	13	38	44	25	25	56	30	39
		b	19	69	44	0	13	25	56	50	25	33	46
		c	0	0	6	6	13	6	0	6	6	5	100
		d	25	13	0	19	0	19	0	6	0	9	77
		e	38	6	13	63	38	6	19	13	13	23	51
Jewish	9	a	22	22	44	33	0	55	33	44	44	33	71
		b	44	55	33	11	11	33	55	33	33	35	68
		c	0	11	0	22	11	11	0	11	22	10	87
		d	22	11	22	11	11	0	0	11	0	10	87
		e	11	0	0	22	66	19	11	0	0	12	70

TABLE 27.7
Percentages of Initial Ratings and Shifts for Various Political
and Geographical Groups in Experiment 2

Principles

Group	N	Rating	1	2	3	4	5	6	7	8	9	Mean %	Shifted
Democratic	17	a	41	29	47	41	18	47	47	53	47	41	49
		b	35	53	53	12	18	41	47	24	35	35	57
		c	0	0	0	6	12	6	6	18	0	5	75
		d	12	12	0	18	6	6	0	6	6	7	91
		e	12	6	0	24	47	0	0	0	12	11	53
Republican	15	a	13	27	40	20	7	53	20	27	47	28	45
		b	40	47	53	13	33	33	47	53	53	41	34
		c	0	7	0	7	0	0	0	7	0	2	100
		d	27	7	0	13	7	0	7	0	0	7	89
		e	20	13	7	47	53	13	27	13	0	21	69
Northern	36	a	22	19	39	28	14	44	39	19	50	31	41
		b	39	58	44	17	19	28	47	53	33	38	46
		c	3	8	3	8	8	6	3	14	8	7	77
		d	14	11	8	11	14	11	3	6	3	9	83
		e	22	3	6	36	44	11	8	8	6	16	62
Southern	15	a	20	20	33	27	13	40	33	53	47	32	51
		b	33	47	47	7	27	53	47	33	47	38	41
		c	0	0	7	7	13	0	0	7	0	4	80
		d	20	20	0	13	0	0	7	0	0	7	100
		e	27	13	13	47	47	7	13	7	7	20	56

that principle were +4 for PQI, −2 for QI QII and +2 for PQII. In every comparison the negative deviations predominated, the sums of the deviations being −17, −14, and −32 for PQI, QI QII, and PQII respectively. These results show that the shifts tended to be in the direction of more rigorous application of the principle, that is, in the direction of fewer exceptions to it. As in Experiment 1, most changes in rating were to an adjacent rating which yielded a deviation score of one unit: 52% of the positive deviations were +1 and 46% of the negative deviations were −1. As the shifts increased in absolute value, the frequencies decreased. Thus 18, 15 and 14% of the positive deviations were for shift scores of +2, +3, and +4 respectively and 22, 19, and 12% of the negative deviations were for shift scores of −2, −3, and −4 respectively. The shifts tended to be slightly more frequent and somewhat larger (in absolute value) for PQII than for PQI or for QI QII, again suggesting increases in inconsistency on successive tasks.

For 51 of the 89 data were available on religion, political party affiliation and geographical region of upbringing (northern or southern part of the United States). There were 19 Protestants, 16 Catholic, and 9 Jewish students, as well as 7 who stated no religious preference. There were 17 Democrats, 15 Republicans, and 19 who gave no political affiliation. The locale in which the student was raised was given as the north by 36 and the south by 15. In comparing the various subgroups' responses one should keep in mind that the percentages are based on small numbers of Ss.

Table 27.6 and 27.7 give the percentages of the initial ratings of the principles in the abstract for the 51 Ss as well as for the various religious, political, and geographical subgroups. The tables also gives the percentages who shifted from their initial rating of a principle in either contextual situation. For the total group of 51 Ss the initial rating of a (no exceptions) was almost twice as frequent on the average as that of e (always exceptions). For the total group and for each of the subgroups, the b and a ratings received the highest frequency and the c and d ratings the lowest frequency of initial choices. The rank order of the initial ratings, arranged in decreasing frequency, was b, a, e, d, and c in every group except the Democrats, for whom the a and b ranks were interchanged and in a few groups for whom the c and d frequencies were equal. In short, Ss favored the ratings of b (sometimes exceptions) and a (no exceptions) while few chose d (often exceptions) and even fewer chose c (exceptions as often as no exceptions), perhaps because they disliked such an ambiguous middle-of-the-road position. Initial ratings in the latter two categories showed the most change subsequently, that is, for the total group and for each sub-group the percentage of shift was the largest for initial ratings of c or d. In contrast, the smallest frequencies of shifts occurred for the initial ratings that were most prevalent, a and b. This was true for the 51 Ss and for the various subgroups with the exception of the Jewish and the Democrat subgroups. The Jewish Ss showed 71 and 68% shift for ratings initially a and b respectively and 70% for ratings initially e whereas the Protestant and Catholic subgroups had between 34 and 46% shift in a and b and 51 and 74% respectively in e. The Democrats had 49 and 57% shift in a and b and 53% in e whereas the Republicans had 45 and 34% shift in a and b and 69% in e. That the initial categories of c and d should have been shifted is perhaps not surprising since they stated that exceptions should often be allowed but what is somewhat surprising is that the a rating of no exceptions should have shifted, with 44% shift for the total group and from 39 to 71% for the subgroups. In general, about 50% of the total group and of each of the subgroups remained consistent (did not shift) with the exceptions of the Jewish subgroups in which only 28% were consistent.

Comparisons of the various subgroups' initial ratings of the nine principles yield some interesting observations. The Catholic subgroup's ratings of Principle 4 (evolution) differed from that of the other religious subgroups. Whereas only 13% of the Catholics rated it as a (no exceptions) and 63% as e (always exceptions), 37% of the Protestants gave it each of these ratings, 33% as e (always exceptions), 37% of the Protestants gave it each of these ratings, 33% of the Jews rated it as a and only 22% as e; these findings suggest that the Catholics were more opposed to the evolution principle than the other Ss. Principle 5 (religious conversion) might be expected to be favored by the Catholics, which it was, with 38% of them rating it as a (no exceptions), a rating given to it by only 5% of the Protestants and by 0% of the Jewish Ss. Moreover, 66% of the latter (and 57% of those professing no religious affiliation) rated this principle as e as if to indicate their disapproval of it; possible explanations of this finding are that the Jews resent the long history of attempts to convert them or that they (and perhaps the Ss of the no religious affiliation subgroups) prefer to stand as iconoclasts.

While 41% of the Democrats rated Principle 1 (segregation) as a, only 13% of the Republicans did so. Surprisingly, the northern and southern subgroups showed very similar initial ratings of this principle. That 47% of the Democrats gave an a rating to Principle 7 (bribery) whereas only 20% of the Republicans did so may reflect the fact that there was a Republican administration when the experiment was conducted. While 53% of the Democrats gave an *a* rating to Principle 8 (work equality for women) only 27% of the Republicans did so. Also, only 19% of the Northern subgroups gave this principle an a rating whereas 53% of the Southern subgroup did so; perhaps the Northerners had a conception of women working in factories and the Southerners of farm and domestic workers.

Finally, the 15 most inconsistent Ss were interviewed individually to see how they would react when their different ratings were pointed out to them. The interview, which took place after the last rating task, began by asking S various questions about his religious, political, and racial beliefs. Then the experimenter pointed, one at a time, to the various principles on which S had been inconsistent in the ratings and asked him to explain the changes in ratings. Most commonly offered during the interviews as an explanation of inconsistencies was that the principle's meaning was altered by the situational context, that is, even though the principle was recognized, the specific situation changed its meaning. Additional reasons given for inconsistent responses were failure to understand the stories, carelessness, and lack of interest. Some Ss said that they were unable to account for the shifts and a few seemed to have been surprised and embarrassed that they had been inconsistent. However, when confronted with a shift from *b* to *c* or *d* or the other way around, some Ss said that they felt that these ratings carried the same meanings and that their use of them did not involve any inconsistency.

Experiment 3. This variation, which became the paradigm for future experimentation whenever time permitted, introduced ranking tasks in addition to the ratings of the principle. Before and after the usual rating tasks, S was asked to rank the nine principles in the abstract from the most important (first rank) to the least important (ninth rank) in the following ways:

As he thought they should be ranked in our society (personal ranking).

As he thought present-day society operationally supports the principles (societal ranking).

Initially S ranked the principles in these two ways and rated the principles in abstract (PI); later he rated them in the first context (QI) and still later in the second context, and then again in the abstract (PII); finally he again gave them personal and societal rankings. This experiment was administered with the assistance of Norman Harper to 40 Ss at the University of Miami who were questioned concerning their religious and political affiliation, what part of the country (north or south) they had spent most of their lives, and whether they were for or against integration. After the final testing session, each S was interviewed to get his reactions to inconsistencies in his responses.

The numbers of different rankings of the principles initially and at the conclusion are presented in Table 27.8 for personal rankings and in Table 27.9 for societal rankings. Of the 40 Ss, three did not give either personal or societal rankings in the first part, and still another did not give societal rankings in the second part. Some principles received very different personal and societal rankings and the changes from the initial to the final rankings tended to be greater for the personal rankings than for the societal rankings, which

TABLE 27.8

Numbers of Various Personal Rankings in Experiment 3

Rank	Situation*	Principles								
		1	2	3	4	5	6	7	8	9
First	PI	1	4	13	5	1	4	3	0	8
	PII	4	3	5	2	2	7	1	2	13
Second	PI	2	8	8	1	4	9	2	3	2
	PII	4	4	11	4	5	7	4	0	0
Third	PI	3	5	6	2	3	10	6	5	0
	PII	8	8	6	2	5	2	3	2	2
Fourth	PI	4	4	1	4	4	4	6	9	3
	PII	1	4	5	2	3	9	6	5	4
Fifth	PI	5	3	2	5	1	3	9	7	4
	PII	4	4	3	3	8	5	5	6	1
Sixth	PI	5	6	1	7	7	5	0	3	5
	PII	6	4	2	8	6	5	3	5	0
Seventh	PI	2	2	5	5	9	1	5	3	7
	PII	1	4	4	9	3	1	10	6	1
Eighth	PI	5	4	2	4	9	3	5	5	2
	PII	2	5	2	4	6	2	4	8	6
Ninth	PI	12	2	1	7	1	2	1	4	9
	PII	10	2	1	4	2	2	3	5	11

*PI refers here to the personal ranking at the beginning of the experiment and PII to the personal ranking at the end of the experiment.

were fairly stable. For example, in the initial rankings, Principle 1 (segregation) received one first-place (most important) and 12 ninth-place (least important) personal rankings and in the final part, four first-place and 10 ninth-place personal rankings; in contrast, each time it received 12 first-place and only two or three ninth-place societal rankings. Thus the extreme personal rankings were almost the reverse of the extreme societal rankings for this principle. It seemed that while the Ss did not initially think that segregation should be important in our society, but assigned it somewhat more importance after the intervening rating tasks, each time they considered that

TABLE 27.9

Numbers of Various Societal Rankings in Experiment 3

Rank	Situation*	Principles								
		1	2	3	4	5	6	7	8	9
First	SI	12	2	2	1	2	11	4	0	1
	SII	12	3	2	1	1	12	2	0	2
Second	SI		5	3	0	0	10	6	1	2
	SII	4	2	3	3	4	7	3		5
Third	SI	2	7	5	2	5	0	8	2	4
	SII	1	7	6	5	3	4	6	1	2
Fourth	SI	1	4	7	4	3	6	6	3	1
	SII	3	3	4	1	6	2	4	6	5
Fifth	SI	3	6	7	3	7	1	3	4	1
	SII	0	3	7	2	8	6	4	4	1
Sixth	SI	4	4	2	3	8	3	2	6	3
	SII	10	3	8	3	3	0	0	6	2
Seventh	SI	1	3	2	5	3	2	4	7	8
	SII	2	4	3	5	6	1	7	1	3
Eighth	SI	2	4	4	5	5	1	0	7	7
	SII	0	6	1	3	3	2	6	7	
Ninth	SI	2		3	12	2	1	2	4	
	SII	3	4	1	11	2	0	3	3	8

*SI refers to the societal ranking at the beginning of the experiment and SII to the societal ranking at the end of the experiment.

society gives strong operational support to the principle. Similarly, Principle 3 (religious minority groups) received 13 first-place personal rankings initially but only five such rankings subsequently, whereas it received two first-place societal rankings each time. Principle 6 (subversive activities) received four first-place personal rankings initially and seven subsequently whereas it received 11 or 12 first-place societal rankings each time. And Principle 9 (Lincoln's beliefs) had eight first-place personal rankings initially and 13 subsequently but only one or two first-place societal rankings each time. Some other interesting observations concerning different rankings can be made from the tables. For example, Principle 5 (religious conversion) received one fifth-place personal rankings initially but eight such rankings subsequently whereas it received seven or eight fifth-place societal rankings. In short, there were some marked differences between the personal and societal rankings and the former were more variable from the initial to the final rankings.

TABLE 27.10
Numbers of Ss Who Gave Various Ratings in Experiment 3

Principles

Situation	Rating	1	2	3	4	5	6	7	8	9	Total
Abstract	a	2	14	14	7	5	21	12	7	17	99
	b	10	17	19	4	21	16	16	19	15	
PI	c	2	2	1	7	4	0	8	8	2	137
	d	16	5	2	7	5	2	3	4	3	34
	e	10	2	4	15	5	1	1	2	3	47
											43
First Context	a	7	18	14	10	6	14	16	12	21	
	b	7	18	16	14	13	18	18	17	14	118
QI	c	5	2	2	4	7	4	4	4	1	135
	d	11	2	5	2	7	3	1	5	2	33
	e	10	0	3	10	7	1	1	2	2	38
											36
Second Context	a	9	11	13	10	7	23	17	8	8	106
	b	13	19	20	6	19	12	20	23	18	150
QII	c	2	4	3	6	5	2	2	3	4	31
	d	7	5	1	6	4	3	1	5	5	37
	e	9	1	3	12	5	0	0	1	5	36
Abstract	a	1	10	12	9	6	20	15	7	15	95
	b	9	21	19	9	18	16	20	24	16	152
PII	c	5	3	2	3	4	1	1	2	5	26
	d	12	3	4	9	8	2	3	5	1	47
	e	13	3	3	10	4	1	1	2	3	40

The numbers of various ratings for the nine principles are presented in Table 27.10 together with the totals for all the principles. It can be seen that in every rating situation, the ratings, arranged in decreasing order of frequency, were *b, a, d, e,* and *c*. In Experiment 2 the rank order of the initial rankings had been *b, a, e, d,* and *c*. Thus Ss in the present experiment also favored rank *b* (sometimes exceptions), with *a* (no exceptions) next, while few selected *c* (exceptions as often as no exceptions), the middle-of-the-road position.

Of the 40 Ss, none was consistent for all nine principles throughout the four rating tasks or even throughout the first three rating tasks. There were only two Ss who said initially that they were against integration. One of these rated Principle 1 (segregation) as *eaaa* in the four rating tasks respectively; later, when confronted with these ratings, he said that the first rating was an error and that he had intended it to be *a*. The other S rated this principle as *e* throughout. Such varied patterns of responses were also found among those who had said that they were for integration. In Principle 1 (as was also the case for Experiment 2) there was a tendency for the ratings to become less flexible from PI to QI and then to QII; however, there was a slight increase in flexibility from PI to PII. The numbers of signed deviations for this principle were as follows for the various comparisons:

	+1	+2	+3	+4	−1	−2	−3	−4
PIQI	6	2	3	0	4	4	2	3
QIQII	5	0	0	0	2	5	2	1
PIQII	5	2	0	0	4	4	6	2
PIPII	6	2	4	0	4	3	1	1

Thus for PIQI there were 11 positive deviations with a weighed sum of 19 and 13 negative deviations with a weighed sum of −30, suggesting less flexibility or more rigor in applying the principle in the first context than for the initial ratings of the principle in abstract. Similarly, for QIQII there were 5 positive deviations and 10 negative deviations with weighed sums of 5 and −22 respectively. And for PIQII there were 7 and 18 negative deviations with weighed sums of 9 and −38 respectively. Thus the differences between the weighed sums of positive and negative deviations were −11, −17, and −29 respectively, suggestive of an increasing tendency toward less flexibility in successive contexts. However, for PIPII there were 12 positive and only 9 negative deviations with weighed sums of 22 and −17 respectively, indicating a slight tendency for a less-rigorous final rating of this principle in abstract. Similar trends held for the nine principles as a whole.

Of the 40 Ss, 18 were Protestant, 10 Catholic, and 12 Jewish; half of the group were Democrats and the others Republicans; 27 were from the north, 11 from the south, and two could not be classified geographically.

The means of the absolute deviation scores were obtained for each principle for the group of 40 Ss and for the various subgroups. These are presented in Table 27.11 for QIQII and also for PIQIQII; the latter were obtained as the sum of the means of the absolute deviations for PIQI, PIQII, and QIQII. For the group as a whole the mean deviations for QIQII ranged from 1.1 for Principle 7 (bribery) to 2.6 for Principle 4 (evolution) and averaged 1.8 units; those for PIQIQII ranged from 1.5 for Principle 7 to 5.1 for Principle 4 and averaged 2.6 units. As in Experiment 2, the Jewish subgroups showed somewhat more shifts, on the whole, than the other religious subgroups, averaging 2.0 units for QIQII, compared to 1.6 for the Protestant and 1.8 for the Catholic subgroups, and 2.8 units for PIQIQII compared to 2.6 for the other religious subgroups. However, the same trend did not hold for all principles. In particular, the Catholic subgroup had the largest deviation for QIQII on Principle 2 (religious activities in public schools) and the smallest deviation for each of QIQII and PIQIQII on Principle 3 (religious minority groups). Every Catholic S showed zero deviation in QIQII on Principle 3, with *aa, bb, cc,* and *dd* ratings given by four, four, one and one S respectively. In PIQIQII the Catholics showed a 1.0 deviation on this principle compared to 2.6 for the Protestants and 3.2 for the Jews.

TABLE 27.11
Mean Absolute Deviation Scores in Experiment 3

Principles

Comparison	Group		1	2	3	4	5	6	7	8	9	Mean
QIQII	All Ss	40	1.8	1.4	1.9	2.6	1.5	1.3	1.1	1.4	2.0	1.8
	Protestant	18	1.3	1.2	1.6	2.3	1.4	1.0	1.3	1.2	1.9	1.6
	Catholic	10	2.3	1.8	0.0	2.8	1.3	1.0	1.0	1.1	2.0	1.8
	Jewish	12	2.3	1.6	2.2	2.8	1.8	1.6	1.0	2.3	2.3	2.0
	Democrat	20	1.8	1.4	2.6	2.6	1.8	1.3	1.2	1.6	2.0	1.9
	Republican	20	1.8	1.5	1.4	2.5	1.1	1.3	1.0	1.3	2.1	1.6
	Northern	27	1.8	1.6	1.9	2.8	1.5	1.4	1.0	1.5	2.1	1.9
	Southern	11	1.5	1.2	1.7	2.3	1.4	1.0	1.3	1.0	2.0	1.6
PIQIQII	All Ss	40	3.1	2.1	2.4	5.1	2.8	1.9	1.5	2.3	2.9	2.6
	Protestant	18	2.8	2.6	2.6	5.1	2.6	2.1	1.2	2.1	2.3	2.6
	Catholic	10	4.0	1.8	1.0	5.4	2.4	1.4	2.0	2.6	2.8	2.6
	Jewish	12	2.5	1.5	3.2	4.8	3.5	2.0	1.5	2.2	3.7	2.8
	Democrat	20	2.5	1.3	2.3	5.3	3.0	2.1	1.6	2.5	3.1	2.6
	Republican	20	3.5	2.8	2.4	4.9	2.6	1.7	1.4	2.0	2.6	2.6
	Northern	27	3.4	2.3	3.0	5.5	3.0	1.9	1.6	2.8	3.1	2.9
	Southern	11	2.0	1.6	0.9	4.7	2.0	2.2	1.5	0.9	2.4	2.0

There seemed to be no consistent differences between the Democrats and the Republicans. In contrast, the northern Ss had a higher deviation than the southern Ss on every principle with the exception of Principle 6 (subversive activities); the differences were 1.4, 2.0, 1.0, and 1.7 on Principles 1 (segregation), 3 (religious minority groups), 5 (religious conversion), and 8 (work equality for women) respectively, with an average difference of about one unit.

When S's different ratings of a principle were shown to him, the reactions were similar to those found in Experiment 2. They included the comment that the context or situation or specific story had been taken into account, surprise and even embarrassment that one had been so inconsistent, the remark that a rating had been made in error and that another was intended, and the defense that some of the different ratings (b, c, d) had similar meanings so that their choice did not represent inconsistency.

Experiment 4. This variation was administered, with the assistance of Norma Sams and Vicki Sullivan, to four groups at the University of Miami, each composed of about 100 students. On the first day the control group was asked to give personal and societal rankings of the nine principles in the abstract and also to rate their applicability. One week later they were asked to perform the same tasks. Experimental group I was given the same tasks as the control group on the first day and a week later; in addition, they were asked to rank and rate the principles in the first context on the fourth day and in the second context on the next day. For Experimental group II the procedure differed only in that the principles in the first and second context were both given on the same day, the second immediately after they had completed the tasks for the first context. Experimental group III had the same procedure as Experimental group II but at the onset the Ss were instructed that they were to assume the role of impartial judges throughout.

The results showed little difference between Experimental groups I and II, suggesting that the time interval between the two contextual situations had little influence. There were more marked differences between Experimental group III and the other experimental groups, suggestive of the influence of the initial instructions to assume the role of judges. Also, there were differences between the control and experimental groups, which point to the role of the intervening contextual situations and the corresponding tasks.

Some Ss consistently maintained the same personal or societal rankings for all their ranking tasks.

The percentages of each group who ranked the principles identically throughout were as follows:

	Societal	Personal
Control	29	34
Exp. I	29	34
Exp. II	27	36
Exp. III	42	42

One might have expected that a higher percentage of control group Ss would have given identical ratings since they had only two rather than four opportunities to do the personal and societal rankings. Yet they do not have a larger frequency of stability than the experimental groups and less than Experimental group III. The differences in societal ranking between the latter group and the other groups were statistically significant at the .05 level. Moreover, Experimental group III was as stable in the societal as in the personal ranking whereas the other groups were less stable for the societal ranking. These results suggest that the instructions to be impartial judges led to more stability and to greater identification of self and society.

Initially ranked as most important for society was Principle 6 (subversive activities) and at least important for society was Principle 4 (evolution). Similarly, in Experiment 3 Principle 6 had initially received the highest number of most important societal rankings and the smallest number of least important societal rankings whereas the reverse had been the case for Principle 4. For each of Principles 4 and 6 the deviation from the first societal ranking to the final societal ranking was correlated to the corresponding deviation for the personal rankings. The correlations were as follows:

	Principle 4	Principle 6
Control		
Exp. I	.084	.169
Exp. II	.414	.410
Exp. III	.338	.468
	.856	.688

The differences between the control groups and the experimental groups were significant at the .02 level. These results suggest that the intervening experience with the contextual situations led to more identification of self and society than in the control group, which did not have this experience. The difference between the third experimental group and the other two was also significant at the .02 level, suggesting that the instructions to be impartial judges fostered such identification; when the instructed Ss shifted on the personal rankings, they tended to shift by the same amount and in the same direction on the societal rankings.

Turning to the rating tasks, we find that no deviation or a deviation of only one unit was shown by at least 60% of the Ss in each group from the first to the final rating of the principles in abstract and by at least 55% of the Ss in each group from the first to the second contextual situation. The most stability in rating from the first context to the second was found for Principle 6, which initially had been ranked as most important, and the least stability for Principle 4, which initially had been ranked as least important. A deviation of no more than one unit for the contextual ratings was shown by 100% of each of Experimental groups I, II, and III for Principle 6 but only by 55, 33, and 47% of these groups respectively for Principle 4. In short, it seemed that importance tended to be directly related to stability in rating of applicability. Of all the principles, Principle 6 tended to be applied most strictly, that is, with the largest percentages of no or few exceptions. From the first to the second context there were increases in more rigorous applications of the principles for Experimental groups I and II. This trend had also been found in the previous experiment and indicated less flexibility in the outgroup situations which predominated in the second text. However, the reverse trend was found for Experimental group III, which showed less rigorous applications of the principles in the second context. Possibly, the instructions to be impartial judges led to more flexibility or leniency in considering one's outgroups.

In the interview at the end of the experiment, before being shown their choices, Ss were asked if there had been contradictions or inconsistencies in their answers. About three-quarters of the Ss replied no, some gave ambiguous answers, and relatively few said yes, and those who answered yes were not necessarily those with wide discrepancies in ranking or ratings. The replies may be indicative of the stress that is placed on consistency and uniformity in our society. When they were shown their replies, the reactions were similar to those obtained in previous experiments.

In future experimentation it would be of interest to use another control group which received the contextual situations but not the principles in abstract. Another modification would be to give a control group and some of the experimental groups the contexts without explicit statement of the principles involved in them. Ss might be asked what principle was involved and/or the extent to which they thought the principle should be applied or they might be asked to what extent they agreed with the principle. Another modification would be to have Ss submit lists of principles which were most important and least important for themselves and as operationally supported by society. They would then be asked to rate these principles. It would be of interest to discover whether or not the most important would be applied more strictly than the less important principles.

Experiment 5. Variations have been conducted in which the contextual situations that usually were given first were presented after the contextual situations that usually were given second, that is, Situations 1 to 9 followed Situations 10 to 18. One such variation was individually administered (by teachers in ASL's social psychology class at SUNY-Albany) to 18 high school girls in their junior or senior year, with half of them receiving the contexts in each order. Another modification was to ask S to comment, with each situation, on whose side she was on and why. A further modification was to insert the word *no* in Principle 1 so that it read: *There should be no segregation between Negroes and whites;* this was to make the principle less shocking and more relevant to the Ss. Each S first ranked the principles in the abstract from most important to least important (personal ranking) and then rated them; then she received the principles in one of the contexts, rated them and commented on them; this was followed by another personal ranking of the principles in abstract, then the principles in the other context were rated and commented on, finally the principles in the abstract were ranked and rated. Ss who received the usual order of the contexts are said to constitute Group QIQII and those who received them in the new order are said to constitute Group QIIQI.

There were three rankings of the principles so that each S had two opportunities to shift her initial rankings. Altogether there were 237 shifts in rank, with 51% occurring in Group QIQII and 49% in Group QIIQI. Thus the Ss in one group were not significantly more likely to change their rankings than the Ss in the other group. For both groups, Principles 1 and 6 were most stable with regard to rankings.

Ss in both groups tended to be more flexible in QII, that is, to give ratings which allowed more exceptions in QII than in QI, regardless of the order of presentation. This differs from the trend found in previous experiments (except for the Ss in Experiment 4 who were told to be impartial judges). One wonders whether the questions asked in each contextual situation about whose side they were on and why might have been a factor in determining the present trend. Ss in Group QIQII were more likely to answer these questions. Also, more of them mentioned phenomenal contradictions with reference to Principle 9; three Ss in Group QIQII said that Lincoln was contradicting himself in the two speeches (with one adding that he did so in much of his writing) but no S in Group QIIQI said this although one remarked that she did not believe that Lincoln made Statement 18. Some reasons for shifts were revealed by the comments about whose side they were on and why. For example, an S in Group QIQII rated Principle 1 as *b* and than as *e*, and commented in the first context that no one should be denied education on the basis of his race and in the second that she didn't think the two races should mix. Yet Ss sometimes shifted their ratings but made similar comments in each context; for example, an S in Group QIIQI rated Principle 1 as *c* and then as *a*, saying at first that the girl had the right to choose the person she wanted to be with and saying subsequently that the Negro woman should have equal rights; and another S in Group QIIQI rated Principle 4 first as *b* and then as *e*, saying each ime that it was very confusing and she didn't know whether to believe the Bible or evolution theories. The comments suggested (as did remarks in previous experiments) that some Ss regarded Principles 4 and 9 as different from the others. As one S pointed out, all principles except Principles 4 and 9 provided implications for actions while these two were concerned only with belief or credibility in light of particular information. Future experimentation should consider replacing these two with principles which are more parallel to the rest.

Experiment 6. Various modifications of the basic experiment have been used for laboratory exercises. One shortened variation of the basic experiment used only five principles; Principle 1 (but with the word no added as in the previous experiment) and Principles 2, 3, 6, 7. They will be referred to as Principles 1^1, 2^1, 3^1, 4^1, and 5^1 respectively. In an attempt to simplify and clarify the five-point rating scale, a new four-point scale was used.

A. No exceptions should ever be made in application of the principle.
B. Occasional exceptions should be made in application of the principle.
C. Frequent exceptions should be made in application of the principle.
D. The principle should never be applied.

The experiment was administered at SUNY-Albany with the assistance of Thomas Lickona to 31 college freshmen and sophomores, about half of whom were females. The five principles were read to S and he was asked to select and write down three principles: the principle which was most important to him, that is, the one which he most strongly supported; the principle which was moderately important to him; and the principle which was least important to him. For each of the three principles which he selected S was asked to apply the four-point rating scale. Then the first contextual situations (QI) involving these principles was presented and S was asked to explain whose side of the conflict he was on, and why, and he was also asked to rate the principles. Because of scheduling difficulties, the remainder of the experiment was run with no break for 17 Ss, after a one-day break for 11 Ss, and after a three-day break for three Ss. The second set of contextual situations (QII) involving the three principles was presented in the same manner at the first. Then S was shown his three ratings of each principle and asked to explain any changes. The results for all Ss were combined since they did not seem to depend on the time-interval between the first and second contextual situations.

Principle 1^1 was selected by 27 of the 31 Ss and the remaining principles by 15 to 18 Ss. For the Ss who selected each principle, we list the percentages who selected it as most, moderately, and least important; the percentage who shifted their rating and the mean absolute deviation are also given.

	1^1	2^1	3^1	4^1	5^1
% most important	52	20	13	59	11
% moderately important	37	40	44	41	6
% least important	11	40	44	0	83
% shifted ratings	19	40	63	47	39
Mean absolute deviation	.26	.73	.87	.58	.59

Principle 1^1, which 14 of 27 Ss ranked as most important, yielded the smallest percentage who were inconsistent on the three ratings and the smallest mean absolute deviation. However, the next smallest percentage and extent of shift was found for Principle 5^1, which 15 out of 18 Ss had ranked as least important. Principle 3^1, which 7 out of 16 Ss had ranked as least important, showed the highest percentage and extent of shift. Thus, while there was not a linear relationship between importance and inconsistency, there was a suggestive trend. This was studied further by obtaining the results for the most important, the moderately important, and the least-important principles.

Shifts in ratings were shown by 32, 35, and 45% of the 31 Ss and the mean absolute deviations were .39, .45, and .55 for the most, moderately, and least-important principles respectively. These results show a tendency for consistency in rating to vary directly with importance of the principle to S.

Initial Rating	Most Important	Moderately Important	Least Important
% A	68	39	23
% B	32	58	26
% C	0	3	35
% D	0	0	16
Mean	1.3	1.6	2.5

The percentages of initial ratings of A, B, C, and D were also obtained for the most, moderately, and least important principles. With a score of 1, 2, 3, and 4 assigned to ratings of A through D respectively a mean rating was obtained. The most frequent ratings were A, B, and C for the most, moderately, and least important principles respectively. The rating of A (no exceptions) decreased and the rating of C (frequent exceptions) increased from the most to the least important, the rating of B (occasional exceptions) was largest for the moderately important principles, while the rating of D (never applied) occurred only for the least important principles. Also the mean ratings increased from the most to the least important principles. These results suggest that the more important the principle, the more likely it was to be applied strictly, that is, without exception. In short, as we found in previous experiments, the more important the principle to S, the fewer exceptions he would allow in its application and the more consistent he would be in his ratings of it in different contexts.

On the whole the Ss were quite consistent in the ratings. Nine Ss made no rating changes at all, ten Ss shifted on only one principle, nine Ss on two principles, and three Ss on three principles. Altogether there were 44 shifts of which 19 were toward more rigor and 25 toward greater flexibility, that is, more exceptions. From the first to the second context there were 18 shifts of which 12 were in the direction of more exceptions. Thus QII, the context with more outgroup situations, yielded less strict application of the principle. This was the same trend found in Experiment 5 but differed from the trend in other experiments (except for the Ss of Experiment 4 who were told to be impartial judges). One wonders whether the questions about whose side they were on and why, which were common to both the present experiment and Experiment 5, might have been a factor in determining the trend.

Some of the comments made about whose side they were on and why revealed apparent reasons for shifts. For example, an S who successively rated Principle 3[1] as AAC said in the first context that he was on the side of the Christians because the Mohammedan authorities have openly violated the principle of separation of church and state; in the second context he said he was on the side of the school because hymns and carols do not constitute religious teachings and are drawn from many cultures and not one; an S who successively rated Principle 5[1] as CCB said in the first context that he was on the civil servants' side explaining that just because they accepted gifts does not mean that they were bribed, but in the second context he said that he was on the government's side because public opinion might result in a loss of respect for public officials. Ss sometimes shifted one rating unit and yet did not change the side they were on or their reason. And there were Ss who changed sides but did not shift their ratings; for example, one S who never shifted his ratings rated Principle 4^1 as B throughout but he said in the first context that he was on the side of the subversives because he did not believe in the Communist doctrine and in the second context that he was on the side of the United States government because the government should protect him; he added in the first context that in general he believes that a government has the right to protect itself but not to destroy its opponents and in the second context that if all the people did was to be members of the Communist party they should not have been executed. Occasionally there was a refusal to take sides; for example, one S who rated Principle 2^1 as B throughout said in the first context that he was on neither side because the church and state are one in the Moslem country and in the second context that he was on the Mohammedans' side because if equal time could not be given to other religions then there should be no religious activity; for Principle 5^1, which he successively rated as DBB, he sided in the first context with the civil servants and in the second with neither side, saying in the first context that a person should be able to accept a gift without fear that it would be considered a bribe and in the second that the workers should be dismissed if and only if it could be proven that the gifts were given because of favoritism to certain companies.

Explanations of inconsistencies were similar to those obtained in previous experiments. In general, Ss said that they changed their ratings because the contextual situations contained factors which had not occurred to them when they had rated the principle in the abstract or because of factors specific to one of the contexts. For example, an S who rated Principle 1^1 as ABB changed because while A is morally and theoretically correct, occasional exceptions may be made when violence serves no ultimate purpose; another S who rated Principle 2^1 as AAC changed because he felt that in the second context an exception should be made because if they did not want to attend public schools they did not have to; the same S, who rated Principle 3^1 as CCA, changed because in this country freedom of choice is guaranteed and implies many other freedoms such as the freedom of conversion; another S rated Principle 4^1 as ABB and changed because he didn't like Communist governments and had not thought of that before; another S who rated Principle 5^1 as DBB, said that some government workers, such as inspectors and those who give out jobs to contractors, should not be allowed to accept gifts because of public opinion. An S who shifted in three principles, rating Principles 1^1, 3^1, and 5^1 as BCC, ABB, and CBB respectively, explained that he was inconsistent because once an example was given the situation was changed and involved people or factors different from those of which he had initially thought.

Concluding Remarks

In each experiment less than 2% of the Ss refused to indicate how they would apply the principles. Although a few individuals did say that a given principle was not applicable in a situation, they still applied it. The behavior of the Ss in some of our prewar studies was quite different. In one of the prewar studies Ss were given a situation, asked for their impressions of it, and asked how they would deal with it if they had to decide the case. Many Ss readily answered in terms of their ideologies, their attitudes toward certain aspects of the situation, or rules or principles which they stated. But there were some Ss who refused to make a decision. They wanted to know more about the situation, what it meant to the people in it, and what the consequences of the outcomes would be for the people in the situation and for the community at large. A few of them said that they wanted to make a just decision and that they could not do this until they heard from the people involved or had more information. It was clear from their comments that they were not oriented to principles or ideologies but wanted to understand what was happening. The Ss who asked for more information were sometimes given a principle and were told that it was involved here and that they should apply it to the case. Some Ss did this but a few insisted that the principle did not help, that it did not apply, that it was not just to use it, and that it was no substitute for more information or for finding out what had actually happened. Those Ss who applied the principle were later confronted with their different judgments of a pair of situations involving it. They said that maybe the principle was invalid or inapplicable, or that the situations could be dealt with better by using different principles, or that the people involved could discuss the issues and reach a decision that would be fair to them and to the community.

When these findings were discussed with Wertheimer, his comments were similar to those which he often made regarding the ways one can approach a problem situation (cf. Luchins & Luchins, 1970c). One can react to the structure of the situation, focus on the evidence, and see what solutions or judgments it suggests or one can face it in terms of principles, rules, habits, or ideologies and therefore focus on certain aspects of the situation and perhaps be blind to its structural requirements. We have to find out the factors, social conditions, attitudes, and assumptions that lead Ss to face the situation in order to see what it requires instead of reacting to it in terms of principles, rules, habits, or ideologies. He pointed out that giving a person a principle to apply might produce a miscentering; the situation might not be faced freely to see what it required. Moreover, in experiments where principles were given, we needed to know more about how the principles were understood and applied. Why did Ss apply the principles as they did, did they think that they fit or were suitable in the situation or did they consider that the use of other principles or values would be more relevant? Since some Ss might apply the principle without thinking about such matters, we needed also to find out what would happen if Ss were told that they should act as judges who want to deal justly and righteously with the people and the situations. Would Ss react differently if they understood what it meant to be just and righteous in terms of the structural requirements of the case instead of acting in terms of social and personal factors? (Cf. Experiment 4 in which some Ss were told to be impartial judges.)

Wertheimer also suggested the use of some of the methods that extremize the Einstellung effect. What would happen if two people who were set by their convictions or who were set experimentally to use different principles (which went in the same direction or in opposite directions) were asked to judge a situation that fitted none, one, or both of the principles? Would the results be different when real beliefs were involved than when people were set experimentally to adhere to certain principles? This discussion also led to experimentation with the methods of clarification used in teaching an Adult Education class composed of American Bundists (Luchins, 1946) by having them face a situation from one and then from another strongly held value or principle. We were interested in what would happen if these were incompatible, for example, to judge a situation in terms of the Sermon on the Mount and the Nazi race theory. Would they agree in a particular situation that the Nazi doctrine actualizes the principles of the Sermon on the Mount or would they see that they were incompatible?

Results in the preliminary experiments suggested that many Ss felt more at ease when allowed to talk in generalities than when asked to point out just where in the statement or situation was the evidence on which they based their judgments. Some could not do so or said that their judgment was based on a combination of acts or on their impression of the whole situation. In discussing these findings with Wertheimer, ASL said that they might be the result of Prägnanz and that they also fit Bacon's indictment of the human mind as the source of error. Bacon noted that the mind is strangely eager to be relieved from suspense and seeks to establish and/or to use a principle. The idols of the tribe, cave, marketplace, and theater are readily used to rise above the evidence; it is human nature to do such things. Bacon had proposed methods of true induction to help men overcome these sources of error. Wertheimer agreed that the sources of error denoted by the idols play a role but he objected to the assumptions that it is human nature to make such errors. The errors are due to field conditions; we have to find these conditions and discover what factors extremize their operation. Bacon's methods might help one overcome these errors but they might blind one to the structure of the problem and the social situation which it is in (cf. Luchins & Luchins, 1970 a, b, c).

Wertheimer's general comments indicated the need to study the social atmosphere of the experimental situation and the social field of which it was a part. His lectures on thinking and concept formation also stressed the need to study the structure of the social situation in which acts of thinking, learning, and problem solving take place. He presented examples from anthropology and sociology to illustrate the role of the social field in such acts. (These lectures will be presented in another monograph.) Some of the results in the preliminary experiments were related to his lectures in which he had discussed the laws of traditional logic. What seemed offhand to be irrational or illogical behavior if viewed in terms of traditional logic often had a reasonable basis, when it was regarded in terms of the person's attitudes and assumptions. That people make or accept inconsistent or contradictory statements does not necessarily mean that they are behaving unreasonably but perhaps requires a new and different logic to deal with such statements.

28
Confidence, Trust, Domination, and Social Influence

We have described elsewhere (Luchins & Luchins, 1970c) the relationship of the effect of Einstellung in learning by repetition to our research on social influences. During the time of formulating the working hypotheses for understanding the Einstellung effects (Luchins, 1942, 28-33), Wertheimer sometimes related some of them to the research on social influences and social learning. We shall reconstruct here some of his preliminary formulations. He noted that it seemed probable from what happened in the experiments that the creation of two different kinds of social atmospheres would produce sharply different results. An atmosphere of slavishness, of fearfulness, a test atmosphere would work in the direction of increasing agreement with incorrect judgments. On the other hand, a free atmosphere, in which the individual was not subject to influences of this kind, would work against incorrect judgments. This observation has been repeatedly validated during the past 30 years of research. We also found that the social atmosphere often vitiated the effects of factors introduced to save the subjects from making nonveridical judgments. Wertheimer's stress on field conditions, on the social atmosphere, does not mean that he did not recognize the role of personality factors. He said that it is necessary for both practical and theoretical reasons to investigate the basic differences in the attitudes and personality characteristics of the subjects in these different social atmospheres. He objected to attributing social influences to this or that trait or to calling those who showed the influences gullible or conformers. He said that we must try to understand the subject's response and not just label it. He also said that we must take into account the characteristic structural features of the whole situation, factors in the social field, in the personality of the subjects, in the larger time-space manifold of which the experiment and subjects were subparts. That we cannot readily know the whole situation does not mean that we must not seek to learn more about it; it means we have to be modest in our assertions about what is actually the case.

He raised the question of the role of the factors of the subject's confidence in the experimenter and in the social field; agreement may have been due to his innocent reliance, faith, and trust that the experimenter in particular or that people in general are not deceitful. This does not mean that an attitude of mistrust or suspicion would have led to better results; mistrust and suspicion often lead one to be blind to situations, even to be duped in the very situation and with the very people of whom one is suspicious. He referred to

412

the negative effects of the debunking attitude fostered by certain methods of propaganda analysis. He went on to say, Suppose a child discovered that the white stuff that tastes so good (sugar) could actually be poison. What happens to the child when he gets the idea that nature and people are deceptive, that they are not what they appear to be? What consequences does it have for him and his social field when he becomes mistrustful and fearful of people and things in the physical and social world? The study of such cases in psychopathology might suggest what the field conditions are that lead to the loss and regaining of confidence in oneself, in one's fellowmen and in the physical world. He referred to the above-described study on prestige (its giving and taking) and said that a similar study should be done for confidence. In what things, people, and events do individuals have confidence, have no confidence, go from having confidence to having no confidence, and vice versa? What are the factors that are involved? What happens to the individual and what consequences does it have for the social field? When or how does confidence lead to narrowness, to slavish, blind reliance; when does it lead to freedom, to courage to act productively and intelligently, and when does it open one's eyes to possibilities of which he would ordinarily not be aware? Why do some people inspire confidence and others inspire mistrust; what does it mean that a person is trusted and reliable or that he is not trusted and is unreliable? What is the difference between simulating confidence and trust and actually having them, between simulating being a reliable and honest person and actually being one, between being a confidence man and a man in whom people have confidence?

ASL once objected to Wertheimer's optimistic attitude, saying that people are always trying to play tricks on each other. Even little children do this and do it in a cruel way. He related a story about a group of children who repeatedly told a feebleminded boy to go around the corner to see if it was raining and the children would laugh. This went on for weeks. One day a new boy on the block went along with the feebleminded child and concurred with his report that it was not raining. When the children laughed the new boy told them that it sometimes rained on one block but not on the other, that it was possible for it to rain on one side of the street and not on the other, and that this had happened on their block a few weeks ago. The gang was upset that he had spoiled their fun. They were interested not in finding out about the rain but in fooling the dull child. Maybe the dull child complied with their request because he had noticed that such things could happen; maybe he was not a gullible victim of their tricks but his behavior had a reasonable basis. Wertheimer said that the story illustrates that sometimes we might influence someone and although we get the response we want, it might mean something else to the so-called gullible person, he might be doing it for a different reason. He noted that in an animal experiment the experimenter may think that he is making the animal comply but the animal may be doing the things that get the experimenter to give him food or water; the experimenter is complying.

A student once asserted that one can just as well learn to be truthful as deceptive, trusting as mistrusting. Wertheimer objected, saying that of course it could be done if enough force was used but what would be the consequences for the person and for the social field if people were arbitrarily forced to behave this way, to act as if they were robots with no minds of their own? Deception and mistrust destroy certain kinds of relationships between people; truth and trust cement them. It has different consequence for the present or future functioning of the system if trust or mistrust is maximized, if people gain or lose their ability to act as free productive individuals because of it. Wertheimer conjectured that it would be more difficult to live in a social world in which there was no truth and no trust; it would destroy the social field and/or bring about personality malfunctioning. He conjectured that to begin with there is a tendency for truth and trust and that it is perhaps too readily destroyed by social conditions. He told the story about the psychologists (Wayne Dennis and his wife) who were studying little children and who were supposed to be cold, distant, and unresponsive to the control group's babies but they were not able to do this because of the way the babies looked at them. One student objected to the assumption that from the beginning there is a feeling of mutuality, of faith, trust, and honesty in people. If this were so, why is it that soldiers and even mothers have killed babies? Wertheimer said that such behavior is due to special conditions: to being narrowed down by ideological or other reasons or by various attitudes and assumptions, to a miscentering which blinded them to the child; if they were not blinded, they would have reacted to the child as did the experimenters who could not ignore the call or look of the babies. He conjectured that trust and truthfulness are natural and that mistrust and deceit are due to certain social conditions and psychopathology. He related this conjecture to the need for a reasonable world, a world in which there are rho-connections, in which things are not arbitrary (cf. Luchins & Luchins, 1970b). In the face of counter examples from daily life, he maintained that truth and mututal trust are necessary conditions for social and individual behavior. Such behavior cannot be fully understood if we regard them in terms of pleasure-pain to the ego or the organism. He noted that the concepts of empathy and identification put the dynamics of such behavior in the ego and still sought to explain it in terms of pleasure-pain. How true is it that people are monads with closed windows, blindly seeking pleasure? It is not true that man is egocentric. Truth and confidence are related to the requirements of a system, to such matters as proper and improper effects in the system, to chaos versus order, to reasonableness versus arbitrary, stupid, blind behavior. In this and other discussions it seemed that Wertheimer assumed that trust, confidence, truthfulness as well as distrust, suspicion, and untruthfulness were functions of the social field, that they produced different effects and had different consequences for the persons and the social field in which such behavior occurred. He objected to the assumption that people are by nature blind and indifferent to such matters. He added that the assumption was related to the Western man's conception of people as essentially evil and self-centered.

When these discussions were reported to ASL's Adult Education class, some students objected to Wertheimer's value judgments and to his assumption that one must have faith in nature and society. Some argued that one had to have faith in himself; if one is sure of himself, is self-sufficient, has a feeling of self-worth, he is able to function; it is all in the person's attitude, his outlook. ASL told them about studies of experimental neurosis in order to illustrate Wertheimer's idea that people need a reasonable world in which things are not arbitrary. They argued that there was no necessity, that it was all chance, that a piece of chalk might just as well fly up as fall down when released, that the sun might just as well rise in the West as in the East. It was all a matter of experience, of conditioning. Still other students said that what Wertheimer was suggesting was not a scientific problem; poets, novelists, and theologians dealt with faith. Someone referred to James' book on religious experience, saying that James describes faith as a kind of self-realization in which there is a feeling of unity with the cosmos; it is a subjective, private matter, a feeling of bliss, a blinding flash of light that sets one apart from others, a transcendence of self, a merging with the absolute, the infinite. A few students then said that faith is related to an other-worldly attitude; it makes one lose touch with daily life's problems and with society. It leads to a loss of perspective and of critical thinking; it is self-hypnosis, an escape from social reality, for example, the economic depression, Fascism, Nazism. Instead of facing life's problems, people seek ecstacy and salvation in mysticism; they might as well seek it in drugs, liquor, and sex. [Paraphrasing a communication of Maslow to the Archives of Psychology, we can say that the students were interested in cold topics and dismissed the hot ones as unscientific, as unworthy of study.]

When ASL reported this discussion to Wertheimer, he remarked that the students talked like psychologists. One need not get involved with theological problems of salvation in discussing the faith by which men live. When you cross on a green light you do not expect to be run down by a car. Wertheimer said that faith does not always lead to an escape from the physical world or the social situation; it sometimes leads to concern about particular people, concrete objects, and events. Lack of faith might sometimes lead to an escape. He suggested that we keep a record of when we do things on faith or with confidence that certain things would happen if such and such occurred or was done. A student who joined in the discussion said that such a diary would not reveal situations or events in which there was a sudden consciousness of one's soul or self, an experience of being flooded with joy or enlightenment, and therefore would not show that there was such a thing as faith. Another student said that we must not mix up theological discussions of faith based on religion with the ordinary acts that involve faith and confidence in people, nature, and society. When someone said that it is all a matter of conditioning, the student said that if we accept Hume's conception of an association, then faith replaces necessity in the connection between events. [Association of ideas is accompanied by a conviction which has its roots in feeling, a kind of natural belief that "unperverted by any theoretical reflections, asserts itself victoriously in man's practical procedures, and is completely adequate for the attainable ends of life and for the knowledge related to" them (Windleband, 1958, 477).] Wertheimer remarked that the questions of faith, confidence, truth, etc. must not be rejected because they have been related to theology. They do not come from and they are not uniquely theological issues; maybe it is the other way around. A refugee scholar said that, in some religions, faith is not the kind of soul-filling experiences that are described by James and by other writers about religion, but involves concrete particular actions in this world.

The discussion changed when Wertheimer asked for recent examples of loss of faith and confidence in people. The refugee scholar said that people are beginning to doubt the value of knowledge, are questioning the purpose of knowledge, are showing a distrust of reason and of science, and are losing confidence that science and scholarship lead to the betterment of mankind. The student mentioned the recent loss of faith and confidence in Communism among some of his acquaintances. He then described the reactions of some Communists and fellow travelers to the report in the *New York Times* of the Hitler-Stalin pact. The *Daily Worker* denounced it as a lie. There was a general disbelief until the *Daily Worker* corroborated the story. Some accepted its explanation or the explanation in the *New Masses* but some became disillusioned and still others became virulent anti-communists. He then noted that the Communist Party seemed to be working with the Nazi Bund in its support of the American First's anti-war program. Do they trust Hitler? The new party line forbids one to criticize Hitler; yet when one says this he is called a fascist. The student predicted that when Hitler invades Russia the poor fellow whose duty it is to bring the report to Stalin will be shot.

Wertheimer suggested that it would be of interest to study the people who lost their faith or confidence in Communism or Nazism or maintained it despite the Hitler-Stalin pact. Why have some people lost faith in their particular ideology and others have not? Was the loss of faith restricted only to the particular ideology? How do these people regard themselves and the social field in contrast to their previous views? The refugee conjectured that personality factors, particularly psychoanalytical factors, would be found to be crucial. Wertheimer agreed that they played a role but suggested that the nature of the structure of their worlds and the roles and function of their faith in Communism and Nazism in their worlds might have been determining factors. The meaning of their confidence in the political party might have been different. He also conjectured that those who still had faith might have faith for different reasons and that their relationship to the political party's ideology might no longer be the same. He suggested that we study Communists and fellow travelers who have altered and who have not altered their faith in Communism. It is of interest to see how and in what ways their relation to Communism, to the political parties, and to other things in the social field have changed due to the change or lack of change in their adherence to Communism. More generally, he suggested that it would be of interest to study people who had faith or confidence in a person or an event and then lost it or maintained it when the person or the event did not live up to expectations. A student suggested that falling in and out of love and the making and breaking of friendships provided a fertile field for the study of the role of trust and confidence in others. The next day ASL used this suggestion to motivate the organization of class projects on confidence. What follows is a summary of various projects that have been used over the years. In one project the students adopted the methods that have been used to study values. They asked subjects, Whom or what do you trust? Give specific examples of people, events, objects. Why do you trust them? Did you always trust them? Whom or what did you trust before? Why do you no longer trust them? In this way the subject was interviewed about the different people, objects, or events he trusted and to find out how it came about that they were trusted or mistrusted and how it affected him, them, and his relationship to them. In the same way subjects were interviewed about confidence, faith, reliability, etc. In another project the students asked people: What does the word *confidence* mean? Give examples. What does it mean not to have confidence? Give examples. In the same way they asked for meanings and examples of the other terms.

In later years, while doing group therapy, ASL told his patients to keep a record of instances of trust, mistrust, truthfulness, dishonesty, deceit, confidence, lack of confidence, etc., and to try to find out how it developed and what the consequences were for the person and his social field. Later they were asked to collect cases of transition from trust to distrust, confidence to lack of confidence, etc., and vice versa. These instances were discussed in the group. During the discussions the patients described their reactions to similar things that happened to them. Some of their examples indicated to them that they had been abused and fooled by others because of being too trusting, that they got into trouble by being too honest and for expecting others to be honest. One thing was clear in these discussions, that characteristics of confidence, trust, truthfulness could have good or bad consequences for people. Some patients found in their experiences only bad consequences and therefore had a suspicious attitude to the world and people; it was difficult to get them to relate to others and it required special effort by the therapist and group members to get them to believe that others were truthful to them. Some patients behaved like Wertheimer's naive children who trusted and had confidence to the extent that they seemed to have no egos. The patients' reports raise this question: Are such people overly sensitive to the requirements of the world? Is it because they tend to focus on certain requirements to the exclusion of other features that they get into trouble?

A technique which we used in group therapy as well as in our course on psychotherapy was to tell the members to make a survey of situations in which they accepted or relied on what they were told without questioning, and situations in which they questioned what they were told. They were then asked to say for each situation whether they ever disagreed and doubted, agreed and did not doubt, and to give reasons for their responses. They were also asked to rate the frequency of doubting and not doubting in each situation, namely, never, rarely, less often than not, equally often as not, more often than not, frequently, always. Most students' reports indicated a preponderance of situations of trust and acceptance and fewer of mistrust and doubt. The patients whom they interviewed gave a larger number of situations of distrust and doubt than of trust and acceptance and they tended to be more extreme in their trust and mistrust, their doubting and their accepting.

Some students undertook to study the effects of lies. They asked themselves and others such questions as these: Someone lied to you; what was your spontaneous reaction to it and to the person; how did it affect your relation to him? Someone let you down or disappointed you; someone who acted like a friend actually did it to exploit or get something out of you. In each case, what was your spontaneous reaction and how did it affect your relationship with the person? In some reports the students indicated no change in their relationship; the act was regarded as not of too great consequences to them, they took it as a fact of life, they tried to understand the other person's reasons. Sometimes, in boy-girl relationships there were other features about the relationship that redeemed the person; they did not want to break up the relationship, it was more important to them that it continue than that they take the person to task. Sometimes they were ashamed to let it be known that they were fooled or disappointed or that they had suspected that the other person was a liar. A discussion of some of the students' findings with Wertheimer led to the suggestion that friendships be studied. Ask the subject: Who is your best friend? Why and in what ways is he or she different from other friends or from people who are not your friends? How did you become best friends; who or what brought you together? In what ways did it change your values, outlooks, beliefs, actions? Was this person always your best friend? If not, who was your best friend before and why is he or she no longer your best friend? How was your previous best friend different from and similar to your present best friend? How did it affect you and your attitude toward people when the friendship broke up? Is your relationship to your present best friend different and was it affected by your previous experience? In this way, study the successive best friends that a person had, the structure of the world of each friendship, the features that remained the same, the features that varied, and what each friendship did to the development of the present interpersonal relationship. Were there certain friendships that had a wider effect on the person's behavior in the social field than others? How does a friendship of this kind differ from relations with acquaintances? Are people who have more or fewer friends affected more or less by their friendships? Generally speaking, what is the structure of the friendship? What does it do to the individuals involved? Does it strengthen them as individuals, tend to make them lose their individuality, to submerge both selves in the friendship, does one dominate or lean on the others? What does it do to the social field of which they are parts, does it blind them to what is going on around them, does it make them sensitive to things in the social field which they had never noticed before? Does it make them stronger or weaker to face events in the social field?

The study of friendships was never undertaken. However, a few years later Maslow suggested to his student Natalie Reader that she study friendships. She and other students were excited about the study and she did some interesting work on it but it never developed into a big project. In a discussion with Wertheimer, he asked, Why are psychology students reluctant to study topics such as friendship? Why do they want to study only the bad things in life? Is psychology concerned only with what is bad? One reason for the apparent reluctance to study friendship was that there was no neat procedure and that it did not lead to clear-cut decisions as in experiments. It is of interest that students in Adult Education Courses were more enthusiastic about undertaking such projects than students in college classes. Our college students were more interested in projects which used the series of pictures and they manipulated the situation so that the subjects had faith or trust in the experimenter and/or the confederate. We close this section with one of these projects.

In discussing other field conditions that may have helped to produce wrong judgments, Wertheimer pointed out that the experimenter's right-wrong verdict might have produced the incorrect responses because the subject felt himself in the role of a pupil who was not asked to face a problem or situation freely but was expected to do what the test or teacher wanted. His response was determined by the relationship between the pupil and teacher and between the pupil and the assigned task as well as by school-demanded performances and personal attitudes. On tests the correct answer is what the teacher says is correct, therefore, the subject gave the answer to get 100% or to pass the test. In preliminary experiments with several series of pictures we were able to develop in subjects a distrust of the confederate because his answers had been wrong. When the face-bottle series was subsequently given, they did not agree with the confederate's responses; but when we told the subject that he had 0% (or a score based on the number of times he agreed with the confederate) it was possible to increase agreement. This experiment led to the formulation that if enough pressure was applied it was possible to force agreement with the incorrect answer given by a person whom one did not trust. For some subjects the agreement was superficial, just public compliance, but a few subjects became so narrowed down by the fear of failure that they even gave the same incorrect responses the next day when they were shown the series without the confederate and no mention was made of tests, etc. Apparently these subjects were robbed of the freedom to face the evidence. Results such as these raised questions about the role of power and freedom in social-judgment situations and about the nature of actions, questions which will be discussed at length in a subsequent monograph.

Experimental Outgrowths: Confidence in the Confederate

We previously alluded to an experiment with a series of pictures (face-bottle series) which studied the effects of agreement with the confederate's response under four different conditions. Under condition P_1 the confederate reported in the first picture of the series what was actually drawn there and, despite the changing nature of the pictures, he continued giving the same response to all the subsequent pictures of the series even when the second percept was clearly portrayed; thus he started out being correct but ended up being incorrect. Under condition P_2 the confederate reported in the first picture what was drawn in the last picture of the series and he persisted with it throughout the series; thus he started out being incorrect but ended up being correct. Under condition P_1-P_2 the confederate started with the first percept but later shifted to the second percept; thus he started out being correct and he ended up being correct. In some variations, under condition P_1-P_2 the confederate shifted abruptly from one percept to the other while in other variations he gradually modified the first percept until by the middle of the series he began to report the emergence of the second percept, so that he shifted with the evidence. In other variations the confederate shifted from the first percept to an irrelevant percept, one not supported by any of the drawings in the series. In still other variations the confederate gave irrelevant responses throughout the series. In addition to the face-bottle series some variations used three or four other series (see Luchins, 1950, for the pictures in the various series). The confederate consistently responded to all the series as under one of the described conditions or as under combinations of these conditions. We were interested in seeing what would be the effects on a subject of consistently experiencing that the confederate started out being correct and ended up being incorrect or vice versa or that he started and ended up being correct. Would the Ss have more confidence in the confederate if he ended up being correct than if he ended up being incorrect? What effects would this have on their responses to the later series of pictures? Would conditions under which they learned to mistrust the confederate show more or less blinding effects than those where they learned to rely on him? Would the results support Wertheimer's conjecture that a suspicious attitude may sometimes be as bad in terms of the blinding effects as unquestioning reliance and trust?

Variations of these studies were conducted in 1952 by social psychology students at McGill University as part of a class project. We report here on some of these experiments. The Ss were told that it was not a test of intelligence nor a projective test and that all they had to do was to look at the pictures and tell what they saw. Experiment I was administered with the assistance of Eleonara M. Lamprecht to thirty subjects who were 20 to 40 years old. Each S was paired with a confederate of about the same age and was tested in the manner used in the previously described studies. Ten Ss were studied under each of conditions P_1, P_2, and P_1-P_2. Four series of pictures were presented to each pair in the following order: I, old man-lady in a bath tub; II, rooster-lady; III, trees-sheep; IV, face-bottle; they consisted of 16, 16, 11, and 21 drawings respectively. Under condition P_1 the confederate reported seeing an old man, a rooster, trees, and face, throughout Series I through IV, respectively. Under condition P_1-P_2 he shifted from the first to the second percept at about the middle of each series; the shifts occurred on Cards 9, 8, 6, and 11 of Series I through IV respectively so that the shift occurred on the eighth card on the average.

TABLE 28.1
Percentages of Responses to Series of Pictures in Experiment 1

		SERIES†			
Condition	Responses*	I	II	III	IV
P_1	P_1	41	18	28	32
	PP_1	3	2	0	10
	I	6	9	1	7
	N	15	30	8	15
	PP_2	3	5	8	5
	P_2	32	36	54	31
	A	41	18	28	32
P_2	P_1	35	26	16	19
	PP_1	1	3	3	5
	I	7	4	0	14
	N	19	13	5	15
	PP_2	6	6	8	4
	P_2	32	47	67	43
	A	32	47	67	43
P_1-P_2	P_1	38	36	32	33
	PP_1	1	2	0	8
	I	9	3	2	2
	N	11	20	1	2
	PP_2	4	6	4	4
	P_2	37	40	60	41
	A	50	66	85	71

†Series I, old man-lady in a bath tub; II, rooster-lady; III, trees-sheep; IV, face-bottle
*P_1 first percept, PP_1 part of first percept, I irrelevant or other response, N no response, PP_2 part of second percept, P_2 second percept, A agreement with confederate.

Table 28.1 summarizes the responses under each of the conditions. In the relatively few cases where S gave two responses, for example, face and bottle, they were listed under both classifications. Parts of the first percept (for example, features of a face) were classified as PP_1 and parts of the second percept (for example, the neck of a bottle) as PP_2. Classified under N (no interpretation) were cases of no responses as well as where S said only that the picture was changing or that he saw nothing or that he could not see what the confederate said. Other responses which were not the first or second percepts or parts of them were classified together with irrelevant response as I. N responses decreased from conditions P_1 to P_2 to P_1-P_2, averaging 19, 15, and 12% respectively and so did I responses, which averaged 7, 6, and 4% respectively. These results show that responses other than the first or second percept tended to decrease from condition P_1 to P_2 to P_1-P_2.

On the average most Ss gave up the first percept on Card 6 under condition P_1 but on Card 5 under condition P_2 and on Card 8 under condition P_1-P_2 (on which the confederate tended to shift). Thus the Ss persisted longer with the first percept when the confederate gave this percept and abandoned it earlier when he gave the second percept.

The emerging percept was reported earlier under condition P_2 where the confederate gave it throughout the series than under the other conditions. In Series I the emerging percept was first mentioned by any S on Card 8 under condition P_2 but not until Card 10 under the other conditions even though the confederate had shifted to this response by Card 9 under condition P_1-P_2. In Series II the emerging percept was first reported by any S on Card 4 under condition P_2 but not until Card 8 under condition P_1-P_2, and not until Card 10 under condition P_1. The emerging percept was first reported on Card 2 in Series III under condition P_2 but not until Cards 4 or 5 under the other conditions. In Series IV it was first reported on Card 5 under condition P_2 but not until Card 11 under the other conditions. On the average, it was reported on cards 5, 8, and 9 under conditions P_2, P_1-P_2, and P_1, respectively. Similarly, most Ss reported the second percept by Cards 9, 11, and 12, respectively. Thus the second percept was reported earlier when the confederate gave this response throughout than when he gave it in part of the series, and it was reported still later when he gave the first percept throughout.

Agreement seemed to be a function both of the series and the conditions of testing. In Series I there were more reports of the first percept under condition P_1 where the confederate gave this response throughout than under the other conditions. However, this changed dramatically in Series II where fewer reports of the first percept were made under condition P_1 than under the other conditions. The table shows that in Series II about one-fifth, one-quarter, and one-third of the responses were of the first percept under conditions P_1, P_2, and P_1-P_2, respectively. In this series the majority of Ss gave up the first percept by Card 3 under condition P_1 but not until Card 5 under condition P_2 and Card 6 under condition P_1-P_2. From Series I to II there was 15% increase of N responses which consisted partly of failures to responses but mainly of remarks by S that he did not see what the confederate reported. It seemed that some Ss lost their confidence in the confederate or became suspicious of or distrusted his judgment when he persisted with the first percept, and did not listen to him even in those cards in Series II which contained this percept. Under each condition the frequency of reports of the first percept was less in the remaining series than in Series I. However, under conditions P_1 and P_1-P_2 there was some increase from Series II to the remaining series whereas under condition P_2 there was a decrease. In Series III and IV about one-fifth of the Ss reported the first percept under condition P_2 whereas about one-third did so under the other conditions. It seems that Ss' confidence in the confederate when the percept which he gave was supported not by the first half but by the second half of the series led them not to report the percept which was present in the first half. Thus there were blinding effects under both conditions P_1 and P_2. These results fit Wertheimer's conjecture that both suspicion and confidence can lead to blinding effects.

Under condition P_2 only about one-third agreed with the confederate in Series I, which is less than this series received under any of the other conditions. This is not surprising since initially there was no support for the confederate's response in the drawings when he named the emerging percept whereas there was initial support when he named the first percept. After Series I the confidence which Ss had in the confederate might be expected to increase from condition P_1 to P_2 to P_1-P_2. The results in the subsequent series are in line with this expectation since they show that in each of Series II, III, and IV the frequency of agreement increased from condition P_1 to P_2 to P_1-P_2, averaging about one-third, one-half, and three-quarters agreement, respectively. In each series the most agreement occurred for the second percept under condition P_1-P_2. The second percept was noticeable earlier in Series III, the shortest and simplest of the series, than in Series IV, the longest and most complex of the series. Concomitantly, agreement with the second percept was greater in Series III than in Series IV and increased from Series II to IV to III under condition P_2 as well as under condition P_1-P_2. In short, the social influence of the confederate diminished under condition P_1 after he had been proven wrong in the first series, whereas his influence under the other conditions continued and led to earlier reports of the second percept and to more agreement with his responses.

There were varied reactions to the confederate. Some Ss seemed to ignore the confederate and made no comments about his responses. Others questioned the confederate, commented on his answers, admitted that they were influenced by his answers or asked him if he did not see what they saw. Under condition P_1 an S said to the confederate in Series II: Don't you see my lady? I don't see a rooster. Another S, a male, said to a female confederate at the end of Series I, If you still see a man in this, you are definitely perverted, and, at the end of Series II, Don't you see the face? If you say this is a rooster, you are definitely crazy. Some Ss tried to point out to the confederate the outline of what they reported. Some told the confederate under condition P_1 that he was being influenced by what he had seen earlier. One S said: Obviously you did not see what was happening. You just stuck to what you said. You are conservative and don't like to change your mind once it is made up. Another said in Series III: You and your trees! Don't you see the animal? It is a sheep. I thought you had more imagination than that. Under condition P_1 Ss seemed to feel superior to the confederate whom they regarded as unimaginative and in a rut because he could not see the changing percept. Indeed, some of the confederates, both male and female, seemed to be uncomfortable or tense about having to appear to be so unimaginative and in the later pictures of each series sometimes gave their answers in a low voice, sounding somewhat unhappy. Under condition P_2 some Ss expressed amazement and puzzlement at the confederate's answers. Some said that the confederate had a terrific imagination or must have seen the pictures before or had more experience with pictures of this sort. In Series I one S said at Picture 10: Maybe I will have to agree with you but I don't see anything yet. A few Ss seemed to be upset or irritated when they could not see what the confederate said and relieved when they finally could see it. One S told the confederate that she had irritated her, asked her to show her in the early drawing of each series where the percept was, and finally told her, O.K., You win again. Under condition P_1-P_2 there was also some surprise that the confederate saw the emerging percept in each series before there was much evidence for it in the drawings. One S told the confederate at the end of Series IV: How the devil you could see that it was just one milk bottle at one stage of the game is beyond me; but you were right—that is the sad part about it. (Some Ss insisted that the second percept in the last series was a flask or a vase and not a milk bottle.)

The subjects seemed to have been influenced by the changing nature of the series. Under all conditions most Ss looked for changes in each series after Series I. They made comments such as: I wonder what this is going to turn into; What's hidden in this one? In the third picture of Series IV, one S said, Already you can tell it will change to something else; it starts earlier in this set. Another said on the first card of Series IV, This man is going to change into an ostrich if the change keeps up this way, and on the fourth card he said, apparently referring to the change, There the fun starts! At the end of the experiment, when they were asked what they thought its purpose was, some Ss referred to the changes and to the influence of the first percept on perception of the emerging percept, for example, The purpose is to notice the transformation from one to the next picture, to see the influence of the first picture on the later ones. Other purposes attributed to the experiment were the following: visual acuity, to see how keen your observance is, how soon you can recognize something that is disguised, how long it takes a person to see what comes up in these pictures after the first one had disintegrated, how persistent your set is, how different people react to pictures or to changes, how soon different people see change, get their ideas on the transformations from one thing to another. Only a few Ss explicitly referred to social influences. One S remarked during the experiment that if two people are in a social situation and one makes a suggestion, at which point the experimenter interrupted him; at the end of the experiment he said that he knew it was being done for social psychology and therefore probably had something to do with social influences.

Experiment 2 was administered with the assistance of Doris R. Marshall and Corina A. Achong, with the former serving as the confederate, to 35 female Ss, aged 15 to 20, most of them high school students and the others college lower classmen who had taken no courses in psychology. The series and the order in which they were presented were essentially the same as in Experiment 1, the differences being that two pictures were added to Series III and one picture deleted from Series IV so that the series consisted of 16, 16, 13, and 20 cards, respectively. There were five control Ss to whom the series were individually administered without a confederate present. Ten Ss were tested under each of conditions P_1, P_2 and P_1-P_2. Under condition P_1 the confederate reported that she saw trees, a man, and a bench throughout Series III. Under condition P_1-P_2 she shifted at Cards 8, 9, and 6 in Series I through III, respectively. Otherwise these conditions were the same for the first three series as for Experiment 1. However, throughout Series IV under conditions P_1 and P_2 the confederate gave an irrelevant response, tree, not supported by any of the drawings in that series. Under condition P_1-P_2 she shifted at Card 9 of Series IV from the first percept to the irrelevant response. In the recording of responses, those involving parts of the first percept (PP_1) were classified under the first percept (P_1). Table 28.2 summarizes the various responses.

TABLE 28.2
Percentages of Responses to Series of Pictures in Experiment 2

SERIES

Condition	Response	I	II	III	IV
Control	P_1	32	55	37	28
	I	31	6	0	13
	N	4	1	0	11
	PP_2	3	6	8	8
	P_2	30	31	55	40
P_1	P_1	53	54	41	22
	I	10	7	13	16
	N	4	2	0	11
	PP_2	11	16	21	9
	P_2	22	21	25	29
	A	53	54	41	14
P_2	P_1	35	39	30	37
	I	15	0	0	1
	N	9	11	0	22
	PP_2	4	6	5	1
	P_2	37	44	65	32
	A	37	44	65	7
P_1-P_2	P_1	42	49	45	34
	I	7	6	0	18
	N	3	1	0	3
	PP_2	4	4	13	5
	P_2	44	41	42	35
	A	83	84	84	37

Only responses to the first three series could be compared with those in Experiment 1. Under condition P_1 there were now more reports of the first percept, that is, more agreement with the confederate, and fewer reports of the second percept than in Experiment 1. Moreover, under this condition the results were now quite similar in Series I and II, unlike what happened in Experiment 1 where there was a drop in P_1 responses and an increase in N responses (usually remarks that they could not see what the confederate reported) from Series I to II. In Series I, II, and III, respectively the frequencies of P_1 responses were now 9, 34, and 13% larger under condition P_1 than the sum of P_1 and PP_1 responses in the previous experiment; the frequencies of P_2 responses were now 10, 19, and 17% less than the corresponding frequencies in the previous experiment. Under condition P_1 three or four Ss continued to give the first percept on Card 10 and 11 of Series II whereas no S gave it on these cards in Experiment 1; the second percept was now not given by any S until Card 12 whereas it was mentioned on Card 8 in Experiment 1. Similarly, under this condition in Series III the first percept was given until Card 7 whereas it had stopped at Card 5 in the previous experiment; the second percept was not given until Card 7 whereas it had been reported by Card 4 in Experiment 1. In short, the confederate seemed to be more influential under condition P_1 than in the previous experiment. Possible reasons were that she was one of the experimenters and older than the Ss whereas in Experiment 1 the confederates were the same age or slightly younger than the Ss with whom they were paired. However, under condition P_2 there was about the same frequency of reports of the second percepts and more reports of the first percept than in the previous experiment. Thus agreement with the confederate was now greater under condition P_1 than P_2, unlike what happened in Experiment 1. However, as in the previous experiment the most agreement occurred under condition P_1-P_2.

In Series IV under condition P_1 one S agreed with the confederate's irrelevant response, tree, in Card 1 through 5, four Ss agreed in Cards 4 and 5, six in Cards 7 and 8 (which were quite ambiguous), and one or two Ss agreed through Card 12, with 14% agreement on the average. Under condition P_2 agreement with the irrelevant response did not begin until Card 4 and ended at Card 13 with at most one or two Ss agreeing on any card and with an average of 7% agreement. Thus the greater agreement with the confederate under condition P_1 continued through Series IV even though she gave an irrelevant response there. When the confederate gave the first percept, face, under condition P_1-P_2 every S agreed on the first five cards but by Card 9 only two Ss agreed. One of these gave the face response to Card 10 where the confederate reported tree, but on the next four cards she said that she saw one or two stumps of a tree with a man's face behind them; one other S gave the tree response on Cards 11 through 13 and another on Cards 10 and 11, with an average of 9% agreement; on the average agreement with the irrelevant response in Series IV decreased from conditions P_1 to P_1-P_2 to P_2.

Comparisons with the Control group may be of some interest even though it consisted only of five Ss. Under condition P_1 on the average there were relatively more reports of the first percept and fewer of the second than in the Control group. Under condition P_2 the first percept was less frequent and the second more frequent than in the Control group. Under condition P_1-P_2 both the first and second percepts were somewhat more frequent than for the Control Ss. In short, whatever percept was given by the confederate tended to have a somewhat higher frequency of reports than when there was no confederate.

On the average, in the first three series the first percept was given up by the majority of Ss on Card 7 in the Control group but not until Card 9 under condition P_1 and on Cards 6 and 8 under conditions P_2 and P_1-P_2 respectively. On the average the second percept was introduced on Card 10 in the Control group and under condition P_1 but on Cards 6 and 7 under conditions P_2 and P_1-P_2 respectively. The majority of Ss reported the second percept on Card 10 in the Control group but not until Card 12 under condition

P_1, on Card 8 under condition P_2, and on Card 10 under condition P_1-P_2. These results show that when the confederate gave the first percept, Ss held on to it longer and introduced the second percept later than when there was no confederate or when the confederate gave the second percept through all or part of the series. Under condition P_1-P_2 the results lay between the extremes under condition P_1 and condition P_2.

Reactions to the pictures and to the confederates' responses were as varied as in Experiment 1. When the pictures were clearly structured, Ss usually reported what was in them but when the pictures were ambiguous they were influenced in varying degrees. When the confederate gave responses which were not supported by the drawings some showed hesitation or amazement. Some turned the pictures this way and that way, trying to discover if they too could see a hidden picture, or asked, Where do you see that? Some remarked, Maybe I am dumb but I can't see that; others said confidently, I don't see that, I see so and so; and still others said diffidently, I can only see so and so. Other Ss seemed to disregard the confederate's answers and some took the overheard responses partly into account.

Ss' answers to questions at the end of the experiment were similar to those found in the previous study. Again most Ss reported that the purpose of the experiment had to do with how much one observed in a short time or with noticing changes in pictures or with how different people see pictures. Very few referred to social influences. An exception was a 14-year-old high school student who said that its purpose was to see if when you heard someone else say something you would say the same thing; she claimed that she answered what she thought she saw and indeed she had never agreed completely with the confederate, for example, when the latter said that she saw an old man's face she might say: I see an old man with a beard, a big nose, heavy bushy eyebrows, and a hat, and when the overheard response was not supported by the drawing she did not hesitate (as did many Ss) but immediately reported what was depicted.

Experiment 3 was administered with the assistance of Etta Binder and Shirley Rosenberg to 40 girls and with the assistance of Mervyn Rosenzveig and Arthur Weinthal to 40 boys. The Ss were between 11 and 13 years of age and were tested at the Montreal YMCA, YMHA, and Neighborhood House. Ten girls and ten boys were control Ss tested without a confederate. Similar numbers were tested under each of conditions P_1, P_2, and P_1-P_2, with the role of the confederate alternated among the experimenters. We were interested in what would happen if the confederate gave an irrelevant response throughout an intermediate series but returned to giving the first or second percept in a subsequent series. Therefore a new series, beauty-hag, consisting of 11 pictures, was presented in addition to the four series used in the previous experiments. The order of presentation was altered and was as follows: I^1, tree-sheep; II^1, face-bottle, III^1, rooster-lady, IV^1, beauty-hag, V^1, old man-lady in a bathtub; they correspond to Series III, IV, II and (following the new series) I of Experiments 1 and 2. Under each condition the confederate gave irrelevant responses to the beauty-hag series. We were also interested in the effects of having the confederate gradually introduce percepts under all the conditions and in all the series, which might make the responses seem more natural and appropriate. Under condition P_1 in Series I^1 the confederate's responses were trees or man, which were modified during the subsequent pictures with

TABLE 28.3
Percentages of Responses to Series of Pictures by
Girls in Experiment 3

Condition	Response	SERIES				
		1^1	II^1	III^1	IV^1	V^1
Control	P_1	69	47	43	63	32
	PP_1	6	5	2	0	3
	I	1	12	16	7	26
	N	1	1	2	0	0
	PP_2	0	4	1	0	10
	P_2	23	31	36	30	29
P_1	P_1	48	51	53	48	34
	PP_1	37	16	8	14	17
	I	0	5	4	12	17
	N	0	5	0	0	1
	PP_2	1	4	6	5	9
	P_2	13	20	28	22	24
	A	88	66	59	36	50
P_2	P_1	32	22	39	35	31
	PP_1	19	7	12	9	12
	I	7	21	1	25	16
	N	5	8	6	8	10
	PP_2	0	0	0	2	0
	P_2	36	43	41	27	31
	A	55	50	50	42	43
P_1-P_2	P_1	55	66	58	55	59
	PP_1	0	0	0	7	0
	I	0	1	1	14	7
	N	0	0	0	0	1
	PP_2	2	5	4	5	0
	P_2	42	29	38	19	33
	A	87	95	94	42	89

such remarks as, The man's there but he's moved behind the tree; in Series II^1, the confederate's responses varied from face to man's face with glasses and, as the bottle emerged, to remarks that the man was wearing an earring. (In some cases the confederate persisted with the earring responses to the last picture where the bottle was labeled milk and one S agreed even there that the picture was that of a man wearing an earring.) Under condition P_1 the confederate slightly varied the first percept in Series III and gave varying irrelevant responses to Series IV^1; in Series V^1 as the picture of the old man disintegrated, the confederate referred to his hat, his cigarettes, and finally, to just a man when the picture was clearly that of a woman in the bathtub. Under condition P_2 the second percept was introduced in a subtle, gradual form; in Series I^1 the confederate first referred to an animal which was changed to a sheep by Card 3; in Series II^1 the confederate first spoke of a modern kind of jug which was soon changed to a bottle and, about four or five cards from the end, to a milk bottle; in Series III[1] features of a face were mentioned until gradually the percept of a lady was introduced; in Series IV[1] changing irrelevant responses were given as under condition P_1; in Series V[1] the confederate's first response was face and then the feminine pronoun was incorporated in such answers as now she's got arms, now she's sitting on something, until the lady in the bathtub was mentioned at about Card 7. The confederate's responses under condition P_1-P_2 were a combination of those described under the two other conditions. Occasionally under all conditions the confederate prompted the S by outlining in the drawing what was purported to be seen or by remarking, Don't you see that?

We consider first the results for the girls which are summarized in Table 28.3. For them the confederate's shift from the first to the second percept under condition P_1-P_2 took place on Cards 7, 15, 10, and 12 of Series I[1], II[1], III[1], and V[1], respectively and, on the average, on Card 11. (There was no such shift in Series IV[1] where the confederate made irrelevant reports throughout under all conditions.) Compared to the previous results there were now more PP_1 and PP_2 responses, parts of the first and second percepts, perhaps because the confederate gradually varied these responses. Compared to the Control group of Experiment 2, the combined percentages of responses of the first percept and parts of it were larger in the present Control group. Yet under condition P_1 this combined percentage was even larger than for the Control group in Series I[1], II[1], III[1], and V[1] where the confederate named the first percept and about equal to that for the Control group in Series IV[1] where the confederate gave irrelevant responses; the combined percentages of responses of the second percept and parts of it were less than for the Control group. These results attest to the influence of the confederate under condition P_1. Under this condition there was a decrease in reports of the first percept in the final series, with P_1 responses constituting about one-third of the answers compared to about one-half in the earlier series and P_1 plus PP_1 responses constituting about one-half compared to about two-thirds in the earlier series. These results suggest that the confederate's repeatedly giving irrelevant responses in the fourth series made the Ss less inclined to agree with her there or even in the subsequent series where she reverted to the first percept.

Under condition P_2 there were more reports of the second percept than in the Control group for those series in which the confederate named this percept; and in every series there were more reports of the second percept and fewer reports of the first percept than under condition P_1. These results attest to the influence of the confederate's responses under condition P_2. In the last two series there was a drop in reports of the second percept, suggesting that the confederate's naming of irrelevant responses in Series IV[1] may have led to some loss of her influence in that series and in the subsequent series where she reverted to the second percept.

Under condition P_1-P_2 in each series there were about as many reports of the first percept as under condition P_1 and more reports of the second percept; compared to condition P_2, there were far more reports of the first percept and somewhat fewer reports of the second. These results testify to the influence of the confederate in generating responses of the first and second percepts when the reports she gave shifted with the evidence. There were smaller differences between responses to the final series and the first three series than under conditions P_1 and P_2, which suggests that Ss tended to retain their confidence in the confederate. In general, agreement with the confederate tended to decrease from conditions P_1-P_2 to P_1 to P_2, the same trend that was found in Experiment 2.

In testing the boys, the experimenter introduced himself as a member of the motion picture industry who was interested in finding out just how clear a picture has to be so that we can see it properly. The confederate was introduced as a friend who would also help view the pictures. Otherwise the procedure was the same as for the girls tested in Experiment 3 except that the confederate's shifts under condition P_1-P_2 took place on Cards 6, 11, 10, and 9 for Series I^1, II^1, III^1, and V^1, respectively so that on the average the shift was on Card 9, two cards earlier than for the girls. A record was kept only of whether a response was the first percept or the second percept, with other responses lumped together; in Series IV^1, where the confederate gave various irrelevant responses, a record was kept mainly of whether S agreed or disagreed. Table 28.4 summarizes the responses.

TABLE 28.4
Percentages of Responses to Series of Pictures by Boys in
Experiment 3

SERIES

Condition	Responses	I^1	II^1	III^1	IV^1	V^1
Control	P_1	46	20	44	51	31
	I	21	55	27	26	42
	P_2	33	25	29	23	27
P_1	P_1	61	42	44	33	47
	I	13	35	28	58	27
	P_2	26	23	28	29	26
	A	61	42	44	0	47
P_2	P_1	39	18	24	40	28
	I	23	50	37	35	41
	P_2	38	32	39	25	31
	A	38	32	39	0	31
P_1-P_2	A	75	71	69	0	73
	D	25	29	31	100	27

The boys who served as Control Ss gave fewer of the first percept and more responses other than the first and second percept than did the girls who were Control Ss. This was particularly striking in Series II^1 where the sum of P_1 and P_2 percepts accounted for less than half of the boys' responses but for about four-fifth of the girls' responses. On the average the sum of the first and second percepts accounted for 56% of the Control boys' answers but over 80% of the Control girls' answers, with the boys tending to give more varied responses. This was also the case under each of conditions P_1, P_2, and P_1-P_2. It would be of interest to investigate whether these differences are related to sex differences or to differences in instructions, experimenters, etc., and whether they would be found for other children and for older males and females.

Under condition P_1, in the four series where the confederate gave the first response there was an increase in reports of the first percept and a slight decrease in reports of the second percept compared to the Control group. Under condition P_2 in the four series where the confederate gave the second percept there was a slight increase in reports of the second percept and a decrease in reports of the first percept compared to the Control group. Under condition P_1-P_2 the first percept was a less frequent response than under condition P_1 but slightly more frequent than under condition P_2. There was no agreement with the confederate's irrelevant responses in Series IV[1] under any of the conditions whereas some of the girls did show agreement. However, the experience with this series did not seem to affect the influence of the confederate in the subsequent series. Aside from the series where the confederate gave irrelevant responses, agreement with him decreased from condition P_1-P_2 to P_1 to P_2, which was the same trend found for the girls.

On the average, the first percept was given up by the majority of the boys on Card 6 in the Control group, not until Card 9 under condition P_1, on Card 5 under condition P_2, and on Card 6 under condition P_1-P_2. The second percept was first introduced on Cards 7 or 8 in the Control group, not until Cards 11 or 12 under condition P_1, on Card 7 under condition P_2 and on Card 10 under condition P_1-P_2. Most Ss reported the second percept on Card 12 in the Control group, not until Card 13 under condition P_1 and on Card 11 under the other conditions. In short, the first percept was maintained longer and the second introduced later under condition P_1 than under the other conditions or in the Control group. Under conditions P_2 and P_1-P_2 the first percept was given up and the second introduced earlier or on the same card as in the Control group.

Compared to the girls, most boys in the Control group gave up the first percept three cards earlier on the average, in Card 6 rather than Card 9. Similarly, under condition P_1-P_2 the first percept was given up by most boys five cards earlier than by the girls, in Card 6 rather than Card 11. Contributing factors might have been the fact that the confederate shifted two cards earlier on the average and a possible tendency for the boys to be less set for the first percept. However, other aspects of the results were the same for the two groups. For both girls and boys under condition P_1-P_2 the second percept tended to be introduced at about the same time that the confederate shifted, that is, on the card on which he shifted or on one card away from it. Under each condition on the average the second percept was introduced on the same cards for the boys and girls (Cards 10 for the Control group and Cards 11, 7, and 10 for conditions P_1, P_2, and P_1-P_2, respectively) and most Ss reported it on the same cards (Cards 12, 13, 11, and 11, respectively).

Most children remarked that the pictures were not accurately drawn or not well drawn. One girl said that we would never be able to use them for anything. After the third series there was a tendency for the children to become bored with the pictures and to begin to give monosyllabic responses instead of full descriptions. In one case the child turned to the experimenter and said, Don't you find this boring? Responses to the unstructured pictures tended to be imaginative and occasionally the Ss declined to respond at all. While the

Control Ss showed little emotional reaction to the pictures, under the pressure exerted by the confederate the children often became disturbed by their inability to see the reported percept. Their reactions were generally more intense than those of the Ss of the previous experiments who were older.

Generally speaking, the results support some of Wertheimer's conjectures concerning social influences. They show that we can train people to develop confidence in the confederate or mistrust of him. They support his contention that social influences are not always malign in nature; they may make people aware of or make them focus on the features of the situation that are relevant and that will bring about genuine behavior, productive thinking, action that is fit and appropriate in terms of the structure of the situation. They may also bring about behavior of another kind, blind, inappropriate behavior in terms of the situation's structural requirements. Since such behavior takes place in a social context, social influences may focus one on the social aspects of the situation so that he disregards the evidence, the object of judgment, the structural requirements of the problem. This may result in a miscentering, producing a cognitive grasp of the situation which leads one to act arbitrarily, blind to the structural requirements of the evidence. We have seen this happen in the early research done with Wertheimer as well as in the present studies. But in the latter studies we have also seen that the social influences may alert one or point to the requirements of the evidence. On the one hand, the vectors of the social forces may go in the same direction as the vectors arising out of the structure of the problem or the judgment situation; on the other hand, they may be opposed to each other. By manipulating the social field and/or the subject's attitudes, assumptions, and previous experiences, it is possible to bring about agreement and disagreement with the social forces when they are in line with and not in line with the evidence. We need to study the structure of the social atmosphere that produces the two kinds of orientation in order to find out what factors bring about the so-called genuine behavior and the so-called blind behavior. To Wertheimer the problem of social influences is not whether people can be made to agree or disagree with social reality or physical reality but what are the factors that sensitize and desensitize people to the structural requirements of judgment situations. Moreover, what can be done to bring about recovery from such blindness? He believed that social relations (as well as science) depend on doing justice to the requirements of the situation, that is, they stand upon Truth. [Wertheimer's conceptions of Truth are discussed in a subsequent monograph.]

We have concluded this discussion on social influences on judgment and perception with some replications of experiments which were conducted when ASL was Wertheimer's research assistant. This was done with the hope that they would stimulate discussion of and research on the factors in the social field and in the personality of the individuals that, on the one hand, bring about the blind, mechanized repetition of what others say or do and, on the other hand, that bring about behavior which Wertheimer calls genuine thinking, real doing in opposition to crippled doing. One kind of crippled doing is behavior in which one acts like an automaton, in which one acts with no mind of his own but mechanically repeats what he is told or shown. Since this kind of behavior has been related to what occurs in hypnosis and since social influences are often related to hypnotic behavior, it is appropriate to mention here that Wertheimer's neglect of hypnotic phenomena in the discussions of social influences was not due to his rejection of its relevance to the understanding of social influences. Dr. Erwin Levy, a psychiatrist, who was Wertheimer's assistant in Germany, wrote the following in a recent letter to ASL:

> Toward the end of his life W[ertheimer] was engaged in work which was highly important to him but which he did not want to talk about because it was in statu nascendi and he did not want his thinking disturbed by others until he was ready. This concerned, first, a theory of hypnosis of which he refused to say anything other than that he had it; secondly, and much more important, a definition of "radix" which he said was very complex, and connected with it a new approach to the law of sufficient reason. I could not persuade him to tell me more about these things and they have not been published; much must be buried in his notes which no one except his daughter can read because they are written in a by-now probably obsolete German shorthand.

Dr. Levy's letter suggests an interesting research problem. What clues about hypnosis can be found in the varied ways in which we studied social influences under Wertheimer's general supervision? Are his comments in this and in the subsequent monographs relevant to discussions of hypnotic phenomena?

29
Power

[Wertheimer repeatedly rejected the idea that social influences involve power of one person over another. He believed that discussions of social influences that centered on the question of who has power over whom might lead to a one-sided view of what actually takes place between the participants in social judgment and value-creating situations. In his course Problems of Social Psychology he proposed alternative ways to look at what goes on in such situations. Perhaps because of the stress on the idea of power by certain visitors and students, in the Spring of 1941 he conducted a seminar in which Karen Horney, Kurt Riezler, Hans Speier, Bernard Glueck, Jr., and Abraham Maslow made formal or informal presentation on topics related to power. There were frequent interruptions of the main speaker for questions and comment by the other professors, by the visitors who had been Wertheimer's associates and assistants in Germany (among whom were Rudolph Arnheim and Erwin Levy), and by graduate students and laymen. ASL took verbatim notes of what the professors said in order to present them to his students for discussion and for research planning. The reconstructed seminars are based on these notes as well as the discussion in ASL's classes.]

In the first session Wertheimer remarked that in daily life the word *power* is often used and went on to ask the students to write answers to the question; What is power? He also asked them to give examples of it. [The seminar members' written answers were not available to us; however, the same questions were asked in ASL's Yeshiva College and Adult Education classes. Their answers made reference to the power of natural phenomena such as electricity, wind, water, power from internal combustion engines, and steam power. They also referred to the strength of people or animals, to the power of governmental agencies, of parents, of kings, of workers, of capitalists, of fascists, of religious and social institutions. In addition to these examples they mentioned will power and the power of the intellect. A few wrote that science is power, that knowledge is power. Some students gave examples of social power in terms of controlling, influencing, or coercing people and wrote that it is represented in authority, leadership, prestige, domination, aggression, and violence. Other students wrote that power is the ability to do or to make things, to produce changes in nature or in society or in individuals or groups of people. A few students referred to a person's ability to influence, to command, and to dominate and to the force of his mind or of his character or of his will. Also mentioned were the legal right of a government, of the military, of the police or of other social institutions to obtain obedience to rules and regulations.]

After collecting the papers on which the students had written their answers Wertheimer again asked, What is power? Someone said that before class he had been thinking about power but could not get a clear idea about it and therefore he could not answer Wertheimer's question. In response to additional questions by Wertheimer he admitted that when he uses the word in daily life he feels that he knows what he is saying but he has difficulty in defining it. When he talks of the power of certain social classes, of dictators, of presidents, of leaders, of people, and of the masses he feels that he knows what he is talking about but when he has to specify just what power is in these cases the idea becomes elusive. Thereupon someone said that the word power is ambiguous, it has many synonyms, each of which stands for a different thing. [Some of the synonyms are faculty, capacity, efficacy, energy, capability, potentiality, force, might, ability, strength, susceptibility, influence, domination, sway, command, government, agency, authority, rule, jurisdiction, effectiveness, caliber, cause.] The student proposed that it would be best not to use the word unless we mean industrial power; hand, water, steam, or electrical power. A visitor pointed out that the same difficulty would arise; it is not easy to define electrical power. The word power is a subjective quality; there is no power in electricity or in the winds of a storm; we attribute power to them. Since it is an emotion-laden word, it is used by propagandists to stir up our feelings. He challenged the proposal that the definition of power be restricted to the utilization of natural power because the industrial aspect of power has also a political and social aspect. When machines replaced the worker and the automobile replaced the horse, great changes occurred in interpersonal relations and in social and political institutions. Hitler's military successes were a result of modern industrial power; they made the foot soldier obsolete and created a new political state of affairs in Europe. Another visitor insisted that in order to know what we are talking about we need to settle on a definition. Therefore, he proposed that power be defined as having such control of objects, people, or other kinds of living beings in the social and physical environment that it was possible for the possessor to act on them or to produce outcomes with them that would not occur if he did not have such control. This led to several remarks about socioeconomic power structures. During this discussion a student pointed out that underlying all attempts to control or to influence is the will of the individual to master his physical and social environment. He went on to outline Adler's theory. Human beings have feelings of inferiority; man suffers from his realization of the biological inferiority of the human race. This awareness of biological inferiority has led man to form groups, to develop an intellect and to invent tools in order to supplement his physical power, to defend himself and to become master of nature. Each individual is aware that others are stronger than he is; this results in setting him against others. Because of organ inferiority and because of feeling small and powerless in relation to his older siblings and adults, the child develops feelings of inferiority that lead him to seek power and control over others. He concluded that there is a striving in all men for significance, for competency, for mastery and that it is due to an innate drive, the Will to Power. Maslow pointed out that Adler had changed his theory, that he had been stressing social interest and not the individual's blind drive for mastery, that what is popularly called the Will to Power is an abnormal characteristic, due to faulty social conditions. Another student pointed out that it was Freud who stressed the innate basis of power. He has postulated a death instinct which is a blind force, like Schopenhauer's blind Will that wants what it wants. This blind force will eventually destroy man and then reason and consciousness will disappear just as they accidentally came into existence due to the capriciousness of the blind Will.

Horney objected to the concept of the death instinct. She said that she agreed with Freud that early attitudes and experiences contribute to the development of one's character but one's behavior is not a mere repetition of them. Present behavior, particularly interpersonal relations, must be understood as a result of a developmental process that is conditioned to a smaller or larger degree by past attitudes and experiences. The totality of childhood experiences starts the development of a certain character structure. The direction of its growth and development is established in childhood and often continues throughout life. Someone interrupted to say that early experiences do not really endure and that the individual has a certain temperament due to his biological nature which can be noticed even in a newborn baby. This temperament gives the enduring quality to the personality. When someone objected to the idea that personality is biologically determined, the student said that an infant is not a piece of putty that is molded at will by society. It is a physical system with certain Gestalt qualities that can be seen in its expressive behavior. Maslow pointed out that to say that a trait is biologically determined is not equivalent to saying that it is unchangeable. Thereupon Horney said that the character structure may change, even drastically, if environmental factors are radically altered. However, there may be factors in the present environment that foster the persistence of the character structure. She went on to say that hostility is not due to an innate death instinct but is a product of environmental and interpersonal factors. She related the expression of power to the compulsive nature of the personality. The striving may be for its own sake or for the sake of hidden motives. There is in compulsive striving a sort of extrovert striving, an outgoing aggression. One must not confuse it with sadistic behavior. In compulsive striving the emphasis is on defense; it is defensive in nature.

After someone pointed out the similarity of Horney's formulations to Adler's, a heated exchange occurred between Horney and a Freudian psychologist who rejected Horney's and Adler's theories as superficial. It was terminated by Wertheimer's summary statement. He said that in contemporary discussions about power there are two extremes in viewing the problem. In one view, power is an instinct. When two roosters meet they fight it out to determine who will be *cock of the walk*. It is the same with people; they are forever struggling to be first, to master all that is before them. It is natural to compete, to seek to dominate. In the other view, there are human relations of various kinds and how the heck does power enter them? He then suggested the following references: Machiavelli, *The Prince;* Hobbes, *The Leviathan;* Weber's work (see Parsons' *Structure of Social Action* for summary of Weber); Pareto, *Mind and Society;* Sorel, *Reflections on Violence;* Znaniecki, *Social Action* (chaps. 8,9,11); Leopole, *Prestige;* Dollard et al., *Frustration and Aggression;* Nietzsche, *Will to Power;* Timasheff, *Introduction to Sciology of Law;* LeFevre,

Liberty and Restraint; J. J. Duvyvendaak, *The Book of Lord Chang;* J. F. Brown, *Psychology and Social Order;* Kimball Young, *Source Book for Social Psychology;* Murphy and Murphy, *Experimental Social Psychology;* Fosdick, *Liberty;* K. Lewin, *Autocratic and Democratic Situations;* Anshen, *Freedom and Its Meaning;* Maslow's investigations on dominance *Journal of General Psychology* 1937-1938, *Psychological Review* 1938, *Journal of Social Psychology* 1939; Horney, *Neurotic Personality of Our Times.* (Some students were surprised at the reading list. Never before had Wertheimer started a seminar in this way. Someone surmised that the list was given because of the request of the professors who would be presenting their ideas for discussion.) Before dismissing the class Wertheimer remarked that it might be useful to differentiate among these three kinds of people who have power: (1) he has power but it has nothing to do with his psychological make-up, it is a function of the position he occupies, (2) he gives the impression that he has power (he seems to have power) but he is really not interested in it; (3) he is interested in having power. Wertheimer asked the class to think of concrete cases of these three kinds of people. What effects do they have on the social situation in which they are?

After-Class Discussion: Freud's Views

Some students followed Wertheimer into the cafeteria where they engaged him in a discussion about the manifestation of power in strikes, lockouts, the demonstrations by WPA workers, the activities of the America Firsters, the Bundists, the Communists, and the war in Europe. A student said that there have always been war and civil strife; it seems to be natural. Perhaps Mussolini was correct when he said during the invasion of Abyssinia that during war men are at their best. Wertheimer asked whether bombing the unarmed or the primitively armed people of Abyssinia was man at his best. Would someone really feel proud of killing little children and unarmed people? The student said that in war who was being killed was not important; one was symbolically slaying evil creatures or defending oneself from people who want to kill him. The Germans were not killing civilians in their bombing of London or of Rotterdam but were killing their enemies; it was a matter of kill or be killed. A man who was armed with a spear or a rock could kill you just as well as a man using a bomb. The student went on to say, Is it not a shame to kill bedbugs or mosquitos, they too are living things? But if you do not kill them they bite you; you try to get them before they get you. It is a law of nature that each species lives on the other.

Wertheimer asked whether this was a correct view of nature. After a pause he said that there are examples of interdependence, of symbiosis and cooperation in animals and men, that such behavior springs from their nature; aggression is not natural, it is brought about by certain field conditions. A student remarked that some years ago the League of Nation's International Institute of Intellectual Cooperation sponsored a discussion about war between scientists.[1] The scientists dealt with the question of why men go to war and

---

1. The student's account of the Einstein-Freud correspondence was inaccurate. Einstein was asked by the League of Nation's International Institute to write a letter to any scientist he wished, asking any single question he deemed of vital importance. He chose to write Freud and ask if war could be abolished as a phenomenan of human interaction. Einstein presented no specific ideas of his own on the subject. (DEL) (DEL is a political science student.)

tried to formulate concrete ways to abolish war. Einstein was one of the people who participated in the discussion. He said that man's nature was not the cause of war and that something could be done to abolish war. A visiting political science student remarked that Einstein was a theoretical physicist. Just as his ideas in physics were of no practical significance, his ideas about war were just theoretical. (This was said in 1941 before the atomic age and space flights.) The student went on to say that he was more inclined to agree with Freud's response to Einstein's letter. When Wertheimer voiced his objections to Freud's basic assumptions about human nature, the student said that Wertheimer refused to accept the existence of evil. Man was not a noble being that was corrupted by social situations. People as well as states claim that what is right is what serves them; man does not seek the truth but power over people and nature. What is called by one person or state arbitrary conduct or cruel oppression is called justice or love by another person or state. Man is a rationalizing animal that seeks good reasons to justify what he wants to do; man acts because of his blind desires and then looks for excuses to explain his actions. His intellect enables him to turn black into white or vice versa in order to serve his unconscious motives. When Wertheimer asked what would be the effect on man and groups if everybody acted blindly and willfully, the student said that the people who were successful in life were those people who were conscious of the power structure. The first thing these people do when they enter a social situation is to size up the power structure. Just like one evaluates his strength when he does certain physical tasks, they evaluate their power vis-a-vis the various people in the situation. They unconsciously know when and where to exert their influence and power. People who make incorrect assessments of the power structure are failures in interpersonal relations and in social situations; some even end up in jails and insane asylums. When Wertheimer asked him whether he really believed this, he answered that he was describing a scientific thesis. He would like to believe that it was not valid but the international scene and even the academic world proved its validity. Scientists have been talking about a naturalistic ethics for over a hundred years but nature seems to have no ethical principles. Victory goes to the creature that has might; might makes right. Wertheimer proposed that he look for examples as well as counter examples of the thesis that might makes right.

After Wertheimer left, the political science student summarized Freud's answer to Einstein's letter of inquiry about what can be done to stop war. Freud wrote that he had assumed that Einstein had written to him as a philanthropist and not as a scientist, that he was not being asked to propose practical solutions but to describe what was psychologically involved in war. Freud then proceeded to reformulate Einstein's question. Einstein had wanted to know the differences between justice, law, right, on the one hand, and force, power, might, on the other. Freud suggested that the basic problem was the relationships among violence and right, justice, law. Freud went on to say that, in the beginning, superior muscular strength had decided in human groups whose will should prevail. When tools were invented, the winner was the individual who had better weapons or was more skilled in their use. This replaced muscular strength by intellectual strength but the purpose of the fight was the same, to assert one's will. Due to this change some people in each group or some groups in relation to other groups were compelled to abandon their claims or their objections to what others were doing. Freud pointed out that to kill an opponent had the advantages of deterring others from doing what he did and of not giving him an opportunity to renew his opposition. It also satisfied an instinctual desire. When the victor began to use the conquered people to render service to him, he gave up some security for the service of the conquered because there was now the danger of revenge and revolt. Violence gave way to right or law when the superior strength of a single individual could be countered by the banding together of several weak individuals. The power of those who were united not only held in check the violence of the mighty individual but compelled him to do the group's will. Thus, right or justice is the might of the group, of the community, but it is still violence. It is directed against anybody who resists the group. The purpose and method are the same but it is no longer the violence of a single individual. This new form of violence, right, or justice, needs certain psychological conditions in order to exist; the group must be stable and lasting. In order for the group to be permanent, it must   organized and have regulations which keep down rebellion. There must be in the group individuals who enforce these regulations and see that the laws are respected. The true source of the group's strength lies in its members' recognition of a community of interests which arise out of the emotional ties between the group members. Thus individual violence is overcome by transforming the individual's power to a larger unity. The security of the group rests on each member surrendering his personal freedom to use his strength for violent acts. Because of the unequal strength of various members and groups and because of its history, the community's or state's justice or laws are differentiated. There is a hierarchy of power within the group, there are different rules for slaves, conquered, strangers, natives, women, children, etc. What brings about social unrest is that certain rulers or ruling groups set themselves above the law and seek to dominate by violence. The oppressed individuals or certain people lower in the hierarchy then seek to change the unequal distribution of justice; they seek equal justice for all.

Someone remarked that Freud's conjecture is similar to Hobbes'. The speaker said that in one way they were similar; to both Freud and Hobbes, a group was a collection of individuals. Hobbes used Galileo's laws of motion to explain social behavior whereas Freud used the biological concepts of instinct. Freud described in greater detail the nature of the forces that repelled and attracted individuals by postulating the concepts of Libido and Death Instinct. To both, man was an emotio-conative creature who had enough intellect to realize that for utilitarian purposes he had to give up his freedom. Hobbes described the renouncing of individual violence in terms of a social contract but Freud claimed that it was due to the unconscious libidinal ties to the father or to the male leaders of the primitive human hordes. When these libidinal ties were broken, the group became a mob in which each person freely expressed his instincts (see seminars on value for a defense of Hobbes).

Someone interrupted to say that Freud did not answer Einstein's letter; he was just speculating. The student who had been reporting on Freud's answer said that Freud had pointed out that human history revealed that as communities used violence against each other, larger and larger social units resulted. In each of these larger units there was law, an island of safety from violence. The Roman Empire brought peace to the Mediterranean, the kings of France organized the various dukedoms and kingdoms into a flourishing state. [How accurate is this, historically speaking?] Thus, war produced some good effects. It created large units within which powerful central governments made violence impossible. But these governments were often not successful, the states had often disintegrated. Freud told Einstein that wars would be prevented when mankind united and set up a central world authority to which was handed over all conflicts of interests between states. But such a central authority needed power to enforce its decisions; without power such an authority was useless. Just as a community was held together by the compelling force of violence and the emotional ties among its members and identifications with a leader, the central authority needed force and emotional ties.

Someone interrupted to say that diverse groups had jointed together in the League Against War and Fascism. Maybe such groups, just like the diverse early Christian sects, would bring people together in some super-community and stop wars. When he said that capitalistic and communistic nations have a community of interests that could be used to unite them into a super-state with central authority, someone pointed out that the communists have said that the history of mankind was a history of class warfare, one group fighting and exploiting another. At present there is a conflict between only two groups, the capitalists and the workers. Once the workers overthrow the capitalistic governments, there will no longer be war between men; man's energy will then be directed to fight disease, poverty, ignorance. Men will be united as members of mankind and together they will try to conquer the forces of nature in order to put them to use for the progress of mankind.

The student who had been reporting on Freud's answer said that he ended his letter on a less optimistic note. Freud wrote that laws need violence, that men are easily led to war. They enthusiastically go to war because it is a social release for their pent-up instinctual energy. Somebody interrupted to give examples of the lowering of restrictions against premarital and extramarital sexual behavior by various respectable people and institutions during war time. The reporter said that Freud did not say that war was popular because it was an opportunity for sexual gratification but because it was an expression of the death instinct. There is in man love and hate just like there is the polarity of attraction and repulsion in physics. Neither of the instincts is good nor bad, both work together; it is not possible for one instinct to exist without the other. The instinct of self-preservation is of an erotic nature but it must have aggressiveness to fulfill its purpose. The instinct of love when directed toward an object needs some contribution from the death instinct, the instinct of mastery, in order for the person to possess the object. There is in man a lust for aggression and destruction. It is at work in every living being and is striving to bring man to ruin and to reduce life to its original nature, inanimate matter. It is not possible to get rid of man's aggressive nature but we may bring Eros to work against it. Whatever encourages the growth of libidinal ties between men operates against war. War will also be lessened by producing a community of shared interests. Someone pointed out that the death instinct is superior in strength to Eros, that in the end death will win. Therefore we can never end violence, we can only mitigate it with love and identification with certain ideals or leaders. Someone pointed out that Freud has brought back the Church's idea of the evil inclination in man. The age of Reason preached the perfectability of man and rejected the idea of the evil inclination; therefore Freud's theory is a step backwards.

The reporter pointed out that Freud had described what he had studied. His ideas were not based on the assumption of Satan's existence or original sin. Maybe we have to accept the existence of evil and plan to do something about it. He then went on to say that Freud also wrote that there is an innate inequality among men. Men fall into two classes, leaders and followers, and the latter are in the majority. The followers need an authority to make decisions for them, someone to whom they can look up to and submit. In view of this, we need to pay more attention to the education of those individuals who are men of independent mind, who cannot readily be intimidated and are eager in their pursuit of truth. Those people should give direction to the masses. Someone said that Hitler, Stalin, and Mussolini would approve of this suggestion; they have programs to train and to detect such individuals. How would this help to eradicate war or violence? Plato had a plan whereby the people with superior, rational, souls would be selected to be rulers but Freud seemed to say that willful ones should be selected for special training. The reporter ignored this and said that the ideal is to have a community of men who have subordinated their instincts to reason. Freud concluded his letter by saying that the evolution of human culture has resulted in physical changes in man. There has been a progressive displacement of the instinctual aims and a restriction of instinctual impulses. Sensations that were pleasurable to our ancestors are intolerable to us (cf. Hebb & Thompson, 1955). With the evolution of culture there is a strengthening of the intellect. The intellect is beginning to govern instinctual life and is leading to the internalization of the aggressive impulses. Pacifists are people who have advanced more in this direction and therefore they repudiate war. The question is: How long do we have to wait until most of mankind advances to the intellectual and emotional state in which war is abhorrent to them?

Someone said that he was surprised to learn that Freud was not pessimistic and asked when the letter was written. When the reporter replied, September 1932, the same student said that he wondered what Freud would say today. In 1932 many people had believed that Hitler would not succeed, that his speeches were just campaign rhetoric. But all that he had preached had come into being. Germany had once been the cultural center of Europe and of science. These cultured people, among them scientists who were not members of Hitler's party, had joined him in the most destructive war in human history. The Mongol invaders of Russia, of the Arabian Peninsula, and of India and China had not been more brutal. They were not cultured but the Germans were. ASL's student said that Freud was caught up in the peace movement of the 1930s and did not fully appreciate his own theoretical insight about the nature of the Death Instinct. Maybe life is but a battle of wills, of blind power exerted by individuals and groups. The other students attacked him for harping on an ancient excuse for war. The Bible says that there always were wars and there will always be wars. But there are other religions that deny this, that stress that men are by nature good. ASL's students wanted to know where in the Pentateuch is it written that there will always be wars and that human nature is evil. Other students said that people who objected to the reality of evil were like the proverbial ostrich that puts its head in the sand to avoid danger. Human history and current events validate the thesis that life is a battle of wills. One could take a pessimistic view of this fact of life and say, as Schopenhauer did, that it is better to be dead than alive or one could say, as Nietzsche did, that it is a glorious battle and that we should enter it to do and to die, for out of the battle will arise the Supermen with a new and superior code of law.

30
Concept of Power in a Non-Western Culture

A Chinese student presented an outline of Chinese philosophy. ASL came toward the end of the session and heard Wertheimer say that in Chinese philosophy power is a nuisance; force and intimidation are considered to be the lowest kind of way to get someone to do something. One sets before someone a model of moral behavior and tries to win him over by the virtuous nature of the model. Someone said that he was struck by the absence of theology and abstractions in Chinese philosophy. It seems that both Confucius and Lao Tzu were more concrete and pragmatic in their approach to life than Western philosophers. However, this virtue was a defect in their civilization. It stressed the development of certain human relations instead of the control and understanding of physical nature. Even the abstract Lao Tzu, whose idea of the Tao seems near to the mystical ideas of Plato and abstract ideas of science, did not seek to control or to influence nature. In fact, Lao Tzu preached resignation. He taught that Tao conforms to the way of Nature. If things are allowed to operate in their natural way they move harmoniously because they do not obstruct the spontaneous and natural operation of Tao. "Tao invariably does nothing and yet there is nothing that is not done." He advised people to do nothing because it would then allow the Tao to do things naturally. Some comments followed in which the idea was attacked as mysticism. The Tao was an inscrutable, ineffable power at work in nature, it was not a moral force as God is but a power that acted without self-assertion or dominance. It was a sort of natural spontaneity of Nature with none of the intellectual or emotio-conative characteristics of Western philosophy's concepts of will and reason. Wertheimer ended the session by suggesting that the students compare the idea of power in different cultures. He suggested that the class study the two Chinese sages' ideas and compare them with the dominant ideas about power in the Western world.

Out-of-Class Discussion: Confucianism

When the students after class were asked for a summary of what the Chinese student had reported, no one seemed to be able to give a summary. ASL was a member of the *Nut Club* of Mr. Daniel Cranford Smith, who lived in the penthouse apartment of the New School. This group often discussed social and political problems. One of its members was a Chinese mandarin. When ASL told him about the seminar he was sorry that he had not attended. He was interested in Wertheimer's formulation and said that it fitted the ·philosophy of Confucius. But it did not fit that of Lao Tzu, who preached withdrawing from all rule or government; his ideal man was an asocial individual and some aspects of his philosophy were even antisocial. Confucius, however, was a humanist who was vitally concerned with daily life and taught that one must be concerned with people and interpersonal relations. Confucius was concerned with man's destiny and with the problems of men and society, particularly the ethical aspects of these problems. Confucius started an ethical revolution and his ideas won without might and violence. They are not abstract moral ideas like that in the philosophies of Plato, Kant, Spinoza, or the various naturalistic philosophers. They center on concrete problems. When someone pointed out that the sayings of Confucius seem to be more like folk wisdom than the logical systems we call philosophy, the Chinese scholar said that Confucius was not building an abstract or logical system. His concern was with the actual moral conduct of man, not with their intellectual capacities. In response to someone's question he said that Confucius developed an ethical and political philosophy that had to a great degree ruled the lives of the Chinese people for over 2,000 years. He taught that a leader or ruler should govern his people benevolently, the welfare of his people should be his most important consideration, and he should be tied to his people by love and kindness. In general, he stressed faithfulness to oneself and to others, sincerity, naturalness, and propriety. He advocated the moral cultivation of man, the pursuit of Tao.

Mr. Smith asked why Confucius had stressed rituals. The speaker said that Confucius was a humanist, and his concern with human social relations was reflected in his stress on rituals. Ritual, li, was a form of social practice or regulation. Confucius asks, "When one refers to rites, does one mean merely the offering of jade or silk?" The answer is No. The rituals are ways of harmonizing men's emotions and desires. They bring about harmonious relations among men and contribute to the harmony of the heavens; rituals are not magical methods of coercing, controlling, or appeasing nature. He went on to say that Confucius was not otherworldly but stressed human relations, jen. Jen taught people to be good rulers, citizens, husbands, wives, brothers and sisters, daughters and sons, neighbors and friends. The jen involved justice, fairness, kindness, mutual affection, filial devotion and fraternity; it involved benevolence human heartedness. To live in terms of jen implies to live in the harmonious relations among all the members of groups and the families of men It is expressed in mutual affection and respect for the recipients of the action. Domination and exploitation are seen as negating the harmony needed for Chinese culture. Confucius also taught that one must not go to extremes in his conduct but should seek the medium, to be moderate in one's behavior, thoughts and feelings. One must do things in a smooth and not in a violent way. One must try to know, but not to control the environment. The stress is on knowing one's fate, not overcoming it.

Mr. Smith said that this view may be one of the reasons why the Chinese did not develop an industrial scientific society even though they had a more advanced society in the fourteenth century than Europe. When he inquired about Confucius' idea of government, the speaker said that Confucius taught that governments should be composed of superior men, men educated in terms of his system of morality and who would use moral suasion not punishment, who would use ritual, propriety, and not regulations. Such men would create a government that was naturally correct. A good ruler governs without exerting himself, and without those who are governed being aware that they are being governed. A government's function was first to teach the people to understand virtue, then to provide for the people's welfare and finally to prepare them for defense against internal and external enemies. In such a society people would feel free, there would be no need for intimidation or punishment. People would act in a harmonious, smooth way.

Mr. Smith asked whether this meant that Confucius believed that human nature was essentially good and that if people were left alone they would do what was good or right. The speaker said that virtue had to be cultivated. Confucius did not preach a vague or abstract ideology but a system of education, of moral training that involved men's actions in particular social situations. One is not born a superior man, one learns to be superior; one is not born virtuous but learns to be virtuous by practicing the virtues.

Before-Class Discussion

A few students were waiting to speak to Wertheimer. While waiting they commented on the Chinese student's presentation. They regarded the remarks as representing ideas of a tradition-bound culture which suppressed the human spirit. When ASL reported to them what he had learned in the *Nut Club* it reinforced their objection to Confucianism. Someone said that it was not a unique philosophy of life. The ancient Jews and the pious ghetto Jews as well as the members of certain peasant societies in Europe, Africa, and Asia also worship traditions and tried to cover every aspect of their daily lives with traditions and rituals. It is not an ethical view of life but a ritualistic view of life. Real ethics begins with the development of autonomous rational control of one's behavior. Wertheimer had sat down while the students had been talking. He asked them to examine what the practice of a tradition does in a social situation. When someone said that it suppresses the natural spirit of man and restricts the options people have for decision-making, he asked for examples where this is so. No one spoke. He then asked for examples where this is not so. No one spoke. Before he left he asked the students these questions: What is the function of specific traditions in concrete social situations? What do they actually accomplish for individuals and for the group?

After he left someone said that science cannot tolerate traditions; it accepts no authority except itself. This led to examples of the heavy hand of tradition holding up the progress of science. The students felt confident that science would lead to peace, prosperity, and happiness if men used its discoveries and discarded old ideas and traditions. When ASL's student pointed to the use of science in war, they said that it was not science that was at fault but capitalism. The discussion ended on this point.

Another Informal Discussion

Some students were seated in the lounge before class. A student said that he had been surprised that a session was devoted to such an unscientific idea as Taoism. He saw no value in what the Chinese student had said. ASL remarked that Confucius' ideas about the education of the superior man as well as the government by superior men did result in the development of a great culture. The student said that it led to the development of leisure-class gentlemen who could write poetry and pursue the arts but not to scientists who developed modern technology and not to social philosophers who developed a democratic state. It led to the mandarins who exploited the masses while they practiced the virtues of the superior man. Confucius codified and glorified ancient Chinese folk wisdom, leading to such a veneration of custom that China had remained a backward country in which most of the people were enslaved. ASL remarked that Confucius cannot be blamed for China's present-day backwardness. That China did not forge ahead in modern times was not entirely due to Confucius' teaching. People overlook the fact that China was for centuries more developed technologically and morally than any European country of the fourteenth century. Someone asked, Why is it that the barbaric people of Western Europe, and not the cultured people of China or the Mediterranean, developed the modern technological world? Is it because the latter venerated the past and did not develop discontinuity with their past? A student pointed out that the Humanists of the Renaissance in Europe also venerated the past and developed cultured gentlemen who exploited the peasants and workers as they practiced Greek Paganism. It was only with the advent of science that men dared to break the cake of custom and win control over physical nature. At present we have begun to do the same with social and personal behavior. ASL said that according to a Chinese scholar whom he met in the *Nut Club,* Confucius lived in a time when morality was being challenged. His writing appealed to the moral feelings of people. What he taught shaped Chinese civilization so that it emphasized morality and not force or power. Modern science has glorified the power of man to control nature. We have succeeded where the magicians of our primitive ancestors failed but we live in a time of moral confusion. Perhaps we need an American Confucius.

Someone said that the ruling classes of China used Confucius' teaching to develop an ideology that helped them remain in power for 2,500 years. He went on to say that morals are just rationalizations of the mighty, that putting them into a code and studying them does not lead to virtue. It is only with the advent of science that we realize what has to be done to make people virtuous. When a student said that science had nothing to do with morality, that morals belonged to the prescientific way of dealing with human behavior, ASL's student said that Comte, who venerated science, had said that human life was not merely a matter of achieving, by means of power, a place in the economic and social hierarchies of a society. Comte said that beyond these hierarchies was a moral order. A person may be low on the socio-economic order but he may be high in the moral and spiritual order because of his devotion to the community. This is similar to Confucius' doctrine. Thus to both Comte and Confucius the moral order did not exist in a transcendental realm; it was an earthly order, not a spiritual order. Some philosophers and scientists, just as the Chinese sages, have said that man's supreme goal should not be the seeking of primacy in power and wealth; man should seek a meritorious life in the service of the community. Someone argued that the doctrine is an opiate which makes men accept their low position in society. ASL's student said that it also makes the wealthy and powerful seek merit. It leads the wealthy and the powerful to help the poor and the weak. The former speaker said that people need not depend on the good graces of the wealthy who are rich due to having exploited the masses. The wealth belongs to the people, the people have the power to take what is due to them without myths about merit.

Wertheimer, who had sat down among the students, asked them why the powerful are sometimes mindful of the powerless, if it is all a matter of power. Can a society, a peasant society, or a modern industrial society, endure if it is not regulated by what is commonly called morality? The speaker remarked that Savonarola, Calvin, the Puritans, and even Hitler and Mussolini have appealed to morality. Are they examples of superior men? Someone said that from a certain point of view they are superior men; it depends on one's frame of reference. Wertheimer asked in what way Hitler is a superior man. The student said that Hitler has succeeded in conquering the Western world. ASL's student asked whether Al Capone is a model of what Confucius meant by a superior man. Wertheimer asked the students to compare the behavior of Confucius to that of Hitler. ASL said that Confucius would not use force but moral suasion. Confucius did not succeed by exerting force but because of the merit of his ways; he did not impose his ideas on people. The previous speaker said that Confucius himself did not use force but when his ideas were accepted by the government, the officials forced people to believe them. This is true of all successful social movements; they all use violence at some point in the process of acquiring power. Even primitive Christians who conquered in the name of love and used techniques of non-resistance also destroyed pagan temples and fought with members of different religious sects. The student challenged us to name a social movement that had achieved recognition only by spiritual worth. What spiritual worth does Stalin or Trotsky have? One succeeded and the other failed; therefore, Stalin is glorified and Trotsky is vilified. Had Trotsky succeeded it would be the other way around.

Wertheimer asked whether there are situations where morality does prevail against arbitrary power. He agreed that there are people who seek power and asked, Are there people who seek moral excellence? We need to look for cases of both kinds of people. This is not a question for debate but for empirical investigation. He then suggested that we study actual social situations to discover the conditions in which groups and individuals act morally and conditions in which they just seek power and are blind to the consequences of their actions.

Someone remarked that Wertheimer's good people may be found among simple peasant societies, in small communities of pious people, in what Cooley has called primary groups, where everybody regards everybody else as his sister and brother and the members are concerned for each other's welfare while pursuing their own goals. But such people are unsuited for modern society where each person must maximize his gains. The student said that it does not exist in our schools because competition and grade grabbing is taught in order to train children for the struggle for power in the socioeconomic hierarchy. ASL's student asked, What moral excellence is achieved by a person who has earned a PhD, does it make one a better man? Suppose someone sincerely sought the truth and human welfare while earning his PhD in psychology and was not mindful of the power politics of his department or of the academic world, would he get a job, let alone get the PhD degree? Wertheimer insisted that the existence of people who just seek power does not preclude the existence of people who seek moral excellence and who are not at all concerned with power. After a pause he said that their behavior has different effects on the social field.

The conversation went back to Confucius when someone said that his philosophy had created a tradition-bound society. It did not give freedom to the individual critically to evaluate the values that were handed down. It stressed permanency and not progress, stability and not change. The student concluded that traditions are to social behavior what habits are to personal behavior; they mechanize and blind. Wertheimer asked why the student viewed tradition negatively. Why set up an opposition between freedom and tradition? ASL's student pointed out that in the early days of the scientific revolution, traditional customs were supported by the Church and the State and they interfered with the growth of science and industry. Science and industry had a radically new orientation toward life. Until the scientific revolution, men looked to the past and glorified it just as Confucius had done. But due to the success of science, people rejected the past and looked toward the future. The scientific method gives modern man a means to develop rational customs, morals, and values. Someone added that modern man no longer leaves the evolution of customs to chance but plans them according to the laws he has discovered. Another student said that, generally speaking, science rejects customs. They are obstacles to the progress of science because of the tendency for people to do what is customary and traditional. Many mistakes have been made because scientific ideas and methods of one era became traditional. The enemy of science is tradition just as the enemy of productive thinking is habit.

Someone pointed out that he learned in his sociology and psychology courses that we must not be ethnocentric when we study cultures of primitive societies. Yet the teachers of these courses used the standards of the technological scientific world to criticize the culture of groups that do not base their behavior on science and technology but on traditional cultures. We have no right to criticize and to reject as unsound the morals and values of people who believe in a Deity, astrology, magic, and even demonology. We may not in the name of science force these people to change their views or ridicule their behavior. A student pointed out that in order for a society to progress it has to get rid of the dead wood of customs.

Wertheimer challenged the thesis that customs are just the dead hand of the past, the dead wood of history. He suggested that they have functional value and are not always nonfunctional. A student insisted that religious rituals and beliefs interfere with the acceptance of modern and scientifically tested ideas and even goods and services. People who practice their old customs are usually kept from fully participating in the culture of the societies in which they live. Moreover, they have a very narrow and constricted view of men and of society. He gave as examples the Amish and the Shtetle Jews of Eastern Europe, especially the Chassidic sects. Wertheimer remarked that maybe their way of life is not as narrow as it seems to us and that their behavior may not be as mechanical and unthinking as it appears. All the cows of a herd may look alike to someone who had never seen cows but the herdsman sees the differences. One of the previous speakers suggested that we study custom-bound groups in our society from the frame of reference of the members of the groups. Thereupon a student described some of the problems of helping the refugees in Williamsburgh, Brooklyn because they are trying to maintain their old-world traditions in America. Their customs and practices are outlandish and keep them from becoming Americans. He went on to say that everything these people do is done in terms of their religion. From the moment they awaken in the morning to the time they go to sleep, they spend all of their free time studying their religious books and discussing religious concepts. They are so engrossed in ritual that they do not know what is going on around them. They need to be enlightened; only when they will be liberated from this way of life will they be able to make a contribution to American society, just as previous immigrants have. This led to some remarks about the need to separate the ethical teachings of religion from its rituals; the former does not depend nor need the latter. ASL's student questioned the separation of ethical ideals from action. He asked the students to study the effects of religious people's rituals on their behavior in the community and on their interpersonal relations. He pointed out that the Amish have a very low rate of crime and of mental illness, that they help their neighbors as well as each other. What are the concrete effects of the ritualized behavior of the Chassidic groups in Williamsburgh; what does it accomplish? Someone said that generally speaking religion has produced more that is bad than good. After a pause, Wertheimer asked, What is a truly religious person? After another pause he said, Why do psychologists study the bad and mean things that people do? Why not study the behavior of good people, of saintly, wise, holy people? Someone said that it is difficult to define what these words mean. Society is plagued with war, fascism, labor strife, delinquency, crime, and mental illness; there is a great need to study the people who cause trouble to society. Religion is a personal matter and, as long as it does not interfere with society's functioning, it is not the business of psychology to study it. ASL's student said that religion, rituals, and customs of primitive people are studied by anthropologists. Why do we not study such behavior in modern societies? Someone said that modern societies must abolish religion because its values are counter to the values of science and technology on which they are based. He claimed that a person who is a scientist cannot be religious. In response to a question he said that psychology must not get lost in the metaphysical problems of religion. Morals are the social norms of a group; one's peer group decides what is moral. When Wertheimer questioned the last statement, the student said that a person discovered or learned what was morally correct by seeing what his peers said was correct.

The conversation returned to Confucius when a student said that he had been taught that the goal of education was not intellectual but moral development. John Dewey as well as old-fashioned educators had also said that the aim of education was character development. Although Confucius' and Dewey's aims are the same, their curricula are different. He went on to suggest that we compare what a mandarin learns in China with what a pupil in a progressive school learns in the USA and with what a Catholic, a Lutheran, a traditional Hebrew school student learns. Wertheimer suggested that maybe we should compare the products of the different schools, compare a Chinese government official who had been trained by Confucius' method and curriculum with a sixteenth-, seventeenth-, and eighteenth-century English government official who had been educated in an English university. ASL's student suggested that the behavior of the adult alumni of the various parochial schools in Europe should be compared with the products of each country's secular educational systems in order to see whether they created superior individuals or bigoted people.

Wertheimer remarked in response to a student's objections, that some people have been saying that a university has to exercise moral leadership, that it is not a place of value-free intellectual discussion. It has to deal with the moral imperatives of the social field; it must deal with real-life problems and not just general principles and abstract ideas. Someone remarked that European university students were more politically minded than American students and that in Latin America the universities were the headquarters of the revolutionaries. He went on to say that the university was not the place for such activities. It led to chaos in Germany; the students who joined the Nazis fought on the campus and in the classroom with the Communists and Social Democrats, classes were disrupted, and teachers and students were intimidated by the various political groups. It destroyed the German universities; it made rowdyism, anti-intellectualism and anti-semitism stylish. Wertheimer left but the students continued talking. Someone said that they were overlooking the fact that the other political parties were doing this too, they did it more subtly because they controlled the schools. Even in America the controlling groups teach their ideology in school. A school teacher said that this keeps mankind divided into ideological camps. When all schools will teach the truth and not ideologies, people will not hate each other and there then will be no wars, no exploitation. ASL's student said that when all schools will teach the same things they will create like-minded individuals. He challenged the assumption that all human troubles stem from cultural differences. When someone said that they do, he asked him why he objects to Hitler's attempt to make people like-minded. What difference is there between Hitler's or a scientist's dictatorship that claims that it has the truth? Will not each create a society of like-minded people? He pointed out that sociologists seem to favor like-mindedness because the discussion of religious, racial, and national differences are taught in courses on social disorganization and the textbooks' titles contain the words *social disorganization*. It seems that everybody, even the sociologist, wants a monolithic society. The students argued that a society based on science will be a society based on truth but the dictators do not believe in the truth; they seek to exploit and to enslave the minds of men. ASL remarked that Hitler also said that he was interested in the truth. Everybody cries that they are for morality and truth as they seek to impose their definition of it on mankind.

The discussion changed when someone said that modern society teaches one to be a consumer; not only the rich, as in Veblen's description, but even the worker. He said that John Marshall, the economist, had once said that our economy does not exist to satisfy man's needs but to create needs to satisfy; this leads to industrial and social progress. This view of the function of industry seem to go against Confucius' and Lao Tzu's teaching. This may explain why Western man has progressed and China has not. Our schools teach children to want, not to be content with their lot. We have upward mobility in our society; industry as well as the people are moving forward. Growth and not stability is stressed. ASL's student said that Confucius was also concerned with growth, growth in morals. A student said that Confucius' doctrine was a myth that taught most people to accept their places as low men on the totem pole. Our society's stress on material growth makes people demand the goods and services that are being denied to them. Everybody has the same right to be on top of the totem pole. Spiritual, moral growth was a valuable ideal in the days when men lived in a world of scarcity. Modern technology and science have given us a world of abundance and therefore we have no need for the moral values that have been taught in the past. A new morality has to develop that is based on the new economic facts of life. Someone pointed out that everybody cannot be first, there is not enough place there for everybody. Why should we strive to be first? He added that since Teddy Roosevelt's days, people have been warning the Americans that they are plundering the planet by wasting natural resources, but the plundering goes on as if there is an everlasting supply and the only obstacle is man's incapacity to consume it. The way modern society wastes and destroys natural resources we will soon eat ourselves out of existence. We have become an ahistorical people. Not only have we renounced the past but we have also rejected the future as we indulge ourselves in the present. Do you realize how much iron and petroleum the war is using up? We act as if there is an inexhaustible supply, we do not think of the future generations who will suffer because of our present-day waste. A refugee scholar added that this is why modern technological society is teaching people to have an awful outlook on life. It is a surface shallow existence in which there are only discrete momentary experiences that appear in a void; for fleeting moments they are together and then disintegrate. Our experiences are like Epicurus' atoms moving in the void, accidentally coming together and separating and not being affected by having been together. It is a world with no structure and therefore absurdly vain, a world of sounds and furies. No one commented on these remarks.

31
Non-Doing and Passive Resistance

Before the class was called to order a student told Wertheimer that the concept of Tao was similar to the Physiocrats' idea of natural law. Like the Physiocrats, Lao Tzu had said that the social ills of the times were due to the facts that civilization and society were artificial and that man's tampering destroyed the natural goodness of things. Since the Tao was the motivating force of the universe that allowed all things to develop by themselves naturally and spontaneously, Lao Tzu therefore advocated withdrawal from governmental activities. ASL's student said that the Physiocrats advocated social reforms and were active as government advisors and ministers. Lao Tzu's behavior reflects the oriental mentality of passivity, the Physiocrats' reflect the occidental mentality of action. When the other professors sat down and the session started, the student repeated a question that he had asked Wertheimer, How can a person believe that it is best to do nothing in the face of trouble? Someone suggested that if one does not know what to do it is best to do nothing. The Physiocrats, the Philosophical Radicals, the Utilitarians, believed that they knew the natural economic laws and created a mess. Contemporary reformers say that the earlier reformers were mistaken but that they now know the natural laws. Perhaps it would be best if everybody followed Lao Tzu's advice and withdrew from attempting to predict and to control nature, society, and man. Let nature take its course, take it easy, do not worry, do not become trapped in ambitions, savor what is really happening around you here and now, do not get lost in abstractions.

Someone remarked that the concept of Tao was used differently by Confucius. The Tao, the way of heaven, was a moral force, a force that stood on the side of the individual who struggled for the right. Lao Tzu objected to Confucius' conception of the Tao. He said that when one pursued the Tao one did what was instinctive, natural. Lao Tzu was opposed to the ideas of virtue, the social ideas and education of Confucius. Lao Tzu said that everybody should be in harmony with the fundamental laws of the universe. Artificial institutions and all striving for that which is out of reach create disharmony. Do nothing, the perfect man does nothing, the great sage originates nothing, he just contemplates the universe. A student protested that it was not possible to do nothing, to live was to act. This led to several comments about

451

the ill effects of doing nothing. Hoover had said that prosperity was around the corner while the people starved. Hitler rearmed the Rhineland, conquered Austria, Czechoslovakia, the Low Lands, and France because no one stopped him. The Sitzkrieg in the winter of 1939-40 was not the answer to the Blitzkrieg of the fall of 1939; when a wolf is attacking you, you have to fight. Evil does not go away, it has to be fought. Some people think that by not looking, by not paying attention and ignoring evil, it will go away. Such non-action actually furthers it. Hitler succeeded because of non-action. The peace movements and the Oxford Oath in England created a situation in which Hitler was able to rearm the Rhineland, to invade Austria and the Sudetenland with impunity. Hitler will eventually conquer the world, if people do not stop him. The doctrine of not seeking to be powerful, of not interfering with nature, is a suicidal doctrine.

A visitor said that he agreed that tolerance of intolerance leads to intolerance. He explained that Hitler was aided and encouraged in all that he had done by the very capitalistic countries that preached peace. The Oxford pledge was signed by people who had hoped that Hitler would invade Russia. That was why they let him rearm Germany and annex Austria and the Sudetenland. When he looled them and attacked Western Europe, they still hoped that he would attack Russia.

Riezler proposed that there are instances where doing nothing is more doing than doing something. Wertheimer asked for concrete examples of this thesis. Someone said that in teaching problem solving it is best to let the child discover the answer by himself; it develops self reliance, understanding and mental maturity. A visitor said that in psychoanalysis the therapist is passive. He may even sit behind a screen so that he does not interfere with the patient's associations. Wertheimer asked, Suppose someone was going to jump out of the window, what would you do? Suppose a person called for help while he was being attacked by a bully, what would you do? After a few students commented, Wertheimer said that we should study concrete situations in order to see what were the effects in them of action or non-action. Are there situations that call for action, if no one acts irreparable damage occurs? Why do some people not answer the call in such situations and why do some people answer the call? A student said that people have to be motivated to act. One should not expect anyone to do anything if he was not motivated; whether or not one acted depended on the personality of the individual, his habits and motives. Wertheimer said that psychologists tend to focus on personality factors but how about the nature of the situation, the field conditions, the person's attitudes and assumptions about what is happening?

A visitor said that people are trained to mind their own business, not to interfere in a lover's quarrel, in a spat between husband and wife, in a street fight between two urchins. Even when someone violates a city ordinance we do not reprove him but leave it to the police. According to certain moralistic views one should reprove his neighbor and one should accept reproof by his neighbor. We no longer follow the biblical injunction to give and to take such correction. Ours is a more permissive society. It is not that people do not care but that they leave it to the people whose business it is to deal with such things. He gave an example from Allport's *Institutional Behavior* in which a guard at Sing Sing Prison saw a canoe turn over in the Hudson River and saw that the occupants were drowning. When one of the prisoners volunteered to swim to their help the guard threatened to shoot anyone who left the yard. The guard's job was to see to it that the prisoners did not escape.

The rest of the session was spent discussing whether not acting may be an excuse to avoid responsibility for one's actions. Wertheimer proposed that instead of talking abstractly the students should study particular situations in order to find out what happened in them, to find out the reasons or processes that led to action and non-action. Moreover, the social situations in which the acts took place should be studied in order to understand their structural requirements.

32
Examples of Social Conflict

In the next session Wertheimer read a newspaper account of a strike in a Brooklyn electrical appliance company. He asked the class, Suppose someone asked you to help settle the dispute, what would you do? Someone said that both the factory owner and the strike leaders were correct from their respective points of view, each person protected his interests. There had to be a clash of interest because they were members of different classes; factory owners' profits depend on keeping the worker's wages down, workers' wages depend on getting a larger share of the owners' profit. The factory owners have been conditioned by the economic system to seek profits and the workers to seek higher wages.

A visitor pointed out that one must look at the situation objectively. Modern society is a society in which various classes are antagonistic toward each other. This reflects a historical drama that not only exists in modern capitalistic society but has existed throughout history. The history of mankind is a history of classes struggling against each other for supremacy. The class struggle is the dynamism of history, it will eventually lead to a classless society in which there willl be no human antagonism. Wertheimer asked whether such talk will help settle the dispute between the workers and the owner of the Brooklyn appliance company. Someone said that it is of help, it points out that they must fight it out, that it is a matter of might, that no reasonable solution can be found. When someone said that such strikes create hardships for the workers and that the workers will never make up the loss in pay from the paltry raise they will eventually get, a visitor said that this is a selfish point of view. It is immoral for a worker to defy his union; his personal interests are not above the interests of the working class. A worker who crosses a picket line is an enemy of the people. ASL asked him who had benefited from the recent WPA teachers' strikes. Twice in two years they lost one day's salary because they went on strike to protest the reduction of the staff. No worker was reinstated and each time they lost 20% of their salary. Moreover, it was a real hardship on some teachers who were supporting families on their weekly $21. Some idealistic unmarried teachers who were sons of middle-class parents and who had left home to go on relief in order to get WPA jobs were all for the strike but the sons and daughters of the poor were not happy about the strike. Would it have been immoral for them to cross the picket line? The visitor remarked that he was surprised to hear such anti-labor views expressed by an intelligent person.

Wertheimer asked, Suppose that the owner of the appliance factory closed his plant and the workers were thrown out of work. Would it help the workers? Suppose the owner gave into their demands and went bankrupt in a few months. Would they have won the strike? The visitor said that the bosses always say that they will close their plants or go bankrupt if they give the workers a raise but they do not. Someone asked, How can one find out whether the boss is telling the truth? The visitor said that the owner's desire for profit will keep him from revealing the facts, his profit motive blinds him. Someone asked whether the workers' greed also blinds them. The visitor said that Wertheimer is ignoring the facts of economic existence. It is unfortunate that owners have to go bankrupt and become workers when they are not able to compete with other capitalists. All societies have been divided into classes with one class exploiting another. But the bourgeois has added a uniquely new feature in this struggle, it cannot maintain its position without creating methods of production which in turn will give rise to a socialistic society. In order to be more effective and win in the struggle for markets, the bosses have to cut prices. This makes them plan the work more efficiently. Only the efficient factories survive, the inefficient bosses become workers. Eventually capitalistic competition will lead to a society in which nearly everybody will be workers. The remaining few factory owners will then be expropriated by the workers who will create a classless society in which men will no longer be arrayed in different and antagonistic classes. They will be one; mankind's energy will then be directed to conquering nature and not each other.

Someone interrupted to say that if this is the inevitable course of history, why do some people advocate revolutions and dictatorship of the proletariat? Since it is the natural law of history, why do anything? It is bound to come to pass. The visitor said that the suffering of the workers and farmers stirs the moral conscience of certain individuals. These people become revolutionaries in order to quicken the historical process just as we try to influence evolution by breeding. To some extent Marxists are like the Positivists and the Utilitarians, the Eugenicists and others who have realized that modern industrial-scientific societies have to reject the ideologies of pre-scientific societies, of the theological and military societies of the past. Modern science makes it possible for man to study the social system of his society, to understand its laws and to develop a new society. Scientific Socialism preaches a new ideology in which profit is not the goal in life but in which cooperation between individuals and groups to abolish poverty and disease is the goal. Wertheimer agreed that many people are attracted to Communism because of these noble ideals but he challenged the notion that a particular worker and his boss cannot appreciate each other's situation and cannot solve their problems productively. He compared the visitor's statement that they are different-minded people because of basic different ideologies to the relativistic argument of Hitler, who has said that Jews and Germans have radically different codes of conduct due to their *Folkgeist*. It is similar to the sociologists who say that a member from one class or culture cannot appreciate the behavior and values of a member from another class or culture.

Someone described the strike at Ford. Henry Ford had said that he would close his plant before he would recognize the union. The only reason that he was forced to recognize it was because the workers were backed up by the force of the government, the NLB forced him to recognize the union. Similarly the recent Woolworth Store strike was won by the group that had the power of the NLB on its side. The student then rejected Wertheimer's assumption that people can be persuaded by the evidence to give in to the demands of others. Each man, group, or institution looks out for its own interests or profit; everybody tries to maximize his profit, tries to get ahead of the next fellow, one grabs as much as he can. He asked Wertheimer to give him an example of an owner of a factory who really had the welfare of his workers at heart. When Wertheimer mentioned Robert Owen, the student dismissed him as an Utopian thinker who had no understanding of economics. Wertheimer said that it might be instructive to study the relations between workers and bosses in small factories and stores that are at present being unionized and in which labor and owners are engaged in collective bargaining. Does such bargaining always represent demands that are expressions of the might, the will of certain people, and are they always blind to the evidence? Maybe there are some cases in which both the worker and owner do act blindly, each looking out for his interests, but perhaps there are also cases where the owner and the workers appreciate each other's situations and try to create conditions so that both are able to advance their interests without destroying anybody. The workers and the bosses in such cases do not focus merely on their interests but on what is necessary to keep the factory or store open for business. The visitor said that such class-alienated workers and bosses are rare. Someone suggested that if such cases are studied it would be found that the workers are deluded by paternalistic owners who are actually exploiting them.

Wertheimer said that such statements assume that people are egocentric and that they are incapable of facing the evidence. A student remarked that according to Freud violence and not right rules the social scene. When Wertheimer objected to the idea that social life is based on violence and coercion, a visitor said that all life consists of one person coercing the other to do what he wishes; a coercionless society is inconceivable. Coercion comes into being whenever two or more people who are different from each other live together. It is characteristic of social behavior that the actions or thoughts of one person compel or restrain another. The coercion may be moral or physical, direct or indirect. If one does not recognize coercion it is because the coercion is automatic, because it has been incorporated into his personality. When the forces within the personality structure do not automatically determine the action and one is aware of the forces on the outside that compel and restrain him, it is recognized as coercion. In response to a question he said that we often react differently when we are coerced by people who have the legitimate right to do it—our parents, judges, policemen. This does not mean that sanctioned or unsanctioned coercion is different, it is the same thing, it is force, violence. We accept sactioned coercion because of our habituation to certain social norms and culturally designated authorities. The prolonged period of human infancy helps develop subordination and dependence of the young on the old; it creates attitudes of obedience and submission to the parents which are generalized to all authority figures. Wertheimer objected to his Freudian view of human relations but the speaker went on to conclude that all civilization rests on the coercion of the young by the old. Tradition and mores rest on the coercion an individual experiences in infancy; they are imposed by coercion.

Wertheimer said that it is stylish to say that social life consists of using violence to force and to coerce others. To some people this view is a myth. How true is it? What kind of evidence is there for it and against it? What are its sociological premises? After a pause, he said that this view stems from an atomistic view of social situations. The actual structure of the social situation is ignored, it is assumed to be a situation where one will battles another will. The visitor said that Wertheimer is taking a moralistic view, that he is assuming that there is a natural moral order. The facts, however, show that might makes right. A student asked, Why do people seek to justify their behavior by the use of such concepts as mutuality, requirements of the situation? Is there in man a need to justify his behavior in terms of a moral order? If there is, it is learned and not innate. Perhaps it is a social mechanism to get obedience. ASL's student asked, Why does all illegitimate power try to become legitimate? Perhaps one cannot renounce the myth without destroying society.

After-Class Discussion

Some students followed Wertheimer to the cafeteria. ASL told them that the *Nut Club* had recently been contrasting Gandhi's and Mao's revolutionary activities. The discussion had led ASL to prepare for his class a lecture on passive resistance and noncooperation. Wertheimer asked him what he was going to say. ASL said that he is uncertain. It is a very attractive idea but it may not be workable. The visitor said that it has resulted in violence; it is a form of coercion. Wertheimer said that there was a difference between the people who practice nonviolence and were hurt or killed by their enemies and people hurting and killing their opponents. A student said that violence is violence. If one sits down in the market place, if one refuses to comply with the laws, it is not civil disobedience, it is not an act against the government but against one's fellowmen. It restricts and keeps people from doing what they need to do. Such disobedience brings into play the agents of social control. Thus nonviolence actually instigates violence. Wertheimer asked whether the violence in Nazi concentration camps is instigated by the prisoners. Someone said that perhaps there is something on the stimulus side that makes the guards react violently. ASL said that no one who was in such a camp would say this. [He was wrong; Bruno Bettleheim in 1947 described how the behavior of a prisoner could produce certain violent or nonviolent responses from the Gestapo officers. One may wonder whether the methods that Bettleheim had used would have saved the Jews who were not as lucky as he was to be able to leave for the USA before World War II. He was in Dachau and Buchenwald before then.]

When Wertheimer left, the discussion turned to the history of passive resistance and the following points were made. It is a method used by Oriental people. There are examples in Ancient India and Judea where people of a village would squat in the square during market days or in the temples in order to get redress for their grievances. The Judeans even used it against the Roman Legions; sometimes they committed mass suicide in the face of superior force. A man in India who had suffered a wrong from his neighbor might sit down on his neighbor's doorstep with the intention to fast unto death. The neighbor would usually redress the wrong because of the belief that the man's ghost would haunt him. In India it is related to a religious ritual, the hartal, in which people abstained from all life activities in order to expose the wrongdoer to moral or spiritual saction; people have used it against despotic kings and government officials. Recently Ghandi had prepared to starve to death on behalf of the Untouchables. His suffering was to shame his disciples and lead to public censure if not spiritual retribution. It is said he meditated on a legend of Buddha in which Buddha offered himself to a hungry tigress. Buddha changed the hartel from an act of retribution to an act of love for the person for whom one sacrificed himself. ASL's student said that the Judeans would commit mass suicide in order not to be converted to paganism by the Romans and in the Middle Ages entire communities of Jews committed suicide to escape forced conversion by the Crusaders. The Stoics, the primitive Christians, the Cathari, the Albigenses, the Anabaptists, and the Quakers used passive resistance in face of demands by the state or the church authorities. Some Christian groups, such as the Quakers, since World War I have used nonresistance as a means of attempting to stop or prevent war. In the post-World War I era, college students organized war resistance organizations whose members pledged to refuse to answer the call to arms by their respective countries. But despite the popularity of the movements in the USA and England, at present (1941) many people are breaking their pledges and volunteering to fight.

Social philosophers and literary men have also preached civil disobedience. Godwin believed that a virtuous man might rely on his own reason to defy force and to shame those who use force. Shelley in his *Masque of Anarchy* and Thoreau in his *Essay on Civil Disobedience* give passionate expression to anarchistic protests against violence. A student pointed out that the factory workers' sit-down strikes and the farmers' mortgage strikes in the thirties were forms of civil disobedience. Someone added that the theories of the general strike of Benbow and Owen are also examples of it. The general strike has played a great role in the labor movement. At first it was suggested that there be a universal withdrawal of all labor from industry in order to get reforms from reactionary governments. This was never done but it has been used as a myth to galvanize the workers in France (cf. Sorel). On the eve of World War I the left wing of the Socialist Parties of Europe had advocated a general strike but it did not eventualize because of the fear that the governments would shoot the striking workers or that the workers of the other countries would not strike against the war. When someone said that general strikes have not been successful, ASL pointed out that the 1905 general strike in Russia led to the promise by the Czar to set up the First Duma. The general strike of the German Socialists and Unions in 1920 succeeded against the *Kapp Putsch*. However, the English general strike of the 1930s was a failure.

Someone said that passive resistance does not mean withdrawing from the social field but not cooperating with the forces in it. It is a method of blocking the actions of certain groups or people in it; it is violence in the sense that it interrupts the vital activities of society. It also interferes with many people's freedom of action. It is an instance where a group disrupts the social field by not doing what the social field demands. It may be a more effective way of disrupting modern technological society than by acting against it. The last

remark led someone to describe a recent sit-down WPA strike at 13 Astor
Place. He described how it interfered with the education of thousands of
people. ASL said that it was a failure and hurt no one except some of his
colleagues who had locked themselves in the building; the police removed
them and they were jailed. The teachers outside marched to the jail and picketed all night. Hundreds of people lost a night's sleep, a few people were
fined and fired from their jobs but not one demand of the workers was met.
It did not even get a decent write up in the newspapers. [He had discussed
the strike with Wertheimer, who said that one good feature was that the
police and the government allowed the strike and that this could never have
happened in Hitler's Germany.] Someone said that the teachers were too
mild, the Workers Alliance and the WPA workers were not militant enough,
were not forceful. When ASL said that this would have resulted in violence,
the student said that some people have justified violence while resisting the
authorities when the government uses terrorism against them. Someone objected to the use of violence because it is wrong to use it; it should not and
cannot be used by those who are devoted to peace and brotherhood. The
moral stance of nonviolence will eventually win over those who use violence
against them.

The visitor said that despite the high ethical values of the advocates of nonviolence their behavior engenders violence. Why does it happen; is there an
aggressive instinct in man? Someone said that people get carried away with
the virtue of their cause; it also gives some people a thrill when they act violently in such situations, others lose the ability for rational debate, discussion,
or persuasion. Another student conjectured that when one upsets the social
field by passive resistance it calls forth emotional reactions by the people
whose behavior is being blocked and this reaction creates a social atmosphere
which in turn agitates the passive resisters. The visitor said that once the social field is disorganized, mob behavior is inevitable. The mob knows no
reason, in it each person acts out his aggressive tendencies. Someone said that
violence should be used only when the time is ripe for it. He went on to explain that this is the reason why the Marxists have rejected the use of violence
except in certain situations.

Later on, some students walked with Wertheimer to the subway. They
made the following comments. Nonviolence seems to be another form of violence unless one disentangles himself from the social field; passive resistance
does not work unless one leaves the field. Where can a man of modern society go to escape the wrath of the people in the social field when he refuses to
cooperate? Years ago it was easy to walk off into the woods or desert and to
live alone; today one has to stay in the community where he becomes an irrit-
ant to those who are affected by his behavior. Only by going off into the desert, living alone, can one practice nonviolence; as long as one is a member of
a community or group he has certain responsibilities toward it. If he is too
weak to assert his demands forcefully he can do it by not cooperating and thus
making people aware that he is not happy about the way he is treated. But he
should not give it a fancy name; it is a form of violence. ASL said that he
often wonders what would happen if all the Anti-Nazis in Germany would refuse to cooperate with Hitler. Would he order them all to be shot? Would he
shoot thousands of defenseless people? Wouldn't the soldiers revolt against
such an order? The way for the defenseless population to rise up against Hi-

tler is to march, wave after wave, in front of the Nazi's machine guns and under the airplanes, unmindful of the bullets. Wouldn't the soldiers stop shooting before all the people were killed? Wertheimer said that people who say this do not understand the Nazis; Hitler cannot be stopped this way. Such methods may work in other countries. The people in England would protest against the government and the party in power would be thrown out of office if the British army shot the passive resisters of India. In response to ASL's question, he said that the Nazis have a different conception of man. They have rejected the idea of Homo sapiens. Passive resistance will not work with Hitler. ASL said that if they killed thousands of people in a day there would be a health hazard even for the Germans. Wertheimer said that they would figure out a way to handle it; they are efficient.

When the students left, ASL said to Wertheimer that some seminar members are against participation in the war; they claim that it is a fight between capitalists and fascists. Wertheimer said that they are mistaken; they are blind to the character of the Nazis. ASL said that it seems that he is advocating the use of force. How is this different from what the Nazis are doing? He said that the use of counter-force to save oneself from being destroyed by someone is not the same thing as to use force to kill and enslave people who are not attacking you. ASL remarked that the Nazis claim that they are threatened, Hitler may really believe that the capitalists, the Jews, and the Communists want to destroy Germany. How do we know that he is not correct and that we are correct in assuming that he is out to get us? Wertheimer told ASL to read the newspaper.

Obedience: An Informal Discussion

A few students sat with Wertheimer discussing the nature of obedience. Someone had said that the statement about the coercive nature of social life implied that obedience was an act of conforming, submitting to, and complying with the force of authority. Wertheimer asked, Why do people obey others? Someone said that it is due to force of habit. The person who obeys is a socialized person, a disciplined person; to disobey is to act in terms of one's will, to act impulsively. Wertheimer asked whether obedience means to conform blindly, to do or die as commanded by one's superiors. Are there cases of obedience and disobedience that have a reasonable basis?

A student said that according to Freud social life is impossible if one lives according to the pleasure principle. An essential condition for existence is obedience to rules and to authorities which makes life possible. Social life would not exist if it depended on the impulse of individuals. Because of fear of punishment or because of expectation of the rewards of complying, people curb their impulses and obey the laws. Wertheimer asked us to focus on specific cases in which a person obeys or disobeys a rule or law of a policeman, of a teacher, of a parent. The same student said that in all such situations the reason for obedience would be fear of punishment or expectation of reward. Wertheimer remarked that there are cases in which people obey because of understanding or realizing what is required in the situation and not because of reward or punishment or profit to their dear egos. The same student told Wertheimer that he was assuming that men had an instinct to obey. Wertheimer told him that such arguments beloud the question of what actually happens when a person obeys in a particular situation. Perhaps people obey for a variety of reasons; the same person may obey for different reasons in different situations.

ASL said that obedience and conformity are at present bad words. They imply that an individual is not acting spontaneously. Wertheimer suggested that we collect sentences in which we hear the word *obedience* and study the situations in which they are used. Would we find that they were always used to mean that one was arbitrarily being compelled to do something, that one was dominated by someone else?

A visitor pointed out that whenever the state is involved, obedience rests on force. Because social life was desirable people gave up their rights to use their own force and gave the state the right to use it. The people have to obey the state that they have created because it ensures peace. That is why people are offended or feel threatened by civil disobedience. When someone sees another person defy the laws, customs, legitimate authorities, he feels as if he were attacked. Man is not born with an ego, he develops it in a society and man's ego reflects the social norms of his society. Man is a social product, he is never a separate individual. Before birth he is part of an adult's body, after birth interpersonal relations replace the physical connections between him and others. The moment he is born people expect him to act in a certain way. If he does not, they impose sanctions. Members of his society assume that the baby will act in a certain way; deviations are not allowed. Wertheimer asked whether a baby's behavior may effect changes in his family. When someone said that an infant does not effect changes because he is powerless to assert himself, Wertheimer asked him to observe parents caring for little babies and children to see what actually happens; the parent teaches the infant or the child but it often happens that in the process the child transforms the parent.

Someone said that if it was true that people obeyed because of ego involvement then how was it possible to have civil disobedience? A student pointed out that in every society there are patterns of disobedience. One obeys as well as disobeys in terms of his society's norms; disobedience that is not in line with these patterns is called psychotic behavior or criminal behavior.

Wertheimer was called away but before he left he suggested that we discuss a particular case of disobedience. Thereupon a student said that Socrates believed that law and order must be maintained, that was why he drank the hemlock instead of escaping. He accepted the sentence because he did not wish to show disrespect to the court even though he believed that its sentence was unjust. Would a modern revolutionary who practiced civil disobedience act as Socrates did? A student suggested that we turn to real cases in the contemporary field. Someone said that he knows children and youths who violate home and school regulations and accept the consequences of their actions when they are caught; they do not say that their parents or the school authorities have no right to punish them. The session ended with the question, How does one go about studying obedience or disobedience if we do not have theoretical clarity about what we mean? ASL remarked that Wertheimer would ask if we really need a formal definition. In everyday life we seem to know what we are talking about when we use the words. Just what are the structures of the acts of obedience and disobedience and are there essential differences between these acts?

33
Power: Domination

The session was started by Riezler who said that power could be classified according to means. [Kurt Riezler's remarks are presented in the informal way in which they were made.] In response to Wertheimer's questions he said that the term *means* often suggests that it is not important which means you use for your end. However, different means may produce different kinds of domination. When someone said that domination is domination, Riezler replied that just to say that it is domination is not enough; domination is a kind of relation between humans. Let us start with two extreme cases: In one case, A treats B like a tool; there is no human relation to B, he is a mere object; A does not want to dominate B but to use him. Here there is no will to power. In the other case let us assume that an ideal marriage exists in which there is no domination but devotion. He drew $A \rightleftharpoons B$ on the blackboard. Here A is centered on B and B is centered on A; both are devoted to the task of building a We. The relation is so mutual that it is of no value to talk about domination. The participants are so centered on the We that the two individuals do not count. Between these two extreme cases are all sorts of relations. A and B may have a common world but A demands that he be the center of the world. In such a case there is domination; the other person is centered on A and is allowed to see the world only through him. In such a case it seems that there is a will to power; A wants other persons to have their lives oriented at all times in terms of his perspective. When Riezler paused, someone remarked that both of his cases are examples of domination. In the former case an individual dominates but in the latter the group or We dominates. Riezler said that it is important in the latter case to distinguish between whether A is centered on his ego or on an external task. One should not talk of a will to power in the case where A is devoted to his task, for example, certain Romans served as dictators for two years in order to save their country and then returned to their farms. Such a man had the soldiers centered on him for the sake of the task and not because of his will to power. In contrast to them is Hitler. Here there is not such devotion to a task but self-inflation. Hitler sees himself as Germany. No one who helps Germany can be against him. The

schema is like this; he drew the following [We A B]. A visitor said that the two cases are not extremes of a continuum and added that a person may have a feeling of power, a desire or will to dominate inanimate objects: a car, a stream, or animals. Why assume that humans want only to dominate other humans. The will in man is blind; it wants what it wants.

One of Wertheimer's former students suggested that in discussions of domination we have to take into account the requirements of the social field and the moral values which are involved. Another former student said that we cannot understand what A or B does by focusing on either A or B but must understand the structure of the We and its place, role, and function in the social field. He then referred the class to the career of Dr. Samuel Hahnemann who had retired and had lived in seclusion until an American lady insisted on seeing him to discuss his ideas with him. The result of these discussions was that he went back to the practice of medicine and founded the homeopathic medicine movement which spread over the world. One could say that the woman had dominated Hahnemann. To say it is not to look at the results of their relationship; it led to the most productive period of his life. Someone said that perhaps it would have been better for the man to remain in retirement, it might have been better for medicine had he not started homeopathy. He went on to say that the judgment of an act involves metaphysical questions of morals and values; therefore, it is more scientific to study the psychodynamics of the person in order to understand his behavior. He concluded that all people have a tendency to assert themselves, a will to power; it is due to the expression of the death instinct. This led to a criticism of Freud's theory and of the instinct concept.

Wertheimer remarked that we must take into account whether or not the dominator tries to rob people of their ability and their opportunity to face the situation. Is the dominator blind or not to the situation in which he behaves? Someone said that the dominator may say that he is trying to open the eyes of people and not to blind them and the people whom he dominates may agree with him; but a person outside of the group may say that he is robbing them of their ability. This is seen in the evaluation of a teacher's behavior in the class by the teacher and by educational reformers. He went on to say that one could find similar examples in political events. Some dictators say that they are not blinding their people and the people agree. When Wertheimer asked him whether there is any way to find out whether or not a dictator's statement is valid, the student said that it all depends on one's frame of reference; no decision is possible. Wertheimer insisted that there may be cases where the dominator seeks to blind and the people realize this. Some of the people in such situations may object but others may not mind it. After a pause he said that there are cases where a person is not really trying to dominate or to blind them but the people feel that they are being robbed of opportunities to face the situations and they may revolt against him. What is the difference between such a situation and the others? Is one allowed to throw all the cases in the same pot? He went on to suggest that we study internal and external conditions that bring about the various kinds of cases. This can be done if one faces concrete situations in order to see what actually takes place in them. Someone pointed out that in terms of a certain time and place one may be dominating or feel that he is dominating but in terms of another time and place he may not. This means that we have to know the space-time manifold in which the action takes place. History decides, not man.

The session ended with a remark by another former student of Wertheimer. There are cases of power in which none of the theories hold. He gave examples of the behavior and the exercise of power of high school teachers in the USA and in Germany.

Out-of-Class Discussion

Some students who had attended Riezler's lectures on the philosophy of history were seated with Wertheimer in the cafeteria. A student remarked that Riezler had once said that power is due to a person being in a position to give the lead, that it is manifested in actualizing oneself in the world and that the self-actualization involves world-building activities. He also said that it is neither a force nor willful behavior; the person enjoys being the center of the other people's world, being a world builder for others. Someone said that this is a fancy way of saying that someone dominates others. The first student said that Riezler gave in his lecture two examples of domination; domination or servitude in a We, and domination and servitude not in a We. In the former power may be an emotion related to world building but in the latter it may be forced, blind slavery. When Wertheimer asked for examples of both kinds of domination, the student said that Riezler had illustrated it with examples of conquered people who were not allowed to live as a group, who were not allowed to develop a We but had to serve as individual slaves for the conquerors. A visitor said that Riezler is assuming that people have a tendency or a desire to create a common world and that the process of world building gives rise to possibilities for self-actualization, but he does not deny that it is possible to think of and to treat people as tools, as beings that have nothing in common with you. Modern society makes it possible for each person to act independently of others, each may act for himself with no concern for a common world. In ancient times certain codes of law did not allow any human relationship to develop between master and slave. Modern technological society was now doing what the legal codes had done in the past. We are related by its administrators to the machines and structures of the industrial world. We are tied together in an impersonal way by the bureaucrats of modern society just like the slave was once tied to the master.

Wertheimer asked whether it was possible to have the kind of slavery that Riezler had described. ASL said that it was possible if the rulers kept rotating the people before they developed personal ties. When ASL said that it would be of interest to study this experimentally, Wertheimer said that it would be cruel to do this, that it would require much force to keep the subjects from developing ties to each other. A student said that he did not think that it would need much force; just as we train people to live together, we can condition them to perform their tasks in isolation. Wertheimer objected to the assumption that people start out as neutral objects. He went on to say that certain situations demand a We. Moreover, in some situations the person is never present as an I but is always part of a We; he acts, feels, and behaves in terms of his membership in the We. People become We-Cripples when they are drawn toward genuine group membership but cannot achieve it because of external or internal causes. Such a state of We-Crippledness is unlivable for many people and they seek to develop a new relationship. One may see himself as no longer with the others in a common world but besides or against the others. In such an isolated person there arises a genuine I that is against the others, as in paranoia (Schulte, 1924 in Ellis, 1938). After a pause Wertheimer said that children as well as adults often develop a living relationship to animals, objects, and places and when the animal, object, or place is no longer available or accessible to them, their world collapses and they act like bereaved people. When ASL interrupted to say that it would be of interest to conduct an experiment in which children or adults are in the same room but are kept from developing We relations, Wertheimer said that it is not necessary to subject people to such cruel treatment. There are jails, mental hospitals, schools, and factories where people are not allowed to develop human relations. Why not start with studying the social atmosphere of such institutions? [Perhaps these remarks may have led to what is described in Luchins, 1959.]

After Wertheimer left, the students from Riezler's course defended his position by outlining Riezler's lecture. (ASL had also attended the course and what follows are from his verbatim lecture notes.)

Riezler rejected individualism as well as the group mind approach to the study of man. The character of a man is a set of possibilities; some people have a larger and others have a smaller range of possibilities. There are two kinds of possibilities, those that represent the inner nature of man, the character of the individual, and those that are the external possibilities, the social and physical conditions. He used the term *potentialities* for man's inner possibilities:

Potentiality refers to tendencies, it is directed to actuality, to release of tension. Character is a dynamism, it is a certain order of urges; it is not a mere sum of potentialities, some potentialities are more relevant than others. The more you actualize your inner self the more your moving is real and pure acting. The problem of the nature of the dynamism is not solved by the natural sciences where force is defined by laws that state that if A then B. When you move from A to B you are the same person in both places.

The relation between the two sets of possibilities is very concrete in one's daily life. The concordance or discrepancy between the two makes our concrete behavior. You can be in a situation in which you cannot use your inner possibilities. The external condition may demand certain things from you but you do not do them because of your inner possibilities, for example, an orator who has no audience and a shy person who has an audience. To say that a stone cannot speak is senseless because the stone never had the possibility. Instead of a stone take an orator whose tongue has been cut out; this is a case of privation. There are also cases of being acted upon in which one cannot actualize his talent.

Acting is actualizing your own possibilities. There are two kinds of human movement: (1) from potentiality to actuality, (2) you are acted upon if you cannot do it. In the former kind you say that it is your act.

You are always on the way from your potential self to the actual self that you have to be. In short, in going from the past to a future, your nature, character, is actualized. You are what you have been and what you will never be. You always remain a man who has a future.

This led to a question concerning the role of the past in the present, which he dealt with as follows:

Not every part of one's past is relevant. We remember and forget parts of the past; we cannot forget and cannot remember other parts because our relation to our past is a living

process. Certain parts of our past are sinking down into our nature and change our potentialities. You digest your past as it melts into your nature. This process of building up a
past is an essential process in your history. In history we select what we want to remember
and to forget. We try to change the past and distort it to our present purposes. [Riezler
gave as an example the attempt of Hitler to use Woton and Siegfried.] These are newly
discovered pasts, they are not the real roots of the German people. If Hitler could succeed
to give the people this new past he would be able to give them a new future because the
past would change the German people.

After someone interrupted to say that this must be what happens in
psychoanalysis, he said:

As we proceed in life we select and create a new past and try to forget our old one.
Psychoanalysis has studied the chunks of the past that have not been melted, that are open
wounds. It is true that there are such things as repression and inhibitions but they are not
essentially human. Freud's claim for his doctrine of man is considered true and good because there is no competition of other doctrines from other sciences. Science has forgotten
man. The study of human passions and the impact between human passions have been neglected. In Pascal, La Bruyere and other French moralists you can find real deep knowledge
about the logique du coeur. Spinoza's ethics is one of the last attempts to study human
passions. The doctrine of passions was once very essential to philosophy, now no one mentions it.

In modern times, like in the political action of the past, all revolutions must have a past.
Since they do not want a traditional past, they try to make a new one. Nazi Germany emphasizes Paganism, which is not a correct past of Germany. Mussolini goes back to Romantic Rome of 2,000 years ago and he behaves like the heir of Ancient Rome but this past has
nothing to do with the inner attitudes of the life of modern Italy as well as of Ancient
Rome. It is frightfully artificial and will break down in two days if given a chance. When
the heat of the revolution dies away the power of the real past appears again.

Each person and nation in history not only has a past but also has a future. We are always on our way from ourselves to ourselves, from potentiality to actuality. We are moving
from something that happened to us yesterday to something that will happen tomorrow;
one movement may be parallel to the other. It could be that tomorrow we will be nearer to
our actualization. We may think that we are moving to prosperity but in reality we may be
moving to a depression. The consequences of man's activity may be just the opposite of
what he expects.

A student said that these remarks are inspirational, they are like poetry and
therefore he will not even try to criticize them. ASL's student pointed out that
the student is saying that he will not entertain them because they are not like
the hypotheses we usually deal with in psychology; but they can be tested em-
pirically. Is it true that one's past is changed by the kind of present or future
one faces? He said that in ASL's general psychology course the students wrote
a detailed case history while the development of personality was discussed.
What would the same students write 4, 8, 16, 25 years later? [This study still
waits to be completed.] Someone then said that Riezler seems to imply that
there is a certain direction or trend in a person's or nation's history and that
it is so persistent that it will reassert itself even when conditions have changed
the course of the person's or the nation's history. ASL said that the hypothesis
has implications for attitude and personality change. It is easier to change certain attitudes and traits than others. Why is this so? Wertheimer would say
that it is because certain traits and attitudes are central and others are
peripheral. Is it that certain experiences sink into the character more readily
than others because of structural features of the experience and the person?
Or is it that situational factors force the person to continue on the changed

course? Someone said that Riezler's theory is related to Wertheimer's concepts of the radix of the personality structure and he dismissed Gestalt psychology as mystical personalistic philosophy (Allport, 1937).

A few students from Riezler's class remained to discuss the similarities between Wertheimer's and Riezler's theories. They agreed that both assumed that man and nature are essentially good, that all evil is due to outer forces which do not allow a person or a nation to function naturally. This is like the belief of some men in the early days of science who read into nature a benevolent God; they substituted ideas from science for ideas from theology. Wertheimer sat down at this point. When the student finished talking he asked whether some people actualize themselves and some do not. The student said that the word *actualize* implies some innate urge in man; there is no such thing. Wertheimer asked whether some people achieve something that gives them a feeling of self-actualization. Are there such cases? What gives rise to this feeling? In what way is this feeling different from a feeling of emptiness in oneself and in one's existence, from a feeling of being forced to be what one does not want to be, from a feeling of being prevented from being what one wants to be?

ASL's student said that there are many people who apply to medical school and are not accepted. Why not study these people to see what happens to them? He suggested that we study people who try to contribute to the groups of which they are members but no one listens to them, that we study people who apply for university positions and who are good teachers and who do good research but who do not get appointed. He added that there are many people who feel attracted to certain professions and trades but are forced by circumstances to do things that they do not like. Why not compare these people's careers and their life spaces with those who are able to pursue the professions and trades of their choices. He went on to suggest that even successful and unsuccessful love affairs, marriages, and businesses could be studied.

The conversation changed when someone said that there are several ideas of Riezler's that can be studied in a very exact way, even though they have been formulated in a poetical manner, but that they should first be reformulated into scientific terminology. Wertheimer questioned whether they must first be reformulated into scientific terminology but he told the student to do it and to mail the translation to him. When he left, the students from Riezler's class listed some of his theses in their original terminology so that the others could translate them into scientific terminology:

> We are always being for ourselves and being for others. As a self-contained being, man is in relation to himself but as an object he is only in relation to others. If you cannot be for others, you feel a lack; you may try to pretend that you are for others. You mirror yourself in the opinion of others. You take what you are and give what you are to others. When you feel that you are something for others, you feel that you are of worth to yourself. In the impact of man on the world there are two modes of being, being for others and being for yourself; both modes are in concordance with each other; if not, we have pain.

The students rejected these statements as incomprehensible. (Years later when ASL read these formulations to his VA clinical psychology trainees they told him that similar statements were made by Harry Stack Sullivan)

34
More about the We

Riezler presented in the seminar on power, in a rather informal manner, several theses that he had previously presented in his lectures. The following formulation is presented with little editing in order to preserve Riezler's manner of speaking.

If A and B fall in love, a We originates. The We is a center of acting and being acted upon; it is not the sum of A and B but a new world originates in which both live. The world changes when they fall in love, A and B develop new loyalties; it is not a loyalty to the beloved but to the new unity, We. It is essential for the We that A and B exchange ideas with each other. Being for others and for ourselves is important for our lives and is the very essence of man. From the moment you are born you are born for others as well as for yourself.

Why is the report of the happenings of a stone not history? Because it lacks a peculiar type of unity. A historical subject is a unity of being acted upon and acting on, the purpose of which is to build a totality in the world; this holds for individuals, institutions, and nations. The subject, the individual, is not a box where contents change but a unity. The only thing demanded for the unity of an object is that the different qualities do not contradict each other. An individual, however, is more than an object. The concept of acting and acting upon is involved in the conception of individuality. These two modes of acting are not arbitrarily correlated to each other, they cannot exist if they are separated. Their relation is not a common X like yellow and hard but the *logos*. The *logos* is the structure of an individual but not of an object; the *logos* is that which in itself is a real unity. Riezler differentiated between unity as the logical one and the numbers of a series. This formulation led to the objection that it is a theological notion and not a scientific concept. It also led to the question of the relation of the individual to the group. Students wanted to know whether this meant that there was a group mind. Wertheimer said nothing, although he seemed to disagree.

Riezler went on to say that we must conceive of the individual in a way that allows us to realize that the individual actualizes himself in a group. The individual is like a prisoner who cannot escape from his cell; the cell is not closed, it has windows. Man is not like Leibnitz's monads. A visitor said that all this may be of value to sociology and philosophy but it is not psychology. Riezler answered that sociology is in need of a doctrine of man and that a doctrine of man cannot start with the solitary individual of psychology; the relation to others is man's very fundament. He reiterated that the two modes of being (being for and in oneself and being for others) are interdependent, both are different ways in which you are. Reality contains both modes and relates one to the other, both are interconnected and grown together with the self. The growing together makes the concreteness of the very life of the individual. There is a mutual give and take between the two modes; the other fellow and not the stars affect your world building. He stressed that one has to be something to others in order to be something to oneself and that one must be something to oneself in order to be for others; if you lack either you try to disguise it; vanity, the passions, and instincts are rooted in this.

He returned to discuss the case of true friendship or true love that he had mentioned before. A and B form a We, yet A B remain A B, although a new radix, a new center of the field of force develops, a We. He drew ⬛(A)(B)⬛ and said that we now have three unities of acting and being acted upon. They are not an and-summation of three items. We is not A and B, it has laws and norms of its own which are not the sum of the laws and norms or common qualities of A and B. For the We different norms are valid than for A and B. To understand the We, we need to look at the We itself without preconceptions. After a pause he said that when we are in love things do not look brighter because of our love but because the things belong in a new world. We discover new things and the values of old things change in the new world. In the beginning we like it, there is no limit to the world building, but in due time we may find differences and difficulties in the We and we may try to conceal them from each other. The private world of A and of B may not entirely submerge in the We, there are all kinds of shades of submerging. Loyalty may not be loyalty to A and B, but loyalty of A and B to the We's norms, A may do something against B because A is obeying the norms of the We. On the strength of the impact of the two modes of being we have a We. By giving ourselves to a We we get ourselves back in a new way.

He said in response to an argument that all this may be considered to be irrational and poetical. However, such remarks do not answer the problem. He added that what is irrational is irrational according to the ratio that is used. He went on to say that a We helps us escape the prison of our existence, it centers us outside of ourselves. Sometimes we may be entirely melted into a We so that there appears what is called a group mind; at other times our relation to a We may be superficial. In the former case our lives may feel endangered when we are separated from the We; in the latter case separation from the We helps us get rid of superficial links to others, it may give us freedom so that we can build an infinite horizon with others.

In the next session Riezler began with the remark that the forces in the history of man, of groups and nature are said to be gold, power, ambition, love, ideas. He then asked, What is ambition? He rejected an answer that it is due to the will or a power motive. There is a big difference between ambition and the will to power. Even in politics most people want to be something for others; they try to appear in the eyes of others to be for them and they are not merely seeking power. He gave as an example the use of medals and other decorations. The inner function of the decoration is the nation, the group; it puts one in a certain status, it is a sign that you are something for others.

The discussion turned to conflict situations. Riezler said that they are situations in which there is no We with a unified center, for example, a We made up of Hitler and Chamberlain or of Roosevelt and Hoover. The whole mentality of the various members are irreconcilable and they fight it out. After he gave as an example the fight between Arabs and Jews in Palestine, he went on to describe types of situations: one individual in another, for example, both are interrelated and share the same spot; one against the other; one besides the other. Such situations are not only possible in history but are possible in our lives. He went on to say that it is impossible to conceive of a world in which we have only one of these types of situations. He added after a pause that there cannot be a world of mere love, hatred, or indifference. If you build up such a world in your fantasy, your whole life breaks down.

After a pause Riezler said, Suppose Robinson Crusoe meets Friday and the latter gives himself away to Robinson Crusoe's power. Friday becomes a tool, a dead thing, a slave; Robinson uses him for his purposes just like a hammer. There is no We, no new centering of the life space in a common world embracing both in which and for which they exist. There is no give or take between each man's world. Suppose there are instances which cause them to develop a world. Robinson gives rules for the world and Friday follows the lead, both need each other. Thus we have a We which Robinson controls, he decides how the We will be built up; he is the master but he builds his world so that it includes Friday and gives Friday a feeling of having a world.

Someone argued that there is no difference between the two ways in which Friday was treated, both are cases of domination. Riezler answered that it makes a big difference whether domination creates a single world or not. There were cases in history where the master and servants did not make a We. In ancient Sparta nine thousand Spartans dominated the Peloponnesian peninsula. They subjugated the Helots and made no attempt to build a common world with them. The Spartan constitution, which was praised as the best in the world, showed that they dedicated their lives to dominate others. Their occupations and education had to be organized so that they could dominate. Therefore, they had to sleep with arms. They had no art and entertainment but had military efficiency. Thus the masters themselves were fettered by rules, they had no freedom. The Spartan was the slave of his master situation. This is one effect of the lack of a We. [This picture of Sparta could be challenged as the description that was handed down by the enemies of Sparta. It is of interest that some Greeks saw a similarity in the way of life of the Spartans with groups in India and Judea and that Plato admired them but Aristotle did not.]

ASL pointed out that, according to Wertheimer, leadership involves followership and followership involves leadership. In view of this, the Spartans created a We relation with their slaves and this created a different social atmosphere than a democratic kind of We. Riezler did not respond to the arguments that the Spartans did develop a We relationship and that everybody is a slave of a We if he is committed to maintain it. He went on to describe the nobility of Venice. Venice was a small city that succeeded in being free for 1,000 years (700-1795). Although the Venetians dominated the Mediterranean Sea, the city's nobility was never more than 1,600 men; it was an absolute nobility, no one could enter it. The nobility enjoyed their power and never had a revolution. Why didn't the other classes rise up against them? It is said that the nobility had *savoir faire,* that they were flexible in meeting all situations, that they nearly succeeded in creating a group mind. The nobility could always rely on the other classes, and could always make a display of power. The community was so strong that it could fight the Pope, who used the strongest church weapons against the Doge of Venice but no one paid attention to them. It is said that the nobility exploited the people but the members of the other classes in the beginning did get something out of the nobility and built a common We. [See also chapter 36.]

He went on to describe India's Caste system. In extreme cases there were different classes with their own norms and rules. Each class was separate from the other but it resulted in a stable organization. Why? In the people's conception of the universe there was a place for each class to be separate, yet all were embedded in one order in the universe. The rise from one class into another was in accordance with the principle of transmigration of souls; if you follow the rules of your class in this world, you will go into a higher class in the next. They were taught that one must have no feelings of inferiority, etc., in this world. To a certain degree the universe was the We group, every man belonged to a We-class and all classes belonged in a universal We. A student said that it was a system of social appeasement and that it was an example of how religion offered people pie in the sky in order to teach them to tolerate injustice. Someone objected to the student's generalization that this is the function of religion; he told the student to read the Pentateuch and the Code of Hammurabi. Riezler concluded that every power tries to exist by creating a scheme of a world in which a place for master and slave is made and in which each is embraced into a totality. The power may justify itself in a religious conception. This is done not because it is more efficient but because the master wants to be a master in the eyes of others; he is not content with merely forcing them, he wants to be acknowledged as the master. A man is something for himself when he is something for others; if others look at you as the center of their world then you are the master, their acknowledgment is the very reality of being a master.

35
Karen Horney: Power Drive

In the next session Karen Horney started the discussion by remarking that there is a power drive in people and that it may be adequate or inadequate in a person's pursuit of his goals. She then went on to point out that in a frustrating situation one may react by feeling crushed, with a resigned attitude, or by withdrawal behavior, becoming suspicious, or by becoming weakly hostile, or by being partly crushed and feeling rebellious. She added that one may develop an aggressive power drive due to the dread of being helpless; this is an inadequate power drive. When she paused for comments, someone disagreed with her assumptions that inadequate power is due to a neurotic personality structure. The inadequacy may not be due to the person but to field conditions. The structure of the situation and how the person's reaction fits into it must be studied in order to determine the adequacy of the power. Maslow pointed out that it is important to distinguish between power status, feeling of power, and power behavior. After these statements, Speier said that three definitions of adequacy have been proposed in discussions of power; definitions in terms of the strength of the individual, in terms of a clear response to a demand of the situation, and in terms of the social norms of the group, that is, different groups may evaluate differently the adequacy of a response. Wertheimer remarked that Horney had said that there are compulsive power drives and that they are due to the experiencing of weakness, fears, anxieties in a person's childhood. He agreed that there are such cases but the power drives may also be brought about by entirely different reasons. He asked, Must infantalism always lie behind them?

The discussion changed when Maslow made some remarks about his study of the relations among self-esteem, dominance behavior, and status dominance. He began by saying that self-esteem is a good relationship with oneself; people who have self-esteem lack inferiority feeling and do not show shyness and withdrawal behavior. Dominance behavior is not clearly related to self esteem, the correlation is about .50. He noted that status dominance emerges from social relationships, that there is no one-to-one relationship between self-esteem and dominance behavior. In response to a question, he said that status dominance is determined most of the time by the situation; legal power may enter here. He went on to say that the craving for power is not the same as for self-esteem or dominance behavior. In response to questions he said that it is related to ego security-ego insecurity. It is not a natural or innate characteristic of man because there are cultures where there is no desire for power.

The discussion turned back to Horney's conjecture when someone said that her thesis is supported by Maslow's work. Wertheimer interrupted to object to Maslow's and Horney's assumption that the drive for power is in the individual. It must be considered in relation to the structure of the political and social field which the person is in. Someone argued that if Hitler and Lincoln were put in the same situation, they would not act the same way. Wertheimer said that the will to power means different things in the situation of Hitler and Lincoln. He reiterated that we have to understand the structure of the situation in order to understand behavior which superficially looks like a will to power. Horney objected, You cannot explain such things on the basis of the whole situation because the essential thing is the emotional life of the individual. Moreover, behavior has an unconscious basis.

After a pause, Wertheimer asked, How should we understand power? Power and the will to power are two different things. In old psychology the social field was left out; if it did enter psychology it was spoken of as a situation which satisfied or did not satisfy the needs of the organism. After some students' objections to what he had said, he continued, We need to understand the field condition in which behavior occurs. Of course we must take into account the history of the individual insofar as it has something to do with the dynamics of the case of behavior under consideration.

A heated exchange occurred between Horney and Wertheimer which was interrupted by Riezler who said that it is necessary to differentiate between the will to power as a fact and the theory that it is a biological trait. The session ended with Speier's remark that in all power structures there are domination and authority. In new social structures there may be more domination than authority but the people in control attempt to turn it into authority by education and propaganda.

Power and Power Structure

In the next session someone presented the thesis that some people dominate others because they are less suggestible than those whom they dominate. People differ in the trait of suggestibility; on the one extreme there are people who have no will of their own and do whatever they are told to do and on the other hand there are people who never or rarely accept suggestions. The latter always initiate behavior, they have extraordinary will power, they dominate social situations and influence others to behave according to their will; they are the leaders. A college instructor then made some remarks to the effect that this view is similar to Le Bon's and Sherif's. People dominate others because they have more prestige than those whom they dominate and prestige is the domination of one individual by another. He went on to present Wertheimer's thesis about prestige, which was then discussed. [It is discussed elsewhere in this monograph.]

Speier changed the discussion by saying that some people have expressed utopian ideas about power. He went on to say that there are four types of utopian thinking about power; the Marxian that looks to the future, the

Romantic that looks to the past, the sociological that talks about harmonious small groups, and the anthropological that describe certain traits as models. Someone remarked that there was nothing utopian about the Marxian concept of power. In response to questions Speier said that power cannot be reduced to strength and that authority is the power of a person to punish the disobedient.

The discussion turned to the notion of power structure. Someone proposed that the real power structure of society lies in the hands of an economic elite. They violate the democratic processes of society, control the courts and even tamper with the legal processes and produce injustice. Someone objected to the notion of a power structure; it is a myth used by certain individuals to rally the people around them in their struggle for power. Some students pointed out that in every social group there is a power structure that maintains order and stability; it is often used to resist change. Perhaps it is not monolithic and is more complex and differentiated than some social and political reformers claim.

Speier pointed out that there is multiple participation in various power structures. He used Henry Ford as an example of the different kinds of power structure in which a person may engage. He drew on the blackboard as he spoke. As a consumer Ford may be in a bilateral power structure $\otimes \rightarrow \bigcirc$, as a husband he dominates his wife $\overset{\oplus}{\underset{\bigcirc}{\downarrow}}$, he may be dependent on specific individuals $\overset{c}{\underset{\oplus}{\downarrow}}$, as a church member he is in an authoritarian relationship in which he is subservient $\overset{\bigcirc}{\underset{\oplus}{\downarrow}}$, as an authoritarian boss he is on top $\overset{\otimes}{\underset{\bigcirc}{\downarrow}}$. After some comments by students Speier said that there may be ambiguous power structures in which you are bullied and you bully. Sometimes the person who holds the power is more concerned with it than the dependent ones. Speier called this an example of the segmentation of power. Wertheimer asked, What are the conditions that give rise to such situations? No one answered and Speier went on to talk about the depersonalization of the power function. He illustrated this by a machine that checks the functioning of the workers instead of a foreman. This is a kind of institutionalization of power; the power of a person is controlled by a mechanism. It may be a machine like a time clock or a bureaucracy.

After-Class Discussion

A few students went to the lounge to discuss Speier's remarks. When Wertheimer walked by, a student asked him, Would you say that it's domination because it is not legal; if it is legal to dominate, is it called authority and not domination? Wertheimer asked, What do you think? Someone said that maybe it should be worded differently. If a person enters into a contractual relation with someone there is mutual consent as to what one requires of the other. They each have the authority to demand of the other what is stipulated in the contract. If a person cleverly writes the contract so that he can demand of the other what the other did not really agree to when he signed the contract, it's a form of domination. The issue is whether there is mutual consent and understanding in making the contract.

ASL's student remarked that he was amazed by Speier's attitude toward power. He talks of power as if values do not enter the picture; but people may do things because they desire to accomplish something of social worth. It is not merely a question of his will but his orientation to do what is good. Another student objected to the assumption that man does things because of some absolute eternal requiredness in nature. Wertheimer said that for thousands of years people have talked about such natural requirements and have ordered their lives to meet them. What were they doing? Someone objected that there is no need to talk about values because it implies a moral force, a force behind the order. Man makes the order, there is no requiredness in nature that demands a certain order. Similarly, there is no requiredness in society; so-called legal authority is just another form of domination; legality is a myth of the state used to control and dominate people. Those in control of the state are said to have the legal power and those who seek the position of power are said to be acting illegally. Wertheimer began a passionate attack on the last idea but was called away. When Wertheimer left, a student said that Wertheimer is moralistic and not scientific, and that he is not impressed by such outbursts. ASL's student said that science has always been moralistic. In the seventeenth and eighteenth centuries science did not attack morality but claimed to be a better way to create a moral order and held out great hopes to mankind. People rejected the supernatural order because it had failed to produce the morality it had held out for man. The intelligentsia seized on scientific ideas to demolish the existing moral order based on Christianity because they were sure that science and reason would lead to a better morality. In view of this, what is wrong with Wertheimer raising questions of morality? Someone said that the danger is that it leads to religious ideas. ASL's student then asked, If people tried to imitate a God of Justice and sought to do this in concrete situations would things be better or worse? Someone answered that we should look at the history of Christianity and consider whether it has produced a moral world. Another student said that we must not talk in generalities, we must talk of specific people. Let us examine the behavior of particular people who are religious but who separate the practical ground of human action from the sphere of spirit in order to preserve the purity of the spiritual realm. Let us compare them with persons who try to actualize the realm of spirit in the mundane world as they seek to actualize His law in the minute particulars of their behavior. He wagered that the latter would be more moral than the former. The previous speaker said that the formulation is unfair, it defines religion in a way that loads the dice in favor of a certain conception of religion that is nonexistent. He then said that studies by sociologists have found little or no correlation between church attendance and liberalism, kindness and morality. ASL's student said that church attendance is no proof that one is religious. Perhaps the immoral need a place to go to pray for forgiveness. Even a belief in God may not be the basic criterion because some people may be religious and be agnostic. In fact some religions are not based on theology but on the practice of a certain code of conduct and morality. And the God of the Jews once said that He would rather that His people forget Him but keep His Law. The former student asked whether we need religion to be human. ASL's student said that he is not arguing for religion but trying to point out that a certain world structure may be implied in a certain religion; because one sees himself related to this world structure, he behaves in a certain way.

Wertheimer had sat down toward the end of the discussion. He proposed that we study people who are committed to different religious and social ideologies in order to test the hypothesis that they act differently in concrete situations. Maybe they will have many points of agreement in concrete situations even though they differ in ideology and religion. He suggested that we find out what the effects are of being members of certain religions and political parties. How does it affect a person's behavior in particular situations and in what way does his behavior change when he becomes a follower of a certain religion or political party? What are the actual consequences for his social field, immediately and in the future, when a certain religious or political ideology is accepted or rejected by a person?

On the way to the subway Wertheimer asked ASL's student how he would decide who is a religious person. The student said that he would first find out the characteristics of the God or of the sages whom they claim to be imitating. For example, the Pentateuch describes in Exodus certain characteristics of God. The student said that he would ask a person who claimed to follow His teaching to give examples of the ways in which he imitated these divine attributes. He would list the characteristics of Jesus and ask Christians to give examples of how they imitated them. He would also ask them to rank the various characteristics in order of importance and to rate the frequency with which they apply them during a particular day and he would sample them on different days. The student then told Wertheimer that some people in the seminar separate power or might from right but the concept of God includes both; He is all powerful yet He is just. How did man ever develop such an idea? Wertheimer said that it was a good question and asked the student to write to him his reflections on it. ASL suggested that he make a study of the existing conceptions of God among ordinary people, not theologians, in order to see whether there are people whose gods are unjust. The student said that Wertheimer had once said that even the devil must have some virtues or else people would not follow him. [They outlined a project that he and ASL had planned to do but it was never carried out partly because of the social atmosphere in academic circles at that time. It still waits to be done.]

36
Nobility of Venice: The Exercise of Power

In the next session Riezler discussed in more detail how the nobility of Venice as a class managed to enjoy prestige or to reestablish it after losing it. He said that until the last century it was a closed nobility, it admitted only members of certain families. There never were more than 1,600 members; every member of the nobility became a member of the council on his twenty-first birthday and participated in the election of the Doge. The method of voting involved a lottery which narrowed down the number of candidates and then they voted and held a lottery for the final election. The real council, the men who actually ruled, consisted of a secret committee of ten.

After pausing he said that the relation of the people of Venice was not merely in terms of classes but in terms of a relationship to a world structure. All the people had an identical behavioral environment that had a place in it for the nobility and the people. It can be schematized like this. He drew the following and went on to say that there was a common ideology in which each

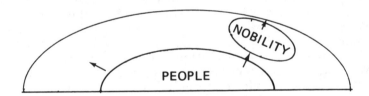

person had his place and that there were no clashes between two ideologies. The nobility tried to maintain this world order. If a nobleman did something to upset the world order he was punished by the nobility. The kind of prestige relations between the nobility and the people was one in which the nobleman's behavior had a formative power for others. The ideal according to which the nobleman formed himself was a gentleman, a gallant fellow.

In response to questions Riezler said that all reports say that there was freedom and sweetness of life in Venice. The noblemen's system of exploitation did not apply to Venice but to Greece and Palestine. They dominated Northern Italy and the Mediterranean and engaged in a combination of war, trade, and piracy which made them prosperous. Someone said that just as the noblemen of Venice created a myth which served as a common ideology, the Nazi's racial myth was being used to unite Europe under the domination of Germany. The difference between people who form a temporary group and people who form a group that lasts for generation after generation is that the latter has a myth. When he said that any myth could be used to perpetuate a group, Wertheimer raised the question of the adequacy of the myth. How does it fit the structure of events as they occur in the daily lives of the people? Perhaps more force is needed to make people accept a myth that does not fit. A visitor objected to the idea that myths may fit or not fit the structural requirements of a group because by definition they are falsehoods used by the power structure to hoodwink the people.

ASL's student pointed out that the legitimate rulers of ancient Italian and Greek cities were descendants of the city's founding families; rulers who were not descendants were called tyrants. However, one did not have to be a biological descendant of the founder; individuals, even slaves, were adopted by the family. Thus the nobility did admit people from the masses. Riezler went on to say that the English nobility is an example of a class that admits commoners into its rank. This led someone to doubt that any caste or upper class is ever entirely cut off from the masses; in all societies people cross class lines. Someone said that although a caste may under certain special conditions admit people into it, there is no public upward mobility in such societies. In a democracy everybody is taught to have the ambition to rise to the top but in stratified societies everybody is taught that he has a certain place and must stay in it. A visitor pointed out that in both kinds of societies there is stratification, that certain families are the ruling classes. This is even true for the USA. Alfred E. Smith could not become president because he was a Roman Catholic. Certain jobs, schools, and places of residence are restricted to members of certain races, nationalities, and religions. It is a cruel illusion to believe that you can rise to the top if you are an Indian, Negro, Catholic or Jew. The ideology of egalitarianism is as much of a myth as the myth of aristocracy. Individuals who have more personal power may get into the ruling elites in both the democratic and aristocratic societies. A student pointed out that social mobility is not an all or none affair; there are different rates of mobility. Social stratification affects the rates and the rates of mobility may have a different effect on the people. Different rates create different social atmospheres. He then suggested that a study be made of the rates of upward mobility in the USA and England in order to see whether democracy does or does not create a different social atmosphere and in turn mold a different type of personality. Someone proposed that marked differences would appear if in each country the study focused on the mobility of each country's races, nationalities, religions within each socioeconomic level.[1]

Someone remarked that there is a difference when a society teaches or does not teach the myth of upward nobility. With the growth of universal education the ideal will become better known to the lower classes and they will de-

1. If egalitarianism is a myth perhaps anti-egalitarianism is an equally persuasive, if not self-fulfilling myth. Thus, for years after 1928 Alfred E. Smith's defeat was accepted as proof that a Catholic could not be elected president. The Kennedy election so shattered this myth that in 1968 Vice Presidential candidate Muskie's Catholicism went virtually unnoticed. (DEL)

mand the freedom that is promised to them but which they do not have. Like labor in the 1930s, the various nationality and racial groups of the USA will fight and win their rights. Another student took the pessimistic view that it would only create greater disillusionment.

After-Class Discussions

1. ASL told Wertheimer that while he was conducting his PhD research in a public school in the slums of Brooklyn, the principal of one of the schools showed him the results of the sixth-grade's term project. The children had built a model of the Williamsburgh Housing Project in the school basement. The principal was experimenting with Dewey's project method of teaching and was pleased that the children had done so well in the achievement tests. He attributed their good scores to learning in a real-life activity. Since the pupils came from impoverished minority groups and might never finish public school, ASL asked the principal why he considered the project to be a real-life experience for such children. The principal said that the aim of education is to teach the children the values of our culture. In our society everybody has a chance to rise to the top if he has the will to fight his way up the ladder of success. Even though neither the children nor their parents have any relation to the social roles enacted in building the houses, they were given a chance to participate in the American Dream.

ASL asked whether it is fair to motivate children to want what they could never achieve. Why deceive the children by motivating them to learn for the sake of socioeconomic advancement when it is closed to them? Wertheimer objected to ASL's pessimistic view but the students agreed with ASL. They gave examples from radio, newspaper, billboards, and magazine advertisements that teach children to want what they cannot buy because they and their parents do not have money. Someone said that Lewin's study of the level of aspiration shows that one lowers his aspirations to fit in with his achievement; one learns not to want to be a millionaire or the president. A visitor argued that the entire culture of the USA is geared toward developing higher and higher expectations. He wondered whether it would be better to give the children a realistic picture of things instead of making the lower classes want what the upper classes have. Teaching children or people goals and not giving them the means to achieve them leads to anomie. People will lose respect for the society and its norms because it teaches goals that cannot be reached by the existing social means.

Someone said old-fashioned societies have used repressive measures to keep people from wanting. As long as a person knows that he is given a chance and that it all depends on his natural ability, he will not be upset if he does not rise to the top. The visitor said that girls who are not pretty and boys who are not handsome are miserable because they cannot get dates. They fully understand that it is their endowment and not society that causes them to be rejected but they are not content with their lot. Neither are some women content with the roles to which their biological makeup condemns them. They feel that their biological constitution bars them from certain positions. What bothers all these people is that they cannot have what the idealized average American has. They do not know that the men and women of the advertisements, of the movies, are not the average Americans. Most people are not handsome, pretty, rich, strong and most things in life are not wonderful, romantic, glorious, etc. Why hold up such false models? He went on to say that our society is training a generation of misfits.

Wertheimer changed the discussion by asking whether it is natural to want blindly. Are greed and envy the basic motives of man? Someone said that according to Freud and Adler these are the basic motives. Moreover, the theory of evolution lends support to their theses. Blind striving is also used to justify grading people in terms of the normal curve. Wertheimer asked what the consequences are for society when everybody believes this. He went on to say that it may produce an unlivable state. When ASL said that he sees no reason why people cannot be conditioned to believe that life is a rat race, Wertheimer insisted that the children will in some way show their rejection of this kind of system if they are given a chance.

2. After class some students met Wertheimer in the cafeteria. One of the students said that with the exception of the psychoanalysts every speaker in the seminar is using a Gestalt theoretical approach. When Wertheimer asked him for examples, the student said that Reizler's conjectures reflect Gestalt theory's ahistorical view of behavior; they stress the requirements of the present. Someone pointed out that Riezler is not stressing the present but the future; men as well as nations are seeking to actualize their potentialities. It reflects Aristotle's idea of development. The present is a situation in which man is growing into some kind of higher being. It is a historical point of view because it stresses purpose in nature; the idea of purpose gives rise to the historical attitude. People who have no future have no history but customs and a past. A student said that the stress on the past is more like saying that things have a cause. It is a more scientific view than the stress on the future, on goals, because teleological explanations are unscientific. A visitor said that the focus on the past does not create a scientific attitude. This is seen in the difference between the legal profession and the scientific profession. Lawyers stress the past, they seek precedents to justify an action in the present but scientists look to the future. That is why politicians who are trained in law cannot understand scientific proposals. Someone remarked that religion stresses the future but it is not scientific. The visitor said that theologians seek ways to arrange things at present so that the Messiah will come and likewise some scientists talk about progress. Theologians are as future-oriented as these scientists. The previous speaker asked whether this means that the religious attitude is the same as the scientific attitude. ASL's student said that years ago scientists stressed progress in opposition to the Humanists, who claimed that Greek civilization was the golden age of man. When science rejected this worship of the pagan past it also rejected the idea of Christian salvation. Man could make a paradise out of this earth by harnessing the forces of nature. The visitor said that the word science was substituted for the Messiah and the word progress for salvation, that it was a mere change in terminology.

The discussion changed after someone said that Adler stresses the future and not the past but this does not make Gestalt theory out of Individual Psychology. Wertheimer remarked that Gestalt psychology is not ahistorical, it is a misunderstanding. Gestalt psychologists have criticized the thesis that present behavior is nothing but a repetition of past experience and that it can be understood by focusing on the past. Someone said that learning by insight means that there is a discontinuity with past experience. Wertheimer said that the difference is not so simple. The student interrupted to say that he favors Gestalt theory because it rejects continuity and stresses discontinuity with the past. Gestalt psychology is on the side of progress, it is against tradition and customs, it stresses spontaneity and creativity. Someone objected to the stress on the future; people behave at present, not in a tomorrow or next year. He cited Köhler's view that the phenomenal future which we experience now is not the actual future toward which we are directed; it is that part of the present phenomenal field which we call the future. The phenomenal past we experience at present is not the real past but part of the present phenomenal field that we call the past. Wertheimer remarked that the problem is how to envision the functioning of the past and the future in the present. He asked the students to think of ways to deal with the problem. Someone remarked that everybody carries into the present his own past experiences and the past of the society's cultural process. What one does is not a unique response but is related to the past and the future of the person and his society; the past is the ground on which one stands. Life becomes a series of unconnected happenings when it is not seen in the context of a personal and social past. The effects of the past are not as negative as Gestalt psychologists claim. He went on to say that according to Korzybski (1933) man is a time-binding creature, the present in which a man lives spans a past and a future. Korzybski's idea of time binding can be translated into field theory's terminology. Someone pointed out that according to traditional psychology the past remains unchanged in the person, it is layered like sedimentary rock, while according to Gestalt psychologists the past is assimilated into an existing structure. Just like the body digests food the psychic system assimilates experiences. The experiences do not remain the same, some are eliminated, others are transformed in various ways with more or less effect on the system's structure. A student objected to the analogy to the assimilation of food; it was a sterile approach to the study of learning, it was a vague idea. The speaker insisted that it was not a vague analogy and that it could serve as a model for research. Wertheimer asked the students how they would study the effects of certain experiences in a person and how they would study the fate of the experience in the person. The students described Wulf's and Bartlett's experiments on memory. Wertheimer suggested that they think of more human, more natural experiences.

3. On the way to the subway ASL told him that in the master's research project that he had done with Hadley Cantril, youths were asked to describe the job or career to which they now aspire and the job or career that they now pursue. After this they were asked whether they always had aspired to it and why. If not, to what had they previously aspired and why had they changed their aspirations? In this way, several youths' career aspirations were traced. They were also asked to describe their present feelings toward and conception of the nature of each of their job aspirations. Nearly everybody had changed his job aspiration at least once. Some changed because conditions outside of them would not allow them to pursue the career, and some because they had changed their minds. Both kinds of subjects reported a change in their conceptions of the job. Students who felt that they were forced to change had had an idealized image of the job and some persisted in idealizing it. Those who changed because of internal factors did not as often persist in idealizing it. Wertheimer wanted to know why the study was put

into the model of Lewin's level of aspiration and then asked ASL whether he really thought that the study dealt with questions that were raised in the discussion after class. Before boarding the train he asked whether there are life situations that can be observed to see what happens to a child's ideas about work.

4. Wertheimer saw some students in the cafeteria and he invited them to sit with him. One student said that Riezler is a Gestalt psychologist because he has rejected a piecemeal approach to the study of behavior of people and groups and has stressed whole qualities. Another student said that he was surprised that RA, a Gestalt psychologist, criticized Riezler's thesis because it did not take into account morality. Gestalt psychology according to Brown (1936) is a science and science is value free. A visitor said that the stress on wholeness is not everything. One must face the question of the nature of the togetherness, its effect on the social structure of which it is a part; the We may be a gang that assassinates and robs people. He referred to certain sects in India who waylay and murder travelers in the name of their god and have enriched themselves by these means. He added that Venice's domination of the Mediterranean was by force; the nations that were dominated did not enjoy it. The same could be said for the *Pax Romana* of the Roman Empire. Somebody asked, Who decides whether an act is an act of domination, those in the We or those outside of the We? When someone said that domination is domination, Wertheimer asked whether a We that has a rule that its members should not dominate each other but only outsiders is the same thing as a We that has a rule that helps outsiders. A student interrupted to say that one of the factors that holds people together in a We is the fear of the outsider. When a We is established a field is created in which there must develop tensions between outsiders and insiders.

Wertheimer remarked that a We may become a means of subjugating others or it may become a source of power for outsiders that helps them to develop and accomplish things. Would you say that the two are the same? In the former people are robbed of their freedom, in the latter people are given freedom. To describe a We as a unity is not enough; what it accomplishes in the social field of which it is a part has to be taken into account. He then went on to challenge the idea that all groups war with each other. Someone said that the theory of evolution is the basis for this conjecture. At first it was a battle for survival between individuals. In order for weak individuals to survive, they banded together in groups because as a group they were stronger than the mighty individuals. Later on weaker groups banded together into larger groups to withstand a more powerful group. At present nation fights against nation. As nations are conquered and become parts of greater and greater empires a day will come when all of mankind will be part of one empire. Then there will no longer be war. ASL's student asked him whether this means that mankind will be better off to let Hitler win and to create a universal state. He answered that evolution is a fact, there is a struggle for existence and only the fit will survive. The ideas of altruism, mercy, and charity are .ideals of a morality created by slaves to enslave the mighty. When Wertheimer asked the student whether he really believed this, he said that as a biologist who had been freed of his religious ideas of morality he does. Wertheimer pointed out that the doctrine of struggle for existence was not a biological fact but an ideological dogma dressed up in biological terminology.

A student said that Huxley's *Brave New World* describes a state where the aim is to keep everybody happy and where sensual pleasure is the aim of life. People do their bit of work and then indulge in sensual experiences, coitus, and hallucinatory pleasures induced by viewing movies which are called feelies and eating soma tablets. There are no sexual taboos; childbirth and the raising of children have been taken over by factories that produce babies and train them to be people who enjoy themselves. But some people, even in this paradise, called it domination. They want to do things the old-fashioned way, to read the old literature and be free not to have to indulge in the variety of sensual experiences. These people are exiled as helpless misfits. The student concluded that domination can appear in a variety of ways. Some groups claim that the scientific world view is the best one because it is not a parochial one and should be taught to everybody. In the name of science, educators impose their scientific ideas and methods on groups which have a nonscientific orientation. How do they know that their methods and ideas are best for mankind; is it not domination?

When Wertheimer said that it is possible to come to a decision by studying the effects of the scientific methods and ideas, the students said that science had enabled man to actualize what he has always wanted, a world of happiness and self-actualization, free from poverty and disease. Science is opposed by those groups that are dominated by ideas of a way of life that is based on irrational customs and values which are counter to the progressive and liberal ideas of science. Wertheimer asked the students how they would change these peoples' ideas. A student said that he would do it by education. Someone pointed out that these people have their own schools, some of these people control the school boards and the mass media so that their ideas are presented to everybody. As long as these people are in control the ideas of science will not prevail. ASL's student said that science has been replacing their customs and ideas because of our modern technological world; even religious institutions have been transformed by the values of modern industry. When new technological-scientific values interfere with a person's religious or traditional beliefs, he usually gives up the old belief. The Sabbath is no longer observed by most people even though they work a five-day week. Not education in science but the cheap automobile has been a big factor in changing old beliefs and practices; the auto had freed youth from adult supervision so that new sexual norms have emerged that are counter to the old religion-based norms. People look forward to going on trips on Sunday instead of to church. Production is organized logically; this means that old roles and rules of behavior have to be given up when one goes to work in a modern factory. Advertising on the radio and in the paper as well as concealed advertising in the movies teach people to want things that are not quite concordant with their religious values. The forces unleased by modern industrial society are dominating all institutions. There is no need to abolish parochial schools or to pass laws that will force old-fashioned sects to change their ways because the larger social field in which they live is transforming them. These people can no longer wander off to the wilderness to escape the forces of change, the frontier is the Pacific Ocean. They have the option to starve or to participate fully in the society that demands the violation of their values as the price for economic survival. He concluded that all this may be called an example of what Riezler and Wertheimer have called domination because men have no free choice in the matter, they have to submit to the economy, to be used like tools for production of goods and as consumers of the products of modern industry. Man has become a certain kind of producer and a certain kind of consumer specified by technology.

Wertheimer remarked that it is possible for man to be free and then played the devil's advocate by defending technology and saying that it makes men happy. The students seemed to agree with him. ASL's student asked whether all that matters is that one's belly is full. How about the age old conception of man as Homo sapiens? Society is robbing man of his soul while filling his belly. The students said that the soul is a prescientific idea, the virtue of not filling one's belly is based on the Malthusian idea of scarcity that modern technology has disproved. Someone added that it is now possible for everybody to have enough to eat without working. Man may now use his energy as he pleases. ASL's student said that the use of machinery instead of human energy uses up natural resources. In order for us not to work, we make it impossible for future generations to live on the earth. There are fixed amounts of fossil fuels and when these are used up man will have to work again. The war is using up so much steel and oil that future generations will not have enough. A student commented that this is the argument of the Bible but man's fate is not in the hands of supernatural powers; it is in his own hands and his goals lie in the infinite horizon. ASL's student argued that modern man is as stimulus-bound as ancient man. Instead of being bound by the stimuli of the natural environment he is tied to the stimuli of his artificial environment. Instead of sacrificing his children to Baal he sacrifices them to the insatiable greed generated by the industrial world.

Someone argued that modern man no longer believes that there is an almighty, providential Deity who created an orderly universe in which each thing has its place and that it is man's duty to achieve a certain ideal or perfect state. Man no longer believes that everything is governed by the Deity's laws and that man, the highest of the Deity's creatures, has a place and has duties to perform which have been allotted to him according to His law. Man had realized that all laws are man-made, the prescientific as well as the scientific. Man is just another biological organism which evolved by random selection. Modern man by accident has unleashed forces that will eventually destroy him and the world. It is not possible to stop these forces. Why should man think that he can outwit the evolutionary forces? Just as there was once an age of reptiles there is now an age of man. Just as the former disappeared, the latter, too, will disappear. ASL's student said that man's modern culture had created the myth of evolution to justify man's greed and shortsighted destruction of his fellowman and the earth. In the past man believed that he was a thinking being, a moral, ethical creature. We are now told that it is a myth, an illusion and that everything is a blind struggle for existence. Are we not being ethnocentric when we say that our beliefs are valid and the prescientific beliefs are superstitious myths? Whose frame of reference is correct? The disillusioned intelligentsia of Europe after World War I must have felt like the Scholastic philosophers when they witnessed the triumph of science over theology. Comte had said that mankind was entering the scientific era; the Positivists, the Liberals, and the Utilitarians thought that we were entering paradise. But, maybe man was entering the final stage of his existence on earth. The irony of all this is that science has ushered in the end of days, the very doctrine of some Christian theologians.

Wertheimer steered the discussion away from a defense of science when he asked whether it is possible to decide whether one's belief is correct in terms of concrete particular situations. He agreed that the validity of the claim to correctness will have to be continuously tested because the situation may change. He went on to ask, What are the consequences for the individuals in concrete life situations if they believe that man is Homo sapiens or if they believe that man is just another machine made by society?

Outgrowths of Riezler's Theses

Some of the seminar members considered Riezler's and Wertheimer's conjectures to be tender minded or unscientific but Maslow seemed to be stimulated by them; aspects of his and his students' work at Brooklyn College reflect a concern with them. The conjectures also became the focus of discussions in ASL's class. The students' reflections and discussions are presented to indicate research problems.

Is it domination when a person is treated like a tool for the sake of the We? Some students argued that it is proper to do this if the person's life depends on it but others said that a person should never be treated like a tool; he is an end in himself. The former students challenged the latter to define a person in a way that does not regard him as a cultural product and yet does not lead to the idea that a person has innate ideas or a soul. Some theorists who stress that man is a cultural product see him as a tool, a part of a machine; to say that he is a subpart of a system does not mean that man is not a tool, a means for the system's ends. Someone therefore proposed that the system be conceived of as an organic whole. This led to the objection that it leads to a mystical view of life and nature. When someone said that the individual is a self-actualizing creature, students argued that the same thing had been said by Plato, Aristotle, Kant, and religious philosophers. Someone pointed out that mystical and religious conceptions of man lead to a view of man controlled by heteronomous forces but the scientific conception leads to a view of man controlled by autonomous forces. The students wondered whether the scientific view makes a god out of each man, each man orders the world at will. This led to the question of whether there is a harmony in the world or a chaos of clashing wills.

In order to focus the discussion on particular cases, ASL gave them an example from Wertheimer's lecture on the soul. Suppose a person is drugged or drunk and had to be moved like an object in order to be kept from being run over by a car? Is it domination? They all said that it was not. Suppose you keep him drugged so that you could use him as an object? They all said that it would now be domination. What is the difference in these two cases? Some said that keeping him drugged robs him of his freedom to think and act for himself. When ASL asked them for life situations that are like these two cases, they gave examples in which an infant, child, or adult was in a situation that was fraught with danger to his life or body and somebody intervened to save him from destruction. Nearly all agreed that these were not cases of domination but a few students argued that such help is potentially dangerous because the person who is helped may become dependent on the other; he may feel that he is of lower status, the persons who do the helping may feel superior to or may not have faith in the person they helped. When some students argued that the person may have suffered loss of life or bodily harm, they argued that one does not know what would have happened. It is wrong to restrain a person, one must have unqualified faith in the other person, one must not interfere with his behavior because it stunts his self-growth. The students pointed out that in certain situations it is clear that we must act; when a child is walking in front of an approaching truck or in front of a mad dog he has to be pulled out of danger. In such situations it is not possible for him to learn from his mistakes or discover what has to be done; the situation does not allow a second chance, the truck will run over the child or the mad dog will bite him. The minority insisted that it is not moral to interfere, each person must be allowed to make his own bed and lie in it. [When ASL reported this argument to Wertheimer he wanted to know who the students were that had such a sophisticated view that deadened them to react to situational requirements. ASL argued that the requirements that were seen might be in the observer's view and not in the situation. He agreed but pointed out that there were clear-cut situations when everybody would agree that such and such an action was required (cf. Luchins, 1963).]

When the minority pointed out that their position was similar to Wertheimer's ideas on productive thinking, ASL asked them what right do we have to decide that a person must always see or learn by himself. Maybe the person does not want to. He may just want or need a solution to an immediate problem; why not give it to him? Someone answered that one must take into account both the person's short-term needs and his long-term needs and then do what is best for his self-growth. ASL asked, If a person is oriented by short-run needs is it domination to force him to have a long-term view of the situation? Why force people to live in the kind of world you like? Some students argued that the situation may require it and the person himself later on would appreciate that it was best for him. It is not domination if what is done is determined scientifically and not on a whim. A student said that there are people who are happy in their narrow, little world; they want to do what they are doing and regard it as an act of unfriendliness when you do not help them or make it impossible for them to do what they are doing. Is it fair for a future- or long-run-oriented person not to help him or to restrain him?

A visitor pointed out that people do not live in closed worlds, their actions may have bad effects on others. ASL asked, Suppose it does not affect anybody except the particular person? The visitor asked for examples in which a person's action has no effect on others. ASL proposed that students should keep a record of such situations. A few weeks later the diaries were discussed in class. In nearly all the examples, the class found that there was direct or indirect effect on others, even though it was a private act such as smoking, drinking, eating, reading a book, daydreaming, walking, or sitting down. There were students who objected to the denial of privacy to a person. They said that it was based on the assumption that one must do things for the sake of society, the church, state, family. The actual cases of the diaries may have really had no effect on anybody; why stress the relatedness of man at the expense of the individual? These students were told by others that the idea of an individual as a separate entity is not valid. One of them added that science never proves a statement. As long as one can find no contradiction one may hold on to his conjecture; conjectures are a matter of faith. Someone pointed out that according to Wertheimer a decision can be made in some life situations and that they are mixing up theoretical arguments about the logic of science with the pragmatic application of the scientific method to solve concrete problems. Someone interrupted to say that Hitler is using science to build his war machine; is it moral to do this? Would you say that as long as his scientists' work does not affect others there is no question of morality? ASL remarked that Wertheimer has stressed that in judging an act it is important to know the structure of the situation in which it occurs and whether the situation is a closed or open system. Generally speaking it can be argued that all situations are related to each other in some larger system. This philosophical view does not preclude the need to find out whether or not what one is doing, in a particular place and time, does or will affect the functioning of other people or other groups. The effects may be so minimal that they can be disregarded: according to the theory of relativity rulers used for measurement are affected by the context in which they are used but the effects on them on earth are so small that they can be disregarded. Thus for certain situations and certain times we do not have to be too concerned with the whole system in which the action occurs. Someone thereupon asked, How does one become aware of the effects of what one is doing on other places and people? Books have been written about the morality of the sexual act which stress the inherent goodness of any practice as long as those who engage in it do it willingly but all sexual behavior involves the death instinct and therefore it is not essentially good. Some anthropologists tell us that what is called a moral sex act in one society is immoral in another because of the different requirements of the different cultural patterns. If we accept their view then the social system determines what is moral and not nature. If one acts in terms of his own natural inclination he is acting blindly; such behavior leads to social disorganization. Even Freud has stressed that men have to live in terms of the Reality Principle and not the Pleasure Principle, that an infant has to develop an ego in order to survive. The aim of psychoanalysis is not the gratification of the instincts but their suppression.

Someone pointed out that Wertheimer would describe acting in terms of one's momentary desires as an act in which there is a concentric narrowing of the visual field. He went on to ask, How would Wertheimer open the eyes of a person who is narrowed down by his desire? Wertheimer assumes that a person has a natural tendency to do what fits or does not fit. If it is true, how does one open the eyes of a person who is blinded by an overwhelming passion or is obsessed with reaching a certain goal? Suppose two or more people say to an individual while he is about to commit murder that he must not do it; if he does it he will be killed for the crime but he says that he does not care and continues with the crime. Of what value was it to try to open his eyes? It would have been better to restrain and even kill him if necessary. Someone said that it is being assumed that a person can be deflected from criminal behavior by being told the consequences of the criminal act. This will not work, that is why no criminal code ever used it. The student who gave the example referred the class to the Talmud for examples where it was used. He went on to say that when parents tell children, Don't touch, it'll burn you, it does stop the child, admonitions work. The class then talked about how to conduct experiment with children and adults in a school, factory, or a mental hospital in order to study the effectiveness of admonitions.

Someone challenged the assumption that the person and not the situation must change; deviant behavior may be a challenge to the people in the situation to create new social structures which will accommodate the deviate. Some students insisted that society cannot change for each person but the proponent said that violence and mental illness are the prices for lack of change. ASL asked whether a perpetually changing social order is livable, whether it is possible to have a society which accommodates each person doing what he wants.

A few days later ASL asked his class for situations in the social field where the problems that had been raised by Reizler and Wertheimer could be studied. They said that one finds instances of love, dominance, and violence in parent-child relations, in sibling relations and in husband-wife relations. They proposed to study cases which appeared to everybody to be instances of love or of domination. What factors in the personality and in the social field produce these We groups? They thought that such cases could be found in the case workers' reports to family courts. They planned to study the cases to see what factors bring about the development of a harmonious family out of a disharmonious one, what actually decreases wife and child beating. When ASL asked them where they would get harmonious families someone said that certain religious groups, such as the Amish and the Chassidic Jews, seem to have harmonious families because of the ideology that ties them together. The husband and wife as well as the children are actually not submitting to each other but to the laws of their sect, thus there is no feeling of domination. Someone told of his experience with Amish and with the Chassidic Jews and argued that the wife and children are dominated by the husband; they are not cases of love but of dominance. The students raised the question whether it is proper to interpret their behavior from our frame of reference. We need to find out how the people themselves feel about how they are being treated. The following method of interviewing was suggested. Each person would be asked to imagine that life is a stage on which one enacts a certain play. They would then be asked, What role do you play? After this the same person would be asked to describe the role of everybody else in his family. After this the same person would be asked to describe the role he thinks the others think that he is playing. The students went on to say that it is important to do this before making a judgment from one's point of view (cf. Luchins, 1951). Someone objected to the study because the students were ignoring the fact that the family through the ages has been a means to exploit women and children. A student argued that there is little reference in the writings of ancient man or in the myths and legends of primitive people to the universality of the exploitive nature of the family. Maybe it is a thesis of social reformers who attack the family because they know that it is the institution that transmits the culture of a society. If you want to change society, get control of the family; to do this you must first destroy the present-day family because it reflects the old order. He went on to say that Engels and Marx had written a paper about the origin of the family in which they developed the thesis that the family was through history a means of exploiting children and women and they advocated that it be abolished in the new society. The USSR abolished the family in the early revolutionary days but reestablished it soon after. Why? Perhaps the family is the most efficient way for a society to reproduce and to raise individuals. When someone referred to the methods described in *Brave New World* as better, the student said that it was satire and not a fact. Thereupon the same person referred to the Oneida Community and the cooperatives in Palestine that have abolished the family and were flourishing. The family may have in the past played a role in reproducing members of society but modern society no longer needs the family. Even though it is the most efficient way to produce babies and rear them, we do not need babies at present. Malthus has pointed out that the food supply does not increase at the same rate as the population's growth; therefore we have war, civil strife, poverty, and disease. The social costs of these social ills outweigh the fact that a husband and wife can raise a child at a cheaper price than a governmental agency. Because of modern knowledge about sex, the recreational aspect of coitus can be divorced from the procreative aspect. Someone said that recent studies have shown that children who are raised in institutions are intellectually stunted, are crippled personalities. The previous speaker said that the results of the cooperatives in Palestine speak against the generality of the conclusion; growing up in an orphan asylum is not the same thing as growing up in a commune where all are brothers and sisters.

Someone said that in his experience as a psychiatric case worker he has come across families in which the parents did not love each other but loved their children. Perhaps it is possible to set up families in which males and females live together because they love the children who are entrusted to them by the community. Maybe society can set up a Eugenics Boards to select from the males and females who want to reproduce biologically those who are the best in terms of society's needs. Only these people would reproduce. A healthy woman could give birth to five to ten children and a healthy male could father thousands of babies. The babies would be distributed to the people who want to have a family. Here, too, proper selection would be made; only those who were best suited to raise them would be given babies. Someone said that it would not be a satisfactory arrangement because people want to perpetuate themselves biologically and this need would increase as man gave up his belief in spiritual immortality. This need might be one reason for the success of the foster home movement. He pointed out that orphanages are being closed because there is a great demand for children by people who feel that they need a family. If they cannot have a family composed of individuals from their flesh and blood, they get them via adoption. Someone asked, Why should foster children be entrusted only to people who are married? Another student said that the raising of children is such an important function that we cannot entrust it to the personal and irrational feelings of people who want a family. Marriage is a way to bind people by contract to care for each other and the child.

One of the previous speakers said that the instability of modern life is due to the persistence of the old morality and institutions in modern scientific society. The violence and the domination in society are due to the frustration of people who have modern ideas and goals but are forced to live in terms of the old methods. We need new patterns and new norms to meet modern man's needs. Someone said that through the ages people have been saying this but in the past the discussions took place among philosophers or the idle rich who sought to justify their way of life. Due to modern methods of education and communication the discussions are no longer confined to the salons or boudoirs of the intelligentsia. In the past many people who deviated did not tell others to do what they did. They practiced their vices in private and did not attack in public the morals of society. At present people who deviate are not content to practice in private, they believe that they must convert the whole world to believe in the righteousness of what they do. Why do they seek to abolish the family, marriage, or this or that institution or moral code? Why do they not practice in private their beliefs and let others practice theirs? Someone said that deviates are not tolerated. Because society nourished us, it had a right to publicly defend and to teach its time-tested patterns of behavior, which give society the stability that is of value even to deviates.

Someone said that he would like to ask reformers, If I hire you to help me raise my child do I not have the right to ask you to teach my morality and not to impose your belief on my child? Some students said that no one has a right to think that his morality is correct, nor does he have the right to tell teachers that they may not teach a certain moral code which they believe is correct. A student said that a child is not born with a code of morals. In order to get along in a society he has to learn its code. If everybody taught his personal code to children there would be chaos. Everybody would be imposing his private view on the child. What right does one have to do this?

ASL ended the discussion by asking the students to survey their friends to find out how prevalent are the beliefs that had been expressed in class. He asked them to predict the percentage of people who would say that the family is an institution that exploits children and women; the percentage of women and children who would say that they feel dominated, enslaved, inferior; the percentage who would advocate abolishing the family and marriage; the percentage who would say that there are not basically different sex roles for the males and females or different social roles for children of different ages. [The data are not available at present. However, the results were included the next year in lecture notes which contain the following summary. Less than 20 percent said that the family exploits children and women, but some said that the social field creates families that are exploitative, brutal, and dominant. Most had a positive feeling toward the family as an institution; very few wanted to abolish the family and marriage. Nearly everybody believed that male and females have certain roles that they do best because of their biological nature but the fact that they differ does not mean that they are inferior or superior; for example, a man is not superior because he has a more active role and the women a more passive role in sexual relations. Similarly it is no sign of being superior because one is less able to do certain things that another can do. Children are less able than adults to do certain things and this calls for different roles for them. ASL referred them to Allport's study on public and private attitudes and asked whether their friends would privately or publicly answer the questions differently. He suggested that they describe Allport's study to their friends and use it as a basis for obtaining their private and public reactions to each question and whether or not they believe or indulge in practices that are at variance from the public ideal. Students in ASL's social psychology classes between 1960-1970 did not think that as many people would be for the old morality and old institutions. They claimed that modern youths are not hypocrites; their public attitudes are not at variance with their private attitudes. Modern youths are more frank and open as they seek to gratify their needs. One graduate student said that it is due to the fact that never before have so many people gone to college; they are just beginning to realize that they have the power to change society.]

Informal Discussion with Wertheimer

When ASL told Wertheimer and a few students who were seated with them about the discussion in class, someone remarked that it reflects the confusion that has developed in men's minds about what is man. In the past people seemed to know who they were but now they do not. He blamed it on education: children are taught in school that they are all equal but they are not told that certain positions in society have sexual, racial, religious, and nationality requirements and that not all children have the possibility to reach the top. They are not taught that there are individual differences. A student said most of the differences are culturally determined; there are no I.Q., personality, or sex differences which are due to biology; the differences are actually social norms. Modern educators believe in democracy and therefore do not teach cultural norms which cause discrimination. She went on to give several examples of discrimination against women that have no basis in biology. Someone remarked that she forgot to mention that the same social discrimination makes stevedores, ditch diggers, miners, soldiers, street cleaners out of men and not women. In the USSR women hold such menial jobs, proving that it is a cultural and not a biological factor that places them in such positions. Some students maintained that the idea of equality is also a cultural fact. A society could teach that all men are equal or unequal; it is all a matter of conditioning. Wertheimer remarked that maybe we are overlooking the differences just as some people have overlooked the similarities. The studies on individual differences do not prove that all men and women are the same. Suppose that for certain traits defined by certain tests men and women, on the average, did not show clear-cut differences. Does it mean that there are no differences? After a pause he said that maybe the question cannot be decided by tests or averages. He asked what we mean when we say that all men are equal. Someone said that in discussions of sex differences it seems to mean that women want to be equal to men in everything men do but they do not want to do dangerous, menial tasks. ASL said that maybe women believe that machines and not men should do them. Another student said that men do not want to do the menial tasks done by women. Someone else asked, What do the women really want? Wertheimer stopped the speculation by saying that it is a matter for investigation, not debate. Thereupon ASL's student said, Let's find out what percentage of men and women want to do such female jobs as housekeeping, secretarial work and what percentage of both sexes want to do what is now man's work, street cleaning, ditch digging. Also, why do some women want to do men's work and why do some men want to do women's work? In the discussion that followed Wertheimer asked what happens to a position when women instead of men occupy it. Secretarial work has until recently been a man's job, now it is a female's job; what differences have occurred in the position? What happens to a female's position when men take over? Teaching in the elementary schools in the USA and social work have until recently been woman's work. What happens in a school or agency when all or most employees are men? What changes of the social field brought about these changes and what changes have they in turn wrought in the social field? He then turned the discussion back to the question of equality by saying that there may be biological reasons that limit the roles that males and females play in society. He asked, What are the consequences of the fact that only women can be mothers? ASL pointed out that some students in his class have rejected the idea that every female has to be a mother. Why can't a woman hand over the baby at birth to a man to raise while she goes back to work? In response to an objection, he pointed out that some pioneers and peasant women used to take out a few hours from work to give birth and go back to plowing or harvesting. Surely a modern woman could take off a few hours to be delivered of her baby and go back to her office or factory. The fact that they do not is due to our social system. It forces a woman to be a mother after it is no longer biologically necessary. Moreover, from early childhood we teach girls that their ultimate goal is to give birth and to raise children. This idea keeps women from actualizing themselves. A student said that women are lucky; they can actualize themselves in a biological manner which needs no special training but a man cannot. In sex the female has a biological advantage over the male who has to learn how to perform the act. Moreover, the female readily learns to outwit male domination by raising sons to dominate in her name; women rule the world because they rear the children. Throughout the ages they have used their biology directly or indirectly to give them power. Women do not need clubs to assert their power, their very passivity conquers. When challenged for examples, the student asked whether the so-called biblical patriarchs really ruled and he contended that Sarah not Abraham, Rebecca not Isaac, Rachel not Jacob dominated the family.

Wertheimer asked the students for examples in which they have used or heard the word *equality* used. After a pause he asked them to consider the meaning of the expression, *equality before the law.* It does not mean that the court gives everybody the same sentence; when people cry for equal treatment they do not mean that they want to be treated the same way. After a pause he said, Maybe women who want equality do not want to be like men or to imitate men but simply want justice. When ASL asked whether it is just that only men should be miners, soldiers and ditch diggers, Wertheimer asked whether it was arbitrarily decided that men and not women should do such tasks. Someone said that when a society's men go off to war and get killed the women stay home in order to give birth to babies who will maintain the society. Someone added that men are more expendable than women; one man may impregnate hundreds of women in a year but during that time a woman can give birth usually to only one child. He asserted that until societies no longer need the women's reproductive organs for production of its members, men and women will have different roles.

A visitor said that modern women are taught in school that they are equal to men. Those girls who take all this seriously and model themselves after certain males find that they cannot play such roles without sacrificing the mother role which has been taught to them from birth. Since the mother and career role are taught to girls, we are creating females who have conflicts; they cannot play both roles at the same time. Maybe we ought to teach the boys to be baby-sitters and housekeepers so that they too could play the mother role after the wife gives birth and goes back to work. When someone remarked that the male earns the family's income, the visitor said that perhaps some men would prefer the mothering role just as some women may prefer the breadwinner role. Why should people be forced to play roles which they do not like and in which they cannot fulfill themselves? ASL said that in his neighborhood there are many poor families where the wife works and the unemployed husband does the housekeeping. It is not unusual because the factories tend to hire women because they are paid less. A woman factory worker is as good as a male worker because machines obviate the need for muscle power and make the work more pleasant. In view of this, more men will be doing the housekeeping. Someone added that due to the war economy there is a shortage of labor. Wives as well as husbands work and share with the housekeeping. Perhaps after the war they will continue doing this. Someone pointed out that lower-class women and children have for a long time been doing men's work in factories and mines; the Industrial Revolution freed them from their traditional roles. Middle- and upper-class women have just begun to demand to be freed of these old roles. A student said that people who were sold into slavery also were freed of their old sex-based roles. ASL said that he once heard a factory hand say that she worked to be able to be a housekeeper before she dies. Do the upper-class women want to be factory hands and charwomen?

Wertheimer brought the question back to equality by saying that to some people equality means doing the same thing, being like the other person; to other people equality means equal opportunity to pursue one's interests. Is this all that there is to it? ASL said that in the *Pledge of Allegiance* to the flag children learn about equality, liberty, and justice for all. Someone said that people do not think of philosophical ideas about justice, equality, or liberty but think of situations in which they live. They see that they are not equally free to do what they wish to do and that some people have more power than they have. In view of this they realize that they better do what they are told; they learn at an early age that might makes right. Why not teach people the facts of life instead of myths? When Wertheimer said that justice and freedom are not myths, a student said that someday society will be a system that is regulated by technologists and scientists. It will be a society in which no one will have to work; everybody will then be free to do as he pleases, to gratify himself or to actualize himself as he sees fit. Wertheimer asked whether such a world of individual monads living in a technologically predetermined harmony would have people in it who possess Homo sapiens' characteristics. The student answered that the Homo sapiens concept is related to prescientific notions of what is man; the age of science calls for a new type of man to evolve. Wertheimer left for class.

37
Hero Worship

In the first half of the session Hans Speier summarized his paper on hero worship. He started by saying that the term *hero* is loosely used; one talks of a hero of labor, of science, of a boy's or a girl's hero. He will use the term in a narrower sense; what is heroic is the description of the behavior of heroes in national epics. In epics the hero is a man who is engaged in overt fighting, especially in individual conflict. In view of this conception of the heroic, a martyr is not a hero nor is a fighter in a modern war. After saying that regardless of the culture all people need a hero, he defended his definition against objections from a visitor. Speier said that he studied epics because there was in them a primitive feature of the heroic. The visitor questioned the assumption that epics are primitive in the sense that they are the original undifferentiated stuff out of which has evolved the more complex thought or literature of modern man. It is wrong to assume that primitive societies are like the one-celled animals out of which, the evolutionists say, arose complex organisms. Someone interrupted to say that hero worship may exist where there are no heroes and heroes may exist where there is no hero worship. He then asked why people worship heroes. Speier said that hero worship is the admiration of the exuberance of life, of strength. It is a sort of envy; it is not rooted in people's respect for courage; the prototype of the hero is more like a madman than a knight. After a pause Speier said that this type of man invites biological study. He is strong not great; is proud not good; strives for power not for justice. He is exuberant to the point of wantonness; he is impetuous in attack. A *Held* in German is a man who bears arms and can fight, in India the Agr refers to the animus of an animal in a man and in Greek he is someone who is able to cope with life and its violent dangers. In all cultures the hero has outstanding strength and not morals. In heroic poetry he is compared to animals with the stress on his great animal powers. In Germanic legends he is half giant; Roland was fifteen feet tall and ate 1,000 loaves of bread. The hero is appalling, not sickly. He is not only strong but violent and brutal; he shows an assertive and not a violent kind of brutality; it is a brutality that comes from strength. He lives vicariously among the wild life and shows the wild exuberance of an animal. Another trait of the hero is cunningness, for example, he wears women's clothing to elude his pursuers and

494

kills his enemies in their sleep. He has practical intelligence, his deeds are not outcomes of diligence or sweat. What counts is not the accomplishment of the task but its adventurousness. Speier added in response to comments that the descriptions also include joy, apprehensiveness, and grief. The hero has no security but fortitude; however, he is a man who has no basic anxiety, he is secure. In response to questions Speier said that heroic security occurs when men encounter risks. It is not security in the modern sense, to die fighting is heroic. The hero may also die because he is sick or is overwhelmed by death. Only lower-class people and women die of old age and starvation. Natural death is blind and deprives man of freedom of action in life. The hero's death is visible. In response to a question he said that the hero fights for something concrete and not for abstractions, for his family, his home, his friend and for his manhood.

Someone asked, Who wrote the epics? Were they weakings who were glorifying things which they could not do? Perhaps the epics were projections of their aggressiveness or a reaction to frustration. A visitor wondered why such epics had survived and said that the historical context must be understood in order to understand them. One cannot take items out of the context of the historical era to which they refer. [The hero of the epic *La Chanson de Roland* was a rather unimportant prefect of the Breton March who was slain in 778 when the rear guard of Charlemagne's army was ambushed by the Basques in the Pyrenees while it was returning from Spain. However, the epic places the ambush at Roncesvalles and transforms the Christian Basques into Saracens and magnifies the importance of the battle. Roland appears in many other chansons of the *Charlemagne Cycle* which were the most loved of the literature of the Middle Ages. ASL asked his WPA class whether they had read the chansons. Many of the students had read them and remembered Roland as a person who fought evil and did good deeds. They insisted that Speier's description of a hero did not characterize Roland. They also wanted to know why the chansons had become popular and how a rather insignificant battle and a relatively unimportant leader in Charlemagne's army were transformed into the Roland of the chansons.]

When a student asked why he claimed that we do not have heroes at present, Speier said that they could not appear in modern capitalistic technological societies. They appeared under social conditions where there was decentralized power, as in the Balkans. They emerged in conditions of Great danger, such as attacks from animals and from strong men and when there was starvation; consciousness of danger gives rise to the hero. In answer to a question, he added that the concept of justice limits hero worship and that in modern times the hero is somebody who rises from the lower classes and goes far above his class; people worship his career, he is a conspicuous demonstration that one can get along in this world. The modern hero is restless rather than active. Modern hero worship is a form of gossip, a form of vicarious enrichment of one's narrowed, stagnant, arrested life. There is a conflict between the arrested conditions of one's life and one's desires and therefore gossip helps satisfy one's desires vicariously. In response to a question he said that the feeble are the modern worshipers of heroes. The rest of the session was spent in a discussion with Horney and Maslow, who pointed out similarities and differences between Speier's hero and various psychoanalytic concepts.

Wertheimer's Critique of Speier's Thesis

Wertheimer began the session by asking for remarks about what had been said last time and went on to make the following summary, pausing for comments which were rarely made. (The summary was justified because there were many new faces.) Speier wants to know what is a hero. In his study he had found that a hero is near to certain biological characteristics and that his behavior has nothing to do with morals; the qualities of a hero are strength of physique and the manifestation of violence, assertiveness, destructiveness, ferociousness. He is not resentful and is free of envy and avarice. He is cunning, enjoys life, does not want to work. He is an adventurer who has no basic anxiety, there is a healthy absence of anxiety, he feels no anxiety in battle. He does not die in bed, he lives for glory and not for morals. Brutality adds to the hero's greatness. This idea of a hero is counter to modern ways of fighting in which there are long-range guns. The hero is only possible under certain conditions where there is great physical insecurity and physical danger. At present we worship a person's career and not his strength. Modern hero worship is rooted in envy, it is a substitute participation in dangerous life. Today the feeble are the hero worshipers, it is a miserable form of expanding their egos.

When Wertheimer paused for comments, a visitor said that at present there is great insecurity. Hitler's hordes have conquered Europe and North Africa, they dominate the world. Perhaps after the war there will be many heroes whose deeds will be celebrated in songs and stories. But, if Speier is correct there will be no heroes. [ASL asked his class to name a hero of World War I. No one could do so. He asked, Why is it that the heroes of old were celebrated in the epics for hundreds of years but at present a hero is given a ticker-tape parade on Wall Street and makes the headlines and for a few days is in all the papers and on all the radios but after a few months he is forgotten? More people at present may know of a person's heroic deed but they remember it for a shorter time. Is it because modern society is more oriented to the present, that modern men are interested in current news and not history?]

ASL's student hypothesized that epics reflect the character of the culture that has created them. Cultures that glorify brutality and sensuality or idealize the emotio-conative kind of man celebrate the behavior of Speier's hero but societies that glorify kindness, mercy, love, and other Homo sapiens' characteristics do not. Hero worship is related to a society's ideal man and is not always the admiration of the exuberance of biological life. He went on to say that the epics were not trustworthy because a people's ideal norms were usually not the same thing as their real norms. If one wants to study heroes in primitive groups one should live with them and find out just who is a hero and why.

Wertheimer remarked that one can criticize Speier for basing his hero on literature and not on actual people in real situations. But one can defend his methods by saying that we cannot study directly the heroes of olden times. ASL's student pointed out that legends and epics are handed down orally and that there is a selection process as they are passed on; each generation emphasizes aspects that fit their conceptions and needs. Moreover, even the epics that are handed down in written form mean a different thing in the tradition of each generation that reads them. The same Biblical stories mean a different thing to a Christian of the twentieth century than of the first century. Also the gentile Christian converts read into them different things than the Jewish Christians; the Gospel's reference to Jews and their behavior did not mean the same things to Jewish and non-Jewish Christians. He went on to say that depending on what one chooses one can prove that the Biblical Jews worshipped devils or angels and that their heroes were saints or sinners.

Wertheimer said that he would be all for the methods used by Speier if he had confined himself to one type of hero but he did not. When a sociologist said that Speier had wanted to get a prototype, Wertheimer said that it was all right to do this if one constructed a basic type from which the other types were qualifications or were limited cases. When the sociologist said that such an undertaking is difficult, Wertheimer agreed and said that this does not mean that one was free arbitrarily to set up a type that is blind to the structure of the phenomena with which one is dealing. After a pause Wertheimer remarked that Speier's paper claims that civilization is anti-heroic because morals play a role in civilization. How valid is this? A visitor said that we no longer live in an era that produces heroes because man has become an object that is engineered into a certain shape. Humanity has been engineered out of existence by modern scientific technology, it has changed his ethics and character, modern man is more like a robot. A machine cannot be a hero; neither can a man who is modeled in terms of it be a hero. Moreover, modern methods of advertising create all sorts of psuedo-heroes. Heroes are made to order by press agents. Someone pointed out that since modern society is egalitarian, everybody is as good as the next person and therefore there cannot be a hero in the old sense of the term. Hero worship exists among the frustrated and maladjusted; a healthy person is his own hero. Perhaps the spread of psychoanalytic ideas will eventually create a healthy society in which people will not be hero worshipers. People will be secure, they will have a feeling of autonomy and be spontaneous as well as democratic. Someone pointed out that although men have lived in cities for 5,000 years there are no epics in which urban people are heroes. What does urban life lack, that the countryside has, that produces the heroic? Someone suggested that life in the cities is relatively safer from wild animals and thieves. There is also more social control; it curbs the behavior that Speier has described as heroic. The city gives one a peaceful not an heroic life. [How true is this today, and was it ever true?]

Wertheimer asked, Why are we interested in the question of what is a hero? We want to find out what is a human being and what is society. It is important to know this for certain social and political situations. After a pause he said that the hero is not out of place in modern society. There are modern societies in which there are heroes. Someone said that a Nazi is a hero in Germany, a Fascist is a hero in Italy, but in our country they are not heroes. When we look at Hitler objectively he is the greatest man Europe has produced; from our moral point of view we may say that what he does is wrong and evil but we can still admire him for his greatness. Speier's hero is like Hitler. ASL defended the feasibility of the student's conjecture by pointing out that Napoleon had for many years been a hero to him even though he knew of the immoral things that Napoleon had done. He wondered whether 100 years from now many people would regard Hitler as their hero. A student remarked that myths will be created about him just as about Roland and perhaps even some Jews and Negroes will worship him as a hero.

Someone pointed out that people at present admire the wild behavior of actors, actresses, gangsters, and the playboys of the upper classes as well as the antics of college students. They are heroes in Speier's sense of the term; people admire their exuberance, their lusty living. He went on to defend Speier's operational definition of the hero. Wertheimer interrupted to say that one is not free to delimit and to define hero in any way one wishes because the definition colors the results. He then said, Maybe in modern society this type of hero does not play a great role. Are modern types of heroes variations of Speier's type or is it the other way around? Was Speier's description adequate for the type he had in mind? Someone said that since there are at present no heroes of Speier's type we cannot make comparisons with modern men nor is there a need to compare Speier's prototype with people of modern times. A visitor said that if one picks up the newspaper or goes to a movie he could find Speier's heroes. Many people admire them, they are fascinated by them, that is why yellow journalism and Hollywood are so successful. Wertheimer said that he does not deny that there are cases like Speier's type of hero, but they occur only under certain kinds of social conditions, in places and periods of social deterioration; it is a sign of decadence. [A graduate student in 1970 said that one can find many examples of Speier's hero in contemporary social movements. Does this mean that our society is more decadent than that of 1940 in which Speier could not find his type of hero?]

Wertheimer remarked, Speier's procedures involve certain axioms which are widely believed but are not correct. In speaking of so-called primitive societies we think that vitality and other biological factors exist with less morals among them than among us. It is assumed that the lower down we go in the evolutionary scale the less morals will be found. In my opinion the reverse is true. We cannot talk of the vital force of a man without knowing how the man relates to the society's religious and moral standards. To Speier force is force whether it is used by a gangster or a judge. He points out common types and disregards their connections to ethics and morals. He is using piecemeal-subtractive abstraction. We get an oversimplified picture if we compare identical elements or similar traits and do not consider the hero's relation to his society. After a pause for comments he said, Speier gave cases in which heroes slew monsters or giants; why wasn't the giant or monster the hero for the people? The monster was usually dangerous not only for the hero but for the community. The hero in some epics fights for light not for darkness; there is some relation of the hero's behavior to good, to bad. There are instances where the hero is a bad man but his behavior is due to his education, to the type of society where ethics is in a labile state. In response to an objection he retorted, We call a boy a hero when he saves a drowning child and not when he drowns children. He went on to say that technology does not play the decisive role in determining what is heroic. When one drives a car or an airplane it becomes part of his system of coordinates and under certain conditions one may act heroically with these modern machines just as the hero in the epic acted heroically with his sword. One may act heroically as he fights a plague or a disease in a country just as in the epic the hero fought a monster or a giant. A visitor pointed out that some people drive their cars in a manner that fits the heroic as described by Speier.

After a long pause Wertheimer remarked that to find the prototype hero one must consider which cases are artifacts of a specific sort of society. The type of hero Speier has used does not fit in with any society. A visitor protested that Speier was using the pure case approach of modern science, his prototype did not have to exist in any society. ASL's student said that Galileo's pure case approach to motion led to the prediction and control of actual cases of motion. Does Speier's prototype explain the actions of real heroes? The visitor replied that it is an ideal type that both primitive and modern men esteem. They want to control their fates, they do not want to be pawns of their societies. Someone pointed out that in all epics the hero had a master, a king, or a god to whom he was loyal unto death. The visitor said that although the hero was not really free to express himself as Speier implied, the hero suggested the possibility that such a man can exist; that is why people cherish the epics. He added that this kind of hero does exist today because we have developed social conditions that allow free-wheeling and free-dealing behavior. The Renaissance's *Homo Universale* has been transformed by the theories of the Enlightenment and Darwinism into the kind of man described by Speier. This man's attitude is expressed in Henley's *Invictus* and in Nietzsche's *Thus Spake Zarathustra*. Perhaps modern man will eventually create a society in which more people will be able to be like Speier's hero. ASL's student said that a society of such heroic individuals will be composed of collections of persons pursuing their own interests. What will keep the society together when each man acts that way? Someone said that modern technology could create a society in which the necessary activities would be done by machines. It could create a harmonious system in which each person will be a monad that moves at will yet does not destroy society. ASL's student said that it takes all kinds of people to have a society and rejected the idea that everybody should be molded into the heroic type described by Speier. The previous speaker then said that Huxley's *Brave New World* could be rewritten so that provisions were made in it for such heroes. In addition to manufacturing workers, they could manufacture a variety of heroes, Speier's as well as Wertheimer's so that there would be a variety of people, sensual-hedonistic, emotio-conative, and cognitive people.

Wertheimer continued with his criticism. In the development of man and in the history of society there have been situations which we can call the heroic. Such situations have a place in daily life, certain situations need a hero. Someone interrupted to say that Hitler has said to the German people that they have before them an important task and he appealed to them to be heroic. He has made them feel like heroes but had he made them moral? Wertheimer replied that Hitler may have appealed to the heroic but one aspect of his appeal is invalid. He has centered the Germans on the idea that they are in perpetual danger and that they have to be perpetually heroic. This results in artificial action, imputed behavior. Someone interrupted to say that according to Wertheimer a hero steps forward to do the great deed once or twice but he does not want to keep on being heroic. In view of this, the heroic act is something extraordinary, people admire the strange and/or unusual greatness of the deed. ASL's student said that Wertheimer's hero does what is required in the situation, he is not egocentric, he does not act because he figures out that it will earn him a medal but feels the need to do something in a situation. He concluded that Wertheimer's model is based on ethics not psychology. Wertheimer insisted that the admiration of greatness without regard to the question of ethics is due to decadence, due to the peoples' blindness to the moral issue that is involved in the action. [A SUNY-Albany student pointed out that according to Wertheimer the admiration by people of the actions of modern youth of the New Left or New Right is a sign of decadence but these youths are idealistic and do what they do in order to awaken people to realize that we live in an immoral society. Their behavior is immoral yet it is done to awaken people's moral sense.]

Speier responded to Wertheimer's criticism in the following manner. There is a fundamental difference in approach, Wertheimer's approach is different from mine. He is in search of morally admirable behavior and wherever he finds it he says that it is heroic behavior. But such centering on the relation of the hero to the structure of society leads to a picture of the perfect statesman, the man who acts wisely and efficiently. This is not the typical hero. Wertheimer objects to the idea that physique comes before morals. But, that it does is a matter of fact. He raises the question of ethical standards. Of course there are ethics in the heroic society but there is a lack of centralized power, the cells of peace and security are loosely organized. In it each wars against the other although there are friendships for common goals and there are certain relations of hosts to guests. There exist, however, constant feuds between hostile and strange brotherhoods. They have a double standard, one for the brotherhoods and another for enemies and strangers. I refrained from discussing ethical standards because I did not want to use our standards. If you do study their ethics you find that the hero has to save his honor and not to solve tasks and that mercy is bad. People focus on the grand performance in the victory of the hero and do not look at the victim's wounds. Several students agreed with Speier that one must not judge the hero of epics in terms of today's moral standards.

Wertheimer remarked to Speier, Let's exclude the question of absolute ethics; you excluded in your discussion all community relationships. You said that in the in-group there is ethics and therefore the hero does not respond arbitrarily but in terms of the group's ethics. I was not thinking of the ideal of mercy but said that what the hero does has something to do with his in-group's morals. Didn't the group approve the grandeur of the hero's success? I think that the study of the sheer admiration of an act without its relation to the community is a kind of false abstraction. Only in times when the community has become estranged from all ethics do we find such sheer worship of brutality. After a pause, he said that what Speier presented is not a general case, not the prototype. ASL's student said that Wertheimer talks about decadence which perplexes him. Is it possible that a primitive society could be decadent? Modern novels imply that only civilized societies are decadent. Moreover, according to the theory of evolution men once lived in the age of savagery. Wertheimer objected to the conjecture that such behavior is the behavior of primitive people. In every age there are savages; even in our modern world we have savages who use scientific methods instead of the methods of the Stone Age. Speier remarked that we must differentiate between hero, knight and martyr. In the hero, sheer physical behavior is admired, in the knight, justice and joy are admired and in the martyr, self-sacrifice is admired. The session ended at this point. [ASL discussed Speier's last remark with Wertheimer, who objected to the formulation and suggested that a study be made of heroes, knights, and saints. Would even a superficial analysis support Speier's statement? This waits to be done.]

38
Closing Remarks of the Seminar on Power

On the last day Wertheimer started the session with the following remarks. We have been concerned with the relation of sociology and psychology to the question of power. The big theories of Riezler's paper missed the point, they are peripheral. It made a division between the institutional and the human side of power. He was interested in the human side but how could we study the human side without the institutional side? In the discussions we heard two extreme views about institutions; that institutions are things in themselves and that institutions are nothing without the dynamic reality of human action. Institutions have reality in the people. If it is only an institution and no men are in it, it is a dead issue. Wertheimer paused for comments and then said that he would make a few preliminary remarks. There is a big difference between sociology's and psychology's view of the problem. This difference is in fact the difference between the position of traditional psychology where all behavior is viewed as individual psychology and the position of modern social psychology where everything is social and there is no individual personality. It is wrong to talk of an individual or of an institution per se. One must realize that the individual has to be viewed as part of a physical and social environment; there are requirements going to and from the environment and the individual. Both make up a system, a whole in which no part can be taken out and studied in isolation from the system. The important thing is their interaction in the system, not the parts per se.

Someone interrupted to say that according to Gestalt theory a person is what he is because of his place, role, and function in the system. Since the person's behavior is determined by the system, there is no human freedom. Wertheimer said that some discussions of human freedom confuse it with determinism. Even if all things were determined, the problem of freedom would still exist. He added, We do not live in a free space but in a structured social field with different conditions for our actions and movements. These conditions play a living role. When society builds roads it is true that restrictions on our movements are imposed by the society but do not the roads give us freedom? On the whole the function of a road is not merely to impose limitations but to make certain things possible. Society in this way serves the individual.

A student insisted that society restricts the free expression of men's natural inclinations, citing Freud. Wertheimer remarked that we should not mix up

501

freedom with arbitrary action. What people want is sometimes due to their being a part of a social group. It is not just forced behavior but behavior that is required by the social field. He referred to pages 83-108 of Lewin's book on measurement of psychological force as he made these points. The question of force can only be dealt with if it is related to the total structure of the forces in the social field. Lewin uses the word valence, it is the factor in the life space of an individual that attracts and repels him. It represents the quality of the situation to the individual. Forces and valences create a field of force. What becomes a valence depends on the field's tension system. The state of the system tries to change itself in the direction to alleviate tension, it changes in the direction of becoming a good gestalt. In response to questions he described the principle of Prägnanz and then went on to say that there are two kinds of tensions. One type always exists in living systems; these tensions make the situation dynamic and these tensions by themselves do not endanger the system. He characterized them as tensions spelled with a small t. The other type of tensions endangers the field's structure; he characterized them as Tensions spelled with a capital T. Someone interrupted to say that his conjecture is similar to that of Adler's and Maslow's that a person seeks security. Wertheimer answered, Yes, security, but in terms of the structural requirements of the situation; the behavior, the actions, of the person involve fitting into a situation. Someone argued that this means conformity to a power structure and pointed out that Maslow's dominant person actualizes himself without conforming, he listens to himself instead of doing what he was taught to do, he acts on his own impulses and does what seems right to him. He is not playing a role but being a person. In contrast, in Wertheimer's conjecture the person focuses on the structure of the total system. The student argued that no person can ever know the system's structure, all he knows is what is in his mind. In learning to be attuned to the needs of himself as a person, he learns to be a free person and courageously to do what is right. All great men, even scientists, are free because they listen to their souls and not to society. Fitting in makes sense when we are dealing with arithmetic but not when it is applied to political situations. Stephen Decatur once said, My country right or wrong, my country. [May she always be in the right, but our country right or wrong.] This reflects Wertheimer's conjecture that a person is a part of a field and must do what it tells him. It leads to condoning immoral acts; no religion has as its slogan, My God, right or wrong, my God. Someone pointed out that in theology God is good and right but man is evil and needs to be bound by customs. Wertheimer pointed out that in some Oriental religions man is good, human nature is good but conditions create evil actions. A visitor interrupted to say that what is natural is good, that modern man has yet to learn to appreciate his biological, physical nature. He rejected Wertheimer's comment that there are dangers in stressing man's physical basis that he has in common with all animals. When one says that the aim of life is body well-being, it can be objectively shown to be correct but when one says that the aim of life is some metaphysical goal, it cannot be proven to be correct. Aristotle once said that man has to actualize his rational soul; this is similar to religious beliefs that are not based on fact. It can be demonstrated that man wants to be secure in the sense that he is not kept from satisfying his tissue needs. The social field exists to gratify his biogenic needs, all social or personality needs directly or indirectly depend on tissue gratification.

Someone pointed out that all social fields have power structures which seek to maintain themselves and are not concerned with individual people. It makes no difference whether the Democrats, Republicans, Socialists, or Fascists rule, the individual is neglected in the name of the group's needs. A student remarked that there is a different flavor to the power structure and a different social atmosphere when one of these parties rule. Wertheimer objected to the assumption that all power structures are the same, that power is power no matter who exercises it. We live in a field with a certain characteristic power structure which has certain effects instead of other effects on the individuals in it. After a pause he added that power is not concentrated only in the individual but is also in the field. A visitor interrupted to ask how he would study power. He said that he would begin with the power structure of the field. This would help us get an understanding of the place where the person's behavior goes on. Someone suggested that we start with extreme cases where a person is a part of a field and has no feeling of individuality and cases where a person has marked feelings of individuality but no awareness of being a part of a social field. What personal and social factors bring about such cases and what can be done to change a person of one type to a person of the other?

Wertheimer said that it is important to answer questions such as these. Under what condition is anarchy possible, what are the features or conditions of jungle law; what are the essential features of the idea of utopian social structures? He added, Under what personal and social conditions do they appear, disappear? What are the dynamics and the directions of development of such systems? In response to an objection he said that it is not a question of 100 percent functioning of such a system but a question of the realization of the dynamic forces working in some direction.

He suggested an experiment in which two groups, A and B, are involved in four kinds of relations. In 1, the members of Group A must tell the truth to each other and the members of Group B must also tell the truth to each other but the members of Group A must tell lies to members of Group B and vice versa. In 2, the members of Group A as well as of Group B must tell the truth to each other and the members of Group A must also tell the truth to members of Group B and vice versa. In 3, the members of Group A as well as of Group B must tell lies to each other but they must tell the truth to members of the other group, that is, members of Group A tell the truth to members of Group B and members of Group B tell the truth to members of Group A. In 4 the members of Group A as well as of Group B must tell lies to each other and members of Group A must tell lies to members of Group B and vice versa. He diagrammed the four relations as follows:

1.	A:	tell truth	tell lies	B: tell truth
2.	A:	tell truth	tell truth	B: tell truth
3.	A:	tell lies	tell truth	B: tell lies
4.	A:	tell lies	tell lies	B: tell lies

He said, Here are four relations; which are possible, which are not possible? After a pause he asked which are dynamically more stable and which are unstable and which would need more bayonets and spies to enforce the rule. After a pause he said that maybe some power structures go in one direction, of more spies and bayonets.

In response to a question he made the following remarks about the determination of power. The degree of strength of a factor in the field is important. Power may be conceived as the amount of driving force of an individual or situation, a force which goes in a certain direction, exercising a change of behavior or attitude in others. The direction of the change is important. We need to know what effect it has on the character of the structure of the persons and of the social situation. We must differentiate between two types of power; power may function due to the requirements of the field, not neglecting the requirements of the field and the individuals in it; power may be real domination, blindly and willfully neglecting the requirement of the field and the individuals, narrowing down the individuals' behavior so that it superficially seems that it is required. The biggest crime is to rob people of the possibility of being able to act in terms of the requirements of the field, robbing them of the required knowledge or misrepresenting something.

In response to a question about the nature of legitimate power, Wertheimer said that action may be brought about by the inner requirements of man or by external rules or habits. Legitimate power is related to these different ways of bringing about action. Before Wertheimer could finish, a visitor objected to the term *inner requiredness,* saying that we have all been habituated to think that there is such a thing as natural lawfulness. Man first makes a law and after a while begins to think that it is natural. When someone breaks these laws he upsets our habits and the feeling of order that they provide; therefore, we strike out against him. Even a tyrant who seizes the power structure by violating the laws is a product of his society's conditioning, therefore, he seeks to rationalize and to justify his willful seizure of power. This is seen in the Chinese Doctrine of the Heavenly Mandate. As long as the emperor is successful in controlling the state's power structure he is said to have the Dictate of the Heavens or Heavenly Mandate. Wertheimer asked whether a revolution's success may in some way be due to its meeting the requirements of the social field and the needs of the individuals in it. During a pause ASL asked, Suppose we arbitrarily took the position that there was lawful requiredness or that there was none. What consequences does it have for man and his lot on earth? A student said that because people assume that good comes from good and evil from evil, they would say that the assumption of required lawfulness would lead to an orderly and good society but the assumption of non-requiredness of laws would not.

Wertheimer remarked that in concrete life situations a law that is imposed in the direction of justice is different from a law that is imposed to satisfy the ego of a king or of a class. ASL's student pointed out that some sociologists say that all laws are arbitrarily made by individuals. This scientific conclusion is used by some people to act arbitrarily in terms of their egos. They say that modern man has realized that he and not nature makes the laws. Man is proud of the fact that he has freed himself of old superstitions. He has become a god. But, the traditional Deity first made the Law before he started creating things and He abides by the Law; to violate it is to annul creation. Since the Deity must abide by the Law, why does modern man think that he could act capriciously? When ASL noted that in ancient times the gods acted capriciously, a student remarked that just as it took thousands of years for man to develop the idea of a God of righteousness it will take thousands of years for the modern god-like men to evolve into righteous beings. Someone said that the notion of God is not an experimental or logical concept. If one wants to be a scientist he has to avoid notions that elude the methods of science. The previous speaker asked whether one can use science to justify one's arbitrary behavior. Someone asked, What is meant by the word *arbitrary;* maybe it is all a matter of taste.

Wertheimer asked, Is it possible to say that force is force, that it is arbitrary whether society inhibits the kidnapper or whether it aids the kidnapper who is stealing the baby? He added that such assertions reflect a piecemeal approach. They ignore the place, role, and function of the act in its context. Thereupon, Speier and Wertheimer got into a discussion that made everybody forget that the class had overrun its time. Speier said, I doubt that a political situation can be said to be required or not required. This may be logically possible but not in actuality. Maybe only in retrospect can it be known what was required; we cannot determine it while we are acting. In order to know whether it is required we need to know the whole situation. No one can do this; therefore, we cannot know what is required. Wertheimer said that luckily it is not necessary to know the whole situation. The question comes down to this, Is there a tendency in man not to be blinded by his interests? Even if in 90 percent of the cases he seems to be blinded, it may still hold. After a pause he said that we need to discover the conditions that bring about the ability to do what is required and the conditions that destroy this tendency. In response to a student's example of willful and blind behavior, he said that the character of the individual is not an and-summation of the individual's actions and experiences but the result of his acting in a particular social field, the result of the dynamic interrelation of a person in a place. In different places the dynamics of the field calls for different responses. [After the war ASL met at Yeshiva College a refugee sociologist who had for many years known Wertheimer in Frankfurt. The sociologist said that he had sometimes attended the New School's seminars. He thought that Wertheimer's behavior seemed to be less concentrated than at the University of Frankfurt and that he appeared to have a boy scout's attitude toward things. When he inquired about ASL's reactions, he told him that he was too busy testing Wertheimer's ideas and reading about what was discussed in class to be aware of Wertheimer as a person. Wertheimer's ideas seemed to some students to be romantic and idealistic but some of the college instructors were impressed to the extent of echoing Wertheimer's ideas in their classes. Many of their students liked the ideas; a few saw the discrepancy between their instructors' actions and their advocacy of Wertheimer's conjectures. These students had different opinions of the instructors than Wertheimer. It seemed to them that the behavior of some of these instructors fitted the model of man that Wertheimer condemned; their playing power politics exemplified the egocentric behavior criticized by Wertheimer. Why did Wertheimer not see what they were doing even when aspects of their actions involved him? Does this mean that his theory is incorrect? ASL told the sociologist that maybe the seminars were a kind of group psychotherapy for the students, and that Wertheimer's conjectures meant different things to different people. But they were a gold mine for research ideas. Maslow, in particular, pursued some of these ideas, contributing his own ideas in the process of developing them. It is not out of place to mention that we had been corresponding with him at the time of his death about the social psychology seminars and had hoped to obtain his comments on the seminars to which he contributed so much.]

Bibliography

Adcock, F. E., Charlesworth, M. P., Cook, S. A. 1923-39. *The Cambridge Ancient History*, Cambridge: The University Press.

Adler, A. 1938. *Social Interest*. London: Farber & Farber.

Allport, F. H. 1933. *Institutional Behavior*. Chapel Hill: University of North Carolina Press.

Allport, G. W. 1937. *Personality: A Psychological Interpretation*. New York: Holt.

Allport, G. W. and Vernon, P. E. 1930. *A Study of Values*. Boston: Houghton Mifflin.

Aristotle. 1920. *Collected Works* (Oxford trans.). New York: Oxford University Press.

Asch, S. E. 1952. *Social Psychology*. New York: Prentice Hall.

Augustine, S. 1931. *The City of God*. Translated by J. Healey. New York: Macmillan.

Ayer, A. J. 1946. *Language, Truth and Logic*. New York: Oxford University Press.

Bacon, F. 1872. *The Works of Francis Bacon*. vols. 5 and 8. Edited by James Spedding et al. New York: Hurd and Houghton.

Bartlett, F. C. 1932. *Remembering*. Cambridge: The University Press.

Benedict, R. 1935. *Patterns of Culture*. Boston: Houghton Mifflin.

Bidney, D. 1967. *Theoretical Anthropology*. New York: Schocken.

Boas, F. 1938. *The Mind of Primitive Man*. New York: Macmillan.

Bojer, J. 1929. *The Power of a Lie*. New York: Century.

Bradley, F. H. (1876) 1962. *Ethical Studies*. London: Oxford University Press.

Brandt, L. W. and Metzger, W. 1969. Reality: What does it mean. *Psychol. Rep.* 25: 127-35.

Brecht, A. 1958. *Political Theory*. Princeton, N. J.: Princeton University Press.

Brod, M. 1970 *Paganism, Christianity and Judaism*. Alabama: University of Alabama Press.

Brown, J. F. 1936. *Psychology and the Social Order*. New York: McGraw-Hill.

Butterfield, H. 1957. *The Origins of Modern Science*. New York: Free Press.

Cantril, H. 1950. *The "Why" of Man's Experience*. New York: Macmillan.

———. 1965. *The Pattern of Human Concern*. New Brunswick, N. J.: Rutgers University Press.

Cassirer, E. 1954. *An Essay on Man*. Garden City, N. Y.: Doubleday.

Collingswood, R. G. 1967. *The Idea of History*. New York: Oxford University Press.

————. 1965. *Idea of Nature*. London: Oxford University Press.
Commoner, B. 1963. *Science and Survival*. New York: Viking.
Cooley, C. H. 1902. *Human Nature and the Social Order*. New York: Scribners.
Copleston, F. C. 1961. *Medieval Philosophy*. New York: Harper and Row.
Dilthey, W. 1914-1958. *Gesammelte Schriften*. 12 vols. Leipzig: Teubner.
Dodd, C. H. 1935. *The Bible and the Greeks*. London: Macmillan.
Doob, L. W. 1935. *Propaganda*. New York: Holt, Rinehart & Winston.
Dostoyevsky, F. 1966. *The Brothers Karamazov*. New York: Airmont Book.
Duncker, K. 1945. On Problem Solving. Translated by L. S. Lees. *Psychol. Monogr.* 58, no. 5.
Edel, A. 1955. *Ethical Judgment*. New York: Free Press.
Ellis, W. D. 1938. *Source Book of Gestalt Psychology*. New York: Harcourt-Brace.
Finkelstein, L., 1950. *The Jews: Their History, Culture and Religion*. New York: Harper.
Foot, P., ed. 1967. *Theories of Ethics*. London: Oxford University Press.
Freeman, E. 1937. *Social Psychology*. New York: Holt, Rinehart & Winston.
Freud, S. 1933. *New Introductory Lectures*. New York: Norton.
Fromm, E. 1941. *Escape From Freedom*. New York: Holt.
Garber, W. 1941. Ph.D. Dissertation, Graduate Faculty, New School for Social Research.
Gide, C. and Rist, C. 1947. *Economic Doctrines*. Boston: D. C. Heath.
Goldstein, K. 1939. *The Organism*. New York: American Book.
Gomperz, T. 1912. *Greek Thinkers*. New York: Scribners.
Guvatkin, H. M. and Whitney, J. P. 1924-1936. *The Cambridge Medieval History*. Cambridge: Cambridge University Press.
Harnak, A. 1908. *The Mission of Christianity in the First and Third Century*. Translated by James Moffat. New York: Putnam.
Harrison, G. R. 1956. *The Role of Science in Our Modern World*. New York: William Morrow.
Hart, H. L. 1963. *Law, Liberty and Morality*. New York: Vintage Books.
Hartshorne, H. and May, M. A. 1928. *Studies in Deceit*. New York: Macmillan.
Hebb, D.O. 1949. *Organization of Behavior*. New York: Wiley.
Hertz, J. H., ed. 1958. *The Pentateuch*. London: Soncino Press.
Hill, T. E. 1959. *Contemporary Ethical Theories*. New York: Macmillan.
Hirsch, S. R. 1962. *Horeb*. London: Soncino Press.
Hitler, A. 1943. *Mein Kampf*. Translated by R. Manheim. Boston: Houghton Mifflin.
Hobbes, T. (1651) 1950. *Leviathan*. New York: Dutton.
Hodges, H. A. 1944. *The Philosophy of Dilthey*. London: Trubner.
Horney, K. 1937. *The Neurotic Personality of Our Time*. New York: Norton.
Hovland, C. I., et al. 1958. *The Order of Presentation in Persuasion*. New Haven: Yale University Press.
Hull, L. W. H. 1959. *History and Philosophy of Science*. New York: Longmans.
Huxley, A. 1938. *The Brave New World*. New York: Harper.
Isaacs, S. 1930. *Intellectual Growth in Young Children*. New York: Harcourt, Brace, and World.
Jaspers, K. 1957. *Man in the Modern Age*. Garden City, N. Y.: Anchor Books.
————. 1963. *Philosophy and the World*. Chicago: Henry Regnery.
Kahler, E. 1969. *The Meaning of History*. New York: The World Pub. Co.
Koffka, K. 1925. *Growth of the Mind*. New York: Harcourt Brace.
————. 1935. *Principles of Gestalt Psychology*. New York: Harcourt Brace.
Köhler, W. 1925. *Mentality of Apes*. London: Kegan, Paul, Trench, Truber.
————. 1929. *Gestalt Psychology*. New York: Liveright.
————. 1938. *The Place of Value in a World of Facts*. New York: Liveright.
Korzybski, A. 1933. *Science and Society*. Lakeville, Conn.: Inst. Gen. Semantics.

Kuenzli, A. E. 1959. *The Phenomenological Problem.* New York: Harper & Row.

Latane, B. and Darley, J. M. 1970. *The Unresponsive Bystander.* New York: Appleton Century Crofts.

Lewin, K. 1935. *Dynamic Theory of Personality.* New York: McGraw-Hill.

Lewin, K. 1938. The conceptual representation and measurement of psychological forces. Durham, North Carolina: Duke University Press.

Lewis, H. B. 1941. Studies in the principles of judgments and attitudes: IV. *J. Soc. Psychol.* 14: 229-56.

Lorge, I. 1936. Prestige, suggestion and attitudes. *J. Soc. Psychol.* 7: 386-402.

Lowie, R. H. 1920. *Primitive Society.* New York: Boni and Liveright.

———. 1929. *Are We Civilized? Human Culture in Perspective.* New York: Harcourt, Brace, and World.

Luchins, A. S. 1939. The Einstellung effect in learning by repetition. Ph.D. Dissertation, New York University.

———. 1942. Mechanization in problem solving. *Psychol. Monogr.* 54, no. 6.

———. 1944. On agreement with another's judgment. *J. Abnor, Soc. Psychol.* 39: 97-111.

———. 1945. Social influences on perception of complex drawings. *J. Soc. Psychol.* 21: 257-73.

———. 1946. A course in group psychotheraphy: methods, contents and results. *J. Clinical Psychol.* 3: 231-39.

———. 1947a. Situational and attitudinal influences on Rorschach responses. *Am. J. Psychiat.* 103: 780-84.

———. 1947b. Methods of studying the progress and outcomes of a group psychotherapy program. *J. Consult. Psychol.* 4: 173-83.

———. 1947c. A conflict in norms: metric versus English units of linear measurement. *J. Soc. Psychol.* 25: 193-206.

———. 1948. The use of specialized audio-aids in a group psychotherapy program for psychotics. *J. Consult. Psychol.* 12: 313-20.

———. 1950. Restructuring social perceptions: a group psychotherapy technique. *J. Consult. Psychol.* 14: 446-51.

———. 1951. Patients view the therapist: a training and research device. *J. Consult. Psychol.* 15: 24-31.

———. 1954. On the theories and problems of adolescence. *J. Gen. Psychol.* 85: 47-63.

———. 1955a. A variational approach to social influences. *J. Soc. Psychol.* 42: 113-19.

———. 1955a. A variational approach to social influences on perception. *J. Soc. Psychol.* 42: 113-19.

———. 1955b. Integration of clinical and experimental theoretical psychology through core courses. *Psychol. Rep. Monog.* 4: 221-46.

———. 1964. On the awareness and denotation of contradictions. *J. Gen. Psychol.* 71: 233-46.

———. and Luchins, E. H. 1955a. Previous experience with ambiguous and nonambiguous perceptual stimuli under various social influences. *J. Soc. Psychol.* 42: 249-70.

———. 1955b. On conformity with true and false communications. *J. Soc. Psychol.* 42: 283-303.

———. 1955c. Influence on perceptions of previous experiences with ambiguous and unambiguous stimuli. *J. Gen. Psychol.* 54: 197-211.

———. 1956. Discovering the source of contradictory communications: the influence of complexity of the task. *J. Soc. Psychol.* 49: 49-63.

———. 1957. Discovering the source of contradictory communications: the influence of a cooperative task. *J. Gen. Psychol.* 56: 159-78.

———. 1959. *Rigidity of Behavior*. Eugene, Ore.: University of Oregon Press.

———. 1960. Influence of experience with conflicting information on reaction to subsequent conflicting information. *J. Soc. Psychol.* 53: 303-16.

———. 1961a. On conformity with judgments of a majority or an authority. *J. Soc. Psychol.* 53: 303-16.

———. 1961b. Social influences on judgment of changing evidence. *J. Soc. Psychol.* 54: 13-36.

———. 1961c. Social influences on impression of personality. *J. Soc. Psychol.* 54: 111-22.

———. 1961d. Imitation by rote and by understanding. *J. Soc. Psychol.* 54: 111-25.

———. 1961e. Intentional and unintentional models in social learning. *J. Soc. Psychol.* 54: 321-35.

———. 1961f. Einstellung effect in social learning. *J. Soc. Psychol.* 55: 59-66.

———. 1962. The effect of the degree of freedom of choice on learning and perception. *J. Soc. Psychol.* 56: 187-205.

———. 1963a. The problems of truth in the study of perception. *Psychol. Rec.* 13: 213-2.

———. 1963b. The role of understanding in social influences on judgment. *J. Soc. Psychol.* 61: 133-50.

———. 1963c. Focusing on the object of judgment in the social situation. *J. Soc. Psychol.* 60: 273-87.

———. 1963d. Effects of order of evidence on social influences on judgment. *J. Soc. Psychol.* 61: 345-63.

———. 1963e. Social influences on judgments of descriptions of people. *J. Soc. Psychol.* 60: 231-49.

———. 1963f. The referent of the frame of reference. *Psychol. Rev.* 13: 293-304

———. 1965a. Anchorage and ordering effects of information on personality impression. *J. Soc. Psychol.* 66: 1-14.

———. 1965b. Reactions to inconsistencies; phenomenal versus logical contradictions. *J. Gen. Psychol.* 73: 47-65.

———. 1966a. Consequences for agreeing with another's wrong judgments. *J. Soc. Psychol.* 68: 275-90.

———. 1966b. Learning a complex social role. *Psychol. Rec.* 10: 177-187.

———. 1967a. Social influences on judgments involving the lower senses: odors. *J. Soc. Psychol.* 72: 227-34.

———. 1967b. Social influences in judgments involving the lower senses: weights. *J. Soc. Psychol.* 72: 235-39.

———. 1967c. Conformity: Task vs. social requirements. *J. Soc. Psychol.* 71: 95-105.

———. 1968. Motivation to tell the truth vs. social influences. *J. Soc. Psychol.* 76: 97-105.

———. 1969a. *The Search For Factors that Extremize the Autokinetic Effect*. Albany, N.Y.: SUNY-Albany, Faculty Students Association.

———. 1969b. Einstellung effect and group problem solving. *J. Soc. Psychol.* 77: 70-89.

———. 1970a. *Wertheimer's Seminars Revisited: Problem Solving and Thinking*. 3 vols. Albany, N.Y.: SUNY-Albany, Faculty Students Association.

———. 1970b. Effects of preconceptions and communications on impressions of a person. *J. Soc. Psychol.* 81: 243-252.

———. 1970c. The effects of order of presentation of information and explanatory models. *J. Soc. Psychol.* 80: 63-70.

———. 1970d. Strengthening motivational factors to tell the truth. *J. Soc. Psychol.* 81: 55-62.

Lynd, R. S. 1939. *Knowledge for What*. Princeton, N.J.: Princeton University Press.

Machiavelli, N. 1532 (1950). *The Prince and the Discourses*. New York: Modern Library.

Malamud, I. 1942. M.S. Thesis Graduate Faculty, New School for Social Research.

Maslow, A. H., ed. 1959. *New Knowledge in Human Values*. New York: Harper.

———. 1965. *Eupsychian Management*. Homewood, Ill.: Dorsey.

———. 1970. *Motivation and Personality*. New York: Harper & Row.

———. 1971. *Religions, Values and Peak-Experiences*. New York: Viking.

Mesthene, E. G. 1970. *Technological Change*. New York: Mentor.

Milgram, S. 1965. Some conditions of obedience and disobedience to authority. *Hum. Relat.* 18: 57-75.

Miller, N. E. and Dollard, J. 1941. *Social Learning and Imitation*. New Haven: Yale University Press.

Murchison, C. 1935. *A Handbook of Social Psychology*. Worcester, Mass.: Clark University Press.

Obler, P. C. and Estrin, H. A., eds. 1962. *The New Scientist*. Garden City: Anchor Books.

Parsegian, V. L., et al. 1968. 1970. *Introduction to the Natural Sciences*. 2 vols. New York: Academic Press.

Perry, R. B. 1950. *General Theory of Value*. Cambridge, Mass.: Harvard University Press.

Piaget, J. 1962. *The Moral Judgment of the Child*. New York, Collier.

Plato. 1943. *The Republic*. Translated by B. Jowett. New York: Books, Inc.

Ramsey, P. 1965. *Nine Modern Moralists*. New York: Spectrum Books.

Randell, J. H. 1926. *The Making of the Modern Mind*. Boston: Houghton Mifflin.

Robinson, J. H. 1914. *Readings in European History*. Boston: Houghton Mifflin.

Rokeach, M. 1969. *Beliefs, Attitudes, and Values*. San Francisco: Jossey-Bass.

Russell, B. 1936. *Religion and Science*. New York: Simon Schuster.

Sandys, J. E. 1921. *History of Classical Scholarship*. New York: Macmillan.

Sarton, G. 1964. *A History of Science*. New York: Wiley.

Schlick, M. 1939. *Problems of Ethics*. New York: Prentice Hall.

Secord, P. F. and Backman, C. W. 1964. *Social Psychology*. New York: McGraw-Hill.

Sesonske, A. 1964. *Value and Obligation*. New York: Oxford University Press.

Sherif, M. 1935. A study of some social factors in perception. *Arch. Psychol.*, no. 187.

———. 1936. *Psychology of Social Norms*. New York: Harper & Row.

———. 1937. An experimental approach to the study of attitudes. *Sociometry*, 1: 80-98.

———. 1948. *An Outline of Social Psychology*. New York: Harper & Row.

———. 1957. *Emerging Problems in Social Psychology*. Norman, Okla.: University Book Exchange.

———. and Cantril, H. 1947. *The Psychology of Ego-Involvements*. New York: Wiley.

———. and Sherif, C. W. 1969. *Social Psychology*. New York: Harper & Row.

Smith, A. 1936. *Wealth of Nations*. New York: Modern Library.

Sorokin, P. 1937. *Contemporary Sociological Theories*. New York: Harper.

Spranger, E. 1928. *Types of Men*. Halle: Niemeyer.

Stammler, R. 1925. *The Theory of Justice*. New York: Macmillan.

Stern, W. 1923-24. *Person und Sache*. 3 vols. Leipzig: Barth.

Strauss, L. 1953. *Natural Right and History*. Chicago: The University of Chicago Press.

Sumner, W. G. and Keller, A. G. 1927. *The Science of Society.* 4 vols. New Haven, Conn.: Yale University Press.

Taylor, A. E. 1927. *Plato: The Man and His Work.* New York: Dial Press.

Thorndike, E. L. 1935. *The Psychology of Wants, Interests and Attitudes.* New York: Appleton-Century.

Thorndike, L. 1917. *The History of Medieval Europe.* Boston: Houghton & Mifflin.

Wagner, D. O. 1934. *Social Reformers.* New York: Macmillan.

Waltz, K. 1954. *Man The State and War.* New York: Columbia University Press.

Werner, H. 1940. *Comparative Psychology of Mental Development.* New York: Harper & Row.

Wertheimer, M. 1905. Experimentelle Untersuchungen zur Tatbestandsdiagnostik. *Arch. ges Psychol.* 6: 59-131.

———. 1910. Musik der Wedda. *Sammelbande d. internat. Musikgesellschaft.* 11: 300-309.

———. 1934. On truth. *Soc. Res.* 1: 135-46.

———. 1935. Some problems in the theory of ethics. *Soc. Res.* 2: 253-67.

Wiener, N. 1964. *God and Golem.* Cambridge, Mass.: MIT Press.

Windelband, W. 1958. *A History of Philosophy.* New York: Harper.

Witken, H. A. et al. 1954. *Personality Through Perception.* New York: Harper-Row.

Witken, H. A. et al. 1954. *Personality Through Perception.* New York: Harper & Row.

Wulf, F. 1922. Über die Veränderung von Vorstellunger (Gedächtnis und Gestalt) *Psychol. Forsch,* pp. 1333-373. Condensed in Selection 10, Tendencies in Figural Variation, in Ellis. *Source Book of Gestalt Psychology.* London: Routledge and Kegan Paul, Ltd., 1938.

Name Index

Achong, C. A., 423
Adler, A., 53, 117, 130, 167, 174, 200, 261,
   275, 276, 434, 435, 480, 502
Allport, F. H., 223, 267, 269, 274, 452
Allport, G. W., 68, 69, 106–8, 223, 467, 490
Anaxagoras, 150
Anaxamenes, 72, 130
Anshen, Ruth, 436
Arcuri, M., 350
Aristotle, 21, 23, 29, 32, 33, 35–37, 128, 171,
   172, 174, 281, 485
Arnheim, R., 289, 433
Asch, S. E., 218
Ayer, A. J., 154

Backman, C. W., 105
Bacon, F., 27, 411
Bartlett, F. C., 481
Benedict, R., 42
Benson, S. L., 351
Bentham, J., 37
Bernard, C., 118
Bernays, E. L., 278
Bettleheim, B., 457
Binder, E., 426
Blake, R., 156
Blum, S., 11
Brannon, A., 317
Brightman, E. S., 72
Brod, M., 22
Brophy, G. R., 310
Brown, A. D., 351
Brown, J. F., 272, 278, 436, 482
Brown, Margaret, 98, 105–7, 186, 213
Bruno, 26
Burstein, G., 101

Cantril, H., 11, 46, 64, 65, 89, 94, 133–36,
   219–22, 231, 233, 237, 249, 277, 278,
   286, 292, 326, 327, 481
Carmichael, S., 376–80, 385
Christensen, 206, 207
Collingswood, R. C., 22, 272
Comte, A., 67, 85, 445, 484
Condorcet, A. N., 40
Confucius, 443–51
Cooley, C. H., 446
Counts, G., 280, 284

Darley, J. M., 207
Darwin, C., 169, 174
Dashiell, J. F., 292
Decatur, S., 502
Descartes, R., 26–28, 332
Dewey, J., 72, 73, 155, 181, 448, 479
Diderot, D., 27
Dilthey, W., 66–69
Dollard, J., 262–65, 267, 332, 435
Dolzeal, H., 302
Doob, L., 277
Dostoyevsky, F., 152
Duncker, K., 73, 238, 240
Dunlap, K., 166
Durkheim, E., 63, 72, 121
Duvyvendaak, J. J., 436

Edison, T., 28
Einstein, A., 437–39
Ellis, W. D., 289, 349, 465
Engels, F., 488
Epicurus, 29, 37, 72, 128
Euclid, 76

The indexes were prepared by Mr. Dell H. Warnick, a graduate student in social psychology
at S.U.N.Y.-Albany.

513

Subject Index